EUROPEAN CAPITAL MARKETS LAW

European capital markets law has developed rapidly. The European legislature has enacted four framework directives and numerous implementing directives to improve investor confidence in the integrity and functioning of capital markets, while in recent years the financial crisis has given impetus to the development of a European supervisory structure. This book systematises the European directives and examines both the underlying concepts and the interdisciplinary features of this field of law. National differences, such as the possibility of private enforcement, are explored by looking at selected EU Member States, including Austria, France, Germany, Italy, Spain, Sweden and the United Kingdom.

The first chapter deals with the foundations of capital markets law in Europe. The second chapter explains the basics and chapter three examines the rules ensuring market integrity—focusing on insider dealing, market manipulation and short selling. Chapter 4 explores the disclosure system; the roles of intermediaries, such as investment firms, financial analysts and rating agencies are described in the fifth chapter; and Chapter 6 deals with compliance in investment firms. Throughout the book there is a strong emphasis on legal practice and frequent reference is made to the key decisions of supervisory authorities and courts.

The book will be useful to students of capital markets law but will also appeal to a broader audience of researchers and practitioners, including attorneys and supervisory authorities.

European Capital Markets Law

Edited by
Rüdiger Veil

Translated by
Rebecca Ahmling

·HART·
PUBLISHING

OXFORD AND PORTLAND, OREGON
2013

Published in the United Kingdom by Hart Publishing Ltd
16C Worcester Place, Oxford, OX1 2JW
Telephone: +44 (0)1865 517530
Fax: +44 (0)1865 510710
E-mail: mail@hartpub.co.uk
Website: http://www.hartpub.co.uk

Published in North America (US and Canada) by
Hart Publishing
c/o International Specialized Book Services
920 NE 58th Avenue, Suite 300
Portland, OR 97213-3786
USA
Tel: +1 503 287 3093 or toll-free: (1) 800 944 6190
Fax: +1 503 280 8832
E-mail: orders@isbs.com
Website: http://www.isbs.com

British Library Cataloguing in Publication Data

Data Available

ISBN: 978-1-84946-440-6

Typeset by Forewords Ltd, Oxon

Printed and bound in Great Britain by
TJ International Ltd, Padstow

Preface

The European Union has been working on integrating securities markets and harmonising admission to these markets since 1979. The first directives only covered stock exchange law and prospectus liability, laying down minimum requirements for the information to be supplied to shareholders. In 1999 the European Commission came to the conclusion that further steps would be necessary in order to create a single European financial market. Only four years later the European legislature enacted four framework directives and numerous implementing regulations and directives to improve the functioning of capital markets and investor confidence. In 2009 these legislative acts were complemented by a regulation on rating agencies and in 2012 by a regulation on short sellings. Finally, the financial crisis gave the necessary incentive for the Member States to develop a new supervisory structure—with the result that since 1 January 2011 the newly founded European Securities and Markets Authority (ESMA) is responsible for supervising financial markets.

This book is valuable for a wide audience. It offers students the possibility to examine European capital markets law as an independent field of law. National particularities, such as the different instruments of private enforcement, are depicted through examples chosen from various Member States, including Austria, France, Germany, Italy, Spain, Sweden and the United Kingdom. The book places a strong emphasis on legal practice, presenting more than 20 decisions by the Belgian, Danish, English, French, German and Swedish supervisory authorities and courts, in order to improve understanding of how the complex theoretical problems are being dealt with in legal practice.

At the same time, the book also offers insights equally relevant to legal research and practice. In future, legal research in capital markets law will evolve increasingly around the European provisions. This book must therefore be seen as a first step in this direction. It attempts to put the provisions in the numerous directives into a system, examine the underlying concepts and describe the intra- and interdisciplinarity of this field of law. The conclusions will also be of interest to lawyers and supervisory practice—information on the new European supervision as of 1 January 2011 still being scarce.

As a textbook, the book must focus on the most important areas of capital markets law. The first two chapters deal with the foundations of capital markets legislature in Europe. They also examine the supervisory structures and explain how European law has to be interpreted. In the following chapters the rules ensuring market integrity are explained. The work deals especially with insider dealing and market manipulation and shows the concepts of the regulation on short sellings. Another focus is the transparency regime which is explored extensively in nine sections—all legislative measures are based on the assumption that disclosure obligations are necessary to ensure investor protection. The following chapter explains the European legal framework for intermediaries, such as investment firms, financial analysts and rating agencies. A separate chapter describes the organisational requirements for investment firms. It focuses on the regulatory aim of protecting investment firms from potential civil and administrative sanctions as well as reputational damages that result from a violation of the European rules of conduct and the aim to ensure investor protection. However, other control functions, such as risk management, and questions of corporate governance are beyond the scope of this book.

The results described in this book regarding the implementation of the European directives into English, French, German, Italian, Spanish and Swedish law are all based on comparative research in these countries by the Institute for Corporate and Capital Markets Law (ICCML) at Bucerius Law School, Hamburg. We had the possibility to conduct interviews in France, Italy, Spain and Sweden. In France, we interviewed the legal practitioners Nicolas Bombrun and Marie-Chrystel Dang Tran (both Latham & Watkins, Paris), David Revcolevschi (Freshfields Bruckhaus Deringer, Paris) and Bruno Zabala (CMS Bureau Francis Lefebvre, Paris), as well as Frédéric Pelèse and Brune David as representatives of the French supervisory authority Autorité des marchés financiers (AMF). We would also like to thank Professor Alain Couret who offered us valuable insights.

In Italy we conducted interviews with the legal practitioners Nicola Barra Caracciolo and Roberto Casula (both Freshfields Bruckhaus Deringer, Milan), Antonio Coletti and Isabella Porchia (both Latham & Watkins, Milan), Gianfranco Veneziano and Mario Cusmai (both Bonelli Erede Pappalardo, Studio Legale, Milan) and Franco Grilli Cicilioni, Sabrina Borocci, Michele Bissoli and Francesca Casini (all Clifford Chance, Milan). Additionally, Carlo Milia from the Italian supervisory authority Commissione Nazionale per le Società e la Borsa (CONSOB) answered our questions on Italian capital markets law from the supervisory authority's point of view.

Swedish capital markets law from the legal advisors' perspective was described to us by Cecilia Bjelle (Baker McKenzie, Stockholm), Björn Kristiansson (Hannes Snellmann Attorneys, Stockholm) as well as Jan Lombach und Joachim Falkner (both White & Case, Stockholm). The Swedish supervisory authority's (Finansinspektionen) perspective was presented to us by Camilla Hagmann Falkler and Denny Jaakko. We were also able to pose any questions that arose to Professor Jan Kleineman, Professor Gustaf Sjöberg (University of Stockholm), Thomas Ordeberg (Swedish ministry of finance) and Fredric Korling (University of Stockholm).

In Spain Jose Luis Blanco and Paco Iso (both Latham & Watkins, Madrid), Emilio Diaz-Ruiz and Javier Redonet Sanchez del Campo (both Uria Menendez, Madrid), Alfonso de Marcos and Armando Albarrán Jiménez (both Freshfields Bruckhaus Deringer, Madrid) and Professor Guillermo Martin Guerra and Professor Alonso Ureba (both Ramón & Cajal, Madrid) offered us their expert opinions as legal practitioners of Spanish capitals market law. Further interviews were conducted with Professor Candido Paz-Ares who also provided us with a suitable contact at the Spanish supervisory authority Comisión Nacional del Mercado de Valores (CNMV) and participated in our conversations with Xavier Pedro Zahn Garcia and four other members of the CNMV.

The interview partners in France, Italy, Spain and Sweden were introduced to us by Andreas Austmann, Joachim von Falkenhausen, Udo Henkel, Volker Land, Sebastian Maerker and Professor Christoph H. Seibt. The interviews with the representatives of the foreign supervisory authorities were made possible by Thomas Eufinger and Stefan Haupt, both from the German supervisory authority (BaFin). I would like to thank them very much for their support.

Financial support for the research project was granted to us by the law firm Freshfields Bruckhaus Deringer and the Foundation to support the Institute for Corporate and Capital Markets Law (ICCML) at Bucerius Law School. Special thanks go to the members of the foundation Aon Holding Deutschland GmbH, Aurubis AG, CAT oil AG, Deloitte

& Touche GmbH, D + S Europe GmbH, Edel AG, Freshfields Bruckhaus Deringer LLP and Latham & Watkins LLP.

The co-authors Hendrik Brinckmann, Philipp Koch, Lars Teigelack, Nikolai Vokuhl, Fabian Walla and Malte Wundenberg provided this book with the necessary expertise they gained during their comparative research studies. I would like to thank them very much for their valuable participation. Particular thanks are due to my colleagues Christian Bumke and Axel Kämmerer who have discussed issues and commented on draft chapters.

This book would not have been possible without the support of Rebecca Ahmling. In October 2010 she took on the task of translating the book into English. It has been a Herculean task, particularly so since the manuscript had to be constantly adjusted to various European capital markets law reforms. Rebecca Ahmling has always studied our texts carefully and discussed the translations with us in depth. I am greatly indebted to her dedication and expertise.

Furthermore I would like to thank the research assistants Juliane Jacobsen, Marcus P. Lerch and Jan Wildhirth and the student assistants Oxana Grushetska, Maximilian Kunzelmann and Lena Templer for their valuable support. Special thanks go to Marcus P. Lerch who has been responsible for the coordination of the editorial work. He has mastered this task with care and patience. The arduous work on the manuscript has been managed carefully by Iris Kessler and Ursula Vogeler.

The book is based on European legislation as of August 2012, whilst considering literature mainly before 2011. Recent articles on the reforms of European capital markets law, however, are considered.

Suggestions regarding the book are welcome and can be posted to me at ruediger.veil@ law-school.de.

Rüdiger Veil
Hamburg, August 2012

Summary Contents

Detailed Contents

1
Foundations of Capital Markets Legislature in Europe

Contents

3
Market Integrity

Contents

Contents

5

Intermediaries

7
Conclusion

Contents

List of Contributors

Rüdiger Veil, born in 1966, studied law at the University of Gießen and Humboldt-University Berlin. He completed his doctoral thesis in 1995 and his habilitation in 2002. Rüdiger Veil is a full professor at Bucerius Law School, Hamburg; he holds the Alfried Krupp-Chair for Civil Law, German and International Business Law and is the managing director of the Institute for Corporate Law and Capital Markets Law (ICCML).

Rebecca Ahmling, born in 1984, is a native speaker of English and German. She studied law at Bucerius Law School in Hamburg and at Université Laval in Québec. She received a doctoral degree (Dr. iur.) from Bucerius Law School with a thesis on the powers of the European Court of Justice to fill gaps in EU legislation by way of analogy. She is currently completing her practical legal training in Munich.

Hendrik Brinckmann, born in 1980, studied law at Bucerius Law School in Hamburg and at the University of Sydney. He obtained his doctoral degree (Dr. iur.) in 2009. His doctoral thesis deals with financial reporting in capital markets law. Currently he is working as an attorney in the area of corporate and capital markets law with Flick Gocke Schaumburg in Berlin.

Philipp Koch, born in 1983, studied law at Bucerius Law School in Hamburg and at Universidad Peruana de Ciencias Aplicadas in Lima. He went to Universidad Autónoma de Madrid and Université Paris I Panthéon-Sorbonne as a research fellow and completed his practical legal training in Hamburg and Frankfurt. Currently, he is a doctoral student and research assistant at the Alfried Krupp-Chair for Civil Law, German and International Business Law at Bucerius Law School in Hamburg.

Lars Teigelack, born in 1982, studied law at Bucerius Law School in Hamburg and the University of Pennsylvania in Philadelphia. He received his doctoral degree (Dr. iur.) from Bucerius Law School in 2009 with a thesis on the influence of behavioral finance on the German regulation of financial analysts. Lars Teigelack is a capital markets and corporate law attorney in the Frankfurt office of White & Case in Frankfurt/Main.

Nikolai Vokuhl, born in 1978, studied law at Christian-Albrechts-University in Kiel and served his practical legal training in Hamburg and Frankfurt. He holds a Master of Laws (LL.M.) from the University of California, Los Angeles (UCLA) and a doctoral degree (Dr. iur.) from Bucerius Law School. His doctoral thesis deals with the conflict between the capital maintenance rules for corporations and the protection of investors on the capital market via a civil law liability of the corporations. He worked as an attorney in the area of corporate and capital markets law at the Frankfurt office of Freshfields Bruckhaus Deringer. Currently, he is working as corporate legal counsel at Amazon.

Fabian Walla, born in 1983, studied law at Bucerius Law School in Hamburg and Cornell Law School; he holds a doctoral degree (Dr. iur.) from Bucerius Law School. His doctoral thesis deals with the German and European capital markets supervision. Fabian Walla worked as research assistant at the Institute for Corporate and Capital Markets Law (ICCML) at Bucerius Law School and was a research fellow at the Stockholm Centre for Commercial Law. He completed his legal training in Lüneburg, Hamburg and Tokyo. Currently, he is working as a corporate law and litigation attorney at the Hamburg office of the law firm Gleiss Lutz.

Malte Wundenberg, born in 1979, studied law at Bucerius Law School and NYU Law School; he holds a Dipl. Kfm. degree ("Master") in business administration and a doctoral degree (Dr. iur.) from Bucerius Law School. His thesis is entitled "Compliance and the Principles-based Supervision of Banking Groups". Malte Wundenberg is an assistant professor (Habilitand) at the Institute for Corporate and Capital Markets Law (ICCML) and was a research fellow at the University of Cambridge.

List of Abbreviations

AB	Aktiebolag (Swedish stock corporation)
ABGB	Allgemeines Bürgerliches Gesetzbuch (Austrian Civil Code)
ABL	Aktiebolagslag (Swedish Stock Corporation Act)
Abl.	Amtsblatt (Official Journal)
AC	Appeal Cases (law reports)
AcP	Archiv für die civilistische Praxis (journal)
AG	Aktiengesellschaft (German stock corporation)/ Die Aktiengesellschaft—Zeitschrift für das gesamte Aktienwesen, für deutsches, europäisches und internationales Unternehmens- und Kapitalmarktrecht (journal)
AIM	Alternative Investment Market
AktG	Aktiengesetz (German Stock Corporation Act)
All ER	All England Law Reports (journal)
a.m.	ante meridiem
Am. Bus. Law J.	American Business Law Journal (journal)
Am. Econ. Rev.	American Economic Review (journal)
AMF	Autorité des marchés financiers (French Financial Markets Authority)
Analisi giur. Ec.	Analisi Giuridica dell'Economia (journal)
AnSVG	Anlegerschutzverbesserungsgesetz (German Investor Protection Improvement Act)
AO	Abgabenordnung (German Act on the Administrative Procedures in Taxation)
APER	Code of Practice of Approved Persons (FSA Handbook)
APRR	Autoroutes Paris-Rhin-Rhône
Ariz. L. Rev.	Arizona Law Review (journal)
ÅRL	Årsredovisningslag (Swedish Annual Report Act)
Art.	Article(s)
ASB	Accounting Standards Board
avr.	Avril (French: April)
BaFin	Bundesanstalt für Finanzdienstleistungsaufsicht (German Federal Financial Supervisory Authority)
BAKred	Bundesaufsichtsamt für Kreditwesen (German Federal Banking Supervisory Office)

Banca Borsa tit. Cred.	Banca, borsa e titoli di credito (journal)
BAV	Bundesaufsichtsamt für das Versicherungswesen (German Federal Agency for Financial Services Supervision)
BAWe	Bundesaufsichtsamt für den Wertpapierhandel (German Federal Supervisory Office for Securities Trading)
BB	Betriebs-Berater (journal)
BBC	British Broadcasting Corporation
Begr.	Begründung (explanatory notes on German statutes)
BEHV - EBK	Verordnung der Eidgenössischen Finanzmarktaufsicht über die Börsen und den Effektenhandel (Swiss Regulation on Stock Exchanges and Securities Trading)
BBLJ	Berkeley Business Law Journal
BFuP	Betriebswirtschaftliche Forschung und Praxis (journal)
BGB	Bürgerliches Gesetzbuch (German Civil Code)
BGBl.	Bundesgesetzblatt (German Federal Law Gazette)
BGH	Bundesgerichtshof (German Federal Court of Justice)
BGHSt	Entscheidungen des Bundesgerichtshofs in Strafsachen (Cases of the German Federal Court of Justice for Criminal Cases)
BGHZ	Entscheidungen des Bundesgerichtshofs in Zivilsachen (Cases of the German Federal Court of Justice for Civil Law Cases)
BilMoG	Gesetz zur Modernisierung des Bilanzrechts (German Accounting Law Modernisation Act)
BKR	Zeitschrift für Bank- und Kapitalmarktrecht (journal)
BörseG	Börsengesetz (Austrian Stock Exchange Act)
BörsG	Börsengesetz (German Stock Exchange Act)
BörsO FWB	Börsenordnung (German Stock Exchange Rules for the Frankfurter Wertpapierbörse)
BörsZulVO	Börsenzulassungs-Verordnung (German Stock Exchange Admission Regulation)
BrB	Brottsbalk (Swedish Criminal Code)
BR-Drucks.	Bundesrats-Drucksache (printed papers of the German Bundesrat)
BT-Drucks.	Bundestags-Drucksache (printed papers of the German Bundestag)
Bull. Civ.	Bulletin civil
Bull. Joly Bourse	Bulletin Joly Bourse
BuM	Beton- und Monierbau AG
BVerfG	Bundesverfassungsgericht (German Federal Constitutional Court)
c/	Contre (French: v.)

CA/C.A.	Cour d'appel (French Court of Appeal)
CAC	Cotation assistée en continu (French benchmark stock market index)
Cal. L. Rev.	California Law Review (journal)
CAR	Contemporary Accounting Research (journal)
CASS	Client Asset Sourcebook (FSA Handbook)
Cass. Com.	Cour de cassation, chambre commerciale (French Supreme Court of Judicature, Commercial Chamber)
CBFA	Commission bancaire, financière et des assurances (Belgian Banking, Finance and Insurance Commissio)
Cc	Code civil (French Civil Code)
CC	Código Civil (Spanish Civil Code)
C. com.	Code de commerce (French Commercial Code)
CCZ	Corporate Compliance Zeitschrift (journal)
CDS	Credit Default Swaps
CEO	Chief executive officer
CEPR	Centre for Economic Policy Research Policy Insight
cert. denied	Certiorari Denied
CESR	Committee of European Securities Regulators
CESR Recommendation	Recommendations of the Committee of European Securities Regulators
CFO	Chief Financial Officer
ch./Chapt.	chapter/chamber (French: chamber)
ChD	Chancery Division (law reports)
Cir.	Circuit
CJA	Criminal Justice Act
CML	Capital Market Law Review
CMLJ	Capital Markets Law Journal (journal)
CMLRev.	Common Market Law Review (journal)
C. mon. fin.	Code monétaire et financier (French Monetary and Financial Code)
CNMV	Comisión Nacional del Mercado de Valores (Spanish National Stock Market Commission)
COB	Commission des opérations de bourse (French Stock Exchange Commission)
COB	Compliance Officer Bulletin
COBS	Conduct of Business Sourcebook (FSA Handbook)
Colum. Bus. L. Rev.	Columbia Business Law Review (journal)
Colum. J. Transnat'l L.	Columbia Journal of Transnational Law (journal)
COM	Commission
Consob	Commissione Nazionale per le Società e la Borsa (Italian Securities and Exchange Commission)
CP	Código Penal (Spanish Criminal Code)

CSC	Carr Sheppards Crosthwaite Ltd.
CSSF	Commission de Surveillance du Secteur Financier (Luxembourg Financial Supervisory Authority)
DAI	Deutsches Aktieninstitut (German Equities Institute)
DAX	Deutscher Aktienindex (German stock market index)
DB	Der Betrieb (journal)
Dec	December
DEPP	Decision Procedure and Penalties (manual)
Die Bank	Die Bank – Zeitschrift für Bankpolitik und Praxis (journal)
Dir.	Directive
DiskE	Diskussionsentwurf (discussion papers for German statutes)
DL	decreto-legge (Italian legislative decree)
D.Lgs/d. leg.	Decreto legislativo (Spanish legislative decree)
DM	Deutsche Mark (former German Currency)
DÖV	Die Öffentliche Verwaltung (journal)
Dr. soc.	Droit de sociétés (journal)
DRS	Deutsche Rechnungslegungsstandards (German Accounting Standards)
DRSC	Deutsches Rechnungslegungs Standards Committee e. V. (German Accounting Standards Committee)
DStR	Deutsches Steuerrecht (journal)
DTR	Disclosure and Transparency Rules (FSA Handbook)
Duke L. J.	Duke Law Journal (journal)
EAEC	European Atomic Energy Community
EAG	Europäische Atomgemeinschaft
EBA	European Banking Authority
EBK	Eidgenössische Bankenkommission (Swiss Federal Banking Commission)
EBLR	European Business Law Review (journal)
EBOR	European Business Organization Law Review (journal)
EC	European Community
EC Treaty	Treaty establishing the European Community
ECB	European Central Bank
ECFR	European Company and Financial Law Review (journal)
ECJ	European Court of Justice
ECL	European Company Law (journal)
ECMH	Efficient Capital Market Hypothesis
ECOFIN	Economic and Financial Affairs Council
ECR	European Court Reports
ECSC	European Coal and Steel Community

ECV	Emittenten-Compliance-Verordnung of 2007 (Austrian Issuer Compliance Regulation)
EEC	European Economic Community
EEC Treaty	Treaty establishing the European Economic Community
EFSF	European Financial Stability Facility
EFTA	European Free Trade Association
EHA	Ministerio de Economía y Hacienda (Spanish Ministry of Economy and Finance)
Eidg.	Eidgenössisch (Swiss federal)
Einl.	Einleitung (introduction)
EIOPA	European Insurance and Occupational Pensions Authority
EOB	execution-only-business
ERT	Europarättslig Tidskrift (journal)
ESC	European Securities Committee
ESCB	European System of Central Banks
ESFS	European System of Financial Supervisors
ESMA	European Securities and Markets Authority
ESMA Regulation	Regulation (EU) No. 1095/2010 of the European Parliament and of the Council of 24 November 2010 establishing a European Supervisory Authority (European Securities and Markets Authority), amending Decision No. 716/2009/EC and repealing Commission Decision 2009/77/EC)
ESME	European Securities Markets Expert Group
ESRB	European Systemic Risk Board
EU	European Union
EuR	Europarecht (journal)
EUV/EU-Vertrag	Vertrag über die Europäische Union (TEU)
EuZW	Europäische Zeitschrift für Wirtschaftsrecht (journal)
EWCA Crim	England and Wales Court of Appeal Criminal
EWS	Europäisches Wirtschafts- und Steuerrecht (journal)
f.	and the following page/article/section
ff.	and the following pages/articles/sections
FCA	Financial Conduct Authority
Feb.	February
FESCO	Forum of European Securities Commission
FFFS	Författningssamling (Official Journal of Swedish Regulations)
FG	Festgabe (German commemorative publication)
FI	Finansinspektionen (Swedish Financial Supervisory Authority)
Fin. Analysts J.	Financial Analysts Journal

FinAnV	Verordnung über die Analyse von Finanzinstrumenten (German Regulation on the Analysis of Financial Instruments)
FinDAG	Gesetz über die Bundesanstalt für Finanzdienstleistungsaufsicht (German Law on the Financial Services Supervisory Authority)
FMA	Finanzmarktaufsichtsbehörde (Austrian Financial Market Authority)
FMABG	Finanzmarktaufsichtsbehördengesetz (Austrian Financial Markets Supervisory Authorities Act)
FMG	Financial Markets Group
Fn.	Footnote
Frankfurter Kommentar zum WpÜG	Frankfurter Kommentar zum Wertpapiererwerbs- und Übernahmegesetz, see Haarmann/Schüppen, Frankfurter Kommentar zum Wertpapiererwerbs- und Übernahmegesetz (commentary)
FRUG	Finanzmarktrichtlinie-Umsetzungsgesetz (German Financial Market Directive Implementation Act)
FS	Festschrift (German commemorative publication)
FSA	Financial Services Authority
FSA Handbook	Handbook of Rules and Guidance
FSAP	Financial Services Action Plan
FSMA	Financial Services and Markets Act 2000
FSMT	Financial Services and Markets Tribunal
FTD	Financial Times Deutschland
FWB	Frankfurter Wertpapierbörse (Frankfurt Stock Exchange)
GBP	Pound sterling
GesRZ	Der Gesellschafter (journal)
GG	Grundgesetz (German Constitution)
GLJ	German Law Journal (journal)
GmbH	Gesellschaft mit beschränkter Haftung (German limited liability company)
GmbH & Co. KG	Gesellschaft mit beschränkter Haftung & Compagnie Kommanditgesellschaft (German Limited Partnership with a Limited Liability Company as General Partner)
GRC	Governance, Risk-Management und Compliance
GWR	Gesellschafts- und Wirtschaftsrecht (journal)
Hdb.	Handbuch (handbook)
HGB	Handelsgesetzbuch (German Commcercial Code)
HM Treasury	Her Majesty's Treasury
IAS	International Accounting Standards

ICCLR	International Company and Commercial Law Review (journal)
IFLR	International Financial Law Review (journal)
IFRS	International Financial Reporting Standards
IIMG	Inter-Institutional Monitoring Group
IKB	IKB Deutsche Industriebank AG
IMFS	Institute for Monetary and Financial Stability
Int'l J. Discl. & Gov.	International Journal of Disclosure and Governance
IOSCO	International Organization of Securities Commissions
IPO	Initial Public Offering
IT	Information Technology
Jan.	January
janv.	Janvier (French: January)
J. Acc., Aud. Finance	Journal of Accounting, Auditing and Finance
J. Acc. Econ.	Journal of Accounting and Economics
J. Acc. Res.	Journal of Accounting Research
JBFA	Journal of Business Finance & Accounting
J. Bus.	Journal of Business
J. Corp. Law	Journal of Corporation Law
J. Corp. L. Stud.	Journal of Corporate Law Studies
J. Exp. Psych., Hum. Perception & Performance	Journal of Experimental Psychology: Human Perception and Performance
J. Fin.	Journal of Finance
J. Fin. Econ.	Journal of Financial Economics
J. Fin. Quant. Analysis	Journal of Financial and Quantitative Analysis
J. Fin. Reg. & Comp.	Journal of Financial Regulation and Compliance
JIBFL	Journal of International Banking and Financial Law
JIBLR	Journal of International Banking Law and Regulation
J Int Bank Law	Journal of International Banking Law
J. Invest. Comp.	Journal of Investment Compliance
JLE	Journal of Law and Economics
JOA	Journal of Accountancy
J. Pol. Econ.	Journal of Political Economy
juill.	Juillet (French: July)
JuS	Juristische Schulung (journal)
JT	Juridisk Tidskrift vid Stockholms Universitet (journal)
JZ	Juristenzeitung (journal)
KapInHaG	Kapitalmarktinformationshaftungsgesetz (German Capital Markets Information Liability Act)
KapMuG	Gesetz über Musterverfahren in kapitalmarktrechtlichen Streitigkeiten (German Capital Markets Model Case Act)

KG	Kommanditgesellschaft (German limited partnership)
KMG	Kapitalmarktgesetz (Austrian Capital Market Act)
Kölner Kommentar zum AktG	Kölner Kommentar zum Aktiengesetz, see Zöllner/Noack, Kölner Kommentar zum Aktiengesetz (commentary)
Kölner Kommentar zum KapMuG	Kölner Kommentar zum KapMuG, see Hess/Reuschle/Rimmelspacher, Kölner Kommentar zum KapMuG (commentary)
Kölner Kommentar zum WpHG	Kölner Kommentar zum WpHG, see Hirte/Möllers, Kölner Kommentar zum WpHG (commentary)
Kölner Kommentar zum WpÜG	Kölner Kommentar zum Wertpapiererwerbs- und Übernahmegesetz, see Zöllner/Noack, Kölner Kommentar zum Wertpapiererwerbs- und Übernahmegesetz (commentary)
Kreditwesen	Zeitschrift für das gesamte Kreditwesen (journal)
KuMaKV	Verordnung zur Konkretisierung des Verbotes der Kurs- und Marktpreismanipulation (German Regulation for the Implementation of the Prohibition on Market and Price Manipulation)
KWG	Gesetz über das Kreditwesen (German Banking Act)
L. & Pol'y Int'l Bus.	Law and Policy in International Business (journal)
Law & Hum Beh.	Law and Human Behavior Law (journal)
Law & Soc'y Rev.	Law and Society Review (journal)
Lewis & Clark L. Rev.	Lewis & Clark Law Review (journal)
LG	Landgericht (German regional court)
LHF	Lag om handel med finansiella instrument (Swedish Act on Trading in Financial Instruments)
lit.	litera (letter)
Lit.	literature
LLP	Limited Liability Partnership
LMV	Ley del Mercado de Valores (Spanish Securities Market Act)
LR	Listing Rules
LSA	Ley de Sociedades Anónimas (Spanish Stock Corporation Act)
LSE	London Stock Exchange
LVM	Lag om värdepappersmarknaden (Swedish Securities Market Act)
MAD	Market Abuse Directive
MaComp	Mindestanforderungen an Compliance (BaFin's Minimum Requirements for Compliance)

MaKonV	Verordnung zur Konkretisierung des Verbotes der Marktmanipulation (German Implementing Regulation on the Prohibition of Market Manipulation)
MAR	Code of Market Conduct/ Market Abuse Regulation (FSA Handbook)
MaRisk	Mindestanforderungen an das Risikomanagement (German Minimum Requirements for Risk Management)
MDax	Mid-Cap-Deutscher Aktienindex (German Mid-cap Stock Index)
Mich. L. Rev.	Michigan Law Review (journal)
Mich. YBI Legal Stud.	Michigan Yearbook of International Legal Studies
MIF	Marchés d'Instruments Financiers (Markets in Financial Instruments)
MiFID	Markets in Financial Instruments Directive
MoU	Memoranda of Understanding
MTF	Multilateral Trading Facility
MTN	Medium Term Notes
Münchener Kommentar zum AktG	Münchener Kommentar zum Aktiengesetz, see Götte/ Habersack, Münchener Kommentar zum Aktiengesetz (commentary)
Münchener Kommentar zum HGB	Münchener Kommentar zum Handelsgesetzbuch, see Schmidt, Münchener Kommentar zum Handelsgesetzbuch (commentary)
MVSV	Mindestinhalts-, Veröffentlichungs- und Sprachenverordnung (Austrian Ordinance on Minimum Contents, Publication and Language)
M&A	Mergers and Acquisitions
n.	Numero (Spanish: number)
NASDAQ	National Association of Securities Dealers Automated Quotations
NBER	National Bureau of Economic Research
NJW	Neue Juristische Wochenschrift (journal)
Notre Dame L. Rev.	Notre Dame Law Review (journal)
Nov.	November
nov.	Novembre (French: November)
Nr./Nr	Nummer (German: number)
NV	naamloze vennootschap (Dutch limited liability company)
Nw. U. L. Rev.	Northwestern University Law Review (journal)
N.Y.L. Sch. L. Rev.	New York Law School Law Review (journal)
N.Y.U. L. Rev.	New York University Law Review (journal)
NYSE	New York Stock Exchange
NZG	Neue Zeitschrift für Gesellschaftsrecht (journal)

öAktG	österreichisches Aktiengesetz (Austrian Stock Corporation Act)
ÖBA	Zeitschrift für das gesamte Bank- und Börsenwesen (journal)
OGAW	Organismus für gemeinsame Anlagen in Wertpapieren (Undertakings for Collective Investment in Transferable Securities (UCITS))
OJ	Official Journal
Oct.	October
OLG	Oberlandesgericht (German higher regional court)
OMX	Aktiebolaget Optionsmäklarna (Swedish Stock Broker Association)
OPA	Oferta pública de adquisición/ Offre publique d'achat (public acquisition offer)
OPE	offre publique d'échange (public exchange offer)
OTC	Over-the-counter
OWiG	Gesetz über Ordnungswidrigkeiten (German Administrative Offences Act)
ÖZW	Österreichische Zeitschrift für Wirtschaftsrecht (journal)
öUWG	Unlauterer-Wettbewerbs-Gesetz (Austrian Act against Unfair Practices)
p.	page(s)
para.	paragraph(s)
PD	Prospectus Directive
PDG	Président-directeur général (Chief Executive Officer)
plc.	public liability company
PR	Prospectus Rules
PRIN	Principles for Businesses (FSA Handbook)
Prop.	Regeringens proposition (explanatory notes)
PS	Policy Statements
Q. J. Econ.	Quarterly Journal of Economics
RD	Real Decreto (Spanish: royal decree)
RDBF	Revue de droit bancaire et financier (journal)
RDBB	Revista de Derecho bancario y bursátil (journal)
RDC	Regulatory Decisions Committee
RdS	Revista de Derecho Social (journal)
RE	Regolamento Emittenti (Italian Issuers' Regulation)
Reg.	Regulation(s)
RegE	Regierungsentwurf (German government drafts of statutes)
Rev. Fin. Studies	Review of Financial Studies

Rev. soc.	Revue des sociétés (journal)
RG AMF	Règlement général Autorité des Marchés Financiers (General Regulations of the French Stock Market Authority)
RINGA	relevant information not generally available
RIS	Regulated Information Service
Riv. Dir. Civ.	Rivista di diritto civile (journal)
Riv. soc.	Rivista delle società (journal)
RIW	Recht der Internationalen Wirtschaft (journal)
RMV	Revista de derecho del mercado de valores (journal)
RNS	Regulatory News Service
RRM	Regolamento del Registro Mercantil (Spanish regulation on Company Registries)
RTDcom.	La Revue trimestrielle de droit commercial (journal)
RTDF	La Revue trimestrielle de droit financier (journal)
s.	sentence
SA	Société Anonyme (French stock corporation)
Sanct.	Sanction
SDAX	Small-Cap-Deutscher Aktienindex (small-cap German stock index)
SE	Societas Europaea
SEA	Securities Exchange Act
SEC	Securities and Exchange Commission
Sec./sec./sect.	section
SEK	Swedish Krona (Swedish Currency)
Sept.	September
SETS	Stock Exchange Electronic Trading Service
SFS	Svensk författningssamling (Swedish law gazette)
SI	Statutory Instruments
SIM	Società di Intermediazione Mobiliare
SME	Small and Medium Enterprises
SOU	Statens offentliga utredningar (Swedish government reports)
S.p.A.	Società per azioni (Italian stock corporation)
SSRN	Social Science Research Network
Stan. J. L. Bus. & Fin.	Stanford Journal of Law, Business and Finance
Stan. L. Rev.	Stanford Law Review
StGB	Strafgesetzbuch (German Criminal Code)
subsec.	subsection
SUP	Supervision
SvJT	Svensk Juristtidning (journal)

SYSC	Senior Management Arrangements, Systems and Controls (FSA Handbook)
SZW	Schweizerische Zeitschrift für Wirtschafts- und Finanzmarktrecht (journal)
TAR	The Accounting Review (journal)
TCI	The Children´s Investment Fund Management
T. corr.	Tribunal correctionnel (French criminal court)
TD	Transparency Directive
TEU	Treaty on European Union
TFEU	Treaty on the Functioning of the European Union
TecDAX	Technologie-Werte Deutscher Aktienindex (stock index for the technology sector)
TGI	Tribunal de grande instance (French regional court)
TOD	Takeover Directive
TUF	Testo Unico della Finanza (Italian Consolidated Laws on Finance)
TUG	Transparenzrichtlinien-Umsetzungsgesetz (German Implementing Act on the Transparency Directive)
ÜbG	Übernahmegesetz (Austrian Takeover Act)
U Chi. L. Rev.	University of Chicago Law Review (journal)
Pa. J. Bus. & Emp. L.	University of Pennsylvania Journal of Business and Employment Law
U. Pa. J. Bus. L.	University of Pennsylvania Journal of Business Law
U. Pa. L. Rev.	University of Pennsylvania Law Review
USD	US dollar
UCITS	Undertakings for Collective Investments in Transferable Securities
UWG	Unlauterer-Wettbewerbs-Gesetz (German Law against Unfair Competition)
v/v.	versus
Va. L. Rev.	Virginia Law Review (journal)
VAG	Versicherungsaufsichtsgesetz (German Law on Insurance Supervision)
VMV	Veröffentlichungs- und Meldeverordnung (Austrian Disclosure and Notification Regulation)
vol.	volume
VW	Volkswagen AG
WA	Wertpapieraufsicht (capital markets supervison)

WAG	Wertpapieraufsichtsgesetz (Austrian Securities Supervision Act)
Wash. U. L. Q.	Washington University Law Quarterly (journal)
WEP	West European Politics
wistra	Zeitschrift für Wirtschafts- und Steuerstrafrecht (journal)
WM	Wertpapier-Mitteilungen Zeitschrift für Wirtschafts- und Bankrecht (journal)
WpAIV	Verordnung zur Konkretisierung von Anzeige-, Mitteilungs- und Veröffentlichungspflichten sowie der Pflicht zur Führung von Insiderverzeichnissen nach dem Wertpapierhandelsgesetz (German Regulation on Disclosure of Securities Trading and Insider Dealings)
WpDVerOV	Verordnung zur Konkretisierung der Verhaltensregeln und Organisationsanforderungen für Wertpapierdienstleistungsunternehmen (German Regulation Implementing the Rules of Conduct and Organisational Requirements for Investment Service Companies)
WpHG	Gesetz über den Wertpapierhandel (German Securities Trading Act)
WpHG-E	Gesetzesentwurf zum WpHG (draft proposal for WpHG)
WpHMV	Verordnung über die Meldepflichten beim Handel mit Wertpapieren und Derivaten (German Regulation on the Notification Obligations when Trading with Securities and Derivatives)
WMF	WMF Württembergische Metallwarenfabrik AG
WpPG	Wertpapierprospektgesetz (German Securities Prospectus Act)
WpÜG	Wertpapiererwerbs- und –übernahmegesetz (German Securities Acquisition and Takeover Act)
WpÜG-Angebots-verordnung	Verordnung über den Inhalt der Angebotsunterlage, die Gegenleistung bei Übernahmeangeboten und Pflichtangeboten und die Befreiung von der Verpflichtung zur Veröffentlichung und zur Abgabe eines Angebots (German WpÜG Offer Ordinance)
XETRA	Exchange Electronic Trading
Yale Law J.	Yale Law Journal
Yale J. on Reg.	Yale Journal on Regulation
ZBB	Zeitschrift für Bankrecht und Bankwirtschaft (journal)
ZEuP	Zeitschrift für Europäisches Privatrecht (journal)
ZEuS	Zeitschrift für europarechtliche Studien (journal)

Zfbf	Schmalenbachs Zeitschrift für betriebswirtschaftliche Forschung (journal)
ZfV	Zeitschrift für Verwaltung (journal)
ZgesKredW	Zeitschrift für das gesamte Kreditwesen (journal)
ZGR	Zeitschrift für Unternehmens- und Gesellschaftsrecht (journal)
ZHR	Zeitschrift für das gesamte Handels- und Wirtschaftsrecht (journal)
ZInsO	Zeitschrift für das gesamte Insolvenzrecht (journal)
ZIP	Zeitschrift für Wirtschaftsrecht (journal)
ZJapanR	Zeitschrift für Japanisches Recht (journal)
ZPO	Zivilprozessordnung (German Civil Procedure Code)
ZRP	Zeitschrift für Rechtspolitik (journal)
ZSR	Zeitschrift für Schweizerisches Recht (journal)

1

Foundations of Capital Markets Legislature in Europe

§ 1 History

Bibliography
Armour, John and Ringe, Wolf-Georg, *European Company Law 1999-2010: Renaissance and Crisis*, 48 CMLRev. (2011), p. 125–174; Avgouleas, Emilios, *The Global Financial Crisis and the Disclosure Paradigm in European Financial Regulation: The Case for Reform*, 6 ECFR (2009), p. 440–475; Bréhier, Bertrand and Pailler, Pauline, *La régulation du marché des materières premières*, Bull. Joly Bourse (2012), p. 122–128; Commission, *The Development of a European Capital Market, Report of a Group of experts appointed by the EEC Commission* (Segré Report) (1966); Ferran, Eilis, *Building an EU Securities Market* (2004); Ferran, Eilis and Goodhart, Charles A.E., *Regulating Financial Services and Markets in the 21st Century* (2001); G30, *Financial Reform: A Framework for Financial Stability* (2009); Heinemann, Friedrich, *The Benefits of Creating an Integrated EU Market for Investment Funds*, 19 ZEW Economic Studies (2003), p. 89–93; Horn, Norbert, *Europäisches Finanzmarktrecht* (2003); Lannoo, Karel, *Emerging Framework for Disclosure in the EU*, 3 J. Corp. L. Stud. (2003), p. 329–358; Moloney, Niamh, *EC Securities Regulation*, 2nd ed. (2008), p. 11–26; Moloney, Niamh, *Confidence and Competence: The Conundrum of EC Capital Markets Law*, 4 J. Corp. L. Stud. (2004), p. 1–50; Papadopoulos, Thomas, *EU Law and the Harmonization of Takeovers in the Internal Market*, (2010); Rontchevsky, Nicolas, *L'harmonisation des sanctions pénales*, Bull. Joly Bourse (2012), p. 139–142; Sasso, Lorenzo and Kost de Sevres, Nicolette, *The New European Financial Markets Legal Framework: A Real Improvement? An Analysis of Financial Law and Governance in European Capital Markets from a Micro and Macro Economic Perspective*, 7 CMLJ (2012), p. 30–54; Segarkis, Konstantinos, *Le renforcement des pouvoirs des autorités compétentes*, Bull. Joly Bourse (2012), p. 118–121; Siems, Mathias M., *The Foundations of Securities Law*, EBLR (2009), p. 141–171; Veil, Rüdiger and Koch, Philipp, *Towards a Uniform European Capital Markets Law: Proposals of the Commission to Reform Market Abuse (2012)*, available at: http://ssrn.com/abstract=1998376; Veil, Rüdiger and Lerch, Marcus P., *Auf dem Weg zu einem Europäischen Finanzmarktrecht: die Vorschläge der Kommission zur Neuregelung der Märkte für Finanzinstrumente*, WM (2012), p. 1557–1565 (part I) and 1605–1613 (part II); Vitkova, Diana, *Level 3 of the Lamfalussy Process: An Effective Tool for Achieving Pan-European Regulatory Consistency*, 2 Law and Financial Markets Review (2008), p. 158–174; Willey, Stuart, *Market Abuse Update*, 93 C.O.B. (2012), p. 1–28.

I. Introduction

1   The former Treaty establishing the European Community did not contain any provisions regarding a European capital markets law. Nonetheless, the European Commission and the Council of the European Union soon claimed to be competent in the harmonisation of the national laws, seeking to fulfil the aim of an internal market. The legislative procedure took place in five phases[1] which shall be the focus of this book.

II. Segré Report (1966)

2   The development of a European capital markets law commenced in 1966, when a group of independent experts,[2] commissioned by the EEC Commission, published its report on a European capital market. The Committee was presided over by Claudio Segré and was supposed "to establish and specify what needs to be done to develop a European capital market, having regard ... to the aims of the Treaty of Rome".[3] The 350-page report, named after the committee's president, brought to light significant structural problems on the national capital markets and criticised the disequilibrium between availability of capital and demand as well as limited markets. It recommended a variety of measures as solutions to these problems. The report emphasised the importance of integrating the securities markets and harmonising the access to the European capital market.

3   The recommendations on "structure of equity markets"[4] and the "conditions for the development of a capital market integrated at European level"[5] occupied an important place in the report. It found clear words in stating that disclosure of information to the public would be one of the main aims.[6] An "information policy" would have to consider three aspects: firstly "campaigns to familiarize the public with security investment and stock-exchange machinery"; secondly "a permanent flow of information on the operations of companies in addition to the annual publication of their accounts"; and thirdly "especially comprehensive information whenever an appeal is made for the public's savings—that is, on the occasion of a security issue or the introduction of securities on a stock exchange".[7]

4   While the Segré Report further contained information regarding the current central aspect of legal enforcement, the Committee's recommendations on this point remained vague. The report regarded an external information control as necessary in order to enforce observation of certain "minimum requirements concerning the

---

[1] N. Moloney, *EC Securities Regulation*, p. 11, distinguishes between four phases in the European capital markets legislation.
[2] The members of the group were A. Batenburg, J.D. Blondeel, G. Della Porta, A. Ferrari, R. Franck, L. Gleske, J. Guyot, A. Lamfalussy, H. Möller, G. Plescoff, C. Segré and P. Tabatoni.
[3] Commission, Segré Report, p. 11.
[4] Ibid., p. 203 ff.
[5] Ibid., p. 238–239.
[6] Ibid., p. 237.
[7] Ibid., p. 238.

scope and quality of information",[8] for example. It then, however, went no further than to demand that the systems for external information control be developed and harmonised. So far information control had been exercised by the banks and stock exchange supervisory authorities in all Member States and in some EEC countries by independent administrative bodies. The Committee did at least formulate the solution of "an agency at Community level, to be competent for issues floated within the territory of the Community and to be endowed with powers similar to those of the Securities and Exchange Commission in the United States, the Banking Commission in Belgium or the Bank Control Commissariat in Luxembourg".[9] However, it would take fifty years for this aim to be accomplished.

III. Phase 1: Coordination of Stock Exchange and Prospectus Laws (1979–1982)

5   The Segré Report contained detailed suggestions on the introduction of securities on the national stock markets and their trading.[10] It even presented a model prospectus adapted to the specific circumstances of different categories of securities and issuers.[11] In view of this, it is not surprising that the first legislative measures concerned the law on stock exchanges and prospectuses. However, it took thirteen years before the first laws were enacted.

6   Directive 79/279/EEC[12] on securities admitted to official stock exchange listing, Directive 80/390/EEC[13] on the requirements for the drawing up, scrutiny and distribution of the listing, and Directive 82/121/EEC[14] on information to be published were the first steps the Council took on the way to a harmonisation of the Member States' statutory provisions. All three directives were based on the Treaty establishing the European Economic Community, especially Article 54(3)(g) and Article 100.[15] Their aim was to eliminate the considerable differences in the Member States' provisions.[16] However, this was hoped to be achieved through the concept of minimum harmonisation: "These differences should be eliminated by coordinating the rules and regulations without necessarily making them completely uniform, in order to achieve an adequate degree of equivalence in the safeguards required in

---

[8] Ibid., p. 238.

[9] Ibid., p. 235.

[10] Ibid., p. 250–251.

[11] Ibid., p. 238, 252 ff.

[12] Council Directive 79/279/EEC of 5 March 1979 coordinating the conditions for the admission of securities to official stock exchange listing, OJ L066, 16 March 1979, p. 21–32.

[13] Council Directive 80/390/EEC of 17 March 1980 coordinating the requirements for the drawing up, scrutiny and distribution of the listing particulars to be published for the admission of securities to official stock exchange listing, OJ L100, 17 April 1980, p. 1–26.

[14] Council Directive 82/121/EEC of 15 February 1982 on information to be published on a regular basis by companies the shares of which have been admitted to official stock exchange listing, OJ L048, 20 February 1982, p. 26–29.

[15] On the legal basis for capital markets law in the former European Community (EC) and today's European Union (EU), cf. § 3 para. 4–10.

[16] Cf. S. Heinze, *Europäisches Kapitalmarktrecht*, p. 19–20.

each Member State to ensure the provision of information which is sufficient and as objective as possible for actual or potential security holders."[17]

IV. White Paper on Completing the Internal Market (1985)

7   In 1985 the White Paper from the Commission to the European Council on "Completing the Internal Market" was published. It can be seen as the next key moment in the development of a European capital markets law.[18] According to the Commission, the liberalisation of financial services represented a major step towards Community financial integration and the widening of the Internal Market.[19] The liberalisation of capital movements in the Community was also regarded as of utmost importance.[20]

8   Whilst the Commission only cited the UCITS Directive 85/611/EEC,[21] which became effective a few months later, but no other specific future legislative measures, it did, however, unequivocally highlight the parameters which, in its opinion, were relevant for the further legislation on capital markets law in Europe. The Commission pointed out, for example, that the supervision of ongoing activities of financial institutions should be guided by the principle of "home country control"[22] and that the barriers between stock exchanges needed to be lifted in order to increase the stock exchanges' liquidity.[23]

V. Phase 2: Harmonisation of the Laws on Securities Markets (1988–1993)

9   A few years later the harmonisation of the laws on securities markets began with the enactment of Directive 88/627/EEC[24] on transparency. On the basis of the former Article 54 EC Treaty it was the Council's reaction to the deficiencies in the national provisions. The directive was enacted in the belief that a policy of adequate information for investors in the field of transferrable securities is likely to improve investor protection, to increase investors' confidence in securities markets and thus to ensure that securities markets function correctly. A coordination at Community level was supposed to equalise investor protection, thus enabling a greater interpenetration

---

[17] Cf. Recitals of the Directive 80/390/EEC.

[18] Completing the Internal Market: White Paper from the Commission to the European Council (Milan, 28–29 June 1985) COM(85) 310 final, 14 June 1985.

[19] Ibid., para. 101.

[20] Ibid., para. 124.

[21] Council Directive 85/611/EEC of 20 December 1985 on the coordination of laws, regulations and administrative provisions relating to undertakings for collective investment in transferrable securities (UCITS), OJ L375, 31 December 1985, p. 3–18.

[22] Completing the Internal Market: White Paper from the Commission to the European Council (Milan, 28–29 June 1985) COM(85) 310 final, 14 June 1985, para. 103.

[23] Ibid., para. 107.

[24] Council Directive 88/627/EEC of 12 December 1988 on the information to be published when a major holding in a listed company is acquired or disposed of, OJ L348, 17 December 1988, p. 62–65.

Rüdiger Veil

of the Member States' transferrable securities markets, helping to establish a true European capital market.

10   Directive 89/298/EEC[25] on issue prospectuses, which was enacted a few months later on the same legal basis, was to contribute to the "Community information policy relating to transferrable securities"[26] for investors. The directive instructed that a prospectus containing information of this nature must be made available to investors when transferrable securities are offered to the public for the first time in a Member State, regardless of whether or not they are to be subsequently listed.[27]

11   Directive 89/592/EEC[28] on insider dealing was based on Article 100a of the former Treaty establishing the European Economic Community. It was related to the secondary market for securities and ordered the Member States to introduce provisions prohibiting insider dealings as these are likely to undermine the investors' confidence and may therefore prejudice the smooth operation of the market. The directive contained no regulations as to how compliance with these rules should be supervised. Also, the rights conferred on the competent national authorities were only outlined. The directive only stated that "the competent authorities must be given all supervisory and investigatory powers that are necessary for the exercise of their functions, where appropriate in collaboration with other authorities".[29]

12   The developments in this field ended temporarily with the enactment of Directive 93/22/EEC[30] on investment services in the securities field. This directive was regarded by the Council of the European Communities as an essential instrument to achieving the aim of completing the Internal Market as described in the Commission's 1986 White Paper. The directive was to ensure the freedom of establishment and the free movement of services regarding investment firms. One of its main aims was investor protection. It demanded the introduction of "prudential rules" on records to be kept of transactions executed and the companies' organisation (Article 10) alongside the enactment of provisions obliging investment firms to inform clients (Article 11).

VI.   Financial Services Action Plan (1999)

13   The next incentive for the development of a European capital markets law was the Commission's presentation of a Financial Services Action Plan (FSAP) in 1999.[31]

---

[25] Council Directive 89/298/EEC of 17 April 1989 coordinating the requirements for the drawing up, scrutiny and distribution of the prospectus to be published when transferrable securities are offered to the public, OJ L124, 5 May 1989, p. 8–15.

[26] Cf. Recitals of the Directive 89/298/EEC.

[27] Directive 80/390/EEC only coordinated the information to be published for the admission of securities to official stock exchange listing.

[28] Council Directive 89/592/EEC of 13 November 1989 coordinating regulations on insider dealing, OJ L334, 18 November 1989, p. 30–32; concerning its history, cf. V. Edwards, *EC Company Law*, p. 309 ff.

[29] Cf. Art. 8(2) Dir. 89/592/EEC.

[30] Council Directive 93/22/EEC of 10 May 1993 on investment services in the securities field, OJ L141, 11 June 1993, p. 27–46.

[31] Communication from the Commission of 11 May 1999 entitled "Implementing the Framework for Financial Markets: Action Plan", COM(1999) 232 final (hereafter FSAP); cf. also N. Moloney, *EC Securities Regulation*, p. 15.

The Commission aimed to use the introduction of the euro in order to supply the European Community with a modern financial system.[32] This system was intended to reduce the costs of capital and intermediation.

14 The FSAP emphasised various priorities of a standardised Europe-wide financial market. These included joint provisions for integrated markets for securities and derivative instruments as well as for an EU-wide raising of capital. Several measures of varying priority were to achieve these aims. Some referred to existing directives—such as Directive 79/279/EEC on securities admitted to official stock exchange listing, Directive 80/390/EEC on the requirements for the drawing up, scrutiny and distribution of the listing, and Directive 82/121/EEC on Regular Reporting—and were to amend these.[33] Additionally, new directives were to be adopted, addressing, for example, market manipulation.[34]

15 Ultimately, in order to be able to keep up with the rapid development of the capital markets and implement new regulations quickly, the FSAP recommended the introduction of suitable mechanisms.[35] Above all, the FSAP imagined this could consist of the introduction of a securities committee, which should participate in the development of European provisions on securities.[36]

VII. Lamfalussy Report (2000)

16 Only a year later the Economic and Financial Affairs Council (ECOFIN) appointed a committee chaired by Alexandre Lamfalussy.[37] The committee was to evaluate the developments of the European capital market and devise a new legislative procedure in order to guarantee a more rapid implementation of new regulative proposals regarding the law of securities and their uniform application through national authorities. Furthermore, the committee was to determine the key priorities for further legislation.

17 On 9 November 2000 the committee published its initial report.[38] This interim report made the following criticisms: the "EU passport for issuers" was still not a reality; rules on disclosure differed greatly between Member States; and there was no agreed definition of market manipulation.[39] In order to eliminate these deficiencies the Committee suggested that the transposition of the key priorities of the FSAP should be completed by 2003, rather than by the initial completion date in 2005.[40] The Committee regarded the biggest problems in developing a European capital markets law as lying in the fact that the process of adopting legislation was too slow and the interpretation and application of provisions differed strongly between

---

[32] FSAP, p. 3.
[33] Cf. FSAP, p. 22.
[34] Cf. FSAP, p. 23.
[35] FSAP, p. 16 ff.
[36] FSAP, p. 30.
[37] Further members were C. Herkströter, L.A. Rojo, B. Ryden, L. Spaventa, N. Walter and N. Wicks.
[38] The Committee of Wise Men, *Initial Report of the Committee of Wise Men on the Regulation of European Securities Markets* (2000).
[39] Ibid., p. 16.
[40] Ibid., p. 22 ff.

Rüdiger Veil

the Member States.[41] The committee recommended that these problems should be eliminated on four levels, orientating themselves on the comitology procedure and taking into account the conceptual ideas described in the FSAP.[42]

18 On 15 February 2001 the Committee published its final report.[43] It recommended a procedure on four levels, as had been outlined in the initial report in order to help accelerate the legislative process for the securities markets.[44] The details of this process, named the Lamfalussy process after the chair of the Committee, are described in the section on the regulation of capital markets.[45] A short description of the different levels has to suffice here. The first level is where the so-called framework directives are developed. On the second level the Commission enacts technical implementing measures for the framework directives. On this level, a special Committee of European Securities Regulators (CESR) was created—in accordance with the recommendations of the Lamfalussy Group. It had advisory functions in the legislative process where the Commission adopted technical implementing measures for the framework directives. Furthermore, it was the CESR's responsibility to improve the cooperation between the national supervisory authorities, to solve disputes between them and to evaluate the implementation of European law.

VIII. Phase 3: Reorganisation of the Laws on Prospectuses and Securities (2003–2007)

19 The three directives enacted between 1979 and 1982 and Directive 88/627/EEC were repeatedly subject to considerable amendments after their enactment. The European legislature therefore decided in 2001 to combine and newly codify the directives for reasons of clarity and efficiency. This resulted in Directive EC/2001/34[46] of 28 May 2001 on the admission of securities to official stock exchange listing and on information to be published on those securities. However, no relevant changes to the law were made by this directive.

20 In November 2002 British economists and auditors published a report, assigned to them by the European Commission. It provided economic proof[47] of the FSAP's legal understanding that the achievement of a European internal market would significantly reduce financing costs, thus paving the way for future developments. The measures announced by the FSAP for the implementation of a European internal market began in 2003. Their implementation continued until 2007. During the first two years four framework directives were developed which today are the core of European capital markets law: the Market Abuse Directive (MAD, 2003), the

---

[41] Ibid., p. 18 ff.

[42] Ibid., p. 24 ff.

[43] The Committee of Wise Men, *Final Report of the Committee of Wise Men on the Regulation of European Securities Markets* (2001).

[44] Final Report, p. 27 ff.

[45] Cf. § 4 para. 8–37.

[46] Directive 2001/34/EC of the European Parliament and of the Council of 28 May 2001 on the admission of securities to official stock exchange listing and on information to be published on those securities, OJ L184, 6 July 2001, p. 1–66.

[47] Cf. L. Burn in R. Panasar and P. Boeckman, *European Securities Law*, para. 108.

Prospectus Directive (PD, 2003), the Markets in Financial Instruments Directive (MiFID, 2004) and the Transparency Directive (TD, 2004). By 2007 so-called implementing measures, mainly directives, but partly regulations, had been enacted to all of these directives. These implementing measures followed the proceedings of Level 2 of the Lamfalussy process.

21 The first directive to be enacted was the MAD.[48] It was the European legislator's reaction to the fact that the Member States' legal framework regarding the protection of market integrity was incomplete at this time. Legal requirements varied from one Member State to another, often leaving economic actors uncertain over concepts, definitions and enforcement. The MAD was further intended to fill loopholes in Community legislation which could be used for wrongful conduct and which would have undermined public confidence and prejudiced the smooth functioning of the markets.[49] In some Member States there was no legislation addressing the issues of price manipulation and the dissemination of misleading information.[50]

22 The MAD was the first directive to contain provisions on market manipulation. It further requested the Member States to forbid insider dealings. These provisions were far more detailed than those of the former Directive 89/592/EEC on insider dealing. The reform of the rules on ad hoc disclosure obligations were a further important step. [51] These obligations were not restricted to insider *facts*, but rather covered all inside *information*, i.e. also a prognosis on possible future facts. In other words disclosure of information now had to take place sooner; a deliberate step by the legislature in order to prevent the abuse of insider knowledge.[52] Additionally, the directive introduced a compulsory disclosure of directors' dealings, which likewise intended to prevent the abuse of inside information and market manipulation. Furthermore, the MAD was the first directive to provide prudential rules for financial analysts. Last but not least, the directive attended to the topic of supervision. The Member States were called upon to designate one single competent authority responsible for supervising compliance with the provisions adopted pursuant to the MAD, as well as international collaboration. The authority was to be of an administrative nature, guaranteeing its independence of economic actors and avoiding conflicts of interest.[53] The directive further requested a common minimum set of effective tools and powers for the competent authority of each Member State in order to guarantee supervisory effectiveness.[54]

23 Many of the Directives' provisions were in need of concretisation. Thus, in order to provide the necessary legal certainty and guarantee a uniform application, the European Commission enacted various implementing measures, after a consulta-

---

[48] Directive 2003/6/EC of the European Parliament and of the Council of 28 January 2003 on insider dealing and market manipulation (Market Abuse), OJ L096, 12 April 2003, p. 16–25.

[49] Recitals 11, 13 MAD.

[50] Cf. Recital 11 MAD.

[51] The former directives 79/279/EEC and 2001/34/EC confined themselves to dictating the obligation to publish new facts which would be likely to have a significant effect on the prices of financial instruments.

[52] Cf. N. Horn, *Europäisches Finanzmarktrecht*, p. 47.

[53] Recital 36 MAD.

[54] Recital 37 MAD.

tion with the CESR: Directive 2003/124/EC[55] on definitions, Directive 2003/125/EC[56] on investment recommendations and the disclosure of conflicts of interest, and Directive 2004/72/EC[57] with further specifications on insider legislation. Finally, the Commission enacted Regulation (EC) No. 2273/2003[58] on exemptions for buy-back programmes and stabilisation of financial instruments.

24 A further landmark in the European capital market legislation was the PD 2003/71/EC[59] from 2003. The Directive coordinates the requirements for the drawing up, scrutiny and distribution of the prospectus to be published for the admission of securities for offers to the public or the trading on regulated markets. The aim of the Directive was once more to ensure investor protection and market efficiency.[60] The European Commission enacted further implementing measures to this directive: Prospectus Regulation (EC) No. 809/2004[61] contains details regarding the content of the prospectus and is directly applicable in the Member States. [62]

25 The third framework directive to be enacted was the Directive 2004/39/EC[63] on markets in financial instruments (MiFID) from 2004. It mainly covered aspects of market organisation and prudential rules for investment firms and—as the directives before it—also required implementing measures. These were defined in Implementing Directive 2006/73[64] as the organisational requirements and operating conditions for investment firms. Additionally, Regulation (EC) No. 1287/2006[65] lays down provisions on record-keeping obligations for investment firms and the admission of financial instruments to trading.

[55] Commission Directive 2003/124/EC of 22 December 2003 implementing Directive 2003/6/EC of the European Parliament and of the Council as regards the definition and public disclosure of inside information and the definition of market manipulation, OJ L339, 24 December 2003, p. 70–72.

[56] Commission Directive 2003/125/EC of 22 December 2003 implementing Directive 2003/6/EC of the European Parliament and of the Council as regards the fair presentation of investment recommendations and the disclosure of conflicts of interest, OJ L339, 24 December 2003, p. 73–77.

[57] Commission Directive 2004/72/EC of 29 April 2004 implementing Directive 2003/6/EC of the European Parliament and of the Council as regards accepted market practices, the definition of inside information in relation to derivatives on commodities, the drawing up of lists of insiders, the notification of managers' transactions and the notification of suspicious transactions, OJ L162, 30 April 2004, p. 70–75.

[58] Commission Regulation (EC) No. 2273/2003 of 22 December 2003 implementing Directive 2003/6/EC of the European Parliament and of the Council as regards exemptions for buy-back programmes and stabilisation of financial instruments, OJ L336, 23 December 2003, p. 33–38.

[59] Directive 2003/71/EC of the European Parliament and of the Council of 4 November 2003 on the prospectus to be published when securities are offered to the public or admitted to trading and amending Directive 2001/34/EC, OJ L345, 31 December 2003, p. 64–89.

[60] Recital 10 PD.

[61] Commission Regulation (EC) No. 809/2004 of 29 April 2004 implementing Directive 2003/71/EC of the European Parliament and of the Council as regards information contained in prospectuses as well as the format, incorporation by reference and publication of such prospectuses and dissemination of advertisements, OJ L149, 30 April 2004, p. 3–143.

[62] To the legal effects of regulations cf. § 3 para. 13.

[63] Directive 2004/39/EC of the European Parliament and of the Council of 21 April 2004 on markets in financial instruments amending Council Directives 85/611/EEC and 93/6/EEC and Directive 2000/12/EC of the European Parliament and of the Council and repealing Council Directive 93/22/EEC, OJ L145, 30 April 2004, p. 1–44.

[64] Commission Directive 2006/73/EC of 10 August 2006 implementing Directive 2004/39/EC of the European Parliament and of the Council as regards organisational requirements and operating conditions for investment firms and defined terms for the purposes of that Directive, OJ L241, 2 September 2006, p. 26–58.

[65] Commission Regulation (EC) No. 1287/2006 of 10 August 2006 implementing Directive 2004/39/EC of the European Parliament and of the Council as regards recordkeeping obligations for investment firms, transaction reporting, market transparency, admission of financial instruments to trading, and defined terms for the purposes of that Directive, OJ L241, 2 September 2006, p. 1–25.

26   The fourth framework directive is the TD from 2004.[66] It concerns the harmonisation of transparency requirements in relation to information about issuers whose securities are admitted to trading on a regulated market. The legislator believed that the accurate, comprehensive and timely disclosure of information about security issuers builds sustained investor confidence and allows an informed assessment of their business performance and assets, thus enhancing both investor protection and market efficiency.[67]

27   The directive begins by giving detailed provisions on the "regular flow of information" in the shape of annual financial reports, half-yearly financial reports and interim management statement. It continues with the "ongoing information". This is defined as information about major holdings and the information for holders of securities admitted to trading on a regulated market. In order to guarantee the uniform application of the TD's provisions, the European Commission enacted a directive with implementing measures, all of which concern procedural issues.[68]

IX.   Continuation of Phase 3: Harmonisation of the Right to Take Over (2004)

28   In the 1980s legislative attempts to regulate takeovers at a European level became apparent. A proposal for a 13th directive on takeover bids presented by the Commission in 1989, however, did not find the approval of the Member States, due to differences in their interests and views on regulatory possibilities. In 1997 the Commission presented an amended proposal. This took into account the dissenting opinions and enabled the Council to adopt a common position on 19 July 2000. The European Parliament, however, raised objections, resulting in the involvement of the Conciliation Committee. On 5 July 2001 it presented a common draft which, however, did not win the recognition of the Parliament. A new proposal for a directive, presented in October 2002, once again threatened to fail due to the opposing views on regulatory possibilities in some Member States. However, a compromise presented by Portugal enabled a political agreement, which led to the adoption of the Takeover Directive (TOD)[69] on 30 April 2004.

29   The Directive has a number of aims. The first is to coordinate certain safeguards in the interests of members and others.[70] On the one hand, the directive can therefore be classed as a set of rules subject to company law. On the other hand, however, the directive also contains aspects of capital markets law. The offeror's obligation to announce his decision to launch a bid, for example, is supposed to reduce the pos-

---

[66] Directive 2004/109/EC of the European Parliament and of the Council of 15 December 2004 on the harmonisation of transparency requirements in relation to information about issuers whose securities are admitted to trading on a regulated market and amending Directive 2001/34/EC, OJ L390, 31 December 2004, p. 38–57.

[67] Recital 1 Directive 2004/109/EC.

[68] Commission Directive 2007/14/EC of 8 March 2007 laying down detailed rules for the implementation of certain provisions of Directive 2004/109/EC on the harmonisation of transparency requirements in relation to information about issuers whose securities are admitted to trading on a regulated market.

[69] Directive 2004/25/EC of the European Parliament and of the Council of 21 April 2004 on takeover bids, OJ L142, 30 April 2004, p. 12–23.

[70] Cf. Recital 1 TOD.

sibilities of insider dealings.[71] The offeror's obligation to submit an offer document is also part of capital markets law. The same must be said of the mandatory bid in cases of a change of control of the company.[72]

X. White Paper on Financial Services Policy (2005)

30 The reorganisation of the laws on prospectuses and securities and the enactment of the Takeover Directive meant that the European legislature had fulfilled the obligations put out by the FSAP. In its Green Paper on Financial Services Policy 2005–2010[73] the Commission could therefore restrict itself to recapitulating its achievements. For future legislation it recommended an attempt at "better regulation"[74]. It was the Commission's opinion that the whole process of law making and application had to be transparent, based on an impact assessment aimed at showing the economic benefits of the proposed measures. The legislative procedure was to take place with the participation of all affected groups.[75]

31 In the White Paper published a few months later, the Commission picked up on this approach and underlined the fact that in the future it would act in accordance with the principle of "better regulation". The continual assessment and evaluation of all new legislative measures was regarded an elemental component thereof.[76] Additionally, the Commission announced its plan to try and ensure a transposition of the directives by the Member States within the agreed deadlines.[77] International supervisory structures played a central role in the White Paper. The Commission planned to further harmonise the supervisory standards and practices. The development of a common European supervisory practice was to be facilitated through an informal cooperation of the national supervisory authorities, e.g. through joint inspections or staff exchanges.[78]

32 The Commission explicitly did not plan new provisions regarding rating agencies, financial analysts, Level 2 measures for the Takeover Bids Directive on requirements in the offer document. and capital requirements for regulated markets.[79] However, shortly afterwards the financial crisis required a change of thinking.

---

[71] Cf. Recital 12 TOD.

[72] Recital 9 of the Takeover Directive appears to convey that the European legislator understood the mandatory bid as a safeguard under company law. However, this does not prevent from classifying the national provisions on mandatory bids as part of capital market law. Cf. § 24 para. 37.

[73] Commission, Green Paper on Financial Services policy (2005–2010), 3 May 2005, COM(2005) 177 final.

[74] Ibid., p. 5; also N. Moloney, *EC Securities Regulation*, p. 47 ff.

[75] Commission, Green Paper on Financial Services Policy (2005–2010), 3 May 2005, COM(2005) 177 final, p. 5, 8 f., 21 ff.

[76] Commission, White Paper on Financial Services Policy (2005–2010), 1 December 2005, COM(2005) 629 final, p. 5 ff.

[77] Ibid., p. 6–7.

[78] Ibid., p. 12.

[79] Ibid., p. 14.

XI. The de Larosière Report (2009)

33   The financial crisis revealed serious deficiencies of global financial markets law. In Europe, regulatory deficiencies and deficiencies in the implementation of existing provisions became apparent.[80] In October 2008 the European Commission therefore instructed a group of outstanding experts to submit recommendations on the future regulation and supervision of the European capital markets. On 29 February 2009 this group, chaired by Jacques de Larosière,[81] published a report of close to 100 pages.[82]

34   Most of their recommendations, such as those for the reinforcement of financial stability on a global level, refer to topics that are not covered by this book. However, group's recommendations for a European financial supervisory system are of special interest for the securities markets. The group suggested promoting the previous Level 3 committees of the Lamfalussy process, especially the CESR, to public authorities.[83] The existing national supervisory authorities were to continue the current supervision, keeping most of their powers, while the European authorities would coordinate the application of high uniform supervisory standards and guarantee intensive cooperation with the other supervisory authorities.

XII. Phase 4: Towards a European Supervision (since 2009)

35   On 23 September 2009 the Commission communicated a comprehensive bundle of legislative measures on the basis of the de Larosière Report. It contained measures for recognising and preventing systematic risks for Europe's entire financial system ("macro-prudential supervision") as well as measures to improve the supervision of individual financial service providers and capital market participants ("micro-prudential supervision").[84] The latter was intended to create a European System of Financial Supervisors (ESFS), consisting of three European authorities with legal personality.[85]

36   These plans were accomplished in 2010, when the European Banking Authority (EBA), the European Insurance and Occupational Pensions Authority (EIOPA) and the European Securities and Markets Authority (ESMA) were established.[86] Since 1 January 2011 the ESMA has participated in the legislative procedures and is responsible for supervising the securities markets together with the national authorities.

---

[80] The legislative response to the financial crisis in the USA is the Dodd–Frank Wall Street Reform and Consumer Protection Act; on this reform cf. D. Skeel, *The New Financial Deal. Understanding the Dodd–Frank Act and its (Unintended) Consequences* (2011).

[81] Further members of the group were L. Balcerowicz, O. Issing, R. Masera, C. Mc Carthy, L. Nyberg, J. Pérez und O. Ruding.

[82] Cf. de Larosière, *The High-Level Group on Financial Supervision in the EU*, Report (2009).

[83] Cf. Ibid., p. 53.

[84] Cf. Communication from the Commission on European financial supervision, 27 May 2009, COM(2009) 252 final.

[85] COM(2009) 503 final, Art. 3(1).

[86] See in more detail § 11 para. 37–78.

Rüdiger Veil

XIII. Phase 5: Regulation of Credit Rating Agencies (2009–2012)

37   Phase 5 partly coincides with phase 4 of the legislative procedure beginning with the plan to introduce regulation for credit rating agencies. The European Commission first addressed this question in April 2002. In April 2006 it reached the conclusion that no legislative initiatives were needed.[87] It was suggested by the International Organization of Securities Commissions (IOSCO) that rating agencies should regulate themselves—and by many this was regarded as sufficient. The European Commission supported this understanding. It was only the outbreak of the financial crisis that lead to a change of thinking as people realised that the credit rating agencies were partly to blame for the incorrect evaluation of credit risks. Due to their important role on global securities and banking markets, the European legislature now wanted to ensure that credit rating activities were conducted in accordance with the principles of integrity, transparency, responsibility and good governance in order to ensure that resulting credit ratings used in the Community are independent, objective and of adequate quality.[88]

38   On 16 September 2009 the European Parliament and the Council enacted Regulation (EC) No. 1060/2009 on credit rating agencies.[89] It mainly contains prudential rules for ratings and subjects the credit rating agencies to supervision. In June 2010, in the course of its plans for preventing a future financial crisis and strengthening the financial system, the European Commission presented amendments to the Regulation. These aimed at attaining a more effective and centralised supervision of the agencies at a European level by the ESMA and more transparency regarding issuers. The European Parliament adopted the Commission`s proposal on 15 December 2010.[90] In November 2011 the Commission presented a further amendment to the regulation, introducing a civil liability for incorrect credit ratings and stricter disclosure obligations for rating agencies.[91]

XIV. Continuation of Phase 5: Revision of the Framework Directives (since 2009)

39   Only a few years after the enactment of the four framework directives the European Commission initiated several consultations in order to assess the implementation of the directives and find possibilities of simplifying and improving them.[92] These consultations were addressed to all financial market participants as well as the gov-

---

[87] Cf. Communication from the Commission on Credit Rating Agencies, 11 March 2006 (2006/C 59/02).

[88] Cf. Recital 1 Regulation (EC) No. 1060/2009 of the European Parliament and of the Council of 16 September 2009 on credit rating agencies.

[89] Regulation (EC) No. 1060/2009 of the European Parliament and of the Council of 16 September 2009 on credit rating agencies, OJ L302, 17 November 2009.

[90] Regulation (EU) No. 513/2011 of the European Parliament and of the Council of 11 May 2011 amending Regulation (EC) No. 1060/2009 on credit rating agencies, OJ L145, 31 May 2011, p. 30–56.

[91] Commission, Proposal for a Regulation of the European Parliament and of the Council amending Regulation (EC) No. 1060/2009 on credit rating agencies, COM(2011) 742/2.

[92] For an overview of the various activities see the "news" on the Commission's website, http://ec.europa.eu/internal_market/securities/news_en.htm.

ernments and supervisory authorities in the Member States and other interested persons. The main aspects were regulatory deficiencies and the investigative and sanctioning powers of the supervisory authorities which continued to differ greatly between the Member States. The consultations were preceded by talks between the Commission and the CESR as well as the Commission and the European Securities Markets Expert Group (ESME). Both the CESR and the Expert Group published statements on some of the topics.

40   The consultations soon led to first results: In 2010 the European Parliament and the Council of the European Union enacted Directive 2010/73/EU on amendments to the PD and the TD, based on the Commission's proposal.[93] According to the Commission's proposal the main aim of the amendments is to improve investor protection. The Member States had to implement the directive by July 2012.

41   More recently the Commission presented a proposal with extensive alterations to the regulatory approach to market abuse, particularly with regard to the impact of administrative and criminal sanctions. The existing MAD 2003/6/EC is to be replaced by the Regulation on insider dealing and market manipulation (market abuse)[94] and the Directive on criminal sanctions for insider dealing and market manipulation.[95,96] The Commission hopes the new approach will "send a message to the public and potential offenders that these [manipulative behaviours] are taken very seriously".[97] Even if the proposal is accepted by the Parliament and the Council, it will not enter into force before 2015.

42   A second proposal,[98] submitted only five days later, concerns the TD, which aims to reduce the administrative burden for small and medium-sized issuers and to harmonise the regime for notification of major holdings. As with regard to market abuse the Commission further wants to introduce stricter sanctions, such as obligatory rules on naming and shaming, harsh administrative pecuniary sanctions and a loss of voting rights.[99] Due to the necessary implementation of the directive in the Member States actual changes to the legal situation are not to be expected before 2014.

[93] Directive 2010/73/EU of the European Parliament and of the Council of 24 November 2010 amending Directives 2003/71/EC on the prospectus to be published when securities are offered to the public or admitted to trading and 2004/109/EC on the harmonisation of transparency requirements in relation to information about issuers whose securities are admitted to trading on a regulated market, OJ L327, 11 December 2010, p. 1.
[94] Proposal for a Regulation of the European Parliament and of the Council on Insider Dealing and Market Manipulation (Market Abuse) of 20 October 2011, COM(2011) 651 final.
[95] Proposal for a Directive of the European Parliament and of the Council on Criminal Sanctions for Insider Dealing and Market Manipulation of 20 October 2011, COM(2011) 654 final.
[96] For further information see Commission, Commission Staff Working Paper Impact Assessment, 20 October 2011, SEC(2011) 1217 final; N. Rontchevsky, Bull. Joly Bourse (2012), p. 139–142; K. Segarkis, Bull. Joly Bourse (2012), p. 118–121; R. Veil and P. Koch, *Towards a Uniform European Capital Markets Law: Proposals of the Commission to Reform Market Abuse* (2012); S. Willey, 93 COB (2010), p. 1, 7–15.
[97] Recital 6 Proposal for a Directive of the European Parliament and of the Council on Criminal Sanctions for Insider Dealing and Market Manipulation of 20 October 2011, COM(2011) 654 final.
[98] Proposal for a Directive of the European Parliament and of the Council amending Directive 2004/109/EC on the harmonization of transparency requirements in relation to information about issuers whose securities are admitted to trading on a regulated market and Commission Directive 2007/14/EC, 25 October 2011, COM(2011) 683/2.
[99] For further information see Commission, Commission Staff Working Paper Impact Assessment, 25 October 2011, SEC(2011) 1279 final.

Rüdiger Veil

43   The Commission further plans to reform the MiFID 2004/39/EC. It justifies its proposals for a Directive on markets in financial instruments repealing Directive 2004/39/EC[100] and for a Regulation on markets in financial instruments[101] largely with the argument that the financial crisis revealed weaknesses regarding the regulation of derivatives. The increasing complexity of these financial instruments requires an increased investor protection. The Commission further claims reforms to be necessary due to the fact that developments on the markets and in technology have led to a number of provisions in the MiFID being outdated.[102]

XV. Continuation of Phase 5: Regulation on Short Sales (2012)

44   Legislative activity also became apparent regarding the topic of short sales. On 15 September 2010 the European Commission accepted a draft proposal for a Regulation on short sales and certain aspects of credit default swaps (CDSs), the aim of which was to improve transparency and reduce risks.[103] It was the experience gained from the financial crisis that led to these measures. The new regulation[104] entered into force in November 2012. Its main aim is to prevent the development of systemic risks by introducing transparency requirements.

XVI. Continuation of Phase 5: Regulation on OTC Derivatives (2012)

45   Derivatives are playing an increasingly important role on the financial markets, the most relevant being over-the-counter (OTC) derivatives, which make up about 80% of all derivatives. The nominal value of the entire OTC derivative market was almost US$615bn in December 2009.[105] The financial crisis in general, and especially the insolvency of Lehman Brothers and the bail-out of AIG, revealed a number of deficiencies in the markets for OTC derivatives that provided the incentive for the Commission to introduce a number of regulatory measures. The proposal for the amended MiFID,[106] for example, aims to subject derivatives to the rules of trading on

---

[100] Proposal for a Directive of the European Parliament and of the Council on Markets in Financial Instruments repealing Directive 2004/39/EC of the European Parliament and of the Council, 20 October 2011, COM(2011) 656 final; for further information see B. Bréhier and P. Pailler, Bull. Joly Bourse (2012), p. 122–128; R. Veil and M.P. Lerch, WM (2012), p. 1557–1565 and 1605–1613.

[101] Proposal for a Regulation of the European Parliament and of the Council on Markets in Financial Instruments and amending Regulation [EMIR] on OTC Derivatives, Central Counterparties and Trade Repositories, 20 October 2011, COM(2011) 652 final.

[102] Explanatory Memorandum, Proposal for a Directive of the European Parliament and of the Council on markets in financial instruments repealing Directive 2004/39/EC of the European Parliament and of the Council, 20 October 2011 COM(2011) 656 final, p. 2.

[103] See § 15 para. 9.

[104] Regulation (EU) No. 236/2012 of the European Parliament and of the Council of 14 March 2012 on short selling and certain aspects of credit default swaps, OJ L86, 24 March 2012, p. 1.

[105] Commission, *Making Derivatives Markets in Europe Safer and More Transparent*, 15 September 2010.

[106] See para. 43.

a regulated market.[107] The new Regulation on OTC derivatives[108] aims to make the European derivatives markets safer and more transparent, particularly by addressing counterparty credit risks. All transactions with OTC derivatives in the EU are now to be registered. Standardised OTC derivatives are further to be cleared by central counterparties.

XVII. Conclusion

46   Looking back on the historical developments in European capital markets law over the last fifty years, it becomes apparent that all steps in EU legislation were preceded by impressive reports written by independent experts: The Segré Report in 1966, the Lamfalussy Report from 2000 and the de Larosière Report published in 2009 significantly influenced European legislation on capital markets law. The Segré Report pointedly described deficiencies and the problem of limited and illiquid markets. The de Larosière Report criticised the shortcomings of the supervisory system. These expert opinions were all the legislative bodies needed to be convinced that a regulation in these areas had become necessary. However, there were no preliminary conceptual considerations regarding the regulation of capital markets to which they could have referred. While the reports contained various reasons for a regulation, none of the expert committees had actually drafted a theory on how to regulate capital markets. The current legal situation and future amendments must therefore be seen as the Commission's own attempt to create a regulatory system. The process is ongoing; in particular, the recent financial crisis has required adjustments. At the same time it has offered the opportunity to build a coherent European capital markets law.

---

[107] Cf. R. Veil and M.P. Lerch, WM (2012), p. 1557, 1561–1565.
[108] Regulation (EU) No. 648/2012 of the European Parliament and of the Council of 4 July 2012 on OTC derivatives, central counterparties and trade repositories, OJ L201, 27 July 2012, p. 1.

Rüdiger Veil

§ 2 Concept and Aims of Capital Markets Regulation

Bibliography

Avgouleas, Emilios, *What Future for Disclosure as a Regulatory Technique? Lessons from Behavioural Decision Theory and the Global Financial Crisis*, in: MacNeil, Iain and O'Brian, Justin (eds.), The Future of Financial Regulation (2010), p. 205–225, Bachmann, Gregor, *Der Grundsatz der Gleichbehandlung im Kapitalmarktrecht*, 170 ZHR (2006), p. 144–177; Bumke, Christian, *Regulierung am Beispiel der Kapitalmärkte*, in: Hopt, Klaus J. et al. (eds.), *Kapitalmarktgesetzgebung im europäischen Binnenmarkt* (2008), p. 107–141; Hazen, Thomas Lee, *Treatise on The Law of Securities Regulation*, 6th ed. (2009); Heinze, Stephan, *Europäisches Kapitalmarktrecht—Recht des Primärmarktes* (1999); Langevoort, Donald C., *Structuring Securities Regulation in the European Union: Lessons from the US Experience*, in: Ferrarini, Guido and Wymeersch, Eddy (eds.), *Investor Protection in Europe— Corporate Law Making, the MiFID and Beyond* (2006), p. 485–505; Loss, Louis and Seligman, Joel, Securities Regulation, Vol. I, 3rd ed. 1998; Mehringer, Christoph, *Das allgemeine kapitalmarktrechtliche Gleichbehandlungsprinzip* (2007); Coffee, John C. and Seligman, Joel, Securities Regulation, 9th ed. (2003).

I. Concept

1   Capital markets law has developed into an separate field of law in Europe. Nevertheless, a precise definition of what it entails is still missing. In the legal literature, the emphasis is mainly placed on the fact that capital markets law refers to the organisation of the capital markets, the trading of securities and the respective behaviour of the market participants, i.e. investors, issuers and financial intermediaries.[1] The European Commission appears to favour a similar understanding. The Internal Market and Services Directorate General describes European capital markets law as follows: The EU directives "regulate the initial and on-going conditions for service providers (investment firms), establish requirements for the issuance of securities ... and co-ordinate the conditions applicable to investment funds. ... The legislation on issuance of securities lays down minimum requirements for the information that must be disclosed to the public and facilitates cross-border issuance of securities."[2]

2   As opposed to this, the United States does not speak of capital markets law but rather of securities regulation,[3] the regulatory scope, however, being the same:[4] securities regulation focuses on rules regarding issues of securities and trade on secondary markets. Takeover law is also often regarded as part of securities regulation and is examined closely in most textbooks. The organisation of the markets and the functions of broker dealers are regarded as further elements of securities regulation. Other financial intermediaries, such as financial analysts and rating agencies, are hardly mentioned in textbooks. In this regard a change is, however, to be expected,

---

[1] N. Moloney, *EC Securities Regulation*, p. 3; P. Buck-Heeb, *Kapitalmarktrecht*, § 1 para 5.

[2] Cf. European Commission, *The EU Single Market—Securities*.

[3] The two most relevant statutes are the "Securities Act of 1933" and the "Securities Exchange Act of 1934". On the development of these, cf. L. Loss and J. Seligman, *Securities Regulation*, Chap. 1A.

[4] Cf. Th.L. Hazen, *The Law of Securities Regulation*, § 1.0[1]; J.C. Coffee and J. Seligman, *Securities Regulation*, Part I, Chap. 1, Sec. 1.

the financial crisis having proven the necessity of a regulation of financial intermediaries. The US legislature has already learned its lesson and now subjects financial
intermediaries to a stricter liability via the newly introduced Dodd–Frank Wall
Street Reform and Consumer Protection Act.

II.   Regulatory Aims

1.   Efficiency of Capital Markets

3   The provisions enacted by the European legislature in the field of capital markets
law aim to achieve a single European market for financial services. As underlined
by the reports of all committees appointed by the European Commission,[5] the goal
is to ensure the efficiency of the capital markets and to protect investors.[6] The European legislature stressed in the recitals to the directives on capital markets law that
ensuring "the smooth functioning of securities markets and public confidence in
markets"[7] is essential. Efficient capital markets could help to improve the allocation
of capital and reduce costs.[8]

4   The aim of ensuring the functioning of securities markets has three dimensions.[9]
The first is the *institutional efficiency*, which describes the basic requirements for an
efficient mechanism of the market segments. It requires a free access to the capital
market for the issuers as well as for the demand and offers by the investors. If a large
part of the investible capital is directed to a specific market segment, this market
will be liquid. The investors can then assume that they will be able to resell their
securities. It is therefore important to take measures to enhance investor confidence
and market integrity.[10]

5   The second dimension is that of *operational efficiency* of the capital markets, i.e.
the reduction of transaction costs. This is achieved on the one hand by reducing
the issuers' costs resulting from the initial public offering (IPO) (admission fees,
prospectus costs, etc.) and ensuing disclosures. On the other hand operational efficiency depends on the investors' costs for security investments.[11] These costs can be
reduced by introducing (periodic and ad hoc) disclosure obligations for the issuer
who is usually the *cheapest cost avoider*.

6   The third dimension, *allocational efficiency*, describes the allocational function of
capital, i.e. matching the most urgent investment opportunities with the investible
financial capital (of private households, institutional investors and companies
looking to invest) in order to achieve the highest return while ensuring a sufficient

---

[5] See § 1 para. 2, 16 and 33.
[6] Cf. C. Bumke, in: K.J. Hopt et al., *Kapitalmarktgesetzgebung im europäischen Binnenmarkt*, p. 107, 118; S. Heinze, *Europäisches Kapitalmarktrecht*, p. 7; S. Kalss et al., *Kapitalmarktrecht*, Vol. I, § 1 para. 21.
[7] Recital 2 MAD and Recital 10 PD.
[8] Recital 1 TD.
[9] More details on transparency and capital market efficiency in § 16 para. 4–13.
[10] The European legislature understood market integrity as a means to ensure the investors' trust in the market, cf. Recital 2 and 12 MAD.
[11] In more detail G. Franke and H. Hax, *Finanzwirtschaft des Unternehmens und Kapitalmarkt*, p. 56.

certainty for investors. This requires investor confidence in the market, which necessitates transparency and disclosure.

7   The functioning of the markets and investor protection are two "communicating vessels"[12] that support each other.[13] This explains why the European legislature wants to achieve "a high level of investor protection".[14] The additional aims of capital market regulation, such as the equal treatment of all market participants[15] and fair competition,[16] can all be seen as different shapes of these two central regulatory aims.[17]

2.   Regulatory Approaches

8   There are two different regulatory approaches to capital market regulation. The first and foremost concept—*transparency*—constitutes the basis for most of the European legislature's provisions.[18] The Recitals of the MAD, for example, request a "prompt and fair disclosure of information to the public".[19] The same approach is taken by the TD, which states in its Recitals that "the disclosure of accurate, comprehensive and timely information about security issuers builds sustained investor confidence and allows an informed assessment of their business performance and assets".[20] Transparency must thus be regarded as the central element of capital market regulation.[21] It is for this reason that the European requirements concerning a disclosure system are described in such detail in this book.

9   The second central regulatory approach is to introduce a system of enforcement.[22] It is supposed to prevent and avert the risk of abuse and at the same time secure the quality of relevant information. Possible approaches to enforcement include private self-monitoring, private external monitoring and administrative supervision. The European Union's legislative activities differ strongly between these three areas. The private self-monitoring carried out by investment firms and intermediaries (investment firms, financial analysts and rating agencies) consists mainly of provisions on company organisation and the prevention of conflicts of interests.[23] The external monitoring by experts and auditors is also clearly defined through European rules on corporate and accounting law, whilst administrative supervision mostly remains a matter of the Member States, even after the latest reforms.[24]

---

[12] K.J. Hopt, *Der Kapitalanlegerschutz im Recht der Banken*, p. 52.

[13] C. Bumke, in: K.J. Hopt et al. (eds.), *Kapitalmarktgesetzgebung im europäischen Binnenmarkt*, p. 107, 119.

[14] Recital 5 and 7 TD; cf. also Recital 16 PD.

[15] This especially refers to an equal access to information for all investors, cf. S. Heinze, *Europäisches Kapitalmarktrecht*, p. 7; G. Bachmann, ZHR 170 (2006), p. 144; Mehringer, *Das allgemeine kapitalmarktrechtliche Gleichbehandlungsprinzip* (2007).

[16] Cf. S. Weber, *Kapitalmarktrecht*, p. 382 ff.

[17] C. Bumke, in K.J. Hopt et al. (eds.), *Kapitalmarktgesetzgebung im europäischen Binnenmarkt*, p. 107, 119.

[18] Recital 15 and 24 MAD; Recital 18 PD.

[19] Recital 24 MAD.

[20] Recital 1 TD and Recital 18 PD.

[21] E. Avgouleas, *What Future for Disclosure as a Regulatory Technique? Lessons from Behavioural Decision Theory and the Global Financial Crisis*, in: I. MacNeil and J. O'Brian (eds.), *The Future of Financial Regulation*, p. 205, 209. In more detail § 16 para. 4–13.

[22] C. Bumke, in: K.J. Hopt et al. (eds.), *Kapitalmarktgesetzgebung im europäischen Binnenmarkt*, p. 107, 126, 130 ff.

[23] Regarding financial analysts cf. § 26 para. 79–87 and for rating agencies § 27 para. 27–33.

[24] For the newest developments regarding supervision see § 11 para. 37–38.

§ 3 Legislative Powers for Regulating Capital Markets in Europe

Bibliography

Bleckmann, Albert, *Probleme der Auslegung europäischer Richtlinien*, ZGR (1992), p. 364–375; Heinze, Stephan, *Europäisches Kapitalmarktrecht—Recht des Primärmarktes* (1999); Hopt, Klaus J., *Harmonisierung im europäischen Gesellschaftsrecht*, ZGR (1992), p. 265–295; Kindler, Peter, *Die sachliche Rechtfertigung des aktienrechtlichen Bezugsrechtsausschlusses im Lichte der Zweiten Gesellschaftsrechtlichen Richtlinie der Europäischen Gemeinschaft*, 158 ZHR (1994), p. 339–370; Mathijsen, P.S.R.F., *A Guide to European Law*, 10th ed. (2010), Part III; Moloney, Niamh, *EC Securities Regulation*, 2nd ed. (2008), p. 6–11; Steiner, Josephine and Woods, Lorna, *EU Law*, 10th ed. (2009), Part III.

I. Legal Foundations of the European Union

1 Today's European Union is the result of many small and large steps of unification taken by the Member States. For an understanding of the European legislation on capital markets, however, an overview of those treaties that contain legal foundations for legislative acts in capital markets law is sufficient.[1]

2 The European integration process commenced in 1957 with the enactment of the so-called Treaties of Rome, i.e. the Treaty establishing the European Economic Community (EEC) and the Treaty establishing the European Atomic Energy Community (EAEC or Euratom). The first legislative acts were thus based on the legal foundations that could be found in the EEC Treaty.[2] The next turning point in the European integration process was the Treaty on European Union (EU) of 7 February 1992 (the so-called Treaty of Maastricht). This Treaty formed the "roof" over the three pillars of the Communities, the first of which comprised the EC (former EEC), the EAEC[3] and the ECSC.[4] Therefore, the European legislature referred to the rules on competence laid down in the EC Treaty when it enacted the four framework directives in capital markets law. Various small amendments of the Treaties ensued as a result of the Treaty of Amsterdam[5] (1995) and the Treaty of Nice[6] (2003).

3 By 1995 the EU already consisted of 15 Member States. Successive enlargements followed, leading to today's total of 27 Member States (since 2007). This growth soon prompted discussions as to whether a new constitution for the EU had become necessary in order to secure the Union's ability to act. It took until 13 December 2007, however, for this Herculean task to be achieved. On this day, the Member States'

---

[1] See in more detail M. Horspool and M. Humphreys, *European Law*, para. 2.1 ff.; P.S.R.F. Mathijsen, *A Guide to European Union Law*, p. 13 ff.; A. Haratsch et al., *Europarecht*, ch. 1, para. 7 ff.

[2] Cf. § 1 para.6.

[3] Cf. J. Schwarze, in: J. Schwarze (ed.), *EU-Kommentar*, Art. 1 EGV para. 10.

[4] In 2002 the Treaty of Paris, establishing the ECSC expired, and the ECSC's activities and resources were absorbed by the European Community.

[5] The Treaty of Amsterdam did not bring any fundamental changes to the structure of the European Union, cf. A. Haratsch et al., *Europarecht*, ch. 1 para. 26.

[6] On the amendments to the EU and EC Treaty see A. Haratsch et al., *Europarecht*, ch. 1 para. 28–29.

Rüdiger Veil

governments signed the Treaty of Lisbon, which entered into effect on 1 December 2009, making the Treaty on the Functioning of the European Union (TFEU)[7] and the Treaty on European Union (TEU) the new legal foundations of the EU.

II.   Rules on Competence

1.   Coordination of Provisions on the Protection of Shareholders and Creditors

4   Most of the capital market directives were based on the European legislature's competence to ensure the freedom of establishment by coordinating the national provisions on the protection of creditors, shareholders and investors.[8] This competence was orginally defined in Article 54(3)(g) EEC Treaty, then implemented into Article 44(2)(g) EC Treaty by the Treaty of Amsterdam and can now be found in the identical Article 50(2)(g) TFEU. It provides the Council and the Commission with the possibility to coordinate "to the necessary extent the safeguards which, for the protection of the interests of members and others, are required by Member States of companies or firms … with a view to making such safeguards equivalent throughout the Union", thus fulfilling the freedom of establishment.

5   The provision only allows a *coordination* of national rules, i.e. an approximation of the national laws as opposed to a full unification.[9] This can be achieved in two ways—either by reducing national protective provisions by regulating a maximum level of shareholder and third-party protection,[10] or by increasing the level of protection provided by the national laws. The latter requires that the approximation takes place by defining a minimum level of shareholder and third-party protection.[11] In both approaches the relevant provisions—which may also be rules on capital markets law—must be aimed at shareholder and third-party protection.[12]

6   The European legislature based two of the four framework directives[13]—the PD 2003/71/EC[14] and the TD 2004/109/EC[15]—on Article 44(2)(g) of the EC Treaty.[16] Use was made of the same rule on competence for the Takeover Directive (TOD) 2004/25/EC.[17] All three directives aim at unifying the protective provisions in the Member States, thus making these directives legal acts subject to the concept of minimum harmonisation.

---

[7] The Treaty establishing the European Community (EC Treaty) was amended by the Treaty of Lisbon and renamed "Treaty on the Functioning of the European Union" (TFEU), receiving a new structure.

[8] It referred to the Community's competence to establish a European internal market, see below para. 9.

[9] Cf. P.-C. Müller-Graff, in: R. Streinz, *EUV/EGV*, Art. 44 EGV para. 17.

[10] Cf. A. Bleckmann, ZGR (1992), p. 364, 372–373; P. Kindler, 158 ZHR (1994), p. 339, 352.

[11] Cf. K.J. Hopt, ZGR (1992), p. 265, 285–286.

[12] Cf. J. Bröhmer, in: C. Callies and M. Ruffert, *EUV/EGV*, Art. 44 EGV para. 12; M. Habersack, *Europäisches Gesellschaftsrecht*, § 4 para. 53; P.-C. Müller-Graff, in: R. Streinz, *EUV/EGV*, Art. 44 EGV para. 18.

[13] Cf. on the particularities of framework directives § 4 para. 13–15.

[14] See § 1 para. 24.

[15] See § 1 para. 26.

[16] Both directives were based on Art. 95 EC Treaty.

[17] See § 1 para. 28.

2. Coordination of Start-Up and Pursuit of Self-Employment

7   Additionally, Article 53(1) TFEU (formerly Article 47(2) EC Treaty and prior to that Article 57(2) EEC Treaty), which allows the European Union to issue directives to make it easier for persons to take up and pursue activities as self-employed persons, has become increasingly important. Once again, the provision only allows a coordination of the rules laid down by law, regulation or administrative action. Whether this coordination is restricted to a minimum harmonisation or enables unification is controversial.[18] In either case, the coordination must aim at making it easier for persons to take up and pursue activities as self-employed persons in other Member States.[19] This can only be achieved if the differences between the Member States' laws are reduced.

8   Directive 93/22/EEC[20] on investment services was enacted on the basis of Article 57(2) EEC Treaty. This provision, later adopted in Article 47(2) EC Treaty also served as the legal basis for the MiFID and its implementing measures.[21]

3. Establishing an Internal Market

9   The European legislature also enacted a number of provisions on capital markets law on the basis of Article 95 EC Treaty. This allowed the Council to "adopt the measures for the approximation of the provisions laid down by law, regulation or administrative action in Member States which have as their object the establishment and functioning of the internal market", independent of the respective subject matter.[22] The European legislature may, however, only take measures necessary for improving the establishment and functioning of the European internal market.[23]

10   The framework directive 2003/6/EC[24] on Market Abuse was based on Article 95 EC Treaty, just as the PD 2003/71/EC[25] and the TD 2004/109/EC[26], which, however, were additionally based on Article 44(2)(g) EC Treaty. Most recently, the European Parliament and the Council enacted Regulation (EC) No. 1060/2009[27] on credit rating agencies with reference to Article 95 EC Treaty. Meanwhile the provision has been adopted into Article 114 TFEU.

---

[18] Speaking for: J. Bröhmer, in: C. Callies and M. Ruffert, *EUV/EGV*, Art. 47 EGV para. 1. Speaking against: M. Schlag, in: J. Schwarze (ed.), *EU-Kommentar*, Art. 47 EGV para. 21.

[19] M. Schlag, in: J. Schwarze (ed.), *EU-Kommentar*, Art. 47 EGV para. 25.

[20] See § 1 para. 12.

[21] See § 1 para. 25.

[22] Cf. Fischer, in: C.-O. Lenz and K.-D. Borchardt, *EU-Verträge*, Art. 114 AEUV para. 9.

[23] Settled case law of the ECJ, cf. ECJ, of 5 October 2000, Case C-376/98 (*Germany/Parliament and Council*) [2000] ECR I-8419, para. 106–107, also W. Kahl, in: C. Callies and M. Ruffert, *EUV/EGV*, Art. 95 EGV para. 16.

[24] See § 1 para. 21.

[25] See § 1 para. 24.

[26] See § 1 para. 26.

[27] See § 1 para. 37.

III. Legislative Instruments

1. Overview

11   The institutions of the European Union can make use of a number of legislative instruments under the TFEU. In order to carry out their task they may adopt regulations, directives or decisions, make recommendations or deliver opinions.[28] The TFEU defines this type of legislation as legal acts.[29] Legal acts adopted in a legislative procedure are defined as legislative acts.[30] The distinction between legislative and non-legislative acts thus does not result from the nature of the legal act (regulation, directive, etc.) but rather from the procedure to be followed for its adoption according to the legal basis.[31]

12   The ordinary legislative procedure consists of a joint adoption of a regulation, directive or decision by the European Parliament and the Council, following the proposal of the Commission.[32] While a legislative act may delegate the power to adopt non-legislative acts of general application, supplementing or amending certain non-essential elements of the legislative act, to the Commission, the essential elements of a field of law shall remain reserved for the legislative act itself.[33]

2. Regulation

13   A regulation is described by the TFEU, as by the former EC Treaty, in two short sentences: "A regulation shall have general application. It shall be binding in its entirety and directly applicable in all Member States."[34] Hence, the regulation need not be implemented into the Member States' national laws in order to become effective, but will rather become immediately enforceable as law. When a regulation comes into force, it overrides all national laws dealing with the same subject matter, i.e. the conflicting national provisions are not applicable—but not, however, void.[35] It is a characteristic of a regulation that it contains provisions in a general and abstract form.[36]

14   In capital markets law, regulations have not so far played much of a role. Rather, European capital market legislation has mainly made use of directives. The European legislature has enacted four framework directives. Even on Level 2 of the Lamfalussy Process[37] regarding implementing measures the European Commission has mostly adopted directives. Only in a few cases has it reverted to regulations. With regard to rating agencies, the European Parliament and the Council have employed regulations.[38] These are immediately applicable in the Member States. In the cases in

---

[28] Cf. Art. 288(1) TFEU and Art. 249(1) EC Treaty.
[29] Cf. Art. 289(3) TFEU.
[30] Cf. Art. 289(3) TFEU.
[31] Cf. T. Oppermann et al., *Europarecht*, § 10 para. 79.
[32] Cf. Art. 289(1) in conjunction with Art. 294 TFEU.
[33] Cf. Art. 290 TFEU.
[34] Cf. Art. 288(2) TFEU and ex Art. 249(2) EC Treaty.
[35] Cf. T. Oppermann et al., *Europarecht*, § 10 para. 91.
[36] Cf. H. Hetmeier, in: C.-O. Lenz and K.-D. Borchardt, *EU-Verträge*, Art. 288 AEUV para. 7.
[37] See § 4 para. 16–21.
[38] See § 1 para. 38.

which the Member States enacted implementing provisions on rating agencies, this took place in accordance with the respective regulation.

3. Directive

15   A directive is defined as "binding, as to the result to be achieved, upon each Member State to which it is addressed, but [leaving] to the national authorities the choice of form and methods".[39] This definition, which already existed in the former EC Treaty and has been adopted in the TFEU, suggests that a directive is a measure to harmonise the national laws. It fits more "smoothly" into national law than a regulation, which is aimed at a full unification of the national laws.[40] At the same time, a directive can also contain precise and detailed provisions, thus depriving the Member States of the possibility of choice of form and methods. Meanwhile, this can, for example, be said of the directives on capital markets law. Whereas for the first directives in this field[41] few provisions sufficed, the latest directives, i.e. the four framework directives[42] and their implementing directives, are far more specific. Only the provisions on enforcement in all four directives remain imprecise enough to leave the national legislatures with a large margin of appreciation.[43]

16   Directives are addressed to the Member States and not to individuals. For the Member States the regulatory aims as laid down in the recitals or the introductory articles are binding. They can be achieved most effectively as described in the further provisions of the directive, as a consequence making these binding for the national legislatures too. The Member States must therefore ensure that their national laws are adapted to correspond with the legal situation laid out by the directive.[44] If this is already the case in individual Member States no further implementing measures need to be taken.

17   The legal practice of transposing directives on capital markets law differs strongly between the Member States. Various Member States, such as the United Kingdom and France, have started to transpose detailed rules one-to-one, claiming to want to avoid additional bureaucratic hurdles. At the same time, this approach averts the danger of an incorrect implementation of the directive.[45]

18   Generally, the provisions of a directive do not have a direct effect. However, the European Court of Justice has developed the doctrine of direct effect which states that directives can have direct legal force should they not have been implemented correctly by the transposition date.[46] This doctrine of direct effect has not yet been applied in capital markets law. This is mainly due to the fact that the four framework directives only aim at structuring the capital markets without conveying rights to the investors, should capital market duties have been breached.[47]

---

[39] Cf. Art. 288(3) sec. 1 TFEU and ex Art. 249(3) EC Treaty.
[40] Cf. T. Oppermann et al., *Europarecht*, § 10 para. 94.
[41] See § 1 para. 5–6.
[42] On the significance of framework directives see below para. 32.
[43] Cf. H. Hetmeier, in: C.-O. Lenz and K.-D. Borchardt, *EU-Verträge*, Art. 288 AEUV para. 11. On the reform of the sanctions see also § 12 para. 5 and 22.
[44] Cf. T. Oppermann et al., *Europarecht*, § 10 para. 102.
[45] See § 4 para. 47.
[46] On this see A. Haratsch et al., *Europarecht*, para. 339 ff.; T. Oppermann et al., *Europarecht*, § 10 para. 111 ff.
[47] Cf. § 12 para. 6–7.

§ 4 Process and Strategies of Capital Markets Regulation in Europe

Bibliography

Alexander, Kern, *Principles v. Rules in Financial Regulation: Re-assessing the Balance in the Credit Crisis—Symposium at Cambridge University, 10–11 April 2008*, 10 EBOR (2009), p. 169–173; Black, Julia, *The Development of Risk Based Regulation in Financial Services: Canada, the UK and Australia—A Research Report* (2004); Black, Julia, *Forms and Paradoxes of Principles-based Regulation*, 3 CMLJ (2008), p. 425–457; Black, Julia, Hopper, Martyn and Band, Christa, *Making a Success of Principles-Based Regulation*, 1 Law and Financial Markets Review (2007), p. 191–206; Burmeister, Frank and Staebe, Erik, *Grenzen des sog. Gold Plating bei der Umsetzung europäischer Richtlinien in nationales Recht*, EuR (2009), p. 444–456; Brinckmann, Hendrik, *Die geplante Reform des Transparenz-RL: Veränderungen bei der Regelpublizität und der Beteiligungstransparenz*, BB (2012), p. 1370–1373; Djankov, Simeon, McLiesh, Caralee and Ramalho, Rita M., *Regulation and Growth*, 92 Economic Letter (2006), p. 395–401; Dougan, Michael, *Minimum Harmonisation and the Internal Market*, 37 CML Rev. (2000), p. 853–885; Dwyer, William, *Final Rules on Information about Major Shareholdings*, 24 JIBLR (2009), p. 435–438; Ferran, Eilis, *Principles-Based, Risk-Based Regulation and Effective Enforcement*, in: Tison, Michel et al. (eds.), *Perspectives in Company Law and Financial Regulation—Essays in Honour of Eddy Wymeersch* (2009), p. 427–448; Fleischer, Holger and Schmolke, Klaus-Ulrich, *Das Anschleichen an eine börsennotierte Aktiengesellschaft—Überlegungen zur Beteiligungstransparenz de lege lata und de lege ferenda*, NZG (2009), p. 401–409; Fleischer, Holger and Schmolke, Klaus-Ulrich, *Zum beabsichtigten Ausbau der kapitalmarktrechtlichen Beteiligungstransparenz bei modernen Finanzinstrumenten (§§ 25, 25a DiskE-WpHG)*, NZG (2010), p. 846–854; Fleischer, Holger and Schmolke, Klaus-Ulrich, *Die Reform der Transparenzrichtlinie—Mindest- oder Vollharmonisierung der kapitalmarktrechtlichen Beteiligungspublizität?*, NZG (2010), p. 1241–1248; Ford, Cristie L., *New Governance, Compliance, and Principles-Based Securities Regulation*, 45 Am. Bus. Law J. (2008), p. 1–60; Frach, Lotte, *Finanzaufsicht in Deutschland und Großbritannien—Die BaFin und die FSA im Spannungsfeld der Politik* (2008); Gerne-Beuerle, Carsten, *United in Diversity. Maximum vs. Minimum Harmonisation in EU Securities Regulation*, 7 CMLJ (2012), p. 317–347; Gruber, Michael, *Voll- oder Mindestharmonisierung?—Auf der Suche nach dem "richtigen" Regelungskonzept im Europäischen Kapitalmarktrecht*, in: Braumüller, Peter et al. (eds.), *Die neue europäische Finanzmarktaufsicht—Band zur ZFR-Jahrestagung 2011* (2012), p. 1–15; Guitard Marín, Juan, *Abuso de Mercado*, in: Uría Fernández, Francisco (ed.), *Régimen jurídico de los mercados de valores y de las instituciones de inversión colectiva* (2007), p. 301; Hertig, Gerard and Lee, Ruben, *Four Predictions about the Future of EU Securities Regulation*, 3 J. Corp. L. Stud. (2003), p. 359–363; Hopt, Klaus J., *Auf dem Weg zu einer neuen europäischen und internationalen Finanzmarktarchitektur*, NZG (2009), p. 1401–1408; Hopt, Klaus J., *Kapitalmarktrecht (mit Prospekthaftung) in der Rechtsprechung des Bundesgerichtshofes*, in: Heldrich, Andreas and Hopt, Klaus J. (eds.), *50 Jahre Bundesgerichtshof—Festgabe aus der Wissenschaft*, Vol. II—*Europäisches und Internationales Recht* (2000), p. 497–550; Hupka, Jan, *Kapitalmarktaufsicht im Wandel—Rechtswirkungen der Empfehlungen des Committee of European Securities Regulators (CESR) im deutschen Kapitalmarktrecht*, WM (2009), p. 1351–1359; Kämmerer, Jörn A., *Selbstregulierung am Beispiel des Kapitalmarktrechts—Eine normativ-institutionelle Positionsbestimmung*, in: Hopt, Klaus J. et al. (eds.), *Kapitalmarktgesetzgebung im europäischen Binnenmarkt* (2008), p. 145–163; Kaplow, Louis, *Rules versus Standards: An Economic Analysis*, 42 Duke L.J. (1992–93), p. 557–629; Kahl, Arno, *Europäische Aufsichtsbehörden und technische Regulierungsstandards*, in: Braumüller, Peter et al. (eds.), *Die neue europäische Finanzmarktaufsicht—Band zur ZFR-Jahrestagung 2011* (2012), p. 55–75; Koch, Philipp, *Die Ad-hoc-Publizität nach dem Kommissionsentwurf einer Marktmissbrauchsverordnung*, BB (2012), p. 1365–1369; Korling, Fredric, *Investeringsrådgivning och placeringsrådgivning—utbytbara begrepp?*, in: Schultz, Mårten (ed.), *Stockholm Centre for Commercial Law Årsbok I* (2009), p. 95–112; Langenbucher, Katja, *Zur Zulässigkeit parlamentsersetzender Normgebungsverfahren im Europarecht*, ZEuP (2002), p. 265–286; Langevoort, Donald C., *Structuring Securities Regulation in the European Union: Lessons from the US Experience*, in: Ferrarini, Guido and Wymeersch, Eddy (eds.), *Investor Protection Europe—Corporate Law Making, the MiFID and Beyond* (2006), p. 485–505; Leixner, Iris, *Komitologie und Lamfalussyverfahren im Finanzdienstleistungsbereich im Lichte der jüngsten Reformen*, Working Paper 1/2010, available at: http://m.bmf. gv.at/Publikationen/Downloads/Working Papers/WP_1_2010_v2.pdf; Lutter, Marcus, Bayer, Walter and Schmidt, Jessica (eds.), *Europäisches Unternehmens- und Kapitalmarktrecht—Grundlagen, Stand und Entwicklung nebst Texten und Materialien* (2012); May, Peter J., *Performance-Based Regulation and Regulatory Regimes: The Saga of Leaky Buildings*, 25 Law & Policy (2003), p. 381–401; Merkner, Andreas and Sustmann, Marco, *Reform des Marktmissbrauchsrechts: Die Vorschläge der Europäischen Kommission zur Verschärfung des Insiderrechts*, AG (2012), p. 315–324; Möller, Andreas, *Kapitalmarktaufsicht—Wandel und Neubestimmung der nationalen und europäischen Kapitalmarktaufsicht anhand des Beispiels der Aufsicht über die Börsen und den Börsenhandel* (2006); Möllers, Thomas M.J., *Vermögensbetreuungsvertrag, graue Vermögensverwaltung und Zweitberatung—Vertragstypen zwischen klassischer Anlageberatung und Vermögensverwaltung*, WM (2008), p. 93–102; Möllers, Thomas M.J., *Europäische Methoden- und Gesetzgebungslehre im Kapitalmarktrecht—Vollharmonisierung, Generalklauseln und soft law im Rahmen des Lamfalussy-Verfahrens als Mittel zur Etablierung von Standards*, ZEuP (2008), p. 480–505; Möllers, Thomas M.J., *Auf dem Weg zu einer neuen europäischen Finanzmarktaufsichtsstruktur*, NZG (2010), p. 285–290; Möllers, Thomas M.J., *Vollharmonisierung im Kapitalmarktrecht—Zur Regelungskompetenz nationaler Gerichte und Parlamente*, in: Gsell, Beate and Herresthal, Carsten (eds.), *Vollharmonisierung im Privatrecht* (2010), p. 235; Moloney, Niamh, *The Committee of European Securities Regulators and Level 3 of the Lamfalussy Process*, in: Tison, Michel et al. (eds.), *Perspectives in Company Law and Financial Regulation—Essays in Honour of Eddy Wymeersch* (2009), p. 449–476; Moloney, Niamh, *EC Securities Regulation*, 2nd ed. (2008), Moloney, Niamh, *The Financial Crisis and EU Securities Law-Making: A Challenge Met?*, in: Grundmann, Stefan et al. (eds.), *Festschrift für Klaus J. Hopt zum 70. Geburtstag*, Vol. II (2010), p. 2265–2282; Ogowewo, Tunde I., *Is Contract the Juridical Basis of the Takeover Panel?*, 12 J Int Bank Law (1997), p. 15–23; Riesenhuber, Karl (ed.), *Europäische Methodenlehre*, 2nd ed. (2010); Roßkopf, Gabriele, *Selbstregulierung von Übernahmeangeboten in Großbritannien* (2000); Schedin, Hans, *En principbaserad tillsyn och reglering—Finansinspektionen på villospår?*, in: Nord, Gunnar and Thorell, Per (eds.), *Regelfrågor på en förändrad kapitalmarknad* (2009), p. 145–155; Scheel, Benedikt, *Die Neuregelungen der Komitologie und das europäische Demokratiedefizit*, ZEuS (2006), p. 521–554; Schmolke, Klaus-Ulrich, *Der Lamfalussy-Prozess im Europäischen Kapitalmarktrecht—Eine Zwischenbilanz*, NZG (2005), p. 912–919; Schmolke, Klaus-Ulrich, *Die Einbeziehung des Komitologieverfahrens in den Lamfalussy-Prozess—Zur Forderung des Europäischen Parlaments nach mehr Entscheidungsteilhabe*, EuR (2006), p. 432–448; Seibt, Christoph H. and Wollenschläger, Bernward, *Europäisierung des Transparenzregimes: Der Vorschlag der Europäischen Kommission zur Transparenzrichtlinie*, AG (2012), p. 305–315; Siebens, Tom and Gambol, Melissa, *Who's Hiding Behind the Hedges? Developments in the USA and UK May Limit Use of Total Return Swaps to Conceal Equity Stakes in Public Companies*, 4 CMLJ (2009), p. 172–178; Spindler, Gerald and Hupka, Jan, *Bindungswirkung von Standards im Kapitalmarktrecht*, in: Möllers, Thomas M.J. (ed.), *Geltung und Faktizität von Standards* (2009), p. 117; Storm, Philipp, *Alternative Freiverkehrssegmente im Kapitalmarktrecht—Zugleich ein Beitrag zur rechtsökonomischen Analyse emittentenbezogener Regulierung durch einen Marktveranstalter und zum System der Segmentierung* (2010); Tamm, Marina, *Das Grünbuch der Kommission zum Verbraucheracquis und das Modell der Vollharmonisierung—Eine kritische Analyse*, EuZW (2007), p. 756–761; Teigelack, Lars, *Insiderhandel und Marktmanipulation im Kommissionsentwurf einer Marktmissbrauchsverordnung*, p. 1361–1365; Veil, Rüdiger, *Compliance-Organisationen in Wertpapierdienstleistungsunternehmen im Zeitalter der MiFiD—Regelungskonzepte und Rechtsprobleme*, WM (2008), p. 1093–1098; Veil, Rüdiger, *Markt-*

regulierung durch privates Recht am Beispiel des Entry Standard der Frankfurter Wertpapierbörse, in: Burgard, Ulrich et al. (eds.), *Festschrift für Uwe H. Schneider zum 70. Geburtstag* (2011), p. 1313–1324; Veil, Rüdiger, *Auf dem Weg zu einem Europäischen Kapitalmarktrecht: die Vorschläge der Kommission zur Neuregelung der Transparenzregime*, WM (2012), p. 53–61; Veil, Rüdiger, *Stimmrechtsverlust nach dem Kommissionsvorschlag zur Neuregelung der kapitalmarktrechtlichen Beteiligungstransparenz*, BB (2012), p. 1374–1377; Veil, Rüdiger and Lerch, Marcus P., Auf dem Weg zu einem Europäischen Finanzmarktrecht: die Vorschläge der Kommission zur Neuregelung der Märkte für Finanzinstrumente, WM (2012), p. 1557–1565 (part I) and 1605–1613 (part II); Veil, Rüdiger and Koch, Philipp, *Auf dem Weg zu einem Europäischen Kapitalmarktrecht: die Vorschläge der Kommission zur Neuregelung des Marktmissbrauchs*, WM (2011), p. 2297–2306; Walla, Fabian, *The Swedish Capital Markets Law from a European Perspective*, 22 EBLR (2011), p. 211–221; Walla, Fabian, *Die Reformen der Europäischen Kommission zum Marktmissbrauchs- und Transparenzregime—Regelungskonzeption, Aufsicht und Sanktionen*, BB (2012), p. 1358–1361; Walla, Fabian, *Die Europäische Wertpapier- und Marktaufsichtsbehörde (ESMA) als Akteur bei der Regulierung der Kapitalmärkte Europas—Grundlagen, erste Erfahrungen und Ausblick*, BKR (2012), p. 265–270; Walla, Fabian, *Die Konzeption der Kapitalmarktaufsicht in Deutschland* (2012); Weber-Rey, Daniela, *Latest Developments in European Corporate Governance in Light of Better Regulation Efforts*, in: Weatherill, Stephen (ed.), *Better Regulation* (2007), p. 247–270; von Wogau, Karl, *Modernisierung der Europäischen Gesetzgebung*, ZEuP (2002), p. 695–700; Wundenberg, Malte, *Compliance und die prinzipiengeleitete Aufsicht über Bankengruppen* (2012); Wymeersch, Eddy, *The Future of Financial Regulation and Supervision in Europe*, 42 CML Rev. (2005), p. 987–1010; Wymeersch, Eddy, *The Structure of Financial Supervision in Europe: About Single Financial Supervisors, Twin Peaks and Multiple Financial Supervisors*, 8 EBOR (2007), p. 237–306.

I.   Process of Capital Markets Regulation

1.   Definition

1   No generally accepted definition of capital market regulation exists as yet. There are, however, a number of approaches attempting to put the concept into more concrete terms and to distinguish capital markets law from other fields of law. Two questions must always be addressed: firstly, what does regulation mean? Secondly, what are capital markets?

(a)   Market Regulation versus Market Supervision

2   According to the most common international understanding[1] capital market regulation describes any type of legislation, i.e. not only by the parliamentary legislator, but also rule making by public authorities or privately organised committees. As opposed to this, market supervision refers to the application and enforcement thereof. Whilst admittedly the areas of regulation and supervision overlap to a cer-

---

[1] N. Moloney, *EC Securities Regulation*, p. 1009 ff. and 1102 ff.; E. Wymeersch, CML Rev. (2005), p. 987, 988; K.J. Hopt, NZG (2009), p. 1401, 1402; apparently also de Larosière Report, p. 13. Seen differently by D.C. Langevoort, in: G. Ferrarini and E. Wymeersch (eds.), *Investor Protection in Europe*, p. 485, 488; S. Djankov et al., 92 Economic Letter (2006), p. 395, 399, who see *regulation* as the generic term for all substantive provisions on capital markets law and their enforcement.

tain extent with regard to public authorities,[2] the distinction between law making and law enforcement remains advantageous for a clear structuring of the system.

(b)   Capital Markets versus Financial Markets Regulation

3   The regulation of capital markets also has to be distinguished from the regulation of financial markets. Capital markets regulation only covers the area of securities trading, not, however, the areas of banking and insurance markets. Furthermore the regulation generally refers to the market as a whole and to financial intermediaries, such as securities firms, financial analysts and rating agencies, rather than aiming to regulate solely individual types of companies.[3] As opposed to this, financial market regulation is a broader concept and deals with securities trading, banking and insurance markets. Financial market regulation can be divided into "prudential regulation" and "conduct of business regulation".[4]

2.   European Legislation

4   Legislation on capital markets law can be adopted at a national or at a European level, the latter of which is becoming increasingly important.[5] As yet European legislation is restricted to provisions on regulated markets[6] and does not affect aspects of trading on open markets.[7] The Commission's proposals for a regulation on market abuse and a reform of the MiFID,[8] however, aim to include financial instruments traded on other markets and platforms, such as multilateral trading facilities (MTFs), organised trading facilities (OTFs) and over the counter (OTC).

5   Since 2002, the four levels of the so-called Lamfalussy Process,[9] a comitology process based on the former Article 202 EC Treaty, have determined the European approach to legislation on capital markets law. Whilst the process was originally restricted to the regulation of capital markets it was later applied in all areas of financial market regulation.[10]

6   Recently, the Lamfalussy Process has been modified due to the enactment of the Treaty of Lisbon on 1 December 2009 and the formation of the ESMA.[11] However, Article 9 of the Protocol (No. 36) on transitional provisions states that the legal effects of all acts adopted prior to the Treaty of Lisbon entering into force shall be

---

[2] For example E. Wymeersch, 8 EBOR (2007), p[. 237, 242 and the de Larosière Report, p. 13.

[3] S. Weber, in: M.A. Dauses (ed.), *Handbuch EU-Wirtschaftsrecht*, F. III para. 100.

[4] On the distinction between the two categories, see E. Wymeersch, 8 EBOR (2007), p. 237, 242 ff.

[5] K.J. Hopt, in: A. Heldrich and K.J. Hopt (eds.), *Festgabe 50 Jahre Bundesgerichtshof*, p. 497, 501 assumed that in the year 2000, for example, 80% of all provisions on capital markets law in Germany could be traced back to the influence of the European legislature. The harmonisation of European law can be expected to continue in the future. Cf. F. Walla, BKR (2012), p. 265, 269–270.

[6] Regarding the definition of regulated markets cf. § 7 para. 24–31.

[7] On open markets see below para. 62 and § 7 para 20.

[8] Cf. § 1 para. 41 and 43.

[9] The process is named after Baron Alexandre Lamfalussy, chair of the expert committee whose draft propositions are the basis for the present legislative procedure. See § 1 para. 16.

[10] Commission, Decision of 5 November 2003, 2004/5/EC; Commission, Decision of 5 November 2003, 2004/6/EC. This extension was initiated by the German and the British government; cf. A. Möller, *Kapitalmarktaufsicht*, p. 149. On the comitology procedure in general see M. Horspool and M. Humphreys, *European Law*, para. 5.33 ff.

[11] For more details on the concept of European supervision see § 11 para. 37–73.

Fabian Walla

preserved. This means that the legislative powers assigned by provisions enacted in the former Lamfalussy Process can still be applied.[12] Important procedural requirements are laid down in the Comitology Regulation, enacted in 2011.[13] The legislative procedure based on these amendments can be described as the Lamfalussy II Process.[14]

7 The following section will describe the original concept of the Lamfalussy Process prior to outlining the amendments made to the legislation by the Treaty of Lisbon and the new EU supervisory system. This overview is necessary as all four framework directives and the respective implementing measures were enacted between 2002 and 2010 and are therefore based on the Lamfalussy Process.

(a) Legislation in the Lamfalussy Process from 2002 to 2010

8 The Lamfalussy Process was introduced by the Commission to effectively fulfil the Financial Services Action Plan (FSAP).[15] The measures referred to in the FSAP were to be achieved through a more efficient, flexible and faster legislative process and with the help of external expert knowledge.[16] The introduction of two pan-European committees who were to participate in the process of law making was a fundamental component of the plan.

(aa) Committees on Capital Markets Regulation

(1) **European Securities Committee**

9 One of the new committees was the European Securities Committee (ESC).[17] It was composed of high-ranking officials of the Member States and was chaired by a representative of the European Commission. Representatives of the CESR, the ECB and the EFTA states participated as observers. The ESC had an advisory function on Levels 1 and 2 of the Lamfalussy Process and additionally that of a regulatory committee on Level 2.[18]

(2) **Committee of European Securities Regulators**

10 A further Committee, introduced in 2001 as the successor to the Forum of European Securities Commission (FESCO), was the CESR.[19] In early 2009 the Commission confirmed the importance of the CESR and enhanced its powers.[20] The CESR

---

[12] This is pointed out by I. Leixner, *Komitologie und Lamfalussyverfahren im Finanzdienstleistungsbereich*, p. 35.

[13] Regulation (EU) No. 182/2011 of the European Parliament and of the Council of 16 February 2011 laying down the rules and general principles concerning mechanisms for control by Member States of the Commission's exercise of implementing powers, OJ L55 p. 13.

[14] J. Schmidt, in: M. Lutter et al. (eds.), *Europäisches Unternehmensrecht*, p. 252.

[15] COM(1999) 232. See in more detail § 1 para. 30.

[16] S. Kalss et al., *Kapitalmarktrecht*, Vol. I, § 1 para. 50.

[17] Commission, Decision of 6 June 2001 establishing the European Securities Committee (ESC) 2001/528/EC.

[18] The legal foundation for this was Council Decision 1999/468/EC of 28 June 1999 laying down the procedures for the exercise of implementing powers, OJ L184, p. 23, amended by Council Decision of 17 July 2006 amending Decision 1999/468/EC laying down the procedures for the exercise of implementing powers conferred on the Commission (2006/512/EC), OJ L200, p. 12.

[19] Commission, Decision of 6 June 2001 establishing the Committee of European Securities Regulators (CESR), 2001/527/EC.

[20] Art. 3 of the Commission Decision of 23 January 2009 establishing the Committee of European Securities Regulators (2009/77/EC), OJ L25, p. 18.

comprised representatives of all 27 Member States, plus Norway, Iceland and the European Commission. Usually, the representatives were at the same time the heads of the national capital market supervisory institutions.

11   The CESR's duty was to advise the Commission on Level 2 of the legislative process—especially regarding technical details of implementing measures.[21] Furthermore the CESR was to improve the cooperation between the national supervisory authorities, resolve disputes between them and evaluate the implementation of EU legislation. The technical advice submitted by the CESR on Level 2 of the Lamfalussy Process could later help legal practice in the Member States with the construction of measures taken by the Commission.[22]

12   On Level 3 of the Lamfalussy Process the CESR was responsible for publishing recommendations and opinions.[23] This constituted the main area of the CESR's work once all implementing measures foreseen by the FSAP on Level 2 had been enacted.[24]

(bb) The Legislative Process

(1) **Level 1: Framework Directives**

13   Level 1 concerned the enactment of broad but sufficiently precise framework directives or regulations after a full consultation process as laid out in the EC Treaty, i.e. under participation of the European Parliament and the Council, based on proposals by the European Commission.

14   These were only to contain basic principles, to be put into more concrete terms on Level 2 and 3 of the Lamfalussy Process. In reality, however, the four framework directives—especially the MiFID—were in parts already very precise in their specifications for the Member States.[25]

15   A good example for broad and openly formulated provision can be found in the framework directive on Market Abuse. Article 1 No. 1 MAD defines the term of inside information as "information of a precise nature which has not been made public, relating, directly or indirectly, to one or more issuers of financial instruments or to one or more financial instruments and which, if it were made public, would be likely to have a significant effect on the prices of those financial instruments or on the price of related derivative financial instruments". This definition is only put into more concrete terms by the implementing directive.[26]

(2) **Level 2: Implementing Measures**

16   Level 2 of the Lamfalussy Process enabled the Commission to enact implementing measures regarding the framework directives without having to adhere to the usual

---

[21] See below para. 16–21.

[22] See § 5 para. 39–40. On the possible legal effect of technical advices, cf. also T.M.J. Möllers, ZEuP (2008), p. 480, 488 ff.; G. Spindler and J. Hupka, in: T.M.J. Möllers (ed.), *Geltung und Faktizität von Standards*, p. 117, 130–131.

[23] Examples in N. Moloney, in: M. Tison et al. (eds.), *Perspectives in Company Law and Financial Regulation*, p. 449, 453 ff.

[24] CESR, *Press Release*, CESR/06–302, June 2006; N. Moloney, in: M. Tison et al. (eds.), *Perspectives in Company Law and Financial Regulation*, p. 449, 450.

[25] E. Wymeersch, *The Future of Financial Supervision and Regulation in Europe*, 42 CML Rev. (2005), p. 987, 991.

[26] See below para. 21.

legislative procedure.[27] The Commission could enact implementing regulations or directives,[28] depending on the aim of the framework provision. The Commission made use of both regulatory instruments.[29] Both committees—the ESC and the CESR—held advisory functions for the Commission in this process.

17   After long discussions a close cooperation between Parliament and Commission regarding the legislation on Level 2 was ensured.[30] The so-called "sunset clauses" originally contained in the framework directives, suspending the Commission from the possibility of adopting implementing measures during a four-year period following the entry into force of the respective directive, were therefore removed in 2008.[31]

18   The legislation on Level 2 originally followed the Comitology Decision of 1999[32] and later the revised Comitology Decision of 2006.[33] Under the new procedure the Commission submitted its draft to the ESC and the CESR for consultation. The ESC acted as a regulatory committee.[34] Where the measure was in accordance with the ESC's opinion the Commission could submit it to the Parliament and Council, who could oppose the measure if it exceeded the Level 1 implementing powers, if it was not compatible with the aim or content of the framework instrument or if it did not respect the principles of subsidiarity and proportionality.[35] Opposition required a qualified majority vote in the Council or a vote of the majority of the members of the Parliament.[36]

19   If the ESC voted against the Commission's draft or failed to deliver an opinion, the Commission had to deliver the draft measure to the Council.[37] If the Council rejected the measure with a qualified majority vote, the proposal failed; otherwise, it was submitted to the Parliament.[38] The Parliament then considered the proposal, a rejection being possible on the same grounds as in cases in which the ESC supported the measure with a respective vote by the majority of the members of the Parliament.[39]

---

[27] S. Kalss et al., *Kapitalmarktrecht*, Vol. I, § 1 para. 43 are critical regarding the lack of certainty regarding the Commission's competences.

[28] On the legislative instruments § 3 para. 11–18.

[29] As yet, five implementing directives and five implementing regulations have been enacted on the basis of the framework directives. See § 5 para. 2–6.

[30] Cf. K.-U. Schmolke, EuR (2006), p. 432, 437. The exact procedure on level 2 was long controversial. On this see the overview in N. Moloney, *EC Securities Regulation*, p. 1028 ff.

[31] Such provisions could be found in Art. 17(4) MAD, Art. 64(4) MiFID, Art. 24(4) PD and Art. 27(4) TD. Seen critically by K.-U. Schmolke, EuR (2006), p. 432, 447–448.

[32] Council Decision of 28 June 1999 laying down the procedures for the exercise of implementing powers conferred on the Commission, 1999/468/EC, OJ L184, p. 23.

[33] Council Decision of 17 July 2006 amending Decision 1999/468/EC laying down the procedures for the exercise of implementing powers conferred on the Commission (2006/512/EC); OJ L200, p. 11. On the historical background see in detail I. Leixner, *Komitologie und Lamfalussyverfahren im Finanzdienstleistungsbereich*, p. 15–16.

[34] For more details on the procedure on level 2, see N. Moloney, *EC Securities Regulations*, p. 1048 ff.

[35] Art. 5a(3) lit. a, b Council Decision 1999/468/EC as of 17 July 2006.

[36] Art. 5a(3) lit. b Council Decision 1999/468/EC as of 17 July 2006.

[37] Art. 5a(4) lit. b Council Decision 1999/468/EC as of 17 July 2006.

[38] Art. 5a(4) lit. b, c Council Decision 1999/468/EC as of 17 July 2006.

[39] Art. 5a(4) lit. e, g Council Decision 1999/468/EC as of 17 July 2006.

20   The implementing measures led to a further harmonisation in the European Union due to their very specific provisions. The downside to this was the fact that the autonomy of Member States was restricted further.[40]

21   Implementing Directive 2003/124/EC, for example, defines in detail what constitutes inside information as mentioned in Article 1 No. 1 of the MAD mentioned above. It specified that inside information "shall be deemed to be of a precise nature if it indicates a set of circumstances which exists or may reasonably be expected to come into existence or an event which has occurred or may reasonably be expected to do so and if it is specific enough to enable a conclusion to be drawn as to the possible effect of that set of circumstances or event on the prices of financial instruments or related derivative financial instruments".

(3) Level 3: Guidelines and Recommendations

22   Level 3 was concerned with the CESR's task of developing guidelines and recommendations for a consistent interpretation of capital markets law throughout Europe in order to ensure a level playing field of all European capital markets.[41] The guidelines and recommendations which continue to be in force[42] are not binding,[43] but rather a significant interpretational help for the national supervisory authorities and the market participants.[44]

23   Although non-binding, a certain indirect legal effect ensues from these measures. In German legal literature, for example, it is argued that the disregard of the CESR's recommendations may facilitate the proof of liability for civil law liability claims. Another example is that a criminal offence may be classed as an unavoidable mistake of law if CESR recommendations were adhered to, yet will usually be seen as avoidable if they were disregarded.[45]

(4) Level 4: Supervision of the Enforcement by Member States

24   On the last level of the Lamfalussy Process the European Commission monitored and evaluates the enforcement of the Community's rules on capital markets law by the Member States. The Commission was to commence an infringement proceeding against a Member State when a breach of European law became apparent. In order to facilitate the supervision, the Member States had an extensive duty to report on the progress of implementation. Additionally, the CESR established a peer-review panel, responsible for supervising the consistent application of European capital markets law throughout the Member States.[46]

---

[40] This is pointed out by W. Groß, *Kapitalmarktrecht*, Vorb. BörsG para. 18.
[41] S. Kalss et al., *Kapitalmarktrecht*, Vol. I, § 1 para. 48.
[42] See below para. 27.
[43] Lamfalussy Report, p. 47; cf. also T.M.J. Möllers, ZEuP (2008), p. 480, 491 ff.
[44] See § 5 para. 39–40.
[45] J. Hupka, WM (2009), p. 1351, 1355 ff.; T.M.J. Möllers, NZG (2010), p. 285, 286; on the civil law effects see G. Spindler and J. Hupka, in: T.M.J. Möllers (ed.), *Geltung und Faktizität von Standards*, p. 117, 135 ff. For a more general approach see S. Kalss, in: K. Riesenhuber (ed.), *Europäische Methodenlehre*, p. 397.
[46] N. Moloney, in: M. Tison et al. (eds.), *Perspectives in Company Law and Financial Regulation*, p. 449, 459.

(cc)   Evaluation

25   The Lamfalussy Process was revised and evaluated[47] in 2007 and found not to be in urgent need of reform.[48] The aim of a more efficient, flexible and faster legislative process largely appears to have been achieved.[49]

26   The use of expert knowledge and a faster and more flexible legislative process are essential in an area subject to such continual changes as capital markets. The downside of this is that the legislative process in capital markets law still lacks democratic legitimacy[50]—despite the European Parliament now being more involved in the legislative process on Level 2.[51]

(b)   The Lamfalussy II Process

27   The four levels of legislation in the Lamfalussy Process continue to exist, although the legislative procedure has been subject to a number of changes through the Treaty of Lisbon and the formation of the ESMA.[52] The Commission has declared its intention "to continue to consult experts appointed by the Member States in the preparation of draft delegated acts in the financial services area, in accordance with its established practice".[53] The new procedures have not changed the fact that framework acts, enacted in the ordinary legislative procedure by the European Parliament and the Council, still constitute the foundation of the European legislation in this field. On Level 3 and 4 the ESMA has taken over from the CESR, enacting nonbinding guidelines and recommendations on the interpretation of the European legislative acts and supervising the implementation of the European requirements in the Member States together with the Commission.[54] Substantial changes can be found on Level 2 of the procedures with regard to the measures for rendering the framework legislation more precise. In order to understand the Lamfalussy II Process one must consider the important new distinction introduced by the Treaty of Lisbon between legal acts such as the non-legislative delegated acts described in Article 290(1) TFEU and the implementation of legally binding acts as described in

---

[47] Commission, *Review of the Lamfalussy process strengthening supervisory convergence* (November 2007); Inter-Institutional Monitoring Group, *Final Report Monitoring the Lamfalussy Process* (October 2007).

[48] N. Moloney, in: M. Tison et al. (eds.), *Perspectives in Company Law and Financial Regulation*, p. 449, 472; similarly N. Moloney, *The Financial Crisis and EU Securities Law-Making: A Challenge Met?*, in: S. Grundmann et al. (eds.), *Festschrift für Klaus J. Hopt*, p. 2264, 2281. For an overview of the points of criticism, especially of the work of the committees on Level 3, see I. Leixner, *Komitologie und Lamfalussyverfahren im Finanzdienstleistungsbereich*, p. 24 ff.

[49] T.M.J. Möllers, ZEuP (2008), p. 480, 502 ff.; K.-U. Schmolke, NZG (2005), p. 912, 918. See also the various reports published by the Inter-Institutional Monitoring Group (IIMG), established by the Commission. With regard to this, the criticism expressed in the literature at the outset of this procedure is unsubstantiated. On this see G. Hertig and R. Lee, 3 J. Corp. L. Stud. (2003), p. 359, 364 ff.

[50] S. Kalss et al., *Kapitalmarktrecht*, Vol. I, § 1 para. 50; K. Langenbucher, ZEuP (2002), p. 265, 283 ff.; B. Scheel, ZEuS (2006), p. 521 ff.; K.-U. Schmolke, EuR (2006), p. 432, 443. Cf. also K. von Wogau, ZEuP (2002), p. 695, 699–700 for a summary of the European Parliament's doubt at the time. The fact that the Lamfalussy Process conforms with European primary law can, however, not be doubted, cf. K.-U. Schmolke, EuR (2006), p. 432, 441.

[51] See above para. 17.

[52] Similarly I. Leixner, *Komitologie und Lamfalussyverfahren im Finanzdienstleistungsbereich*, p. 32.

[53] Declaration No. 39 annexed to the Final Act of the Intergovernmental Conference which adopted the Treaty of Lisbon, OJ C115, 9 May 2008, p. 350. The details, however, remain unclear.

[54] See under § 11 para. 64–65.

Article 291(1) TFEU.[55] The distinction between the two categories from the perspective of primary law remains unclear.[56]

28   In 2011, the Commission presented extensive proposals for amendments to the MAD, the MiFID and the TD.[57] The MAD is to be replaced by a Market Abuse Regulation,[58] and the MiFID by a regulation (MiFIR) and a MiFID II Directive,[59] whilst the TD is to remain in force but be revised comprehensively.[60] These reforms in European capital markets law are to be implemented on the basis of the Lamfalussy II Process.

(aa)   The New Level 2

29   Pursuant to the new procedure, Level 2 requires the distinction between acts by the Commission and those drafted by the ESMA. The Commission adopts delegated acts, under consultation with the ESMA. These are complemented by regulatory technical standards that are drafted by the ESMA and are also classed as delegated acts under Article 290 TFEU, requiring endorsement by the Commission as confirmation.[61] Regulatory Technical Standards must thus be seen as a special form of delegated act.[62] The Commission can adopt delegated acts as directives, regulations or decisions. Generally, regulations are most recommendable.

30   The provisions and the requirements for their applicability are then put into more concrete terms by implementing acts as described in Article 291 TFEU. These must also be divided into implementing acts adopted by the Commission and the ESC as Comitology Committee in the sense of the Comitology Regulation, and technical implementing standards drafted by the ESMA that require endorsement by the Commission.

31   On these grounds Level 2 of the Lamfalussy II Process can be seen as a multi-stage process with regard to precision of the legislative acts. The Commission's delegated acts put the framework provisions on Level 1 into more concrete terms. Whilst

---

[55] Cf. I. Leixner, *Komitologie und Lamfalussyverfahren im Finanzdienstleistungsbereich*, p. 35 ff. The Commission's legislation is often referred to as "tertiary legislation", cf. T. von Danwitz, in: M.A. Dauses (ed.), *Handbuch EU-Wirtschaftsrecht*, B.II. para. 72. The distinction between the two is not without problems, cf. R. Streinz et al., *Vertrag von Lissabon*, § 10 sec. 3

[56] Cf. A. Kahl, in: Braumüller et al. (eds.), *Die neue Europäische Finanzmarktaufsicht—ZFR Jahrestagung 2011*, p. 55, 71.

[57] Cf. F. Walla, BB (2012), p. 1358 ff.

[58] Proposal for a Regulation of the European Parliament and of the Council on insider dealing and market manipulation (market abuse), COM(2011), 651 final. See R. Veil and P. Koch, WM (2011), p. 2297 ff.; A. Merkner and M. Sustmann, AG (2012), p. 315 ff.; L. Teigelack, BB (2012), p. 1361 ff.; P. Koch, BB (2012), p. 1365 ff.

[59] Proposal for a Directive of the European Parliament and of the Council amending Directive 2004/109/EC on the harmonisation of transparency requirements in relation to information about issuers whose securities are admitted to trading on a regulated market and Commission Directive 2007/14/EC, COM(2011), 683 final. For details see R. Veil, WM (2012), p. 52 ff.; C.H. Seibt and B. Wollenschläger, AG (2012), p. 305 ff.; R. Veil, BB (2012), p. 1374 ff.

[60] Proposal for a Directive of the European Parliament and of the Council on markets in financial instruments repealing Directive 2004/39/EC of the European Parliament and of the Council, COM(2011), 656 final and Proposal for a Regulation of the European Parliament and of the Council on markets in financial instruments and amending Regulation [EMIR] on OTC derivatives, central counterparties and trade repositories, KOM(2011), 652 final. On the reform see R. Veil and M.P. Lerch, WM (2012), p. 1557–1565 and 1605–1613.

[61] For more details see § 11 para. 66–72. Cf. also N. Moloney, in: S. Grundmann et al. (eds.), *Festschrift für Klaus J. Hopt*, p. 2265, 2271–2272.

[62] Similarly A. Kahl, in: Braumüller et al. (eds.), *Die neue Europäische Finanzmarktaufsicht—ZFR Jahrestagung 2011*, p. 55, 57.

Article 290 TFEU only allows them to "supplement or amend certain non-essential elements of the legislative act", the Commission is granted a certain creative power in fact, allowing it to exert significant influence through its delegated acts. Similarly, the ESMA's regulatory technical standards are also not to "imply strategic decisions or policy choices" pursuant to Article 15 ESMA Regulation, but in practice also grant a certain legislative discretion, albeit not to the same extent as the Commission is supposed to have.

32   *Examples:* The Commission can adopt delegated acts for the purpose of defining the identities and the reasons for persons to be included on an insider list (Article 13(4) Proposal for a Market Abuse Regulation) or as to the financial instruments to be taken into account when calculating the number of voting rights that determine the transparency requirements (Article 13 Proposal for a Transparency Directive). The ESMA is to adopt regulatory technical standards on the procedures to be followed by market operators to prevent market abuse (Article 11(7) Proposal for a Market Abuse Regulation) and to render more precise the provisions on exemptions from the rules on transparency regarding major shareholdings (Article 9(4), (6) Proposal for a Transparency Directive).

33   Implementing acts by the Commission and technical implementing standards by the ESMA which mainly concern procedural requirements also put the requirements for the applicability of a provision into more concrete terms on the next level.

34   *Examples:* The Commission is to adopt implementing measures regarding the specific procedures for reports of breaches (Article 29(3) Proposal for a Market Abuse Regulation).[63] The ESMA is to draft technical implementing standards with regard to the disclosure procedure for inside information (Article 12(9) Proposal for a Market Abuse Directive).[64]

35   The relationship between the different legislative acts on Level 2 of the Lamfalussy II Process is not always reflected, however, on the respective authoritative basis in the reformed framework legislation: Article 14(6) Proposal for a Market Abuse Regulation, for example, allows the Commission to adopt delegated acts specifying the persons who are required to disclose Directors' dealings. As opposed to this, the same legislative act requires the ESMA to develop draft regulatory technical standards to determine the exact duties for financial analysts. This constitutes a further-reaching power than that granted to the Commission in Article 14 of the proposal. The European legislator, despite its intention, has thus not fully achieved the development of a hierarchical relationship between the two forms of Level 2 measures.

(bb) Criticism

36   The new procedure must be regarded positively with regard to the role of the ESMA, enabling the use of its specific expertise. It is further generally wise to allow the Commission and the ESMA—as far as permissible under primary law—to develop delegated acts, in order to reduce the necessity of the tedious European legislative procedures. At the same time, the variety of legal sources in European law together

[63] Draft as of the Presidency compromise of 2 May 2012.
[64] Ibid.

with abundant national provisions will lead to an extremely complex and partially opaque regulatory system. It therefore appears critical to require the further distinction between technical regulatory standards and delegated acts by the Commission. Ultimately, only the enactment of the proposed legislation can show whether the new legislative mechanism is viable in practice.

(cc)   Graph: Lamfalussy II Process

Level 1	**Legislative Acts** **by the European Parliament and the Council** **(Art. 294 ff. TFEU)**	
Level 2	Delegated Acts by the Commission (Art. 290 TFEU)	Regulatory Technical Standards (RTS) drafted by ESMA endorsed by the Commission (Art. 10 ESMA-Regulation; Art. 290 TFEU)
	Implementing Acts by the European Commission and the ESC (Art. 291 TFEU)	Implementing Technical Standards (ITS) drafted by ESMA endorsed by the Commission (Art. 15 ESMA-Regulation; Art. 291 TFEU)
Level 3	**Non-binding Guidelines and recommendations by ESMA** **(Art. 16 ESMA-Regulation)**	
Level 4	**Enforcement by ESMA and the European Commission** **(Art. 17 ESMA-Regulation)**	

37   Figure 1 shows a schematic of the Lamfalussy II process.

II.   Strategies of Capital Markets Regulation

1.   Minimum and Maximum Harmonisation

38   European capital markets law is characterised by "unity and diversity".[65] This is a result of the fact that European legislation in this area consists of a combination of minimum and maximum harmonisation.[66]

---

[65] R. Veil and P. Koch, *Französisches Kapitalmarktrecht*, p. 1; R. Veil and F. Walla, *Schwedisches Kapitalmarktrecht*, p. 1; R. Veil and M. Wundenberg, *Englisches Kapitalmarktrecht*, p. 1; see also C. Gerne-Beuerle, 7 CMLJ (2012), p. 317–342.

[66] On the legal foundations in primary law see M. Gruber, in: Braumüller et al. (eds.), *Die neue Europäische Finanzmarktaufsicht—ZFR Jahrestagung 2011*, p. 1, 4 ff.

Fabian Walla

(a) Definitions

39   Maximum harmonisation describes the concept under which the legislative order of a provision is exclusive, i.e. allowing no deviations from its content in the Member States' national laws.[67] As opposed to this, minimum harmonisation may be assumed in cases in which the provision only contains minimum requirements that must be met by the Member States and may be exceeded.[68] The two concepts can be inherent in both directives and regulations. Whilst regulations will usually aim at a maximum harmonisation, it may in some cases also be possible that a regulation only requires minimum harmonisation.[69] Directives are equally open to both concepts.[70]

40   In order to determine whether a provision is minimally or maximally harmonising, one must interpret the provision, thus determining the underlying interests of the European legislator.[71] If a conclusion cannot be reached simply by interpretation of the legislative act's provisions, reference can often be made to the recitals.

41   An analysis of the Lamfalussy directives currently in force reveals that the MiFID follows the concept of maximum harmonisation,[72] whilst the TD is an example of minimum harmonisation.[73] The concept adhered to in the Prospectus and MAD is unclear and a matter of controversy.[74] The Commission's proposal for a regulation on insider trading and market manipulation and its proposal for amendments to the TD[75] now follow a concept of maximum harmonisation to a large extent.[76]

42   The Commission plans to develop fully harmonised rules on the transparency with regard to major shareholdings in the course of the revision of the TD, Article 3(1) Proposal for a Transparency Directive explicitly stating that a holder of shares, or a natural person or legal entity referred to in Articles 10 or 13, may not be made subject to requirements more stringent than those laid down in the Directive. Regarding periodic disclosure, the Commission still follows the concept of minimum harmonisation, as becomes apparent in Article 3(1) which declares that the home Member State may make an issuer subject to require-

---

[67] H.-H. Hernfeld, in: J. Schwarze (ed.), *EU-Kommentar*, Art. 95 EGV para. 49; C. Tietje, in: E. Grabitz and M. Hilf (eds.), *Recht der europäischen Union*, Vorb. Art. 94–97 para. 39; J. Steiner and L. Woods, *EU Law*, 16.3.1.

[68] C. Tietje, in: E. Grabitz and M. Hilf (eds.), *Recht der Europäischen Union*, Vorb. Art. 94–97 para. 41; in detail M. Dougan, 37 CML Rev. (2000), p. 853 ff. Gold plating is permitted in these cases, cf. para. 49.

[69] H.-W. Micklitz and P. Rott, in: M.A. Dauses (ed.), *Handbuch des EU-Wirtschaftsrechts*, H. V. para. 40.

[70] H.-H. Hernfeld, in: J. Schwarze (ed.), *EU-Kommentar*, Art. 95 EGV para. 39; M. Nettesheim, in: E. Grabitz and M. Hilf (eds.), *Recht der Europäischen Union*, Art. 249 EGV para. 133.

[71] Cf. ECJ of 14 October 1987, Case 278/85 (*Commission/Denmark*) [1987] ECR 4069 para. 16–17. On the methods of interpretation applied in European law see § 5 para. 34–55.

[72] A. Fuchs, in: A. Fuchs (ed.), WpHG Kommentar, § 31 para. 18; K. Rothenhöfer, in: E. Schwark and D. Zimmer (eds.), *Kapitalmarktrechts-Kommentar*, § 31 para. 16; N. Moloney, *EC Securities Regulation*, p. 35; T.M.J. Möllers, WM (2008), p. 93, 98. In Germany the term *Vollharmonisierung*, i.e. "full harmonisation" is most commonly applied. P.O. Mülbert, WM (2007), p. 1149, 1157, seemingly follows the English terminology, speaking of *Maximalharmonisierung*. Cf. also M. Gruber, in: Braumüller et al. (eds.), *Die neue Europäische Finanzmarktaufsicht—ZFR Jahrestagung 2011*, p. 1, 2.

[73] Cf. Recital 7 TD.

[74] For a maximum harmonisation: T.M.J. Möllers, ZEuP (2008), p. 480, 499, who deduces this from the nature of the directive as framework directive in the Lamfalussy-process (with the exception of the Transparency Directive). For a minimum harmonisation: N. Moloney, *EC Securities Regulation*, p. 35.

[75] Cf. § 1 para. 41–42.

[76] Explicitly Art. 3 Directive amending Directive 2004/109/EC (proposal); for the Regulation on insider trading and market manipulation cf. R. Veil and P. Koch, WM (2010), p. 2297 ff.

ments more stringent than those laid down in the Directive.[77] In this context it is unclear whether the maximum harmonisation also refers to the rules on the attribution of voting rights.[78] This question must be answered by interpreting the directive. The fact that a regulation can also be minimally harmonising can be seen in the rules on sanctions contained in the Proposal for a Market Abuse Regulation, which states in Article 26(2) that it only aims to achieve minimum harmonisation.

(b)   Advantages and Disadvantages

43   Neither concept of harmonisation comes without disadvantages. The advantage of a maximum harmonisation lies in the fact that it prevents a legal fragmentation, thereby reducing the transaction costs for market participants.[79] As opposed to this, a minimum harmonisation furthers the competition between the different legal systems in the Member States,[80] thus presenting incentives for regulatory innovations and preventing the law from stagnation.[81] A minimum harmonisation also ensures that the Member States preserve their "national identity" to a certain degree.[82] This complies with the principle of subsidiarity.[83]

(c)   Tendency towards Maximum Harmonisation

44   On the basis of the Financial Services Action Plan, the Commission is encouraging a shift from minimum to maximum harmonisation which is becoming increasingly apparent.[84] It is meanwhile being discussed that areas that were so far dominated by minimum harmonisation—such as transparency of major shareholdings—should also be subjected to maximum harmonisation.[85] The CRA Regulation,[86] the short-selling regulation,[87] the development from directive to regulation with regard to market abuse and MiFID all indicate that, additionally, there is a tendency towards regulations which generally follow the concept of maximum harmonisation instead of directives, which by nature usually allow the Member States a certain leeway.

---

[77] Cf. R. Veil, WM (2012), p. 53, 54.

[78] Cf. C. H. Seibt and B. Wollenschläger, AG (2012), p. 305, 310.

[79] Summarised in H. Fleischer and K.-U. Schmolke, NZG (2009), p. 401, 408; H. Fleischer and K.-U. Schmolke, NZG (2010), p. 1241, 1245; N. Moloney, *EC Securities Regulation*, p. 34.

[80] N. Moloney, *EC Securities Regulation*, p. 10.

[81] H. Fleischer and K.-U. Schmolke, NZG (2009), p. 401, 408; H. Fleischer and K.-U. Schmolke, NZG (2010), p. 1241, 1245–1246.

[82] Cf. also M. Gruber, in: Braumüller et al. (eds.), *Die neue Europäische Finanzmarktaufsicht—ZFR Jahrestagung 2011*, p. 1, 14. On the values of heterogeneity in the national legal systems in Europe see M. Tamm, EuZW (2007), p. 756, 758.

[83] Cf. M. Gruber, in: Braumüller et al. (eds.), *Die neue Europäische Finanzmarktaufsicht—ZFR Jahrestagung 2011*, p. 1, 13

[84] H. Fleischer and K.-U. Schmolke, NZG (2010), p. 1241, 1243; N. Moloney, *EC Securities Regulation*, p. 31 ff.; T.M.J. Möllers, ZEuP (2008), p. 480, 499 ff.; T.M.J. Möllers, in: B. Gsell and C. Herresthal, *Vollharmonisierung im Privatrecht*, p. 235, 250 ff.

[85] See in detail H. Fleischer and K.-U. Schmolke, NZG (2010), p. 1241 ff.

[86] See § 27 para. 11 ff. On the maximally harmonising effects of this regulation cf. also T.M.J. Möllers, NZG (2010), p. 1241 ff.

[87] See § 1 para. 44 and in detail in § 15 para. 9.

Fabian Walla

2. Regulatory Concepts in the Member States

45 The Member States have to implement the European directives into their national laws. Therefore national capital markets law is primarily "European law". Additionally, however, a number of Member States have enacted their own national provisions which address additional aspects of capital markets law or put the means of enforcement into more concrete terms. The fact that there are thus two coexisting systems of capital markets law is a phenomenon existing only in the European Union.

(a) Transformation of European Law

46 The Member States are obliged to transpose the directives that were enacted on Level 1 and 2 of the Lamfalussy Process into their national laws.[88] Unless the respective directive follows the concept of maximum harmonisation,[89] the Member States have a large margin of appreciation concerning the exact form of transposition and may orientate themselves by their national traditions and concepts.[90] This margin of appreciation is reflected in a comparative examination of the different methods of implementation in the Member States regarding capital markets law.

47 Several Member States—France,[91] the United Kingdom[92] and Spain[93] among others—often implement the provisions of directives into their national law "one-to-one", as this procedure, which one could graphically call "copy-out", eliminates the danger of the national provisions violating EU law and prevents difficulties in interpretation. From a European perspective this type of transposition is to be welcomed as it achieves a high level of harmonisation.

48 Other Member States, such as Germany, often deviate from the directive's wording,[94] adapting the provisions to the particularities of their national capital markets law.[95] In Sweden the transposition is sometimes only fragmentary—conformity with European law only being achieved by an interpretation that relies on the help of the legislative materials.[96]

---

[88] See para. 13–35.
[89] On the concepts of minimum and maximum harmonisation see para. 38–44.
[90] M. Nettesheim, in: E. Grabitz and M. Hilf (eds.), *Recht der Europäischen Union*, Art. 249 EGV para. 140; G. Schmidt, in: H. von der Groeben and J. Schwarze (eds.), *EU/EG-Vertrag*, Art. 249 EGV para. 40.
[91] Cf. for example on the MiFID transposition R. Veil and P. Koch, *Französisches Kapitalmarktrecht*, p. 106.
[92] Cf. R. Veil and M. Wundenberg, *Englisches Kapitalmarktrecht*, p. 14 f.
[93] Cf. J. Guitard Marín, in: F.F. Uría, *Régimen jurídico de los mercados de valores y de las instituciones de inversión colectiva*, p. 301, 306.
[94] The copy-out approach is becoming more and more popular in Germany. The German federal government explicitly stated that it was following a one-to-one implementation of the MiFID. Cf. on this R. Veil, WM (2008), p. 1093, 1094.
[95] The provisions of the MAD, the TD and the MiFID are largely implemented in the Wertpapierhandelsgesetz (WpHG), which can be regarded as the "constitution" of capital markets law. Only the transposition of the Prospectus Directive, which was mainly implemented in the Wertpapierprospektgesetz (WpPG) and the Börsengesetz (BörsG), can be seen as an exception from this approach.
[96] This can especially be seen with regard to the transposition of the MAD. On this see F. Walla, in: M. Schultz, *Stockholm Centre for Commercial Law Årsbok II*, p. 427, 432 ff. On the question whether this complies with European law ECJ of 7 May 2002, Case C-478/99 (*Commission/Sweden*) [2002] ECR I-4147.

(b)   Accompanying National Law

49   In many Member States the implemented European provisions are accompanied by autonomous national rules, which often exceed the provisions of European law.[97] This phenomenon is referred to as gold-plating[98] and is permitted in areas of minimum harmonisation.[99] Whilst gold-plating aims at fulfilling the goals of European capital markets law particularly well, one must bear in mind that exceeding the directive's provisions will also obstruct the harmonisation of law in the European Union. Therefore, it is only consistent that the European Commission deems it highly important for Member States to refrain as much as possible from adding national rules to those agreed upon at European level.[100]

50   In some Member States the original legislation on capital markets law continues to exist parallel to the provisions implemented into national law by the European directives on capital markets law.[101]

(c)   The Principles-based Approach to Regulation in the United Kingdom

51   The approach to regulation taken by national law in the United Kingdom is very different from that in the other Member States. The former national supervisory authority, the Financial Services Authority (FSA), established the concept of so-called principles-based regulation,[102] which will be followed by its successor, the Financial Conduct Authority (FCA).[103] The principles-based regulation forms a second level of regulation next to the implemented European directives.

(aa)   Foundations of Principles-based Regulation

52   In this "principles-based" model the FSA made use of abstract standards and objectives, i.e. principles, rather than applying detailed, prescriptive rules.[104] In its Handbook of Rules and Guidelines, the FSA published eleven high-level standards for financial intermediaries[105] and seven listing principles for issuers.[106] In other

---

[97] Examples for this are the provisions in Germany (§ 27a WpHG) and France (Art. L 233-6 and -7 Code de commerce) on the notifications by the owners of holdings, cf. § 20 para. 129 and 132.

[98] On the limits of *gold plating* see F. Burmeister and E. Staebe, EuR (2009), p. 444 ff. and on the concept itself see the interim report of the Inter-Institutional Monitoring Group (IIMG) of 15 October 2007.

[99] See also above para. 39 ff.

[100] Communication from the Commission on the Review of the Lamfalussy process, 20 November 2007, COM(2007), 727 final, p. 5–6.

[101] The Swedish act on investment advice for consumers (Lag om finansiell radgivning till konsumenter, SFS 2003:862), which stayed applicable even after the transposition of the MiFID (cf. Lag om värdepappersmarknaden, SFS 2007:528) can be seen as an example thereof. Cf. F. Korling, in: M. Schultz, *Stockholm Centre for Commercial Law Årsbok I*, p. 95 ff.

[102] On this see FSA, *Principles-based Regulation: Focusing on the Outcome that Matters* (2007) and FSA, *A New Regulator for a New Century* (2000). Cf. also in legal literature: E. Ferran, in: M. Tison et al. (eds.), *Perspectives in Company Law and Financial Regulation*, p. 427 ff.; J. Black, 3 CMLJ (2008), p. 425 ff.; J. Black et al., 1 Law and Financial Markets Review (2007), p. 191 ff.; C.L. Ford, 45 Am. Bus. Law J. (2008), p. 1 ff.; D. Weber-Rey, in: S. Weatherill, *Better Regulation*, p. 247 ff. From a law and economics point of view: L. Kaplow, 42 Duke LJ (1992–93), p. 557 ff.

[103] See under § 11 para. 11.

[104] J. Black et al., 1 Law and Financial Markets Review (2007), p. 191.

[105] FSA Handbook, PRIN 2.1. The FSA Handbook also contains principles for so-called *approved person* and for the *senior management*.

[106] FSA Handbook, LR 7.2.

Fabian Walla

words the statutory objectives are supported by a set of extensive principles of good regulation.[107] Instead of focusing on the process to be followed by the market participants, these principles only define the regulatory objective, leaving the market participants—who, according to this strategy, are better placed than regulators to determine possible and effective processes—to find the most efficient way of achieving that outcome.[108]

53   The aim of this type of regulation can therefore be seen as encouraging innovations by market participants.[109] Additionally, the FSA believed this approach would achieve a more flexible regulatory framework, reduce red tape costs and enable a faster regulatory reaction to market changes, especially regarding market abuse.

54   Despite the latest financial crisis the FSA did not abandon this approach.[110] However, regarding solvency supervision it modified its regulation due to the experiences made during the crisis by supplementing the principles with detailed macro-level rules on prudential regulation.[111]

(bb) Effects of Principles-based Regulation on Enforcement

55   Principles-based regulation strongly affects the enforcement in cases of failure to comply with the principles.[112] The FSA's approach contained the possibility of sanctioning the failure to comply with penalties. In some areas—especially regarding insider trading—it bases most of its enforcement on the breach of principles.[113] This is possible, as the application of principles is not prevented by the applicability of the provisions of the Financial Services and Markets Act 2000 (FSMA),[114] thus enabling a supervisory sanction even if the prohibitory provisions introduced into the FSMA transforming European law are not affected, provided the FSA assumed a violation of the principles.[115] This has led to intense discussions between the FSA and the market participants.[116] Nonetheless, the FSA's informal guidance on the construction of the principles has achieved legal certainty for the market participants to some extent.

56   All in all, the high level of cooperation and communication between the supervisory authority and the market participants in the United Kingdom, which is necessary with this approach, is unrivalled in the EU.

(cc) Evaluation

57   The fact that the detailed provisions on regulation in the other Member States have so far not prevented misconduct may be used as an argument for the FSA's principles-based approach. In provisions which only define the legislative aim but

---

[107] P.J. May, 25 Law & Pol'y (2003), p. 381.

[108] J. Black, *The Development of Risk Based Regulation in Financial Services: Canada, the UK and Australia*, p. 30.

[109] FSA, *Principles-based Regulation—Focusing on the Outcome That matters* (2007), p. 6.

[110] FSA, *Business Plan 2008/2009*, p. 7.

[111] Cf. K. Alexander, 10 EBOR (2009), p. 169, 173.

[112] Cf. F. Walla, *Konzeption der Kapitalmarktaufsicht in Deutschland*, p. 164 ff.; M. Wundenberg, *Compliance und die prinzipiengeleitete Aufsicht, passim*.

[113] R. Veil and M. Wundenberg, *Englisches Kapitalmarktrecht*, p. 11.

[114] Ibid. More details on the distinction between *principles* and *rules* in R. Purves, in: M. Blair et al. (eds.), *Financial Services Law*, para. 5.26 ff.

[115] Cf. for an example § 13 para. 120 and 122.

[116] Cf. L. Frach, *Finanzaufsicht in Deutschland und Großbritannien*, p. 130 ff.

do not contain clear rules on how this is to be achieved, it is much easier for the supervisory authority to ensure that the legislative intention is fulfilled. The FSA could adapt its regulations far more easily to market changes and the market participants' innovations.

58   The advantages of the use of principles, as opposed to detailed rules, recently became apparent concerning the transparency regarding major holdings: as of 1 June 2009 the FSA adopted a principles-based approach with regard to the so-called contracts for difference,[117] in order to prevent the accumulation of undisclosed equity stakes (hidden ownership).[118] As a reaction to the market participants' innovations regarding possibilities of hidden ownership, the provision established disclosure obligations for any economic share-ownership exceeding a specific threshold value. Tendencies towards a principles-based approach in this area of capital markets law are also becoming increasingly apparent in the other Member States.[119]

59   Yet the principles-based approach has considerable disadvantages. These concern in particular the legal uncertainty for market participants, for whom it may be unclear whether they have complied with certain principles. This lack of legal certainty is one of the main points of criticism regarding the FSA's approach. Furthermore, the high level of informal communication that takes place with the administration may lead to a lack of transparency in administration.[120] Last but not least it may be difficult to bring the principles-based approach in line with the fundamental constitutional concepts of the European Union,[121] such as the principle of legal clarity. Further doubts regarding the constitutionality of the principles-based approach arise with regard to the separation of powers, when one considers that enforcement is possible and penalties may be imposed on the sole basis of the principles developed by the supervisory authority itself.

(dd) Outlook

60   The FSA's approach to regulation is unique in Europe's capital markets law systems. Yet the introduction of a principles-based regulation at a second regulatory level was also discussed in Sweden.[122] The disadvantages mentioned above have, however, prevented any of the other Member States from following the United Kingdom's approach. It is to be assumed that, inter alia, the conflicting constitutional principles will prevent the other Member States from introducing a similar system in the future.

61   To a certain extent the introduction of a principles-based approach has already occurred in European capital markets law.[123] It is recommendable for other regula-

---

[117] On this see § 20 para. 80.
[118] Cf. FSA, *Consultation Paper 07/20*, para. 2.10 ff.; W. Dwyer, 24 JIBLR (2009), p. 435 ff.; T. Siebens and M. Gambol, 4 CMLJ (2009), p. 172, 176–177; summarised in R. Veil and M. Wundenberg, *Englisches Kapitalmarktrecht*, p. 126 ff.
[119] Cf. § 20 para. 109.
[120] Cf. J. Black et al., 1 Law and Financial Markets Review (2007), p. 191, 201.
[121] On the concept of common constitutional traditions see M. Hilf and F. Schorkopf, in: E. Grabitz and M. Hilf (eds.), *Recht der Europäischen Union*, Art. 6 EUV para. 6 ff.
[122] Finansinspektionen, *Promemoria of 4 March 2008*; seen critically by H. Schedin, in: G. Nord and P. Thorell, *Regelfrågor på en förandrad kapitalmarknad*, p. 145 ff.
[123] On compliance see § 29 para. 3 ff., on the regulation of rating agencies see § 27 para. 25.

tory areas *de lege ferenda*, where the possibility to react quickly and effectively to the market participants' innovations may be necessary. Principles-based legislation is an effective way to deal with market abuse and attempts at circumventing disclosure provisions. However, it must take into consideration the above-mentioned concerns regarding constitutionality.

(d) Self-regulation

62   Many Member States complement public regulation by a more or less developed self-regulation which, however, mainly concerns the dealings on the unregulated markets not covered by the European legislation, such as the Open Market (*Freiverkehr*) in Germany[124] or the Alternative Investment Market (AIM) in the UK.[125] Traditionally, the market organisation in these cases is subject to the stock exchanges and their listing rules.

63   On the regulated markets, self-regulation has lost most of its importance, as the European directives leave hardly any leeway for the market operators and participants. A few areas of self-regulation do, however, still exist: The takeover law in the United Kingdom[126] and the rules on ad hoc disclosure in Sweden,[127] for example, are mainly self-regulatory. Additionally, some Member States have private supervisory institutions, such as the Fondsrådet[128] in Denmark or the Aktiemarknadsnämnden[129] in Sweden, with their own standards-setting powers. The MAD and Implementing Directive 2003/125/EC provide the possibility of self-regulation for certain areas of capital markets law: journalists are exempt from certain rules of conduct pertaining to financial analysts, for example, if they are subject to a comparable self-regulation.[130]

---

[124] On German law see P. Storm, *Alternative Freiverkehrssegmente im Kapitalmarktrecht*, p. 79 ff.; R. Veil, *Marktregulierung durch privates Recht am Beispiel des Entry Standard der Frankfurter Wertpapierbörse*, in: Ulrich Burgard et al. (eds.), *Festschrift für Uwe H. Schneider*, p. 1313.

[125] Cf. P. Storm, *Alternative Freiverkehrssegmente im Kapitalmarktrecht*, p. 44 ff.

[126] Cf. for example T.I. Ogowewo, 12 J Int Bank Law (1997), p. 15 ff.; monographic: G. Roßkopf, *Selbstregulierung von Übernahmeangeboten in Großbritannien*, p. 86 ff.

[127] R. Veil and F. Walla, *Schwedisches Kapitalmarktrecht*, p. 83 ff.

[128] On this see www.finanstilsynet.dk/Om-os/Fondsraadet.aspx?sc_lang=en.

[129] More on this in R. Veil and F. Walla, *Schwedisches Kapitalmarktrecht*, p. 15 ff.

[130] § 26 para. 25–27. The concept of self-regulation in capital markets law is described in detail in J.A. Kämmerer, in: K.J. Hopt et al. (eds.), *Kapitalmarktgesetzgebung im europäischen Binnenmarkt*, p. 145, 151 ff.

§ 5 Sources of Law and Principles of Interpretation

Bibliography

Bleckmann, Albert, *Probleme der Auslegung europäischer Richtlinien*, ZGR (1992), p. 364–375; Conac, Pierre-Henri, *Autorité des marchés financiers*, in: Dictionnaire Joly Bourse et produits financiers, Tome 1 (2009); Langenbucher, Katja, *Zur Zulässigkeit parlamentsersetzender Normgebungsverfahren im Europarecht*, ZEuP (2002), p. 265–286; Langenbucher, Katja (ed.), *Europarechtliche Bezüge des Privatrechts*, 2nd ed. (2008); Möllers, Thomas M.J., *Europäische Methoden- und Gesetzgebungslehre im Kapitalmarktrecht—Vollharmonisierung, Generalklauseln und soft law im Rahmen des Lamfalussy-Verfahrens als Mittel zur Etablierung von Standards*, ZEuP (2008), p. 480–505; Moloney, Niamh, *The Committee of European Securities Regulators and Level 3 of the Lamfalussy Process*, in: Tison, Michel et al. (eds.), *Perspectives in Company Law and Financial Regulation—Essays in Honour of Eddy Wymeersch* (2009), p. 449–476; Riesenhuber, Karl (ed.), *Europäische Methodenlehre*, 2nd ed. (2010); Spindler, Gerald and Hupka, Jan, *Bindungswirkung von Standards im Kapitalmarktrecht*, in: Möllers, Thomas M. J. (ed.), *Geltung und Faktizität von Standards* (2009), p. 117.

I. Sources of Law

1   So far no uniform European capital markets law exists, as most sources of European law on this matter are directives which generally have no direct effect in the Member States. Rather, the directives' provisions first have to be transposed into national law by each Member State. Thus—despite the fact that it is based on legislative acts of the European Union—capital markets law in Europe in most parts remains national law and in practice 27 different national legal systems of capital markets law have to be taken into account. An overview of the national sources of capital markets law in the Member States, i.e. parliamentary acts and regulations enacted by ministries and supervisory authorities, is therefore necessary. Initially, however, the relevant, momentarily effective sources of European capital markets law shall be listed, without closer details to their content.[1]

1.   European Law

(a)   Framework Directives

2   The most important sources of European capital markets law and the regulation of the securities markets are the four framework directives and their respective implementing measures (directives and regulations). All framework directives are currently subject to reforms, only the amendments to the PD having, however, been enacted to date.

3   — Directive 2003/6/EC of the European Parliament and of the Council of 28 January 2003 on insider dealing and market manipulation (market abuse).

— Commission Directive 2003/124/EC of 22 December 2003 implementing Directive 2003/6/EC of the European Parliament and of the Council as regards

---

[1] See § 1 para. 6 ff.

Rüdiger Veil

the definition and public disclosure of inside information and the definition of market manipulation.

— Commission Directive 2003/125/EC of 22 December 2003 implementing Directive 2003/6/EC of the European Parliament and of the Council as regards the fair presentation of investment recommendations and the disclosure of conflicts of interest.

— Commission Directive 2004/72/EC of 29 April 2004 implementing Directive 2003/6/EC of the European Parliament and of the Council as regards the accepted market practices, the definition of inside information in relation to derivatives on commodities, the drawing up of lists of insiders, the notification of managers' transactions and the notification of suspicious transactions.

— Commission Regulation (EC) No. 2273/2003 22 December 2003 implementing Directive 2003/6/EC of the European Parliament and of the Council as regards exemptions for buy-back programmes and stabilisation of financial instruments.

4   — Directive 2003/71/EC of the European Parliament and of the Council of 4 November 2003 on the prospectus to be published when securities are offered to the public or admitted to trading and amending Directive 2001/34/EC; amended by Directive 2010/73/EU.[2]

— Commission Regulation (EC) No. 809/2004 of 29 April 2004 implementing Directive 2003/71/EC of the European Parliament and of the Council as regards information contained in prospectuses as well as the format, incorporation by reference and publication of such prospectuses and dissemination of advertisements; amended by Regulation 486/2012/EU.[3]

— Commission Regulation (EC) No. 1569/2007 of 21 December 2007 establishing a mechanism for the determination of equivalence of accounting standards applied by third country issuers of securities pursuant to Directives 2003/71/EC and 2004/109/EC of the European Parliament and of the Council.

5   — Directive 2004/39/EC of the European Parliament and of the Council of 21 April 2004 on markets in financial instruments amending Council Directives 85/611/EEC and 93/6/EEC and Directive 2000/12/EC of the European Parliament and of the Council and repealing Council Directive 93/22/EEC.

— Commission Directive 2006/73/EC of 10 August 2006 implementing Directive 2004/39/EC of the European Parliament and of the Council as regards organisational requirements and operating conditions for investment firms and defined terms for the purposes of that Directive.

— Commission Regulation (EC) No. 1287/2006 of 10 August 2006 implementing Directive 2004/39/EC of the European Parliament and of the Council as

[2] Directive 2010/73/EU of the European Parliament and of the Council of 24 November 2010 amending Directives 2003/71/EC on the prospectus to be published when securities are offered to the public or admitted to trading and 2004/109/EC on the harmonisation of transparency requirements in relation to information about issuers whose securities are admitted to trading on a regulated market.

[3] Commission delegated Regulation (EU) No. 486/2012 of 30 March 2012 amending Regulation (EC) No. 809/2004 as regards the format and the content of the prospectus, the base prospectus, the summary and the final terms and as regards the disclosure requirements.

regards recordkeeping obligations for investment firms, transaction reporting, market transparency, admission of financial instruments to trading, and defined terms for the purposes of that Directive.

6 — Directive 2004/109/EC of the European Parliament and of the Council of 15 December 2004 on the harmonisation of transparency requirements in relation to information about issuers whose securities are admitted to trading on a regulated market and amending Directive 2001/34/EC.

— Commission Directive 2007/14/EC of 8 March 2007 laying down detailed rules for the implementation of certain provisions of Directive 2004/109/EC on the harmonisation of transparency requirements in relation to information about issuers whose securities are admitted to trading in a regulated market.

— Commission Regulation (EC) No. 1569/2007 of 21 December 2007 establishing a mechanism for the determination of equivalence of accounting standards applied by third country issuers of securities pursuant to Directives 2003/71/EC and 2004/109/EC of the European Parliament and of the Council.

(b)   Takeover Directive

7 The Takeover Directive regulates matters of company and of capital markets law.

— Directive 2004/25/EC of the European Parliament and of the Council of 21 April 2004 on takeover bids.

The European legislature has not enacted any implementing measures as yet. Since 2011 the European Commission has been examining possibilities of amending the Takeover Directive.[4] It cannot yet be said whether, or even if, reforms are planned.

(c)   Regulation on Credit Rating Agencies

8 Additionally in 2009 the following regulation was enacted:

— Regulation (EC) No. 1060/2009 of the European Parliament and of the Council of 16 September 2009 on credit rating agencies.

(d)   Regulation on Short Sellings

9 On 15 September 2010 the European Commission accepted a draft proposal for a Regulation on short sales and certain aspects of credit default swaps (CDSs). The regulation entered into force in November 2012.

— Regulation (EU) No. 236/2012 of the European Parliament and of the Council of 14 March 2012 on short selling and certain aspects of credit default swaps.

The Regulation allows the Commission to adopt delegated acts with regard to a number of questions. The Commission has already made use of this possibility.[5]

---

[4] Cf. Commission Staff Working Document, Report on the implementation of the Directive on Takeover Bids, 21.2.2007, SEC(2007) 268; Report from the Commission to the European Parliament, the Council, the European Economic and Social Committee and the Committee of the Regions, Application of Directive 2004/25/EC on takeover bids, Brussels, 28 June 2012, COM(2012) 347 final.

[5] Commission Delegated Regulation (EU) No. 918/2012 of 5 July 2012 supplementing Regulation (EU) No. 236/2012 of the European Parliament and of the Council on short selling and certain aspects of credit default

(e)   Regulations on the European Supervisory Authorities

10   Since 1 January 2011 three European authorities are responsible for the supervision of financial market participants. The following three regulations contain provisions thereon:

— Regulation (EU) No. 1093/2010 of the European Parliament and of the Council of 24 November 2010 establishing a European Supervisory Authority (European Banking Authority), amending Decision No. 716/2009/EC and repealing Commission Decision 2009/78/EC.

— Regulation (EU) No. 1094/2010 of the European Parliament and of the Council of 24 November 2010 establishing a European Supervisory Authority (European Insurance and Occupational Pensions Authority), amending Decision No. 716/2009/EC and repealing Commission Decision 2009/79/EC.

— Regulation (EU) No. 1094/2010 of the European Parliament and of the Council of 24 November 2010 establishing a European Supervisory Authority (European Securities and Markets Authority), amending Decision No. 716/2009/EC and repealing Commission Decision 2009/77/EC.

(f)   Further Directives

11   The following directives and regulations can also be regarded as legal sources of European financial markets law. They are not considered in this book, however, as they do not concern the regulation of capital markets or treat specific questions, which are outside the scope of this book.

— Council Directive 85/611/EEC of 20 December 1985 on the coordination of laws, regulations and administrative provisions relating to undertakings for collective investment in transferable securities (UCITS).

— Commission Directive 2007/16/EC of 19 March 2007 implementing Council Directive 85/611/EEC on the coordination of laws, regulations and administrative provisions relating to undertakings for collective investment in transferable securities (UCITS) as regards the clarification of certain definitions.

— Directive 2002/65/EC of the European Parliament and of the Council of 23 September 2002 concerning the distance marketing of consumer financial services and amending Council Directive 90/619/EEC and Directives 97/7/EC and 98/27/EC.

— Regulation (EC) No. 1606/2002 of the European Parliament and of the Council of 19 July 2002 on the application of international accounting standards.

swaps with regard to definitions, the calculation of net short positions, covered sovereign credit default swaps, notification thresholds, liquidity thresholds for suspending restrictions, significant falls in the value of financial instruments and adverse events, OJ L274, 5 July 2012, p. 1–15; Commission Delegated Regulation (EU) No. 919/2012 of 5 July 2012 supplementing Regulation (EU) No. 236/2012 of the European Parliament and of the Council on short selling and certain aspects of credit default swaps with regard to regulatory technical standards for the method of calculation of the fall in value for liquid shares and other financial instruments, OJ L274, 9 October 2012, p. 16–17.

2. National Laws of the Member States

12   This book will examine the sources of capital markets law in Austria, France, Germany, Italy, Spain, Sweden and the United Kingdom. The relevant provisions of civil and criminal law in the aforementioned Member States cannot also be taken into account. Notice must, however, be taken of the interpretational aids and the interpretational understanding of the national supervisory authorities. These guidelines and communications play an important role in capital markets law practice.

(a) Austria

13   The Austrian capital markets law is laid down in a number of statutes, the most important of which are the BörseG (Stock Exchange Act), the KMG (Capital Market Act), WAG (Securities Supervision Act), the ÜbG (Takeover Act) and the FMABG (Financial Market Supervisory Authority Act). The main provisions on transparency, such as ad hoc disclosure, the disclosure of major holdings and the disclosure of directors' dealings, can be found in the BörseG. Provisions on insider trading and market manipulation are also contained in the BörseG.

14   Statutes such as the Kuratorengesetz, the Investmentfondsgesetz and the Beteiligungsfondsgesetz concern connected fields of law and also address a number of questions on capital markets law, especially on issuing, offering and managing financial instruments such as bonds and participation certificates.[6] Legal practice in Austria orientates itself on the interpretation by the supervisory authority, the FMA, which publishes its understanding of certain aspects which have proved difficult in practice in newsletters.[7] These only aim to inform the issuers of the interpretation of certain requirements, as can be deduced from the respective provisions of the statutes and regulations. They are therefore not legally binding.[8]

(b) France

15   In France, the most important source of capital markets law can be found in the statutes, especially in the Code monétaire et financier (C. mon. fin., the French Monetary and Financial Code). Provisions on transparency regarding major holdings and all company law can be found in the Code de commerce, the French Commercial Code. In practice, the RG AMF (General Regulations of the French supervisory authority),[9] which were enacted by the Autorité des marchés financiers (AMF—French stock market supervisory authority) and countersigned by the Minister for Economic Affairs, is of particular importance.[10]

16   The statutes are supplemented by various regulations (*ordonnances*), which refer directly to the individual statutory provisions. If the statutory article is "Art. L. ...

---

[6] Cf. S. Kalss et al., *Kapitalmarktrecht*, Vol. I, § 1 para. 81.

[7] These newsletters are also available in English at: www.fma.gv.at/de/startseite.html.

[8] On further non-binding forms of action see S. Kalss et al., *Kapitalmarktrecht*, Vol. I, § 2 para. 21–22.

[9] The French sources of law are available—partly in English—at: www.legifrance.gouv.fr. However, not all of the unofficial translations are up to date. The Règlement général can be found on the website of the AMF (www.amf-france.org) in French and in English. The most important provisions on capital markets law are also printed in R. Veil and P. Koch, *Französisches Kapitalmarktrecht*, p. 115.

[10] Cf. Art. L. 621-6 C. mon. fin.

Rüdiger Veil

C. mon. fin.", for example, the respective regulatory article will be named "Art. R. …
C. mon. fin.". The legislation of these *ordonnances* plays an important role in France.
This is often seen critically, the provisions not always being of a technical nature and
lacking the legislative materials which accompany statutory provisions and facilitate
construction.[11]

17   In an official procedure, the so-called *rescrit*, the AMF can present its interpretation of its *règlement général* and grant exemptions from certain obligations.[12] The
AMF also publishes instructions and recommendations which render the *règlement
général* more precise.[13] Finally, the AMF publishes various forms of statements
(*avis, principes généraux, notes, guides, vade-mecum, communiqués, recommendations, communications du college ou des services, positions*). These texts are partially
treated as legislative acts by the courts.[14]

(c)   Germany

18   The main sources of capital markets law in Germany are the BörsG (Stock Exchange
Act), the WpPG (Securities Prospectus Act), the WpHG (Securities Trading Act)
and the WpÜG (Securities Acquisition and Takeover Act).[15] The WpHG plays a
central role, regulating the tasks and powers of the BaFin, i.e. the German Federal
Financial Supervisory Authority, and containing provisions on insider monitoring,
transparency on major holdings and the monitoring of compliance with the rules
on market manipulation. Additionally, it provides rules of conduct for investment
firms, the monitoring of company accounts and the disclosure of financial reports.
It is reverently referred to as the "Constitution" of capital markets law.[16]

19   These provisions are supplemented by regulations, such as the BörsZulVO (Stock
Exchange Admission Regulation) on the admission of securities to the regulated
market of the stock exchange, enacted by the German Federal Ministry of Finance
in order to further specify the original acts. In total, the WpHG is supplemented
by eight ordinances, the most important of which are the WpHMV (Regulation
on Securities Trading Reports), the WpAIV (German Federal Ministry of Finance's
Regulation on Security Trading Notification and Insider Lists), the MaKonV (Regulation to Further Define the Prohibition against [*sic*] Market Manipulation, i.e.
Market Manipulation Definition Regulation), the FinAnV (Regulation Governing
the Analysis of Financial Instruments) and the WpDVerOV (Ordinance Specifying
Rules of Conduct and Organisation Requirements for Investment Services Enterprises).

20   Five additional regulations were enacted regarding the WpÜG, the most important
being the WpÜGAngebV (Ordinance relating to the contents of the offer document,

---

[11] Cf. Y. Paclot, Bull. Joly Bourse (2009), p. 59.
[12] Cf. Art. 121-1 ff. RG AMF.
[13] Cf. Art. L. 621-6 C. mon. fin.
[14] Cf. P.-H. Conac, *Dictionnaire Joly Bourse et produits financiers*, p. 48–49.
[15] The relevant versions of all statutes and regulations can be found on the website of the German Federal
Ministry of Justice (www.gesetze-im-internet.de). English translations of the WpHG and the WpÜG are available
on the BaFin's website (www.bafin.de).
[16] Cf. K.J. Hopt, in: A. Baumbach and K.J. Hopt, *HGB Kommentar*, Part 16: WpHG, para. 1.

the consideration payable in the case of takeover bids and mandatory offers, and exemption from the obligation to publish and to make an offer).

21 In regular intervals the BaFin publishes notices on the application and interpretation of the capital markets law provisions. These may take on the form of bulletins, newsletters or official statements and have the legal nature of a simple administrative act without a regulatory content, only aiming to communicate the authority's understanding of certain provisions.[17] The objective of the *Emittentenleitfaden* (issuer guideline)[18] is to offer practical help with the provisions on securities trading law, without constituting a legal annotation. It is to aid the access to this field of law and clarify the BaFin's regulatory practice.[19] It is legally non-binding and must be understood as an interpretative administrative provision[20] which may only have the effect of binding the BaFin internally.[21] The courts are not bound by the BaFin's interpretation. The BaFin may exempt from certain obligations, which has particular relevance in takeover law where pursuant to § 37 WpÜG the BaFin can exempt the offeror from the duty to publish and make an offer.[22]

(d) Italy

22 Italy also enacted a statute for the most relevant provisions on capital markets law: the TUF (Italian Consolidated Laws on Finance).[23] The TUF authorises the supervisory authority, Consob, to enact regulations (*Regolamenti*) together with or without the Banca d'Italia. The three main regulations are the RE (Italian Issuers' Regulation) for issuers, the Regolamento Mercati (Italian Financial Markets regulation) for the markets and the Regolamento Intermediari (Italian Regulation on Intermediaries) for financial intermediaries.

23 The *comunicazione* (communications) published by the supervisory authority Consob constitute another level of regulation. They refer to specific legal problems which have been presented to Consob by market participants. Whilst the *comunicazione* are not legally binding, it must generally be assumed that Consob will take enforcement measures if the provisions of the *comunicazione* are not abided by in a later, similar case. In reality, a *comunicazione* is therefore binding. The *comunicazione* will not, however, describe all the circumstances of the case to which it refers. Rather, it will often only contain the answers to the legal problem presented, making it difficult to determine whether the case at hand is sufficiently similar to the one treated in the *comunicazione*.

---

[17] Cf. VGH Kassel, WM (2007), p. 382, 393 regarding a newsletter and G. Dreyling and D. Döhmel, in: H.-D. Assmann and U.H. Schneider (eds.), *Kommentar zum WpHG*, § 4 para. 9; V. Schlette and M. Bouchon, in: A. Fuchs (ed.), *Kommentar zum WpHG*, § 4 para. 27.

[18] The Emittentenleitfaden 2009 (issuer guideline) is available on the BaFin's website (www.bafin.de). An abridged version in English is also available for information purposes. The German version is, however, binding in all respects.

[19] Bafin, *Emittentenleitfaden 2009* (issuer guideline) p. 23.

[20] Cf. BGH, ZIP (2008), p. 639, 641.

[21] P. Mennicke, in: A. Fuchs (ed.), *Kommentar zum WpHG*, Vor §§ 12–14 para. 40; K. Rothehöfer, in: S. Kümpel and A. Wittig (eds.), *Bank- und Kapitalmarktrecht*, para. 3.454.

[22] The BaFin may also, upon written application, permit voting rights from shares in the target company to remain unconsidered when calculating the percentage of voting rights, cf. § 36 WpÜG.

[23] Testo Unico della Finanza (TUF) Decreto legislativo (D.Lgs) del 24 febbraio 1998, n. 58.

Rüdiger Veil

(e)   *Spain*

24   In Spain, parliamentary acts constitute the "apex of the pyramid" concerning sources of capital markets law.[24] These are followed by the so-called RD (Royal Decree), a form of statutory regulation enacted by the government, and the Orden, enacted by the ministries and identifiable by their number and the abbreviation of the issuing ministry. In capital markets law this will mostly be the Ministerio de Economía y Hacienda (EHA), i.e. the Ministry of Economy and Finance. The so-called Circular, enacted by the Spanish national securities markets commission—the CNMV—and published in the official gazette, constitutes the base of this pyramid.

25   The Ley 24/1988, de 28 de julio, del Mercado de Valores (LMV) is the most important Spanish law on capital markets. As a framework law it is restricted to the more general provisions, which are then substantiated by regulations. The LMV has priority over the LSA (Spanish Stock Corporation Act), and the RRM (Spanish Regulation on Company Registries) (cf. Article 111.2 LMV, Article 3 LSA).[25]

(f)   *Sweden*

26   In Sweden the main sources of capital markets law are parliamentary acts (*lagar*), government regulations (*förordningar*) and regulations enacted by the Finansinspektionen (*föreskrifter*).[26] All parliamentary statutes and governmental regulations since 1825[27] are compiled in the official Swedish Code of Statutes (SFS).[28] Statutes and regulations therein are sorted by the year of their enactment, followed by a consecutive numbering for all legislative acts of the respective year. The citation "SFS 2005:551", for example, refers to legislative act 551 from 2005.

27   Swedish statutes are divided into chapters which are then subdivided into sections; shorter statutes only making use of the latter. In this book, the method of quotation for Swedish statutes has been adapted to the more common style, i.e. the section symbol (§) and the term for chapter (*kapitel*) precede the number, whereas Sweden generally uses the reverse order (e.g. Kapitel 29, § 1 ABL instead of the Swedish 29 Kapitel, 1 § ABL).

28   Most provisions on capital markets law can be found in the LHF (Swedish Act on the Trading with Financial Instruments, SFS 1991:980) and in the LVM (Securities Market Act, SFS 2007:528) which as of 1 November 2007 replaced the Lag om börs- och clearingverksamhet (Act on Stock Markets and Clearing, SFS 1992:543) and the Lag om värdepappersrörelse (Act on Securities Transactions, SFS 1991:981).

29   The LHF contains provisions on securities prospectuses, some rules on public takeover bids (especially regarding the requirements concerning offer documents),

---

[24] All Spanish statutes can be found in Spanish on the internet page of the official gazette, the Boletín Oficial del Estado, available at: www.boe.es and at www.noticias.juridicas.com. The internet page of the Spanish supervisory authority CNMV, available at: www.cnmv.es, which has English translations of some of the statutes, may also be of interest.

[25] Cf. A.J. Tapia Hermida, *Derecho del Mercado de Valores,* p. 64.

[26] In more detail R. Veil and F. Walla, *Schwedisches Kapitalmarktrecht,* p. 5 ff.

[27] L. Carlson, *Fundamentals of Swedish Law,* p. 38.

[28] All statutes and governmental regulations are available in Swedish on the website of the Swedish parliament *(Sveriges Riksdag).* Cf. www.riksdagen.se/webbnav/index.aspx?nid=3912. A significant number of statutes has also been officially translated into English and is available at: www.sweden.gov.se/sb/d/3288.

rules on transparency regarding major holdings, provisions for financial analysts and partly the competences of the Finansinspektionen. The LVM contains prudential rules for financial intermediaries and governs ad hoc and periodical disclosure alongside the supervision of regulated market operators, investment firms and issuers by the Finansinspektionen. Additional relevant statutes in the field of capital markets law are the Lag om straff för marknadsmissbruk vid handel med finansiella instrument (Market Abuse Act, SFS 2005:377) which prohibits market manipulation and insider dealings, the Lag om Anmälningsskyldighet Vissa Innehav av Finansiella Instrument (Act on the Disclosure of Ownership regarding Certain Financial Instruments), the Lag om offentliga uppköpserbjudanden på aktiemarknaden (Takeover Act, SFS 2000:1087) and the Lag om investeringsfonds (Investment Fund Act, SFS 2004:46).

30 The parliamentary acts are often complemented by regulations enacted by the government of the supervisory authority.[29] Recommendations published by the self-regulation committees also play an important role in Swedish capital markets law.[30]

(g) United Kingdom

31 In the United Kingdom, the Financial Services and Markets Act 2000 (FSMA) can be classed as the "constitution" of all capital markets law. It is supplemented by the FSA's Handbook of Rules and Guidance (FSA Handbook), which contains implementing provisions and interpretational details.[31] A third source of law must been seen in the rules of common law which play an especially important role in law enforcement.

32 The FSA Handbook is essential for legal practice. It is divided into seven blocks and a glossary which defines several legal terms. It is preceded by the so-called "Principles for Businesses", eleven fundamental rules of conduct and organisation by which all firms regulated by the FSA have to abide.[32] The following chapters and sections of the Handbook are of particular relevance: The Prospectus Rules (PR, for the implementation of the PD), the Code of Market Conduct (MAR, for the implementation of the MAD), the Disclosure and Transparency Rules (DTR, for the implementation of the Transparency and MAD), the New Conduct of Business Sourcebook (COBS, for the implementation of the conduct of business rules in accordance with the MiFID) and the section on Senior Management Arrangements, Systems and Controls (SYSC, for the requirements regarding compliance under the MiFID).

33 Legally binding rules are marked in the Handbook with an "R", whilst sections marked with a "G" are only a guidance to aid interpretation and indicate the FSA's legal understanding.[33] The Handbook further contains a number of so-called eviden-

[29] J. Hjalt, in: D. Campbell (ed.), *International Securities Law and Regulation*, Vol. 3, p. 316–317.
[30] See in detail R. Veil and F. Walla, *Schwedisches Kapitalmarktrecht*, p. 12 ff.
[31] More details on the structure and regulatory system of the FSA Handbooks can be found in A. Winckler, *A Practitioner's Guide to the FSA Handbook*; R. Purves, in: M. Blair et al. (eds.), *Financial Services Law*, para. 5.01 ff.
[32] For principles-based legislation in the field of capital markets law see § 4 para. 51 ff. and § 29 para. 4 ff.
[33] On the legal effects of these interpretational aids see M. Threipland, in: M. Blair (ed.), *Blackstone's Guide to the Financial Services and Markets Act 2000*, p. 140–141.

tial rules which provide a legal presumption on the interpretation of the respective provision. Provisions marked with a "C" indicate safe-harbour rules.

II. Interpretation

1. Importance of Interpretation

34 Regulations enacted by the European legislature become immediately enforceable as law simultaneously in all Member States.[34] National courts and national supervisory authorities must therefore interpret a regulation's provisions when applying them. They may not refer to the national laws and methods of interpretation but must rather apply the European doctrine of interpretation.

35 *Example:* Regulation (EC) No. 2273/2003 provides exemptions from the prohibition of trading in own shares in "buy-back" programmes. According to Article 3 of the regulation, buy-back programmes are not subject to the prohibition if their sole purpose is the reduction of capital (in value or in number of shares). A German court would have to interpret this provision in accordance with the European doctrine of interpretation.

36 Directives, on the other hand, have to be transposed into the Member States' national laws, thus allowing the national civil, criminal and administrative courts to apply national laws in accordance with national methods of interpretation. In these cases the question that may arise will rather be whether the national law is consistent with the directive's requirements. The supreme body for deciding this question is the European Court of Justice (ECJ) which will generally be called upon by a national court for a binding[35] preliminary ruling on the interpretation of Union law.[36] The ECJ will not refer to national law or interpretational methods but will rather follow an autonomous European approach.[37]

37 *Example:* The Belgian supervisory authority (CBFA) imposed fines on the Belgian issuer Spector and its board member van Raemdonck, finding that they had committed insider dealings as prohibited by the MAD and its Belgian national implementing provisions. The respondents brought an appeal before a higher court in Belgium, which had to decide on questions regarding the interpretation of Belgian law whilst considering the MAD, and in this context referred a number of questions to the ECJ.[38] One of the questions referred was regarding the requirements for a "use" of information for a transaction to be classed as insider dealing. In its ruling,[39] the ECJ had to interpret the respective provisions of the MAD.

[34] See § 3 para. 13–14.
[35] Cf. Art. 19(1) EU Treaty and the former provision Art. 220 EC Treaty.
[36] Cf. Art. 19(3) lit. b) EU Treaty.
[37] Cf. ECJ of 5 February 1963, Case 26/62 (*van Gend & Loos*) [1963] ECR 1.
[38] See § 13 para. 80.
[39] ECJ of 23 December 2009, Case C-45/08 (*Spector*) [2009] ECR I-12073.

38   *Facts:* In the case *Daimler/Geltl*[40] the BGH presented the ECJ with two questions on the interpretation of the term "inside information" regarding the ad hoc disclosure rules for a preliminary ruling.[41] The German court was of the opinion that its decision depended on the correct interpretation of the European provisions. The ECJ had to decide on the questions referred to it by interpreting the respective provisions in the MAD and the implementing Directive 2003/124/EC.

39   The CESR could not make binding statements on the interpretation of European law. Even the "Guidelines" published by the CESR (since 2011 by the ESMA on the grounds of Article 16 ESMA Regulation) on Level 3 of the Lamfalussy Process, which aim to achieve a consistent application of its legislation,[42] are not legally binding. They rather constitute non-binding recommendations on how to interpret the provisions due to experiences of the CESR with supervisory practices. The "Guidelines" are addressed to the national supervisory authorities. Whilst they may not be legally binding, the national supervisory authorities will in fact hardly be able to deviate from them.[43] The Bundesverwaltungsgericht (the German Supreme Court of Administrative Law) even ruled that a CESR opinion reflects the national supervisory authority's opinion and that there is thus an assumption of correctness inherent to a CESR recommendation.[44]

40   Civil, criminal and administrative courts in the Member States, however, need not adhere to CESR recommendations. At the same time it is hard to imagine how a court may justify imposing a penalty on a capital market participant if it acted in accordance with the CESR's "Guidelines".[45] This cannot also apply to measures taken by the ESMA. Its guidelines and recommendations[46] are as non-binding for the national authorities and courts as the former CESR Guidelines. As opposed to this, the regulatory and implementing technical standards, enacted by the Commission as delegated law,[47] are binding and must therefore be adhered to by the national authorities and courts.

2.   Principles of Statutory Interpretation

41   Based on the ECJ's case law, legal academics and the legal practice have meanwhile developed principles for the interpretation of European Union law, ensuring its independence from the national laws and its uniform application within the Member States.[48] It consists mainly of the interpretational methods known in the Member States, adapting these, however, to the particularities of the European legal system.[49]

---

[40] See in detail in § 13 para. 57.
[41] BGH, ZIP (2011), p. 72.
[42] See § 4 para. 22–23.
[43] Cf. also S. Kalss et al., *Kapitalmarktrecht*, Vol. I, § 1 para. 104.
[44] BVerwG, ZIP (2011), p. 1313, 1316.
[45] See § 4 para. 23.
[46] See below § 11 para. 64.
[47] See below § 11 para. 66–72.
[48] K.-D. Borchardt, in R. Schulze et al. (eds.), *Europarecht*, § 15 para. 32; T. Oppermann et al., *Europarecht*, § 10 para. 168.
[49] See in detail K. Langenbucher, in: K. Langenbucher (ed.), *Europarechtliche Bezüge des Privatrechts*, § 1 para. 5 ff; M. Pechstein and C. Drechsler, in: K. Riesenhuber (ed.), *Europäische Methodenlehre*, § 8 para. 17 ff.

        Rüdiger Veil

A specific order of importance of the different methods of interpretation cannot be deduced from the ECJ's decisions.[50]

(a) Textual Interpretation

42   Starting point for any statutory interpretation is usually the so-called textual interpretation which examines the language and wording of a provision. The ECJ does not refer to the respective terms in national law,[51] rather developing an independent European understanding.[52] As all legislative acts of the EU are equally authentic in all languages, it is not sufficient to examine a single version of the respective provision. Rather, a representative number of versions will have to be taken into account.[53] Often this will lead to the problem that no definite answer can be found with the help of the textual approach.

(b) Contextual Interpretation

43   The contextual approach to interpretation examines the structure and position of a provision in the statute as a whole in order to deduce the meaning of the provision therefrom. It is closely connected to teleological interpretation.[54] The contextual approach can aim at confirming a result determined through the literal interpretation by referring to a different provision which is based on similar concepts.[55] Contextual arguments, can, on the other hand, also enable rejection of a certain understanding of a provision.[56] If the result is contrary to the underlying concepts of law a different understanding may be favourable.

44   In the ECJ's case law, contextual arguments play an important role in the interpretation of the fundamental freedoms.[57] As opposed to this, the contextual approach to interpretation has played no great role in the field of capital markets law so far. This may change in the future, since meanwhile most fields of capital markets law are subject to European regulations and directives, resulting in a closely knit accumulation of directives and regulations with the result of a more or less full codification where the underlying concepts are largely comparable.

45   *Example:* The Takeover Directive requires that the decision to make a bid be made public without delay. Yet the directive contains no definition of the term "decision". However, the recitals of the Takeover Directive indicate that the European legislature understood the decision to make a bid as a price-sensitive informa-

---

[50] Cf. M. Pechstein and C. Drechsler, in: K. Riesenhuber (ed.), *Europäische Methodenlehre*, § 8 para. 39.

[51] Cf. ECJ of 22 November 1977, Case 43/77 (*Industrial Diamond Supplies/Riva*) [1977] ECR 2175 para. 15 ff.; ECJ of 2 April 1998, Case C-296/95 (*EMU Tabac and Others*) [1998] ECR I-1605 para. 30.

[52] K. Langenbucher, in: K. Langenbucher (ed.), *Europarechtliche Bezüge des Privatrechts*, § 1 para. 10.

[53] K.-D. Borchardt, in: R. Schulze et al. (eds.), *Europarecht*, § 15 para. 36.

[54] Therefore contextual and teleological interpretation are not always treated as different approaches, but seen as one (contextual-teleological interpretation). In this sense: K.-D. Borchardt, in: R. Schulze et al. (eds.), *Europarecht*, § 15 para. 45.

[55] R. Bieber et al., *Die Europäische Union*, § 9 para. 16; T. Oppermann et al., *Europarecht*, § 10 para. 172.

[56] T. Oppermann et al., *Europarecht*, § 10 para. 172.

[57] Cf. ECJ of 30 April 1974, Case 155/73 (*Sacchi*) [1974] ECR 409 para. 7–8; ECJ of 31 March 1971, Case 22/70 (*Commission/Council*) [1971] ECR 263 para, 12; cf. also M. Pechstein and C. Drechsler, in: K. Riesenhuber (ed.), *Europäische Methodenlehre*, § 8 para. 24 ff.

tion, thus requiring disclosure in order to prevent insider dealings.[58] Therefore, the concepts of the MAD regarding the disclosure of inside information can be of assistance for interpreting the term "decision" in the context of the Takeover Directive. The obligation to disclose a prognosis on sufficiently probable future facts is of especial interest in this respect.[59] The conclusion regarding the contextual interpretation of the term "decision" must therefore be that a decision to make a bid in the sense of the Takeover Directive must already be assumed even before it has been made, as soon as it is sufficiently probable.[60]

46 A contextual interpretation can also be of help when a directive or a regulation makes use of a certain term without defining it. Whilst the Commission now mostly defines the relevant terms in the implementing measures on Level 2 of the Lamfalussy Process, it is not possible to provide accompanying definitions for every term. In these cases a reference to another directive may be of help. Ideally, it may contain a definition itself or at least one may refer to that discussion regarding the interpretation of the term.

47 *Example:* According to the TD, notification requirements concerning the acquisition or disposal of major proportions of voting rights also depend on the voting rights attached to shares which are held by a "controlled undertaking". The "controlled undertaking" is defined in Article 2(1)(f) of the TD, which, however, does not clarify what is to be classed as an "undertaking". Therefore, the use of the term "undertaking" in the Seventh Council Directive 83/349/EEC can be used as a guidance on how to interpret the term in the TD.[61]

(c) Historical Interpretation

48 For various reasons the interpretation of a provision according to its history is less important in primary law.[62] The main problem is that it will often be difficult to determine the underlying concept the legislature followed.[63] With regard to secondary legislation, historical interpretation is more fruitful.[64] The intentions of the legislative bodies involved in the legislative procedure can be deduced from the recitals of the legislative act.[65]

49 *Example:* In the judgment regarding the above-mentioned *Spector* case the ECJ justified its interpretation of the prohibition on insider dealing with the fact that the European legislature's aim in enacting the MAD was to fill gaps left by the old Directive on insider dealing. Because the Commission had originally submitted a

---

[58] In more detail below § 24 para. 29 ff.

[59] See § 13 para. 36–41 and § 19 para. 45–48.

[60] This does not, however, mean that the application will be based on this interpretation of the provision, as historical or teleological aspects may lead to a different result. On this problem see § 24 para. 30–31.

[61] On the problems of interpretation see § 20 para. 69–73.

[62] Cf. T. Oppermann et al., *Europarecht*, § 10 para. 174.

[63] Cf. K. Langenbucher, in: K. Langenbucher (ed.), *Europarechtliche Bezüge des Privatrechts*, § 1 para. 11.

[64] Cf. ECJ of 27 June 2006, Case C-540/03 (*Parliament/Council*) [2006] ECR I-5769 para. 38; ECJ of 6 May 2003, Case C-104/01 (*Libertel/Benelux-Merkenbureau*) [2003] ECR I-3793; J. Schwarze, in: J. Schwarze (ed.), *EU-Kommentar*, Art. 220 EGV para. 28.

[65] Cf. the ECJ's legislation in other areas of law: ECJ of 15 May 1997, Case C-355/95P (*TWD*) [1997] ECR I-2549. Cf. K.-D. Borchardt, in: R. Schulze et al. (eds.), *Europarecht*, § 15 para. 44; and specifically on capital markets law: S. Kalss et al., *Kapitalmarktrecht*, Vol. I, § 1 para. 87.

Rüdiger Veil

different proposal during the legislative process, the ECJ assumed that the European Parliament favoured an objective approach regarding the notion of insider dealing without any element of purpose or intent.[66]

50   Historical interpretation is facilitated by the fact that the European Commission presented drafts on the later legislative acts in the field of capital markets law. These contained general remarks and explained the underlying concepts regarding the individual provisions. The European Parliament then submitted its opinion on these drafts.

51   In addition, the CESR published various papers and reports on the proposed legislation which can also help with the interpretation.[67] *Technical advice*[68] on the implementing measures answers questions that may arise when applying the draft's provisions. The quality of the drafts, however, varies from case to case.[69] It depends on the individual case whether the technical advice can be used for the interpretation of the provisions. It may, however, indicate why an original draft or individual provisions of such were later rejected and replaced by a different provision.

52   The CESR also issued so-called Feedback Statements. These were developed in the consultation procedure in which the CESR supported the Commission before the enactment of legislation. The Feedback Statement summarised the answers to the questions raised by the CESR, but did not, however, reflect, from whom the respective question came. Therefore, Feedback Statements cannot be used when determining the European legislature's historical intention.[70]

(d)   Teleological Interpretation

53   The teleological approach has a central role in the principles of statutory interpretation in Europe. Determining the spirit and purpose of a provision is often facilitated by the recitals preceding directives and regulations. Whilst most legislation in the field of capital markets law simply sums up the general aims of market efficiency and investor protection,[71] in some cases the purpose of the legislative act is actually described in more detail, enabling a clear teleological answer to the question of interpretation.[72]

54   *Example:* In the aforementioned *Spector* case the ECJ deducted from Recitals 2 and 12 that the directive prohibited insider dealings in order to ensure the integrity of Community financial markets and enhancing investor confidence in those markets, a confidence which depends, inter alia, on investors being placed on an equal footing and protected against the improper use of inside information (para. 47). The Court then explained that Recitals 18, 19 and 30 of the directive provided several examples of situations in which the fact that a primary insider in possession of inside information entered into a transaction on the market could

---

[66] Cf. ECJ of 23 December 2009, Case C-45/08 (*Spector*) [2009] ECR I-12073 para. 33–34.

[67] S. Kalss et al., *Kapitalmarktrecht*, Vol. I, § 1 para. 95 is more sceptical, fearing a lack of transparency due to an abundance of information. Cf. also T.M.J. Möllers, ZEuP (2008), p. 480.

[68] The advice can be found on the ESMA website (www.esma.europa.eu).

[69] Cf. S. Kalss et al., *Kapitalmarktrecht*, Vol. I, § 1 para. 98.

[70] Likewise S. Kalss et al., *Kapitalmarktrecht*, Vol. I, § 1 para. 98.

[71] See § 2 para. 8–9.

[72] Cf. also S. Kalss et al., *Kapitalmarktrecht*, Vol. I, § 1 para. 89.

not in itself constitute "use of inside information" for the purposes of Article 2(1) of the directive (para. 56).

55 Finally, it must be pointed out that the ECJ, when interpreting a provision in accordance with its spirit and purpose, takes into account its *effet utile*.[73] This principle describes the obligation to interpret a provision in such a way that it unfolds the largest possible effectiveness and benefit. The *effet utile* has the function of optimising the interpretation of the Treaties and all other European provisions.[74]

---

[73] Cf. ECJ of 17 January 1980, Case 792/79 R (*Camera Care*) [1980] ECR 119 para. 17–18; ECJ of 6 October 1981, Case 246/80 (*Broekmeulen*) [1981], ECR 2311, para. 16; ECJ of 19 November 1991, Cases C-6/90 and C-9/90 (*Francovich*) [1991] ECR I- 5357, para. 32.

[74] K. Langenbucher, in: K. Langenbucher (ed.), *Europarechtliche Bezüge des Privatrechts*, § 1 para. 33; M. Pechstein and C. Drechsler, in: K. Riesenhuber (ed.), *Europäische Methodenlehre*, § 8 para 37.

Rüdiger Veil

§ 6 Challenges for Academic Research and Teaching

Bibliography

Barber, Brad and Odean, Terrance, *Boys Will Be Boys*, QJ Econ. (2001), p. 261–292; Becker, Gary S., *Der ökonomische Ansatz zur Erklärung menschlichen Verhaltens* (1982); Benicke, Christoph, *Wertpapiervermögensverwaltung* (2006); Bumke, Christian, *Regulierung am Beispiel der Kapitalmärkte*, in: Hopt, Klaus J. et al. (eds.), *Kapitalmarktgesetzgebung im Europäischen Binnenmarkt* (2008), p. 107–141; Cahn, Andreas, *Grenzen des Markt- und Anlegerschutzes durch das WpHG*, 162 ZHR (1998), p. 1–50; Choi, Stephen J. and Pritchard, Adam C. (eds.), *Securities Regulation: Cases and Analysis* (2005); Davis, Paul, *Davies Review on Issuer Liability: Final Report* (2007); Eidenmüller, Horst, *Der homo oeconomicus und das Schuldrecht: Herausforderungen durch Behavioral Law and Economics*, JZ (2005), p. 216–224; Findeisen, Maximilian, *Über die Regulierung und die Rechtsfolgen von Interessenkonflikten in der Aktienanalyse von Investmentbanken* (2007); Fischhoff, Baruch, Slovic, Paul and Lichtenstein, Sarah, *Knowing with Certainty: The Appropriateness of Extreme Confidence*, 3 J. Exp. Psychol., Hum. Perception & Performance (1977), p. 552–564; Fleischer, Holger, *Behavioral Law and Economics im Gesellschafts- und Kapitalmarktrecht—Ein Werkstattbericht*, in: Fuchs, Andreas et al. (eds.), *Festschrift für Ulrich Immenga* (2004), p. 575; Fleischer, Holger, *Empfiehlt es sich, im Interesse des Anlegerschutzes und zur Förderung des Finanzplatzes Deutschland, das Kapitalmarkt- und Börsenrecht neu zu regeln?*, Gutachten F zum 64. Deutschen Juristentag (2002); Göres, Ulrich L., *Interessenkonflikte von Wertpapierdienstleistern und -analysten bei der Wertpapieranalyse* (2004); Hammen, Horst, *Analogieverbot beim Acting in Concert?*, Der Konzern (2009), p. 18–23; Hirte, Heribert, *Ad-hoc-Publizität und Krise der Gesellschaft*, ZInsO (2006), p. 1289–1299; Horn, Norbert, *Die Aufklärungs- und Beratungspflichten der Banken*, ZBB (1997), p. 139–152; Kahneman, Daniel and Tversky, Amos, *Prospect Theory: An Analysis of Decision under Risk*, Econometrica (1979), p. 263–292; Kahneman, Daniel, Knetsch, Jack L. and Thaler, Richard H., *Fairness and the Assumptions of Economics*, 59 J. Bus. (1986), p. 285–300; Kamin, Kim A. and Rachlinski, Jeffrey J., *Ex Post Ex Ante: Determining Liability in Hindsight*, 19 Law & Hum. Behav. (1995), p. 89–104; Klöhn, Lars, *Kapitalmarkt, Spekulation und Behavioral Finance* (2006); Klöhn, Lars, *Der Beitrag der Verhaltensökonomik zum Kapitalmarktrecht*, in: Fleischer, Holger and Zimmer, Daniel (eds.), *Beitrag der Verhaltensökonomie (Behavioral Economics) zum Handels- und Wirtschaftsrecht*, ZHR Beiheft 75 (2011), p. 83–99; Köndgen, Johannes, *Wieviel Aufklärung braucht ein Wertpapierkunde?*, ZBB (1996), p. 361–365; Lang, Norbert, *Doppelnormen im Recht der Finanzdienstleistungen*, ZBB (2004), p. 289–295; Leisch, Franz C., *Informationspflichten nach § 31 WpHG* (2004); MacNeil, Ian G., *The Law on Financial Investment* (2005); Merkt, Hanno and Rossbach, Oliver, *Zur Einführung—Kapitalmarktrecht*, JuS (2003), p. 217–224; Merkt, Hanno and Binder, Jens-Hinrich, *Kapitalmarktrecht als Gegenstand des Studiums im Schwerpunktbereich—Grundlagen, Inhalte, Perspektiven*, JURA (2006), p. 683–692; Odean, Terrance, *Volume, Volatility, Price, and Profit. When All Traders Are Above Average*, 53 J. Fin. (1998), p. 1887–1934; Reich, Norbert, *Informations-, Aufklärungs- und Warnpflichten beim Anlagengeschäft unter besonderer Berücksichtigung des "execution-only-business" (EOB)*, WM (1997), p. 1601–1609; Rubel, Jörgen, *Erfüllung von WpHG-Pflichten in der Insolvenz durch Insolvenzverwalter oder Vorstand?*, AG (2009), p. 615–622; Skeel, David A., *The New Financial Deal: Understanding the Dodd–Frank Act and its (Unintended) Consequences* (2011); Sunstein, Cass R., *What's Available? Social Influences and Behavioral Economics*, 97 Nw. Univ. L Rev. (2003), p. 1295–1314; Sethe, Rolf, *Anlegerschutz im Recht der Vermögensverwaltung* (2005); Svenson, Ola, *Are We All Less Risky and More Skillful than Our Fellow Drivers?*, 77 Acta Psychologica (1981), p. 143–148; Teigelack, Lars, *Finanzanalysen und Behavioral Finance* (2009); Tversky, Amos and Kahneman, Daniel, *Judgement under Uncertainty: Heuristics and Biases*, 185 Science (1974), p. 1124–1131; Veil, Rüdiger and Dolff, Christian, *Kapitalmarktrechtliche Mitteilungspflichten des Treuhänders*, AG (2010), p. 385–391; Veil, Rüdiger, *Enforcement of Capital Markets Law in Europe—Observations from a Civil Law Country*,

11 EBOR (2010), p. 409–422; Veil, Rüdiger, *Wie viel "Enforcement" ist notwendig?—Zur Reform des Instrumentenmix bei der Sanktionierung kapitalmarktrechtlicher Mitteilungspflichten gemäß §§ 21 ff. WpHG*, 175 ZHR (2011), p. 83–109; Weichert, Tilman and Wenninger, Thomas, *Die Neuregelung der Erkundigungs- und Aufklärungspflichten von Wertpapierdienstleistungsunternehmen gem. Art. 19 RiL 2004/39/EG (MiFID) und Finanzmarkt-Richtlinie-Umsetzungsgesetz*, WM (2007), p. 627–636.

I.   Capital Markets Law as a Topic of Legal Research

1   In most Member States, capital markets law only became an independent field of law with the implementation of the capital markets law directives.[1] Since then an animated and intense academic discussion has evolved around this field of law, which is inspired by and orientates itself on US law.[2] The latter fully regulated the capital markets thirty years earlier than the European legislature's first tentative steps in this direction.[3] Europe has not yet caught up with this "head start" by the Americans.[4] The four framework directives are largely based on the example of the Securities Regulation in the United States. Legal research in this area is thus not possible without comparative law.

2   International research is confronted with a number of difficulties resulting from the intradisciplinary character of capital markets law. Whilst on the one hand it must be characterised as public law and is sanctioned by measures under criminal law, it also affects the legal relationship between private parties, thus also presenting the civil courts with the necessity to apply capital market rules. These aspects of civil law play a particularly important role in Austria and Germany.

3   Additionally, unlike any other field of law, capital markets law requires an interdisciplinary exchange of concepts. The provisions regarding the disclosure of relevant information and the continuing legislative activities at both the European and national level could not be explained without the findings of economics. The efficient capital market hypothesis and the economic reasons for disclosure obligations are described in more detail elsewhere in this book.[5] This chapter rather presents the overall underlying question whether capital markets law provisions are based on the concept of a *Homo oeconomicus* or whether they should follow the findings of empirical research and behavioural finance.

---

[1] On the history of European capital markets legislation see § 1 para. 5 ff.

[2] Cf. N. Moloney, *EC Securities Regulation*, p. 24 ("critical importance of transatlanatic regulatory dialogue"); on the example function of US-American law cf. H. Fleischer, *Gutachten F zum 64. Deutschen Juristentag*, p. F 16; on the europeanisation and internationalisation of capital markets law see C. Bumke, in: K.J. Hopt et al. (eds.), *Kapitalmarktgesetzgebung im Europäischen Binnenmarkt*, p. 107, 126–127.

[3] On the development of US-American capital markets law see J.C. Coffee and J. Seligman, *Securities Regulation*, chap. 1 section 5.

[4] The United Kingdom is an exception, capital markets law developing sooner here than in the other European Member States, cf. R. Veil and M. Wundenberg, *Englisches Kapitalmarktrecht*, p. 5 ff.

[5] See in detail § 16 para. 4–13.

Rüdiger Veil

1.   Intradisciplinarity

(a)   Legal Nature

4   Capital markets law mainly aims to ensure the functioning of capital markets.[6] The provisions reflect *public interest*. A further characteristic is that the supervisory authorities interact with the market participants in their function as bodies with sovereign powers. This can be seen, for example, in the national authorities' power to supervise the compliance with rules provided in the national and European capital markets acts.[7] Capital markets law is classed as an area of public law,[8] the supervisory authorities being granted administrative powers: all Member States permit their supervisory authorities to adopt administrative measures, such as a correction of false or misleading disclosed information, a temporary prohibition of an unlawful activity, a suspension of trading of financial instruments or other acts, in order to ensure the functioning of the markets.[9]

5   The sanctions are also of an administrative nature; most breaches of rules are sanctioned criminally or with administrative fines.[10] Whilst the European legislative acts do not require rules on criminal sanctions to be introduced by the Member States,[11] most Member States have nevertheless opted to criminally sanction violations of the rules on insider dealings and market manipulation. Furthermore, all jurisdictions provide the possibility to impose fines.[12] Generally this will also lie within the responsibility of the supervisory authorities.[13]

6   The European legislative acts do not aim to regulate legal relationships under civil law. The public nature of the provisions does not, however, prevent the national legislatures and courts from referring to these administrative capital markets law requirements in national civil law proceedings when defining civil law provisions and determining the duties of the parties of a contract. In these cases the provisions obtain a dual nature.[14] In German law, the most prominent example for this are the conduct of business rules for investment firms contained in the MiFID. The obligations of banks towards their clients regarding investment recommendations under MiFID,[15] for example, also become relevant in civil law. They put the contractual

---

[6] See § 2 para. 3–7.

[7] Capital markets law is therefore often named supervisory law. See § 11 para. 1.

[8] Cf. for Germany H.-D. Assmann, in: H.-D. Assmann and U.H. Schneider (eds.), *Kommentar zum WpHG*, Einl. para. 94; for Austria S. Kalss et al. (eds.), *Kapitalmarktrecht*, § 1 para. 105.

[9] Cf. D. Zetzsche, in: E. Schwark and D. Zimmer (eds.), *Kapitalmarktrechts-Kommentar*, § 4 WpHG para. 36.

[10] In Germany a number of publications has adopted a criminal law approach to capital markets law; cf. C. Schröder, *Handbuch Kapitalmarktstrafrecht*; T. Park, *Kommentar zum Kapitalmarktstrafrecht*; D. Ziouvas, *Das neue Kapitalmarktstrafecht—Europäisierung und Legitimation*.

[11] See § 12 para. 4 and 22.

[12] In more detail at § 11 para. 21 ff.

[13] The Commission's amendments to the three framework directives aim to unify the sanctioning regime in Europe (see § 1 para. 39–43).

[14] For Germany see N. Reich, WM (1997), p. 1601, 1604; N. Lang, ZBB (2004), p. 289, 294; T.M.J. Möllers, in: H. Hirte and T.M.J. Möllers (eds.), *Kölner Kommentar zum WpHG*, § 31 para. 9; T. Weichert and T. Wenninger, WM (2007), p. 627, 635; for Austria S. Kalss et al. (eds.), *Kapitalmarktrecht*, § 1 para. 105.

[15] See § 25 para. 4–9.

obligations of banks into more concrete terms.[16] Further examples include the rules of conducts in the European provisions on financial analysts[17] and rating agencies.[18]

7   The civil law courts may also be confronted with capital markets law by way of private enforcement. Different forms of private enforcement are common in numerous Member States.[19] In some jurisdictions the legislature included the possibility for investors to claim damages from the issuer or other responsible parties for breaches of disclosure obligations.[20] Other Member States sanction breaches of the provisions on the notification of major shareholdings with a loss of rights that may become relevant in civil law proceedings.[21] All these forms of private enforcements allow civil law courts to apply provisions of a public law nature.

(b)   Interpretation

8   The provenance of capital markets law provisions is important for their interpretation.[22] A provision of public law must be interpreted in accordance with the rules of interpretation common for provisions of this nature.[23] At the same time, a criminal or civil law court will apply criminal or civil law methods of interpretation if the dual nature of the provisions allows this.[24] In some Member States criminal and civil law methods of interpretation have one important difference: the prohibition to draw an analogy to criminal and administrative penal provisions[25] does not apply in civil law. This gives rise to the question whether in these Member States civil law courts are restricted in their methods of extensive interpretation.

9   In German and Austrian legal literature this problem is discussed under the term *gespaltene Auslegung*, i.e. a dual interpretation of capital markets law provisions. Some regard such a dual interpretation as possible,[26] arguing that the interpretation of civil law rules follows civil law principles, which allow gaps to be filled by way of analogy. A dual interpretation depending on whether a criminal or civil understanding of the provision is required would, however, lead to a strong legal

---

[16] In Germany, it is unclear whether the provisions can be applied on a one-to-one basis in contract law or whether they merely have an indirect effect on civil law. For a direct applicability J. Köndgen, ZBB (1996), p. 361–362; N. Lang, ZBB (2004), p. 289, 295; F. Leisch, *Informationspflichten nach § 31 WpHG*, p. 85; C. Benicke, *Wertpapiervermögensverwaltung*, p. 461 ff.; T.M.J. Möllers, in: H. Hirte and T.M.J. Möllers (eds.), *Kölner Kommentar zum WpHG*, § 31 para. 6–7; for an indirect effect on obligations under civil law N. Horn, ZBB (1997), p. 139, 149–150; I. Koller, in: H.-D. Assmann and U.H. Schneider (eds.), *Kommentar zum WpHG*, vor § 31 para. 3; R. Sethe, *Anlegerschutz im Recht der Vermögensverwaltung*, p. 748 ff.
[17] See § 26 para. 28 ff.
[18] See § 27 para. 38.
[19] Cf. R. Veil, 11 EBOR (2010), p. 409, 417 ff.
[20] See § 7 para. 10 ff.
[21] See § 20 para. 91–95.
[22] On the interpretation of European law see § 5 para. 34–55.
[23] Cf. S. Kalss et al. (eds.), *Kapitalmarktrecht*, para. 108.
[24] Cf. D. Zimmer, in: E. Schwark and D. Zimmer (eds.), *Kapitalmarktrechts-Kommentar*, § 1 WpHG para. 8.
[25] In Germany, the prohibition of analogy is of a constitutional nature. Cf. Art. 103(2) GG.
[26] On German law see A. Cahn, ZHR 162 (1998), p. 1, 8–9; also H. Hammen, Der Konzern (2009), p. 18, 21; H. Hirte, in: H. Hirte and T.M.J. Möllers (eds.), *Kölner Kommentar zum WpHG*, § 21 para. 7; on Austrian law see S. Kalss et al. (eds.), *Kapitalmarktrecht*, para. 110–111.

uncertainty for market participants and is therefore not convincing.[27] The ECJ thus acted correctly rejecting it in its ruling in *Grøngaard/Bang*.[28]

10   In cases in which violations of capital markets law are sanctioned both under criminal and under civil law, the supervisory authorities and the courts in some Member States may reach different results when interpreting these provisions. An example for this can be found in German legal practice in *Daimler/Geltl*.[29] In the proceedings regarding an administrative fine, the OLG Frankfurt/Main developed a different understanding of the term "inside information" than the courts responsible for the test case under civil law.[30] The risk of different interpretations by different authorities should, however, not really interfere with the functioning of the market or the mergers and acquisitions practice. Most interpretational questions are predetermined by European law, thus giving the ECJ the final power of interpretation.[31] Civil law courts must therefore be welcomed as "supervisory instances" over the supervisory authorities.[32]

11   In the United Kingdom capital markets law is predominantly supervisory law and as such mainly subject to the FSA's understanding and sanctioning practice. The concept of administrative enforcement of capital markets law has proven successful in the United Kingdom. Nevertheless, the legislature recently introduced a civil liability.[33] The prerequisites are, however, high,[34] one of the reasons possibly being that individual claims for damages are still hardly known in the UK.[35]

(c)   Coordination with other Areas of Company and Business Law

12   Capital markets law is closely connected to other areas of company and business law, the most important being accounting law,[36] which is largely harmonised and partly even unified at a European level, and company law,[37] which still falls mainly

---

[27] On German takeover law see BGHZ 169, p. 98, 106 (*WMF*); on German capital markets law see H.-D. Assmann, in: H.-D. Assmann and U.H. Schneider (eds.), *Kommentar zum WpHG*, Einl. para. 95; A. Fuchs, in: A. Fuchs, *Kommentar zum WpHG*, Einl. para. 79; R. Veil and C. Dolff, AG (2010), p. 385.

[28] Cf. ECJ of 22 May 2005, Case C-384/02 [2005], ECR I-9939 para. 28 (obiter dictum): "the interpretation of a directive's scope cannot be dependent upon the civil, administrative or criminal nature of the proceedings in which it is invoked".

[29] See § 5 para. 38, § 13 para. 57 and § 19 para. 85.

[30] The case had to be decided on by two different divisions of the Oberlandesgericht (OLG, Higher Regional Court) Stuttgart before it was brought before the Bundesgerichtshof (BGH, German Federal Court) for appeal. See § 13 para. 59.

[31] The BGH presented a number of questions on the interpretation of Art. 1(1) MAD and its implementing directive 2003/124/EC to the ECJ. Cf. BGH, ZIP (2011), p. 72.

[32] Cf. R. Veil, 11 EBOR (2010), p. 409, 420 ff.

[33] The legal foundation is The Financial Services and Markets Act 2000 (Liability of Issuers) Regulation 2010. See § 12 para. 21 and § 19 para. 124.

[34] The Ministry of Financy assigned P. Davies, London School of Economics, the task of examining the current regime of liability for incorrect capital market information and developing possible improvements. In the Final Report he submitted in 2007 P. Davies recommended, keeping liability restricted to wrongful intent and not extending it to negligence or gross negligence. The legislature largely took account of this recommendation in its amendments. See § 19 para. 124.

[35] An exception only being cases of prospectus liability. See § 17 para. 50–74.

[36] On the current unification and harmonisation of accounting law see J. Baetge et al. (eds.), *Bilanzen*, p. 26 ff. (on the directives) and 62 ff. (on the IFRS) as well as the compilation of European legislative acts in fn.39.

[37] On the current developments concerning the harmonisation of company law cf. T. Raiser and R. Veil, *Recht der Kapitalgesellschaften*, § 59 para. 9 ff.

into the regulatory autonomy of the Member States. Insolvency law also plays a role regarding capital markets law and can lead to difficult legal questions.[38]

(aa) Accounting Law

13 Capital markets law and accounting law are closely connected: accounting law traditionally aims to ensure that investors are informed about the issuer's profitability and profit prospects. The European legislature has enacted various legislative acts on this matter.[39] The capital markets law directives can therefore simply refer to these legislative acts under accounting law. Rules on financial reporting are thus based on the European provisions on company accounting,[40] references thereto in capital markets law having only informational purposes.[41]

(bb) Company Law

14 Capital markets law and company law are also closely related, although this may sometimes not at first be apparent. It is especially noticeable that certain provisions, which can nowadays be found in capital markets law, were first contained in company law. With the implementation of the European legislative acts, the Member States transferred the provisions into their capital markets law.

15 This phenomenon can be observed in numerous Member States.[42] The German provisions on the notification of major shareholdings, for example, originate from the provisions in the AktG (German Stock Corporations Act) of 1965 on the notification obligations of certain shareholders (cf. §§ 20–22).[43] This explains why the regime on notification obligations regarding major shareholdings under capital markets law sanctions breaches of these provisions with a loss of the rights attached to shares—when implementing the European provisions into the WpHG (German Securities Trading Act), the legislature based the new rules on the respective provisions in the Stock Corporation Act.[44] Furthermore, the loss of rights in German capital markets law explains why issuers are given the right to demand proof of the reported shareholding, although this is not provided for in the TD.[45]

---

[38] See the German provisions on the duties of the insolvency administrator (§ 11 WpHG); H. Hirte, ZInsO (2006), p. 1289; J. Rubel, AG (2009), p. 615; B.-A. Lau, *Die börsennotierte Aktiengesellschaft in der Insolvenz* (2008).

[39] Regulation 2002/1606/EC of the European Parliament and of the Council of 19 July 2002 on the application of international accounting standards (IAS Regulation), Official Journal L 243, 11 September 2002, p. 1. There are also a number of relevant directives: Fourth Council Directive 78/660/EEC of 25 July 1978 based on Article 54(3)(g) of the Treaty on the annual accounts of certain types of companies (Annual Account Directive), OJ L222, 14 August 1978, p. 11 and the Seventh Council Directive 83/349/EEC of 13 June 1983 based on Article 54(3)(g) of the Treaty on consolidated accounts (Consolidated Account Directive), OJ L193, 18 July 1983, p. 1; see also Directive 2006/43/EC of the European Parliament and of the Council of 17 May 2006 on statutory audits of annual accounts and consolidated accounts, amending Council Directives 78/660/EEC and 83/349/EEC and repealing Council Directive 84/253/EEC, OJ L157, 9 June 2006, p. 87.

[40] See § 18 para. 6–8.

[41] This function is the underlying concept for the principle of "fair value", according to which assets and debts must be balanced according to their market value. An asset is recognised in the balance sheet if it is probable that there will be future economic benefits for the company. For an overview of the differences between the national rules on accounting and the IAS/IFRS see H. Adler et al. (eds.), *Rechnungslegung nach Internationalen Standards*, Abschnitt 1 para. 249 ff.

[42] On the disclosure provisions in the United Kingdom see R. Veil and M. Wundenberg, *Englisches Kapitalmarktrecht*, p. 89; on the transparency regarding major shareholdings in France see R. Veil and P. Koch, *Französisches Kapitalmarktrecht*, p. 79–80.

[43] These provisions can currently be found in §§ 21 ff. WpHG. See § 20 para. 20.

[44] Cf. R. Veil, ZHR 175 (2011), p. 83 ff.

[45] Cf. § 27 WpHG; C. Dolff, *Der Rechtsverlust gem. § 28 WpHG aus der Perspektive eines Emittenten* (2011).

16   Capital markets law and company law have different aims. This may lead to conflicts between both. In these cases the European legislature and the national courts must solve this conflict, taking into account the additional problem that only capital markets law is entirely European whilst large areas of company law remain a matter of national law which has varying forms in the different Member States.

17   Two examples may help to understand this. The first concerns disclosure obligations. It is in the interest of the capital market if price-relevant information is disclosed as soon as possible. Yet the issuer may have a legitimate interest in temporarily keeping the information secret. Solving this conflict is made difficult by the fact that stock corporations are organised in different ways throughout the Member States. British stock corporations, for example, have a one-tier-system with a board of directors, whilst German stock corporations have a two-tier-system with a management and a supervisory board. These different systems coincide with different rights and obligations. The European legislature took this into account when introducing the rules on ad hoc disclosure, allowing a suspension of disclosure for stock corporations with a two-tier system if price-relevant facts, such as a capital increase, depend on the supervisory board's decision. Without such a suspension, autonomy of the supervisory board's decision would not be ensured.[46]

18   The second example comes from the rules on inside information. It is a central aim of the MAD to prevent inside information from being passed on. The ECJ has ruled that information may only be passed on if this is indispensable for the legal obligations of a director. Due to a lack of harmonisation the ECJ decided that this must be determined according to the respective provisions of national law, thus taking into account the national regulatory concepts on company law in the Member States.[47]

19   It can further be difficult to distinguish between capital markets and company law with regard to the sanctions imposed. The handling of cases in which a shareholder acquired shares on the basis of incorrect information and now demands to rescind the contract or claim damages remains unclear.[48] The relationship between investor protection under capital markets law and creditor protection under stock corporation law has occupied legal practice and research for over a hundred years: are payments to shareholders as a result of incorrect prospectuses compatible with the principle of capital maintenance? Can payments be made from the nominal capital? These questions have been addressed by European law, the Directive on the maintenance of capital[49] prohibiting the reduction of a company's capital by distributing it to shareholders.[50]

---

[46] See § 19 para. 86–91.
[47] See § 13 para. 87.
[48] See in detail § 17 para. 74 and § 19 para. 117.
[49] Second Council Directive 77/91/EEC of 13 December 1976 on coordination of safeguards which, for the protection of the interests of members and others, are required by Member States of companies within the meaning of the second paragraph of Article 58 of the Treaty, in respect of the formation of public limited liability companies and the maintenance and alteration of their capital, with a view to making such safeguards equivalent, OJ L26, 31 January 1977, p. 1.
[50] Cf. N. Vokuhl, *Kapitalmarktrechtlicher Anlegerschutz und Kapitalerhaltung in der Aktiengesellschaft*, p. 46 ff.; E. Wild, *Prospekthaftung einer Aktiengesellschaft unter deutschem und europäischem Kapitalschutz*, p. 183 ff.

2. *Homo oeconomicus* or **Behavioural Finance?**

(a) Basic Assumption: Rationality

20   Capital market legislation aims to influence the market participants' behaviour. It must therefore apply certain concepts that aim to predict the reactions of market participants to certain rules. The economic analysis of law refers to the concept of a *Homo oeconomicus*,[51] thereby assuming that a model person acts rationally and aims to maximise his own economic benefits.[52] It will always choose the alternative most suited to his preferences, whilst the benefits for others will not play any role in his decision. The underlying premise of the economic analysis of law is that the *Homo oeconomicus* can obtain and process all relevant information available.[53]

(b) Behavioural Anomalies

21   The assumption of rationality does not coincide with reality. The behavioural finance-research[54] of the past decades has shown numerous behavioural anomalies, which have unsettled the economic behavioural model. Even though these empirical studies do not always explicitly examine the behaviour of capital market participants, the conclusions must nonetheless lead to a critical examination of the concept of a *Homo oeconomicus*.

(aa) Bounded Rationality

22   The assumption of rationality assumes that man has unlimited possibilities to take in and process information. Often one will, however, be confronted with decisions that were made quickly, without having had the possibility to process all the information available. In these cases, man works with rules of thumb, so-called heuristics. In a complex situation that requires a decision, he will search for an anchor which he will use as a starting point to evaluate the possible alternatives. This anchor value will have a disproportionate influence on the decision.[55] Decisions can thus be manipulated by directing the decision-maker towards a certain anchor value.

(bb) Overconfidence

23   A rational person should be able to determine correctly his knowledge and skills. Empirical studies have, however, proven that people systematically tend towards overconfidence. Most car drivers, for example, maintain they are better and safer

---

[51] G. Becker, *Der ökonomische Ansatz zur Erklärung menschlichen Verhaltens*, p. 15; on the criticsm regarding New Institutional Economics cf. R. Richter and E. Furubotn, *Neue Institutionenökonomik*, p. 3–4.

[52] According to the so-called "expected utility theory" individuals will always opt for the alternative that maximises their expected utility. It can be determined by multiplication of the benefits of the option and its probability. Cf. L. Klöhn, *Kapitalmarkt, Spekulation und Behavioral Finance*, p. 86 ff. with further references.

[53] H. Eidenmüller, JZ (2005), p. 216, 217.

[54] Cf. the literature listed in the bibliography and cited below: D. Kahneman and A. Tversky; A. Shleifer, *Inefficient Markets. An Introduction to Behavioural Finance* (2000); H. Shefrin, *Beyond Greed and Fear. Understanding Behavioural Finance and the Psychology of Investment* (2000); R. Shiller, *Irrational Exuberance*, 2nd ed. (2005); J. Goldberg and R. von Nitzsch, *Behavioral Finance*, 4th ed. (2004); on the discussion regarding the possibilities of taking into account these insights when interpreting the law see L. Klöhn, *Kapitalmarkt, Spekulation und Behavioral Finance*, p. 80 ff.; L. Teigelack, *Finanzanalysen und Behavioral Finance*, p. 88 ff.

[55] Cf. A. Tversky and D. Kahneman, 185 Science (1974), p. 1124.

           Rüdiger Veil

drivers than their passengers.[56] Statistically, however, only 50% of all drivers can actually be better than average. Overconfidence is more pronounced with men than with women.[57] The problem of overconfidence must particularly be taken into account for provisions that aim to warn market participants, as an overconfident person will tend to ignore the warning.

(cc) Fairness

24 According to the concept of rational behaviour a person will only be interested in maximising his own economic benefits. Participants in numerous studies, however, showed behaviour in which they were prepared to accept personal economic losses, in order to punish others for their behaviour if this was felt to be unfair (ultimatum game).[58] If a statute determines that certain facts are "relevant" for human decisions, aspects of fairness may also have to play a role.

(dd) Prospect Theory/Framing/Risk Aversity

25 The concept of rationality assumes that individuals will distinguish between alternatives according to the expected utility, the model person always choosing the alternative with the highest expected utility. As opposed to this, the *prospect theory* assumes that a decision will always depart from a certain reference point. Outcomes lower than this reference point will be considered as losses, higher outcomes as gains.

26 *Framing* means presenting the same option with equal expected utility in different formats to make it appear either as a loss or as a gain, thus proving that people's decisions can be influenced. Depending on the type of framing the participants of different study groups developed different risk attitudes. Small but certain gains are usually preferred as opposed to the possibility of larger (or no) gains, showing a certain aversion to risk. As opposed to this, in the scenario of a certain loss or the possibility of an even higher (or no) loss, people will usually opt for the possibility of preventing the loss.[59] By manipulating the point of reference, decisions can therefore be influenced.

(ee) Hindsight Bias

27 Events that have already occurred tend to be seen as more probable than before they took place. The evaluation of a certain decision depends on how the respective person processed the information available to him before the event. The actual result, not known at the time, plays a role in this process. However, for most people it is difficult to separate out actual developments, creating the impression the result had actually been foreseen. In these cases the person who made the wrong decision is blamed for not having foreseen the result.

---

[56] Cf. O. Svenson, 77 Acta Psychologica (1981), p. 143.

[57] B. Fischhoff, P. Slovic and S. Lichtenstein, 3 J. Exp. Psych., Hum. Perception & Performance (1977), p. 552; on the phenomenon of overconfidence on the capital market see T. Odean, *Volume, Volatility, Price and Profit When All Traders Are Above Average*, 53 J. Fin. (1998), p. 1887; on gender-specific overconfidence on the capital markets see B. Barber and T. Odean, *Boys Will Be Boys*, Q. J. Econ. (2001), p. 261.

[58] Cf. D. Kahneman, J. L. Knetsch and R. H. Thaler, 59 J. Bus. (1986), p. 285.

[59] Cf. A. Tversky and D. Kahneman, Econometrica (1979), p. 263.

28   This behavioural anomaly is of legal relevance in cases where the question of a liability based on negligence has arisen,[60] the most prominent example being the introduction of the business judgment rule for management liability, in order to meet hindsight bias.[61]

(ff)   Representativeness/Availability/Salience

29   Whether the occurrence of an event is regarded as probable depends strongly on the information that was available to the respective person. With information that is easily accessible or salient, such as newspaper reports on shark attacks and aeroplane crashes, the probability of an occurrence is overestimated.[62] Contrary to the model of the rationally acting person, people tend to not make use of all the information to which they would have access, rather relying only on the information easily available to them.[63]

(c)   *Relevance of the Results of Behavioural Economics for Capital Markets Law*

30   The results of the research on behavioural finance can be of legal use on two levels. Firstly it appears possible to take the results into account when interpreting the law. This is especially so with regard to the concept of a "reasonable investor",[64] as used in rules on inside information and disclosure,[65] and the general terms of care and conscientiousness in the provisions on financial intermediaries such as financial analysts and rating agencies.[66] Courts are already making use of this possibility, the Bundesgerichtshof, for example, having stated that a reasonable investor must take into account the fact that market participants behave irrationally.[67]

31   Secondly the results of behavioural economics studies could provide an incentive for the legislature to amend the rules of capital markets law in order to take certain anomalies into account. It could, for example, develop a new system of liability including a liability for financial analysts who distort the results of a financial analysis,[68] introduce new measures, such as trade prohibitions, protecting investors of their own or the analyst's behavioural anomalies,[69] or introduce investment licenses in order to raise investor awareness of irrational behaviour and achieve more rational decisions.[70]

---

[60] Cf. K. Kamin and J. Rachlinski, Law & Hum Behav. (1995), p. 89.

[61] Cf. H. Fleischer, *Handbuch des Vorstandsrechts*, § 7 para. 45 ff.; T. Raiser and R. Veil, *Recht der Kapitalgesellschaften*, § 14 para. 66; H. Merkt and S. Göthel, *US-amerikanisches Gesellschaftsrecht*, para. 843 ff.

[62] Cf. C.R. Sunstein, 97 Nw. U. L. Rev. (2003), p. 1295 ff.

[63] Cf. A. Tversky and D. Kahneman, 185 Science (1974), p. 1124, 1127.

[64] L. Klöhn, *Kapitalmarkt, Spekulation und Behavioral Finance*, p. 210 f., 247–248; L. Teigelack, *Finanzanalysen und Behavioral Finance*, p. 162 ff.; see also § 16 para. 26.

[65] See § 13 para. 61.

[66] See § 14 para. 20–24; § 26 para. 29.

[67] Cf. BGH, ZIP (2012), p. 318, 323.

[68] Cf. L. Teigelack, *Finanzanalysen und Behavioral Finance*, p. 287 ff.

[69] Cf. ibid., p. 294 ff.; on the discussion regarding the introduction of black out or quiet periods see M. Findeisen, *Über die Regulierung und die Rechtsfolgen von Interessenkonflikten in der Aktienanalyse von Investmentbanken*, p. 205; U.L. Göres, *Interessenkonflikte von Wertpapierdienstleistern und -analysten bei der Wertpapieranalyse*, p. 95.

[70] Cf. L. Teigelack, *Finanzanalysen und Behavioral Finance*, p. 270 ff.; on the discussion regarding the different categories of investors and the introduction of investor tests see S. Choi, 88 Cal. L. Rev. (2000), p. 279 ff.

Rüdiger Veil

32   The legal discussion on taking the results of behavioural finance studies for inter-
      preting capital markets law into account is still in the early stages.[71] The problem
      that anomalies do not occur with all market participants remains to be solved. Their
      behaviour has furthermore not yet been studied in its entirety. One must further
      keep in mind that the main aim of capital markets law is to ensure the functioning
      of the markets as a whole. A financial analysis, for example, is made public to an
      unlimited number of people. In such a scenario it appears justifiable, or even neces-
      sary, to accept certain deviations from the model behaviour of a *Homo oeconomicus*
      without adapting the concept when developing rules on the construction, presenta-
      tion and distribution of a financial analysis. This may be seen differently regarding
      the provisions regulating the relationship between individual investors (customers)
      and their banks. One will also have to ask the question as to how far legal rules on
      capital markets are allowed to be paternalistic.[72] The legal discussion has as yet not
      found an answer to this question.[73]

II.   The Relevance of Capital Markets Law for University Teaching in Europe

33   The growing importance of capital markets law has had a strong influence in law
      faculties in Germany in the past ten years. Most of them, meanwhile, offer courses
      on capital markets law as an individual field of law.[74] However, legal literature on
      capital markets law remains scarce.[75] As yet, there is no literature on European capital
      markets law by a German author.[76] As opposed to this, numerous handbooks[77] and
      legal commentaries,[78] intended for the legal practice have been published. Various

---

[71] Cf. H. Fleischer, in A. Fuchs et al. (eds.), *Festschrift für Ulrich Immenga*, p. 575 ff.; L. Klöhn, *Kapitalmarkt, Spekulation und Behavioral Finance*, p. 153; L. Teigelack, *Finanzanalysen und Behavioral Finance*, p. 161 ff.; L. Klöhn, in: H. Fleischer and D. Zimmer (eds.), ZHR Beiheft 75 (2011), p. 83–99.

[72] On the different concepts of paternalism see C.R. Sunstein and R.H. Thaler, 70 U Chi. L. Rev. (2003), p. 1159 ff.; S. Choi and A. Pritchard, 56 Stan. L. Rev. (2003), p. 1 ff.; L. Klöhn, *Kapitalmarkt, Spekulation und Behavioral Finance*, p. 150 ff.

[73] For a solution following the principle of proportionality see L. Teigelack, *Finanzanalysen und Behavioral Finance*, p. 237 ff.

[74] See the introduction for students of the specialised subject courses at universities H. Merkt and O. Ross-bach, JuS (2003), p. 217 ff. and H. Merkt and J.-H. Binder, JURA (2006), p. 683.

[75] Only two publications entirely on capital markets law exist as yet: Buck-Heeb, Petra, *Kapitalmarktrecht*, 5th ed. (2011); Grunewald, Barbara and Schlitt, Michael (eds.), *Einführung in das Kapitalmarktrecht*, 2nd ed. (2009). Other publications combine descriptions of capital markets law with company law: Langenbucher, Katja, *Aktien- und Kapitalmarktrecht*, 2nd ed. (2008); Kübler, Friedrich and Assmann, Heinz-Dieter, *Gesellschaftsrecht*, 6th ed. (2006); Raiser, Thomas and Veil, Rüdiger, *Recht der Kapitalgesellschaften*, 5th ed. (2010).

[76] Grundmann, Stefan, *Europäisches Gesellschaftsrecht*, 2nd ed. (2011) also covers certain aspects of capital markets law, especially prospectus liability and takeover law.

[77] Cf. Assmann, Heinz-Dieter and Schütze, Rolf A. (eds.), *Handbuch des Kapitalanlagerechts*, 3rd ed. (2007); Habersack, Mathias, Mülbert, Peter O. and Schlitt, Michael (eds.), *Unternehmensfinanzierung am Kapitalmarkt*, 2nd ed. (2008); Kümpel, Siegfried and Wittig, Arne (eds.), *Bank- and Kapitalmarktrecht*, 4th ed. (2011); Lenen-bach, Markus, *Kapitalmarktrecht*, 2nd ed. (2010).

[78] Cf. Assmann, Heinz-Dieter and Schneider, Uwe H. (eds.), *Kommentar zum WpHG*, 6th ed. (2012); Hirte, Heribert and Möllers, Thomas M.J. (eds.), *Kölner Kommentar zum WpHG* (2007); Schäfer, Frank A. and Hamann, Uwe (eds.), *Kapitalmarktgesetze*, looseleaf; Schwark, Eberhardt and Zimmer, Daniel (eds.), *Kapitalmarktrechts-Kommentar*, 4th ed. (2010).

legal journals, amongst others two peer-reviewed journals on company and business law,[79] regularly publish articles on capital markets law.[80]

34 Capital markets law has also found its way into the lecture rooms of other Member States. Italian law faculties offer lectures exclusively on capital markets law (*diritto di valori mobiliari*) and a number of textbooks have been published on this matter,[81] resulting in a lively academic discussion.

35 Austrian law faculties also offer lectures on capital markets law. There are sufficient publications both for educational and practical interests, including a large textbook[82] and legal commentaries on the Austrian capital markets law provisions.[83] Legal journals are the basis for discussions on current legal problems.[84]

36 In France, universities offer lectures on French capital markets law, textbooks provide additional sources for research[85] and questions relevant in legal practice are discussed in French legal journals.[86] It must further be mentioned that France has very extensive commentaries on important judgments.

37 In Sweden capital markets law is commonly taught in combination with banking law under the more general title "financial market law". Little legal literature can be found, only one title being of interest to students.[87] A number of legal commentaries, however, enable easy access to Swedish capital markets law.[88] There are also numerous doctoral theses on practical aspects of capital markets law, such as on prospectus liability and disclosure obligations.

---

[79] Both journals—Zeitschrift für das gesamte Handels- und Wirtschaftsrecht (ZHR) and Zeitschrift für Unternehmens- und Gesellschaftsrecht (ZGR)—mainly publish articles on company law, regularly, however, including articles on capital markets law. Especially K.J. Hopt is known for numerous key publications in both ZHR and ZGR on the development of capital markets law disclosure regime in Germany (cf. 140 ZHR (1976), p. 201; 140 ZHR (1977), p. 389; ZGR (1980), p. 225; ZGR (1991), p. 17; 159 ZHR (1995), p. 135; ZGR (1997), p. 1; 166 ZHR (2002), p. 375).

[80] The most important journals are Wertpapiermitteilungen (WM), Zeitschrift für Bank- und Börsenrecht (ZBB) and Zeitschrift für Bank- und Kapitalmarktrecht (BKR), as well as Zeitschrift für Wirtschaftsrecht (ZIP), Neue Zeitschrift für Gesellschaftsrecht (NZG), Betriebsberater (BB) and Der Betrieb (DB). Capital markets law is also being examined from the perspective of criminal law, the most relevant journal for publications in this area being Zeitschrift für Wirtschafts- und Steuerstrafrecht (wistra).

[81] Cf. Annunziata, Filippo, *La disciplina del mercato mobiliare*, 4th ed. (2008); Costi, Renzo, *Il mercato mobiliare* (2010).

[82] Cf. Kalss, Susanne, Oppitz, Martin and Zollner, Johannes (eds.), *Kapitalmarktrecht I* (2005).

[83] Cf. Brandl, Ernst and Saria, Gerhard (eds.), *Praxiskommentar zum WAG* (2008); Zib, Christian, Russ, Alexander and Lorenz, Heinrich (eds.), *Kapitalmarktgesetz Kommentar* (2008); on WAG see the statutes and materials compiled by Winternitz, Christian P. and Aigner, Lukas (eds.), *Wertpapieraufsichtsgesetz* (2007).

[84] The following are the most important journals: ecolex (Fachzeitschrift für Wirtschaftsrecht); GesRZ (Der Gesellschafter); ÖBA (Österreichisches Bankarchiv); ÖZW (Österreichische Zeitschrift für Wirtschaftsrecht).

[85] Cf. Couret, Alain and Le Nabasque, Hervé (eds.), *Droit financier*, 2nd ed. (2012); Bonneau, Thierry and Drumond, France (eds.), *Droit des marchés financiers*, 2nd ed. (2005); Valette, Jean-Paul, *Droit de la régulation des marchés financiers* (2005).

[86] Capital markets law publications can mainly be found in Revue trimestrielle de droit financiér (RTDF), Revue de droit bancaire et financier (RDBF) and Bulletin Joly Bourse (Bull. Joly Bourse).

[87] Afrell, Lars, *Lärobok i kapitalmarknadsrätt*, 2nd ed. (1998).

[88] Andersson, Sten, Johansson, Svante and Skog, Rolf (eds.), *Aktiebolagslagen. En kommentar på Internet* (2009); Beckman, Mats, *Lagarna på värdepappersområdet. En kommentar till insiderstrafflagen m. fl. lagar* (2002); Bergmann, Cecilia, Bogdan, Michael and Eriksson, Anders (eds.), *Karnov Lagkommentar på Internet, Lag (2007:528) om värdepappersmarknaden* (2009); Bergmann, Cecilia, Bogdan, Michael and Eriksson, Anders (eds.), *Karnov Lagkommentar på Internet, Lag (1991:980) om handel med finansiella instrument* (2009); Bergmann, Cecilia, Bogdan, Michael and Eriksson, Anders (eds.), *Karnov Lagkommentar på Internet, Lag (2006:451) om offentliga uppköpserbjudanden på aktiemarknaden* (2009); Samuelsson, Per, Afrell, Lars and Cavallin, Samuel (eds.), *Lagen om marknadsmissbruk och lagen om anmälningsskyldighet. En kommentar* (2005).

Rüdiger Veil

38   In Spain, capital markets law is usually still taught in combination with commercial and company law. Equally, legal literature still centres around these topics, only offering individual chapters on capital markets law.[89]

39   The situation is similar in England, where capital markets law plays almost no role in legal training and where no textbooks on this matter exist. This field of law is only referred to in a few textbooks on company law.[90] There are, however, some handbooks, legal commentaries[91] and journals[92] on aspects of capital markets law. One of the most important textbooks on European capital markets law is the publication of an English legal academic.[93]

III.   Outlook

40   Capital markets law in Europe is still mainly regulated under the national laws of the Member States, merely being influenced by European law. It is, however, becoming apparent that the development of a fully unified European capital markets law is only a matter of time. European legislation is going to play an ever-larger role, the latest measures on rating agencies and short sellings already having been enacted by way of regulation instead of directive.[94] The upcoming reforms regarding three of the four framework directives[95] will probably also lead to a change from directives to regulations and from minimum to maximum harmonisation, detailed provisions prohibiting the Member States from enacting their own, stricter rules, rather requiring them to adopt the directives' provisions into their national law on a one-to-one basis.

41   A similar prognosis is possible concerning legal enforcement: the ESMA is not empowered to supervise the Europe-wide trading of securities. It does, however, already have considerable powers, such as the release of recommendations and guidelines and the preparation of technical regulatory standards. This enables the

---

[89] Cf. Menéndez, Aurelio, *Lecciones de Derecho Mercantil*, 6th ed. (2008); Tapia Hermida, Alberto J., *Derecho del Mercado de Valores*, 2nd ed. (2003); Zunzunegui, Fernando, *Derecho del Mercado Financiero*, 3rd ed. (2005).

[90] Prospectus liability and takeover law, market abuse and disclosure are all examined in the publications Boyle, Anthony J. and Birds, John (eds.), *Boyle & Birds' Company Law*, 7th ed. (2009); Davies, Paul L., *Gower and Davies' Principles of Modern Company Law*, 8th ed. (2008); Mayson, Stephen W., French, Derek and Ryan, Christopher, *Mayson, French & Ryan on Company Law*, 27th ed. (2010); Sealy, Len and Worthington, Sarah, *Cases and Materials in Company Law*, 9th ed. (2010).

[91] Blair, Michael, Walker, George and Purves, Robert (eds.), *Financial Services Law*, 2nd ed. (2009); Lord Millett, Todd, Michael and Alcock, Alistair (eds.), *Gore-Browne on Companies*, looseleaf, 44th ed. (2012); Lomnicka, Eva Z. and Powell, John L. (eds.), *Encyclopedia of Financial Services Law*, looseleaf (2011); Morse, Geoffrey, *Palmer's Company Law*, looseleaf (2011); Haynes, Andrew, *Financial Services Law Guide*, 3rd ed. (2006); Blair, Michael et al. (eds.), *Annotated Guide to the Financial Services and Markets Act 2000*, 2nd ed. (2005); MacNeil, Ian, *The Law on Financial Investment*, 2nd ed. (2005). Cf. also Blair, Michael, *Blackstone's Guide to the Financial Services & Markets Act 2000*, 2nd ed. (2010), (overview over all main areas regulated by the FSMA).

[92] For example the following journals: Capital Markets Law Journal; Law and Financial Markets Review; Company Lawyer.

[93] N. Moloney, *EC Securities Regulation*, 2nd ed. (2008); the publication Panasar, Raj and Boeckman, Philip, *European Securities Law* (2010) also cited in this book, examines capital markets law from the perspective of a legal practitioner and is restricted to a description of the legal situation in 14 Member States.

[94] On the Rating Regulation see § 1 para. 37 and § 27 para. 11; on the Regulation on Short Sellings see § 1 para. 44 and § 15 para.9.

[95] See § 1 para. 39–43.

ESMA to ensure a consistent application of European provisions by the national authorities throughout Europe.[96]

42   The course for a European capital markets law has thus been set. At the same time, the task of developing a unified law is not an easy one as it will be necessary to pay sufficient notice to the different legal cultures of the Member States and their strategies to regulate markets. The principles-based approach to legislation taken in the United Kingdom has proven to be an efficient method of regulation regarding compliance throughout Europe. It has the advantage that the supervisory authorities are more flexible with regard to attempts at circumvention the legal requirements.[97] Some continental European countries, however, prefer the legal certainty that accompanies detailed provisions. It is further doubtful whether the principles-based approach can be brought in line with the constitutional law in these states.

43   In future, legal research needs to take on a more European dimension. This process has already begun with numerous legal journals publishing articles on capital markets law transnationally.[98] The aim of this book is to take part in this discussion by depicting the methodological questions of European capital markets law, systemising the provisions of the numerous directives and developing an understanding of the underlying principles, whilst taking into account the national concepts and relevance of the regimes in Austria, France, Germany, Italy, Spain, Sweden and the United Kingdom.

---

[96] See § 11 para. 42–43.

[97] See § 4 para. 51–61 on the advantages and disadvantages of these regulatory strategies and § 29 para. 4 ff. on the MiFID's principle-based approach to regulation.

[98] These are mainly: European Company and Financial Law Review (ECFR); European Business Organization Law Review (EBOR); European Business Law Review (EBLR).

Rüdiger Veil

2

Basics of Capital Markets Law

§ 7 Capital Markets

Bibliography

Blair, Michael and Walker, George, *Financial Markets and Exchanges Law* (2007); Commission, *Commission Staff Working Paper Impact Assessment*, 20 October 2011, SEC(2011) 1217 final; Ferran, Eilis, *Building an EU Securities Market* (2004); Fleckner, Andreas M., *Stock Exchanges at the Crossroads*, 74 Fordham L. Rev. (2005–2006), p. 2541–2620; Fleischer, Holger and Bedkowski, Dorothea, *Aktien- und kapitalmarktrechtliche Probleme des Pilot Fishing bei Börsengängen und Kapitalerhöhungen*, DB (2009), p. 2195–2200; Fleischer, Holger, *Empfiehlt es sich, im Interesse des Anlegerschutzes und zur Förderung des Finanzplatzes Deutschland das Kapitalmarkt- und Börsenrecht neu zu regeln?*, Gutachten F zum 64. Deutschen Juristentag (2002); Fuller, Geoffrey, *The Law and Practice of International Capital Markets*, 2nd ed. (2009); Harris, Larry, *Trading & Exchanges* (2003); Schiessl, Maximilian, *Auf der Suche nach dem "Ankeraktionär"—"PIPE"-Transaktionen und Organpflichten*, AG (2009), p. 385–392; Rechtschaffen, Alan N., *Capital Markets, Derivatives and the Law* (2009); Schwartz, Robert and Francioni, Reto, *Equity Markets in Action* (2004); Seibt, Christoph H., *Sanierungskapitalerhöhungen: Dogmatische Überlegungen und Praxisgestaltungen*, Der Konzern (2009), p. 261–272; Storm, Philipp, *Alternative Freiverkehrssegmente im Kapitalmarktrecht* (2010); Veil, Rüdiger, *Marktregulierung durch privates Recht am Beispiel des Entry Standard der Frankfurter Wertpapierbörse*, in: Burgard, Ulrich et al. (eds.), *Festschrift für Uwe H. Schneider zum 70. Geburtstag* (2011), p. 1313–1324; Veil, Rüdiger and Lerch, Marcus P., *Auf dem Weg zu einem Europäischen Finanzmarktrecht: die Vorschläge der Kommission zur Neuregelung der Märkte für Finanzinstrumente*, WM (2012), p. 1557–1565 (part I) and 1605–1613 (part II); Woepking, James, *International Capital Markets and Their Importance*, 9 Transnat'l L. & Contemp. Prob. (1999), p. 233–246.

I.   Overview

1.   Trading Venue

1   A market is a system in which supply and demand meet. A capital market is thus a market where companies and business enterprises can raise equity or borrow capital and where these are publicly traded. Borrowed capital is generally raised by issuing

bonds,[1] whilst equity is raised by issuing shares.[2] These markets are also called cash markets in order to underline the fact that turnover transactions take place here. In Germany, commitments can be made on cash markets for a period of two days.[3] The contract must be fulfilled within this period.

2   European law defines a "trading venue" as regulated markets, multilateral trading facilities (MTFs)[4] or systematic internalisers[5] acting in their capacity as such.[6] The concept of regulated markets will be described in more detail later. For now it must suffice to mention that regulated markets and multilateral trading systems only differ in few aspects, the most decisive being that only regulated markets are subject to supervision by authorities.[7] The European legislative acts on capital markets law also only apply to regulated markets.[8]

3   Over-the-counter (OTC) trading describes a form of trading that takes place directly between two investors, i.e. off-exchange. The term is further employed in a more extensive sense, describing trading not done at a designated trading venue, such as regulated markets or MTFs.[9]

4   The concept of capital markets may not, however, be equated with that of money markets, exchange markets and derivatives markets.[10] The core of the money market consists of banks procuring liquidity by borrowing and lending to each other, using short-term loans and credits. The exchange market is where cheques and bills denominated in foreign currencies can be traded with foreign banks.[11] It is usually an interbank market. The derivatives markets—closely connected to the capital markets[12]—trade in futures and options.[13]

5   In March 2011, the European equity market turnover was approximately €1,885bn; of this, approximately 52% was conducted on traditional stock exchanges, 14% on MTFs and 34% via bilateral OTC arrangements.[14]

---

[1] See § 8 para. 15–17.

[2] Cf. M. Lenenbach, *Kapitalmarktrecht*, para. 1.14 ff.

[3] Cf. M. Oulds, in: S. Kümpel and A. Wittig (eds.), *Bank- und Kapitalmarktrecht*, para. 14.41.

[4] On this concept see Art. 4(1) No. 15 MiFID. The Commission estimates that MTFs currently account for approximately 10% of total European equity trading volume. Cf. European Commission, *Commission Staff Working Paper*, p. 94–95.

[5] On this concept see Art. 4(1) No. 7 MiFID.

[6] Cf. Art. 2 No. 8 Commission Regulation (EC) No. 1287/2006 of 10 August 2006 implementing Directive 2004/39/EC.

[7] The requirements regarding the supervision of complicance with the rules for a regulated market are laid down in Art. 43 MiFID. As opposed to this multilateral trading systems are subject to the general supervision of investment firms (cf. Art. 17 MiFID).

[8] See below para. 17.

[9] Commission, *Commission Staff Working Paper*, p. 102.

[10] Cf. P. Buck-Heeb, *Kapitalmarktrecht*, § 2 para. 82 ff.

[11] Cf. ibid., para. 85; M. Oulds, in: S. Kümpel and A. Wittig (eds.), *Bank- und Kapitalmarktrecht*, para. 14.58 ff.

[12] Cf. G. Fuller, *The Law and Practice of International Capital Markets*, para. 1.214; M. Oulds, in: S. Kümpel and A. Wittig (eds.), *Bank- und Kapitalmarktrecht*, para. 14.147.

[13] Cf. A.N. Rechtschaffen, *Capital Markets, Derivatives and the Law*, p. 19; S. Kümpel, *Bank- und Kapitalmarktrecht*, para. 8.142.

[14] Commission, *Commission Staff Working Paper*, p. 94 (referring to Thomson Reuters Monthly Market Share Report, March 2011).

Rüdiger Veil

6   With regard to the financing of states and companies, bonds play an impor-
     tant role.[15] According to the Commission, corporate and financial bonds, unlike
     shares, are not, however, traded on secondary markets. The "trading landscape"
     is "dominated by government bonds".[16]

7   The European derivatives market has also been subject to considerable develop-
     ments in the last few years.[17] Exchange traded derivatives are generally confined
     to more standard products such as options and futures, whilst OTC derivatives
     are not and may include products such as swaps and forward rate agreements.[18]

8   Until recently, capital markets were marketplaces where traders came together to
     contract. Nowadays, however, the large capital markets are mostly virtual markets.[19]
     The electronic securities trading system Xetra, created for the Frankfurt Stock
     Exchange, collects all buying and selling orders of authorised dealers in a central
     computer system. If number and price of a buying and a selling order coincide,
     the orders are automatically brought together. Xetra thus provides a platform for
     trading securities, accessible from all over the world. 90% of the total share turnover
     in Germany already takes place via Xetra, a fifth of this being orders from private
     investors.[20] The London Stock Exchange's order books are also managed electroni-
     cally, ensuring a high liquidity of the trading platform SETS, where the securities of
     all large companies are traded.[21]

2.   Primary and Secondary Markets

9   Both economy and law distinguish between primary and secondary capital mar-
     kets.[22] The primary market is the part of the capital markets that deals with issuing
     new securities. Shares will generally be issued by stock corporations and acquired by
     investors. However, the shares may also be put up for sale by a major shareholder.[23]
     In practice, both the stock corporation and the existing shareholders will put shares
     up for sale.[24] In Germany, the primary market is carried out as OTC trading.[25]

10   Shares can be issued by the issuer himself or through securities underwriting, the
     latter being predominant in practice.[26] In these cases a syndicate of banks under-
     writes the transaction, subsequently selling the newly issued shares to the public.[27]

---

[15] Cf. ibid., p. 96: "In terms of total debt outstanding, financial institutions and corporates raised a total of $8,604.8 billion on the European debt market, compared to $14,761.3 billion raised on the international debt market as of December 2009."

[16] Ibid.

[17] Cf. ibid., p. 98 with reference to data on global OTC derivatives markets, mainly generated from statistics compiled by the Bank for International Settlements (BIS).

[18] Ibid., p. 98.

[19] Cf. N. Moloney, *EC Securities Regulation*, p. 766; M. Lenenbach, *Kapitalmarktrecht*, para. 1.10.

[20] Cf. the information available on the homepage of Deutsche Börse AG, available at: www.boerse-frankfurt. de/DE/index.aspx?pageID=44&NewsID=77.

[21] Cf. information on the homepage of the London Stock Exchange, available at: www.londonstockexchange. com/products-and-services/trading-services/sets/sets.htm.

[22] Cf. G. Franke and H. Hax, *Finanzwirtschaft des Unternehmens und Kapitalmarkt*, p. 53.

[23] This is also termed a secondary offer, the offer by the company being termed a primary offer, cf. R. Panasar, P. de Carlos and J. Redonet, in: R. Panasar and P. Boeckman, *European Securities Law*, para. 2.32.

[24] Cf. ibid.

[25] Cf. M. Lenenbach, *Kapitalmarktrecht*, para. 1.24.

[26] Cf. ibid., para. 1.22.

[27] Cf. § 10 para 2.

---

11   Issuing shares through securities underwritings confers numerous advantages as opposed to issuing shares directly. Banks will generally have better business relations with institutional investors willing to buy shares. Banks are furthermore familiar with the usages and customs of the capital markets and will thus be able to determine the best time to raise capital and determine the issuing price in a so-called bookbuilding procedure[28] more easily. This includes direct contact with the institutional investors.[29] The underwriting fee the issuer must pay the bank for its services may be considerable.[30]

12   The secondary market, also known as the aftermarket, is the financial market where previously issued securities and financial instruments are bought and sold. The secondary market allows investors to dispose of previously acquired securities, making these investments once again available to the public. The market participants of secondary markets are usually the investors or the investors and financial intermediaries, such as banks.[31]

3.   Stock Exchanges

13   The large secondary markets are highly organised stock markets.[32] The organisation of Europe's stock exchanges is still largely a matter of national law: neither the Markets in Financial Instruments Directive (MiFID) nor the other European legislative acts contain organisational requirements. Whilst a number of European stock exchanges have merged during the last few years,[33] this has not led to the development of a leading pan-European stock exchange: the most significant European stock exchanges remain the London Stock Exchange (LSE) and the Frankfurter Wertpapierbörse (FWB). According to the World Federation of Exchanges, the LSE undertook 5.5% and the FWB 4.1% of global stock trading in 2008.[34]

14   Whilst the LSE was originally also responsible for the supervision of securities trading, the reforms in 2000 transferred this task to the Financial Services Authority (FSA). The LSE is now only responsible for the admission of new securities to the markets it runs,[35] including the Main Market and the Alternative Investment Market (AIM). The LSE is organised as a public limited company (plc).

15   As opposed to this, the organisation of the German stock exchanges is complex and can only be understood from a historical perspective. The exchanges are

[28] Cf. A. Meyer, in: R. Marsch-Barner and F.A. Schäfer (eds.), *Handbuch börsennotierte AG*, § 8 para. 30 ff.; B. Singhof and M. Weber, in: M. Habersack et al. (eds.), *Unternehmensfinanzierung am Kapitalmarkt*, § 3 para. 75; M. Willamowski, *Bookbuilding*, (2000).
[29] On so-called pilot fishing cf. H. Fleischer and D. Bedkowski, DB (2009), p. 2195; on finding anchor shareholders cf. M. Schiessl, AG (2009), p. 385; on the dealing with new investors cf. C.H. Seibt, *Der Konzern* (2009), p. 261. On the different types of investors see § 9 para. 7–13.
[30] Usually the issuer will owe a certain percentage of the volume of shares issued or its proceeds as commission. Cf. C.P. Claussen, *Bank- und Börsenrecht*, para. 355; H. Haag, in: M. Habersack et al. (eds.) *Unternehmensfinanzierung am Kapitalmarkt*, § 23 para. 30: between 3% and 5%, for larger values more.
[31] Cf. S. Heinze, *Europäisches Kapitalmarktrecht*, p. 5.
[32] Cf. M. Lenenbach, *Kapitalmarktrecht*, para. 1.30.
[33] Cf. N. Moloney, *EC Securities Regulation*, p. 773.
[34] The NASDAQ held 32.1% and the NYSE Euronext 29.6% of the global stock trading. Cf. World Federation of Exchanges (WFE), Annual Report 2008.
[35] Cf. R. Panasar and S. Glasper, in: R. Panasar and P. Boekmann, *European Securities Law*, para. 21.11.

Rüdiger Veil

institutions under public law with only partial legal capacity.[36] German law distinguishes between the operating institution with legal capacity (*Börsenträger*)—e.g. the Deutsche Börse AG—and a stock exchange—e.g. the Frankfurt Stock Exchange—which acts as market operator. As the stock exchange has only partial legal capacity,[37] it cannot acquire property or conclude contracts with its employees and does not possess any financial resources.[38] Rather, the Deutsche Börse AG as the operating institution is required to provide the financial, personal and material measures necessary for the further development of stock exchange procedures.[39] The operating institution is entrusted with public power and is obligated to establish and operate the stock exchange. The Börsenaufsichtsbehörde (Stock Exchange Supervisory Authority) is a federal state authority, entrusted with the supervision of the stock exchange's bodies—i.e. the Börsenrat (Stock Exchange Council), the Börsengeschäftsführung (Stock Exchange Management), the Sanktionsausschuss (Sanction Committee) and the Handelsüberwachungsstelle (Trading Surveillance Office)—as well as the operating institution.[40] The Börsenaufsichtsbehörde will, in particular, issue instructions to the Handelsüberwachungsstelle regarding establishment and operation.[41]

16   The stock exchanges are subject to special rules intended to ensure the correct determination of stock prices, enabling them to represent the actual market situation. Additionally, the exchange prices must be made public. The stock exchange's management can suspend or prohibit trading if regulated stock exchange dealings are in its opinion endangered or no longer guaranteed. It can, finally, instruct certain companies to determine the stock exchange prices. These lead brokers are then obligated to work towards regulated market proceedings.

II.   Regulated Capital Markets

1.   Scope of Application of the Legislative Acts on Capital Markets Law

17   The European legislative acts only aim at organising the regulated markets.[42] The aim of the Prospectus Directive (PD), for example, is to harmonise the requirements for the drawing up, approval and distribution of the prospectus to be published when securities are offered to the public or admitted to trading on a *regulated market* situated or operating within a Member State.[43] The Market Abuse Directive (MAD) demands from the Member States that they apply the prohibitions of insider dealings and market manipulation and the requirements on the disclosure of inside information and director's dealings to all actions concerning financial instruments that are admitted to trading on a *regulated market* or for which a request for admis-

---

[36] Cf. § 2(1), (2) BörsG.
[37] It does not have full legal capacity, cf. H. Beck, in: E. Schwark and D. Zimmer (eds.), *Kapitalmarktrechts-Kommentar*, § 2 BörsG para. 37.
[38] Cf. ibid., para. 38–39.
[39] Cf. § 5(1) BörsG.
[40] Cf. § 3(1) BörsG.
[41] Cf. § 7(1) BörsG.
[42] On the other markets under European law see above para. 2.
[43] Cf. Art. 1(1) PD.

sion to trading on such a market has been made.[44] The Transparency Directive (TD) establishes requirements in relation to disclosure of periodic and ongoing information about issuers whose securities are already admitted to trading in a *regulated market* situated or operating within a Member State.[45] And the MiFID applies "to investment firms and *regulated markets*".[46]

18   The Member States are thus only required to transpose the provisions of the four framework directives and their implementing measures for their regulated markets. On all other markets, they can, but are not obligated to, apply these provisions. Some Member States have made use of this possibility—Germany, for example, has extended the provisions on insider dealings and market manipulation to the so-called open, non-regulated, market.[47]

19   The Member States may, however, refrain from such an extension of the European provisions or allow the market operators to develop their own rules.

20   In Germany, for example, a stock exchange may empower the operating institution to develop an open market for securities neither admitted to trading on the regulated market nor integrated therein.[48] All German stock exchanges have made use of this competence. The FWB has introduced an open market and developed rules similar to those of the regulated market.[49] The London AIM is also a non-regulated market, for which the LSE has, however, also developed rules similar to those developed for regulated markets.[50] Further examples are the LSE's Professional Securities Market and the Luxembourg Stock Exchange's EuroMTF.[51]

21   Not all of Europe's capital markets must be regarded as regulated markets in the sense of the European legislative acts.[52] The shares of all larger companies are, however, generally traded on regulated markets.

22   In future, European provisions on market abuse may also apply to other markets and platforms if the Commission's proposal for a regulation on insider dealing and market manipulation is enacted.[53] If a consensus is reached in Parliament and Council regarding the Commission's proposal amending the MiFID[54] these alternative markets will furthermore be subject to transparency obligations.

23   The Commission justifies these and other proposals for amendments to the MiFID in view of the fact that the financial crisis revealed shortcomings in the rules regarding the functioning and transparency of the financial markets.[55] The reforms are to ensure that the trading of derivatives also takes place on regulated trading

---

[44] Cf. Art. 10 MAD.
[45] Cf. Art. 1(1) TD.
[46] Cf. Art. 1(1) MiFID.
[47] Cf. § 12 No. 1 and § 20a(1) No. 1 WpHG.
[48] Cf. § 48(1) BörsG.
[49] Cf. R. Veil, in: *Festschrift für Uwe H. Schneider*, p. 1313, 1316 ff. for the Entry Standard of the Frankfurter Stock Exchange.
[50] Cf. London Stock Exchange, AIM Rules for Companies, February 2010.
[51] Cf. L. Burn, in: R. Panasar and P. Boeckman, *European Securities Law*, para. 1.16.
[52] Cf. P. Storm, *Alternative Freiverkehrssegmente im Kapitalmarktrecht*, p. 44 ff.
[53] Cf. § 1 para 41.
[54] Cf. § 1 para 43.
[55] Cf. Recital 4 MiFID-II Draft; Cf. R. Veil and M.P. Lerch, WM (2012), p. 1557–1558 and 1562–1563.

venues.[56] The Commission further plans to introduce so-called organised trading facilities (OTFs) as a new trading venue.[57] These trading venues are to encompass investment firms' *broker-crossing* systems, i.e. internal matching systems that execute client orders against each other, and systems for trading clearing-eligible and sufficiently liquid derivatives.[58]

2.   Definition

24   The first two framework directives, i.e. the PD and the MAD, refer to Directive 93/22/EEC with regard to the concept of regulated markets.[59] As opposed to this, the MiFID contains its own definition of the term,[60] which in turn is referred to in the TD[61] and, as of 1 November 2007, also applies to the PD and the MAD, pursuant to Article 69 MiFID.

25   A regulated market as defined in the MiFID "means a multilateral system operated and/or managed by a market operator, which brings together or facilitates the bringing together of multiple third-party buying and selling interests in financial instruments—in the system and in accordance with its non-discretionary rules—in a way that results in a contract, in respect of the financial instruments admitted to trading under its rules and/or systems, and which is authorised and functions regularly and in accordance with the provisions of Title III".

26   This definition proves to be laborious. A regulated market must be authorised,[62] distinguishing it from a MTF.[63] This gives rise to a number of questions: What is a "system"? What does "the bringing together of multiple third-party buying and selling interests" mean? What do the "non-discretionary rules" refer to? And finally, when does a system not function "regularly"?

27   Recital 6 of the MiFID indicates that the notion of a system should encompass all those markets that are composed of a set of rules and a trading platform as well as those that only function on the basis of a set of rules, whilst the term buying and selling interests is to be understood in a broad sense and includes orders, quotes and indications of interest.

28   Recital 6 further lays down that the interests be brought together in the system by means of non-discretionary rules set by the system operator, meaning that they are brought together under the system's rules or by means of the system's protocols or internal operating procedures (including procedures embodied in computer software). The term "non-discretionary rules" means that these rules leave the investment firm operating an MTF with no discretion as to how interests may interact.

---

[56] Commission, Explanatory Memorandum of the Proposal for a Regulation of the European Parliament and of the Council on Markets in Financial Instruments and amending Regulation [EMIR] on OTC Derivatives, Central Counterparties and Trade Repositories, 20 October 2011, COM(2011) 652 final, p. 6.

[57] Cf. Art. 2(1) subsec. 7 MiFIR Draft; cf. R. Veil and M.P. Lerch, WM (2012), p. 1557, 1562–1563.

[58] Cf. Recital 7 MiFIR Draft.

[59] Cf. Art. 2(1)(j) PD and Art. 1 No. 4 MAD.

[60] Cf. Art. 4 No. 14 MiFID.

[61] Cf. Art. 2(1)(c) TD.

[62] Art. 43 MiFiD determines the requirements for a regulated market to be granted authorisation.

[63] Cf. L. Klöhn, in: K. Langenbucher (ed.), *Europarechtliche Bezüge des Privatrechts*, § 6 para. 21.

29   The reference to Title III of the MiFID finally indicates that a regulated market is subject to certain requirements regarding market management,[64] persons exercising significant influence over the management of the regulated market[65] and market organisation.[66] The operator of the regulated market must perform tasks relating to the organisation and operation of the regulated market under the supervision of the competent authority.[67]

30   In Germany, the concept of a regulated—or organised—market is thus defined as "a multilateral system operated or managed in Germany, another Member State of the European Union or another signatory to the Agreement on the European Economic Area, authorised, regulated and supervised by public bodies, which, in the system and in accordance with pre-determined provisions, brings together or facilitates the bringing together of multiple third-party buying and selling interests in financial instruments admitted to trading on such a system in a way that results in a contract for the acquisition of these financial instruments".[68] The United Kingdom has not developed its own definition of a regulated market, rather implementing the MiFID's definition more or less one-to-one.[69] The fact that a regulated market must be authorised, regulated and supervised by a competent authority thus can only be deduced from the reference to Title III of the MiFID.[70]

31   Formerly, the Committee of European Securities Regulators (CESR) published a list of all regulated markets within the European Union and the European Economic Area (EAA).[71] This is now being continued by the European Securities and Markets Authority (ESMA) and in August 2012 contained a total of 94 regulated markets,[72] the most widely known being NYSE Euronext (Amsterdam/Paris/Lisbon/Brussels), the FWB, the LSE and NASDAQ/OMX (Stockholm/Helsinki/Copenhagen/Talinn/Riga/Vilnius). The list can also be used to identify which national supervisory authority is responsible for the separate markets.

3.   Market Segments

32   Most important regulated markets are divided into segments,[73] the FWB, for example, distinguishing between Prime Standard and General Standard listing. The Prime Standard segment is a sub-segment of the regulated market segment, with a

---

[64] Cf. Art. 37 MiFID.
[65] Cf. Art. 38 MiFID.
[66] Cf. Art. 39 MiFID.
[67] Cf. Art. 36(2) MiFID.
[68] Cf. § 2(5) WpHG. The provisions uses the term "organised market" as a synonym for the term "regulated market" used in the European legislative acts. Cf. H.-D. Assmann, in: H.-D. Assmann and U.H. Schneider, *Kommentar zum WpHG*, § 2 para. 161.
[69] Defined in the FSA Handbook's Glossary of Definitions; on the functions of the Glossary see § 5 para. 31–33.
[70] The Glossary defines a regulated market as "a multilateral system operated and/or managed by a market operator, which brings together or facilitates the bringing together of multiple third-party buying and selling interests in financial instruments—in the system and in accordance with its non-discretionary rules—in a way that results in a contract, in respect of the financial instruments admitted to trading under its rules and/or systems, and which is authorised and functions regularly and in accordance with the provisions of Title III of MiFID".
[71] Art. 47 MiFID obligates the Member States to draw up a list of the regulated markets and forward that list to the other Member States and the Commission.
[72] Cf. ESMA, *MiFID Database*, available at: http://mifiddatabase.esma.europa.eu.
[73] Cf. P. Storm, *Alternative Freiverkehrssegmente im Kapitalmarktrecht*, p. 149 ff.

Rüdiger Veil

range of obligations that exceeds the rules provided for by the European legislative acts. These include the disclosure of corporate action timetables and the organisation of annual analyst conferences. The admission to the Prime Standard listing is a prerequisite for the inclusion in one of the FWB indices, including DAX (large cap), MDAX (mid cap), TecDAX (technology issuers) and SDAX (small cap).[74]

[74] Cf. the information available on the homepage of Deutsche Börse AG, available at: http://deutsche-boerse.com/dbag/dispatch/de/allInstruments/gdb_navigation/listing/10_Market_Structure/15_transparency_   standards/10_prime_standard.

§ 8 Financial Instruments

Bibliography

Casper, Matthias, *Der Optionsvertrag* (2005); Davies, Paul L., *Davies and Gower's Principles of Modern Company Law*, 8th ed. (2008), p. 872–875; Ferran, Eilis, *Principles of Corporate Finance Law* (2008), p. 430–432; Fleckner, Andreas M., *Finanztermingeschäfte in Devisen*, ZBB (2005), p. 96–111; Choi, Stephen J., *A Framework for the Regulation of Securities Markets Intermediaries*, 45 BBLJ (2003), p. 45–81; Fuller, Geoffrey and Collett, Elizabeth, *Structured Investment Vehicles—The Dullest Business on the Planet?*, 3 CMLJ (2008), p. 376—388; Fuller, Geoffrey, *The Law and Practice of International Capital Markets* (2009); Haisch, Martin L. and Helios, Marcus, *Rechtshandbuch Finanzinstrumente* (2011); Heinze, Stephan, *Europäisches Kapitalmarktrecht. Recht des Primärmarktes* (1999); Hu, Henry T.C., *Swaps, the Modern Process of Financial Innovation and the Vulnerability of a Regulatory Paradigm*, 138 U. Pa. L. Rev. (1989–1990), p. 333–436; Reiner, Günter, *Derivative Finanzinstrumente im Recht* (2002); Rechtschaffen, Alan N., *Capital Markets, Derivatives and the Law* (2009); Schmidt, Martin, *Derivative Finanzinstrumente*, 3rd ed. (2006).

I. Introduction

1   The PD harmonised the requirements for the drawing up, approval and distribution of the prospectus to be published when securities are offered to the public or admitted to trading on a regulated market.[1] The TD established requirements in relation to the disclosure of periodic and ongoing information about issuers whose securities are already admitted to trading on a regulated market.[2] Both legislative acts hence contain provisions on the disposal of and trade in securities. A precise definition of the term "securities" is thus essential for determining the directives' scope of application.

2   The other framework directives operate largely with the term financial instruments. The MAD, for example, demands from the Member States that they apply the prohibitions regarding insider dealings and market manipulation and the requirements on the disclosure of inside information and director's dealings to actions concerning financial instruments that are admitted to trading on a regulated market or for which a request for admission to trading has been made.[3] Financial instruments are not only transferrable securities, but also money market instruments, equity, interest rate and currency swaps.[4]

3   The following section deals with securities as the key element for the understanding of capital markets. Other financial instruments will also be examined in this context. Whilst this book places emphasis on the regulation of capital markets, the derivatives markets are closely connected thereto and have been of increasing importance since 2008.[5] It is therefore necessary to make a few remarks to this regard.

---

[1] Cf. Art. 1(1) PD.
[2] Cf. Art. 1(1) TD.
[3] Cf. Art. 10 MAD.
[4] Cf. Art. 1 No. 3 MAD. In more detail: § 13 para. 47.
[5] Cf. § 7 para. 7.

Rüdiger Veil

II. Securities

1. Definitions in the Directives

4   The first two framework directives, i.e. the PD and the MAD, referred to Directive 93/22/EEC with regard to the definition of a security.[6] As opposed to this, the MiFID contains its own definition,[7] which in turn is referred to in the TD and, as of 1 November 2007, also applies to the PD and the MAD, pursuant to Article 69 MiFID.[8]

5   "Transferable securities" thus means "those classes of securities which are negotiable on the capital market, with the exception of instruments of payment, such as:

6   (a)   shares in companies and other securities equivalent to shares in companies, partnerships or other entities, and depositary receipts in respect of shares;

7   (b)   bonds or other forms of securitised debt, including depositary receipts in respect of such securities;

8   (c)   any other securities giving the right to acquire or sell any such transferable securities or giving rise to a cash settlement determined by reference to transferable securities, currencies, interest rates or yields, commodities or other indices or measures."

9   The MiFID defines the concept of securities typologically by enumerating some exemplary instruments that can be qualified as securities, instead of providing an abstract definition of the term.[9] The definition does, however, contain the prerequisites of the instrument being transferable and negotiable.[10] Hence, the security's terms cannot be customised but must rather contain standardised features.[11] A personal liability of the holder is also not permitted.[12] Only under these prerequisites is it possible to determine the exchange price of a security. It is irrelevant whether or not the security is certified.

2. Shares

10   Shares are the prototype of tradable securities on the capital markets.[13] They are thus the first mentioned security in the MiFID's definition. Neither the understanding of shares nor that of shareholders is clearly described in the legislative acts of capital markets law. The TD merely defines the shareholder as any natural person or legal

---

[6] Cf. Art. 2(1)(a) PD and Art. 1 No. 3 MAD.

[7] Cf. Art. 4 No. 18 MiFID.

[8] Cf. Art. 2(1)(a) TD.

[9] The former Investment Services Directive also made do with a typological list of securities. Cf. S. Kalss et al. (eds.), *Kapitalmarktrecht*, § 1 para. 4; S. Heinze, *Europäisches Kapitalmarktrecht*, p. 40–41.

[10] Cf. Art. 4 No. 18 MiFID: "transferable securities".

[11] Cf. H.-D. Assmann, in: H.-D. Assmann and U.H. Schneider, *Kommentar zum WpHG*, § 2 para. 7; S. Kalss et al. (eds.), *Kapitalmarktrecht*, § 1 para. 4.

[12] Cf. S. Kalss et al. (eds.), *Kapitalmarktrecht*, § 1 para. 4.

[13] A.N. Rechtschaffen, *Capital Markets, Derivatives and the Law*, p. 43; H.-D. Assmann, in: H.-D. Assmann and U.H. Schneider, *Kommentar zum WpHG*, § 2 para. 14.

entity who holds shares of the issuer.[14] The issuer is understood to be a legal entity, whose securities are admitted to trading on a regulated market.[15]

11   In the absence of specifications in the European provisions the term must be construed in accordance with the national rules of the Member States, this being the usual regulatory concept in the company law directives. Article 2(b) of the Directive on Shareholder Rights[16] refers to the "applicable law" with regard to the term "shareholder", meaning the law of the Member States where the company has its registered office.[17] The public limited companies of the Member States are listed in Article 1 of the Second Council Directive 77/91/EEC.[18]

12   Shares can be issued as par shares or non-par shares.[19] A German stock corporation can thus issue shares with a face value of €1 or higher or instead issue shares representing a fraction of ownership in a company. Non-par shares of a company must participate equally in its share capital.[20] In Germany, preferred stocks to which no voting rights are attributed are also commonly used.[21] These can also be traded on the regulated capital market, as is the case for Volkswagen (VW) preferred stock which have substituted VW common stock since 2009.

13   Generally, shares are freely transferable. Whether the transfer of shares can be restricted depends on the national company law of each Member State. In Germany a restriction (*Vinkulierung*) is only possible for registered shares and has an immediate legal effect (in rem).[22] Therefore, the transfer of shares with restricted transferability is only possible with the consent of the issuer. This does not prevent registered shares with restricted transferability from being tradable on the capital markets. Smooth trade can, however, only be ensured if the company's consent can easily be obtained.[23]

14   The details regarding the different forms of shares and the prerequisites for transferring them go beyond the aims of this present book and must remain a matter for work on company law in the Member States.[24]

---

[14] Cf. Art. 2(1)(e) TD.

[15] Art. 2(1)(d) TD; cf. also Art. 2(1)(h) PD.

[16] Directive 2007/36/EC of the European Parliament and of the Council of 11 July 2007 on the exercise of certain rights of shareholders in listed companies, OJ L184, 14 July 2007, p. 17.

[17] Cf. Art. 1(2) Directive on shareholder rights.

[18] Second Council Directive 77/91/EEC of 13 December 1976 on coordination of safeguards which, for the protection of the interests of members and others, are required by Member States of companies within the meaning of the second paragraph of Article 58 of the Treaty, in respect of the formation of public limited liability companies and the maintenance and alteration of their capital, with a view to making such safeguards equivalent, OJ L26, 31 January 1977, p. 1.

[19] Cf. E. Werlauff, *EU Company Law*, ch. 9.3.

[20] Cf. § 8(3) AktG.

[21] Cf. §§ 139 ff. AktG.

[22] Cf. § 68(2) AktG.

[23] H.-D. Assmann, in: H.-D. Assmann and U.H. Schneider, *Kommentar zum WpHG*, § 2 para. 14; P. Versteegen, in: H. Hirte and T.M.J. Möllers (eds.), *Kölner Kommentar zum WpHG*, § 2 para. 20.

[24] On English law: P. Davies, *Davies and Gower's Principles of Modern Company Law*, 8th ed. (2008), ch. 13; on Italian law: F. Di Sabato, *Diritto delle società*, 2nd ed. (2005); on Austrian law: S. Kalss, in: S. Kalss et al. (eds.), *Österreichisches Gesellschaftsrecht* (2008), para. 3/90 ff.; on Spanish law: R. Uría and A. Menéndez, *Curso de Derecho Mercantil I*, 2nd ed. (2006).

Rüdiger Veil

3. Bonds

15   Bonds play an important role in financing companies (corporate bonds) or states (public loan[25]).[26] Similar to shares, they can also be traded on secondary markets.[27] The term is defined neither in the MiFID nor in the other European legislative acts, the only European requirement thus being that the bonds may not be customised.[28] The legal nature of a bond under civil law and the requirements for it to be effectively issued are therefore to be determined pursuant to the national provisions of the respective Member State.

16   In general, a bond may be defined as a debt security, in which the authorised issuer[29] owes the holders a debt. Thus a bond is like a loan: the issuer is the borrower (debtor), the holder is the lender (creditor). The holder (investor) has a creditor stake as opposed to an equity stake in the company. In the case of the issuer's insolvency its claim is thus senior to the residual claims of the shareholders. The interest rate (coupon) the issuer has to pay to the bond holders is usually fixed throughout the life of the bond. The interest rate that the issuer of a bond must pay is influenced by a variety of factors, in particular the creditworthiness of the issuer, the length of the term and the mode of repayment.[30] Most bonds are annual, meaning that interest is paid at fixed yearly intervals. However, other agreements may also provide that the coupon is only paid on maturity of the bond. The terms of bonds vary, short-term bonds having an average maturity of four years, whilst long-term bonds have a maturity of more than eight years. On maturity, the issuer is obligated to repay the nominal amount to the principal.

17   The details of the arrangement, especially regarding a possible collateralisation of the repayment, are contained in the terms and conditions of the loan. Whether these are subject to a judicial control depends on the applicable national law. Under German law, the courts have qualified the terms and conditions of a loan as general terms (so-called *Allgemeine Geschäftsbedingungen* (AGB)), thus subjecting their content to a close judicial examination in accordance with the provisions thereon in the BGB (German Civil Code).[31]

4. Derivatives

18   Derivatives are contracts that are to be fulfilled at fixed terms and at a specific future date. This distinguishes them from normal (spot) transactions.[32] Futures and options

---

[25] The term public loan is to be understood more extensively than the term government bonds, which are issued by corporations under public law and the federated states. Cf. A.N. Rechtschaffen, *Capital Markets, Derivatives and the Law*, p. 146.

[26] G. Fuller, *The Law and Practice of International Capital Markets*, para. 1.62; A.N. Rechtschaffen, *Capital Markets, Derivatives and the Law*, p. 18.

[27] See § 7 para. 12.

[28] See above para. 9.

[29] Cf. Art. 2(1)(h) PD.

[30] Cf. M. Lenenbach, *Kapitalmarktrecht*, para. 1.15.

[31] Cf. BGHZ 119, 305, 312 ff.

[32] The conditions for transactions are different in each Member State. In Germany, a normal transaction must be fulfilled within two trading days.

refer to a specific financial product (so-called underlying).[33] Futures are irrevocable for both parties. As opposed to this, an option grants the holder the right, but not the obligation, to buy (call option) respectively sell (put option) the underlying asset at a predetermined price. Certain options (premium deals) may require the buyer or seller to pay a premium (abandon) if it decides to withdraw from the contract.

19   The variety of derivatives is impressive. They can be divided into four categories:[34] (i) swaps; (ii) options; (iii) futures and forwards; (iv) stock loans and repos. Depending on the type of underlying, the MiFID distinguishes between derivatives relating to securities and relating to commodities.[35] Futures obligate the seller to deliver the underlying asset, e.g. shares, to the buyer at a certain price.[36] As opposed to this an option contract grants the buyer (beneficiary) the right but not the obligation to demand fulfilment by the other party (writer).[37] An option and a future can be either physically settled or cash settled. Under a cash settled option, physical delivery of the security is not required. The difference in price between the stock price and the fixed price in the option (strike price) is settled in cash.

---

[33] A.N. Rechtschaffen, *Capital Markets, Derivatives and the Law*, p. 19; M. Oulds, in: S. Kümpel and A. Wittig (eds.), *Bank- und Kapitalmarktrecht*, para. 14.43 ff.

[34] G. Fuller, *The Law and Practice of International Capital Markets*, para. 1.215.

[35] Cf. Annex I Sec. C No. 3 MiFID.

[36] Cf. G. Fuller, *The Law and Practice of International Capital Markets*, para. 1.226; C. Kumpan, in: E. Schwark and D. Zimmer (eds.), *Kapitalmarktrechts-Kommentar*, § 2 WpHG para. 37; M. Oulds, in: S. Kümpel and A. Wittig (eds.), *Bank- und Kapitalmarktrecht*, para. 14.43.

[37] Cf. G. Fuller, *The Law and Practice of International Capital Markets*, para. 1.220; C. Kumpan, in: E. Schwark and D. Zimmer (eds.), *Kapitalmarktrechts-Kommentar*, § 2 WpHG para. 37.

Rüdiger Veil

§ 9 Market Participants

Bibliography

Ferran, Eilis, *After the Crisis: The Regulation of Hedge Funds and Private Equity in the EU*, 12 EBOR (2011), p. 379–414; Gringel, Christoph, *Die Regulierung von Hedgefonds zwischen Anleger- und Fondsinteressen* (2009); Hammen, Horst, *Börsenorganisationsrecht im Wandel*, AG (2001), p. 549–567; Israel, Alexander and Holzborn, Timo, *Die Neustrukturierung des Finanzmarktrechts durch das Finanzmarkt-Richtlinien-Umsetzungsgesetz (FRUG)*, NJW (2008), p. 791–796; Kahan, Marcel and Rock, Edward B., *Hedge Funds in Corporate Governance and Corporate Control*, 155 U. Pa. L. Rev. (2007), p. 1021–1094; Klein, April and Zur, Emanuel, *Entrepreneurial Shareholder Activism: Hedge Funds and other Private Investors*, 64 J. Fin. (2009), p. 182–229; Kumpan, Christoph and Leyens, Patrick C., *Conflicts of Interest of Financial Intermediaries*, 5 ECFR (2008), p. 72–100; Möllers, Thomas M. J., *Investor Protection in the System of Capital Markets Law: Legal Foundations and Outlook*, 36 N.C. J. Int'l L. & Com. Reg. (2010–2011), p. 57–84; Olsson, Katarina, in: af Sandeberg, Catarina and Sevenius, Robert (eds.), *Börsrätt*, 2nd ed. (2008), p. 183; Payne, Jennifer, *Private Equity and its Regulation in Europe*, 13 EBOR (2012), p. 559–585; Napoletano, Vincenzo, in: Alpa, Guido and Capriglione, Francesco (eds.), *Commentari al Testo Unico delle disposizioni in materia di intermediazione finanziaria*, p. 634; Quaglia, Lucia, *The "Old" and "New" Political Economy of Hedge Fund Regulation in the European Union*, 34 WEP (2011), p. 665–682; Segna, Ulrich, *Die Rechtsform deutscher Wertpapierbörsen*, ZBB (1999), p. 144–152; Sepe, Marco in: Alpa, Guido and Capriglione, Francesco (eds.), *Commentari al Testo Unico delle disposizioni in materia di intermediazione finanziaria* (1998), p. 590; Schmidt, Reinhard H. and Spindler, Gerald, *Finanzinvestoren aus ökonomischer und juristischer Perspektive* (2008); Wentrup, Christian, *Die Kontrolle von Hedgefonds* (2009).

I. Introduction

1   The capital markets function as trading venues for investors and issuers of financial products. On the primary markets investors buy and issuers sell; on the secondary markets the investors can act as buyers or as sellers.[1] Trading securities on regulated markets[2] requires the participation of financial intermediaries, legal provisions preventing investors from personally concluding contracts on the stock market. In Germany, for example, trading requires the authorisation of the stock exchange's management.[3] Only persons professionally buying and selling for their own account or in their own name for the account of others or acting as intermediaries will be admitted to trading on the stock exchange.[4] In legal practice it is mostly banks that are admitted to trading, whilst private investors, not acting professionally, cannot be admitted.[5]

2   The so-called financial intermediaries[6]—primarily investment firms, financial analysts and rating agencies—play an important role, filtering the relevant information

---

[1] On the distinction between primary and secondary markets see § 7 para. 9.
[2] On the concept of regulated markets see § 7 para. 24–30.
[3] Cf. § 19(1) BörsG.
[4] Cf. § 19(2) BörsG.
[5] Cf. H. Beck, in: E. Schwark and D. Zimmer (eds.), *Kapitalmarktrechts-Kommentar*, § 19 BörsG para. 18.
[6] On this term cf. L. Klöhn, in: K. Langenbucher (ed.), *Europarechtliche Bezüge des Privatrechts*, § 6 para. 121.

from the flood of information which constitutes the "blood in the capital market's veins"[7] and submitting investment recommendations on its basis. Intermediaries are also in the interest of issuers whose costs for capital are reduced by letting the financial analysts evaluate the information.[8] As opposed to this, rating agencies such as Standard & Poor's, Moody's and Fitch restrict themselves to evaluating the relative creditworthiness (solvency) of companies or debt securities in order to provide investors with the information necessary for well-informed investment decisions.[9]

3   Capital markets cannot exist without independent supervision. This is no European insight, but rather the predominant worldwide understanding. In Europe, the supervision of the capital markets is executed by the national supervisory authorities, ensuring compliance with the prohibitions and requirements for the capital markets and imposing sanctions for breaches thereof. As of 1 January 2011 the ESMA[10] complements this supervisory system. The authorities do not themselves participate in the market transactions, only ensuring the functioning thereof. In cases of public takeovers they are responsible for administering the entire proceedings.

4   The following section gives an overview of all market participants that are subject to European rules, i.e. especially issuers and investors but also other persons, such as market makers. The functions and competencies of the supervisory authorities are described in more detail in another section.[11] Investment firms, financial analysts and rating agencies are also examined separately.[12] A description of the numerous bodies of the stock exchanges and self-regulatory bodies in the different Member States is beyond the scope of this book. Therefore, a reference to the respective national legal literature on stock exchange law in Austria,[13] France,[14] Germany,[15] Italy,[16] Spain,[17] Sweden[18] and the United Kingdom[19] must suffice.

II.   Issuers

5   The European legislative acts waste few words on issuers. The PD defines the issuer

---

[7] M. Lenenbach, *Kapitalmarktrecht*, para. 2.277.

[8] See § 26 para. 2.

[9] See § 27 para. 2.

[10] See § 11 para. 37–76.

[11] In more detail § 11 para. 10–27.

[12] See § 25 on investment firms, § 26 on financial analysts and § 27 on rating agencies.

[13] Cf. S. Kalss et al., *Kapitalmarktrecht*, Vol. I, § 12 para. 1 ff.

[14] Cf. A. Couret et al., *Droit Financier*, para. 44–54.

[15] Cf. H. Hammen, AG (2001), p. 549; A. Israel and T. Holzborn, NJW (2008), p. 791; U. Segna, ZBB (1999), p. 144; also F.A. Schäfer and U. Hamann, *Kapitalmarktgesetze* (with a commentary on the BörsG); E. Schwark and D. Zimmer (eds.), *Kapitalmarktrechts-Kommentar* (with a commentary on the BörsG).

[16] Cf. M. Sepe, in: Alpa, Guido and Capriglione, Francesco (eds.), *Commentari al Testo Unico delle disposizioni in materia di intermediazione finanziaria*, p. 590 ff. (on the organisaton of the stock exchange and its management under private law); V. Napoletano, in: Alpa, Guido and Capriglione, Francesco (eds.), *Commentari al Testo Unico delle disposizioni in materia di intermediazione finanziaria*, p. 634 ff. (on the historical development of the stock exchanges).

[17] Cf. A.J. Tapia Hermida, *Derecho del Mercado de Valores*.

[18] Cf. K. Olsson, in: C. af Sandeberg and R. Sevenius, *Börsrätt*, p. 183 ff.; on the self-regulatory bodies: J. Lycke, in: C. Bergmann et al. (eds.), *Karnov Lagkommentar, Lag om värdepappersmarknaden, Prelimenary Remarks*.

[19] Cf. R. Panasar and S. Glasper, in: R. Panasar and P. Boeckman, *European Securities Law*, para. 21.01 ff.

as a legal entity which issues or proposes to issue securities.[20] The TD extends this definition to "a legal entity governed by private or public law, including a State, whose securities are admitted to trading on a regulated market, the issuer being, in the case of depository receipts representing securities, the issuer of the securities represented".[21] The MAD contains no definition of an issuer, rather only defining the term "financial instruments". Therefore, any person can come into question as the issuer of a financial instrument in the sense of the directive.

6   The PD refers to the constellation of a securities issuer acting directly as a market participant by selling securities on the primary market.[22] Regarding securities traded on the secondary market, the issuer is no longer directly involved[23] as the transaction takes place between the individual seller and buyer. However, the issuer remains liable for the securitised claims.[24] The issuer, for example, remains obligated to the buyer of bonds to repay the loan on maturity.[25] Trading in securities on the secondary market is ensured by subjecting the issuer to numerous disclosure obligations in the MAD and the TD. The issuer must therefore be regarded as an indirect market participant on the secondary market.[26]

III. Investors

7   Investors can be divided into private investors and institutional investors.[27] Institutional investors encompass banks, insurance companies, investment funds, hedge funds, sovereign wealth funds and pension funds. All must be classed as indirect capital market participants[28] due to the fact that neither private nor institutional investors are generally permitted to participate directly in the conclusion of contracts on capital markets.[29]

8   The commonly used term "financial investor" is not a legal one. Financial investors are investors who do not act strategically, but rather only pursue financial interests. Whilst a strategic investor will also follow financial aims, he must be distinguished from the financial investor who follows no long-term business strategy for making profits but rather aims at making profits from investment to investment.[30]

---

[20] Cf. Art. 1(1)(j) PD.

[21] Cf. Art. 2 (1)(d) TD II.

[22] Shares can be issued by the issuer himself or through securities underwriting. See § 10 para. 1–2.

[23] An issuer can become his own investor by acquiring own issued shares. However, the acquisition of shares of the own company is subject to stricter rules in the Second Company Law Directive on the capital of public limited companies. For more details see M. Habersack, *Europäisches Gesellschaftsrecht*, § 6 para. 47 ff. The prohibitions of insider dealings and market manipulation must also be taken into account unless the requirements for the exemptions for a stabilisation of financial instruments or buy-back programmes are fulfilled. For these requirements of the safe harbour provisions see § 13 para. 96–98 and in more detail § 14 para. 49–73.

[24] Cf. M. Lenenbach, *Kapitalmarktrecht*, para. 2.271.

[25] On the duties of the issuer of a bond see § 8 para. 16–17.

[26] Cf. S. Kümpel and A. Wittig, *Bank- und Kapitalmarktrecht*, para. 8.253 and 8.254.; M. Lenenbach, *Kapitalmarktrecht*, para. 2.271.

[27] Cf. M. Lenenbach, *Kapitalmarktrecht*, para. 2.274.

[28] Cf. S. Kümpel and A. Wittig, *Bank- und Kapitalmarktrecht*, para. 8.265 and 8.267.

[29] See above para. 1.

[30] R.H. Schmidt and G. Spindler, *Finanzinvestoren aus ökonomischer und juristischer Perspektive*.

9   Private equity companies and hedge funds are typical financial investors.[31] Hedge funds usually make use of certain types of financial instruments and certain trading practices, such as short selling, in order to attain leverage.[32] Only a few hedge funds are activistic. Activist hedge funds aim to improve the governance of companies and increase their value. They are thus especially interested in publicly listed companies in which the principal-agent conflict is especially apparent. In order to achieve their aims, hedge funds must acquire a critical 3–10% of company shares. Generally, they will need, and search for, assistance to achieve this.

10   Whilst specific rules for investors, especially strict rules for hedge funds,[33] meanwhile exist at a European level or have—as is the case for sovereign wealth funds[34]—shifted into the centre of attention of the European legislature, these will be not examined any closer in this context. They do not belong to the field of capital markets law.[35] The rules on the harmonisation of investment funds,[36] which were introduced at a European level more than two decades ago, also constitute a separate regulatory area[37] which cannot be described in detail here. It is far more relevant to examine the types of investors that were envisaged by the four framework directives of capital markets law.

11   Most legislative acts in capital markets law do not distinguish between private and public investors. The disclosure obligations laid down in the MAD apply to the benefit of all investors, the European legislature seeing private and institutional investors as equally worthy of protection.[38] The prohibitions of insider dealings and market manipulation apply to "any [natural or legal] person".[39] The disclosure provisions in the TD are also intended to enable all investors to make investment decisions. The European legislature especially wanted the information to be accessible at afford-

---

[31] In more detail M. Kahan and E.B. Rock, 155 University of Pennsylvania L Rev. (2007), p. 1021–1094; A. Klein and E. Zur, 64 J. Fin. (2009), p. 182–229; C. Gringel, *Die Regulierung von Hedgefonds zwischen Anleger- und Fondsinteressen*; C. Wentrup, *Die Kontrolle von Hedgefonds*.

[32] Leverage means the use of financial instruments or borrowed capital to increase the potential return of an investment.

[33] Directive 2011/61/EU of the European Parliament and of the Council of 8 June 2011 on Alternative Investment Fund Managers and amending Directives 2003/41/EC and 2009/65/EC and regulations (EC) No. 1060/2009 and (EU) No. 1095/2010, OJ L174, 1 July 2007, p. 1.

[34] Cf. Communication from the Commission to the European Parliament, the Council, the European Economic and Social Committee and the Committee of the Regions of 27 February 2008—a common European approach to Sovereign Wealth Funds, COM(2008), 115 final. For literature on sovereign wealth funds see M. Audit, *Les fonds souverains sont-ils des investisseurs étrangers comme les autres?*, Recueil Dalloz (2008), p. 1424–1429; F. Bassan, *Host States and Sovereign Wealth Funds, between National Security and International Law*, EBLR (2010), p. 165–201; R. Beck and M. Fidora, *Sovereign Wealth Funds—Before and Since the Crisis*, EBOR 10 (2009), p. 353–367; B. de Meester, *International Legal Aspects of Sovereign Wealth Fund Investments: Reconciling International Economic Law and the Law of State Immunities with a New Role of the State*, EBLR (2009), p. 779–817; M. Preißer, *Sovereign Wealth Funds* (2013).

[35] On the concept of capital markets law see § 2 para. 1–2.

[36] Cf. Council Directive 85/611/EEC on the coordination of laws, regulations and administrative provisions relating to undertakings for collective investment in transferable securities (UCITS), OJ L375, 31 December 1985, p. 3.

[37] Directive 85/611/EEC was subject to numerous amendments and finally recast by Directive 2009/65/EC of the European Parliament and of the Council of 13 July 2009 on the coordination of laws, regulations and administrative provisions relating to undertakings for collective investment in transferable securities (UCITS), OJ L302, 13 July 2009, p. 32.

[38] Cf. Recital 25 MAD.

[39] Cf. Art. 4 in conjunction with Art. 1 No. 6 MAD on the prohibitions of insider dealings and Art. 5 MAD on the prohibition of market manipulations.

                                                             Rüdiger Veil

able prices for retail investors.[40] The disclosure of "regulated information" is thus also intended to provide private investors with the necessary information for well-founded investment decisions. [41]

12   Only the PD distinguishes between "qualified investors" and other investors, qualified investors requiring less protection. The obligation to publish a prospectus, for example, does therefore not apply to offers of securities addressed solely to qualified investors.[42] Accordingly, a qualified investor must, however, be defined restrictively, encompassing only legal entities that are authorised or regulated to operate in the financial markets, including: credit institutions, investment firms, other authorised or regulated financial institutions, insurance companies, collective investment schemes and their management companies, pension funds and their management companies, commodity dealers, as well as entities not so authorised or regulated whose corporate purpose is solely to invest in securities.[43]

13   The Markets in Financial Instruments Directive (MiFID) also distinguishes between different types of investors. Annex II lists who must be regarded as professional clients for the purpose of the directive. "Retail clients" are clients who are not professional clients.[44] The MiFID assumes that professional clients require less protection, having sufficient experience, knowledge and expertise to make their own investor decisions and correctly assess the risks connected thereto. The implementing directive 2006/73/EC thus abstains from protecting professional investors as recipients of investment advice or other investment services. The information obligations laid down in Article 19(2)–(5) MiFID therefore only apply to retail investors and potential retail investors.[45]

IV.   Other Persons as Norm Addressees

14   The rights and obligations of the management and the persons responsible therein are mainly determined by company law.[46] As opposed to this, capital markets law is aimed at organising the capital markets, and is thus not addressed directly at the management, as can be seen with regard to the obligation to publish an interim management statement.[47] This constitutes an obligation of the issuer and not a management obligation. However, in a few cases the members of the administrative board, management and supervisory board are subjected to obligations under

---

[40] Cf. Recital 25 TD.

[41] Regulated information means all information which the issuer, or any other person who has applied for the admission of securities to trading on a regulated market without the issuer's consent, is required to disclose under the TD (see § 18 para. 23 ff. and § 20 para. 17 ff.) or pursuant to Art. 6 MAD (see § 19 para. 25 ff. and § 21 para. 12 ff.). Cf. Art. 2(1)(k) TD.

[42] Cf. Art. 3(2)(a) PD.

[43] Cf. Art. 2(1)(e) and (i) PD.

[44] Cf. Art. 4(1) No. 12 MiFID.

[45] Cf. Art. 27 ff. Directive 2006/73/EC; on this see § 25 para. 4.

[46] The obligations of the management, administrative and supervisory body of a stock corporation have so far not been harmonised by the European legislature. The draft of a Fifth Directive which was first submitted in 1972 and last amended in 1991 must be considered to have failed. Cf. T. Raiser and R. Veil, *Recht der Kapitalgesellschaften*, § 60 para. 28.

[47] Cf. Art. 6 TD. See § 18 para. 50 ff.

capital markets law, the most prominent example being the obligation to notify the competent authority of directors' dealings.[48] This must, however, be seen more as an obligation of the respective persons as indirect market participants than as members of the company's bodies. The prohibitions of insider dealings are also addressed to the members of the administrative or supervisory board and the management of the issuer. The MAD classes these persons as primary insiders.

15   As opposed to this, so-called market makers must be classed as direct market participants whose rights and obligations are to be determined by the national stock exchange laws of the Member States. Only few provisions thereon can be found in the European legislative acts. Just as any other market participant, market makers are subject to the prohibitions of manipulation and insider dealings as well as disclosure obligations regarding major holdings. With regard to their special functions, the application of these provisions does not, however, seem entirely justified, as is also indicated in the Recitals of the MAD: "The mere fact that market-makers with inside information confine themselves to pursuing their legitimate business of buying or selling financial instruments should not in itself be deemed to constitute use of such inside information."[49] The TD extends this understanding, exempting market makers from the obligation of the notification of the acquisition or disposal of major holdings under certain conditions.[50] It also contains a definition of a market maker: "A person who holds himself out on the financial markets on a continuous basis as being willing to deal on own account by buying and selling financial instruments against his proprietary capital at prices defined by him."[51]

---

[48] Cf. Art. 6(4) MAD and the implementing provisions in Directive 2004/72/EC.
[49] Cf. Recital 18 MAD.
[50] Cf. Art. 9(5) TD. On this see § 20 para. 28–29.
[51] Cf. Art. 2(1)(n) TD.

Rüdiger Veil

§ 10   Access to the Markets and Market Exit

Bibliography
Habersack, Mathias, Mülbert, Peter and Schlitt, Michael, *Unternehmensfinanzierung am Kapital-markt*, 2nd ed. (2008); Langenbucher, Katja, *Aktien- und Kapitalmarktrecht*, § 13 and § 20; Lutter, Marcus, Bayer, Walter and Schmidt, Jessica, *Europäisches Unternehmens- und Kapitalmarktrecht*, 5th ed. (2012); Moloney, Niamh, *EC Securities Regulation*, 2nd ed. (2008), p. 67–78; Panasar, Raj and Boeckman, Philip, *European Securities Law* (2010).

I.   Issuance of Shares

1   A stock corporation must generally increase its capital in order to issue shares.[1] Both the increase in capital and the placement of the securities usually require the involvement of banks that have the necessary business contacts to institutional investors and are familiar with the customs and expectations of the capital markets. Banks organise roadshows and conferences with analysts. Due to banks' expertise they are further able to judge the ideal time for the issuance better than the investor. They can further coordinate the cooperation with legal advisors, and together with these they correspond with the supervisory authorities.[2] Banks further fulfil a number of obligations after the issuance, including serving as the paying agency for the issued shares, ensuring trade for less liquid shares[3] and, if necessary, carrying out price-stabilising measures.

2   An issuer will generally assign a number of banks the task of monitoring the issuance,[4] the financial risk of larger transactions being too big for an individual bank. This association of banks is called a banking syndicate and is led by one of the participating banks (leading bank or leading underwriter). A banking syndicate takes over all the shares from the capital increase and offers these to existing shareholders or interested third parties. The rights and obligations of the banks are laid down in an underwriting agreement.[5] This also contains provisions on the liability for the prospectus.[6]

---

[1] The requirements for a capital increase can be found in the national company laws of the Member States. Some aspects have, however, been harmonised by Art. 25–29 Directive 77/91/EEC (Capital Directive). Cf. M. Lutter et al. (eds.), *Europäisches Unternehmens- und Kapitalmarktrecht*, § 20 para. 156–178.

[2] Very descriptive on the basic rules regarding communication with the supervisory authorities: R. Panasar et al., in: R. Panasar and P. Boeckman (eds.), *European Securities Regulation*, para. 2.59: "There are three basic rules that market participants should follow when dealing with the regulator: (i) be nice to them; (ii) do not upset them; and (iii) do not be unpleasant to them. In addition, there is one overarching principle: tell the truth."

[3] This function is also named Designated Sponsoring.

[4] Cf. R. Panasar et al., in: R. Panasar and P. Boeckman (eds.), *European Securities Regulation*, para. 2.04. The commission the issuer owes for these services can be considerable. Generally the parties will agree that the issuer owes a certain percentage of the issuing volume or the proceeds of the issue. It can range between 3 and 5%. Cf. H. Haag, in: M. Habersack et al. (eds.), *Unternehmensfinanzierung am Kapitalmarkt*, § 23 para. 30.

[5] Cf. R. Panasar et al., in: R. Panasar and P. Boeckman (eds.), *European Securities Regulation*, para. 2.124–2.147; G. Fuller, *The Law and Practice of International Capital Markets*, para. 6.11–6.15; A. Meyer, in: R. Marsch-Barner and F.A. Schäfer (eds.), *Handbuch börsennotierte AG*, § 8 para. 104–191.

[6] On prospectus liability see § 17 para. 61–64.

---

3   One of the most difficult tasks is the determination of the issue price. In practice, three different procedures are known: the fixed price procedure, the auction procedure and the book-building procedure—the last one being the most important.[7] In book-building procedures shares are not offered at a fixed price, the prospectus rather only containing a price range. During a so-called order-taking period the investors then have the opportunity to submit orders, listing the maximum number of shares they are willing to buy and the maximum share price they are prepared to pay. When the order-taking period is over, the banking syndicate will evaluate the information, allowing the management of the company to fix an issuing price.

4   The details of the transaction support and the underwriting are beyond the scope of this book, being a matter that is largely influenced by contractual practice and varies widely between the Member States due to the different legal requirements in corporate law with regard to capital increases.

II.   Admission to Trading of Shares

5   The success of an issue of shares depends on how well the conditions for a later trade of the shares were fulfilled. It is not sufficient for the company to offer its shares publicly.[8] It must rather also apply to have its shares traded on a regulated market[9] or another market,[10] pursuant to the national stock exchange provisions in the Member States and the stock exchange operator's regulations. Such details would also exceed the scope of this book.[11]

III.   Market Exit

6   Market exit is also termed "delisting" and constitutes the revocation of the admission of shares to trading on a stock exchange. The revocation can either be carried out by the stock exchange operator or at the request of the issuer. The legal requirements can be found in the national stock exchange laws of the Member States and the stock exchange operator's regulations. No provisions thereon exist at a European level as yet.[12]

7   There are numerous reasons for a delisting.[13] The issuer may be interested in avoiding the costs resulting from the admission to the stock exchange due to the

---

[7] Cf. G. Fuller, *The Law and Practice of International Capital Markets*, para. 6.17–6.18; A. Meyer, in: R. Marsch-Barner and F.A. Schäfer (eds.), *Handbuch börsennotierte AG*, § 8 para. 30–34.

[8] On the term public offer see § 17 para. 19.

[9] On the term regulated market see § 7 para. 24.

[10] On the term open market see § 7 para. 20.

[11] Cf. on German law P. Buck-Heeb, *Kapitalmarktrecht*, para. 94–110; on the law in the United Kingdom K. Hughes, in: R. Panasar and P. Boeckman (eds.), *European Securities Regulation*, para. 5.01–5.114; R. Panasar and S. Glasper, in: R. Panasar and P. Boeckman (eds.), *European Securities Regulation*, para. 21.1.5; on French law A. Couret et al., *Droit financier*, para. 53–54.

[12] The PD, however, requires an issuer to publish a prospectus if it publicly offers the shares and requires their admission to trading on the stock exchange. Cf. § 17 para. 4.

[13] Cf. K. Langenbucher, *Aktien- und Kapitalmarktrecht*, § 20 para. 2–7.

numerous disclosure obligations and compliance requirements. The issuer can then either abstain from trading his shares on the stock exchange entirely or apply for the admission of his shares at a market with lowers requirements (downgrading).[14] The stock exchange operator may revoke the admission to the stock exchange, if the trade of the shares is no longer ensured or the issuer has breached important obligations.

8   For the shareholders of an issuer the delisting involves considerable disadvantages. Whilst they can legally still sell their shares, they have no market to operate over. This gives rise to the question of whether shareholders are protected in the event of a delisting. A uniform answer to this question for the whole of Europe is not possible as the European legislature has not addressed this question and the legal situation in the Member States is too disparate to be described in this book.[15]

---

[14] For example the stock trading on the AIM (London) or on the open market (Frankfurt) instead of on the regulated market.

[15] In Germany the BGH regards investor protection as necessary and ruled that the general shareholders' meeting must decide on the question of a delisting by simple majority. The investors must further have the opportunity to withdraw from the company against an appropriate cash settlement. Cf. BGHZ 153, p. 47.

§ 11   Capital Markets Supervision in Europe

Bibliography

Abrams, Richard K. and Taylor, Michael W., *Assessing the Case for Unified Sector Supervision*, Financial Markets Group Special Papers No. 134, London (2002); Aoki, Hiroko, *Neuregelung von Aufsicht, Rechtsdurchsetzung und Finanzdienstleistungen in Japan*, ZJapanR (2003), p. 13–24; Aoki, Hiroko, *The New Regulatory and Supervisory Architecture of Japan's Financial Markets*, ZJapanR (2001), p. 101–115; Arnone, Marco and Gambini, Alessandro, *Architecture of Supervisory Authorities and Banking Supervision*, in: Masciandaro, Donato and Quintyn, Marc (eds.), *Designing Financial Supervision Institutions—Independence, Accountability and Governance* (2007), p. 262–308; Bebchuk, Lucian A. and Roe, Marc J., *A Theory of Path Dependence in Corporate Ownership and Governance*, 52 Stan. L. Rev. (1999–2000), p. 127–170; Cary, William L., *Federalism and Corporate Law: Reflections upon Delaware*, 83 Yale Law J. (1973–74), p. 663–705; Casey Jean-Pierre and Lannoo Karel, Centre for European Policy Studies, *Financial Regulation and Supervision Beyond 2005* (2005), p. 10; Caspari, Karl-Burkhard, *Allfinanzaufsicht in Europa*, (2003); Centrum für Europäische Politik, *Rechtsgutachten—Errichtung Europäischer Behörden für die Banken-, Versicherungs- und Wertpapieraufsicht* (2009), available at: www.cep.eu/fileadmin/user_upload/Kurz-analysen/EU-Finanzaufsicht/Rechtsgutacht-en_Finanzaufsicht.pdf; Cihák, Martin and Podpiera, Richard, *Experience with Integrated Supervisors: Governance and Quality of Supervision*, in: Masciandaro, Donato and Quintyn, Marc (eds.), *Designing Financial Supervision Institutions—Independence, Accountability and Governance* (2007), p. 309–341; Coffee, John, *Law and the Market: The Impact of Enforcement*, 156 U. Pa. L. Rev. (2007), p. 230–308; Conac, Pierre-Henri, *Autorité des marchés financiers*, in: *Dictionnaire Joly Bourse et produits financiers*, Vol. 1 (2009); Conac, Pierre-Henri, *The Reform of the French Financial Supervision Structure: "Twin-Peaks" on the Menu*, in: Grundmann, Stefan et al. (eds.), *Festschrift für Klaus J. Hopt zum 70. Geburtstag* (2010), p. 3027–3042; de Kezel, Evelien, *The Liability of the Dutch Financial Supervisors in an International Perspective*, 6 ECL (2009), p. 211–216; Elsen, Jochen Robert and Jäger, Lars, *Revision der Prospekt-RL—Überblick wesentlicher Neuerungen*, BKR (2010), p. 97–101; Ferran, Eilís, Building an EU Securities Market (2004); Ferran, Eilís, *Capital Market Competitiveness and Enforcement*, available at: http://papers.ssrn.com/sol3/papers.cfm?abstract_id=1127245; Frach, Lotte, *Finanzaufsicht in Deutschland und Großbritannien—Die BaFin und die FSA im Spannungsfeld der Politik* (2008); Frank, Alexander, *Die Rechtswirkungen der Leitlinien und Empfehlungen der Europäischen Wertpapier- und Marktaufsichtsbehörde* (2012); Gower, Laurence C.B., *Capital Market and Securities Regulation in the Light of the Recent British Experience*, in: Buxbaum, Richard M. et al. (eds.), *European Business Law—Legal and Economic Analysis of Integration and Harmonization* (1991), p. 307–325; Granner, Georg, System und Organisation der neuen europäischen Finanzmarktaufsicht, in: Braumüller Peter et al. (eds.), *Die neue europäische Finanzmarktaufsicht—ZFR-Jahrestagung 2011* (2012), p. 27–53; Hopt, Klaus J., *Auf dem Weg zu einer neuen europäischen und internationalen Finanzmarktarchitektur*, NZG (2009), p. 1401–1408; Jackson, Howel E., *Variation in the Intensity of Financial Regulation: Preliminary Evidence and Potential Implication*, 24 Yale J. on Reg. (2007), p. 253–290; Jackson, Howell E., *The Impact of Enforcement: A Reflection*, 156 U. Pa. L. Rev. (2007), p. 400–411, Jackson, Howell E. and Roe, Marc J., *Public and Private Enforcement of Securities Laws: Resource-based Evidence*, Public Law & Legal Theory Research Paper Series Paper No. 0–28 and John M. Olin Center for Law and Business Law & Economics Research Paper Series Paper No. 638 (Apr 2009); Kalss, Susanne, *Die Gestaltung der Kapitalmarktaufsicht in Österreich*, ZfV (1998), p. 252–258; Kahl, Arno, *Europäische Aufsichtsbehörden und technische Regulierungsstandards*, in: Braumüller, Peter et al. (eds.), *Die neue europäische Finanzmarktaufsicht—ZFR-Jahrestagung 2011* (2012); p. 55–75; Kämmerer, Jörn Axel, *Das neue Europäische Finanzaufsichtssystem (ESFS)—Modell für eine europäisierte Verwaltungsarchitektur*, NVwZ (2011), p. 1281–1287; Karmel, Roberta, *The Case of a European Securities Commission*, 38

Fabian Walla

Colum. J. Transnat'l L. (1999), p. 9–44; Lamandini, Marco, *When More Is Needed: The European Financial Supervisory Reform and its Legal Basis*, 6 ECL (2009), p. 197–202; Lehmann, Matthias and Manger-Nestler, Cornelia, *Die Vorschläge zur neuen Architektur der europäischen Finanzaufsicht*, EuZW (2010), p. 87–92; Luttermann, Claus, *Juristische Analyse von Ökonomie, Staat und Gesellschaft*, ZRP (2010), p. 1–4; Manger-Nestler, Cornelia, *Rechtsschutz in der europäischen Bankenaufsicht*, Kreditwesen (2012), p. 528–532; Masciandaro, Donato, *Regulating the Regulators: The Changing Face of Financial Architectures Before and After the Crisis*, 6 ECL (2009), p. 187–196; Masciandaro, Donato, Nieto, Maria and Quintyn, Marc, *Will They Sing the Same Tune? Measuring Convergence in the New European System of Financial Supervisors*, Centre for Economic Policy Research Policy Insight No. 37 (2009); Masciandaro, Donato and Quintyn, Marc, *Reforming Financial Supervision and the Role of Central Banks: A Review of Global Trends, Causes and Effects (1998–2008)*, Centre for Economic Policy Research Policy Insight No. 30 (2009); Merkt, Hanno, *Kapitalmarktrecht— Ursprünge, Genese, aktuelle Ausprägung, Herausforderungen*, in: Grundmann, Stefan et al. (eds.), *Festschrift für Klaus J. Hopt zum 70. Geburtstag*, Vol. II (2010), p. 2207–2245; Möller, Andreas, *Kapitalmarktaufsicht—Wandel und Neubestimmung der nationalen und europäischen Kapitalmarktaufsicht anhand des Beispiels der Aufsicht über die Börsen und den Börsenhandel* (2006); Möllers, Thomas M.J., Christ, Dominique and Harrer, Andreas, *Nationale Alleingänge und die europäische Reaktion auf ein Verbot ungedeckter Leerverkäufe*, NZG (2010), p. 1167–1170; Moloney, Niamh, *The Financial Crisis and EU Securities Law-Making: A Challenge Met?*, in: Grundmann, Stefan et al. (eds.), *Festschrift für Klaus J. Hopt zum 70. Geburtstag*, Vol. II (2010), p. 2265ff.; Müller, Markus, *Systemwettbewerb, Harmonisierung und Wettbewerbsverzerrung, Europa zwischen einem Wettbewerb der Gesetzgeber und vollständiger Harmonisierung* (2000); Ogowewo, Tunde Idolo, *Is Contract the Juridical basis of the Takeover Panel?*, 12 J. Int. Bank. Law. (1997), p. 15–23; Pan, Eric J., *Harmonization of US–EU Securities Regulation: The Case for a Single European Securities Regulator*, 34 L. & Pol'y Int'l Bus. (2003), p. 499–536; Park, Tido (ed.), *Kapitalmarktstrafrecht*, 2nd ed. (2008); Partsch, René, *Die Harmonisierung der Europäischen Finanzaufsicht*, ZBB (2010), p. 72–76; Potacs, Michael, *Effet utile als Auslegungsgrundsatz*, EuR (2009), p. 465–487; Pötzsch, Thorsten, *Reform der Europäischen Finanzaufsichtsstrukturen*, in: Grundmann, Stefan et al. (eds.), *Festschrift für Klaus J. Hopt zum 70. Geburtstag*, Vol. II (2010), p. 2367ff.; Raschauer, Bernhard, *Verfahren der Rechtssetzung im europäischen Finanzmarktrecht*, in: Braumüller, Peter et al. (eds.), *Die neue europäische Finanzmarktaufsicht—ZFR-Jahrestagung 2011* (2012), p. 17–26; Romano, Roberta, *Empowering Investors: A Market Approach to Securities Regulation*, 107 Yale Law J. (1997–98), p. 2359–2430; Seibt, Christoph H., *Der (Stimm-)Rechtsverlust als Sanktion für die Nichterfüllung kapitalmarktrechtlicher Mitteilungspflichten im Lichte des Vorschlags der Europäischen Kommission zur Reform der Transparenzrichtlinie*, ZIP (2012), p. 797–803; Seibt, Christoph H. and Wollenschläger, Bernward, *Europäisierung des Transparenzregimes: Der Vorschlag der Europäischen Kommission zur Transparenzrichtlinie*, AG (2012), p. 305–315; Storr, Stefan, *Agenturen und Rechtsschutz*, in: Braumüller et al. (eds.), *Die neue europäische Finanzmarktaufsicht—ZFR-Jahrestagung 2011* (2012), p. 77–93; Taylor, Michael, *Twin Peaks. A Regulation Structure for the New Century* (1995); Thieffry, Gilles, *Towards a European Securities Commission*, 18 IFLR (1999), p. 300–307; Thieffry, Gilles, *The Case for a European Securities Commission*, in: Ferran, Eilís and Goodhart, Charles A.E. (eds.), *Regulation Financial Services in the 21st Century* (2001), p. 211–234; Tiebout, Charles M., *Pure Theory of Local Expenditures*, 64 J. Pol. Econ. (1956), p. 416–424; Tröger, Tobias H., *Corporate Governance in a Viable Market for Secondary Listings*, 10 Pa. J. Bus. & Employ. L. (2007–08), p. 89–186; Veil, Rüdiger, *Enforcement of Capital Markets Law in Europe—Observations from a Civil Law Country*, 11 EBOR (2010), p. 408–422; Walla, Fabian, *Die Reformen der Europäischen Kommission zum Marktmissbrauchs- und Transparenzregime—Regelungskonzeption, Aufsicht und Sanktionen*, BB (2012), p. 1358–1361; Walla, Fabian, *Die Europäische Wertpapier- und Marktaufsichtsbehörde (ESMA) als Akteur bei der Regulierung der Kapitalmärkte Europas—Grundlagen, erste Erfahrungen und Ausblick*, BKR (2012), p. 265–270; Walla, Fabian, *Die Konzeption der Kapitalmarktaufsicht in Deutschland* (2012); Weber, Martin, *Die Entwicklung des Kapitalmarktrechts im Jahre 2009*, NJW (2010), p. 274–281; Westrup,

Jonathan, *Independence and Accountability: Why Politics Matters*, in: Masciandaro, Donato and Quintyn, Marc (eds.), *Designing financial supervision institutions—independence, accountability and governance* (2007), p. 117–150; Wittig, Arne, *Stärkung der Finanzaufsicht*, DB (2010) Standpunkte, p. 69–71; Wymeersch, Eddy, *Regulation European Markets: The Harmonisation of Securities Regulation in Europe in the new Trading Environment*, in: Ferran, Eilís and Goodhart, Charles A.E. (eds.), *Regulation Financial Services in the 21st Century* (2001), p. 189–210; Wymeersch, Eddy, *The future of financial regulation and supervision in Europe*, 42 CML Rev (2005), p. 987–1010; Wymeersch, Eddy, *The Structure of Financial Supervision in Europe: About Single Financial Supervisors, Twin Peaks and Multiple Financial Supervisors*, 8 EBOR (2007), p. 237–306.

I.   Introduction

1   The supervisory authorities ensure compliance with capital markets law provisions. Capital markets law is therefore regularly classified as a matter of supervisory law.[1] European law only contains few provisions on the structure and powers of the national supervisory authorities. It therefore comes as no surprise that the national supervisory concepts vary greatly from one Member State to another as the national supervisory authorities possess very different powers to intervene and sanction.[2]

II.   European Requirements

1.   Institutional Organisation

2   Regarding the institutional organisation of a supervisory system for capital markets, European Union law merely requires that the Member States designate *a single administrative authority* competent to ensure that the provisions of the MAD, the PD and the TD are applied.[3] The regulatory approach of the Lamfalussy directives thus renounces the former approach to be found in older European legislative acts which spoke only of the *competent authority*.[4] The new wording is stricter, requiring the designation of governmental (administrative) institutions, as opposed to the wider definition which also encompassed bodies under private law entrusted with public powers.[5] Only the PD requires that the competent authority be completely independent from all market participants.[6] The suggestion to subject the Member States to stricter rules regarding the national supervisory structure has not as yet

---

[1] S. Kalss et al., *Kapitalmarktrecht*, § 2 para. 1.

[2] See § 12 para. 4–7.

[3] Art. 21(1) PD; Art. 11(1) MAD; Art. 24(1) TD.

[4] Art. 8(1) Directive on Insider Dealings; Art. 9(1) Directive coordinating the conditions for the admission; Art. 18(1) Directive coordinating the requirements for the drawing up, scrutiny and distribution of the listing particulars to be published for the admission of securities to official stock exchange listing; Art. 9(1) Interim Report Directive; Art. 12(1) Directive on the information to be published when a major holding in a listed company is acquired or disposed of. Art. 22(1) Investment Services Directive already used the term "competent authorities".

[5] S. Weber, in: M.A. Dauses (ed.), *Handbuch des EU-Wirtschaftsrechts*, F. III para. 101.

[6] Art. 21(1) subsec. 3 PD.

Fabian Walla

been brought forward—not even in the course of the most recent debates on reforms regarding European capital markets law.[7]

3   The European directives moreover allow the Member States to delegate the supervisory tasks of public authorities to other entities.[8] This is, however, only permitted under certain conditions, namely that the entity to which the tasks are to be delegated at is to be organised in such a manner as to avoid a conflict of interest.[9] The directives contain no further requirements regarding the institutional and internal organisation or the areas of responsibility of the national authorities. The decision whether the supervision of securities trading should be joined with bank and insurance supervision, resulting in one authority being responsible for the entire financial supervision, thus remains with the Member States.[10]

2.   Powers

4   European law, however, contains relatively detailed provisions with respect to the national authorities' powers, the directives enumerating a minimum of powers and sanctioning possibilities with which the authorities must be provided. These are complemented by a general clause ensuring that the rules laid down by the directives can be enforced effectively.

(a)   Minimum Powers

5   The directives on capital markets law contain a catalogue of minimum requirements regarding the investigatory powers and possible sanctions of the national supervisory institutions. They require that the national authorities must at least have the right to access any document and to receive a copy, demand information from any person involved, carry out on-site inspections or request the temporary prohibition of professional activity. The authority must further be empowered to require the cessation of any practice that is contrary to the directives' provisions.[11]

6   A comparison of the four framework directives shows that the MiFID, in particular, has a tendency towards more detailed requirements at a European level. Article 41(2) MiFID, for example, obligates a competent authority that demands suspension or removal of a financial instrument immediately to make public its decision and inform the competent authorities of the other Member States. However, the MAD, the PD and the TD only contain provisions according to which the competent authority "may" disclose any measures taken to the public.[12] The MiFID further lays down that the supervisory authorities may allow auditors or experts to carry out verifications or investigations and may also require authorised investment firms and regulated markets' auditors to provide information.[13] However, even

---

[7] See under § 4 para. 28.
[8] In UK takeover law the tasks were delegated to the Takeover Panel. On the legal status of this body see T.I. Ogowewo, 12 J Int Bank Law (1997), p. 15 ff.
[9] Art. 21(2) PD; Art. 48(2) MiFID.
[10] See in more detail below paras.10 ff.
[11] Cf. Art. 21(3) PD; Art. 12(2) MAD; Art. 24(4) TD; Art. 50(2) MiFID.
[12] Art. 21(3) PD; Art. 14(4) MAD; Art. 28(2) TD and also Art. 51(3) MiFID.
[13] Art. 50(2)(m) and (h) MiFID.

these more detailed rules should not mislead: exhaustive European requirements regarding supervision do not yet exist.

(b) Additional General Clauses

7   In addition to these minimum requirements the capital markets law directives contain general clauses ensuring that the competent authorities have the powers "necessary"[14] for enforcement. The Member States must ensure that the "appropriate" administrative measures can be taken to ensure an "effective, proportionate and dissuasive" enforcement.[15] Whether this is the case must be determined according to national law.[16] At the same time, general clauses must be understood as the legislature's aim to ensure effective enforcement,[17] thus constituting a form of the *effet-utile*-principle[18] in secondary legislation.[19]

(c) Proposals for Reforms

8   The current European reforms aim to harmonise the supervisory powers throughout Europe,[20] whilst still following the original regulatory concept of specific minimum powers, accompanied by an abstract clause granting general supervisory powers.

III. National Organisation of Capital Markets Supervision

9   Taking into account the basic legal requirements of European law, the disparate nature of the supervisory practice and culture throughout the European Union is hardly surprising.[21] A comparative study is indispensable in order to achieve an overview of capital markets supervision as practised in Europe. It must contain an examination of the different institutional concepts concerning supervision and the respective internal organisation. The powers of intervention ascribed to the supervisory authorities of the different Member States must also be taken into consideration.

---

[14] Art. 21(3) PD; Art. 24(4) TD ("Each competent authority shall have all the powers necessary for the performance of its functions"); Art. 50(1) MiFID ("Competent authorities shall be given all supervisory and investigatory powers that are necessary for the exercise of their functions"). Art. 12(1) MAD ("The competent authority shall be given all supervisory and investigatory powers that are necessary for the exercise of its functions").

[15] Art. 14(1) MAD.

[16] ECJ of 23 December 2009, Case C-45/08 (*Spector*) [2009] ECR I-12073, para. 71.

[17] R. Veil, 11 EBOR (2010), p. 409, 411.

[18] On this principle of interpretation in the light of recent ECJ rulings see M. Potacs, EuR (2009), p. 465, 466 ff.

[19] The ECJ is entitled to put general clauses into more concrete terms, having, however, failed to make public its understanding of these terms as yet. In *Spector* the ECJ did, in fact, rule that when determining an administrative financial sanction the general clauses in the MAD cannot be interpreted as an obligation for the competent national authorities to take the possibility of a subsequent criminal sanction into account, cf. ECJ of 23 December 2009, Case C-45/08 (*Spector*) [2009] ECR I-12073, para. 74.

[20] See § 4 para. 27–37.

[21] N. Moloney, *EC Securities Regulation*, p. 1104.

Fabian Walla

1. Institutional Concepts

10 The various institutional concepts regarding the development of a supervisory system show the different understandings that are predominant in the Member States, the two "classic" concepts being as follows:

— supervisory authorities with exclusive competence regarding capital markets supervision (so-called "sectoral supervision");

— concentration of the entire financial markets supervision, securities trading, banking and insurance supervision, under one supervisory body (so-called "integrated supervision").

As a result of the financial and sovereign debt crisis of the past few years, a supervisory concept has developed in which prudential supervision and conduct of business supervision are carried out by separate institutions, in order to prevent systemic risks in the field of prudential supervision.

(a) Model of Integrated Supervision

11 In the first decade of the twenty-first century integrated supervision of securities trading appeared to prevail throughout the whole of Europe,[22] Sweden[23] and Denmark[24] being amongst the first to follow this concept. The establishment of an integrated supervision in the United Kingdom, i.e. the FSA, in 1997 confirmed this tendency towards a single supervisory authority, the entire supervision of the bank, insurance and securities sectors being "under one roof".[25] The United Kingdom has, however, recently given up this former integrated approach to supervision, abolishing the FSA and dividing the tasks between two new institutions:[26] the Prudential Regulation Authority (PRA)[27] is a subsidiary of the Bank of England and carries out the prudential regulation of financial firms, including banks and significant investment firms and insurance companies. The conduct of business supervision regarding all market participants and the prudential regulation over regulated firms not supervised by the PRA is now carried out by the Financial Conduct Authority (FCA).[28]

12 After the formation of the FSA, Germany was the most prominent example of change towards integrated supervision. As of 1 May 2002 the former Bundesaufsichtamt für den Wertpapierhandel (BAWe), Bundesaufsichtamt für das Kreditwesen (BAKred) and Bundesaufsichtamt für das Versicherungswesen (BAV), i.e. the supervisory authorities for securities, banking and insurances, were combined in the Bundesanstalt für Finanzdienstleistungsaufsicht (BaFin), as required by the FinDAG.[29] Austria

---

[22] For example K.-B. Caspari, *Allfinanzaufsicht in Europa*, p. 5–6.

[23] The Swedish supervisory authority Finansinspektionen (FI) was established in 1991. On its organisation and functions see R. Veil and F. Walla, *Schwedisches Kapitalmarktrecht*, p. 8 ff.

[24] The Danish supervisory authority Finanstilsynet was established on 1 January 1988.

[25] E. Wymeersch, 42 CML Rev (2005), p. 987, 990.

[26] Cf. E. Ferran, 31 Oxford J Legal Studies (2011), p. 455 ff.

[27] Cf. Bank of England/FSA, *The Bank of England, Prudential Regulation Authority—Our Approach to Banking Supervision* (2011).

[28] Cf. The Financial Conduct Authority, *Approach to Regulation* (2011).

[29] Gesetz über die integrierte Finanzaufsicht (Integrated Financial Supervision Act), BGBl. I (2002), p. 1310. Cf. F. Walla, *Die Konzeption der Kapitalmarktaufsicht in Deutschland*, p. 19 ff.

followed suit and introduced a new supervisory authority, the Finanzmarktaufsicht (FMA), in 2002.[30] Identical developments can be found in Belgium, Finland and in the new Member States Poland, Slovenia, Hungary, Latvia, Estonia, Malta and Cyprus.[31] Ireland, Slovakia and the Czech Republic also concentrated their supervision, the responsible authorities, however, being the national central banks. States outside the European Union, such as Switzerland, Norway, Kazakhstan, Iceland and Lichtenstein, together with Australia, Columbia, South Korea, Ruanda, Nicaragua and Japan,[32] have also adopted this approach.[33] The degree to which the three supervisory sectors are integrated varies largely from state to state.[34]

13   Integrated supervision does not, however, prevent the Member States from organising prudential supervision for banks separately, which often remains in the competence of the national central banks, as is currently the case in Germany. The legal literature has named this the *twin-peak approach*.[35]

14   The concept of integrated supervision was justified by the fact that developments in the capital markets would in future make difficult a distinction between the banking and insurance sector and the other financial services,[36] as insurance companies, banks and other financial services companies increasingly compete for the sale of financial products.[37] A distinction between the supervisory authorities could therefore lead to regulatory arbitrage.[38] Additionally it was assumed that the number of financial conglomerates active in all three economic sectors would in future increase.[39]

(b)   Model of Sectoral Supervision

15   Other Member States, such as France with its Autorité des Marchés Financiers (AMF)[40] or Spain with its Comisión Nacional del Mercado de Valores (CNMV), have adhered to the concept of sectoral supervision. Similarly, Greece, Portugal, Slovenia, Lithuania and Romania all have an additional authority exclusively responsible for the supervision of capital markets. The European supervisory structure also follows this approach.[41] The main advantages of this concept are the possibility of referring to the expertise which has grown historically and preventing a single supervisory

---

[30] Finanzmarktaufsichtsgesetz (Financial Market Supervision Act), BGBl. 2001/97. On the developments of Austrian capital markets supervision before the establishment of the FMA S. Kalss, ZfV 1998, p. 252, 264 ff.

[31] See table in E. Wymeersch, 8 EBOR (2007), p. 237, 256.

[32] For more details see H. Aoki, ZJapanR 2003, p. 13, 15 ff. and H. Aoki, ZJapanR 2001, p. 101, 106 ff.

[33] This enumeration is based on the research of D. Masciandro, 6 ECL (2009), p. 187 and E. Wymeersch, 7 EBOR (2007), p. 237, 256–257.

[34] E. Wymeersch, 7 EBOR (2007), p. 237, 268. Cf. V. Schlette and M. Bouchon, in A. Fuchs, *Kommentar zum WpHG*, Vor §§ 3–11(3)8 who criticised the lack of integration between the supervisory sectors of the German model of integrated supervision.

[35] On the justification of this model M. Taylor, *Twin Peaks: A Regulatory Structure for the New Century*, passim.

[36] See the explanatory notes of the FinDAG, Allgemeiner Teil, p. 31 or the statements of HM Treasury regarding the establishment of the FSA as quoted in E. Wymeersch, 8 EBOR (2007), p. 237, 253.

[37] K.-B. Caspari, *Allfinanzaufsicht in Europa*, p. 7–8.

[38] A. Möller, *Kapitalmarktaufsicht*, p. 67; K.-B. Caspari, *Allfinanzaufsicht in Europa*, p. 11–12.

[39] K.-B. Caspari, *Allfinanzaufsicht in Europa*, p. 7.

[40] On this R. Veil and P. Koch, *Französisches Kapitalmarktrecht*, p. 6 ff. On recent reforms of the solvency supervision in France see P.-H. Conac, in: S. Grundmann et al. (eds.), *Festschrift für Klaus J. Hopt*, p. 3027 ff.

[41] See para. 37 ff.

institution becoming too powerful.[42] Additionally one may assume that individual authorities will be far more able to specialise in their respective field of activity.

(c) Hybrid Models

16   Numerous Member States have developed hybrid forms of these two models. In Bulgaria, for example, capital markets supervision and insurance supervision are combined, whilst in Luxembourg the authority for capital markets supervision is also responsible for banking supervision. The Netherlands has organised banking and insurance supervision separately from capital markets supervision, the latter, however, being executed by the national central bank. Italy's supervisory concept is very specific: the Commissione Nazionale per le Società e la Borsa (Consob) constitutes the supervisory body exclusively responsible for the supervision of capital markets.

(d) Distinction between Prudential Supervision and Conduct of Business Supervision

17   The recent developments in the United Kingdom prove that the financial and sovereign debt crisis have led to an intense examination of the different concepts of financial and capital markets supervision in order to find an effective supervisory concept for determining and preventing systemic risks.[43] In the United Kingdom a separation of prudential supervision of banks, significant investment firms or insurance companies and conduct of business supervision with regard to banks, insurance companies and the securities markets was regarded as the favourable solution. The aim is to strengthen prudential supervision in order to prevent the destabilisation of the financial system in the future.[44] It remains to be seen whether other Member States will be as quick to follow this approach as was the case with regard to the introduction of the FSA. Germany, for one, has opted against fundamental reforms of the supervisory structure for the time being, rather merely introducing a new consultative body, the Ausschuss für Finanzstabilität[45] (Financial Stability Committee), which is to determine risks to the stability of the financial markets.

(e) Generally Preferrable Supervisory Model?

18   Intensive economic and legal studies have not been able to prove the superiority of any one supervisory concept.[46] Hopt[47] therefore concludes that the decision

---

[42] Cf. R. Romano, 107 Yale Law J. (1997–98), p. 2359 ff.

[43] Cf. HM Treasury, *A New Approach to Financial Regulation: The Blueprint For Reform* (2011); FSA, *The Turner Review—A Regulatory Response to the Global Banking Crisis* (2009).

[44] The Bank of England, *Prudential Regulation Authority, Our Approach to Banking Supervision* (2011), p. 5.

[45] The committee was introduced by the Gesetz zur Überwachung der Finanzstabilität (Finanzstabilitätsgesetz—FinStabG).

[46] R.K. Abrams and M.W. Taylor, FMG Special Papers No. 134, passim; D. Llewellyn, in J. Carmichel, A. Fleming and D. Lewellyn (eds.), *Aligning Financial Supervisory Structures*, p. 25 ff. According to M. Cihàk and R. Podpiera, in D. Masciandro and M. Quintyn (eds.). *Designing Financial Supervision*, p. 309 ff., empirical studies have been able to prove the advantages of the model of integrated supervision. According to M. Arnone and A. Gambini, in D. Masciandro and M. Quintyn (eds.), *Designing Financial Supervision*, p. 262 ff. empirical studies have proven that an organisational connection between solvency supervision and organisational supervision is recommendable.

[47] K.J. Hopt, NZG (2009), p. 1401, 1402.

regarding the institutional organisation of capital markets supervision is solely political, depending mainly on national path dependence,[48,49] The effectiveness of supervision depends entirely on the exact competencies of the supervisory authority.

2.   Internal Organisation

19   There is a further diversity of methods with regard to the internal organisation of the national supervisory institutions. Most national authorities are managed by a collegiate body. The head of this body, however, has a very different function in each Member State. Germany, for instance, adheres to a concept in which the president of the managing body holds a strong position.[50] It must further be noted that in some Member States sanctions are imposed by an independent authority, e.g. by the Commission des Sanctions of the French AMF,[51] unlike in Germany and Sweden, where the enforcement is not executed by a separate body within the authority. The supervisory authorities are also not always independent of government, an especially large governmental influence on supervision existing in France.[52]

3.   Administrative Powers

20   As described above, the framework directives of European capital markets law contain a catalogue of minimum powers for the national authorities together with additional general clauses.[53] Nevertheless, the sanctions provided for in the different Member States differ widely. Therefore, the current proposals for amendments to European capital markets law, aim to harmonise these national supervisory powers.

(a)   Administrative Fines

21   All Member States provide the possibility for the supervisory authority to impose administrative fines for non-compliance with capital markets law provisions.[54] In Germany, administrative fines (*Bußgelder*) refer to administrative offences (*Ordnungswidrigkeiten*). The severity of the fines for market manipulation and insider dealings varies greatly between the Member States, from unlimited fines in the United Kingdom, to tens of millions of euros in Italy and merely 1,000 euros for

---

[48] On path dependence of legal systems L.A. Bebchuk and M.J. Roe, 52 Stan. L. Rev. (1999–2000), p. 127, 137 ff. With regard to the national supervisory systems the national central banks in particular have a certain path dependence, cf. D. Masciandaro, M. Nieto and M. Quintyn, CEPR Policy Insight No. 37, p. 5.

[49] D. Masciandaro and M. Quintyn, CEPR Policy Insight No. 30, p. 9; J. Westrup, in: D. Masciandaro and M. Quintyn, *Designing Financial Supervision*, p. 117 ff. Similarly E. Wymeersch, 8 EBOR (2007), p. 237, 264.

[50] In 2002, when the German BaFin was established, it was organised as being managed solely by a president. This concept was, however, reorganised in 2008, newly introducing a managing body and giving the head of this body a strong position. On the background of these reforms see RegBegr. BR-Drucks. 671/07, p. 7–8. (explanatory notes).

[51] Cf. P.-H. Conac, in *Dictionnaire Joly Bourse et produits financiers*, p. 19.

[52] R. Veil and P. Koch, *Französisches Kapitalmarktrecht*, p. 7; cf. D. Masciandaro and M. Quintyn, CEPR Policy Insight No. 37, p. 7–8 who attempt to quantify the amount of independence of the national supervisory authorities.

[53] See § 12 para. 4 ff.

[54] Not every Member State has provisions for imposing fines for breaches of all the directives. In Denmark, for example, fines may not be imposed for breaches of the TS and the MAD, whilst breaches of the MiFID are subject to fines.

Fabian Walla

natural persons in Slovenia and Lithuania.[55] Breaches of the MiFID rules can be sanctioned with fines of up to €12,500 in Luxemburg, whilst the Swedish authorities can impose sanctions of up to 50,000,000 SEK (around €,000,000) and in the United Kingdom and Denmark there is no limit on the possible fines.[56] Within the scope of the TD the maximum fines vary between €1,022 in Bulgaria and €10,000,000 in France.[57] Fines for breaches of the requirements of the PD range from €1,350 in Denmark and €2,500,000 in Belgium, France and Poland.[58] Once again, the United Kingdom provides no limit on the height of the fines.[59] The criteria to determine the justified level of a fine within the authorities' margin of appreciation also differs greatly throughout the European Union.[60]

22   The Commission has recognised this disparity within the EU. Thus, in its latest proposals for reforming European Capital Markets Law it aims to harmonise the law by requiring national supervisory authorities to have a power to impose fines of up to €5,000,000.[61] The criteria which the national supervisory authorities are to follow when imposing fines are also to be harmonised.[62]

(b)   Other Administrative Measures

23   There is also no noticeable consistency regarding the other administrative sanctions that can be imposed, although all Member States provide some form of additional sanction for non-compliance with the provisions of the PD, the MAD, the MiFID or the TD. Some Member States provide the possibility that the supervisory authority may dismiss the managing director for misconduct, this sanction being entirely unknown in other Member States.[63] The same can be said of the power for the supervisory authorities to issue public warnings[64] or the public notification of unlawful

---

[55] CESR, *Report on administrative measures and sanctions as well as the criminal sanctions available in Member States under the Market Abuse Directive (MAD)*, CESR/08-099, February 2008, p. 3 ff.

[56] CESR, *Report on the mapping of supervisory powers, supervisory practices, administrative and criminal sanctioning regimes of Member States in relation to the Markets in Financial Instruments Directive (MiFID)*, CESR/08–220, February 2009, p. 14.

[57] CESR, *Report on the mapping of supervisory powers, administrative and criminal sanctioning regimes of Member States in relation to the Transparency Directive (TD)*, CESR/09-058, July 2009, p. 9.

[58] CESR, *Report on CESR members' powers under the PD and its implementing measures*, CESR/07–383, June 2007, p. 66–67.

[59] CESR, *Report on administrative measures and sanctions as well as the criminal sanctions available in Member States under the Market Abuse Directive (MAD)*, CESR/08-099, February 2008, p. 13 CESR, *Report on the mapping of supervisory powers, administrative and criminal sanctioning regimes of Member States in relation to the Transparency Directive (TD)*, CESR/09-058, July 2009, p. 67.

[60] On examples in the MiFiD see CESR, *Report on administrative measures and sanctions as well as the criminal sanctions available in Member States under the Market Abuse Directive (MAD)*, CESR/08-099, February 2008, p. 17.

[61] Art. 26 Abs. 1(l), (m) MAR Draft; Art. 28c TD Draft. Cf. F. Walla, BB (2012), p. 1358, 1360.

[62] Art. 28c TD Draft; Art. 28 MAR Draft.

[63] With reference to this CESR, *Report on administrative measures and sanctions as well as the criminal sanctions available in Member States under the Market Abuse Directive (MAD)*, CESR/08-099, February 2008, p. 2. See also CESR, *Report on the mapping of supervisory powers, administrative and criminal sanctioning regimes of Member States in relation to the Transparency Directive (TD)*, CESR/09-058, July 2009, p. 15; CESR (para. 58), p. 73–74.

[64] See CESR, *Report on the mapping of supervisory powers, administrative and criminal sanctioning regimes of Member States in relation to the Transparency Directive (TD)*, CESR/09-058, July 2009, p. 15 and CESR, *Report on CESR members' powers under the PD and its implementing measures*, CESR/07-383, June 2007, p. 72.

behaviour (naming and shaming).[65] According to the CESR, numerous Member States also provide the possibility for the supervisory authority to prescribe a loss of rights for breaches of the TD's provisions,[66] whilst such rules are non-existent in some Member States and others again, e.g. Germany or in parts Luxembourg and France,[67] have developed rules according to which a loss of rights occurs automatically *ex lege* without the decision of the supervisory authority.[68]

24   The Commission also plans to harmonise these measures, e.g. by regulating the supervisory authorities' powers to declare a loss of voting rights.[69] The requirements regarding naming and shaming are also to be harmonised and made stricter, obliging the national supervisory authorities to publish sanctions imposed against a market participant even before the sanction enters into force.[70]

(c)   Criminal Powers of Supervisory Authorities

25   Some supervisory authorities—in particular the former FSA in the United Kingdom[71] and the Irish supervisory authority[72]—also prosecute criminal offences committed by market participants. This once again clarifies the differences that exist between the national systems of enforcement, the attribution of criminal powers to an administrative authority outside the rules on administrative offences being entirely unknown in the German and Swedish legal system, for example. The Commission has therefore abstained from introducing binding criminal powers for the supervisory authorities in its most recent reform proposals.

4.   Liability of Supervisory Authorities

26   Significant differences between the Member States can also be found in the liability of the national supervisory authorities.[73] Whilst in Germany, the BaFin is protected from any liability towards a third party by § 4(4) FinDAG, the Netherlands[74] and Sweden[75] have no rules restricting the liability of their supervisory authorities.

---

[65] See under § 12 para. 10–20.

[66] CESR, *Report on the mapping of supervisory powers, administrative and criminal sanctioning regimes of Member States in relation to the Transparency Directive (TD)*, CESR/09-058, July 2009, p. 54, 59, 63. CESR lists France as an example. France, Germany and Italy, however, have introduced provisions on a loss of rights *ex lege*.

[67] Cf. R. Veil and P. Koch, *Französisches Kapitalmarktrecht*, p. 97.

[68] In more detail below § 20 para. 92 ff.

[69] In detail R. Veil, BB (2012), p. 1374, 1375 ff.; C.H. Seibt and B. Wollenschläger, AG (2012), p. 305, 313 ff.; C.H. Seibt, ZIP (2012), p. 797 ff.

[70] Cf. F. Walla, BB (2012), p. 1358, 1360; C.H. Seibt and B. Wollenschläger, AG (2012), p. 305, 313. The compromise achieved with the Council has led to a slightly less strict proposal, cf. Art. 30a First Compromise of the Council MAR; Art. 28b First Compromise of the Council TD.

[71] R. Veil and M. Wundenberg, *Englisches Kapitalmarktrecht*, p. 8 with further references.

[72] CESR, *Report on administrative measures and sanctions as well as the criminal sanctions available in Member States under the Market Abuse Directive (MAD)*, CESR/08-099, February 2008, p. 13 (para. 13).

[73] According to D. Masciandaro and M. Quintyn, CEPR Policy Insight No. 37, p. 17 the immunity of the national supervisory authorities is an essential step for a further harmonisation of supervision in Europe.

[74] Cf. E. de Kezel, 6 ECL (2009), p. 211, 213.

[75] The liability of the Swedisch supervisory authority is, however, not relevant in practice, cf. R. Veil and F. Walla, *Schwedisches Kapitalmarktrecht*, p. 18.

The United Kingdom, Ireland, France,[76] Belgium and Luxembourg have rules on a restricted liability for damages caused by their supervisory authorities.[77]

5. Use of Resources and Sanctioning Activity

27 Apart from these differences in the national legal concepts regarding the supervisory institutions, empirical studies have brought to light further differences regarding the resources used by the Member States in capital markets supervision and the activity of the supervisory authorities.[78] The US scholar Howell E. Jackson, in particular, proved that large differences exist not only with regard to the financial and personal resources employed,[79] but also with regard to the supervisory activity compared with the frequency and severity of sanctions.[80] The most significant discrepancies can be found between legal systems adhering to common law rules and those based on civil law.[81] Whilst such complex empirical studies are associated with a relatively high degree of uncertainty concerning their completeness, correctness and the comparability of data, this specific study does at least allow the definite conclusion that differences exist in the severity with which the supervisory institutions use their powers to enforce sanctions. The ensuing question, controversially discussed in the international legal literature,[82] is whether a high or rather a low level of supervision is legally recommendable.

IV. Cooperation between the National Supervisory Institutions

28 Currently, capital markets are primarily supervised by the national authorities. In order to adapt to the growing interaction between the European capital markets and the increasing number of cross-border constellations resulting therefrom, cooperation between the supervisory authorities within the different Member States is inevitable.

1. Cooperation within the European Union

29 The European directives form the legal basis for the cooperation between the supervisory authorities.[83] All four framework directives contain an obligation for the national supervisory authorities to cooperate whenever necessary for the purpose

---

[76] On this R. Veil and P. Koch, *Französisches Kapitalmarktrecht*, p. 17.

[77] On the conflict of laws regarding liability of the supervisory authorities see E. de Kezel, 6 ECL (2009), p. 211, 214 ff.

[78] Cf. N. Moloney, *EC Securities Regulation*, p. 1104–1105.

[79] H.E. Jackson, 24 Yale J. Reg. (2007), p. 253, 266 ff. Also see H.E. Jackson and M.J. Roe, Public Law & Legal Theory Research Paper Series Paper No. 0-28 and John M. Olin Center for Law and Business Law & Economics Research Paper Series Paper No. 638, p. 41 (table 2).

[80] H.E. Jackson, 24 Yale J. Reg. (2007), p. 253, 278 ff.

[81] Ibid., 272.

[82] Supporting a high intensity of supervision J. Coffee, 156 U. Pa. L. Rev. (2007), p. 229 ff.; T.H. Tröger, 10 U. Pa. J. Bus. & Emp. L. (2007–08), p. 89 ff. Dissenting: E. Ferran, Capital Market Competitiveness and Enforcement, passim; H.E. Jackson, 156 U. Pa. L. Rev. (2007), p. 400 ff.

[83] Cf. H. Beck, in: E. Schwark and D. Zimmer (eds.), *Kapitalmarktrechts-Kommentar*, § 7 WpHG para. 7.

Basics of Capital Markets Law

of fulfilling their duties.[84] The obligations between the supervisory authority of the home Member State and the supervisory authority in the host Member State to cooperate on matters referring to the concept of a "single passport", i.e. concerning the supervision of investment firms and the admission of securities prospectuses, are especially detailed. This results in a complex system of cooperation between the Member States in the MiFID's scope of application: generally the country-of-origin principle applies, the authorisation by the home Member State being valid for the entire EU and allowing the investment firm to provide the services or perform the activities for which it has been authorised throughout the Union (Article 6(3) MiFID). Yet the host Member State of a branch of an investment firm is responsible for the authorisation and supervision of the respective branch. In practice, the supervision of subsidiaries constitutes a large part of the supervision of investment firms (Articles 13(9) and 32(7) MiFID).

30   The most detailed rules on an exchange of information between the national authorities are to be found in the MAD and the MiFID: pursuant to Article 59 MiFID and Article 16(2) MAD, a competent authority may refuse to act on a request for cooperation only where this might adversely affect its sovereignty, security or public policy, if it has already initiated its own judicial proceedings in this matter or if a final judgment thereon has already been delivered by the respective national courts. If the request for information is not acted upon within a reasonable period of time the authority whose request was rejected may bring that non-compliance to the attention of the ESMA, where discussions will take place in order to reach a "rapid and effective solution".[85] If a competent authority is convinced that the directives' provisions are being, or have been, breached on the territory of another Member State, Article 16(3) MAD and Article 56(4) MiFID require that it notify the competent authority of the other Member State which must then take appropriate action. According to Article 16(4) MAD and Article 57 MiFID a competent authority of one Member State may also request that an investigation be carried out by the competent authority of another Member State, on the latter's territory. Such an investigation is, however, subject to the overall control of the Member State on whose territory it is conducted. If the other Member State refuses to allow such investigations, this may be brought to the attention of the ESMA for the initiation of a mediation procedure.

31   In the PD's scope of application, Article 22(2) requires cooperation especially concerning issuers with more than one home competent authority because of their various classes of securities. All directives underline the importance of guarding professional secrecy with regard to information exchanged with other authorities.[86]

32   In addition to this mandatory cooperation, a tendency towards a well-functioning informal and voluntary cooperation can be observed.[87] The coordination between the different national authorities was further achieved with the help of the ESMA.[88]

---

[84] Art. 16(1) MAD; Art. 22(2) PD; Art. 25(2) TD; Art. 56(1) MiFID.
[85] Art. 16(3) subsec. 3 MAD.
[86] Art. 16(2) MAD; Art. 22(1) PD; Art. 25(1), (3) TD; Art. 58(5) MiFID.
[87] E. Wymeersch, 42 CML Rev (2005), p. 987, 995.
[88] See para. 42 ff.

2. Cooperation with Third Countries

33 The European legislative acts contain no rules on cooperation with third countries, leaving the Member States dependent on the voluntary cooperation of other states. This will often be carried out through so-called *memoranda of understanding* (MoU) concluded between the supervisory authorities of the Member State and the third country.[89] These agreements will usually contain the obligation for both states to exchange information and consult before taking certain administrative measures.[90] In legal practice such memoranda of understanding are often constructed following the recommendations of the International Organisation of Securities Commissions (IOSCO) from 1991.[91]

34 The MoU between all Member States of the IOSCO from 2002 is especially relevant in practice, obligating the supervisory authorities of the IOSCO to pursue mutual cooperation.[92] It must, however, be underlined that MoU can only legally obligate the supervisory authorities to cooperate but do not confer duties or powers or establish new powers.[93] MoU have no legally binding effect.[94] They can, however, help to improve coordination and cooperation between the national supervisory authorities.[95]

V. Competition between the National Supervisory Institutions

35 The field of capital markets supervision is subject to competition between the national supervisory authorities, especially within the European Union.[96] This is made possible by the far-reaching options of the supervised institutions as to which supervisory authority should be responsible.[97] The concept of a "single passport" for security prospectuses and the admission of investment firms, as introduced by the PD and the MiFID, grant a large amount of flexibility to investment firms, allowing them to choose which supervisory authority should approve their prospectus or decide on their admission as an investment firm.[98]

---

[89] The conclusion of MoU between supervisory authorities within in the European Union remains common practice even after the introduction of the new directives on cooperation, cf. M. Lamandini, 6 ECL (2009), p. 197, 198–199. (referring to banking supervision).

[90] E. Wymeersch, 42 CML Rev (2005), p. 987, 995–996.

[91] IOSCO, *Principles of Memoranda of Understanding*, September 1991.

[92] IOSCO, *Multilateral memorandum of understanding concerning consultation and cooperation and the exchange of information*, May 2002.

[93] H. Beck, in: E. Schwark and D. Zimmer (eds.), *Kapitalmarktrechts-Kommentar*, § 7 WpHG para. 8; H. Bauer, in: W. Goette and M. Habersack (eds.), *Münchener Kommentar zum AktG*, WpÜG Abschnitt 2 § 8 para. 14; E. Wymeersch, 42 CML Rev (2005), p. 987, 996.

[94] H. Schäfer, in: T. Park (ed.), *Kapitalmarktstrafrecht*, Teil 2 para. 70.

[95] G. Dreyling and D. Döhmel, in: H.-D. Assmann and U.H. Schneider (eds.), *Kommentar zum WpHG*, § 7 para. 8.

[96] E. Wymeersch, 42 CML (2005), p. 987, 1004 who assumes the existence of market for supervision in the European Union. Cf. for the impact of competion between national supervisory authorities F. Walla, *Die Konzeption der Kapitalmarktaufsicht in Deutschland*, p. 45 ff.

[97] N. Moloney, *EC Securities Regulation*, p. 1105.

[98] On the plans for extending the scope of the single passport when revising the PD, cf. J.R. Elsen and L. Jäger, BKR (2010), p. 97, 98 ff.

---

36   Whilst in legal practice no competitive atmosphere between the supervisory institutions can as yet be observed,[99] they are aware of the continual competition.[100] This
may either be greeted as a means for increasing their efficiency and innovation[101]
or seen critically, as by the former CESR, as hindering European integration.[102] It
must, however, be taken into consideration that for now this competition exists
and supervisory authorities will make all decisions in view of this. Whether the
ESMA will actually be able to put an end to the competition, as expected by some,[103]
remains to be seen.

VI.   The European Financial Supervisory Scheme

37   International legal literature has long been discussing whether a central European
supervisory institution,[104] following the example of the US Securities and Exchange
Commission (SEC) should be introduced. The latest financial crisis, finally, gave a
strong incentive for introducing a new European supervisory scheme.[105] The Commission laid down the cornerstones of the new supervisory system, based largely
on the work of the expert group under the chair of Jacques de Larosière[106] in its
legislative package of 23 September 2009.[107] On 22 September 2010 the European
Parliament accepted the Commission's proposal, suggesting only few amendments.[108]
It was approved by the Council on 17 November 2010 and entered into force on 1
January 2011.

1.   The European Financial Markets Supervisory System

38   The new European financial markets supervisory system consists of two pillars: The
macro-prudential level aims to avoid systemic risks for the entire European financial
system whilst the micro-prudential level is intended to develop a European system

---

[99] Cf. N. Moloney, in: S. Grundmann et al. (eds.), *Festschrift für Klaus J. Hopt*, p. 2264, 2274. First indications
of competition can be found with regard to exports and imports in the field of the single passport: the United
Kingdom and Sweden have attracted attention as "exporters", whereas Belgium, Finland, Germany, Ireland, Luxemburg, Sweden and Portugal are classed as important importers of regulatory approval, cf. N. Moloney, *EC
Securities Regulation*, p. 1106.

[100] Cf. explicitly BaFin's longtime President, Jochen Sanio, in the prefeace of L. Frach, *Finanzaufsicht in
Deutschland und Großbritannien.*

[101] Centre for European Policy Studies, Financial Regulation and Supervision Beyond 2005, p. 10.

[102] CESR, *A proposed evolution of EU securities supervision beyond 2007*, CESR/07-783, p. 3 ("referees should
not compete").

[103] N. Moloney, in: S. Grundmann et al. (eds.), *Festschrift für Klaus J. Hopt*, p. 2264, 2274.

[104] L.C.B. Gower, in: R.M. Buxbaum et al. (eds.), *European Business Law*, p. 307, 315 ff.; Pan, 34 L. & Pol'y
Int'l Bus. (2003), p. 499, 526 ff.; G. Thieffry, 18 Financial Law Review (1999), p. 14 ff.; G. Thieffry, in: E. Ferran
and C.A.E. Goodhart (eds.), *Regulation Financial Services in 21st Century*, p. 211, 220 ff.; R. Karmel, 38 Colum.
J. Transnat'l L. Law (1999), p. 9, 32 ff.; E. Wymeersch, in: E. Ferran and C.A.E. Goodhart (eds.), *Regulation
Financial Services in 21st Century*, p. 189, 193; summarised in A. Möller, *Kapitalmarktaufsicht*, p. 189 ff.

[105] Cf. Recital 1 ESMA Regulation

[106] See § 1 para. 33.

[107] COM(2009), 499 final; COM(2009), 500 final; COM(2009), 501 final; COM(2009), 502 final; COM(2009),
503 final. Cf. Communication from the Commission of 27 May 2009, COM(2009), 252 final.

[108] On securities supervision: Legislative Proposal of the European Parliament of 22 September 2010 on the
Proposal for a Regulation of the European Parliament and of the Council establishing a European Securities and
Markets Authority (COM(2009)0503, C7-0167/2009, 2009/0144(COD).

Fabian Walla

of supervision for the individual financial service providers and capital market participants. The legal foundation for the introduction of a supervisory system in EU primary law was originally Article 95 of the EC Treaty. Since the enactment of the Treaty of Lisbon the measures are now based on Article 114 TFEU.[109]

(a) Macro-prudential Level

39   The European Systemic Risk Board (ESRB) is responsible for the macro-level supervision,[110] ensuring the general stability of Europe's financial system.[111] The ESRB, however, does not have its own legal personality,[112] rather being a body for cooperation between members of the Commission, the European Central Bank, the European supervisory authorities on the micro-prudential level (ESAs) together with the national supervisory authorities and central banks.[113] The ESRB is to have the power to issue warnings regarding systemic risks and recommendations for their prevention.[114] The ESRB is not, however, to be equipped with legally binding legislative powers or powers of intervention.[115]

(b) Micro-prudential Level

40   At a micro-prudential level, the supervision of the individual financial actors is the responsibility of the European System of Financial Supervision (ESFS),[116] consisting of three central European authorities: the European Banking Authority (EBA), the European Insurance and Occupational Pensions Authority (EIOPA) and the ESMA, all of which have their own legal personality.[117] Together with the national supervisory authorities, these European authorities form a network responsible for the supervision of the financial markets.[118] As opposed to the macro-prudential level, the European authorities of the ESFS all have legally binding legislative powers and powers of intervention.[119] Yet the day-to-day supervision of market participants is

---

[109] COM(2009), 503 final, Recital 10; this is regarded as a sufficient legal foundation of competence in legal literature, cf. M. Lehmann and C. Manger-Nestler, EuZW (2010), p. 87, 88; T. Pötzsch, in: S. Grundmann et al. (eds.), *Festschrift für Klaus J. Hopt*, p. 2367, 2370 ff.; M. Lamandini, 6 ECL (2009), p. 197, 200 with reference to ECJ of 2 May 2006, Case C-217/04 (United Kingdom/European Parliament) [2006] ECR I-3771. In more detail Centrum für Europäische Politik, *Rechtsgutachten of 6.7.2009*, passim.

[110] Regulation (EU) No. 1092/2010 of the European Parliament and of the Council of 24 November 2010 on European Union macro-prudential oversight of the financial system and establishing a European Systemic Risk Board.

[111] See press release of 23 September 2009.

[112] Cf. Recital 15 Regulation (EU) No. 1092/2010 of the European Parliament and of the Council of 24 November 2010 on European Union macro-prudential oversight of the financial system and establishing a European Systemic Risk Board.

[113] Cf. COM(2009), 499 final, Art. 6.

[114] COM(2009), 499 final, Art. 16 ff.

[115] Cf. Art. 15 ff. Regulation (EU) No. 1092/2010 of the European Parliament and of the Council of 24 November 2010 on European Union macro-prudential oversight of the financial system and establishing a European Systemic Risk Board.

[116] COM(2009), 503 final.

[117] COM(2009), 503 final, Art. 3(1). Cf. G. Granner, in: Braumüller et al. (eds.), *Die neue Europäische Finanzmarktaufsicht—ZFR Jahrestagung 2011*, p. 27, 31. ff.

[118] Recital 9 ESMA Regulation.

[119] See below para. 47.

still to be carried out by the national supervisory authorities, with the national level continuing to be the centre of supervision under the new model.[120]

41   A Joint Committee is to ensure a cooperation and coordination between the macro- and the micro-prudential level and between the individual authorities on the micro-prudential level.

2.   The European Securities and Markets Authority (ESMA)

42   The ESMA is based on the ESMA Regulation and assumed all tasks and powers of the former CESR.[121] Accordingly, the ESMA has its seat in Paris.[122] At the end of 2012, the ESMA had 101 employees,[123] a number that was expected to increase to 160 by the end of 2013.[124] The authority's responsibility is to improve the functioning of the internal market by taking into account the interests of the Member States and the differences between the financial markets participants, thereby ensuring an effective and consistent level of regulation and supervision.[125] Additionally, the ESMA is to protect public values such as the integrity and stability of the financial system, the transparency of markets and financial products and the protection of investors.[126] The ESMA should also prevent regulatory arbitrage and strengthen international supervisory coordination[127] alongside consumer protection[128].

(a)   Internal Organisation

43   The supervisory body is to be governed by the Board of Supervisors, which is to give guidance and advice to the ESMA.[129] The ESMA additionally comprises a Management Board, a Chairperson, an Executive Director and a Board of Appeal.[130]

44   The Board of Supervisors is composed of the heads of the national public authorities and further non-voting members, namely representatives of the Commission, the ESRB, the Chairperson of the ESMA and one representative from each of the other two European Supervisory Authorities.[131] The Board of Supervisors appoints the ESMA Chairperson. [132] For up to one month after the selection, the European Parliament may, however, object to the designation of the selected person.[133] Steven Maijoor from the Netherlands was appointed the first Chairman of the ESMA. The Board of Supervisors must further elect an alternate to carry out the functions of

---

[120] See A. Wittig, DB (2010), *Standpunkte*, p. 69.
[121] Recital 8 and 67 ESMA Regulation.
[122] Art. 7 ESMA Regulation.
[123] ESMA, *2013 Work Programme*, ESMA/2012/631, October 2012, p. 17.
[124] Ibid, p. 21.
[125] Recital 11 ESMA Regulation.
[126] Recital 11 ESMA Regulation.
[127] Recital 11 ESMA Regulation; cf. Art. 8(2)(i) ESMA Regulation.
[128] Recital 11 ESMA Regulation; cf. Art. 8(2)(i) ESMA Regulation.
[129] Art. 43(1), (2) ESMA Regulation.
[130] Art. 6 ESMA Regulation.
[131] Art. 40(1) ESMA Regulation. In general, decisions of the Board of Supervisors are taken by a simple majority of its members, each member having one vote, cf. Art. 44(1) ESMA Regulation. With regard to the acts specified in Art. 10–16 ESMA Regulation, however, the Board of Supervisors' decisions must be taken on the basis of a majority as defined in the Treaty of Lisbon, cf. Art. 44(1)2 ESMA Regulation.
[132] Art. 43(3) ESMA Regulation.
[133] Art. 48(2) ESMA Regulation.

Fabian Walla

the Chairperson in his absence and who may not be a member of the Management Board.[134] The Chairperson's main tasks are the representation of the ESMA and chairing the meetings of the Board of Supervisors and the Management Board.[135] After confirmation by the European Parliament, the Board of Supervisors must also appoint an Executive Director in charge of the management of the ESMA and prepare the work of the Management Board,[136] which constitutes the ESMA's day-to-day supervisory activities.[137] The Executive Director may participate in meetings of the Board of Supervisors, but does not have the right to vote.[138] The first Executive Director is Verena Ross, a German national formerly working for the United Kingdom's supervisor.

45   One of the Management Board's tasks is to ensure that the ESMA performs the tasks assigned to it and acts according to its budgetary plan.[139] The Management Board is composed of the Chairperson and six other members of the Board of Supervisors, elected from the voting members of the Board of Supervisors.[140] The Executive Director and a representative of the Commission can participate in meetings of the Management Board but do not have the right to vote.[141] The Management Board further appoints members of the Board of Appeal.[142] The Board of Appeal is a joint body of the three new European Authorities providing legal protection against measures taken by ESMA, EIOPA or EBA.[143]

(b)   Independence

46   The ESMA is independent, acting solely in the interest of the European Union.[144] The autonomy of its bodies[145] and its budgetary autonomy do in fact achieve independence to a very large extent.[146] However, due to the fact that the members of ESMA's supervisory body come from the national capital markets supervisory authorities, a certain adaptation towards the national interests cannot be prevented. This distinguishes the ESMA from the European Central Bank which can be seen as a more independent body.[147]

(c)   Powers of Intervention towards the National Supervisory Authorities

47   Generally the concept of the European supervisory system does not provide for the ESMA to have any direct powers (of intervention) over issuers and market participants. The continuous supervision of market developments is rather to remain a

---

[134] Art. 48(2)3 ESMA Regulation.
[135] Art. 48(1) ESMA Regulation.
[136] Art. 51(2) ESMA Regulation.
[137] Cf. No. 6.3.3 Commission Proposal, COM(2009), 503 final.
[138] Art. 40(6) ESMA Regulation.
[139] Art. 47(1) ESMA Regulation.
[140] Art. 45(1) ESMA Regulation.
[141] Art. 45(2) ESMA Regulation.
[142] Art. 47(8) ESMA Regulation.
[143] See below para. 76.
[144] Cf. Recital 59 ESMA Regulation.
[145] Art. 42, 46, 49, 52, 59 ESMA Regulation.
[146] Cf. M. Lehmann and C. Manger-Nestler, EuZW (2010), p. 87, 89.
[147] Cf. ibid., p. 87, 98; M. Lehmann and C. Manger-Nestler, ZBB (2011), p. 2, 8.

matter of the Member States' national authorities, which are only to be supervised by the ESMA, in order to ensure coordination of international supervision.[148] To this end, peer reviews pursuant to Article 30 ESMA Regulation are an efficient and effective tool for analysing and comparing the national institutions' activities.[149] According to Article 35 of the regulation, the ESMA further has the right to request information from the competent authorities within the Member States in order to perform its supervisory duties. There are, however, two ways of intervening against national authorities or in exceptional cases against market participants.

(aa) Breaches of EU Law by the National Supervisory Authorities

48   When a competent authority has incorrectly or insufficiently applied European Union law, Article 17 ESMA Regulation provides a three-step mechanism[150] for the Authority as a proportionate response thereto:

49   The ESMA itself, the Council, Parliament, Commission or the Securities and Markets Stakeholder Group may initiate investigations regarding the incorrect or insufficient application of EU law obligations by national authorities in their supervisory practice. Within two months after commencement of the investigations, the ESMA may issue a recommendation to the competent national authority on how to overcome the breach.

50   In the case that the competent national authority does not follow the recommendation within a one-month period, the Commission is empowered on a second level to issue a formal opinion taking the ESMA's recommendation into account and requiring the competent authority to take the actions necessary to ensure compliance with Union law.

51   To overcome situations in which these actions are not taken within the given time limit, the ESMA may adopt decisions addressed to individual participants in the financial markets. These may obligate the respective participant to comply with its duties under EU law. This power, however, only exists where it is necessary to remedy such non-compliance in a timely manner in order to maintain or restore neutral conditions of competition on the market or ensure the orderly functioning and integrity of the financial system.[151] The breach must further affect directly applicable provisions of European law. The ESMA is thus empowered to undertake a form of "right of entry" in order to remedy breaches of EU law.[152]

(bb) Decisions on Emergency Situations and Disagreements

52   In cases of so-called "emergency situations"[153] and "disagreements between national supervisory authorities"[154] the ESMA is permitted to address measures to individual national supervisory authorities. The measures must be necessary as a reaction to adverse developments which may seriously jeopardise the orderly functioning and

---

[148] Art. 1(5)(c) and Art. 31 ESMA Regulation.
[149] Cf. Recital 41 ESMA Regulation.
[150] Recital 28 ESMA Regulation; cf. M. Lehmann and C. Manger-Nestler, EuZW (2010), p. 87, 90.
[151] Art. 17(6) ESMA Regulation.
[152] M. Lehmann and C. Manger-Nestler, EuZW (2010), p. 87, 91. Cf. also J.A. Kämmerer, NVwZ (2011), p. 1281, 1284 ff.
[153] Art. 18 ESMA Regulation.
[154] Art. 19 ESMA Regulation.

Fabian Walla

integrity of financial markets or the stability of the whole or part of the financial system in the Union. Should the national authority not comply with the decision, the ESMA may adopt an individual decision addressed to a financial market participant, requiring the necessary action to comply with its obligations.[155]

(1) Emergency Situation

53   The Council is empowered to determine the existence of so-called emergency situations in consultation with the Commission, the ESRB and, where appropriate, the ESAs.[156] The request for such a decision can be made by the ESMA, the Commission or the ESRB. If a competent authority does not comply with the decision of the ESMA, a decision addressed directly to a financial markets participant requiring the necessary action to comply with its obligations under that legislation is only permitted under strict conditions. This is the case in situations requiring rectification in order to restore the orderly functioning and integrity of financial markets or the stability of the whole or part of the financial system in the Union.

(2) Disagreements between Competent Authorities in Cross-Border Situations

54   In cases of disagreements between national supervisory authorities, the ESMA may adopt a decision, addressed to a financial markets participant requiring the necessary action to comply with its obligations under EU law. Prior to this, the ESMA has, however, to act as a mediator between the authorities, setting a time limit for conciliation.[157] Where a competent authority does not comply with the ESMA's decision, the latter may adopt an individual decision addressed to a financial markets participant requiring the necessary action to comply with its obligations under European law pursuant to Article 19(4) ESMA Regulation. Unlike in cases of emergency, this power is not subject to further conditions to be fulfilled.

(3) National Fiscal Responsibilities Limit ESMA Powers

55   The limits to the ESMA's powers are laid down in the safeguard provision in Article 38 ESMA Regulation, which prohibits any decisions adopted by the ESMA from impinging on the fiscal responsibilities of Member States. Where a Member State considers that a decision impinges on its fiscal responsibilities, it may notify the ESMA and the Commission within two weeks after it has been notified of the ESMA decision resulting in this decision being suspended.

56   According to Article 38(2) ESMA Regulation, in cases of a disagreement being resolved by the ESMA, the Authority must then re-evaluate its decision and where it maintains it, the Council must take a decision according to the majority of the votes. It may maintain the decision or revoke it, in which case the decision is terminated.

57   Should a Member State consider that an emergency decision taken under Article 38(3) impinges on its fiscal responsibilities, it may notify the ESMA, the Commission and the Council that the decision will not be implemented by the competent authority and the Council is automatically responsible for deciding on the admissibility of the decision, without prior re-evaluation by the ESMA. This requires a simple majority of its members. If the Council decides not to revoke the Authority's

---

[155] M. Lehmann and C. Manger-Nestler, EuZW (2010), p. 87, 91.
[156] Cf. Art. 18(2) ESMA Regulation.
[157] Art. 19(2) ESMA Regulation.

decision relating to Article 18(3) and if the Member State concerned still considers that the decision of the Authority impinges upon its fiscal responsibilities, it may again notify the Commission and the Authority and request the Council to re-examine the matter again, causing a suspension of the ESMA's decision.[158] Article 38(5) clarifies that any abuse of this possibility is prohibited, as incompatible with the internal market.

(d) Direct Supervision of the Market Participants

58   In some exceptional cases the ESMA regulation does not strictly abide by the concept of a "supervision of supervisors", giving the ESMA direct powers of intervention towards individual market participants. The ESMA has such power in the exceptional cases of "emergency situations" and "disagreements between national supervisory authorities" or in cases in which a national authority violates EU law, provided the strict conditions are all fulfilled and the national supervisory authority has not complied with the directions issued by the ESMA.

(aa) Warnings and Prohibition of Financial Activities

59   The ESMA may also issue warnings in the event that a financial activity poses a serious threat to supervisory objectives.[159] In 2012 the ESMA made use of this possibility for the first time, issuing a warning against dealing with unauthorised firms offering foreign exchange investments.[160] Pursuant to Article 9(5) ESMA Regulation the authority may furthermore temporarily prohibit or restrict certain financial activities if they threaten the orderly functioning and integrity of financial markets or the stability of the whole or part of the financial system in the European Union. This requires either an emergency situation as laid down in Article 18 or that the conditions laid down in European legislative acts are fulfilled.

(bb) Supervision of Credit Rating Agencies

60   As the only authority of the ESFS, the ESMA has general and direct supervisory powers over a group of market participants. The ESMA is responsible for registering and supervising credit rating agencies and has the necessary sanctioning powers—such as withdrawal of registration, the suspension of ratings[161] and the possibility of imposing fines up to €750,000—and the accompanying investigatory powers for this task.[162] The supervision of credit rating agencies was thus the focus of ESMA's work in the first year of its existence.[163] The supervision of credit rating agencies could function as a model for future developments in European capital markets supervision.

---

[158] Cf. Art. 38(4) ESMA Regulation.
[159] Cf. Art. 9(3) ESMA Regulation.
[160] ESMA, *Investor Warning against Trading in Foreign Exchange (Forex)*, ESMA/2011/412, December 2011.
[161] In particular, the powers laid down in Art. 23, 24 Rating Regulation are to be applied to the ESMA.
[162] Cf. COM(2009), 503 final, Explanatory Memorandum No. 6.6. See. § 27 for more details on the supervision of rating agencies.
[163] Cf. F. Walla, BKR (2012), p. 265, 268.

61   The Commission has debated conferring supervisory powers, comparable to those regarding rating agencies, to the ESMA in further fields in the future,[164] such as the supervision of short sales and derivative constructions.[165] These plans have been dismissed for the time being. The ESMA has been, however, granted the direct supervision of the register pursuant to the Over-the-Counter Derivate Regulation[166] in 2012.

(e)   Rule-Making Powers

62   The ESMA replaced the CESR in the former Lamfalussy process,[167] having an advisory function towards the Commission[168], Parliament and Council[169] in their legislative proceedings. ESMA's technical advice plays an important role in the Commission's delegated legislation on Level 2 of the Lamfalussy II process.[170]

63   The ESMA, however, also develops legislation itself under the advice of the Securities and Markets Stakeholder Group, i.e. representatives of financial market participants and consumers together with top-ranking academics.[171] With regard to the rule-making powers one must distinguish between different measures: The ESMA may issue non-binding "guidelines and recommendations" or draft "regulatory technical standards" and "implementing technical standards".

(aa) Guidelines and Recommendations

64   The European authority is empowered to issue guidelines and recommendations which contain abstract and general requirements addressed to market participants or national supervisors.[172] Such guidelines and recommendations are soft law, i.e. non-binding for the market participants, national courts or the ECJ. They are also generally non-binding for the national supervisory authorities. However, in the event that a competent authority does not comply or does not intend to comply, it must inform the ESMA, stating its reasons, which are then made public by the ESMA ("comply or explain" principle).[173]

65   The ESMA guidelines and recommendations are highly relevant for legal practice because they are an important tool to construe the European capital market law and national legislation which is based on EU directives and used by national courts

---

[164] Cf. Commission, Proposal for an ESMA Regulation, Annex.

[165] Cf. No. 3.3.6 Explanation of the Commission Proposal for a Regulation on Short Selling and certain aspects of Credit Default Swaps COM(2010) 482, final. ESMA is, however, only empowered in emergency situations, cf. § 15 para.181. Regarding the supervision of Alternative Investment Fund Manager (AIFM) no direct powers were conferred to the ESMA. The ESMA rather functions as a supervisory authority over the national authorities in this field of capital markets law, cf. Directive 2011/61/EU of the European Parliament and the Council of 8 June 2011 on Alternative Investment Fund Managers and amending Directives 2003/41/EC and 2009/65/EC and Regulations (EC) No. 1060/2009 and (EU) No. 1095/2010.

[166] Regulation of the European Parliament and of the Council on OTC derivatives, central counterparties and trade repositories, 4 July 2012, OJ L201, 27 July 2012, p. 1.

[167] Recital 68 ESMA Regulation.

[168] Cf. Recital 21 ESMA Regulation.

[169] Cf. Recital 45 ESMA Regulation.

[170] See § 4 para. 27–37.

[171] Cf. Art. 37 ESMA Regulation.

[172] Cf. Art. 16 ESMA Regulation.

[173] Art. 16(3)3 ESMA Regulation.

and authorities.[174] There is a presumption that ESMA's soft law complies with the intention of the European legislature.[175] Furthermore, the ESMA may bind itself through its guidelines and recommendations because of the principle of equality under European law. Compliance with ESMA's soft law might also lead to a safe harbour regarding criminal and private law liability.[176]

66 As an example, the recommendations of the ESMA regarding the content of a prospectus for a security[177] are treated by market participants as binding rules when determining the content necessary for a security prospectus. This important role of ESMA's soft law shows the impact the authority's rule-making powers have on the further development of European capital markets law.

(bb) Regulatory and Implementing Technical Standards

67 The ESMA is further empowered to draft "regulatory and implementing technical standards" to ensure consistent harmonisation by means of delegated acts under Article 290 TFEU or implementing measures under Article 291 TFEU which have to be confirmed by the Commission (*endorsement*).[178] They can only be subject to amendments by the Commission in very restricted and extraordinary circumstances[179] and the ESMA must therefore generally be regarded as their author.[180] Regulatory and implementing technical standards are adopted by means of regulations or decisions with a direct effect.[181] In other words, they do not require implementation by the Member States in order to become effective. The legislative acts are comparable to those formerly enacted on Level 3 of the former Lamfalussy process.[182] In order to implement these new powers, the capital markets law directives had to be amended to contain the necessary authorisation. These were introduced by the so-called "omnibus I" directive.[183]

---

[174] A. Frank, *Die Rechtswirkungen der Leitlinien und Empfehlungen der Europäischen Wertpapier- und Marktaufsichtsbehörde*, p. 210, thus classifies ESMA's guidelines and recommendations as "secondary legal sources".

[175] Ibid., p. 191. Cf. also E. Ferran, *Building an EU Securities Market*, p. 100.

[176] Cf. A. Frank, *Die Rechtswirkungen der Leitlinien und Empfehlungen der Europäischen Wertpapier- und Marktaufsichtsbehörde*, p. 171 ff.

[177] ESMA, *Recommendations—ESMA update of the CESR recommendations on the consistent implementation of Commission Regulation (EC) No. 809/2004 implementing the Prospectus Directive*, ESMA/2011/81, 23 March 2011.

[178] Art. 10(1) ESMA Regulation. Comparable with an *endorsement* under IFRS provisions, cf. N. Moloney, in: S. Grundmann et al. (eds.), *Festschrift für Klaus J. Hopt*, p. 2265, 2273.

[179] Cf. Recital 23 ESMA Regulation.

[180] Cf. also A. Kahl, in: Braumüller et al. (eds.), *Die neue Europäische Finanzmarktaufsicht—ZFR Jahrestagung 2011*, p. 55, 57.

[181] Cf. Art. 10(4) and 15(4) ESMA Regulation.

[182] Cf. Centrum für Europäische Politik, *EU-Wertpapieraufsichtsbehörde* (ESMA), p. 1.

[183] Directive No. 2010/78/EU of the European Parliament and of the Council of 24 November 2010 amending Directives 98/26/EC, 2002/87/EC, 2003/6/EC, 2003/41/EC, 2003/71/EC, 2004/39/EC, 2004/109/EC, 2005/60/EC, 2006/48/EC, 2006/49/EC and 2009/65/EC in respect of the powers of the European Supervisory Authority (European Banking Authority), the European Supervisory Authority (European Insurance and Occupational Pensions Authority) and the European Supervisory Authority (European Securities and Markets Authority), OJ L331, p. 120; cf. also the draft of a "omnibus II" Directive: Proposal for a Directive of the European Parliament and of the Council amending Directives 2003/71/EC and 2009/138/EC in respect of the powers of the European Insurance and Occupational Pensions Authority and the European Securities and Markets Authority, COM(2011) 8 final.

68   ESMA's technical standards must be seen as a further tier in the sources of European capital markets law.[184] They range below the framework legislation which constitutes the foundation for all European capital markets legislation on the same level as the Commission's delegated acts and implementing measures. Technical standards can be divided into regulatory technical standards and implementing technical standards.

(1) Regulatory Technical Standards

69   ESMA's regulatory technical standards do not become legally binding until confirmed by the Commission and require a legal foundation in the European directives on capital markets law.[185] The Commission should amend the regulatory standard proposed by the ESMA only in very restricted and extraordinary circumstances.[186] In the event that the Commission does not endorse a draft regulatory technical standard, Article 14 ESMA Regulation provides that the Council be engaged in order to encourage conciliation. The European Parliament or the Council may object to a regulatory technical standard.[187] They also have the competence to revoke the power delegated to ESMA with regard to the regulatory standards.[188] The power to adopt regulatory technical standards conferred on the Commission has further been restricted to a period of four years.[189]

70   Whilst regulatory technical standards are explicitly not to imply strategic decisions or policy choices,[190] they still constitute legally binding acts, granting the ESMA and the Commission a certain legislative leeway.[191] Mostly, regulatory technical standards are to be applied in order to lay down procedural rules; some provisions, however, further grant the ESMA farther-reaching powers regarding the substantiation of provisions through regulatory technical standards. These two different approaches can be found in the Rating Agency Regulation and the PD:[192] whilst Article 21(4)(a)–(c) Rating Agency Regulation allows the ESMA to draft regulatory technical standards in order to lay down procedural rules for the registration of rating agencies, Article 16(3) PD grants the ESMA the right to develop regulatory technical standards in order to "specify situations where a significant new factor, material mistake or inaccuracy relating to the information included in the prospectus requires a supplement to the prospectus to be published". This leeway is much broader than the powers pursuant to Article 21(4)(a)–(c) Rating Agency Regulation. It allows the ESMA to put the rules in the framework legislation into more concrete terms and is thus of great practical relevance.

---

[184] See § 4 para. 31–35.
[185] Legal foundations were mainly introduced in the omnibus directives, see below, para. 58.
[186] Cf. Recitals 23, 24 ESMA Regulation.
[187] Art. 13 ESMA Regulation.
[188] Art. 12 ESMA Regulation.
[189] Art. 11 ESMA Regulation.
[190] Art. 10(1)2 ESMA Regulation. These may only be contained in directives and regulations enacted by the Parliament and the Council, see § 4 para. 31–36.
[191] The Commission has published a Communication on the exercise of its powers, cf. Communication from the Commission to the European Parliament and the Council, Implementation of Article 290 of the Treaty on the Functioning of the European Union, COM(2009) 673.
[192] Cf. F. Walla, BKR (2012), p. 265, 268.

71   The ESMA has made use of its legislative powers eagerly, presenting its first four proposals for technical standards with regard to the Rating Agency Regulation to the Commission for endorsement in 2011.[193]

(2) Implementing Technical Standards

72   The ESMA can further develop implementing technical standards and submit them to the Commission for *endorsement*.[194] They constitute legislative acts on the legal basis of Article 291 TFEU. The Commission is not bound as strongly by ESMA's proposals as in the case of regulatory technical standards.[195] Neither Council nor Parliament has the power to object or revoke the proposals for an implementing technical standard. Rather, in cases involving Article 291 TFEU, the Member States are required to control the Commission's exercise of implementing powers.[196]

73   Implementing technical standards are not to imply strategic decisions or policy choices and are to determine the conditions of application of the European legislative acts on capital markets law.[197] They are to enable the development of standard forms, sample texts and other measures facilitating procedures.[198] As yet, the ESMA has made use of this possibility only once,[199] the exact role of implementing technical standards in legal practice therefore remaining unclear.

(3) Assessment

74   The possibility for the European supervisory authority to develop binding rules that are directly applicable in the Member States must be regarded as one of the most important innovations within the European supervisory scheme.[200] Technical standards will increase the influence of European legislation on capital markets law, leading to a considerable increase in the density of European legislative acts in this field.[201] It is to be expected that certain market standards that were formerly influenced by informal provisions and the administrative practice of the national

---

[193] ESMA, *Final report—Draft RTS on the content and format of ratings data periodic reporting to be requested from credit ratings agencies for the purpose of on-going supervision by ESMA*, ESMA/2011/464, December 2011; ESMA, *Final report—Regulatory technical standards on the information for registration and certification of credit rating agencies*, ESMA/2011/463, December 2011; ESMA, *Final Report—Draft RTS on the assessment of compliance of credit rating methodologies with CRA Regulation*, ESMA/2011/462, December 2011; ESMA, *Final report—Regulatory Technical Standards on the presentation of the information that credit rating agencies shall disclose in accordance with Article 11(2) and point 1 of Part II of Section E of Annex I to Regulation (EC) No. 1060/2009*, ESMA/2011/461, December 2011.

[194] Cf. Art. 15 ESMA Regulation.

[195] Cf. M. Lehmann and C. Manger-Nestler, ZBB (2011), p. 2, 11 on the Regulation establishing a European Banking Authority.

[196] Cf. European Commission, Proposal for a Regulation of the European Parliament and of the Council laying down the rules and general principles concerning mechanisms for control by Member States of the Commission's exercise of implementing powers, COM(2010) 83.

[197] Cf. Art. 15 ESMA Regulation; R. Streinz et al., *Der Vertrag von Lissabon*, § 10 3.

[198] Cf. for example Art. 5(2)2; Art. 13(5)(b)2 PD; Art. 7(4)3 MiFID.

[199] Commission Implementing Regulation (EU) No. 826/2012 of 29 June 2012 laying down implementing technical standards with regard to the means for public disclosure of net position in shares, the format of the information to be provided to the European Securities and Markets Authority in relation to net short positions, the types of agreements, arrangements and measures to adequately ensure that shares or sovereign debt instruments are available for settlement and the dates and period for the determination of the principal venue for a share according to Regulation (EU) No. 236/2012 of the European Parliament and of the Council on short selling and certain aspects of credit default swaps, OJ L251, p. 1. See under § 15 para. 9.

[200] T.M.J. Möllers et al., NZG (2010), p. 285, 289 used the term "explosive".

[201] See under § 4 para. 31–37.

Fabian Walla

supervisory authorities, will in future be regulated by ESMA in the shape of guidelines, recommendations and particularly implementing technical standards.[202]

75 However, technical standards give rise to (i) the question of the democratic legitimacy of this type of executive legislation by an independent European supervisory authority; and (ii) the question as to which effects the ESMA standards will have on the enforcement under private and criminal law. Attention has furthermore been drawn to the fact that the new legislative act could unnecessarily complicate capital markets supervision,[203] causing higher transaction costs and thus posing a risk for the efficiency of capital markets in Europe.

(f) Judicial Review

76 The ESMA Regulation grants the market participants and national authorities legal protection against decisions made by the ESMA on the grounds of Articles 17–19, providing them with the right to make an appeal against any decision addressed to them.[204] The Board of Appeal is a joint body of the ESAs and is composed of six members with a proven record of relevant knowledge and professional experience in the fields of finance and financial markets law.[205] The members of the Board of Appeal are to be independent in making their decisions and not bound by any instructions.[206] Article 61 ESMA Regulation states that in order to contest a decision of the Board of Appeal, action may be brought before the Court of Justice of the European Union, in accordance with Article 263 TFEU.[207] In cases where there is no right of appeal laid down in the ESMA Regulation, proceedings may also be brought before the ECJ directly. This particularly applies with regard to proceedings agains technical standards on the grounds of Article 263(4) TFEU.[208]

(g) Liability

77 The ESMA Regulation clarifies in Article 69(1) that the ESMA is to make good any damage caused by it or by its staff in the performance of duties according to the common general principles in the laws of the Member States. Respective claims for public liability are to be brought before the ECJ.

3. Conclusion

78 The Commission's proposals in the legislative package of 3 September 2009 were greeted with criticism by numerous Member States, who did not agree with giving the European authorities the power to make decisions addressed directly to indi-

---

[202] Cf. B. Raschauer, in: Braumüller et al. (eds.), *Die neue europäische Finanzaufsicht—ZHR-Jahrestagung 2011*, p. 17, 26.
[203] A. Wittig, DB (2010), *Standpunkte*, p. 69, 70. Cf. also S. Storr, in: Braumüller et al. (eds.), *Die neue europäische Finanzaufsicht—ZHR-Jahrestagung 2011*, p. 77, 88 ff.; C. Manger-Nestler, *Kreditwesen* (2012), p. 528, 530 ff.;
[204] Art. 60(1) ESMA Regulation.
[205] Art. 58 ESMA Regulation.
[206] Art. 59 ESMA Regulation.
[207] Art. 47(1) ESMA Regulation.
[208] C. Manger-Nestler, *Kreditwesen* (2012), p. 528, 531.

vidual financial market participants.[209] The legal literature had mixed opinions on this matter: whilst some maintained the Commission's proposal did not go far enough,[210] not sufficiently ensuring the authority's independence and following the concept of sectoral supervision,[211] others claimed the European Union ought to be more restrictive in introducing new harmonising provisions. They pointed out that difficulties in communication arise for the Member States when interacting with an authority at a European level.[212]

79   Even though it is too early to assess accurately the effects of ESMA's initiation, the new supervisory structure was a step in the right direction: increasing cross-border transactions on capital markets and the growing unification of capital markets law at a European level make a European approach to supervision indispensable. The entire European securities supervision may in the long run evolve around the ESMA, giving it comparable powers to the SEC in the United States. Numerous questions of practical relevance will be decided by the ESMA in Paris, whilst the national supervisory authorities will become less important. The legal practice would be well advised to adapt to this new regulatory body as soon as possible.

[209] On banking supervision see F.-C. Zeitler, Die Welt, 13 November 2009. Cf. also T.M.J. Möllers, D. Christ and A. Harrer, NZG (2010), p. 285, 290 (fn. 90).
[210] K.J. Hopt, NZG (2009), p. 1041, 1408; M. Lamandini, 6 ECL (2009), p. 197, 202; similarly R. Partsch, ZBB (2010), p. 72, 76.
[211] D. Masciandaro, M. Nieto and M. Quintyn, CEPR Policy Insight No. 37, p. 16 ff.; T.M.J. Möllers, D. Christ and A. Harrer, NZG (2010), p. 285, 289.
[212] For example R. Veil, 11 EBOR (2010), p. 409, 422.

§ 12   Sanctions

Bibliography

Af Sandeberg, Catarina, *Prospectus Liability in a Scandinavian Perspective*, 13 EBLR (2002), p. 323–334; Armour, John, *Enforcement Strategies in UK Corporate Governance*, in: Armour, John and Payne, Jennifer (eds.), *Rationality in Company Law: Essays in Honour of DD Prentice* (2009); Armour, John, Mayer, Colin and Polo, Andrea, *Regulatory Sanctions and Reputational Damage in Financial Markets*, Oxford Legal Studies Research Paper No. 62/2010, available at: http://ssrn.com/abstract=1678028; Arsouze, Charles, *Réflexions sur les propositions du Rapport Coulon concernant le pouvoir de sanction de l'AMF*, Bull. Joly Bourse (2008), p. 246–257; Coffee, John C., *Law and the Market: The Impact of Enforcement*, 156 U. Pa. L. Rev. (2007), p. 229–311; Davies, Paul L., *Davies Review of Issuer Liability: Final Report* (2007); Eckl, Christian, *Länderbericht Spanien*, in: Hopt, Klaus J. and Voigt, Hans-Christoph (eds.), *Prospekt- und Kapitalmarktinformationshaftung* (2005), p. 945; Ferran, Eilis, *Are US-style Investor Suits Coming to the UK?*, 9 J. Corp. L. Stud. (2009), p. 315–348; Fleischer, Holger, *Erweiterte Außenhaftung der Organmitglieder im Europäischen Gesellschafts- und Kapitalmarktrecht*, ZGR (2004), p. 437–479; García Malsipica, Silvia, *Infracciones y sanciones*, in: Uría, Francisco, *Régimen jurídico de los mercados de valores y de las instituciones de inversión colectiva* (2007), p. 785; Gehrmann, Philipp, *Das Spector-Urteil des EuGH—Zur Beweislastumkehr beim Insiderhandel*, ZBB (2010), p. 48–52; Hellgardt, Alexander and Ringe, Wolf-Georg, *Internationale Kapitalmarkthaftung als Corporate Governance—Haftungstatbestände und Kollisionsrecht in transatlantischer Perspektive*, 173 ZHR (2009), p. 802–838; Hernández Sainz, Esther, *El abuso de información privilegiada en los mercados de valores* (2007); Iribarren Blanco, Miguel, *Responsabilidad civil por la información divulgada por las sociedades cotizadas, Monografía No. 2/2008 asociada a la Revista de Mercado de Valores* (2008); Jackson, Howell and Mark J. Roe, *Public and Private Enforcement of Securities Laws: Resource-Based Evidence*, 93 J. Fin. Econ. (2009), p. 207–238; Jeandidier, Wilfrid, *Droit pénal des affaires*, 6th ed. (2005); Kahan, Dan M., *What's Really Wrong with Shaming Sanctions*, 84 Texas Law Review (2006), p. 2075–2095; Kämmerer, Jörn A., *Bemessung von Geldbußen im Wettbewerbs- und Kapitalmarktrecht: Eine komparative Betrachtung*, in: Grundmann, Stefan et al. (eds.), *Festschrift für Klaus J. Hopt zum 70. Geburtstag* (2010), p. 2043; Kalss, Susanne and Oelkers, Janine, *Öffentliche Bekanntgabe—Ein wirksames Aufsichtsinstrument im Kapitalmarktrecht?*, ÖBA (2009), p. 123–143; La Porta, Rafael, Lopez-de-Silanes, Florencio and Shleifer, Andrei, *What Works in Securities Laws?*, 61 J. Fin. (2006), p. 1–32; Lindblom, Per Henrik, *Lagen omgruppprättegång—bakgrund och framtid*, SvJT (2005), p. 129–191; Mattout, Jean-Pierre, *Information financière et responsabilité des dirigeants*, Droit des sociétés (2004), p. 11; Moloney, Niamh, *How to Protect Investors: Lessons from the EC and the UK* (2010); Opitz, Peter, *Zur Nutzung von Insiderinformationen—Anmerkung zur Entscheidung des EuGH vom 23. 12. 2009—C-45/08*, BKR (2010), p. 71–74; Röhl, Hans-Christian, *Finanzmarktaufsicht*, in: Fehling, Michael and Ruffert, Matthias (eds.), *Regulierungsrecht* (2010), § 18; Rontchevsky, Nicolas, *L'harmonisation des sanctions pénales*, Bull. Joly Bourse (2012), p. 139–142; Satzger, Helmut, *Internationales und Europäisches Strafrecht*, 4th ed. (2010); Schröder, Christian, *Europäische Richtlinien und deutsches Strafrecht—eine Untersuchung über den Einfluß europäischer Richtlinien gemäß Art. 249 Abs. 3 EGV auf das deutsche Strafrecht* (2002); Schwark, Eberhard, *Anlegerschutz durch Wirtschaftsrecht* (1979); Segarkis, Konstantinos, *Le renforcement des pouvoirs des autorités compétentes*, Bull. Joly Bourse (2012), p. 118–121; Stasiak, Frédéric, *Droit pénal des affaires* (2005); Veil, Rüdiger, *Kapitalanleger im Prozess—Publizität, Haftung und kollektive Rechtsverfolgung*, in: NJW-Sonderheft 3. Hannoveraner ZPO-Symposion (2006), p. 3–8; Veil, Rüdiger, *Concepts of Supervisory Legislation and Enforcement in European Capital Markets Law—Observations from a Civil Law Country*, 11 EBOR (2010), p. 409–422; Veil, Rüdiger and Koch, Philipp, *Towards a Uniform European Capital Markets Law: Proposals of the Commission to Reform Market Abuse (2012)*, available at: http://ssrn.com/abstract=1998376; Vogel, Joachim, *Wertpapierhandelsstrafrecht—Vorschein eines neuen Strafrechtsmodells*, in: Pawlik, Michael and Zaczyk, Rainer (eds.), *Festschrift für Günther Jakobs zum 70. Geburtstag* (2007), p. 731; Zimmer, Daniel and Höft, Jan, *"Private Enforcement" im öffentlichen Interesse?—Ansätze zur Effektivierung der Rechtsdurchsetzung bei Streu- und Massenschäden im Kapitalmarkt-, Wettbewerbs- und Kartellrecht*, ZGR (2009), p. 662–720.

I.   Introduction

1   Several approaches are used in Europe to sanction misconduct under capital markets law, ranging from reprimands by self-regulatory bodies without legal consequences to damage claims under civil law and administrative or criminal sanctions imposed by public bodies, such as supervisory authorities or courts. The most common administrative sanctions are fines and the disgorgement of profits,[1] but the publication of breaches and imposed sanctions, so-called *naming and shaming*, can also be seen as an administrative sanction,[2] playing an important role in most Member States. Criminal sanctions consist of imprisonment, fines and the disgorgement of profits the offender obtained through the offence. Under civil law, the investors may claim damages. Furthermore, the loss of voting rights and other rights attached to shares is a common sanction in many Member States, mostly designed as an instrument of private enforcement.[3]

2   Member States have placed varying importance on the different types of sanctions, the European legislature having been very restrictive in laying down precise rules on sanctions for the Member States to impose.[4] The sanctions introduced by the Member States are thus mostly constructed in conformity with the respective national concept for regulating the capital markets. Most Member States thereby follow the concept that capital markets law is a field of public law and is as such subject to supervision by the national authorities.[5] This results in most Member States granting their supervisory authorities far-reaching powers to impose administrative sanctions.

3   Only recently numerous Member States have begun to introduce civil law sanctions, following the example of US capital markets law which regards *private enforcement* as an essential element of capital markets law enforcement. This US approach is based on a number of empirical and comparative studies that have concluded that private enforcement is a far more effective means of capital markets regulation than a system relying mainly on public enforcement.[6] The introduction of substantive provisions granting investors the right to claim damages alone, however, does not

---

[1] See H.-C. Röhl, in: M. Fehling and M. Ruffert (eds.), *Regulierungsrecht*, § 18 para. 59 ff.

[2] On a legal-economic analysis of naming and shaming see J. Armour et al., Oxford Legal Studies Research Paper No. 62/2010, p. 15 ff.

[3] Cf. R. Veil, 11 EBOR (2010), p. 409, 419–420.

[4] See in more detail at para. 4–7.

[5] Cf. for Germany H.-C. Röhl, in: M. Fehling and M. Ruffert, *Regulierungsrecht*, § 18 para. 13 ff., and regarding investor protection E. Schwark, *Anlegerschutz durch Wirtschaftsrecht* (1979).

[6] R. La Porta et al., 61 J. Fin. (2006), p. 1, 27 argue that "several aspects of public enforcement, such as having an independent and/or focused regulator or criminal sanctions, do not matter, and others matter in only some regressions. In contrast, both extensive disclosure requirements and standards of liability facilitation investor recovery of losses are associated with larger stock markets." H.E. Jackson and M.J. Roe, 93 J. Fin. Econ. (2009), p. 207, 237 however, come to different conclusions: "Overall, and most importantly, we caution against using

suffice due to the generally high costs of civil liability claims, shared between a large number of injured parties. In capital markets law there is a high risk that the investors will not claim their damages, a phenomenon termed "rational apathy". The substantive provisions must, therefore, be accompanied by effective procedural provisions, which can, for example, provide for the possibility of class actions as in US law.[7]

II.   Requirements in the European Directives on Capital Markets Law

1.   Criminal and Administrative Sanctions

4   The four framework directives on capital markets law contain only a few requirements regarding the sanctions to be introduced by the Member States:

> "Without prejudice to the right of Member States to impose criminal sanctions and without prejudice to their civil liability regime, Member States shall ensure, in conformity with their national law, that the appropriate administrative measures can be taken or administrative sanctions be imposed against the persons responsible, where the provisions adopted in the implementation of this Directive have not been complied with. Member States shall ensure that these measures are effective, proportionate and dissuasive."[8]

The Member States are therefore free to decide whether they wish to introduce criminal sanctions. According to the four framework directives, the Member States need not even introduce administrative sanctions. The directive does not contain provisions requiring any specific sanction or minimum fine—any measures that are effective, proportionate and dissuasive being sufficient.

5   The Commission has most recently presented its aim to ensure that supervision of capital markets in Europe becomes more effective. The proposal for a Market Abuse Regulation[9] envisages a number of provisions strengthening the powers of the national authorities.[10] The Commission also intends to ensure a more deterrent regime by way of uniform and stronger sanctions.[11] The draft Market Abuse Regulation is limited to administrative measures and sanctions. The Member States are to be required to implement the provisions in Articles 25–29 in their national legal sys-

---

current views of the relative value of private and public enforcement to make public policy. Public enforcement as we measure it does well in the regressions."

[7] The United States have, however, had bad experience with class actions, a main point of criticsm being that the volume of securities class actions "was increasing to epidemic proportions". Furthermore, "the benefits to individual class members were negligible, seldom exceeding a very small percentage of their losses". Thirdly, class actions were "lawyer-driven". Cf. J.C. Coffee and J. Seligman, *Securities Regulation*, ch. 15 A.1. ("The Dilemma of Private Securities Regulation").

[8] Art. 25 PD; Art. 14 MAD; Art. 28 TD; Art. 51 MiFID.

[9] Cf. § 1 para. 41.

[10] See Art. 17 MAR Draft.

[11] Preamble para. 34 MAR Draft: "equal, strong and deterrent sanctions regimes". Cf. on this regulatory approach N. Rontchevsky, Bull. Joly Bourse (2012), p. 139–142; R. Veil and P. Koch, *Towards a Uniform European Capital Markets Law: Proposals of the Commission to Reform Market Abuse* (2012).

Rüdiger Veil/Fabian Walla

tems.[12] The Regulation would thus not have direct effect in the Member States.[13] The Commission has also presented a proposal for a directive on criminal sanctions for insider dealing and market manipulation.[14] Member States are requested to introduce criminal sanctions with respect to the "most serious market abuse offences".[15] This directive would (as all directives) require implementation into national laws.

2. Civil Law Sanctions

6   Provisions on civil law sanctions are rare in the European directives. Neither the MAD nor the MiFID contain provisions on civil law liability for damages suffered by investors. The TD's requirements are only vague:

> "Member States shall ensure that responsibility for the information to be drawn up and made public in accordance with Articles 4, 5, 6 and 16 lies at least with the issuer or its administrative, management or supervisory bodies and shall ensure that their laws, regulations and administrative provisions on liability apply to the issuers, the bodies referred to in this Article or the persons responsible within the issuers."[16]

The Member States are therefore free to decide who is to be held liable for incorrect financial reports, i.e. whether this is to be the issuer, the members of the administrative board, the supervisory board or the board of directors. They can also determine whether responsibility for breaches of the directive's provisions should require intent or also apply to cases of gross or ordinary negligence.[17] The PD only contains the following provisions on the civil law liability for incorrect information given in a prospectus: "Member States shall ensure that responsibility for the information given in a prospectus attaches at least to the issuer or its administrative, management or supervisory bodies, the offeror, the person asking for the admission to trading on a regulated market or the guarantor, as the case may be."[18] It does not, however, stipulate the conditions for such a liability, i.e. whether the issuer is only held liable for wrongful intent or also for negligence.[19]

7   None of the four framework directives provides any further provisions on civil law liability. In particular, they do not require a loss of voting rights for breaches of the notification obligations, which the shareholders could demand by way of contesting the resolution of the general meeting. The reason for this may be that as yet the pro-

---

[12] See Art. 24(1) MAR Draft: "Member States shall lay down the rules on administrative measures and sanctions".

[13] The wording of Art. 25 ("This Article shall apply in all the following circumstances ...") and Art. 26 ("competent authorities shall, in conformity with national law, have the power to ...") MAR Draft seems to imply that the provisions should have direct effect like the other parts of the draft Market Abuse Regulation. Taking into account Art. 24 (1) MAR Draft, however, it is more convincing to interpret the provisions as an obligation for national legislatures to introduce such rules.

[14] Cf. § 1 para 41.

[15] See Art. 1(1) Directive on Criminal Sanctions Draft.

[16] Art. 7 TD.

[17] See § 18 para. 63.

[18] Cf. Art. 6(1) PD.

[19] See § 17 para. 43–44.

cedure for contesting such resolutions has not yet been harmonised at a European level and derivative actions are not known in all jurisdictions.[20]

III. National Sanctioning Systems

8   The CESR's "reports on administrative measures and sanctions as well as the criminal sanctions available in the Member States"[21] show how the Member States operate and the extent of their sanctions. The concepts differ greatly, especially regarding the severity of fines to be imposed. Yet the reports omit to describe the legal practice in the Member States, although it is necessary to examine to what extent fines are imposed in order to determine how far they are deterrent.[22] The reports also contain no information on the sanctions under civil law, such as liability towards investors. This aspect has only recently gained importance in Europe.

9   The following overview will examine the legal situation in France, Germany, Italy, Spain, Sweden and the United Kingdom, noting especially the relevance of sanctions in practice. The results displayed have been gained from publicly accessible sources, such as legal articles, publications and reports made by the supervisory authorities, in addition to interviews conducted with members of the legal and supervisory practice.[23]

1.   France

10   The legal practice in France centres around administrative sanctions (*sanctions administratives*), imposed by the AMF.[24] Criminal sanctions, however, also play an important role.[25] The AMF has a so-called *commission des sanctions*, authorised to impose fines of up to €10 million for certain breaches of capital markets law provisions.[26] The AMF makes use of its powers quite actively, and fines of several hundred

---

[20] In Germany, resolutions of the general meeting are often contested by way of action for annulment. Whilst the reasons for this are numerous, actions prevail, in which minority shareholders attempt to achieve unlawful benefits. See T. Raiser and R. Veil, *Recht der Kapitalgesellschaften*, § 16 para. 168 ff.

[21] CESR, *Report on CESR Members' Powers under the PD and its Implementing Measures*, CESR/07-383, June 2007; CESR, *Report on administrative measures and sanctions as well as the criminal sanctions available in Member States under the market abuse directive (MAD)*, CESR/08-099, February 2008; CESR, *Report on the mapping of supervisory powers, supervisory practices, administrative and criminal sanctioning regimes of Member States in relation to the Markets in Financial Instruments Directive (MiFID)*, CESR/08-220, February 2009; CESR, *Report on the mapping of supervisory powers, administrative and criminal sanctioning regimes of Member States in relation to the Transparency Directive (TD)*, CESR/09-058, July 2009.

[22] ESMA has, however, meanwhile also begun to examine the legal practice. Cf. ESMA, *Prospectus Directive: Peer Review Report on good practices in the approval Process*, ESMA/2012/300, May 2012; ESMA, *Actual use of sanctioning powers under MAD*, ESMA/2012/270, April 2012.

[23] The names of the interview partners can be found in the preface. Their statements are only referred to herein, where they gave a consistent picture of legal practice in the respective jurisdiction.

[24] F. Stasiak, *Droit pénal des affaires*, p. 248; J.-P. Mattout, *Droit des societés*, p. 11, 13. In detail on the AMF's sanctioning powers R. Veil and P. Koch, *Französisches Kapitalmarktrecht*, p. 10 ff.

[25] Cf. W. Jeandidier, *Droit pénal des affaires*, p. 150 para. 121; R. Veil and P. Koch, *Französisches Kapitalmarktrecht*, p. 113.

[26] Cf. R. Veil and P. Koch, *Französisches Kapitalmarktrecht*, p. 10–16.

thousand euros are frequent. The AMF also publishes violations and the imposed sanctions on its website.[27]

11   In contrast, civil law protection for investors as yet plays no important role in France.[28] The French legislature has not introduced any specific provisions on damages for breaches of capital markets law provisions, so that claims can only be brought forward on the basis of the general law of torts.[29] Class actions or similar proceedings do not exist.[30] Claiming damages under civil law in criminal proceedings has, however, recently become more popular.[31] The loss of voting rights for the failure to comply with the notification obligations regarding major shareholdings plays an important role, especially as it can be employed to prevent hostile takeovers.[32] It is for this reason that numerous French companies have introduced additional notification thresholds for investors in their articles of association, the breach of which also leads to a loss of rights.[33]

2.   Germany

12   In Germany, supervisory sanctions for administrative offences prevail: breaches of capital markets law are mainly prosecuted by the BaFin, who will generally impose fines. The maximum fine under securities law is €1,000,000, whilst administrative offences law stipulates a general minimum for fines at €5,[34] granting the BaFin a large discretion. The height of the fines imposed in practice is comparatively low,[35] the BaFin usually levying fines of no more than €20,000.[36] Insider dealing and market manipulation is criminally prosecuted.[37] The criminal courts are responsible for determining the level of the fine or the length of imprisonment. Additionally, a loss of rights usually ensues from breaches of the rules on inside information. The BaFin also has the right to publish imposed sanctions on its website but has not as yet made use of this naming and shaming, maybe also for constitutional reasons.[38]

13   Some violations are additionally subject to an effective civil liability. A number of specific legal foundations exist, according to which investors can claim damages for

---

[27] The AMF publishes the sanctions it has imposed on its website under "Sanctions/Décisions de la Commission des sanctions". See www.amf-france.org.
[28] Cf. C. Arsouze, Bull. Joly Bourse (2008), p. 246, 251.
[29] Cf. R. Veil and P. Koch, *Französisches Kapitalmarktrecht*, p. 21.
[30] Cf. on the legal discussion regarding the introduction of an *action collective* R. Veil and P. Koch, *Französisches Kapitalmarktrecht*, p. 22.
[31] Cf. ibid., p. 21.
[32] Cf. ibid., p. 79.
[33] See § 20 para. 25.
[34] Cf. § 17(1) OWiG.
[35] Seen critically by J.A. Kämmerer, in: S. Grundmann et al. (eds.), *Festschrift für Klaus J. Hopt*, p. 2043, 2059.
[36] According to the BaFin's annual reports the maximum fine to have been imposed for a breach of the notification obligations regarding major shareholdings were €45,000. Cf. F. Walla, *Die Konzeption der Kapitalmarktaufsicht in Deutschland* (2013), p. 123–127.
[37] The criminal sanctions in capital markets law have led to an intense discussion on the legal foundations and dogmatics of criminal law. J. Vogel, *Festschrift für Günther Jakobs*, p. 731 ff. On the discussion regarding the effects of the ECJ's *Spector*-decision (see § 13 para. 80) on national criminal law, cf. P. Gehrmann, ZBB (2010), p. 48 ff.; P. Opitz, BKR (2010), p. 71 ff.
[38] In Germany, it is disputed whether the publication of breaches of notification obligations and the sanctions imposed can serve as a sanction (cf. § 40b WpHG). It is largely understood more as a measure in order to prevent such breaches in the future. Cf. J. Vogel, in: H.-D. Assmann and U.H. Schneider (eds.), *Kommentar zum WpHG*, § 40b para. 4; apparently dissenting: H. Fleischer, ZGR (2004), p. 437, 476–477.

Rüdiger Veil/Fabian Walla

incorrect ad hoc notifications.[39] They are accompanied by the general provisions for damages under tort law. These have been adapted by the Bundesgerichtshof (BGH, German Federal Court of Justice) to match the specific needs of capital markets law, being termed *Informationsdeliktshaftung* (informational tort liability) and granting damages on the basis of the rules laid down in § 826 BGB on intentional damage contrary to public policy.[40] On the basis of the KapMuG (Capital Investors' Test Proceedings Act) legal proceedings are facilitated for investors, giving them the possibility to file suit in so-called test proceedings, similar to class action suits.[41] Sanctions under civil law also include the loss of rights, especially in cases in which an investor fails to comply with the notification obligations regarding changes in major shareholdings.[42]

3. Italy

14   Italian law is characterised by a combination of criminal and administrative sanctions, breaches against the provisions on inside information and market manipulation being sanctioned with both penalties and administrative fines. Criminal and administrative fines can be severe, reaching up to €10,000,000.[43] In some cases minimum fines are also fixed, e.g. €20,000 for market manipulation.

15   Sanctions under civil law are rare. Italian law provides no specific rules thereon, merely applying the general civil law rules. The courts, however, have so far not had to deal with damage claims of investors. A loss of voting rights for breaches of the notification obligations is more common and Consob may even contest resolutions of the general meeting in order to enforce the loss of rights.[44] Even though Consob has not made use of this possibility yet, the possibility of a loss of rights appears to have a considerable deterring effect.[45]

4. Spain

16   In Spain, breaches of capital markets law are primarily sanctioned by administrative measures, criminal provisions playing only a small role.[46] Fines dominate in legal practice.[47] Mild and serious infringements are prosecuted by the CNMV pursuant to Article 97.1.a and b LMV (Spanish Securities Market Act),[48] whilst the Min-

---

[39] Cf. §§ 37b, 37c WpHG; see § 19 para. 118.

[40] Cf. § 826 BGB; see § 19 para. 111.

[41] Statute on test proceedings in disputes regarding capital markets law (Kapitalanleger-Musterverfahrensgesetz—KapMuG), 16 August 2005, BGBl. I (2005), p. 2437. Cf. R. Veil, in: *NJW-Sonderheft 3. Hannoveraner ZPO-Symposion* (2006), p. 3; on the practical relevance of the KapMuG B. Hess, in: B. Hess et al. (eds.), *Kölner Kommentar zum KapMuG*, Einl. para. 44; D. Zimmer and J. Höft, ZGR (2009), p. 663 ff.

[42] The effects of a loss of rights are too strong and are therefore in need of reform, cf. R. Veil, 175 ZHR (2011), p. 83, 91 ff.

[43] Cf. the CESR reports referred to in fn. 21.

[44] According to our Italian interview partners, this provision is a result of the fact that resolutions of the general meeting are not often contested by shareholders.

[45] All legal practitioners interviewed in Italy agreed on this.

[46] Cf. E. Hernández Sainz, *El abuso de información privilegiada en los mercados de valores*, p. 617 ff.

[47] Cf. S. García Malsipica, in: F. Uría, *Régimen jurídico de los mercados de valores y de las instituciones de inversión colectiva*, p. 785, 831.

[48] Serious infringements are listed in Art. 100 LMV; sanctions are listed in Art. 103 LMV. The definition of a mild infraction (*infracciones leves*) can be deduced e contrario from Art. 101 LMV; sanctions are listed in Art. 104 LMV.

istry for Economy and Finance is responsible for prosecuting particularly serious infringements (*infracciones muy graves*).[49] The sanctions are published in a registry kept by the CNMV;[50] serious breaches of the capital markets law provisions are also published in the official Spanish gazette.[51]

17   The only relevant sanctions under civil law are for prospectus liability and incorrect financial reports,[52] as Spanish law contains no special provisions on ad hoc disclosure obligations. Whilst legal literature has partially recommended the introduction of general provisions on civil liability for the incorrect publication of information on secondary markets, the legislature has to date ignored these ideas.[53] Damages can therefore only be claimed under the general civil law rules, especially tort law.[54] Filing claims is made more difficult by a lack of possibility of class actions under Spanish law.[55]

5.   Sweden

18   Swedish law relies entirely on criminal sanctions for breaches of insider prohibitions and the prohibitions on market manipulation. This has been strongly criticised, due to the fact that only few cases have ever led to a conviction.[56] Demands regarding the introduction of administrative fines have not, however, been met so far. In contrast, the rules on transparency of major holdings and the rules of conduct for investment firms are primarily subject to supervisory sanctions such as fines and special charges that can be for a considerable amount, e.g. between 15,000 and 5,000,000 SEK for delayed notification of the acquisition of stock.[57] The supervisory authority in Sweden also publishes the sanctions it imposes on its website.

19   Civil sanctions are less important, although Sweden has procedural rules on class actions which constitute a key element of investor protection.[58] A reason for this may be that there are no specific provisions on investor rights: whilst the general rules of tort law apply, under which a pure economic loss is generally unrecoverable, there is no possibility to place claims against the issuer, not even for the publication of incorrect prospectuses.[59] In these cases investors can only file suit against the managing directors. The possibility of a loss of rights does not exist with regard to the transparency of major holdings.[60]

---

[49] Particularly serious infringements are listed in Art. 99 LMV; sanctions are listed in Art. 102 LMV.
[50] Cf. Art. 98.3 LMV.
[51] Cf. Art. 102 LMV, Art. 103 LMV.
[52] Cf. E. Hernández Sainz, *El abuso de información privilegiada en los mercados de valores*, p. 617 ff. All legal practitioners interviewed in Spain agreed on this.
[53] Cf. M. Iribarren Blanco, *Responsabilidad civil por la información divulgada por las sociedades cotizadas*, p. 40 ff.
[54] Cf. C. Eckl, in: K.-J. and H.-C. Voigt (eds.), *Prospekt- und Kapitalmarktinformationshaftung*, p. 945, 983.
[55] Cf. M. Iribarren Blanco, *Responsabilidad civil por la información divulgada por las sociedades cotizadas*, p. 161.
[56] Cf. R. Veil and F. Walla, *Schwedisches Kapitalmarktrecht*, p. 60–61.
[57] Cf. ibid., p. 99.
[58] Class actions were introduced by the Lag omgrupprättegång (SFS 2002:599); on the legislative history see NJA II 2002, p. 309 ff. and the comprehensive report on the first experiences with this law by P.H. Lindblom, SvJT (2005), p. 129 ff. Cf. also R. Veil and F. Walla, *Schwedisches Kapitalmarktrecht*, p. 33–34.
[59] In detail R. Veil and F. Walla, *Schwedisches Kapitalmarktrecht*, p. 26 ff.
[60] This does not apply to take over law, cf. ibid., p. 97–98.

6. United Kingdom

20   The United Kingdom relies mainly on supervisory sanctions.[61] In this context, the powers of the FCA (as the successor to the FSA) are considerable: there is no upper limit to the fines that may be imposed.[62] Regarding inside information and market manipulation criminal sanctions also play an important role. The FSA is also responsible for their prosecution and will determine which cases are brought before the criminal courts.[63] The FSA regularly publishes the sanctions it has imposed on its website. It has, however, always aimed at a good cooperation with the companies it supervises and has therefore often only imposed very low fines. This has led to the former FSA being described as a "not-enforcement driven regulator".[64] Under the influence of the financial crises, however, the FSA admitted to attributing an important role to enforcement.[65]

21   Civil liability, common with regard to prospectus requirements, is of minor importance with regard to disclosure obligations on secondary markets, which for a long time played a very unimportant role.[66] Only recently were rules provided thereon: the Treasury assigned Professor Paul Davies of the London School of Economics the task of examining the current liability regime regarding incorrect information and developing possible improvements.[67] Most of his recommendations were subsequently adopted by the Treasury.[68] On 1 October 2010 a legal basis for the issuer's liability was finally enacted.[69] The new provisions are extensive in as far as they apply to all information published on the secondary market, even to that not legally required. Yet the UK legislature did not introduce rules for the most difficult problems of capital markets law, such as the proof of causation between the incorrect information and the investment decision.[70] The other requirements for a successful claim are also difficult to fulfil: the investor must prove that the issuer acted intentionally or recklessly. The fact that there is no possibility for class actions means that the costs of the proceedings will be considerable. The legislature has not as yet referred to the proposal to introduce a class action procedure as submitted by the Civil Justice Council in 2008.[71] A loss of rights as a further instrument of private enforcement is also unknown in UK capital markets law.

---

[61] R. Veil and M. Wundenberg, *Englisches Kapitalmarktrecht*, p. 152.

[62] The FSA's procedures for taking statutory notice decisions and the FSA's policy on the imposition and amount of penalties are laid down in the Decision Procedure and Penalties Manual (DEPP) of the FSA Handbook. According to DEPP 6.5.2 the FSA's penalty-setting regime is based on three principles: (i) disgorgement—a form or individual should not benefit from any breach; (ii) discipline—a firm or individual should be penalised for wrongdoing; and (iii) deterrence—any penalty imposed should deter the firm or individual who committed the breach, and others, from committing further or similar breaches.

[63] On the FSA reforms see § 11 para. 11.

[64] Cf. J.C. Coffee, 156 U. Pa. L. Rev. (2007), p. 229 ff.

[65] The "Supervisory Enhancement Program" developed by the FSA in 2008 aimed to intensify the supervision of the market participants and ensure a credible deterrence by developing a rigorous enforcement of breaches of these rules (see www.fsa.gov.uk/pubs/other/enhancement.pdf).

[66] In detail R. Veil and M. Wundenberg, *Englisches Kapitalmarktrecht*, p. 105 ff.

[67] Cf. P. Davis, *Final Report*, 2007.

[68] Cf. HM Treasury, *Extension of the Statutory Regime for Issuer Liability*, July 2008.

[69] Cf. E. Ferran, *Are US-style Investor Suits Coming to the UK?*, 9 J. Corp. L. Stud. (2009), p. 315–348.

[70] On solutions for the problem of the proof of causation see § 19 para. 114 and 119.

[71] The recommendations submitted by the Civil Justice Council are available at: www.judiciary.gov.uk.

IV. Conclusion

22   The studies published by the CESR show that the enforcement of capital markets law varies greatly between EU Member States. This has led the European Commission to conclude that a harmonisation of sanctions is necessary.[72] We agree with this statement only with regard to administrative sanctions. Concerning sanctions under criminal law, however, one must not forget that even after the most recent reforms criminal law remains primarily a national matter for which the EU has only restricted competencies.[73] It furthermore remains unclear whether the EU will successfully achieve a unification of legal practice regarding the fines imposed by the Member States.

23   European rules on administrative measures must take into account the different concepts of civil law sanctions followed in the Member States, especially the notion of a loss of rights, which is a particularly important sanction for breaches of notification obligations with regard to major shareholdings in some Member States. The civil liability of issuers and managing directors' remains insufficiently developed in many EU Member States.

24   These results give rise to the question whether sanctions under civil law ought also to be harmonised. Is it recommendable to have binding provisions regarding a loss of rights for breaches of notification obligations regarding changes in major holdings? And should the EU prescribe that investors may claim damages from the issuer or the managing directors for incorrect disclosure of information? Should class actions be introduced Europe-wide? On reflection of the past ten years it appears doubtful whether a further harmonisation will be necessary. Numerous Member States have independently reached the conclusion that a protection of investors by way of civil law claims bears advantages and have acted accordingly. Most recently, the United Kingdom has introduced specific statutory rules which aim to achieve well-balanced results. The reforms can be seen as the result of a competition between the different legal systems of the Member States. It is desirable that the European legislature continues to further this competition.

---

[72] See para 5.
[73] Cf. Art. 83 TFEU.

Rüdiger Veil/Fabian Walla

3

Market Integrity

§ 13   Insider Dealing

Bibliography

Alcock, Alistair, *Five Years of Market Abuse*, 28 Company Lawyer (2007), p. 163; Alexander, R.C.H., *Insider Dealing and Money Laundering in the EU: Law and Regulation* (2007); Alvisi, Chiara, *Abusi di mercato e tutele civili*, 1 Contratto e impresa/Europa (2007), p. 181; Amati, Enrico, *L'abuso di informazioni privilegiate: l`illecito amministrativo—Art. 187 Abuso di informazioni privilegiate*, 5 Le Nuove leggi civili commentate (2007), p. 1064; Annunziata, Filippo, *La Disciplina del Mercato Mobilare*, 4th ed. (2008); Arden, Justice, *Spector Photo Group and its Wider Implications*, ECFR (2010), p. 342–346; Bachmann, Gregor, *Kapitalmarktrechtliche Probleme bei der Zusammenführung von Unternehmen*, ZHR 172 (2008), p. 597–634; Bainbridge, Stephen M., *Securities Law: Insider Trading* (1999); Band, Christa and Hopper, Martyn, *Market Abuse—A Developing Jurisprudence*, JIBLR (2007) p. 231–239; Bazley, Stuart, *Market Cleanliness, Systems and Controls and Future Regulatory Enforcement*, 28 Company Lawyer (2007), p. 341–343; Bingel, Adrian, *Rechtliche Grenzen der Kursstabilisierung nach Aktienplatzierungen* (2007); Blair, Michael and Walker, George, *Financial Services Law* (2009); Brandi, Tim Oliver and Süßmann, Rainer, *Neue Insiderregeln und Ad-hoc-Publizität—Folgen für Ablauf und Gestaltung von M & A-Transaktionen*, AG (2004), p. 642–658; Brandstetter, Ruth, *Der "Insider-Straftatbestand"—In der Praxis ein Papiertiger*, ecolex (1998), p. 803; Cahn, Andreas, *Das neue Insiderrecht*, Der Konzern (2005), p. 5–13; Cascante, Christian and Bingel, Adrian, *Insiderhandel—in Zukunft leichter nachweisbar? Die Auslegung des Insiderrechts durch den EuGH und die Folgen für die M&A-Praxis*, NZG (2010), p. 161–165; Crespi, Alberto, *Manipolazione del mercato e manipolazione di norme incriminatrici*, 2 Banca Borsa tit. Cred. (2009), p. 107–135; Diekmann, Hans and Sustmann, Marco, *Gesetz zur Verbesserung des Anlegerschutzes (Anlegerschutzverbesserungsgesetz—AnSVG)*, NZG (2004), p. 929–939; Entrena Ruiz, Daniel, *El empleo de información privilegiada en el mercado de valores: un estudio de su régimen administrativo sancionador* (2006); Fleischer, Holger, *Ad-hoc-Publizität beim einvernehmlichen vorzeitigen Ausscheiden des Vorstandsvorsitzenden—Der DaimlerChrysler-Musterentscheid des OLG Stuttgart*, NZG (2007), p. 401–407; Gilotta, Sergio, *Disclosure in Securities Markets and the Firm's Need for Confidentiality: Theoretical Framework and Regulatory Analysis*, 13 EBOR (2012), p. 45–88; Guitard Marin, Juan, *Abuso de Mercado*, in: Francisco Uría (coordinador), *Régimen jurídico de los mercados de valores y de las instituciones de inversión colectiva*, La Ley (2007), p. 301; Hasselbach, Kai, *Die Weitergabe von Insiderinformationen bei M & A-Transaktionen mit börsennotierten Aktiengesellschaften*, NZG (2004), p. 1087–1095; Hausmaninger, Christian, *Pro: „Entkriminalisierung" des Insiderrechts*, ÖBA (2003), p. 637–638; Henderson, Andrew, *First Light: The Financial Services Authority's Enforcement of the Market Abuse Regime*, 20 JIBLR 2005, p. 494–500; Hilgard, Marc C. and Mock, Sebastian, *Stoneridge and its Impact on European Capital Market and Consumer Law*, ECFR (2008), p. 453–466; Hopt, Klaus J. and Wymeersch,

Eddy, *European Insider Dealing* (1991); Iragüen, Jesús Ibarra/Jiminéz-Blanco, Gonzalo, *Abuso de Mercado: Una Panorámica de su Normativa Administrativa y Penal Vigente*, 126 RDBB (2012), p. 49–104; Iribarren Blanco, Miguel, *Responsabilidad civil por la información divulgada por las sociedades cotizadas*, Monografía No. 2 (2008), asociada a la Revista de Mercado de Valores (2008); Kemnitz, Lukas, *Due Diligence und neues Insiderrecht* (2007); Klöhn, Lars, *Der "gestreckte Geschehensablauf" vor dem EUGH*, NZG (2011), p. 166–171; Klöhn, Lars, *The European Insider Trading Regulation after Spector Photo Group*, ECFR (2010), p. 347–366; Kretschmer, Werner and Oppitz, Martin, *Essentialia der Börsegesetznovelle*, ÖBA (1994), p. 610–619; Lahmann, Kai, *Insiderhandel. Ökonomische Analyse eines ordnungspolitischen Dilemmas* (1994); Lasserre Capdeville, Jérôme, *Le délit de communication d'une information privilégiée: vingt ans après*, Bull. Joly Bourse (2009), p. 69–76; Loke, Alexander F., *From Fiduciary Theory to Information Abuse: The Changing Fabric of Insider Trading Law in the UK, Australia and Singapore*, American Journal of Comparative Law (2006), p. 123; Madrazo, Regina, *Información no pública en las sociedades cotizadas españolas. Tipología y tratamiento en los reglamentos internos de conducta*, RMV No. 2 (2008), p. 471–481; Manne, Henry G., *Insider Trading and the Stock Market* (1966); Marsh, Jonathan, *Handling Price Sensitive Information: A Guide to the Legal and Regulatory Obligations*, 23 COB (2005), p. 1–39; Mayhew, David and Anderson, Karen, *Whither Market Abuse (in a More Principles-based Regulatory World)*, 22 JIBLR (2007), p. 515–531; Mehringer, Christoph, *Das allgemeine kapitalmarktrechtliche Gleichbehandlungsprinzip* (2007); Mennicke, Petra R., *Sanktionen gegen Insiderhandel—Eine rechtsvergleichende Untersuchung unter Berücksichtigung des US-amerikanischen und britischen Rechts* (1996); Moalem, David and Hansen, Jesper Lau, *Insider Dealing and Parity of Information—Is 'Georgakis' Still Valid?*, 9 EBLR (2008), p. 949–984; Moosmayer, Klaus, *Straf- und bußgeldrechtliche Regelungen im Entwurf eines Vierten Finanzmarktförderungsgesetzes*, wistra (2002), p. 161–170; Nietsch, Michael, *Die Verwendung der Insiderinformation*, ZHR 174 (2010), p. 556–592; Rider, Barry, Alexander, Kern, Linklater, Lisa and Bazley, Stuart, *Market Abuse and Insider Dealing*, 2nd ed. (2009); Russen, Jonathan, *Financial Services: Authorisation, Supervision and Enforcement* (2006); Schulz, Stephan, *Das Insiderhandelsverbot nach § 14 Abs 1 Nr. 1 WpHG im Lichte der Spector-Rechtsprechung des EuGH*, ZIP (2010), p. 609–613; Sethe, Rolf, *Die Verschärfung des insiderrechtlichen Weitergabeverbots*, ZBB (2006), p. 243–257; Singhof, Bernd, *Zur Weitergabe von Insiderinformationen im Unterordnungskonzern*, ZGR (2001), p. 146–174; Staikouras, Panagiotis K., *Four Years of MADness?—The New Market Abuse Prohibition Revisited: Integrated Implementation Through the Lens of a Critical, Comparative Analysis*, 9 EBLR (2008), p. 775–809; Steinberg, Marc I., *Insider Trading, Selective Disclosure and Prompt Disclosure: A Comparative Analysis* (2001) U. Pa. J. Int'l. Econ. Law 635; Veil, Rüdiger, *Der Schutz des verständigen Anlegers durch Publizität und Haftung im europäischen und nationalen Kapitalmarktrecht*, ZBB (2006), p. 162–171; Veil, Rüdiger, *Weitergabe von Informationen durch den Aufsichtsrat an Aktionäre und Dritte. Ein Lehrstück zum Verhältnis zwischen Gesellschafts- und Kapitalmarktrecht*, ZHR 172 (2008), p. 239–273; Veil, Rüdiger, *Concepts of Supervisory Legislation and Enforcement in European Capital Markets Law—Observations from a Civil Law Country*, 11 EBOR (2010), p. 409–422; Villeda, Gisella Victoria, *Prävention und Repression von Insiderhandel* (2010); Wang, William K.S. and Steinberg, Marc. I., *Insider Trading* (1996); Willey, Stuart, *Market Abuse Update*, 93 COB (2012), p. 1–28; Ziehl, Katrin, *Kapitalmarktprognosen und Insider-Trading* (2006).

I. Introduction

1   In the United States, legislation on capital markets law, including aspects of market abuse, was already on the agenda in 1934, when the federal legislature enacted the Securities Exchange Act and the Securities and Exchange Commission laid down the SEC Rules. Both the US Supreme Court and lower courts extended the provisions—especially Rule 10b-5—thus developing a powerful regime, based on the

notion that all insider dealings are disadvantageous for the market in the longer term.[1] In the 1960s and 1970s, however, debates flared up in the United States[2] and Europe[3] as to whether insider dealings might after all have a positive effect and ought therefore to be legalised. It was argued that an investor who concludes a securities transaction with an insider will generally not suffer any damage as the investor would in any case have carried out the transaction. It was furthermore claimed that insider dealings allow inside information to access the capital markets, thus ensuring an appropriate pricing of securities. Additionally, legalising insider dealings was assumed to solve conflicts arising between principals and agents. This theory was based on the understanding that the possibility of abusing inside information has to be seen as a form of manager remuneration. Due to the fact that inside information is only produced when risks are taken, legalising insider dealings would encourage the managers' willingness to take such risks.

2   Yet these arguments purported by the critics of a regulation restricting insider dealings are not convincing. Whilst it is true that an investor concluding a security transaction will mostly not suffer any damage as it would also have concluded the same transaction with another person, market makers will react to a possible risk of losses with larger margins of sales and purchases. Thus, insiders cause higher transaction costs that must be carried by all market participants. The second argument must also be rejected: it has been proven that an issuer's obligation to disclose information immediately[4] is more likely to ensure efficiency of the capital markets than dealings on the basis of inside information.[5] The opinion that the legalisation of insider dealing would serve as an incentive for the management to take risks and thus be advantageous for the company and its shareholders can also not prevail. By using put options the management could easily gain financial advantages from negative information, thus not necessarily maximising company value. A further problem of legalised insider dealings is the fact that third parties would also be able to profit from inside information, resulting in the so-called "free rider problem".

3   Despite all these arguments various Member States were sceptical towards regulations on insider dealings, some not introducing the first provisions until well into the 1980s. In Germany, the prevailing opinion was that voluntary rules were sufficient. The Federal Minister for Economics engaged an expert committee which published "Recommendations on the Solution of the Insider Problem" in 1970. The report included guidelines on insider dealings, prohibiting members of the management board and supervisory board, major shareholders and employees of a stock corporation from dealing in shares and bonds of the corporation by using inside information.[6] This self-regulatory approach, however, did not prove successful.

4   The legal situation in Europe changed with the enactment of Directive 89/592/

---

[1] Cf. S.M. Bainbridge, *Securities Law: Insider Trading* (1999); W.K.S. Wang and M.I. Steinberg, *Insider Trading* (1996).

[2] Cf. H.G. Manne, *Insider Trading and the Stock Market* (1966), p. 131 ff.

[3] Cf. K.J. Hopt and E. Wymeersch, *European Insider Dealing* (1991).

[4] For more details on this obligation see § 19 para. 25–51.

[5] Cf. K. Lahmann, *Insiderhandel*, p. 169.

[6] For the last version of the recommendations see WM (1998), p. 1105. An analysis of the sanction for breaches of these obligations is made by G.V. Villeda, *Prävention und Repression im Insiderhandel*, p. 46 ff.

EEC of 13 November 1989 coordinating regulations on insider dealings.[7] The
European legislature justified the introduction of a European directive with the fact
that investor confidence was based mainly on the assurance that all investors are
placed on an equal footing and are protected against the improper use of inside
information. The smooth operation of markets depends to a large extent on the
confidence it inspires in investors. By benefiting certain investors as opposed to
others, insider dealing is likely to undermine that confidence and may therefore
prejudice the smooth operation of the market.[8] In the mid-1990s insider dealings
were thus prohibited in Europe.[9]

5   Only eleven years later the changes on the financial markets and in European Community law caused the European legislature to carry out fundamental reforms of the
regime in order to be able to prevent insider dealings and market manipulations
more effectively.[10] To this end the Market Abuse Directive (MAD)[11] was enacted,
replacing the Insider Directive.

6   The MAD's objective is to ensure the integrity of the Community's financial markets and to enhance investor confidence in those markets.[12] The directive conceives
the prohibition of insider dealings as a prerequisite for achieving "full and proper
market transparency".[13] The prohibition is thus justified by the necessity of organising markets and ensuring their proper functioning[14]. The underlying principle
is that of informational equality of all investors,[15] whilst the aspect of managers
breaching their duty of loyalty by taking advantage of inside information, which
plays an important role in the US discussion,[16] is not referred to by European capital
markets law.

II.   Regulatory Concepts

1.   Requirements under European Law

(a)   Prohibitions Laid Down by the Market Abuse Directive

7   The MAD and its Implementing Directives 2003/124/EC[17] and 2004/72/EC[18] con-

---

[7] See § 1 para. 11.
[8] Recitals of Directive 89/592/EEC.
[9] Pursuant to Art. 14(1), the Insider Directive was to be transposed by 1 June 1992.
[10] A reason for the directive was also the aim of combating the financing of terrorist activities; cf. Recital 14
MAD.
[11] See § 1 para. 22.
[12] Cf. Recital 12 MAD.
[13] Cf. Recital 15 MAD.
[14] On this regulatory aim see § 2 para. 3.
[15] Cf. C. Mehringer, *Das allgemeine kapitalmarktrechtliche Gleichbehandlungsprinzip*, p. 102 ff.
[16] Cf. *Chiarella v. US*, 445 US 222 (1980); cf. on the misappropriation theory M.A. Snyder, *The Supreme Court
and the Misappropriation Theory of Securities Fraud and Insider Trading: Clarification or Confusion?*, Capital Univ.
L. Rev. 27 (1999), p. 419–447.
[17] Commission Directive 2003/124/EC of 22 December 2003 implementing Directive 2003/6/EC of the European Parliament and of the Council as regards the definition and public disclosure of inside information and the
definition of market manipulation, OJ L339, 24 December 2003, p. 70.
[18] Commission Directive 2004/72/EC of 29 April 2004 implementing Directive 2003/6/EC of the European
Parliament and of the Council as regards accepted market practices, the definition of inside information in rela-

tain detailed dispositions for the Member States regarding prohibitions on insider dealings. The directive begins with a definition of the term "inside information", this being "information of a precise nature which has not been made public, relating directly or indirectly, to one or more issuers of financial instruments or to one or more financial instruments and which, if it were made public, would be likely to have a significant effect on the prices of those financial instruments or on the price of related derivative financial instruments"[19]. The Committee of European Securities Regulators (CESR) has developed "Guidelines"[20] on the individual elements of this concept, explaining these[21] and giving details on the requirement to keep insider lists.[22]

8 Subsequently, the MAD defines which behaviour the Member States must prohibit with regard to inside information, namely (i) acquiring and disposing of shares to which the information relates, (ii) disclosing inside information to any other person and (iii) recommending or inducing another person, on the basis of this information, to acquire or dispose of the respective shares. The Member States must ensure that all three prohibitions apply to so-called primary insiders, i.e. persons who have direct access to this information "by virtue of their membership of the administrative, management or supervisory bodies of the issuer, by virtue of their holding in the capital of the issuer, by virtue of his having access to the information through the exercise of his employment, profession or duties or by virtue of criminal activities".[23] The Member States must further ensure that the prohibitions also apply to any other person who possesses inside information, provided this person knows or ought to have known that it is inside information.[24] The MAD contents itself with a minimum harmonisation in this field, allowing the Member States to exceed the European provisions and introduce a higher level of protection. Some Member States have availed themselves of this possibility.[25]

9 The MAD contains no provisions on possible sanctions for breaches of the prohibitions. The Member States can therefore decide individually whether they wish to impose criminal sanctions.[26] They must, however, ensure that "in conformity with their national law, the appropriate administrative measures can be taken or administrative sanctions be imposed".[27] The details are once again left to the national legislatures: "The Member States shall ensure that these measures are effective, proportionate and dissuasive."[28] This demand, also to be found in the other framework

tion to derivatives on commodities, the drawing up of lists of insiders, the notification of managers' transactions and the notification of suspicious transactions, OJ L162, 30 April 2004, p. 70.

[19] Art. 1(1) MAD.
[20] On their legal quality and relevance for interpretation see § 5 para. 39–40.
[21] CESR, *Level 3—Second Set of CESR Guidance and Information on the Common Operation of the Directive to the Market*, CESR/06-562b, July 2007.
[22] CESR, *Level 3—Third Set of CESR Guidance and Information on the Common Operation of the Directive to the Market*, CESR/09-219, May 2009.
[23] Art. 2(1) MAD.
[24] Art. 4 MAD.
[25] On the more strict regulatory concept pursued in the United Kingdom see below para. 27–31.
[26] Cf. Art. 14(1) MAD: "Without prejudice to the right of Member States to impose criminal sanctions ...".
[27] Art. 14(1) MAD.
[28] Art. 14(1) MAD.

directives,[29] is to ensure that the European legal framework against market abuse is sufficient.[30]

(b) Accompanying Rules

10   The prohibition of insider dealings is accompanied by numerous other rules in the MAD, the Transparency Directive (TD) and the Markets in Financial Instruments Directive (MiFID), such as the issuer's obligation to make public inside information without delay.[31] The European legislature's aim was to ensure that all investors gain access to price-sensitive information as soon as possible and to counteract the dangers of insider dealings. The provisions on insider dealings and ad hoc disclosure therefore both operate with the concept of inside information. Other transparency rules, such as the obligation to notify and make public directors' dealings[32] and the TD's provisions on the notification and publication of changes in major shareholdings[33] are also aimed at preventing the misuse of inside information. The MiFID's rules of conduct for investment firms also pursue the goal of preventing prohibited insider dealings,[34] especially by demanding the introduction of compliance structures,[35] such as Chinese walls.

(c) Reform

11   On 20 October 2011 the European Commission made public two proposals[36] regarding amendments to the rules on market abuse.[37] The worldwide economic and financial crises made clear the importance of market integrity, and the CESR's study[38] and the de Larosière report[39] underlined the fact that the legal situation in the Member States regarding criminal and administrative sanctions was disparate and hardly provided incentives to act lawfully.[40] The European Commission therefore regarded it as necessary to extend the rules on market abuse to other markets and develop stricter rules on supervision and sanctions.

12   Pursuant to the proposal for a new regulation, the rules on insider dealing are also to apply to financial instruments traded on multilateral trading facilities (MTFs) or

---

[29] See § 1 para. 21 ff.
[30] Recital 38 MAD.
[31] See § 31 para. 25 ff.
[32] See § 21 para. 2.
[33] See § 20 para. 17 ff.
[34] See § 29 para. 1.
[35] See § 43 para. 43.
[36] Proposal for a Regulation of the European Parliament and of the Council on Insider Dealing and Market Manipulation (Market Abuse) of 20 October 2011 COM(2011) 651 final; Proposal for a Directive of the European Parliament and of the Council on Criminal Sanctions for Insider Dealing and Market Manipulation of 20 October 2011, COM(2011), 654 final. Cf. on this reform R. Veil and P. Koch, *Towards a Uniform European Capital Markets Law: Proposals of the Commission to Reform Market Abuse* (2012); S. Willey, 93 COB (2012), p. 1, 12–15.
[37] Furthermore, the European Commission has published a Working Paper as an accompanying document to the two proposals (Commission Staff Working Paper Impact Assessment, 20.10.2011, SEC(2011) 1217 final).
[38] Cf. CESR, *Report on administrative measures and sanctions as well as the criminal sanctions available in Member States under the market abuse directive (MAD)*, CESR/08-099, February 2008.
[39] Cf. J. de Larosière, *The High-Level Group on Financial Supervision in the EU*, Report, 25.2.2009.
[40] Cf. Recital 34 MAR Draft.

organised trading facilities (OTFs).[41] Over-the-counter (OTC) trading has also been included in the scope of the regulation.[42] The Commission further plans to prohibit insider dealings for share derivatives, traded exclusively OTC.[43]

13   The proposal for a Market Abuse Regulation further contains a number of provisions that have the aim to strengthen the powers of the national supervisory authorities.[44] The unification and intensification of the sanctions are to increase the dissuasiveness of sanctions in the future.[45] The draft Market Abuse Regulation focuses on the administrative measures and sanctions. In Chapter 5 it contains regulatory requirements for the Member States,[46] obliging them to implement provisions on the imposition of fines[47] into their national laws. The regulation's respective provisions are thus not to apply directly. According to the draft of a new MAD, the Member States are further to prohibit certain forms of behaviour by criminal law. Rules on criminal sanctions are assumed to demonstrate "social disapproval of a qualitatively different nature compared to administrative sanctions or compensation mechanisms under civil law".[48]

2.   Implementation in the Member States

14   The Member States have transposed the MAD's provisions in different ways, some only recurring to criminal provisions, whilst others implementing administrative as well as criminal prohibitions. The administrative prohibitions generally have lower prerequisites—partly letting negligence suffice—and are therefore more easily enforceable in practice. Not all Member States have transposed the MAD's and the implementing directives' provisions one-to-one.

(a)   Austria

15   In Austria, it was the European provisions that gave the incentive for introducing statutory provisions on insider dealings.[49] Since 1 October 1993 the BörseG (Austrian Stock Exchange Trading Act) contains insider provisions, all of which are of a criminal nature.[50] They so far do not, however, appear to be of any great importance in judicial practice.[51]

16   § 48a BörseG defines the concept of inside information, which corresponds strongly with that in MAD, the only difference being the understanding of the information as *genau* (i.e. exact) instead of *präzise* (i.e. precise).[52] § 48b BörseG contains a number

---

[41] Cf. Art. 2(1)(b) MAR Draft.
[42] Cf. Art. 2(1)(c) MAR Draft.
[43] Cf. Art. 2(2) MAR Draft (as yet derivatives only fall within the scope of Art. 9(2) MAD in exceptional cases).
[44] Cf. Art. 17 MAR Draft.
[45] Cf. Recital 34 MAR Draft: "equal, strong and deterrent sanctions regimes".
[46] Cf. Art. 24 (1) MAR Draft.
[47] Cf. Art. 25–29 MAR Draft; see also para. 127–129.
[48] Cf. Explanatory Memorandum, p. 3–4.
[49] Cf. S. Kalss, M. Oppitz and J. Zollner, *Kapitalmarktrecht*, § 20 para. 7; in more detail W. Kretschmer and M. Oppitz, ÖBA (1994), p. 610 ff.
[50] The criminal sanctions are seen critically by C. Hausmaninger, ÖBA (2003), p. 637–638.
[51] Cf. R. Brandstetter, *ecolex* (1998), p. 803.
[52] Cf. S. Kalss, M. Oppitz and J. Zollner, *Kapitalmarktrecht*, § 20 para. 15.

of prohibitions, analogous to those in the European provisions. The individual cases distinguish between an insider as the offender and third-person offenders.[53] A few deviations from the MAD can also be found here, the most relevant concerning the most serious prohibition: any person taking advantage of inside information with the intention of gaining a pecuniary benefit for himself or herself or a third party by (i) buying or selling the financial instruments concerned or offering to buy or to sell these to a third party, or recommending such action, or (ii) making this information accessible to a third party without having been ordered to do so, will be punished by law to a prison sentence of up to three years and if the benefit gained exceeds €50,000, by a prison sentence of six months to five years (§ 48b(1) BörseG).

(b) France

17 French law first introduced the criminal offence of insider dealing in 1970 and the first supervisory regulations on the prohibition of insider dealing in 1989. The *délit*[54] under criminal law and the supervisory *manquement*[55] are mostly very similar, differing only in certain aspects.[56] The criminal provisions, for example, only refer to financial instruments admitted to trading on a regulated market. Furthermore, they do not prohibit a person from recommending the acquisition or disposal of financial shares to another person. The most important difference is, however, probably the fact that the administrative provisions, unlike the criminal provisions, do not require intent but only negligence (*imprudence*).

18 France has its own classification of insiders, ranging from primary insiders to tertiary insiders. Primary insiders, such as management board members, general directors or members of the administrative or supervisory board, are assumed to know inside information about the issuer.[57] As opposed to this, secondary insiders, i.e. persons with access to inside information due to their profession or duties, are only liable if there is definite proof that they possessed the respective information. Tertiary insiders are all other persons in the possession of inside information, be it members of the family or friends of primary or secondary insiders.[58]

(c) Germany

19 The German legislature did not enact implementing rules to the Insider Directive prohibiting insider dealings until 1 January 1994.[59] These were amended in 2005[60] in order for them to comply with the MAD and to enhance investor protection.[61] It is now prohibited (i) to make use of inside information to acquire or dispose of insider securities for one's own account or for the account of or on behalf of a third

---

[53] § 48b (4) BörseG defines the term insider in accordance with the requirements of the MAD.
[54] Cf. Art. L. 465-1 C. mon. fin.
[55] Cf. Art. 622-1, 622-2 RG AMF.
[56] In more detail R. Veil and P. Koch, *Französisches Kapitalmarktrecht*, p. 43 ff.
[57] Cf. J. Lasserre Capdeville, Bull. Joly Bourse (2009), p. 69, 70.
[58] Cf. ibid., p. 69, 71.
[59] Cf. §§ 12 ff. WpHG.
[60] The amendments to the WpHG were made by the Anlegerschutzverbesserungsgesetz (AnSVG, Law on the improvement of investor protection) of 28 October 2004, BGBl. I, p. 2630.
[61] Cf. H. Diekmann and M. Sustmann, NZG (2004), p. 929.

party, (ii) to disclose or make available inside information to a third party without the authority to do so and (iii) to recommend, on the basis of inside information, that a third party acquires or disposes of insider securities, or to otherwise induce a third party to do so.[62] These prohibitions are addressed to all insiders, whether primary or secondary. The distinction between primary and secondary insiders only becomes relevant with regard to the possible sanctions, i.e. prison sentence, criminal or administrative fine.[63]

20   The German legislature has not implemented the definition of inside information in the MAD and Directive 2003/124/EC one-to-one, but rather developed its own understanding of this term. The BaFin is responsible for supervising the compliance with the three prohibitions. Its *Emittentenleitfaden* (issuer guideline) contains information on the BaFin's administrative practice and details on its understanding of the provisions on insider dealings.[64] These explanations prove an important help for the legal practice when interpreting the provisions.

21   Possible criminal penalties are imprisonment and criminal fines, whilst administrative offences are sanctioned with administrative fines (cf. §§ 38 and 39 WpHG (German Securities Trading Act)). If the facts give rise to the suspicion of a criminal offence, the public prosecutor is the competent authority, responsible for prosecuting and charging suspects before a criminal court.[65] The BaFin is not competent for the prosecution of criminal offences, only being empowered to sanction administrative offences with administrative fines.[66]

(d)   Italy

22   In Italy, the provisions on insider dealings are laid down in Articles 181ff. TUF (Italian Consolidated Laws on Finance). Article 184 TUF contains criminal provisions for primary insiders that prohibit the acquisition and disposal of shares, the disclosure of information and recommendations on the basis of inside information.[67] Article 187-bis I TUF contains supervisory rules that also apply to secondary insiders.[68] Administrative sanctions can be imposed whether or not the insider dealing was a criminal offence resulting in criminal liability.

23   The Italian prohibitions are very closely modelled on the MAD's example with only few deviations. The provisions refer to the concept of privileged information (*informazione privilegiata*), i.e. information of a precise nature that has not been made public, relating directly or indirectly to one or more issuers of financial instruments or to one or more financial instruments and which, if it were made public would be likely to have a significant effect on the prices of the financial instruments. The Italian supervisory authority (Consob) does not follow a clear interpretational

---

[62] Cf. § 14 (1) Nos. 1–3 WpHG.

[63] See para. 117.

[64] Cf. BaFin, *Emittentenleitaden 2009* (issuer guideline), p. 27 ff. on the supervision of insiders and p. 115 ff. on insider lists.

[65] Cf. § 4(5) WpHG.

[66] § 40 WpHG indicates that the BaFin is the supervisory authority responsible for prosecuting and imposing fines for administrative offences under the WpHG.

[67] Cf. F. Annunziata, *La Disciplina del mercato Mobiliare*, p. 422.

[68] The introduction of administrative measures is seen critically by A. Crespi, 2 Banca borsa e titoli di credito (2009), p. 107, 111.

line regarding the understanding of information of a precise nature in the provisions on insider trading and ad hoc disclosure. In a *Communicazione*[69] it justifies the different notions with the fact that a premature disclosure of uncertain information could mislead the market.[70]

(e) Spain

24 In anticipation of the Insider Directive, Spain first introduced provisions on insider dealings in 1988. The ensuing transposition of the MAD and its implementing measures was carried out more or less one-to-one.[71] However, the Spanish legislature adopted a new term—"privileged information" (*información privilegiada*)—as opposed to the term "relevant information" (*información relevante*) required for an ad hoc disclosure obligation.[72] Whether both concepts are to be interpreted in the same way[73] or whether the introduction of a new term involves an incorrect transposition of the MAD, as yet remains unclear.[74]

25 Spanish law distinguishes between administrative and criminal sanctions. The administrative sanctions follow the concept of the prohibitions laid down in the MAD. Article 81.4 LMV (Spanish Securities Market Act) requires an insider to treat inside information confidentially. The sanctions under criminal law are conceived differently. Article 284 CP (Spanish Criminal Code) prohibits the insider from using (*utilizar*) the information in an attempt to distort the prices. Article 285 CP prohibits the use (*uso*) and disclosure (*suministro*) of inside information. A person is only criminally liable under Article 285 CP if his action resulted in a profit or a loss of a minimum of €600,000.

(f) Sweden

26 Swedish law only provides criminal provisions prohibiting insider dealings, and these provisions have been subject to a number of reforms. Since the transposition of the MAD the main provisions can now be found in the Market Abuse Act (Lag om straff för marknadsmissbruk vid handel med finansiella instrument), further statutes containing additional rules on keeping insider lists and certain trading prohibitions.[75] Both the prohibition of insider dealings and the definition of inside information differ from the European understanding. The Swedish legislature has not laid down a specific prohibition to acquire or dispose of shares by using inside information but rather introduced a blanket clause covering all types of prohibitions: an insider may not, on his own account, deal with the respective financial instruments or induce a third party by recommendation or in another way to trade in the

[69] Consob, *Comunicazione n. DME/5078692*, 29 November 2005.
[70] For more details see § 29 para. 47.
[71] Seen critically by J. Guitard Marin, *Abuso de mercado*, p. 306.
[72] On this concept cf. J.I. Iragüen and G. Jiminéz-Blanco, 126 RDBB (2012), p. 49, 54–60.
[73] D. Entrena Ruiz, *El empleo de información privilegiada*, p. 75–76; R. Madrazo, RMV No. 2-2008, p. 471, 473 ff.
[74] M. Iribarren Blanco, *Responsabilidad civil*, p. 90 ff.
[75] Cf. R. Veil and F. Walla, *Schwedisches Kapitalmarktrecht*, p. 38.

Rüdiger Veil

financial instrument.[76] Negligent behaviour is also subject to criminal liability,[77] thus including cases in which the offender negligently mistook the nature of the inside information to be publicly known.

(g) United Kingdom

27   In the United Kingdom, rules prohibiting insider dealings and market manipulation existed before the MAD was implemented.[78] The developments began in criminal law,[79] which has contained sanctions for insider dealings since 1980. Criminal law was significantly influenced by the Insider Directive of 1989 and the MAD which replaced it.[80] Today the criminal provisions prohibiting insider dealings, disclosure and recommendations or inducement can be found in Part V sections 52–64 and schedules 1 and 2 of the Criminal Justice Act 1993.[81] Additionally, the enactment of the Financial Services and Markets Act 2000 (FSMA) led to the introduction of an administrative "civil market abuse regime"[82] in Part VIII section 118 FSMA 2000. This was justified by the fact that the criminal provisions were often not applicable due to the difficulties in proving mens rea.

28   The MAD was mainly implemented in the Financial Services and Markets Act 2000 (Market Abuse) Regulation 2005.[83] Insider dealings and market manipulation are now "under one umbrella".[84] The Code of Market Conduct (MAR), which is part of the FSA Handbook, contains further details regarding section 118 FSMA.[85] The criminal regime on insider dealings remains in force, the British legislature considering an adaptation of the criminal provisions superfluous, due to the fact that Article 14 MAD only refers to administrative measures.

29   The changes in supervisory law have resulted in a complex regime on insider regulation, as the insider rules in the United Kingdom from before the implementation of the MAD did not only refer to inside information but rather to all "relevant information not generally available" (RINGA). The British legislature opted temporarily to uphold the existing, stricter regime. This was achieved in conformance with European law by constructing the former provisions in section 118(4) (Insider Dealings) and sections 118 (8) FSMA (Market Manipulation) as catch-all clauses.[86]

---

[76] Cf. § 2 MAD.

[77] Cf. § 3 MAD. On this see R. Veil and F. Walla, *Schwedisches Kapitalmarktrecht*, p. 48–49.

[78] For an overview of the history of a supervisory market abuse regime see J. Melrose, in: M. Blair and G. Walker (eds.), *Financial Services Law*, para. 6.01 ff.

[79] The roots of the prohibition of insider trading and market manipulation can be traced back to the beginning of the 19th century in common law, cf. A. Alcock, in: M. Lord et al. (eds.), *F. Gore-Browne on Companies*, sec. 42-1 (Update 68). Throughout this book, common law will not be taken into account, neither being linked to the Insider Directive nor to the MAD.

[80] Sec. 5 Company Act (1980).

[81] Introduced in the CJA by the Criminal Justice Act 1993 (Commencement No. 5) Order (SI 1994/242), thereby transposing the Insider Directive into British law.

[82] The terminology varies; the term "civil market abuse regime" is used by the FSA for sec. 118 FSMA. Cf. J. Melrose, in: M. Blair and G. Walker, *Financial Services Law*, para. 6.03.

[83] A comparison of the former insider law and the current market manipulation law can be found in J. Russen, *Financial Services*, p. 181 ff.

[84] E. Lomnicka, *Palmer's Company Law*, para. 11.101.

[85] The Code of Market Conduct was modified by the FSA's Market Abuse Directive Instrument 2005 (FSA 2005/15) in the course of the transposition of the MAD.

[86] The provisions exceeding the MAD's requirements are also defined as *super-equivalent provisions*.

30 The insider regime of the United Kingdom thus consists of a number of elements. Firstly, there are the criminal provisions on the offence of insider dealings in sections 52ff. Criminal Justice Act (CJA), prohibiting insider dealings and the disclosure to and encouragement of third parties. These provisions were not amended in the course of the transposition of the MAD. Secondly, there are the supervisory provisions in section 118(2) and (3) FSMA, based on the MAD, which constitute a "new" insider legislation. Thirdly, there is the catch-all clause in section 118(4) based on the former insider rules, which will remain applicable for a transitional period.

31 A fourth element of great importance is the principles in the FSA's Handbook.[87] These "High Level Standards"[88] are laid down in the Principles for Business (PRIN)[89] in the first part of the Handbook and are defined as "Rules", thus constituting universally applicable provisions, on which the FSA can additionally or exclusively base the imposition of fines.[90] This is especially relevant for cases in which certain aspects of the more specific prohibition of insider dealings are not given or cannot be proven. Section 118 FSMA does not have a limiting effect on the applicability of the principles, thus allowing the FSA to refer to them at any time. The FSA can therefore impose sanctions even if the information has meanwhile been made public and is thus no longer inside information.[91]

III. Concept of Inside Information

1. Overview

32 The concept of inside information is the key element of various rules in capital markets law. It constitutes a requirement for all three prohibitions of insider dealings described in the Market Abuse Directive and for the ad hoc disclosure obligation, also provided for by this directive. Issuers of financial instruments are required to inform the public as soon as possible of inside information which directly concerns the said issuer.[92] The concept of inside information also plays an important role regarding the rules on market manipulation.[93] Due to its utmost importance for three of the most relevant prohibitions in European capital markets law, the examination of the concept of inside information will begin with the European understanding of the term. This will be followed by an exemplary account of the transposition of this concept in the Member States, paying special attention to the judicial experiences with interpreting the term.

[87] On the relevance of principles based regulation in insider law see D. Mayhew and K. Anderson, JIBLR (2007), p. 515 ff.; A. Alcock, 28 Company Lawyer (2007), p. 163, 170 f.; S. Bazley, 28 Company Lawyer (2007), p. 341 ff.
[88] On principles-based capital markets regulation see § 4 para. 51–68.
[89] Similar principles apply to the FSA's *approved persons*. They are laid down in the FSA Handbook's Code of Practice of Approved Persons (APER).
[90] Cf. (with case material) J. Bagge et al. (eds.), *Financial Service Decision Digest*, p. 18–19; D. Mayhew and K. Anderson, JIBLR (2007), p. 515, 519 ff.; C. Band and M. Hopper, JIBLR (2007), p. 231 ff.
[91] An example for this is the FSA's decision in S.J. Pignatelli (breach of Principles 2 and 3 of the FSA's Code of Practice of Approved Persons); see in more detail below para. 120.
[92] See § 19 para. 25.
[93] See § 14 para. 16.

2. Definition of Inside Information under European Law

33 Article 1 No. 1 MAD defines inside information as information of a precise nature which has not been made public relating, directly or indirectly, to one or more issuers of financial instruments or to one or more financial instruments and which, if it were made public, would be likely to have a significant effect on the prices of those financial instruments or on the price of related derivative financial instruments. This definition contains two elements: (i) that of information of a precise nature which has not been made public; and (ii) that of a likelihood of having a significant effect on the prices of financial instruments

34 Both elements are formulated in an abstract manner and give rise to a number of questions regarding their application. The European Commission therefore enacted Implementing Directive 2003/124/EC on the definition and public disclosure of inside information and the definition of market abuse, which aimed to increase legal certainty for the market participants therewith.[94] CESR has issued an extensive statement on the notion of "inside information" which, whilst neither binding for the supervisory authorities nor for the national courts,[95] nevertheless plays an important role in practice as an interpretational guideline.

(a) Information of a Precise Nature

35 Directive 2003/124/EC defines information of a precise nature as information that indicates a set of circumstances which exists or may reasonably be expected to come into existence or an event which has occurred or may reasonably be expected to do so and if it is specific enough to enable a conclusion to be drawn as to the possible effect of that set of circumstances or event on the prices of financial instruments or related derivative financial instruments.[96] CESR rightly points out that the precise nature of information must be assessed on a case-by-case basis, depending on the content of the information and its context.[97] It can prove difficult in this context to determine the moment at which it appears sufficiently probable that a certain event will occur. According to the CESR, this must be determined on the basis of the information available at this time: can it reasonably be expected that this event will occur? This does not, however, answer the question of what is required for the event to appear reasonably probable. This has been highly disputed in Germany. There are two possible approaches to interpretation. The first is to require a certain degree of probability (either a predominant probability, i.e. over 50%, or a high probability). The second possibility is to determine the degree of probability by the effects the event will have on the issuer: events that are particularly likely to have a significant effect on the security price need only be of slight probability,[98] whilst a higher probability is required for events less likely to have a significant effect. This second approach is also called *probability/magnitude*-formula.[99]

---

[94] Cf. Recital 2 of Directive 2003/124/EC.
[95] See § 5 para. 39.
[96] Art. 1(1) Directive 2003/124/EC.
[97] CESR, *Level 3—second set of CESR guidance and information on the common operation of the Directive to the market*, CESR/06-562b, July 2007, No. 1.5.
[98] Cf. BGH ZIP (2011), p. 72, second question referred for a preliminary ruling.
[99] Cf. L. Klöhn, NZG (2011), p. 166, 168.

36   The European Court of Justice (ECJ) opted for the first approach:

> "Article 1(1) of Directive 2003/124, in using the terms 'may reasonably be expected', cannot be interpreted as requiring that proof be made out of a high probability of the circumstances or events in question coming into existence or occurring. To restrict the scope of [the provision] in respect of future circumstances and events to such a degree of probability would undermine the objectives ... to protect the integrity of the European Union financial markets and to enhance investor confidence in those markets. In such a scenario, insiders would be able to derive undue benefit from certain information which, under such a restrictive interpretation, would be held not to be precise, to the detriment of others who are unaware of it. However, in order to ensure legal certainty for market participants, including issuers, ... precise information is not to be considered as including information concerning circumstances and events the occurrence of which is implausible. Otherwise, issuers could believe that they are obliged to disclose information which is not specific or is unlikely to influence the prices of their financial instruments. It follows that, in using the terms 'may reasonably be expected', Article 1(1) of Directive 2003/124 refers to future circumstances or events from which it appears, on the basis of an overall assessment of the factors existing at the relevant time, that there is a realistic prospect that they will come into existence or occur."[100]

37   It remains unclear whether in cases of particularly price-sensitive information a lower degree of probability might suffice. The Advocate General confirmed this:

> "It follows that, where the potential of that information for affecting share prices is significant, it is sufficient that the occurrence of the future set of circumstances or event, albeit uncertain, be not impossible or improbable. In making that assessment, the extent of the consequences for the issuer will be of relevance inasmuch as that will form part of the information available *ex ante*, given that a reasonable investor will base his decisions on the anticipated impact of the information in the light of the totality of the related issuer's activity, the reliability of the information source and every other market variable which might, in the circumstances, affect the financial instrument in question or the related derivative financial instrument."[101]

The ECJ, however, did not follow the Advocate General in this regard: "The question whether the required probability of occurrence of a set of circumstances or an event may vary depending on the magnitude of their effect on the prices of the financial instruments concerned must be answered in the negative."[102] This interpretation appears favourable, the Advocate General's approach causing legal uncertainty for investors and issuers.

38   To determine when information has become "precise" and is thus to be classed as inside information is a particular problem in multi-stage processes, such as capital increases or mergers. In these cases it is either possible to refer to the individual process—e.g. the process of fixing the stock's issue price in the case of a capital

---

[100] ECJ of 28 June 2012, C-19/11 (not yet published), para. 46–49.
[101] Cf. Opinion of Advocate General Mengozzi, delivered on 21 March 2012, Case C-19/11, para. 106–107.
[102] ECJ of 28 June 2012, C-19/11 (not yet published), para. 50.

increase or fixing the share exchange ratio in merger cases—or to the process as a whole, i.e. the final result. The problem in these cases arises from the fact that in two-tier stock corporations, the relevant measures must first be decided on by the management, then by the supervisory board and then by the general shareholders' meeting in order to become effective. Assuming one referred to the moment of the management's decision, the prohibitions on insider dealings would apply at a very early stage. Whilst this would conform with the regulatory aim of ensuring market integrity, it would also require that the issuer discloses information at this early time, unless it had a legitimate interest not to do so.[103]

39   The CESR regarded both interpretations as admissible and recommended an examination of both the respective stage of the process individually and the overall process and the probability of it taking place.[104] In the German discussion, the prevailing understanding was originally that each process must be examined individually, determining whether the information is specific enough to have an effect on the price of securities, although the approval of the supervisory board or the general shareholders' meeting is still outstanding.[105] German literature did not pay much attention to this question, assuming that generally both approaches would lead to the same result:[106] even when referring to the process as a whole, one would have to determine whether this seemed sufficiently probable at the time of the management's decision or only with the supervisory board's consent. This question must also be answered if one refers to the individual process when determining the price relevance of the information. The Bundesgerichtshof (BGH, German Federal Court of Justice), however, came to a different result, and therefore presented the case to the ECJ for a preliminary ruling. The BGH reasoned that in a protracted set of facts, the individual steps that have taken place could also constitute "precise information" in the sense of the MAD and Article 1(1) Directive 2003/124/EC.[107] A preliminary ruling was necessary as the two approaches do not necessarily come to the same results.[108]

40   The ECJ answered the question in the light of the aims of the MAD:

"An interpretation of the terms 'set of circumstances' and 'event' which disregards the intermediate steps in a protracted process risks undermining the objectives [to protect the integrity of the European Union financial markets and to enhance investor confidence in those markets]. To rule out the possibility that information relating to such a step in a protracted process may be of a precise nature for the purposes of point 1 of Article 1 of Directive 2003/6 would remove the

[103] See § 19 para. 63–72.
[104] Cf. CESR, *Level 3—second set of CESR guidance and information on the common operation of the Directive to the market*, CESR/06–562b, July 2007, No. 1.6: "It is also important to note that, if the information concerns a process which occurs in stages, each stage of the process as well as the overall process could be information of a precise nature."
[105] Cf. H.D. Assmann, in: H.D. Assmann and U.H. Schneider (eds.), *Kommentar zum WpHG*, § 13 para. 28–29; A. Cahn, Der Konzern (2005), p. 5, 6; H. Fleischer, NZG (2007), p. 401, 405; BaFin, *Emittentenleitfaden 2009* (issuer guideline), p. 31; cf. BGH ZIP (2008), p. 639, 641; OLG Stuttgart, ZIP (2009), p. 962, 964–965. Dissenting opinion: C. Pawlik, in: A. Hirte and T.M.J. Möllers (eds.), *Kölner Kommentar zum WpHG*, § 13 para. 16; S. Kümpel and R. Veil, *Wertpapierhandelsgesetz*, Part 3 para. 25.
[106] Cf. H. Fleischer, NZG (2007), p. 401, 404.
[107] BGH ZIP (2011), p. 72.
[108] BGH ZIP (2011), p. 72, 74.

obligation, provided for in the first subparagraph of Article 6(1), to disclose that information, even if it were quite specific and even though the other elements making up inside information ... were also present. In such a situation, certain parties who possessed inside information could be in an advantageous position vis-à-vis other investors and be able to profit from that information, to the detriment of those who are unaware of it. The risk of such a situation occurring is all the greater given that it would be possible, in certain circumstances, to regard the outcome of a specific process as an intermediate step in another, larger process. Consequently, information relating to an intermediate step which is part of a protracted process may be precise information. It should be noted that this interpretation does not hold true only for those steps which have already come into existence or have already occurred, but also concerns ... steps which may reasonably be expected to come into existence or occur."[109]

41 This interpretation is convincing. The wording of the Directive 2003/124/EC permits both interpretations. Particular note must therefore be taken of the regulatory aim. The prohibitions on insider dealings constitute the centrepiece of the MAD and it was the explicit aim of the European legislature to effectively prevent insider dealings.[110] The understanding of the concept of inside information must therefore also focus on this aim of ensuring that the prohibitions are as effective as possible.[111] This aim is most easily attained if the individual steps are also regarded as possible inside information. It must then be determined from case to case whether an individual procedure—such as the decision to resign from the position of the chairman of the management as in the case *Daimler/Geltl*—is likely to have a significant effect on the prices of the financial instruments.[112] This understanding of the concept of inside information does not interfere with the supervisory board's autonomy to take part in decisions regarding the company's affairs, as the issuer can refrain from making this information public for exactly this reason.[113]

(b) Potential Influence on the Price of Financial Instruments

42 Directive 2003/124/EC further states that "information which, if it were made public, would be likely to have a significant effect on the prices of financial instruments or related financial instruments" should mean "information a reasonable investors would be likely to use as part of the basis of his investment decision".[114]

43 According to the CESR, the potential influence on the price of financial instruments is to be determined ex ante. The CESR has also commented on the difficult question as to the degree of probability required for a significant price effect to be expected. Whilst the mere possibility that a piece of information will have a significant price effect is not enough to trigger a disclosure obligation, a degree of probability close

---

[109] ECJ of 28 June 2012, C-19/11 (not yet published), para. 35–38.
[110] See para. 6.
[111] On the *effet utile* as a method of interpretation in European law see § 5 para. 55.
[112] Cf. L. Klöhn, NZG (2011), p. 266, 170.
[113] See § 19 para. 71.
[114] Art. 1(2) Directive 2003/124/EC.

Rüdiger Veil

to certainty can also not be required.[115] Quantitative criteria alone, such as specific thresholds (2 or 5%), are not a suitable means for determining the significance of price movement, due to the fact that the volatility of "blue-chip" securities of larger companies is typically less than that of smaller, less liquid stocks. The CESR names three criteria that should be taken into consideration when determining whether a significant effect is likely to occur: (i) whether the type of information is the same as information which has, in the past, had a significant effect on prices; (ii) whether pre-existing analyst research reports and opinions indicate that the type of information in question is price sensitive; and (iii) whether the company itself has ever treated similar events as inside information.[116]

(c) Reference to an Issuer of Financial Instruments

44   The concept of inside information further depends on the term "financial instrument", which relates either to the *issuer* of a financial instrument or to a *financial instrument* itself. Most circumstances relevant for price developments, such as profit drops, the discovery of a new oilfield or the resignation of the management board's chairman, refer to the issuer. As opposed to this, the case *Georgakis* dealt with information relating to an issuer's financial instruments.

45   *Facts (abridged):*[117] Georgakis and members of his family were major shareholders of Parnassos and Atemke, two stock corporations whose shares were admitted to trading on the Greek stock market. On recommendation of their financial consultant, Georgakis and further members of the family decided to support Parnassos' shares price when a decline in prices became apparent, by buying, selling and buying back Parnassos and Atemke shares amongst each other. The ECJ ruled that the decision of the members of the Georgakis group concerning the support of Parnassos shares established a common position within the group regarding the transactions to be effected between its members, with the aim of causing an artificial increase in the price of Parnassos' transferrable securities. For those who participated in its adoption, knowledge of the existence of such a decision and of its content constitutes inside information, being information of a precise nature which has not been made public and relates to transferrable securities.[118] Whilst the ECJ's decision was still based on the former Insider Directive, the Court's considerations can be applied analogously to the interpretation of the notion of inside information as defined in the MAD.[119]

46   The concept of financial instruments also needs to be put into more concrete terms.[120] The MAD lists the following instruments as financial instruments:

---

[115] CESR, *Level 3—second set of CESR guidance and information on the common operation of the Directive to the market*, CESR/06-562b, July 2007, No. 1.12.
[116] Ibid., No. 1.14.
[117] Cf. ECJ of 10 May 2007, Case C-391/04 [2007] ECR I-3741.
[118] Cf. ECJ of 10 May 2007, Case C-391/04 [2007] ECR I-3741, para. 33.
[119] Cf. D. Moalem and J. L. Hansen, 9 EBLR (2008), p. 949, 957 ff.
[120] On the concept of financial instruments in general see § 8 para. 4–9.

47   Financial instruments are: transferrable securities, especially shares,[121] units in collective investment undertakings, money-market instruments, financial-futures contracts, including equivalent cash-settled instruments, forward interest-rate agreements, interest-rate, currency and equity swaps, options to acquire or dispose of any instrument falling into these categories, including equivalent cash-settled instruments, especially options on currency and on interest rates, derivatives on commodities, any other instrument admitted to trading on a regulated market in a Member State or for which a request for admission to trading on such a market has been made.[122]

48   The Directive's definition of inside information also encompasses information which relates indirectly to issuers or financial instruments.[123] The CESR has compiled a list of examples of such information, which includes inter alia future publications of rating agencies' reports and antitrust authority's decisions concerning a listed company.[124]

(d)   Special Rules for Derivatives on Commodities and Front Running

49   In relation to derivatives on commodities the MAD contains special rules, stating that in these cases "inside information" should mean information of a precise nature which has not been made public, relating, directly or indirectly, to one or more such derivatives and which users of markets on which such derivatives are traded would expect to receive in accordance with accepted market practices on those markets.[125] This definition refers to information disclosed in accordance with legal or regulatory provisions, market rules, contracts or customs.[126] With regard to derivatives on pigs, for example, knowledge of an epidemic must be regarded as inside information. The same must be said of changes in the subsidy policy with regard to derivatives on potatoes.[127]

50   The European legislature further wanted to tackle the practice known as front running, i.e. stockbrokers executing orders on a security for their own account while taking advantage of advance knowledge of pending orders from its customers.[128] Therefore, the MAD provides that for persons charged with the execution of orders concerning financial instruments, "inside information" should also mean information conveyed by a client and related to the client's pending orders, which is of a precise nature, which relates directly or indirectly to one or more issuers of financial instruments or to one or more financial instruments, and which, if it were made public, would be likely to have a significant effect on the prices of those financial

---

[121] The original version of the Market Abuse Directive referred to the Council Directive 93/22/EEC of 10 May 1993 on investment services in the securities field with regard to the financial instruments to which it was to apply.

[122] Art. 1(3) MAD.

[123] The issuer is only required to disclose inside information that relates directly to himself. See § 15 para. 37.

[124] CESR, *Level 3—second set of CESR guidance and information on the common operation of the Directive to the market*, CESR/06-562b, July 2007, No. 1.16

[125] Art. 1(1) MAD.

[126] Art. 4 Directive 2004/72/EC.

[127] BaFin, *Emittentenleitfaden 2009* (issuer guideline), p. 36.

[128] Cf. Recital 19 MAD.

instruments or on the price of related derivative financial instruments.[129] Not every order of a client has a significant effect on the price. Front running must, however, be assumed, if the large volume of the client's order gave rise to an incentive for the person executing the order to acquire or dispose of the respective financial instruments, for example.[130]

3. Transposition in the Member States

(a) Overview

51   Not all Member States have transposed the European requirements one-to-one. The national German and Austrian law, for example, contain different elements in their definitions of inside information. Whilst the United Kingdom has adopted the regulatory provisions of the directive one-to-one, the same cannot be said of the criminal sanctions on insider dealings which are based on a different notion of information. French law also operates with two different terms. The criminal jurisprudence has developed a definition for information according to which the information must be of a precise nature, confidential, likely to affect the prices and privileged from an objective point of view. Whether or not the effect on the prices is significant is immaterial.[131] As opposed to that, the concept of information in administrative law[132] follows the definition under European law, requiring that the information significantly influences the prices of the financial instruments.

52   An examination of the legal situation in the Member States can help develop a uniform understanding of the concept of inside information for European law. The United Kingdom and Germany will hereafter serve as examples, as both states provide a wealth of material on this matter.[133] The cases decided on by the supervisory authorities and the courts show impressively how difficult it can be in each individual case to determine whether the respective information must be classed as inside information.

(b) Germany

53   In Germany, inside information is defined in § 13(1) WpHG. Remarkably, the German legislature has thereby not adopted the definition contained in the MAD. Pursuant to the definition in the WpHG, inside information is any concrete information about circumstances which are not public knowledge relating to one or more issuers of insider securities, or to the insider securities themselves, which, should it become publicly known, would be likely to have a significant effect on the stock exchange or market price of the insider security. By requiring *concrete information* the German legislature wanted to comply with Article 1(1) Directive 2003/124/EC, which demands that the information be specific enough to enable a conclusion on

---

[129] Art. 1(1) MAD.
[130] Cf. BaFin, *Emittentenleitfaden 2009* (issuer guideline), p. 34.
[131] Cf. J. Lasserre Capdeville, Bull. Joly Bourse (2009), p. 69, 71.
[132] Cf. Art. 621-1 ff. RG AMF.
[133] On cases in the French legal practice of courts and supervisory authorities cf. R. Veil and P. Koch, *Französisches Kapitalmarktrecht*, p. 38 ff.

the possible effect of that set of circumstances or event with respect to the prices of financial instruments or related derivative financial instruments.

54   Circumstances can above all be defined as facts, i.e. past or present external procedures or situations that can be proven.[134]

55   Whether knowledge of internal plans and intentions of a person can also be classed as inside information was discussed controversially at length, being of relevance especially for so-called cases of scalping.[135] The BGH ruled that the intention to later sell the recommended securities could not be classed as inside information.[136] The concept of information imperatively requires a connection to a third party. A person cannot therefore be regarded as informed about his own intentions.[137]

56   § 13(1) WpHG further extends the term "circumstances" to cases which may reasonably be expected to come into existence in the future, thus allowing certain future developments, such as expected profit losses or mergers, also to be classed as inside information.[138] In *Daimler/Geltl* the court had to decide under which conditions a case can reasonably be expected to come into existence in the future.

57   *Facts (abridged):*[139] In its meeting on 28 July 2005 the supervisory board of DaimlerChrysler AG decided at 9.50 a.m. that the CEO Schrempp should retire from the board as of 31 December 2005 and be replaced by board member Zetsche. A few minutes later DaimlerChrysler AG published an ad hoc notification with this information and its share price rose considerably. Schrempp had already discussed his retirement with the chairman of the supervisory board at length on 17 May 2005 and informed two other members of the supervisory board on 1 June 2005. DaimlerChrysler's communication manager and the executive secretary, who had been informed on 6 July 2005, had been working on the press release, an external statement and a letter to the employees since 10 July 2005. On 27 July 2005 the presiding committee of the supervisory board had decided to recommend a decision on the early retirement of Schrempp and his successor to the supervisory board the following day. Investors who had disposed of shares before the ad hoc information was published claimed a total of €5,500,000 in damages from DaimlerChrysler AG for these events.

58   In the test case—a special form of class action for investors in Germany—the courts had to deal with the concept of inside information.[140] The BGH first ruled that the intent or deliberation of a CEO to retire early from his position by mutual agreement with the supervisory board is price-sensitive information and could thus be subject to the provisions on inside information.[141] Until the supervisory board has agreed to the retirement, the information will, however, only be classifiable as inside information if the board's consent is sufficiently probable. According to the BGH,

---

[134] Cf. H.D. Assmann, in: H.D. Assmann and U.H. Schneider (eds.), *Kommentar zum WpHG*, § 13 para. 33a; E. Schwark, in: E. Schwark, and D. Zimmer (eds.), *Kapitalmarktrechts-Kommentar*, § 13 WpHG para. 29.
[135] See § 14 para. 43.
[136] On *scalping* as a form of market manipulation see § 14 para. 45.
[137] BGHSt 48 (2003), p. 373.
[138] See above para. 35–41.
[139] Cf. OLG Stuttgart, ZIP (2009), p. 962 and BGH ZIP (2008), p. 639.
[140] On further aspects of the obligation to disclose inside information see § 19 para. 85, 89, 97.
[141] Cf. H. Fleischer, NZG (2007), p. 401, 402.

such an overwhelming probability can be assumed if the chances of the supervisory board consenting are over 50%.[142] This interpretation of national law coincides with the CESR's understanding of the respective European provisions, as laid down in its "Guidelines",[143] and also fulfils the provision's aim of preventing insider dealings.

59   The Oberlandesgericht (OLG, higher regional court) Stuttgart, again presented with the case after the decision of the BGH,[144] ruled that the supervisory board's consent became sufficiently probable on 27 July 2005 when a committee of the supervisory board came to a unanimous agreement.[145] However, the plaintiffs appealed the decision and argued this interpretation did not comply with the regulatory aims of the directive.[146] The case was therefore submitted to the BGH a second time, the BGH now coming to a different conclusion and therefore presenting the question, whether in a multi-stage process an intermediate step can be classed as inside information, to the ECJ for a preliminary ruling.[147] The ECJ confirmed this, as described above (para.40). In the case *Daimler/Geltl* inside information could thus already have existed on 17 July 2005. Whether this was actually the case depends on the possible effect of the information on the prices of the financial instruments.

60   German law contains one further important detail regarding the concept of inside information, this being the likelihood of having a significant effect on the stock exchange or market price of the insider security. Such a likelihood is deemed to exist if a reasonable investor took the information into account for his investment decisions (§ 13(1) WpHG). This provision once again differs from the European requirements which, in Article 1 Directive 2003/124/EC, refer to the question of whether a "reasonable investor would be likely to use [the information] as part of the basis of his investment decision".

61   The concept of a reasonable investor is meanwhile common throughout all capital markets law.[148] In rules on insider dealings the reasonable investor is the key element in determining whether information is price sensitive, making it especially important to define the term clearly. The jurisprudence on prospectus liability gives a good general first idea on the interpretation:[149] whether information contained in a prospectus can be regarded as essential depends on whether this information is significant for the investment decision of a reasonable reader of the prospectus.[150] This definition has given rise to the question of whether a reasonable investor is inexperienced or professional. The courts have adopted a compromise by assuming that a reasonable investor knows the conditions and practices of the capital markets and can understand balance sheets, without necessarily being familiar with the details.[151] This definition can be conferred to the

---

[142] BGH ZIP (2008), p. 639 key sentence 2.
[143] See above para. 36.
[144] The BGH reversed the OLG Stuttgart's decision, ZIP (2007), p. 481 and referred the case back to a different civil division of the court in Stuttgart.
[145] OLG Stuttgart ZIP (2009), p. 962, 966 ff.
[146] See above para. 40–42.
[147] BGH ZIP (2011), p. 72.
[148] Cf. R. Veil, ZBB (2006), p. 162, 167.
[149] See § 17 para. 56–57.
[150] Cf. OLG Frankfurt, AG (2005), p. 851, 852.
[151] Cf. on prospectus law BGH NJW (1982), p. 2823, 2824; OLG Frankfurt, AG (2005), p. 851, 852.

secondary markets: a reasonable investor is an investor who acts rationally, is adequately informed, observant and critical.

62   Ultimately, it will be a question of each individual case whether certain information may have a significant effect on the prices of financial instruments. The BaFin refers to the fact whether the respective information will encourage an investor to acquire or dispose of shares and whether this appears profitable to a reasonable investor.[152]

63   In a first step the BaFin examines, ex ante, whether the event itself could potentially be price sensitive in a significant way according to general experience. This must be assumed, for example, for an important cooperation, the acquisition or disposal of major holdings and if the issuer has liquidity problems. In a second step the BaFin takes into account the existing or foreseeable specific aspects of the case at hand that may reduce or increase price sensitivity, paying special attention to the question whether the respective information was already known and taken into consideration on the capital market. Investors will, for example, often already have taken the issuer's results into account for their investment or divestment. Information that is already contained in the share price will, however, no longer newly influence the prices of financial instruments significantly. The effects of information must in a third step also be considered in the light of the issuer's overall activity, the reliability of the information's source and other market variables, such as the volatility of the market, especially with regard to comparable financial instruments of other issuers in the same industry.

64   *Example:* The OLG Düsseldorf[153] had to determine whether the IKB-Bank had been affected by the subprime mortgage crisis in the United States due to its investment history. The OLG Düsseldorf classed the information on subprime-based instruments held by the IKB-Bank and its special-purpose entities as specific information in the sense of § 13(1) WpHG. It ruled, however, that the information was not able to influence significantly the IKB-Bank's share price on 27 July 2007. According to the predominant understanding at the time, subprime-based instruments in the company's portfolio were not particularly significant for investment decisions, the ratings received by rating agencies being deemed far more relevant in determining credit risks.[154]

(c)   United Kingdom

65   The provisions on insider dealings are based on two pillars in the United Kingdom:[155] on criminal provisions and on the prohibitions under supervisory law. Both regimes have their own definitions of inside information.[156] The FSA's final notices and the FSA Tribunal's[157] decisions play an important role in the development of the English provisions on insider dealings, based on an understanding of inside information (RINGA, i.e. relevant information not generally available, and FSA Principles) that

---

[152] Cf. BaFin, *Emittentenleitfaden* 2009 (issuer guideline), p. 33–34.

[153] OLG Düsseldorf, AG (2011), p. 31, 34.

[154] OLG Düsseldorf, AG (2011), p. 31, 35; see also the unpublished ruling of the OLG Düsseldorf of 27 January 2010, I-15 U 230/09 (available at: www.juris.de), and the respective appeal case BGH ZIP (2012), p. 318–326.

[155] See above para. 27–31.

[156] For more details see R. Veil and M. Wundenberg, *Englisches Kapitalmarktrecht*, p. 49 ff.

[157] The FSA Tribunal is the first instance of appeal against decisions of the FSA.

differs from the European concept.[158] At the same time the leading case of *Arif Mohammed*[159] illustrates problems which can also arise under the MAD's definition of inside information.

66 *Facts (abridged):* While working as an auditor, Mohammed obtained knowledge of the fact that an industrial enterprise which was being audited by his auditing company was planning to sell the electronics sector of the company. When this information was later disclosed, the shares prices rose about 19%. Mohammed, who had bought shares on the ground of this information, justified himself with the fact that before the notification of the sale rumours of this had already existed on the market and the information had therefore no longer been inside information. The Tribunal did not share this point of view, arguing that one must distinguish between information that has been made public and is sufficiently precise and information that exists only as a rumour.[160] Furthermore, the progression of the share prices after the disclosure of the information indicated that the rumours had not yet influenced the share prices and could therefore not be regarded as publicly available. The Tribunal did not support Mohammed in the point that the decision to sell had not been specific and precise information,[161] as he had not had any information on the modalities of the sale.[162] The Tribunal regarded an information as sufficiently precise once the insider has more or less certain knowledge of the future sale of the sector, independent of the fact whether the details of the transaction were known to him.

67 The CESR has also stated in its Guidelines that it does not regard rumours to be sufficient to constitute inside information: "CESR considers that in determining whether a set of circumstances exists or an event has occurred, a key issue is whether there is firm and objective evidence for this as opposed to rumours or speculation."[163] The case of *Mohammed*, however, shows that it is difficult to determine whether information is precise in each individual case. In *Tivox AB* the highest Swedish court came to a different conclusion although the case itself was similar:[164]

68 *Facts (abridged):* After a discussion with an auditor of the company, who had participated in the board of directors' meeting and therefore knew of the withdrawal of a credit line for a subsidiary company, a shareholder disposed of his shares in the parent company. The appellate court ruled that the vague recommendation to

---

[158] An overview of case material can be found in: J. Bagge et al. (eds.), *Financial Services Decisions: FSA Notices and FSMT Decisions*, (2007) (analysis of the FSA Notices and Tribunal decisions made before December 2006); C. Band and M. Hopper, JIBLR (2007), p. 231. Cf. also p. K. Stajkouras, 9 EBLR (2008), p. 775. Criminal case material is scarce. Cf. recently *Regina v. Asif Nazir Butt* (2006), EWCA Crim p. 137.

[159] *Arif Mohammed v. Financial Services Authority* (2005), The Financial Services Markets Tribunal para 12. This is the first decision of the Tribunal regarding sec. 118 FSMA, which was, however, still based on the old insider rules which applied the "relevant information not generally available test" now contained—as described above—in sec. 118(4) FSMA as a catch-all clause.

[160] Cf. *James Parker v. Financial Services Authority* (2006), The Financial Services Markets Tribunal para 37.

[161] So far the term "relevant information" was defined in MAR 1.4.9. of the FSA Handbooks as "specific and precise information". Due to the fact that the MAD also requires precise information, the Tribunal's considerations will stay relevant under the new legal situation.

[162] Para. 73 ff. of the judgment.

[163] CESR, *Level 3—second set of CESR guidance and information on the common operation of the Directive to the market*, CESR/06-562b, July 2007, No. 1.5.

[164] Cf. R. Veil and F. Walla, *Schwedisches Kapitalmarktrecht*, p. 44–45.

---

sell, without more information on the circumstances, was not sufficiently precise to be regarded as inside information.

69   Irrespective of the problem of inside information, an issuer must decide on how to react to rumours. CESR has issued a statement on this question, recommending a "no comment-policy"[165] and stating that, in general, as opposed to in exceptional circumstances, issuers are under no obligation to respond to speculation or market rumours which are without substance.[166]

IV. Prohibitions

1.   Overview

70   The MAD obliges EU Member States to introduce provisions according to which recommending or inducing another person, on the basis of inside information, to acquire or dispose of financial instruments to which the information relates, is prohibited.[167] The directive does not, however, describe how breaches of this rule are to be sanctioned. It is therefore not surprising that Member States have developed different sanctioning regimes, some opting for criminal prohibitions whilst others developed administrative sanctions and others again combined both possibilities, in most cases subjecting them to very different prerequisites. Some Member States have left their existing criminal prohibitions unaltered even after the enactment of the Insider Directive, only adapting the supervisory provisions to the requirements of European law.[168] To go into more detail regarding the national implementations would go beyond the scope of this book. Rather, the supervisory rules included in the MAD itself will be examined, the ECJ having defined the requirements that have to be met by the Member States when implementing these provisions in a number of cases.

2.   Prohibition of the Acquisition or Disposal of Financial Instruments

(a)   European Requirements

71   Member States must prohibit any person who possesses inside information from using that information by acquiring or disposing of, or by trying to acquire or dispose of, financial instruments to which that information relates for his own account or for the account of a third party, either directly or indirectly.[169] This prohibition is to ensure the integrity of the financial markets and enhance investor confidence, at the same time ensuring more equality between contracting parties in market transactions.[170]

---

[165] CESR, *Level 3—third set of CESR guidance and information on the common operation of the Directive to the market,* CESR/09-219, May 2007, No. 4.1.

[166] See § 19 para. 93.

[167] Art. 3(b) MAD.

[168] See above para. 15–31.

[169] Art. 2(1) MAD.

[170] Cf. ECJ of 10 May 2007, Case C-391/04 [2007] ECR I-3741 on Art. 2 of the former Insider Directive 89/592/EEC.

72   In the above-mentioned case *Georgakis*[171] all contracting parties of the transactions had access to the same information and no one had been able to benefit from having more information than the others. The ECJ therefore correctly ruled that Georgakis and the members of his family had not breached the rules prohibiting the use of inside information by acquiring or disposing of financial instruments.[172]

(b)   Legal Practice in the Member States

73   Some Member States have transposed the European provisions prohibiting the use of inside information by acquiring or disposing of financial instruments one-to-one, whereas others have developed deviating prohibitions, especially regarding the aspect of the use of inside information. English law, for example, requires causation ("on the basis of"),[173] whereas the German WpHG prohibits "making use of inside information to acquire or dispose of insider securities for own account or for the account or on behalf of a third party",[174] and Austrian law speaks of "taking advantage of inside information".[175]

74   The term "making use of" was chosen by the German legislature in order to express that a purposeful behaviour of the offender, such as the intent of making profits, is not necessary under German law.[176] At the same time, however, the term implies that there must—at least additionally to other factors—be a chain of causation between the acquisition or disposal of the financial instruments to the inside information.[177] This can become relevant if the target company passes on inside information to an investor in the course of a due diligence proceeding.

75   If the investor is only strengthened in his decision to acquire a financial instrument of the respective company a breach of the prohibition of acquisitions of financial instruments cannot be assumed under German law.[178] As opposed to this, the rules prohibiting the use of inside information are breached if the investor makes additional purchases on the stock market.[179]

76   A further question is whether an investor makes use of inside information when it gains knowledge of the inside fact during an OTC acquisition of share packages and thereupon decides to acquire them. In Germany, this is negated, even if the investor took the information into account when assessing the price.[180] The functioning of the market is only affected if the inside information puts individual market participants at an advantage compared to others. OTC acquisi-

---

[171] See above para. 45.

[172] The aim was to fix artificially and simultaneously the prices of certain securities. This constitutes a type of market manipulation as prohibited by the MAD. See § 14 para. 25–30.

[173] Cf. R. Veil and M. Wundenberg, *Englisches Kapitalmarktrecht*, p. 63–64.

[174] Cf. § 14(1) No. 1 WpHG.

[175] Cf. Art. 48b(1) BörseG.

[176] Cf. Begr. RegE Anlegerschutzverbesserungsgesetz, BT-Drucks. 15/3174, p. 34 (explanatory notes).

[177] Cf. P. Mennicke, in: A. Fuchs (ed.), *Kommentar zum WpHG*, § 14 para. 52, 55.

[178] Cf. H.D. Assmann, in: H.D. Assmann and U.H. Schneider (eds.), *Kommentar zum WpHG*, § 14 para. 45; P. Mennicke, in: A. Fuchs (ed.), *Kommentar zum WpHG*, § 14 para. 75; from a European perspective M. Kemnitz, *Due Diligence und neues Insiderrecht*, p. 67 ff.

[179] Cf. BaFin, *Emittentenleitfaden 2009* (issuer guideline), p. 37–38; H. Diekmann and M. Sustmann, NZG (2004), p. 929, 931; on Austrian law S. Kalss, M. Oppitz and J. Zollner, *Kapitalmarktrecht*, § 20 para. 27; dissenting opinion: P. Mennicke, in: A. Fuchs (ed.), *Kommentar zum WpHG*, § 14 para. 75.

[180] Cf. BaFin, *Emittentenleitfaden 2009* (issuer guideline), p. 37–38.

tions are, however, restricted to a specific package, for which the buyer and seller will have the same amount of information once the due diligence procedure has taken place. Such an acquisition is thus not subject to the prohibition even if the investor obtained inside information in the course of it.

77   The prohibition of the use of inside information plays an important role in French mergers and acquisitions (M&A) transactions. In 2003 the supervisory authority published a recommendation (*procédures dites de data room*)[181] with "rules" which were to ensure an equal access for all investors to information and prevent insider dealings (not, however, the disclosure of inside information to others).

78   According to the recommendation, a due diligence is only permitted with regard to the acquisition of a major holding. Investor and issuer must furthermore conclude a non-disclosure agreement. During the due diligence the parties are not permitted to trade with the issuer's financial instruments and must not pass on inside information to third parties. The investor must submit a letter of intent, in order to prove it is serious about the acquisition and to present his financing options. The information that is disclosed in the course of the due diligence must only be such as is necessary to confirm the investor's acquisition interest and to put the details of the transaction into more concrete terms. The information is not to be decisive for the investor's decision to invest in the company. If the investor does not make an offer pursuant to the due diligence, the issuer must disclose all the relevant and potentially price-sensitive information from the due diligence.

(c)   The ECJ's Interpretation and Conclusions for the Legal Practice in the Member States

79   Some of the Member States' rules regarding the prohibition of acquisitions or disposals of financial instruments may need to be revised due to the ECJ's ruling in *Spector*[182] in which the court examined the prohibition closely and gave concrete details on how the Member States' national rules are to be interpreted.

80   *Facts (abridged):* Spector, a listed company under Belgian law, offered a programme via which employees could acquire shares in the company, which Spector planned to acquire on the market. On 21 May 2003 Spector informed Euronext Brussels of its plan to acquire a certain number of its own shares. On 11 and 13 August 2003 board member van Raemdonck acquired 19,773 shares at an average price of €9.97 for Spector. The price for exercising the acquisition option laid at €10.45. Subsequently Spector disclosed the company's business results and company policy, leading to a price increase up to €12.50. The Belgian supervisory authority (CBFA) imposed fines of €80,000 and €20,000 on Spector and van Raemdonck, respectively, for the acquisition of the shares. The court, having to decide on the legality of the fines, submitted a number of questions to

---

[181] Cf. COB, Publication de la recommandation no 2003-01 relative à la transmission d'informations privilégiées préalablement à des opérations de cessions de participations significatives dans des sociétés cotées sur un marché réglementé.

[182] ECJ of 23 December 2009, Case C-45/08 (*Spector*) [2009] ECR I-12073.

the ECJ for a preliminary ruling, especially regarding the requirement of making use of inside information.

81   The ECJ ruled that the fact that a *primary insider* "in *possession* of *inside information*, *acquires* or *disposes of*, or tries to acquire or dispose of, for his own account or for the account of a third party, either directly or indirectly, the *financial instruments* to which that information relates *implies* that that *person* has '*used that information*' within the *meaning of that provision*, but without prejudice to the rights of the defence and, in particular, to the right to be able to rebut that presumption. The question whether that person has infringed the prohibition on insider dealing must be analysed in the light of the purpose of that directive, which is to protect the integrity of the financial markets and to enhance investor confidence, which is based, in particular, on the assurance that investors will be placed on an equal footing and protected from the misuse of inside information."[183]

82   The ECJ lists a number of examples for which the assumption will not apply—the most practically relevant being the constellations of a public takeover bid and a merger proposal. In these cases the use of the inside information "should not in itself be deemed to constitute insider dealing. The operation whereby an undertaking, after obtaining inside information concerning a specific company, subsequently launches a public take-over bid for the capital of that company at a rate higher than the market rate cannot, in principle, be regarded as prohibited insider dealing since it does not infringe on the interests protected by that directive."[184]

83   The ECJ did not refer to the question whether the prohibition as laid down in the MAD requires causation of the inside information for the offender's behaviour. Therefore the most important cases regarding M&A transactions do not have to be interpreted differently in the light of the *Spector* decision.[185] It also remains as yet unclear what the ECJ's description of the prohibition as "objective", i.e. without any requirements regarding wilfulness or negligence, means for the Member States.[186] So far this has constituted an additional element in the prohibition in all national laws, which had to be proven by the supervisory authorities or courts with regard to the offender. It is not to be assumed that the ECJ's interpretation intended to make this proof superfluous.

3.   Disclosure to another Person

(a)   European Requirements

84   The Member States must prohibit any person with inside information from disclosing inside information to any other person unless such disclosure is made in the normal course of the exercise of his employment, profession or duties.[187] This rule was refined by the ECJ's decision in *Grøngaard/Bang*.[188] Whilst the decision relates

---

[183] Ibid., para. 62.
[184] Ibid., para. 59.
[185] Similarly S. Schulz, ZIP (2010), p. 609, 611 and C. Cascante and A. Bingel, NZG (2010), p. 61, 162.
[186] Cf. M. Nietsch, ZHR 174 (2010), p. 557, 567.
[187] Art. 3(a) MAD.
[188] ECJ of 22 November 2005, Case C-384/02 [2005] ECR I-9939.

to the former Insider Directive, the court's interpretation is also applicable to the identical provision in the MAD.[189]

85   *Facts (abridged):* Bang was chairman of the Finansforbund, a trade union in the financial sector. Grøngaard, who had been appointed by the employees, was a member of the administrative board of the company RealDanmark, a relatively large listed financial institution. Subsequent to an extraordinary administrative board meeting of RealDanmark, Grøngaard passed on information to Bang on 28 August 2000, regarding the planned merger negotiations with the Danske Bank, another large Danish financial institution. Between 28 August and 4 September 2009 Bang consulted with his two deputies and one of his employees in the administration of the Finansforbund and passed the information he had received from Grøngaard on to them. On 2 October 2000 the merger between RealDanmark and Danske Bank was made public and RealDanmark's shares price rose by 65%. Grøngaard and Bang were criminally prosecuted under section 36(1) of the Danish Securities Trading Act (vædipapirhandelslov) for disclosing inside information. The Københavns Byret decided to stay the proceedings and made reference to the ECJ for a preliminary ruling.

86   The ECJ examined in particular the fact that the prohibition of disclosing inside information does not apply unconditionally. The provision is not applicable if the insider passes on the information in the normal course of the exercise of his employment, profession or duties. According to the ECJ, this exemption clause must be treated restrictively, and can only be justified if there is a close link between the disclosure and the exercise of the employment, profession or duties and the disclosure of such information is strictly necessary for the exercise thereof.[190] Particular care is required with regard to sensitive information. In these cases, the disclosure is manifestly capable of significantly affecting the price of the transferrable securities in question. The ECJ stated that inside information relating to a merger between two companies quoted on the stock exchange is an example of such particularly sensitive information.

87   Whether the exception from the prohibition can be assumed must, according to the ECJ, be determined by the national court in the light of the applicable national laws. What is to be regarded as coming within the normal ambit of the exercise of an employment, profession or duties, depends to a large extent, in the absence of harmonisation in that respect, on the rules governing those questions in the various national legal systems.[191] In particular, the underlying legal concepts in national labour and company law must therefore be taken into account in order to determine whether a member of the board of directors or the supervisory board was permitted to pass on inside information on the company to a major shareholder or whether a representative of the employees on the supervisory board may pass on information to "his" union.

---

[189] R. Sethe, ZBB (2006), p. 243, 250.
[190] ECJ of 22 November 2005, Case C-384/02 [2005] ECR I-9939. The High Court of Denmark ruled that a member nominated by the employees has the possibility to discuss a merger that would have a considerable effect on the employees with the chair of his union. The defendants in *Grøngaard/Bang* were therefore exempted from liability. Cf. Højesteret Kopenhagen, ZIP (2009), p. 1526, 1527.
[191] ECJ of 22 November 2005, Case C-384/02 [2005] ECR I-9939, para. 39–40.

88   Under consideration of these facts, as part of its examination, "a national court must, in the light of the applicable national rules, take particular account of: the fact that that exception to the prohibition of disclosure of inside information must be interpreted strictly, the fact that each additional disclosure is liable to increase the risk of that information being exploited for a purpose contrary to Directive 89/592, and the sensitivity of the inside information".[192]

(b)   Legal Practice in the Member States

89   The Member States have implemented the prohibition into their national laws one-to-one or following the wording of the Directive very closely. In the United Kingdom, for example, the supervisory prohibition to disclose inside information does not apply if it takes place "in the proper course of the exercise of [the insider's] employment, profession or duties".[193] The FSA Handbook contains extensive explanations and interpretational details on this exemption. It is of particular importance to determine whether the insider had the obligation to maintain confidentiality. The FSA's further interpretational remarks all refer to specific cases, such as the disclosure of information to support a hostile takeover bid.[194] As opposed to this, the interpretational rules developed by the ECJ do not seem to be taken into account in Britain's supervisory practice.

90   France introduced a prohibition to disclose inside information, also called *délit de dîner en ville*, in 1989,[195] which meanwhile applies equally to primary, secondary and tertiary insiders. It plays an unimportant role in legal practice, difficulties in proving the offence often preventing a conviction under criminal law.[196]

91   Contrary to this, the supervisory practice in Germany has dealt extensively with the prohibition to disclose inside information. In the BaFin's opinion the disclosure of information in a due diligence procedure cannot be regarded as prohibited if it was to ensure a specific acquisition of a share package or control. Especially in cases of an acquisition of major holdings the economic interests of both issuer and investor would justify a stronger transparency than for the usual acquisition of shares on stock markets. Therefore, the disclosure of information in these cases would be permitted in the course of due diligence proceedings.[197] The exact cases to which this rule applies as yet remain unclear. Based on a consideration of the statutory notification thresholds,[198] German legal literature suggests shareholdings of between 2 and 5%.[199]

92   This interpretation of the prohibition to disclose inside information does not appear entirely convincing, as the BaFin does not explain why its interpretation deviates

---

[192] Cf. ibid., para. 48.

[193] Sec. 118(3) FSMA.

[194] Cf. R. Veil and M. Wundenberg, *Englisches Kapitalmarktrecht*, p. 65.

[195] Art. L. 465-1 C. mon. fin. In the version of the statute no. 89-531 of 2 August 1989.

[196] Cf. J. Lasserre Capdeville, Bull. Joly Bourse (Jan/Feb 2009), p. 69, 75: one single judgment since 1989 (acquittal).

[197] BaFin, *Emittentenleitfaden 2009* (issuer guideline), p. 41.

[198] The thresholds commence at 5% of the voting rights under the TD II. Some Member States, e.g. Germany, Italy and the UK, however, have introduced lower thresholds, starting at 2 or 3%. On this see § 20 para. 20–26.

[199] For 5% T. O. Brandi and R. Süßmann, AG (2004), p. 642, 648; for 2% in cases of a high market capitalisation K. Hasselbach, NZG (2004), p. 1087, 1089.

from the stricter understanding of the prohibition purported by the ECJ.[200] The ECJ requires a case-to-case examination regarding the sensitivity of the information. Even in cases of 20% shareholdings the board of directors of the issuer must ask itself whether the disclosure of the information to the investor is really necessary.

93 Certain cases, in which the disclosure will generally be permitted, however, still exist. They include the possibility for members of the supervisory board to disclose inside information to a major shareholder outside the general shareholders' meeting if this may heighten the chances of a certain measure, such as a capital increase, being adopted by the shareholders' meeting. As opposed to this, the members of the supervisory board are not permitted to disclose inside information regarding upcoming business and personnel policy measures to individual shareholders. These cases may again have to be treated differently when the issuer is a subsidiary of a parent company. The members of the supervisory board must in these constellations take the controlling company's interest in a unified management of the whole group into consideration. The disclosure of inside information to the controlling company can therefore be permissible.[201]

4. Recommending or Inducing

(a) European Requirements

94 The Member States must prohibit any person with inside information from recommending or inducing another person, on the basis of inside information, to acquire or dispose of financial instruments to which that information relates.[202] This prohibition is a catch-all clause, to which the ECJ has not yet referred to.

(b) Legal Practice in the Member States

95 The Member States have all transposed the prohibition into their national laws. In Germany, for example, it is prohibited "to recommend, on the basis of inside information, that a third party acquire or dispose of insider securities, or to otherwise induce a third party to do so".[203] The prohibition to recommend or induce has the aim of preventing an insider from using a third party or acting collusively with him, in order to circumvent the prohibitions applying to the insider dealing himself by recommending the deals to the third party.[204] "Induce" is defined as any means of influencing the will of a third party.[205] It is sufficient if the insider suggests a specific transaction to a third party, irrespective of whether or not it explicitly discloses his inside information. The prohibition requires causation between the insider's information and the offender's recommendation, i.e. the offender must recommend the acquisition or disposal of shares based on his inside knowledge.

---

[200] Seen critically by G. Bachmann, ZHR 172 (2008), p. 597, 623.
[201] Cf. B. Singhof, ZGR (2001), p. 146, 162; R. Veil, ZHR 172 (2008), p. 239, 268.
[202] Art. 3(b) MAD.
[203] Cf. § 14(1) No. 3 WpHG.
[204] Cf. Begr. RegE Zweites Finanzmarktförderungsgesetz, BT-Drucks. 12/6679, p. 47–48 (explanatory notes).
[205] Cf. Begr. RegE Anlegerschutzverbesserungsgesetz, BT-Drucks. 15/3174, p. 34 (explanatory notes).

5. Exemptions

96 The European legislature admits that in certain circumstances and for economic reasons the stabilisation of financial instruments or trading in own shares in buy-back programmes can be legitimate, and therefore should not in itself be regarded as market abuse.[206] The prohibition should thus not apply to trading in own shares in "buy-back" programmes or to the stabilisation of a financial instrument provided such trading is carried out in accordance with the implementing measures the European Commission enacted regarding the MAD.[207] The CESR has published "Guidance and Information" on this matter.[208]

97 The regulation[209] states that in order to benefit from the exemption, the buy-back programme must comply with the regulation's provisions (Article 4) and with certain conditions for trading (Article 5). A buy-back may take place for three reasons. Firstly, the aim can be to reduce the authorised capital in value or number, which can mainly—as in *Spector*—be achieved through the acquisition of the company's own shares. Secondly, the aim of a buy-back can be to fulfil liabilities resulting from debt financial instruments, such as convertible bonds, exchangeable into equity instruments. Thirdly, a buy-back of shares may be permissible to fulfil liabilities resulting from employee share option programmes or other allocations of shares of the issuer or of an associate company to employees. Stock option programmes for members of the management do not fall within the scope of the regulation. Due to the fact that members of the management have access to inside information, in these cases the danger of an abuse thereof exists. A further requirement for the exemption is that the issuer abides by certain rules during its participation in the buy-back programme, such as refraining from selling its own shares.

98 Similar restrictions apply to any measure stabilising the prices, i.e. "any purchase or offer to purchase relevant securities, or any transaction in associated instruments equivalent thereto by investment firms or credit institutions, which is undertaken in the context of a significant distribution of such relevant securities exclusively for supporting the market price of these relevant securities for a predetermined period of time, due to a selling pressure in such securities".[210] In these cases the insider prohibitions apply, unless stabilisation is carried out only for a limited time (Article 8) and is adequately public (Article 9).

---

[206] Cf. Recital 33 MAD; see also S. Gilotta, 13 EBOR (2012), p. 45, 84–85.

[207] Cf. Art. 8 MAD.

[208] CESR, *Level 3—Third Set of CESR Guidance and Information on the Common Operation of the Directive to the Market*, CESR/09-219, May 2009; cf. also A. Bingel, *Rechtliche Grenzen der Kursstabilisierung nach Aktienplatzierungen* (2007).

[209] Commission Regulation (EC) No. 2273/2003 of 22 December 2003 implementing Directive 2003/6/EC of the European Parliament and of the Council as regards exemptions for buy-back programmes and stabilisation of financial instruments, OJ L336, 23 December 2003, p. 33.

[210] Cf. Art. 2(7) Regulation (EC) No. 2273/2003.

V. Supervision

1. European Requirements

(a) Functions and Powers of the Authorities

99 The application of the provisions enacted for the implementation of the MAD by the legal practice (issuers, investors and intermediaries) must be supervised by the national authorities.[211] The European legislature regarded it as imperative that a single competent authority of an administrative nature, guaranteeing its independence of economic actors and avoiding conflicts of interest, be designated in each Member State to supervise compliance with the provisions.[212] It further regarded a common minimum set of effective tools and powers for the competent authority of each Member State necessary in order to guarantee supervisory effectiveness.[213] The national authorities' powers had differed greatly between the Member States,[214] which is why the European legislature approached this aspect in such detail.

100 In Article 12, the MAD lays down, abstractly, that the competent authorities must be given all supervisory and investigatory powers that are necessary for the exercise of their functions,[215] including at least the right to (a) have access to any document in any form whatsoever, and to receive a copy of it; (b) demand information from any person, including those who are successively involved in the transmission of orders or conduct of the operations concerned, as well as their principals, and if necessary, to summon and hear any such person; (c) carry out on-site inspections; (d) require existing telephone and existing data traffic records; (e) require the cessation of any practice that is contrary to the provisions adopted in the implementation of this Directive; (f) suspend trading of the financial instruments concerned; (g) request the freezing and/or sequestration of assets; and (h) request temporary prohibition of professional activity.[216] The Member States must further ensure that an appeal may be brought before a court against the decisions taken by the competent authority.[217]

101 Additionally the MAD provides detailed rules on cooperation required between the Member States' supervisory authorities, obliging them render assistance to competent authorities of other Member States,[218] especially by exchanging information and cooperating in investigation activities.[219]

(b) Insider Lists

102 The Member States must ensure that issuers, or persons acting on their behalf or for their account, draw up a list of those persons working for them, under a contract

---

[211] Art. 11 MAD.
[212] Cf. Recital 36 MAD.
[213] Cf. Recital 37 MAD.
[214] See § 1 para. 21.
[215] Art. 12(1) MAD.
[216] Art. 12(2)(a)–(h) MAD.
[217] Art. 15 MAD.
[218] Art. 16(1) MAD.
[219] Art. 16(1)–(4) MAD.

Rüdiger Veil

of employment or otherwise, who have access to inside information.[220] These are typically members of the management and their employees as well as persons with access to the data processing. Persons with an advisory function, such as lawyers, accountants, auditors and the members of rating agencies, also fall within the scope of this provision.[221] It may also apply to the members of an agency responsible for the translation of ad hoc notifications or drafts of contracts.[222]

103 The European Commission put these requirements into more concrete terms: pursuant to Directive 2004/72/EC, lists of insiders must at least state the identity of any person having access to inside information, the reason why any such person is on the list and the date on which the list of insiders was created and updated.[223]

104 Issuers and persons acting on their behalf or for their account must regularly update this list and transmit it to the competent authority whenever the latter requests it.[224] There is thus no obligation for an issuer spontaneously to provide its insider list to the competent authority or inform it of updates to the list if the competent authority has not requested it from the issuer.[225] The lists of insiders must be promptly updated whenever there is a change in the reason why any person is already on the list, whenever any new person has to be added to the list or if any person already on the list no longer has access to inside information.[226]

105 A central element of the supervision of insiders through the use of insider lists is the duty to inform insiders of their obligations: the persons required to draw up lists of insiders must "take the necessary measures to ensure that any person on such a list that has access to inside information, acknowledges the legal and regulatory duties entailed and is aware of the sanctions attaching to the misuse or improper circulation of such information".[227] This provision aims to make the respective person aware of his behaviour regarding the dissemination of inside information.[228]

106 According to the CESR, the supervision of insider lists has proven very successful.[229] The details of the varying legal practices in the Member States go beyond the scope of this book. It must suffice to point out that most national provisions stipulate that the relevant information be stored for considerable periods.[230]

(c) Notification Obligation

107 A further central element regarding the supervision of insiders is a notification obligation: Member States have to provide provisions requiring any person profes-

---

[220] Art. 6(3) MAD.
[221] Cf. CESR, *Level 3—Second Set of CESR Guidance and Information on the Common Operation of the Directive to the Market*, CESR/06-562b, July 2007.
[222] Cf. BaFin, *Emittentenleitfaden 2009* (issuer guideline), p. 117.
[223] Art. 5(2) Directive 2004/72/EC.
[224] Art. 6(3) MAD.
[225] CESR, *Level 3—Second Set of CESR Guidance and Information on the Common Operation of the Directive to the Market*, CESR/06-562b, July 2007.
[226] Art. 5(3) Directive 2004/72/EC.
[227] Cf. Art. 5(5) Directive 2004/72/EC.
[228] Cf. BaFin, *Emittentenleitfaden 2009* (issuer guideline), p. 66.
[229] Cf. CESR, *Level 3—Third Set of CESR Guidance and Information on the Common Operation of the Directive to the Market*, CESR/09-219, May 2009.
[230] In Germany storage must be ensured for six years (cf. § 16(2) WpAIV), in the UK for five years (DTR 2.8.5 R).

sionally arranging transactions in financial instruments—i.e. investment firms and credit institutions[231]—who reasonably suspects that a transaction might constitute insider dealing or market manipulation to notify the competent authority without delay.[232]

108 This legally required "whistleblowing" constitutes a central aspect of the supervision of insiders, enabling the supervisory authorities to examine cases of market abuse and strengthen the market participants' understanding of the fact that market integrity is essential for the functioning of capital markets.[233] The European Commission has therefore laid down detailed rules on the content of such a notification and on the procedure to be followed when notifying the national authorities.[234] The CESR further published guidance on which proceedings are subject to notification and what information must be submitted.[235]

2. Legal Practice in the Member States

109 The national authorities strictly supervise the compliance with the prohibitions of insider dealings. In Germany, for example, banks and financial service providers notified the authorities of a total of 1.5 billion transactions in 2011.[236] The BaFin's investigations are mostly preceded by reports of banks, notifications of trading surveillance offices, inquiries by the public prosecutors, or notifications by companies or investors. The BaFin follows empirically proven typical patterns of insider trading.[237]

110 In 2011 the BaFin initiated 29 proceedings and brought charges against 52 persons for alleged insider dealings. Convictions are rare: in 2009 the public prosecutor closed 53 proceedings, in 14 cases concurrently imposing fines.[238] In 2011 only two people were convicted of insider trading.[239] In the same year, the BaFin received 24 inquiries from abroad, mainly from Austria and France. The BaFin itself addressed foreign supervisory authorities in 51 cases, especially the supervisory authorities in Switzerland, Great Britain, Austria and Luxembourg.[240]

111 The most commonly imposed sanction in 2009–2011 was the disgorgement of profits. Additionally, fines were imposed.[241] In the most serious case of insider dealings brought before the courts so far, the LG Bonn convicted an employee of Deutsche Telekom in March 2009 of the unauthorised disclosure of inside information and sentenced him to 15 months of imprisonment on probation and 50 hours of community service. The court additionally demanded he forfeited his profit of €2.4 million.[242]

[231] The term "person professionally arranging transactions" is defined in Art. 1(3) Directive 2004/72/EC.
[232] Art. 6(9) MAD.
[233] Cf. CESR, *Level 3—Third Set of CESR Guidance and Information on the Common Operation of the Directive to the Market*, CESR/09-219, May 2009.
[234] Cf. Art. 7–10 Directive 2004/72/EC.
[235] Cf. CESR, *Level 3—Third Set of CESR Guidance and Information on the Common Operation of the Directive to the Market*, No. 2.4.1 und 2.4.2, CESR/09-219, May 2009.
[236] Cf. BaFin, *Jahresbericht 2011* (annual report), p. 199.
[237] Cf. K. Ziehl, *Kapitalmarktprognosen und Insider-Trading*, p. 48 ff.
[238] Cf. BaFin, *Jahresbericht 2009* (annual report), p. 182.
[239] Cf. BaFin, *Jahresbericht 2011* (annual report), p. 200.
[240] Cf. ibid.
[241] Cf. the compilation of cases in G.V. Villeda, *Prävention und Insiderhandel*, p. 10 ff.
[242] Cf. BaFin, *Jahresbericht 2009* (annual report), p. 183.

112   The legal practice in the United Kingdom in 2009 was very similar. In two cases criminal proceedings were carried out, in which the offenders were sentenced to imprisonment for 12 to 24 months and disgorgement (£100,000–475,000). In four cases the FSA instigated criminal proceedings[243] and in various further cases it made use of its supervisory competencies and imposed fines.[244] In 2010, however, the FSA introduced a new penalty framework. The FSA now focuses on "credible deterrence through targeted enforcement action to combat insider dealing and market abuse".[245] During 2011 the FSA issued 13 final notices, with total penalties of £15.6 million and prohibited four individuals from working in the financial sector as a result of market abuse.[246]

113   Experiences in Sweden regarding the enforcement of the prohibition of insider dealings are especially unusual. Swedish law only provides criminal sanctions. This approach has been strongly criticised for the high bar it sets for criminal liability. An empirical study came to the conclusion that between 1991 and 1999 of the 416 cases initiated by the Finansinspectionen, the public prosecutor pressed charges in only 27, leading to a mere eight convictions. The legal literature therefore recommends the introduction of administrative sanctions as the supervisory authorities are allegedly in the possession of better resources for the enforcement of the provisions on insider dealings than the courts or the public prosecutors.[247]

VI.   Sanctions

1.   Penalties and Fines

114   The Member States have fulfilled the MAD's requirement of providing effective, proportionate and dissuasive sanctions[248] in different ways.[249] Most have introduced a criminal liability for breaches of the prohibition in Article 2 of the directive to acquire or dispose of shares by making use of inside information.[250] They have further empowered their supervisory authorities to impose sanctions for breaches of the additional prohibitions or to take other necessary administrative measures.

---

[243] Cf. FSA, *Annual Report 2009/2010*, p. 38.

[244] Cf. ibid.: "Our work in the past year has focused on … continuing to pursue cases through the civil market abuse regime with more cases in the RDC and Tribunal process than ever before, as well as more Final Notices being issued."

[245] Cf. FSA, *Annual Report 2011/2012*, p. 14; cf. on the FSA's commitment S. Willey, 93 COB (2012), p. 1, 16–17.

[246] Cf. FSA, *Annual Report 2011/2012*, p. 47.

[247] Cf. R. Veil and F. Walla, *Schwedisches Kapitalmarktrecht*, p. 60–61.

[248] See above para. 9.

[249] Cf. CESR, *Report on Administrative Measures and Sanctions as well as the Criminal Sanctions available in Member States under the Market Abuse Directive (MAD)*, CESR/07-693, February 2008.

[250] In 27 out of 28 jurisdictions criminal sanctions can be imposed, cf. CESR, *Report on Administrative Measures and Sanctions as well as the Criminal Sanctions available in Member States under the Market Abuse Directive (MAD)*, CESR/07-693, February 2008, p. 2.

(a)   Regulatory Techniques

115   Most Member States have provided clearly formulated prohibitions, a breach of which may result in a penalty or fine, provided—in most cases—the offender acted wilfully. In some Member States, gross negligence or even simple negligence may suffice. French supervisory law, for example, provides sanction for ordinary negligence.[251] In Sweden, ordinary negligence is even sufficient for the criminal provisions.[252] The German legislature introduced penalties (§ 38 WpHG) as well as fines (§ 39 WpHG) in so-called blanket clauses.

116   Pursuant to § 38(1) No. 1 WpHG, for example, any person who acquires or disposes of an insider security in contravention of a prohibition pursuant to § 14(1) No. 1 WpHG will be liable to imprisonment or to a criminal fine. The provisions refers to the prohibition of insider dealing laid down in § 14 WpHG. This criminal liability of a person can therefore only be determined by a joint examination of the two provisions: § 38 and § 14 WpHG. This and the imprecise terms in insider law have been heavily criticised in the legal literature.[253] The constitutional requirement of clarity is generally only fulfilled if the criminal behaviour can be clearly deduced from the law, often not considered to be the case if the provision first makes reference to additional provisions.

117   Breaches of the prohibition to disclose inside information or to recommend the acquisition of shares to a third party on the basis of inside information are only criminally prosecuted in Germany if the offence is committed by a primary insider. Primary insiders are defined as persons who by virtue of their membership in the management or supervisory body of the issuer, or as a personally liable partner of the issuer or of an undertaking affiliated with the issuer, by virtue of their holding in the capital of the issuer or a company affiliated with the issuer or by virtue of their profession, activities or duties performed as part of his function or due to the preparation or perpetration of a criminal offence are privy to inside information (§ 38(1) Nos. 2a–d WpHG). In all other cases a breach of the prohibition to disclose inside information or to recommend the acquisition of shares to a third party is subject to fines under administrative law (§ 39(2) Nos. 3 and 4 WpHG).

118   The situation is similar in the United Kingdom, where the criminal provisions are, however, more extensive, including (i) dealing in securities that are price-affected securities in relation to the information, (ii) encouraging another person to deal with such securities and (iii) disclosing the inside information to another person.[254] The provision applies irrespective of whether the offender is a primary insider. The MAD's requirements were implemented into administrative law.

119   Summarising these findings, it can be said that criminal as well as supervisory law contain well-differentiated prohibitions in most Member States, apart from

---

[251] See above para. 17.

[252] See above para. 26.

[253] Cf. K. Moosmayer, wistra (2002), p. 161, 168; also seen critically by K. Altenhain, in: H. Hirte and T.M.J. Möllers (eds.), *Kölner Kommentar zum WpHG*, § 38 para. 21; J. Vogel, in: H.D. Assmann and U.H. Schneider (eds.), *Kommentar zum WpHG*, Vor § 38 para. 4b; on the usefulness of criminal law in the prevention of insider dealings in general see G.V. Villeda, *Prävention und Repression von Insiderhandel*, p. 379 ff.

[254] Cf. sec. 52 CJA; see R. Veil and M. Wundenberg, *Englisches Kapitalmarktrecht*, p. 68; for an overview on the FSA's enforcement see A. Henderson, 20 JIBLR (2005), p. 494–500.

the United Kingdom where the regulatory concept also relies on the breach of "principles"[255] for which the FSA can impose sanctions, as has been the case for a number of insider dealings.

120   *Facts (abridged):* Pignatelli received an e-mail from an analyst with potential inside information and forwarded it immediately to numerous other persons, including four hedge fund managers. Due to the fact that the information was already publicly known, this constituted no breach of section 118(3) FSMA. The FSA imposed a fine on Pignatelli nevertheless, basing it on Principles 2 and 3 of the FSA's Statements of Principle for Approved Persons.[256] Principle 2 demands approved persons act with due skill, care and diligence. The FSA claimed that Pignatelli had breached this principle by ignoring the warning signs and consulting his superior before forwarding the e-mail. Principle 3 of the FSA's Statements of Principle for Approved Persons requires a person to observe proper standards of market conduct. According to the FSA, Pignatelli had breached this rule by forwarding the e-mail in a manner that gave other market participants the impression it contained inside information.[257]

121   A further interesting example of an enforcement based on principles is the FSA's decision in *Casoni.*[258]

122   *Facts (abridged):* Casoni, an important analyst working for the Citigroup, drew up a report containing a recommendation to acquire shares. Before his analysis was published, Casoni contacted fund managers, informing them of his report and the details of his evaluation method. The FSA did not determine whether the recommendation to acquire shares had to be regarded as inside information, rather referring to Principle 3 of the Statements of Principle for Approved Persons and coming to the conclusion that by passing on the information Casoni had breached the proper standards of market conduct. This enabled the FSA to impose a fine without having to prove the price sensitivity of the information.

123   The way in which the FSA imposes sanctions based merely on the breach of principles is unique in Europe. For constitutional reasons it appears doubtful whether this type of enforcement could be introduced in the capital markets law of other Member States.[259]

(b)   Legal Frameworks for Penalties and Fines

124   The sanctions for breaches of the prohibitions of insider dealings differ greatly throughout Europe.[260] In Germany, the provisions distinguish between criminal and administrative liabilities. The prohibition to acquire or dispose of shares on the

---

[255] See above para. 31.

[256] FSA, *Final Notice*, 20 November 2006.

[257] Cf. also FSA, *Final Notice to Mr. Christopher William Gower*, 12 January 2011: The FSA imposed a financial penalty of £50,000 for failing to comply with Principle 3 of the FSA's Statements of Principle for Approved Person, considering that Gower had given the impression that inside information had been disclosed.

[258] FSA, *Final Notice*, 20 March 2007; on this see D. Mayhew and K. Anderson, JIBLR (2007), p. 515, 520–521.

[259] Cf. R. Veil, 11 EBOR (2010), p. 409, 415.

[260] Cf. for an overview CESR, *Report on Administrative Measures and Sanctions as well as the Criminal Sanctions available in Member States under the Market Abuse Directive (MAD)*, CESR/07-693, February 2008, appendix "Statistics from 29 Countries".

basis of inside information is sanctioned with an imprisonment of up to five years or with a monetary penalty (§ 38(1), (3) and (5) WpHG). The same sanctions apply if a primary insider discloses or makes available inside information to a third party or recommends, on the basis of inside information, that a third party acquire or dispose of insider securities, or to otherwise induce a third party to do so. Others, so-called secondary insiders, can only be sanctioned with administrative fines up to €200,000 in these cases (§ 39(2) Nos. 3 and 4, (4) WpHG). The court can further disgorge unlawfully acquired profits.[261]

125   English law also distinguishes between criminal and administrative sanctions. On conviction, an offender is liable to a fine or imprisonment for a term not exceeding seven years pursuant to section 61 CJA. The sanctions under administrative law are primarily defined in section 123 FSMA as fines "of such amount as [the FSA] considers appropriate".[262] Forfeiture is also possible under British law.

126   Italy also allows severe criminal sanctions to be imposed, these consisting of an imprisonment of up to six years and monetary penalties of up to €3 million but no more than ten-fold of the profit.[263] Additionally, the profits can be forfeited or an equivalent sum seized.[264] Consob's power to impose fines remains, irrespective of whether the criminal provisions apply. By combining administrative and criminal penalties, Italian law aims at deterring offenders and covering all persons involved in insider deals.[265]

(c)   Reform

127   The proposal for a Market Abuse Regulation[266] aims to achieve unification and introduce stricter sanctions. It lists 22 circumstances for which the national supervisory authorities must be granted sanctioning powers.[267] The possible measures and sanctions are also described in detail[268] and range from "temporary prohibition of an activity" to "administrative pecuniary sanctions" and "suspend trading of the financial instrument". The regulation then continues by listing the circumstances which the supervisory authority must take into account when determining the type of administrative measures and sanctions to be applied.[269] These guidelines were introduced due to the insight that the national authorities made very different use of their sanctioning powers in the past. The European requirements and the guidelines to be developed by the European Securities and Markets Authority (ESMA)[270] aim to unify the law and legal practice in the Member States.

---

[261] Cf. § 73(1) StGB; BGH ZIP (2010), p. 426, 429.

[262] The FSA has imposed high fines in recent years. For example, the owner of a prominent US hedge fund and his fund were fined £7.2 million for engaging in market abuse. The enforcement notices are available at: www.fsa.gov.uk/pages/about/what/financial_crime/market_abuse/library/notices/index.shtml. See on the FSA's commitment to "credible deterrence" of market abuse S. Willey, 93 COB (2012), p. 1, 16–17.

[263] Cf. Art. 184 III TUF.

[264] Art. 187 I and II TUF.

[265] Cf. C. Alvisi, 1 *Contratto e impresa/Europa*, p. 181, 183; E. Amati, 5 *Le Nuove leggi civili commentate*, p. 1064, 1067.

[266] Cf. para. 11–13.

[267] Cf. Art. 25 MAR Draft.

[268] Cf. Art. 26 MAR Draft.

[269] Cf. Art. 27(1) MAR Draft.

[270] Cf. Art. 27 (2) MAR Draft: Guidelines on types of administrative measures and sanctions and level of fines.

128 The national supervisory authorities must be empowered to be able to impose fines of twice the profits obtained. With regard to legal persons, administrative pecuniary sanctions of up to 10% of the total annual turnover in the preceding business year should be possible.[271] The supervisory authorities are further required to make public any measures and sanctions[272] unless such publication would seriously jeopardise the stability of the financial markets.

129 According to the draft directive, the Member States are also required to introduce criminal sanctions for "the most serious market abuse offences".[273] They only have to sanction intentional offences.[274] Furthermore, they are obliged to ensure that legal persons can be held liable.[275]

2. Naming and Shaming

130 The Member States must provide rules permitting the competent authority to disclose to the public every measure or sanction imposed for infringement of the prohibitions of insider dealing, unless such disclosure would seriously jeopardise the financial markets or cause disproportionate damage to the parties involved.[276] The Member States' transpositions of this provision once again differ greatly.

131 In Germany, the BaFin can make publicly known incontestable measures that it has adopted due to contraventions of prohibitions or requirements on its website, provided that this is suitable and necessary to resolve or avoid irregularities in accordance with § 4(1) WpHG, unless such publication would place the financial markets in considerable danger or would cause disproportionate damage to the parties involved.[277] This competence of the BaFin is regarded very critically in Germany for constitutional reasons, which may well be the reason why the BaFin has so far not made use of its powers to make measures taken against an insider publicly known.[278]

132 The same cannot be said of the FSA which is also permitted to publish breaches of the prohibitions on insider dealings in the United Kingdom.[279] A prerequisite is that the FSA has issued the offender with a so-called *warning notice*[280] and submitted a *decision notice* regarding the level of the fine. The respective offender may then refer the matter to the FSA's Tribunal. This procedure is of great practical importance.[281]

133 In France, the AMF also commonly makes public the sanctions—Décisions de la Commission des Sanctions—it has imposed. In Italy the disclosure is regulated by Article 186 TUF requiring that a judgment convicting a person of insider dealings be made public in at least two national daily newspapers, one of which must be a financial newspaper.

---

[271] Cf. Art. 26(1)(m) MAR Draft.
[272] Cf. Art. 26 (3) MAR-Draft.
[273] Cf. Art. 1 (1) MAD II Draft.
[274] Cf. Art. 3 and 4 MAD II Draft.
[275] Cf. Art. 7 MAD II Draft.
[276] Art. 14(4) MAD.
[277] Cf. § 40b WpHG.
[278] Cf. J. Vogel, in: H.D. Assmann and U.H. Schneider (eds.), *Kommentar zum WpHG*, § 40b para. 1.
[279] Sec. 123(3) FSMA.
[280] Sec. 126 FSMA.
[281] In detail E.J. Swan and J. Virgo, *Market Abuse Regulation*, 10.14 ff.

3. Investor Protection by Civil Liability

134 The MAD contains no provisions requiring the introduction of a civil liability, leaving this to the choice of the Member States. In Germany, the WpHG does not contain any provisions for investors to claim damages from insiders. Such claims are therefore subject to the general civil law provisions. The prevailing opinion in the literature is that the law of torts does not apply,[282] as the provisions regarding insider dealing are not aimed at the protection of individual investors. Since the possibility of damage claims for the incorrect publication of inside information was introduced for investors in 2002,[283] this discussion has become less important.[284]

135 The legislature in the United Kingdom has also not introduced a specific legal basis for investor claims in cases of a breach of the insider prohibitions.[285] Whilst an investor may theoretically claim damages under sections 118 and 397 FSMA/sections 52ff. CJA, claiming a so-called "implicit private cause of action", this method has not yet been established before the higher courts.[286] Similar can be said of the further possibility that an investor can base his claims on the general provision subjecting the issuer to damage claims of private persons under supervisory law.[287] This basis for the claim has the further disadvantage that it is subject to numerous restrictions,[288] therefore rarely promising success.

136 Sweden and Spain also provide no specific rules on this matter, leaving the question of damages to the law of torts. There is as yet no debate in the legal literature of these states[289] on how a civil law liability could be developed.

137 As opposed to this, the French courts meanwhile see the possibility of an investor's damages being compensated in cases of insider dealings. In *Sidel* shareholders claimed compensation in criminal proceedings which both the Tribunal correctionnel and the Cour d'appel awarded on the merits, based on Articles 1382 and 1384 Code civil (Cc, French Civil Code). However, the proof of actual damage was not possible, the insider dealing only affecting 30,000 shares, whilst during the relevant period a total of more than 3 million shares were being traded. The courts therefore concluded that the information was not price sensitive.[290]

VII. Conclusion

138 No other area of capital markets law has developed as clearly as the prohibition of insider dealings. This can be ascribed to the fact that the concept of inside informa-

---

[282] Cf. P. Mennicke, *Sanktionen gegen Insiderhandel*, p. 618 ff.; E. Schwark, in: E. Schwark and D. Zimmer (eds.), *Kapitalmarktrechts-Kommentar*, § 14 WpHG para. 4; H.D. Assmann, in: H.D. Assmann and U.H. Schneider (eds.), *Kommentar zum WpHG*, § 14 para. 210.

[283] See § 19 para. 118.

[284] Cf. §§ 37b, 37c WpHG; more details in § 19 para. 118–121.

[285] For an overview of civil law liability cf. J. Marsh, 23 COB (2005), p. 1, 26.

[286] Cf. R. Veil and M. Wundenberg, *Englisches Kapitalmarktrecht*, p. 84.

[287] Sec. 150 FSMA is the legal basis.

[288] In more detail R. Veil and M. Wundenberg, *Englisches Kapitalmarktrecht*, p. 85.

[289] Cf. R. Veil and F. Walla, *Schwedisches Kapitalmarktrecht*, p. 53–54 and 60.

[290] T. corr. Paris, 11e ch., 1re sect., of 12 September 2006, no. 0018992026; CA Paris, 9e ch., sect. B, of 17 October 2008, no. 06/09036.

tion was clearly defined in the implementing measures the European Commission enacted to this end. The CESR's Guidelines constitute a further valuable help for legal practice, giving recommendations on how to deal with the especially difficult multi-level cases, such as capital increases and mergers. A comparison of the Member States' national provisions also proves important. The national supervisory authorities and courts have had to examine important questions on the details of inside information and the application of the prohibitions with regard to M&A transaction. These insights can be helpful in legal practice.

139   The ECJ has further outlined the key prohibitions of insider dealings in its judgments in *Grøngaard/Bang* and *Spector*. The requirements for the assumption of inside information are very strict. Whilst the exact conclusions that can be deduced from *Spector* for the prohibition of the acquisition of shares based on inside information and the disclosure thereof may still be unclear, it appears that the ECJ's interpretation of the provisions does not overly restrict legal practice as due diligence procedures will remain possible.

140   At present, there is no reason why fundamental reforms should be necessary at a European level. Possible grievances are rather the result of unfortunate methods of implementation in the Member States, preventing an effective enforcement of the prohibitions. With regard to this, a need for action remains and not all Member States seem to have picked up on the ECJ's clear words. A further cause for concern is the fact that not all Member States provide for sufficiently severe sanctions. Tightening these provisions would underline the importance of the prohibition of insider dealings for the functioning of the capital markets. The European Commission's proposals for reforms in October 2011 must therefore be seen as a step in the right direction: strengthening the powers of the national supervisory authorities, instead of relying solely on a regime of criminal sanction, appears most promising to this end.

§ 14 Market Manipulation

Bibliography

Af Sandeberg, Catarina, *Marknadsmissbruk—insiderbrott och kursmanipulation?*, Ny Juridik (2002), p. 7–20; af Sandeberg, Catarina, *Strikt ansvar vid insiderbrott—administrativa sanktioner för effektivare brottsbekämpning*, JT (2002–2003), p. 869–884; Aggarwal, Rajesh K. and Wu, Guijon, *Stock Market Manipulations*, 79 J. Bus. (2006), p. 1915–1953; Allen, Franklin and Gale, Douglas, *Stock Price Manipulation*, 5 Rev. Fin. Studies (1992), p. 503–529; Avgouelas, Emilios, *The Mechanics and Regulation of Market Abuse* (2005); Barber, Brad M. and Odean, Terrance, *All that Glitters: The Effect of Attention and News on the Buying Behavior of Individual and Institutional Investors*, 21 Rev. Fin. Studies (2008), p. 785–818; Barber, Brad M. and Odean, Terrance, *Trading Is Hazardous to Your Wealth: The Common Investment Performance of Individual Investors*, 55 J. Fin. (2000), p. 773–806; Chen, Qi and Jiang, Wei, *Analysts' Weighting of Public and Private Information*, 19 Rev. Fin. Studies (2006), p. 319–355; Deshmukh, Sanjay, Goel, Anand M. and Howe, Keith M., *CEO Overconfidence and Dividend Policy: Theory and Evidence*, Working Paper (2009), available at: http://ssrn.com/abstract=1107542; Eichelberger, Jan, *Das Verbot der Marktmanipulation* (2006); Fischel, Daniel R. and Ross, David J., *Should the Law Prohibit Manipulation in Financial Markets?*, 105 Harv. L. Rev. (1991), p. 503–553; Fleischer, Holger, *Stock Spams—Anlegerschutz und Marktmanipulation*, ZBB (2008), p. 137–147; Friesen, Geoffrey C. and Weller, Paul A., *Quantifying Cognitive Biases in Analysts Earnings Forecasts*, 9 Journal of Financial Markets (2006), p. 333–365; Grüger, Tobias W., *Kurspflegemaßnahmen durch Banken—Zulässige Marktpraxis oder Verstoß gegen das Verbot der Marktmanipulation nach § 20a WpHG?*, BKR (2007), p. 437–447; Hellgardt, Alexander, *Europarechtliche Vorgaben für die Kapitalmarktinformationshaftung de lege lata und nach Inkrafttreten der Marktmissbrauchsverordnung*, AG (2012), p. 154–168; Jacobson, Hans and Lycke, Johan, *Marknadsmissbruksdirektivet och dess genomförande i Sverige*, ERT (2005), p. 303–320; Kahneman, Daniel and Tversky, Amos, *Prospect Theory: An Analysis of Decision under Risk*, 47 Econometrica (1979), p. 263–291; Klöhn, Lars, *Kapitalmarkt, Spekulation und Behavioral Finance* (2006); Langevoort, Donald C., *Taming the Animal Spirits of the Stock Market—A Behavioral Approach to Securities Regulation*, 97 Nw. U. L. Rev. (2002), p. 135–188; Leppert, Michael and Stürwald, Florian, *Aktienrückkauf und Kursstabilisierung—Die Safe-Harbour-Regelungen der Verordnung (EG) Nr. 2273/2003 und der KuMaKV*, ZBB (2004), p. 302–314; Lenzen, Ursula, *Unerlaubte Eingriffe in die Börsenkursbildung* (2000); Malmendier, Ulrike and Tate, Geoffrey A., *Who Makes Acquisitions? CEO Overconfidence and the Market's Reaction*, Working Paper (2003), available at: http://ssrn.com/abstract=470788; Samuelsson, Per, *Nya regler om marknadsmissbruk*, JT (2004–2005), p. 256–268; Stotz, Olaf and von Nitzsch, Rüdiger, *Warum sich Analysten überschätzen—Einfluss des Kontrollgefühls auf die Selbstüberschätzung*, ZBB (2003), p. 106–113; Teigelack, Lars, *Finanzanalysen und Behavioral Finance* (2009); Tversky, Amos and Kahneman, Daniel, *Rational Choice and the Framing of Decisions*, 59 J. Bus. (1986), p. 251–278; Veil, Rüdiger, *Der Schutz des verständigen Anlegers durch Publizität und Haftung im europäischen Kapitalmarktrecht*, ZBB (2006), p. 162–171; Waschkeit, Indre, *Marktmanipulation am Kapitalmarkt* (2007); Wesser, Erik, *Har du varit ute och shoppat, Jacob?—En studie av Finansinspektionens utredning av insiderbrott under 1990-talet* (2001); Willey, Stuart, *Market Abuse Update*, 93 COB (2012), p. 1–28; Ziouvas, Dimitris, *Das neue Recht gegen Kurs- und Marktpreismanipulation im 4. Finanzmarktförderungsgesetz*, ZGR (2003), p. 113–146.

I. Introduction

1 The aim of every market manipulation is to influence the present market price in

order to achieve positive results for the manipulator, i.e. increasing the price before sales and lowering it before acquisitions. Prices can be influenced by information-based as well as transaction-based manipulations.[1] Manipulations most commonly occur on illiquid markets with only little regulation; these markets have the least stringent transparency rules and therefore the largest informational asymmetries between the manipulators and other market participants. In these cases, manipulators can exert particular influence on the amount of information available to the public regarding a certain financial instrument. Additionally, each individual order is potentially more likely to cause price movements on relatively illiquid markets.[2] This can particularly effect emerging markets, which do not yet have sufficient liquidity and efficiency.[3] Within the European Union, market segments below the threshold of regulated markets, e.g. the German *Freiverkehr* (open market), are most likely to be subject to manipulation.[4]

2   Manipulated prices influence the functioning of the market and must therefore be prohibited.[5] Investors could lose confidence in a manipulated market and eventually exit the market, a move which would adversely affect the market mechanism.[6] The United States, therefore, introduced comprehensive prohibitions on market manipulation as early as the 1930s. In Europe, a community-wide approach was only adopted in 2003. The MAD was intended to ensure a uniform framework throughout the Community,[7] because some Member States had not enacted legislation prohibiting such manipulations. The directive's rules for the Member States thus aim to protect the reliability and accuracy of price formation. Investors must be able to rely on the fact that the price has evolved through supply and demand and not through manipulation. The prohibition of market manipulation is also intended as a means of hindering the financing of terrorist activities.[8]

3   In October 2011, the Commission made public two proposals[9] regarding amendments to the rules on market abuse.[10] The Commission no longer intends to rely on the Member States to implement the more or less broad provisions contained in a directive, rather setting out the rules itself through a directly applicable regulation. It is currently awaiting the European Parliament's consent to the draft.[11]

---

[1] Cf. R.K. Aggarwal and G. Wu, 79. J. Bus. (2006), p. 1915; H. Fleischer, in: A. Fuchs (ed.), *Kommentar zum WpHG*, § 20a para. 9 ff.; J. Vogel, in: H.-D. Assmann and U.H. Schneider (eds.), *Kommentar zum WpHG*, § 20a para. 39 ff.

[2] R.K. Aggarwal and G. Wu, 79. J. Bus. (2006), p. 1915, 1917; BaFin, *Jahresbericht 2008* (annual report), p. 161.

[3] R.K. Aggarwal and G. Wu, 79. J. Bus. (2006), p. 1915, 1918 quoted studies referring to China and Pakistan.

[4] BaFin, *Jahresbericht 2011* (annual report), p. 197.

[5] Recitals 12, 15 MAD.

[6] J. Vogel, in: H.-D. Assmann and U.H. Schneider (eds.), *Kommentar zumWpHG,* § 20a para. 40.

[7] Recitals 11, 12 MAD; cf. also Communication from the Commission on implementing the Financial Services Action Plan, 11 May 1999, COM(1999) 232 final.

[8] Recital 14 MAD.

[9] Proposal for a Regulation of the European Parliament and of the Council on Insider Dealing and Market Manipulation (Market Abuse) of 20 October 2011 COM(2011) 651 final; Proposal for a Directive of the European Parliament and of the Council on Criminal Sanctions for Insider Dealing and Market Manipulation of 20 October 2011, COM(2011), 654 final. Cf. on this reform R. Veil and P. Koch, *Towards a Uniform European Capital Markets Law: Proposals of the Commission to Reform Market Abuse* (2012); S. Willey, 93 COB (2012), p. 1, 12–15.

[10] Furthermore, the European Commission has published a Working Paper as an accompanying document to the two proposals (Commission Staff Working Paper Impact Assessment, 20.10.2011, SEC(2011) 1217 final).

[11] Cf. § 1 para. 41 and § 13 para. 11–13.

II. Regulatory Concepts

1. Requirements under European Law

4   The MAD begins by requiring that the Member States generally prohibit any person from engaging in market manipulation.[12] It then provides a core definition of market manipulation as one of three different possible activities,[13] also offering three practically relevant examples of this core definition.[14] Other patterns of activity are explicitly exempted from the scope of application of the directive. These include the trading in own shares in "buy-back" programmes and the stabilisation of a financial instrument, provided such trading is carried out in accordance with Regulation 2273/2003.[15] The MAD additionally contains organisational requirements necessary for detecting market manipulation. The Member States are thus required to "ensure that market operators adopt structural provisions aimed at preventing and detecting market manipulation practices".[16] The Member States are also required to introduce a general notification obligation for securities transactions in order to enable the national authorities to supervise compliance with these provisions.

5   The broadly phrased prohibitions and exemptions are implemented through three further legal acts. Implementing Directive 124 establishes several signals that are to be taken into account when investigating potentially manipulative behaviour.[17] Regulation 2273/2003 lays down rules on the so-called safe-harbour provisions for buy-back programmes and stabilisation measures, whilst Implementing Directive 2004/72 describes further accepted market practices.[18]

6   The former CESR has established guidelines[19] (Level 3 Guidance) which elaborate on the requirements for accepted market practices and explain several manipulative activities[20] as well as the application of the safe-harbour rules in greater detail.[21] In addition, the CESR has published various documents summarising the current status of the application of the Directive in the Member States.[22]

---

[12] Art. 5 MAD.
[13] Art. 1(2) subsec. 1(a)–(c) MAD. The draft regulation establishes a fourth-benchmark manipulation, cf. COM(2012) 421 final in reaction to the LIBOR scandal.
[14] Art. 1(2) subsec. 2 MAD.
[15] Art. 8 MAD.
[16] Art. 6(6) MAD.
[17] Commission Directive 2003/124/EC of 22 December 2003 implementing Directive 2003/6/EC of the European Parliament and of the Council as regards the definition and public disclosure of inside information and the definition of market manipulation, OJ L339, 24 December 2003, p. 70.
[18] Commission Regulation 2273/2003/EC of 22 December 2003 implementing Directive 2003/6/EC of the European Parliament and of the Council as regards exemptions for buy-back programmes and stabilisation of financial instruments, OJ L336, 23 December 2003, p. 33 and Commission Directive 2004/72/EC of 29 April 2004 implementing Directive 2003/6/EC of the European Parliament and of the Council as regards accepted market practices, the definition of inside information in relation to derivatives on commodities, the drawing up of lists of insiders, the notification of managers' transactions and the notification of suspicious transactions, OJ L162, 30 April 2004, p. 70.
[19] See § 5 para. 39 as to the legal qualification of these guidelines and their effect on the construction of the Directives and other legal acts.
[20] CESR, *Level 3—First Set of CESR Guidance and Information on the Common Operation of the Directive to the Market*, CESR/04-505b, October 2008.
[21] CESR, *Level 3—Third Set of CESR Guidance and Information on the Common Operation of the Directive to the Market*, CESR/09-219, May 2009.
[22] CESR, *Report on CESR Members' Powers under the Market Abuse Directive and its Implementing Measures*, CESR/07-380, June 2007.

2. Implementation in the Member States

7   Most Member States have implemented the provisions of the MAD into their national law using the so-called "copy-out approach". The United Kingdom has inserted the provisions on market manipulation in the FSMA[23] and the FSA Handbook.[24] Additionally, a criminal law provision sanctions two different forms of market manipulation.[25] Austria,[26] Spain,[27] France[28] and Italy[29] also adopted the provisions of the MAD on a one-to-one basis.

8   German law already provided for a prohibition of a manipulation of prices[30] before the introduction of the MAD. This provision had, however, proven to be ineffective, requiring proof of the intention to affect a market price, which was nearly impossible.[31] As a result, a new provision was inserted in the WpHG (German Securities Trading Act) in 2002 and was put into more specific terms by means of a regulation.[32] These rules had to be amended in the course of the implementation of the MAD and the regulation was replaced entirely.[33] The German legislature, however, still adhered to the wording of the former provision in the BörsG (German Stock Exchange Act). The wording of the German provisions thus differs from that of the MAD.

9   Sweden has chosen a particular approach by replacing the existing provision on the manipulation of prices with the MAD's rule on market manipulation[34] without introducing an additional regulation rendering this provision more specific. The Swedish courts must therefore take into account the European implementing measures and the preliminary notes to the provisions, when interpreting the Swedish provision.[35]

III. Scope of Application

1. Personal Scope

10   The prohibition of market manipulation generally applies to all market participants.

---

[23] Sec. 118(5)–(8).

[24] The chapter is entitled Code of Market Conduct (MAR); the provisions are laid down in 1.6–1.10 MAR; on the legal nature of the FSA Handbook see § 5 para. 33.

[25] Sec. 397 FSMA.

[26] § 48a BörseG.

[27] The general prohibition of market manipulation is contained in a parliamentary act (Art. 83 ter. 1 LMV), while the instances derived from the core definition and the indicators of market manipulation have been laid down separately in a regulation (Art. 2, 3 RD 1333/2005).

[28] Art. 631-1 to -4 RG AMF.

[29] Art. 185, 187-ter TUF; Art. 40, 43 Regolamento Mercati.

[30] § 88 former BörsG.

[31] J. Vogel, in: H.-D. Assmann and U.H. Schneider (eds.), *Kommentar zum WpHG*, Vor § 20a para. 2.

[32] § 20a WpHG (old version) was put into more concrete terms by the Regulation to Further Define the Prohibition of Price and Market Price Manipulations (Verordnung zur Konkretisierung des Verbots der Kurs- und Marktpreismanipulation, KuMaKV).

[33] Market Manipulation Definition Regulation—Regulation to Further Define the Prohibition against Market Manipulation (MaKonV, Verordnung zur Konkretisierung des Verbots der Marktmanipulation).

[34] § 8 Lag om straff för marknadsmissbruk vid handel med finansiella instrument (SFS 2005:377).

[35] See P. Samuelsson et al. (eds.), *Lagen om marknadsmissbruk och lagen om anmälnings-skylighet. En kommentar*, p. 284 ff.; H. Jacobson and J. Lycke, ERT (2005), p. 303, 308–309.

Only journalists, when acting in their professional capacity, are partly exempted from the definition. With regard to journalists, the "dissemination of information is to be assessed taking into account the rules governing their profession, unless those persons derive, directly or indirectly, an advantage or profits from the dissemination of the information in question".[36]

2. Material Scope

11 The *material* scope of the directive covers all market manipulations concerning financial instruments as defined in Article 1 No. 3 MAD.[37] Thus, the Member States have to ensure that market manipulation is forbidden on regulated markets. Germany has exceeded this requirement in certain respects, also applying the prohibition to financial instruments that are admitted to trading on the open market (*Freiverkehr*)[38] or if the application for such an admission or inclusion has been made or publicly announced.[39] The rules further apply to markets for commodities, emission allowances and foreign currencies.[40] Italy has a civil law prohibition regarding price manipulation of securities traded OTC which exceeds the directive's requirements.[41]

12 The draft regulation[42] considerably extends the material scope of the rules on market manipulation. The scope is no longer limited to financial instruments traded on regulated markets; the draft regulation also applies to financial instruments traded on MTFs and OTFs and any related financial instruments traded OTC, which can have an effect on the covered underlying market (e.g. credit default swaps (CDSs)). The reasoning behind this extension is to avoid regulatory arbitrage among trading venues and to ensure investor protection throughout the European Union.[43] Emission allowances are to be classified as financial instruments, thus subjecting financial instruments relating to wholesale energy products to the provisions on market abuse.[44] Finally, the prohibition of market manipulation in the draft regulation also covers the interlinkages between spot commodity markets and related financial markets, i.e. manipulative strategies which use financial instruments to influence spot commodity contracts and vice versa.[45] In this context, the draft regulation excludes monetary and public debt management as well as climate policy activities from its scope.[46]

---

[36] Art. 1(2) subsec. 1(c) MAD.
[37] On this term see § 8 para. 4–9 and § 13 para. 47.
[38] § 20a(1) sentence 2 No. 1 WpHG.
[39] § 20a(1) sentence 3 WpHG.
[40] § 20a(4) WpHG.
[41] Art. 2637 Codice Civile.
[42] See para. 3.
[43] Recital 8 and Art. 2 No. 1(a), (b), No. 3 lit. (a) COM 2011(651) final.
[44] Recital 15 and Art. 2 No. 1(d) COM 2011(651) final.
[45] Recital 15 and Art. 2 No. 3(b), (c) COM 2011(651) final.
[46] Art. 4 COM 2011(651) final.

Lars Teigelack

IV. Prohibitions

1. Regulatory System

13 Market manipulation prevents the market from being complete and transparent. The European legislature is of the opinion that full and proper market transparency is a prerequisite for all economic actors to be able to participate in integrated financial markets.[47] The MAD distinguishes transaction-based and information-based manipulations[48] and labels these two forms "core definitions". *Transaction-based* manipulations[49] are based on the possibility of giving false or misleading signals as to the supply of, demand for or price of financial instruments through an actual transaction. As opposed to this, *information-based* manipulation requires the dissemination of false or misleading information.[50] The third core definition is a combination of both types of manipulation, which must be assumed if transactions or orders to trade employ fictitious devices or any other form of deception or contrivance.[51] Directive 2003/124 specifies the meaning of the latter two core definitions by establishing non-exhaustive *signals* that are to be taken into account when investigating possibly manipulative behaviour.[52] However, these signals do not allow the automatic conclusion that the behaviour in question constitutes market manipulation.

14 The MAD further provides *instances* of manipulative behaviour, which it derives from the three core definitions.[53] The described instances are also non-exhaustive. Even if none of these three instances applies, the respective behaviour can still be considered manipulative within the meaning of Article 1 No. 2(a), (b) or (c) MAD. If one of the instances does, however, apply, the respective behaviour definitely constitutes market manipulation; hence, the instances are not merely signals within the meaning of Articles 4 and 5 of Directive 2003/124.

15 The draft regulation[54] generally maintains this approach, but also prohibits attempted market manipulation.[55] Manipulations are no longer limited to transactions or orders to trade but also include any other behaviour.

2. Core Definitions of Market Manipulation

(a) Information Based Manipulation

(aa) The Core Definition

16 Any behaviour that constitutes a "dissemination of information through the media, including the Internet, or by any other means, which gives, or is likely to give, false or misleading signals as to financial instruments, including the dissemina-

---

[47] Cf. Recital 15 MAD.
[48] This classification was first used by F. Allen and D. Gale, 5 Rev. Fin. Stud. (1992), p. 503.
[49] Art. 1(2)(a) MAD.
[50] Art. 1(2) subsec. 1(c) MAD.
[51] Art. 1(2) subsec. 1(b) MAD.
[52] Art. 4 and 5 and Recital 6 of Directive 2003/124/EC.
[53] Art. 1(2) subsec. 2 MAD.
[54] See para. 3.
[55] Art. 8(2) COM 2011(651) final.

tion of rumours and false or misleading news, where the person who made the dissemination knew, or ought to have known, that the information was false or misleading"[56] is an information-based manipulation. Information-based manipulation may be achieved by publishing incorrect balance sheets or ad hoc notifications or by incorrect statements in the media, e.g. during press conferences dealing with a company's financial statements. The so-called *painting the tape*, i.e. presenting non-existing orders on the price tape in order to feign strong demand, also constitutes a type of information-based manipulation.[57] However, not every information based manipulation is easy to determine.

17   In Germany the "Porsche case" made the headlines with the accusation of information-based market manipulation. Porsche Automobil Holding SE (formerly Dr. Ing. h.c. F. Porsche AG) is accused of intentionally hiding its intent to take over Volkswagen AG (VW).[58] In September 2005 Porsche, which then held 20% of VW's shares, claimed that it definitely had no intention of taking over VW. In the following months, Porsche increased its stake in VW, resulting in a holding of more than 30% of the shares by March 2007. Porsche made a mandatory offer pursuant to the WpÜG (German Takeover Act) and the supervisory board permitted the acquisition of a major shareholding in March 2008. In a press release published a week later, Porsche claimed it had no intention of extending its shareholding to a total of 75%. Only in October 2008 did the CEO announce the plan to acquire further shares in order to hold a total of 75% and thus be able to conclude a domination and profit/loss transfer agreement.[59] Finally, in November 2009 a letter by Porsche's General Counsel was published, stating that Porsche had already "run through" the possibility of a complete takeover of VW during the first acquisition of VW shares in 2005.

18   A further case that caused quite a stir in Germany is that of the former CEO of IKB-Bank AG. In a press release of 20 July 2007, the defendant stated that the risks of dealing with US subprime mortgages would have "practically no influence" on IKB. The depreciation would not exceed a seven-figure sum. On the day of publication, the price of IKB increased above that of the MDax,[60] where IKB was listed. One week later it became apparent that the depreciation would run to billions rather than millions. The court held that the former CEO had knowingly manipulated the press release, and that he had thus misled investors by stating that IKB Bank AG had not been materially influenced by the subprime problems, although further analyses of banks and rating agencies showed that the opposite was true.[61]

---

[56] Art. 1(2) subsec. 1(c) MAD.
[57] J. Vogel, in: H.-D. Assmann and U.H. Schneider (eds.), *Kommentar zum WpHG*, § 20a para. 33 and CESR, *Market Abuse Directive—Level 3—first set of CESR guidance and information on the common operation of the Directive*, CESR/04–505b, May 2005, p. 11 ff.
[58] Cf. Handelsblatt of 30 January 2010.
[59] This contract (cf. § 291 AktG, German Stock Corporation Act) allows a parent company to give instructions to the board of the subsidiary and to obtain the profits gained by the subsidiary.
[60] The MDax Index is part of the Prime Standard Segment of the Frankfurt Stock Exchange (FWB). It includes the 50 shares from classical sectors excluding technology that rank immediately below the companies included in the DAX index.
[61] LG Düsseldorf, GWR (2010), p. 504; upheld by BGH, AG (2011), p. 702.

19   In the United Kingdom, the FSA imposed a fine of £17 million on Shell for continually having delivered incorrect information regarding the reserves of a certain natural resource, thus influencing the share price.[62]

(bb) Digression: Behavioural Finance

20   Any information-based manipulation aims to influence the perception of other market participants. Whether information potentially gives incorrect or misleading signals depends not only on the information itself, but also to a large extent on how the information is understood by the recipient. If investors have persistent problems understanding or processing certain information correctly, a clever manipulator can take advantage of this fact.[63]

21   The literature on behavioural finance has proven that humans generally tend to overestimate their abilities. This phenomenon of *overconfidence* also arises on financial markets, as studies on financial analysts[64], CEOs with regard to takeovers and dividend policies,[65] and private investors with online trading accounts[66] have shown. The result of such overconfidence can be that people do not fall for the manipulator because they believe him, but rather because they believe they can still control events.[67]

22   The human assessment of risks furthermore changes, depending on whether information is framed as a possibility to make profits or prevent losses (*framing effect*), the inclination to take risks being larger when trying to prevent losses. Similarly, humans tend to choose safe profits over possible, but uncertain, higher profits, even if the expected utility in both cases is the same.[68]

23   Finally, humans take in information more easily the more prominently it is presented (*availability bias*). This can lead to the problem that certain information is not acknowledged, simply because of the way it is presented, e.g. disclaimers on possible conflicts of interest of the manipulator or information on particular risks.[69]

24   These three examples show how much influence human weaknesses in processing information can have on investment decisions. The MAD and the national implementing measures, however, do not take this aspect of behavioural finance into account. They rather build on the concept of a *reasonable investor*[70] who bases his

[62] FSA Final Notice, *Shell Transport and Trading Company, plc and The Royal Dutch Petroleum Company NV*, 24 August 2004 (this judgment was made prior to the introduction of the new regime and is now viewed as a sanction for information-based manipulation).
[63] L. Teigelack, *Finanzanalysen und Behavioral Finance*, p. 182 concerning the use of information resulting from a research report. On behavioural finance see L. Klöhn, *Kapitalmarkt, Spekulation und Behavioral Finance*, p. 92 ff.; see also § 6 para. 20–32.
[64] G. Friesen and P. Weller, 9 Journal of Financial Markets (2006), p. 14; O. Stotz and R. von Nitzsch, ZBB (2003), p. 106 ff.; see also Q. Chen and W. Jiang, 19 Rev. Fin. Studies (2006), p. 319, 339, 350.
[65] U. Malmendier and G. Tate, Working Paper (2003), p. 1, 36; S. Deshmukh et al., Working Paper (2009), p. 32.
[66] B. Barber and T. Odean, 21 Rev. Fin. Studies (2008), p. 785; B. Barber and T. Odean, 55 J. Fin. (2000), p. 773.
[67] Cf. L. Teigelack, *Finanzanalysen und Behavioral Finance*, p. 143.
[68] In general D. Kahneman and A. Tversky, 47 Econometrica (1979), p. 263, 268–269; A. Tversky and D. Kahneman, 59 J. Bus. (1986), p. 251, 260.
[69] L. Teigelack, *Finanzanalysen und Behavioral Finance*, p. 131, 143–144.
[70] See § 13 para. 61.

decision on all available information.[71] It has not yet been considered that this reasonable investor may make mistakes when coming to an investment decision. Accepting this danger would lead to new problems, as one can hardly predict which person will make which mistake in processing information in any given situation. Perhaps the concept of a reasonable investor must therefore be regarded as a deliberate decision of the legislature not to want to protect incorrect investment decisions.[72]

(b) Transaction-Based Manipulation

(aa) Core Definition and Signals

25 The MAD further requires that Member States prohibit transaction-based market manipulations, i.e. any transactions or orders to trade

— which give, or are likely to give, false or misleading signals as to the supply of, demand for or price of financial instruments, or

— which secure, by a person, or persons acting in collaboration, the price of one or several financial instruments at an abnormal or artificial level.[73]

26 Article 4 Implementing Directive 2003/124/EC specifies these broadly phrased definitions. The Member States have to ensure that certain non-exhaustive signals, which cannot necessarily be deemed in themselves to constitute market manipulation, are taken into account when transactions or orders to trade are examined by market participants and competent authorities.

27 The signals are, among other things

— the extent to which orders to trade given or transactions undertaken represent a significant proportion of the daily volume of transactions in the relevant financial instrument on the regulated market concerned;

— the extent to which orders to trade given or transactions undertaken by persons with a significant buying or selling position in a financial instrument lead to significant changes in the price of the financial instrument;

— whether transactions undertaken lead to no change in beneficial ownership of a financial instrument;[74]

— the extent to which orders to trade given or transactions undertaken include position reversals in a short period and represent a significant proportion of the daily volume of transactions in the relevant financial instrument on the regulated market concerned;

— the extent to which orders to trade given or transactions undertaken are concentrated within a short time span in the trading session and lead to a price change which is subsequently reversed;

---

[71] Cf. Recital 1 MAD and CESR, *CESR's Advice on Level 2 Implementing Measures for the Proposed Market Abuse Directive*, CESR/02–89d, August 2003, p. 10; overview in R. Veil, ZBB (2006), p. 162 ff.; L. Teigelack, *Finanzanalysen und Behavioral Finance*, p. 83 ff.

[72] L. Teigelack, *Finanzanalysen und Behavioral Finance*, p. 86–87.

[73] Art. 1(2) subsec. 1(a) MAD; the ECJ has ruled that "securing" the price at an abnormal level requires no minimum time period. Even very short-lived distortions constitute trade-based manipulation (ECJ of 7 July 2011, Case C-445/09 (*IMC Securities*) [2011] ECR I-0000).

[74] This refers to so-called *wash sales*; see para. 28.

— the extent to which orders to trade are given or transactions are undertaken at or around a specific time when reference prices, settlement prices and valuations are calculated and lead to price changes which have an effect on such prices and valuations.[75]

28   CESR guidelines[76] give a good overview of forms of trade-based market manipulations. *Wash sales* are a prominent example: if an investor sells shares to a company that it owns, the economic ownership of the security does not change and this may be considered trade-based manipulation. *Marking the close* can happen, if transactions are intentionally entered into at the close of the market, so that investors trading on the basis of the closing price pay a higher price. *Spoofing* describes the procedure in which a manipulator who holds a *long position* submits one or more orders to buy, thus achieving the incorrect impression of a high demand. Shortly thereafter (before executing the order) the manipulator cancels the order, hoping that other market participants submit buy orders due to the seemingly higher demand. The manipulator then sells his securities at this higher price. *Improper matched orders* are orders placed by different parties at basically identical conditions. However, the parties have previously agreed on placing these orders, so that an unnatural strike price can result.

29   In Germany, for example, the sole member of the Board of Directors of Nomia Equity AG had submitted buy and sell orders through two different accounts at high limits. This led to an increase in the share price, and the director sold a large equity stake to his accomplice, a fund manager, at the higher share price.[77]

30   If the parties disclose the exceptional circumstances before the transaction, their behaviour does not constitute market manipulation. Disclosure according to the legal or exchange rules can be sufficient.[78] In these cases, the reliability of the price formation does not need to be protected, as the market is informed of the special circumstances beforehand, and thus cannot be misled.

(bb) Exceptions

31   No trade-based manipulation within the meaning of Article 1 No. 2(a) MAD occurs if the person entering into the transaction or placing the order to trade can demonstrate that it had legitimate reasons for doing so and that these transactions or orders to trade conform to accepted market practices on the regulated market concerned.[79] The Directive phrases the exception as a reversal of the burden of proof. The Member States must therefore prohibit the behaviour, unless the person who entered into the transaction can submit a legitimate reason and show that the transaction conforms to an accepted market practice. There is an intensive discussion in the legal literature as to the legitimate reasons and accepted market practices; however, this largely remains *law in the books* without any particular practical relevance.

---

[75] Art. 4 Implementing Directive 2003/124/EC.
[76] CESR, *Market Abuse Directive—Level 3—first set of CESR guidance and information on the common operation of the Directive*, CESR/04-505b, May 2005, p. 11 ff.
[77] BaFin, *Jahresbericht 2009* (annual report), p. 188.
[78] H. Fleischer, in: A. Fuchs (ed.), *Kommentar zum WpHG*, § 20a para. 53.
[79] Art. 1(2) subsec. 1(a) MAD.

(1) Legitimate Reasons

32 Neither the MAD nor the implementing measures contain information as to what constitutes a legitimate reason. Additionally, neither the CESR nor the ESMA have made any statement in this respect.

33 German legal literature is predominantly of the opinion that any reason that is accepted in capital markets law and is not contrary to market integrity is legitimate.[80] There does not appear to be any jurisprudence on this question as yet. In the United Kingdom, the FSA has listed numerous criteria in its Handbook that indicate the existence or non-existence of a legitimate reason. Legitimate reasons can, for example be assumed if the transaction is based on a legal or supervisory obligation towards a third party. As opposed to this, a legitimate reason is less likely if the transaction was performed in order to give incorrect or misleading signals.[81]

(2) Accepted Market Practices

34 The MAD defines the term as "practices that are reasonably expected in one or more financial markets and are accepted by the competent authority in accordance with guidelines adopted by the Commission".[82] Directive 2004/72 sets forth the factors that national supervisory authorities may consider in accepting a market practice and outlines the consultation process for acceptance.[83]

35 The Member States are to take into account several aspects,[84] such as the level of transparency of the relevant market practice to the market as a whole, the need to safeguard the operation of market forces and the proper interplay of the forces of supply and demand, the risk inherent in the relevant practice for the integrity of related markets, the structural characteristics of the relevant market (i.e. the type of market participants and the extent of retail investors participation), and the outcome of any investigation of the relevant market practice by any other competent authority.[85]

36 German legal literature is in favour of accepting several market practices, including so-called *block trades*, i.e. trades in large quantities of shares, or a buy-back of own shares outside the *safe-harbour* rule.[86] So far, however, these attempts have remained unsuccessful. The German supervisory authority (BaFin) has not yet accepted any market practice. In France one of the two accepted market practices is that the issuer may buy back shares for acquisition financing.[87] Spain and France allow investment firms to buy and sell shares in the name of the

---

[80] H. Fleischer, in: A. Fuchs (ed.), *Kommentar zum WpHG*, § 20a para. 79; J. Vogel, in: H.-D. Assmann and U.H. Schneider (eds.), *Kommentar zum WpHG*, § 20a para. 179.

[81] Against legitimate reasons MAR 1.6.5 [E]; for 1.6.6 [E]; cf. R. Veil and M. Wundenberg, *Englisches Kapitalmarktrecht*, p. 79.

[82] Art. 1(5) MAD.

[83] On the procedure see CESR, *Market Abuse Directive—Level 3—first set of CESR guidance and information on the common operation of the Directive*, CESR/04–505b, May 2005, p. 4 ff.

[84] Italy, Sweden and the United Kingdom, for example, exceed the requirements of European law, allowing the national authorities to take into account additional factors, not mentioned in the directive; see CESR, *Report on CESR Members' Powers under the Market Abuse Directive and its Implementing Measures*, CESR/07-380, June 2007, p. 22.

[85] Art. 2 lit(a)–(g) Directive 2004/72/EC.

[86] H. Fleischer, in: A. Fuchs (ed.), *Kommentar zum WpHG*, § 20a para. 88.

[87] See below para. 56.

Lars Teigelack

issuer on the basis of so-called liquidity contracts. This is also not covered by the *safe harbours*.[88] Austria has also accepted a market practice, allowing so-called *Kompensgeschäfte* in certain debt securities, according to which market participants may, under certain strict conditions for both buyers and sellers, procure a reference price for the security. This would usually be regarded as a *wash sale*.[89] In the United Kingdom the FSA has accepted certain market practices on the London Metal Exchange.[90] It has partly been suggested that practices accepted by one Member State should be allowed throughout Europe, an opinion that the CESR, however, does not share.[91]

(c)   Other Forms of Market Manipulation

37   The Member States must also prohibit transactions or orders to trade which employ fictitious devices or any other form of deception or contrivance.[92] This serves as a catch-all clause for all market manipulations that are not covered by the other two definitions, in order to prevent any behaviour that ought to be prohibited from remaining unsanctioned.[93] Implementing Directive 2003/124 provides for signals that must be taken into account when trying to determine whether behaviour is to be considered manipulative. Pursuant to Article 5, Member States have to ensure that the following signals are taken into account:

— whether orders to trade given or transactions undertaken by persons are preceded or followed by dissemination of false or misleading information by the same persons or persons linked to them;[94]

— whether orders to trade are given or transactions are undertaken by persons before or after the same persons or persons linked to them produce or disseminate research or investment recommendations which are erroneous or biased or demonstrably influenced by material interest.

3.   Examples of Market Manipulation

38   The MAD complements the general definition with two examples of specific practically relevant behaviours that constitute market manipulation.

(a)   Dominant Market Position

39   The first example of market manipulation is conduct by a person, or persons acting in collaboration, to secure a dominant position over the supply of or demand for a

---

[88] For Spain see: www.cesr-eu.org/popup2.php?id=4949; for France see: www.cesr-eu.org/popup2.php?id=3380.

[89] Cf. www.cesr-eu.org/popup2.php?id=3377 and the FMA's Market Practice Regulation (Marktpraxisverordnung), BGBl. II 2005/1.

[90] FSA Handbook, MAR 1 Annex 2.

[91] CESR, *CESR's response to the Commission call for evidence on the review of the Market Abuse Directive*, CESR/09-635, July 2009, p. 7.

[92] Art. 1(2) subsec. 1(b) MAD.

[93] On the German understanding H. Fleischer, in: A. Fuchs (ed.), *Kommentar zum WpHG*, § 20a para. 58.

[94] This can only refer to information that is not already likely to give false or misleading signals as to financial instruments, as this form of information is already included in the core definition in Art. 1(2)(c) MAD.

financial instrument which has the effect of fixing, directly or indirectly, purchase or sale prices or creating other unfair trading conditions.[95] Strictly speaking, this example does not refer to a manipulation on the ground of the information accessible for market participants. To have a dominant market position does not mean that others are misled. This is rather an antitrust problem, affecting market fairness.[96] The reason why the dominant market position was still introduced as part of the definition of market manipulation may be the fact that monopolies are likely to reduce investors' trust in the market.

40 According to the directive, any conduct to secure a dominant position is to be prohibited, irrespective of whether the person intends to abuse this position. The dominant position must, however, have the effect of fixing, directly or indirectly, purchase or sale prices or creating other unfair trading conditions. Such manipulation can occur if many undiscovered short sales have taken place, and the securities of the respective company are thus in great demand on the market.

41 *Example:* In Germany, the case of VW shares, which briefly soared to a price of over €1,000, making VW for a short time the world's most valuable company, has proven controversial.[97] At the same time as declaring Porsche's intention to acquire a total of 75% of VW's shares,[98] Porsche's CEO had informed the public of already having raised its holdings to 43%, with an additional 31% in "options" as a forward cover. These were *cash-settled equity swaps* that did not have to be disclosed at the time.[99] As a result short sellers and index funds had to acquire further VW shares. However, the supply of ordinary VW shares was extremely low at this time, as large numbers of the available shares were held by Porsche itself or by its contractual counterparties via option contracts. The counterparties had acquired shares in order to hedge the risks resulting from the option contract. The federal state of Lower Saxony held a little more than 20% of the shares, so that a supply of merely 6% of available shares was met by 13% of shorted shares.

(b) Transactions at the Close of the Market

42 A second example of market manipulation is the so-called *marking the close*.[100] The MAD defines this as the acquisition or sale of financial instruments at the close of the market with the effect of misleading investors acting on the basis of closing prices.[101] This can be especially profitable when further transactions are concluded on the basis of an upwards distorted closing price.

---

[95] Art. 1(2) subsec. 2 indent 1 MAD.
[96] J. Vogel, in: H.-D. Assmann and U.H. Schneider (eds.), *Kommentar zum WpHG*, § 20a para. 231 ff.
[97] Spiegel online of 28 October 2008, www.spiegel.de/wirtschaft/0,1518,587036,00.html.
[98] See para. 17.
[99] In more detail see § 20 para. 80 and 107–126.
[100] See also CESR, *Market Abuse Directive—Level 3—first set of CESR guidance and information on the common operation of the Directive*, CESR/04-505b, May 2005, p. 11.
[101] Art. 1(2) subsec. 2 indent 2 MAD.

(c)   Abusing the Access to the Media

43   A third example of market manipulation refers to "taking advantage of occasional or regular access to the traditional or electronic media by voicing an opinion about a financial instrument (or indirectly about its issuer) while having previously taken positions on that financial instrument and profiting subsequently from the impact of the opinions voiced on the price of that instrument, without having simultaneously disclosed that conflict of interest to the public in a proper and effective way".[102] This is so-called *scalping*, which might, for example, involve spam e-mails, which promise considerable increases in the share price of specific issuers.[103] Before sending the e-mail, the sender buys shares in the generally illiquid titles, enabling them to profit from the subsequent price movement. Successful *scalping* requires that the opinion of the scalper can influence the share price. It therefore usually happens with regard to illiquid shares for which even slight trading activities can lead to price movements.[104]

44   In Germany the BGH had to deal with a criminal case on scalping in 2003. The defendant was the editor of a money magazine and appeared in stock exchange programmes on television issuing investment recommendations. He had obtained the reputation of being an opinion maker in the "new market" and had entered into consultancy contracts with two equity funds. These usually followed his recommendations without any further enquiries. The defendant and an accomplice raised funds, before acquiring new economy stock and then recommending these to the two funds without, however, indicating that he was holding respective shares himself. Due to the high order volume the prices of the securities rose and the defendant sold his shares at a higher price.

45   Before this case, the prevailing view in legal literature held that the acquisition of securities by a *scalper* prior to the public recommendation thereof violated the rules on insider dealings, the knowledge of the *scalper* of the ensuing recommendation being regarded as inside information. The BGH rightly did not follow this understanding, arguing that personally created facts did not constitute inside information requiring that the information have a connection to a third party and not exist only in the mind of the *scalper*.[105]

46   The *scalper's* recommendation need not in itself be incorrect or misleading. It is rather sufficient if the scalper has not disclosed the conflict of interest arising from his own position. Recommendations of a *scalper* that give false or misleading signals in the sense of the core definition already constitute market manipulation for this reason.

47   In Germany, *scalping* was the supervisory authority's focus in 2008 and 2009. Most *scalping* activities could be observed on the open market where the trans-

---

[102] Art. 1(2) subsec. 2 indent 3 MAD.

[103] On so-called stock spam see H. Fleischer, ZBB (2008), pp.137 ff. and L. Teigelack, *Finanzanalysen und Behavioral Finance*, p. 282–283.

[104] Cf. R.K. Aggarwal and G. Wu, 79. J. Bus. (2006), p. 1915, 1917; one of the most commonly cited examples from the United States is the case *SEC v. Lebed*, 73 SEC Docket 741 (20 September 2000), in which a teenager earned a few hundred thousand dollars through *scalping* on the Internet.

[105] BGHSt 48 (2003), p. 373.

parency requirements are lower, and the information disseminated by *scalpers* is often the only information available to investors.[106]

48   The draft regulation[107] adds two new examples to the existing three. They relate to emission allowances and algorithmic and high-frequency trading. The acquisition or sale of emission allowances or related derivatives on the secondary market prior to an auction is to be considered market manipulation, if it has the effect that the auction clearing price is fixed at an abnormal or artificial level or if bidders are misled.[108] Algorithmic and high-frequency tradings are not prohibited per se, certain forms rather being classified as *trade-based* market manipulations. In general, sending orders to a trading venue without an intention to trade is prohibited if the order is placed with the intention of disrupting or delaying the functioning of the venue's trading system, by making it more difficult for others to identify genuine orders (so-called *layering* or *quote stuffing*) or creating a false or misleading impression about the supply and demand for a financial instrument.[109]

V.   Safe-Harbour Rules

1.   Introduction

49   The MAD stipulates two exceptions from the prohibition of market manipulation. The prohibitions do not apply to trading in own shares in "buy-back" programmes and the stabilisation of a financial instrument, provided such trading is carried out in accordance with the procedure laid down in the implementing measures.[110] This refers to Regulation 2273/2003, which cannot be regarded as mere *book law*: buy-back programmes and stabilisation measures are of considerable practical importance.

50   The exemptions only apply to relevant securities, i.e. transferrable securities as defined in the MAD, which are *admitted* to trading on a regulated market or for which a request for admission to trading on such a market has been made, and which are the subject of a significant distribution.[111] Germany extends this scope of application to financial instruments that are merely *included* in the open or regulated market, but not admitted to trading on a regulated market within the European Economic Area.[112]

51   The draft regulation[113] excludes buy-back programmes and stabilisation from the scope of the provisions on market abuse under similar conditions to the current Regulation 2273/2003. The Commission is required to develop technical imple-

---

[106] BaFin, *Jahresbericht 2008* (annual report), p. 161–162; BaFin, *Jahresbericht 2009* (annual report), p. 186.
[107] Cf. para. 3.
[108] Art. 8(3) lit. (e) COM(2011) 651 final.
[109] Art. 8(3) lit. (c) COM(2011) 651 final.
[110] Art. 8 MAD.
[111] Art. 2(6) Regulation 2273/2003.
[112] § 20a(3) sentence 2 WpHG.
[113] See para. 3.

menting measures specifying the exact conditions. The effect the draft will have on Regulation 2273/2003 remains unclear.[114]

2. Buy-Back Programmes

52 The acquisition of own shares by a company can help signal to the market that the securities are not undervalued. The incentive to buy caused by the company can lead to a stabilisation or increase of the share price. A company may also buy back shares as currency for acquisitions, to prevent takeovers or to meet obligations arising from employee share option programmes or exchangeable bonds.[115]

53 Once the share price deviates from the securities' "real value", one enters the realm of market manipulation, because the price is no longer determined by the free interaction of market forces, but rather by the company steering the market. Nevertheless, buy-back programmes for shares (not bonds) must be exempted from the prohibition of market manipulation under certain conditions due to their great importance for issuers.

54 The exemption applies to any trading in own shares. This means that not only buy-back programmes, but also circumventive actions and the acquisition of derivatives, such as call-options, must meet the requirements of the regulation in order to be exempt from the rules on market manipulation.[116]

55 Buy-back programmes that meet the requirements established by the regulation are only exempt from the prohibition of market manipulation and insider dealing as long as the obligations to disclose inside information[117] and major shareholdings[118] remain applicable.[119] The issuer also has to meet the EU corporate law requirements regarding share buy-backs.[120]

(a) Aim of the Programme

56 Legitimate objectives for buy-back programmes only include the reduction of an issuer's capital (in value or in number of shares), meeting obligations arising from debt financial instruments exchangeable into equity instruments or employee share option programmes, or other allocations of shares to employees of the issuer or of an associate company.[121] Calls to include buy-back programmes for acquisition financing into the *safe harbour* can be heard regularly in legal practice. The CESR has rebuffed this demand, although not all supervisory authorities share this opinion.[122] France, for example, has declared the acquisition of own shares to finance the acquisition of a company on Euronext an *accepted market practice*.[123]

---

[114] Art. 3 COM (2011) 651 final.

[115] Cf. H. Fleischer, in: A. Fuchs (ed.), *Kommentar zum WpHG*, § 20a para. 94 with further references.

[116] J. Vogel, in: H.-D. Assmann and U.H. Schneider (eds.), *Kommentar zum WpHG*, § 20a para. 251.

[117] See § 15 Rn. 25 ff.

[118] See § 16 Rn. 17 ff.

[119] J. Vogel, in: H.-D. Assmann and U.H. Schneider (eds.), *Kommentar zum WpHG*, § 20a para. 250–251.

[120] Recital 4 Regulation 2273/2003.

[121] Art. 3 Regulation 2273/2003.

[122] CESR, *CESR's response to the Commission call for evidence on the review of the Market Abuse Directive*, CESR/09-635, July 2009, p. 7.

[123] Cf. www.cesr-eu.org/popup2.php?id=3379.

(b) Disclosure Obligations

57   In order to profit from the *safe-harbour* rule, an issuer must comply with certain disclosure obligations, both prior to and after implementing the buy-back. Full details of the programme must be adequately disclosed to the public, *prior* to the start of trading and subsequently in case of changes.[124] The "adequate disclosure" of information is to be determined in accordance with the TD and will not be described in any further detail herein.[125]

58   The issuer must further publicly disclose details of all transactions *after* the date of execution of such transactions.[126] This does not mean that the information must be disclosed after each individual transaction, but rather no later than the end of the seventh trading day after the last transaction of the programme.

(c) Trading Conditions

59   The buy-back programme must follow the procedure laid down in the regulation. The provisions on trading conditions are to ensure that the acquisition of own shares by the company does not lead to an artificial price increase by higher acquisition prices or a shortage of shares on the free market.[127] The regulation therefore lays down requirements on the minimum price to be paid on a regulated market,[128] as well as for the purchase of own shares through derivative financial instruments and on non-regulated markets.[129] A shortage of shares on the market is to be prevented by the fact that "the issuer must not purchase more than 25% of the average daily volume of the shares in any one day on the regulated market on which the purchase is carried out".[130] Special requirements apply in cases of extremely low liquidity on the relevant market, where the issuer cannot purchase a sufficient amount of shares.[131]

(d) Restrictions

60   Additionally, the issuer is subject to a number of restrictions, which are to ensure fairness and transparency of the buy-back programme.[132] The issuer may not sell own shares for the duration of the programme and may not trade at all during certain, so-called "closed" periods, if national law provides for such periods, or where the issuer has decided to delay the public disclosure of inside information.[133]

---

[124] Art. 4(2) Regulation 2273/2003.

[125] Art. 2(5) Regulation 2273/2003 refers to Art. 102(1) and 103 Directive 2001/34/EC, which were amended by the Transparency Directive, cf. Art. 32(6) Directive 2004/109/EC.

[126] Art. 4(4) Regulation 2273/2003.

[127] Art. 5 Regulation 2273/2003; also see J. Vogel, in H.-D. Assmann and U.H. Schneider (eds.), *Kommentar zum WpHG*, § 20a para. 258.

[128] Art. 5 (1) subsec. 1 Regulation 2273/2003.

[129] Art. 5 (1) subsec. 2, 3 Regulation 2273/2003.

[130] Art. 5(2) subsec. 1 Regulation 2273/2003.

[131] Art. 5(3) Regulation 2273/2003.

[132] J. Vogel, in: H.-D. Assmann and U.H. Schneider (eds.), *Kommentar zum WpHG*, § 20a para. 262.

[133] Art. 6(1) Regulation 2273/2003; on exemptions from publication requirements to protect an issuer's legitimate interests, cf. § 15 para. 68 ff.

61   *Closed or prohibited periods* in the sense of the MAD are periods during which the issuer's board members or all employees are prohibited to trade in the issuer's shares. Germany does not provide for any such *closed periods*. In the United Kingdom, the two months prior to the publication of the quarterly figures are a *prohibited period*.[134]

62   The restrictions on trading do not apply if the issuer is an investment firm or credit institution and has established effective information barriers (*Chinese walls*) between those responsible for the handling of inside information and those responsible for any decision relating to the trading of own shares.[135] They also do not apply if the issuer has a time-scheduled buy-back programme in place or the buy-back programme is managed by an investment firm or a credit institution with sole discretion as to the transactions.[136] A *time-scheduled* programme sets out the dates and quantities of securities to be traded during the period of the programme at the time of the public disclosure of the buy-back programme.[137] The disadvantage of these programmes is that the issuer can no longer react flexibly to the actual market conditions.[138] At the same time, they guarantee transparency and independence, thus exempting the issuer from the prohibitions.

3.   Price Stabilisation

63   So-called price stabilisation activities constitute a second *safe harbour*. The regulation defines stabilisation as any transaction on primary or secondary markets in the context of a significant distribution of securities supporting the market price.[139] These measures are privileged, because stock issues are often accompanied by numerous disposals of shares by short-term traders. Some investors also subsequently sell as many shares as necessary to cover their costs of acquiring the newly issued shares (so-called *flipping*).[140] The resulting selling pressure reduces the price of the financial instruments. This is regarded as contrary to market interests, and the regulation thus aims to prevent such price drops.[141] Since stabilisation activities lead to an artificial price level, adequate public disclosure is necessary in order to ensure the investors' trust in the market mechanisms.[142]

64   As with buy-back programmes, the safe harbour for stabilisation measures only exempts an issuer from the prohibition of market manipulation. Ad hoc disclosure obligations and the general rules governing investment firms and credit institutions still apply, as only these institutions are allowed to carry out stabilisation measures.

---

[134] LR 12.2.1 in conjunction with Model Code (Annex 1 of LR 9) 1(a).
[135] Art. 6(1) subsec. 1, 2 Regulation 2273/2003.
[136] Art. 6(3) Regulation 2273/2003.
[137] Art. 2(4) Regulation 2273/2003.
[138] J. Vogel, in: H.-D. Assmann and U.H. Schneider (eds.), *Kommentar zum WpHG*, § 20a para. 262.
[139] Cf. ibid., § 20a para. 265.
[140] W. Feuring and C. Berrar, in: M. Habersack et al. (eds.), *Unternehmensfinanzierung am Kapitalmarkt*, § 34 para. 1.
[141] Recital 11 Regulation 2273/2003.
[142] Recitals 16, 18 Regulation 2273/2003.

(a) Scope of Application

65   Only investment firms and credit institutions are permitted to undertake stabilisation activities under the regulation.[143] The safe harbour is open to the *initial* and *secondary public offerings* of relevant securities.[144] This also includes the placement of shares after a capital increase.[145] So-called *block trades*, in which large shareholdings are traded between individual persons, do not fall within the scope of the regulation.[146]

66   In Germany the legal literature discusses the question of whether one must distinguish between *block trades* as private transactions and *block trades* with several bidders which may be regarded as secondary offerings, provided they are announced publicly.[147] The British FSA does not provide a *safe harbour* for *block trades*, reasoning that they constitute entirely private transactions.[148] Neither the CESR nor the ESMA have yet submitted any guidelines on Level 3 of the Lamfalussy procedure.[149]

67   The *safe-harbour* rule further does not apply to a decline in stock prices resulting from the poor economic situation of an issuer. Additionally, stabilisation may under no circumstances "be executed above the offering price".[150] Stabilisation may only aim to stabilise the price, not, however, to increase it. According to the CESR, sales also do not fall within the scope of the directive, as only the purchase of shares can stabilise the price.[151]

(b) Period of Stabilisation

68   The regulation only exempts stabilisation activities from the market manipulation provisions if these activities were limited to a certain time period in advance.[152] The activities must furthermore have an immediate relation to an offering. In an initial public offering of shares and other securities equivalent to shares, the period begins on the date of commencement of trading and ends no later than 30 calendar days thereafter.[153] The *safe harbour* is therefore not open for transactions during the *bookbuilding* phase. In a secondary offering, the relevant period begins on the date of adequate public disclosure of the final price of the relevant securities and ends no later than 30 calendar days after the date of allotment. Special rules exist for bonds

---

[143] Art. 2(7) Regulation 2273/2003.

[144] Art. 2(6) Regulation 2273/2003.

[145] J. Vogel, in: H.-D. Assmann and U.H. Schneider (eds.), *Kommentar zum WpHG*, § 20a para. 273.

[146] Recital 14 Regulation 2273/2003.

[147] H. Fleischer, in: A. Fuchs (ed.), *Kommentar zum WpHG*, § 20a para. 109; J. Vogel, in H.-D. Assmann and U.H. Schneider (eds.), *Kommentar zum WpHG*, § 20a para. 273.

[148] MAR 2.2.6 G.

[149] CESR, *Level 3—Third Set of CESR Guidance and Information on the Common Operation of the Directive to the Market*, CESR/09-219, May 2009, contains no recommendations regarding block trades.

[150] Art. 10(1) (shares or other securities equivalent to shares,) and accordingly (2) (securitised debt convertible or exchangeable into shares) Regulation 2273/2003.

[151] CESR, *Level 3—Third Set of CESR Guidance and Information on the Common Operation of the Directive to the Market*, CESR/09-219, May 2009, p. 11–12.

[152] Art. 8(1) Regulation 2273/2003.

[153] Art. 8(2) Regulation 2273/2003.

and other forms of debt securities, because the quotation of prices usually does not begin immediately after the issuance of the securities.[154]

(c)   Disclosure and Organisational Obligations

69   As for buy-back programmes, European law also demands disclosure of stabilisation activities. Before the opening of the offer period of the relevant securities, adequate public disclosure[155] is required. The issuer must make public the fact that stabilisation may or may not be undertaken and that it may be stopped at any time. The disclosure must further contain information on the beginning and end of the period during which stabilisation may occur and on the conditions under which a so-called greenshoe option may be exercised.[156] These provisions do not, however, apply to offers under the scope of the Prospectus Directive.[157] The Prospectus Regulation already lays down that these and further details are to be made public.

70   Within one week after the end of the stabilisation period, certain details of the transactions or the fact that no stabilisation was undertaken are to be adequately disclosed and the competent authority is to be informed.[158] The issuer is additionally obligated to record each stabilisation order or transaction, ensuring a better supervision by the competent authority.[159]

(d)   Ancillary Stabilisation

71   "Ancillary stabilisation" means the exercise of an overallotment facility or of a greenshoe option by investment firms or credit institutions.[160] In the offering, a greater number of securities is allotted than originally offered. This measure serves to mitigate any potential demand surplus. The additional securities are usually provided by one or more securities loans. If the market price of the instrument declines after the offering, the underwriting bank or banks acquires securities on the market in order to stabilise the instrument's price, and "repays" the securities loans with these shares. If the market price increases or remains stable, the underwriting bank or banks can acquire the shares lent to it at the issue price and sell them with a profit in the market. A conflict of interest may occur if the bank acquires too many shares through the greenshoe option, and now wants to sell those shares.[161]

72   In Germany it is disputed, whether the option may be exercised even in the absence of any excess demand.[162] With respect to another uncertainty, CESR has recently issued a statement according to which the disposal of securities that

---

[154] J. Vogel, in: H.-D. Assmann and U.H. Schneider (eds.), *Kommentar zum WpHG*, § 20a para. 280; cf. Art. 8 (4), (5) Regulation 2273/2003.

[155] Art. 2(5) Regulation 2273/2003.

[156] Art. 9(1) Regulation 2273/2003.

[157] Art. 9(1) sentence 2 Regulation 2273/2003.

[158] Art. 9(2), (3) Regulation 2273/2003.

[159] Art. 9(4) Regulation 2273/2003.

[160] Art. 2(12) Regulation 2273/2003; on the concept of overallotment and *greenshoe* options see Art. 2(13), (14) Regulation 2273/2003 and A. Meyer, in: R. Marsch-Barner and F. Schäfer (eds.), *Handbuch börsennotierte AG*, § 8 para. 63 ff.

[161] J. Vogel, in: H.-D. Assmann and U.H. Schneider (eds.), *Kommentar zum WpHG*, § 20a para. 289.

[162] Ibid., § 20a para. 291.

---

were acquired through stabilisation measures and the subsequent sale of such papers (*refreshing the greenshoe*) do not fall within the scope of the safe harbour. The regulation defines stabilisation measures as measures supporting the market price of securities due to selling pressure in such securities. This can only be achieved through buy orders.[163]

73   Ancillary stabilisation thus depends on additional prerequisites. An overallotment of securities is therefore only permitted during the subscription period and only at the issue price. The greenshoe option can only be exercised in the context of an overallotment, it must be exercised during the stabilisation period, and it may not amount to more than 15% of the original offer. Further disclosure obligations apply after the completion of the offering.[164]

VI.   Supervision

1.   Supervisory Mechanisms

74   The national supervisory authorities are charged with the task of monitoring compliance with the prohibition of market manipulation.[165] The European legal acts make supervision possible by forcing Member States to establish general notification obligations for all transactions and special notification obligations for suspicious transactions.[166] The supervisory authorities employ methods of IT monitoring. Italy, France, the United Kingdom, Austria and to a certain degree Germany use software that can determine deviations from normal order behaviour with the help of algorithms and statistical tests.[167]

2.   Investigatory Powers

75   The MAD contains detailed provisions on the minimum powers of supervisory authorities. These powers include the right to have access to any document and to receive copies, demand information from any person, and if necessary, to summon and hear any such person, to carry out onsite inspections, to require existing telephone and existing data traffic records, to require the cessation of any practice that is contrary to the MAD, to suspend trading in the respective financial instrument, to request the freezing and/or sequestration of assets, and to request temporary prohibition of professional activity.[168]

76   Member States have implemented these powers into their national laws. Problems arise when investigatory powers conflict with the basic constitutional rights of the

---

[163] Art. 2(7) Regulation 2273/2003; CESR, *Level 3—Third Set of CESR Guidance and Information on the Common Operation of the Directive to the Market*, CESR/09–219, May 2009, p. 12.

[164] Art. 11 Regulation 2273/2003.

[165] Only in Sweden does the authority have to cooperate with the stock exchanges; cf. R. Veil and F. Walla, *Swedish Capital Markets Law*, p. 10 ff.

[166] Art. 6(9) MAD; Art. 7 ff. Directive 2004/72/EC; Art. 25(3) MiFID.

[167] Report On CESR Members' Powers Under The Market Abuse Directive and its Implementing Measures (07-380), p. 27 ff.

[168] Art. 12(2) MAD.

market participants. Journalists, for example, may refer to their right to protect their sources. Furthermore, the summoning of persons from third countries may be difficult to enforce.[169] Differences exist between the authorities' powers to require existing telephone and data traffic records. Although all authorities are generally empowered to require these, the practical enforcement thereof differs greatly. The Italian authority can only require the telephone records of supervised companies, whereas judicial authorities are responsible for other persons and for Internet providers.[170] In Sweden, data protection laws prevent the supervisory authority from receiving data from telephone service providers.[171]

77   All Member States have allowed their authorities to suspend trading in the respective financial instruments. The German supervisory authority BaFin views this power very critically and does not make use of it to prevent market manipulation, reasoning that it constitutes too drastic a measure. Trading could only be suspended for a few hours, and this would hardly be sufficient to uncover cases of market manipulation.[172] Not in all Member States can the supervisory authority demand the freezing and/or sequestration of assets. In Germany, for example, the BaFin does not possess this power, and in Spain the applicable procedure is unclear, so that the CNMV has yet not filed such a request.[173]

78   The draft regulation establishes a set of minimum regulatory powers including the right to directly access traders' systems in relation to derivatives on commodities and the right to enter private premises in order to seize documents. The latter power is subject to prior authorisation of the judicial authority of the respective Member State.[174] Member States may hence grant their competent authority greater powers than those mentioned in the regulation.

VII. Sanctions

1.   Requirements under European Law

79   With regard to the sanctions for market manipulations, the MAD merely contains very general provisions.[175] The Member States are to ensure "that the appropriate administrative measures can be taken or administrative sanctions be imposed against the persons responsible where the provisions adopted in the implementation of this Directive have not been complied with".[176] They must further ensure that these measures are "effective, proportionate and dissuasive".[177] They are not,

---

[169] CESR, *Review Panel Report, MAD Options and Discretions*, CESR/09-1120, March 2010, p. 96.
[170] Ibid., p. 97.
[171] Ibid., p. 90.
[172] Ibid., p. 100.
[173] Ibid., p. 100.
[174] Cf. R. Veil and P. Koch, *Towards a Uniform European Capital Markets Law: Proposals of the Commission to Reform Market Abuse* (2012).
[175] See § 12 para. 4–5.
[176] Art. 14(1) MAD.
[177] Art. 14(1) MAD.

however, obligated to impose criminal sanctions for market manipulation, and thus make use of all the investigatory powers of the law enforcement agencies.[178]

80   Further, supervisory authorities are to have the right to publish all sanctions imposed. Member States must provide "that the competent authority may disclose to the public every measure or sanction that will be imposed for infringement of the provisions adopted in the implementation of this Directive, unless such disclosure would seriously jeopardise the financial markets or cause disproportionate damage to the parties involved".[179]

81   The Commission has reached the conclusion that this framework is insufficient for criminal sanctions and has presented a draft directive on criminal sanctions for insider dealing and market manipulation.[180] Further, the draft regulation[181] contains detailed rules on administrative sanctions.[182]

2.   Transposition in the Member States

(a)   Criminal Sanctions

82   Sweden is the only Member State to impose only criminal sanctions for market manipulation, the maximum prison sentence being four years.[183] Critics argue against this approach, reasoning that the supervisory authorities possess better resources than public prosecutors.[184] It thus is no surprise that convictions for market manipulation are relatively rare. Between 1991 and 1999, 416 procedures were initiated, which led to a mere 27 charges and only eight convictions.[185] In 2008 the supervisory authority reported 190 suspected cases of market manipulation.[186] In Italy, penalties for market manipulation range between one and six years of imprisonment. In 2010, Consob only reported 11 cases of market manipulations to the judicial authorities; from 2005 to 2010 the total number of cases was only 53.[187] Spanish law also treats market manipulation as a crime[188] that may be punished with up to 24 months of imprisonment. Only 10 procedures were initiated for both market manipulation and insider dealings in 2010.[189] In France, up to two years of imprisonment can be imposed, in the United Kingdom imprisonment can be up to seven years. In Germany, market manipulation only constitutes a crime when committed intentionally and having an actual effect on the market price.[190] Influencing the price may lead to imprisonment of up to five years or monetary fines.

---

[178] Art. 14(1) MAD.

[179] Art. 14(4) MAD.

[180] COM(2011) 654 final.

[181] Cf. § 1 para. 41.

[182] Art. 24–29 COM(2011) 651 final.

[183] §§ 8, 15 Market Abuse Act.

[184] Cf. C. af Sandeberg, JT (2002–2003), p. 870, 882 ff.; C. af Sandeberg, Ny Juridik (2002), p. 7, 18; seen critically by p. Samuelsson, JT (2003–2004), p. 256, 263 ff.; H. Jacobson and J. Lycke, ERT (2005), p. 303, 311.

[185] E. Wesser, *Har du varit ute och shoppat, Jacob?—En studie av Finansinspektionens utredning av insiderbrott under 1990-talet*, p. 125 ff.

[186] Cf. www.fi.se/Templates/Page7176.aspx.

[187] Consob, *Annual Report (2008)*, p. 96, 98; (2010), p. 109.

[188] Art. 284 CP.

[189] CNMV, *Annual Report (2009)*, p. 155; (2010), p. 187.

[190] §§ 38(2); 39(1) Nos. 1, 2 and (2) WpHG.

83   The concepts of the Member States concerning monetary penalties also differ greatly. Some Member States have laid down maximum limits, others determine the limit according to the offender's income or the profits gained through the manipulation. In Italy, monetary penalties can range between €20,000 and €3 million or an amount of up to ten times the profits.[191] In France, monetary penalties of up to €1.5 million or ten times the amount of the profits may be imposed.[192] In Spain the penalty may vary between 12 and 24 monthly fees, a monthly fee consisting of 30 daily fees.[193] In the United Kingdom, unlimited monetary penalties are available to punish market manipulation.[194] Swedish courts are not permitted to impose monetary penalties, but can demand that profits be forfeited. Germany provides no precise limit to monetary fines. Rather, the sum depends on the offender's income. The highest possible penalty is 360 daily fees of €30,000 each, i.e. a total of €10.8 million. The minimum penalty is five daily fees of €1 each.[195] The courts can additionally declare forfeit the profits gained through the market manipulation.[196] Ninety court proceedings were closed in Germany in 2011, 11 of which resulted in a conviction and 69 of which were dismissed, partly against payment of a monetary remedy.[197]

84   The draft directive[198] obligates the Member States to make certain forms of intentional market manipulation a criminal offence. This also applies to inciting, aiding and abetting or attempting to commit one of these forms of market manipulation.[199] Both the MAD and the new draft directive grant the Member States discretion with regard to the measures taken to ensure that criminal sanctions are effective, proportionate and dissuasive.[200] In addition to criminal proceedings against the actual perpetrator/inciter/accessory, legal persons can also be held liable for the offences committed for their benefit by any person holding a leading position within that entity. The same applies if a person with a leading position has failed to supervise or control a person under his or her authority, and has thereby enabled them to commit one of the aforementioned offences.[201] The Commission was restricted to the instrument of a directive as the European Union does not have the powers to harmonise criminal law by way of a regulation.[202]

(b)   Administrative Sanctions

85   Most Member States choose fines when imposing administrative sanctions. In Spain, a *particularly severe infraction*[203] can lead to fines of up to five times the

---

[191] Art. 185 I TUF.

[192] Art. L. 465-2 and L. 465-3 C. mon. fin.; in more detail R. Veil and p. Koch, *Französisches Kapitalmarktrecht*, p. 16 ff.

[193] Cf. Art. 50 CP.

[194] Sec. 397(3) FSMA.

[195] § 40 StGB.

[196] § 73(1) StGB.

[197] Detailed overview in BaFin, *Jahresbericht 2009* (annual report), p. 187 also with data on 2008 and 2007; BaFin, *Jahresbericht 2011* (annual report), p. 205–210 also with data on 2010.

[198] Cf. § 1 para. 41.

[199] Art. 4, 5 COM(2011) 654 final.

[200] Art. 6 COM(2011) 654 final.

[201] Art. 7 COM(2011) 654 final.

[202] Art. 83(1) TFEU.

[203] An infraction qualifies as particularly severe, if the manipulation had considerable influence on the market price; cf. Art. 99.i LMV.

amount of the profits gained.[204] *Severe infractions*[205] can be sanctioned with a fine of up to double the amount of the profits.[206] Fines in Italian supervisory proceedings range from €20,000 to €5 million.[207] The fine may, however, be tripled or raised to ten times the amount of the profits, if this appears justified by the severity of the offence.[208] In France,[209] administrative fines are limited to €10 million for legal entities and €1.5 million for persons or ten times the amount of the profits. The Austrian supervisory authorities can impose fines of up to €75,000 and declare forfeiture of the profits gained through the offence.[210] All market manipulations constitute administrative offences in Germany, to be sanctioned with a maximum fine of €1 million.[211] Both transaction-based and other manipulations must have been committed intentionally,[212] whereas information-based manipulations are subject to fines even when committed grossly negligently. Theoretically, fines are unrestricted and aim at skimming the offender's excess profits.[213] In practice, this possibility is not, however, made use of. In the United Kingdom, the FSA is permitted to impose unlimited fines, but had unofficially restricted fines for "serious cases" of market manipulation to a maximum of £100,000. The highest fine imposed against a person was a sum of approximately £970,000.[214] In 2010, however, the FSA introduced a new penalty framework. The FSA now focuses on "credible deterrence through targeted enforcement action to combat insider dealing and market abuse".[215]

86   Finally, the publication of sanctions—the so-called naming and shaming—can be considered an administrative sanction.[216] It can lead to considerable reputational damage[217] and enhance transparency by disclosing to the market all the sanctions imposed. Italian, French, British and Spanish authorities make wide use of this measure, whereas German and Austrian authorities are reluctant. Austrian legal literature has raised doubts about the constitutionality of a disclosure of the sanctions imposed, as the offender has no right to be heard prior to disclosure.[218] The German BaFin has not yet disclosed any sanctions. This may, for one, result from liability risks, a publication being likely to cause damage to the respective issuer. It may, however, also be the result of the fact that the German legislature and the BaFin generally view this form of "denunciation" critically.[219]

---

[204] If the exact profits cannot be determined, the factors according to which the fine is imposed can be either 5% of the offender's own funds, 5% of the funds used for the offence or €600,000.

[205] Art. 100.w LMV.

[206] If the profits cannot be determined, the factors according to which the fine is imposed can be either 2% of the offender's own funds, 2% of the funds used for the offence or €300,000.

[207] Art. 187-ter I TUF.

[208] Art. 187-ter V TUF.

[209] Art. 631-1 to 631-4 RG AMF.

[210] § 48c(1), (3) BörseG.

[211] Information-based manipulation § 39(2) No. 11; transaction-based manipulation § 39(1) No. 1; others § 39(1) No. 2 in conjunction with § 39(4) WpHG.

[212] § 39(1) No. 1, 2 in conjunction with § 39(4) WpHG; § 10 OWiG.

[213] § 17(4) OWiG.

[214] Cf. FSA, *Annual Report 2009/2010*, p. 21 on the as yet highest penalties and other examples p. 38.

[215] Cf. FSA, *Annual Report 2011/2012*, p. 14; cf. on the FSA's commitment S. Willey, 93 COB (2012), p. 1, 16–17; consequently the highest fine mentioned in the *Annual Report 2011/2012* is $9,600,000 or €6,000,000 (p. 45).

[216] Cf. § 7 para 1.

[217] CESR, *Review Panel Report, MAD Options and Discretions*, CESR/09–1120, March 2010, p. 115.

[218] Ibid., p. 118.

[219] K. Altenhain, in: H. Hirte and T.C.H. Möllers (eds.), *Kölner Kommentar zum WpHG*, § 40b para. 5; J. Vogel, in: H.-D. Assmann and U.H. Schneider (eds.), *Kommentar zum WpHG*, § 40b para. 6 ff.; M.P. Waßmer, in: Fuchs (ed.), *Kommentar zum WpHG*, § 40b para. 4.

87   The draft regulation contains a new concept regarding administrative measures and sanctions. Article 25 of the proposal lists the circumstances that allow the supervisory authority to impose administrative sanctions.[220] The draft further describes measures and sanctions that can be imposed; the list, however, is non-exhaustive, allowing Member States to introduce further sanctioning powers and higher pecuniary sanctions.[221] Unlike in earlier directives, the Commission has refrained from imposing specific minimum amounts and has again left this task to the Member States, merely requiring the sanctions to be effective, proportionate and dissuasive.[222] As opposed to this, the draft regulation does list a maximum amount, pecuniary sanctions being restricted to twice the amount of profits gained or losses avoided for natural persons and to 10% of last year's annual turnover for legal persons.[223] *Naming and shaming* can be expected to play a much greater role under the draft regulation, as measures and sanctions are to be published without undue delay, unless this would cause disproportionate damage for the parties involved.[224]

(c)   *Investor Protection through Civil Liability*

88   Civil law sanctions for violations of the prohibition on market manipulation play no role in Italy, France, Spain, Sweden and the United Kingdom. In Germany, on the other hand, the possibility of *private enforcement* has received considerably more attention. The courts have in particular had to answer the question whether § 20a WpHG can be regarded as a protective provision under § 823(2) of the BGB (German Civil Code).

89   The BGH had to decide on whether board members of Infomatec AG were liable to pay damages for incorrect ad hoc notifications.[225] The company had falsely reported orders amounting to approximately €55 million. The court ruled out prospectus liability, because ad hoc notifications, as opposed to prospectuses, only aim to inform of individual incidents, rather than giving a comprehensive picture of the company.[226] The court also held that the applicable provision in the former § 88 BörsG did not constitute a protective provision in the sense of § 823(2) BGB. As the rule did not aim to protect individual investors, the actually resulting investor protection was rather a mere reflex, whereas the aim of § 88 BörsG was only to ensure the functioning of the markets at a macro-level.[227]

90   A need for civil liability does not exist, and the court ruling not to admit such liability was thus correct. The German legislature has introduced special provisions establishing liability for incorrect or omitted ad hoc announcements, but not for market manipulation. German commentators have, however, argued that EU law requires the possibility of private enforcement for the protection of the individual

---

[220] Art. 25 lit. (d), (e) COM(2011) 651 for market manipulation and the attempt thereof.
[221] Art. 26 No. 1, 2 COM(2011) 651 final.
[222] Art. 24 No. 1 COM(2011) 651 final.
[223] Art. 26 No. 1 lit. (k), (m) COM(2011) 651 final.
[224] Art. 26 No. 3 COM(2011) 651 final.
[225] See also § 19 para. 112.
[226] BGHZ 160 (2004), p. 134, 138.
[227] BGHZ 160 (2004), p. 134, 139–140; confirmed in BGH XI ZR 51/10, ZIP 2012, 318 – IKB; on § 88 former BörsG also BVerfG, ZIP (2002), p. 1986; also H. Fleischer, in: A. Fuchs (ed.), *Kommentar zum WpHG*, § 20a para. 154.

investor, referring to ECJ decisions regarding antitrust law[228] and more fundamentally referring to decisions regarding European directives granting rights to individuals.[229] One author in particular has recently argued that where no private enforcement is required by EU law (i.e. outside the scope of liability for prospectuses, financial reports, and ad hoc announcements), the prohibition of market manipulation should be interpreted as protecting the rights of individual investors.[230] However, no court has ruled on this as yet, and the absence of a clear statement by the European legislature leaves the question open for discussion.

91 Unlike the German approach, the predominant legal opinion in Austria is that private enforcement by the investors is possible under § 48a of the BörseG, because the provision is said to constitute a protective provision for the benefit of each individual investor.[231] The Austrian OGH has recently confirmed this position.[232]

VIII. Conclusion

92 Most Member States have implemented the European provisions on market manipulation one-to-one. The prohibitions themselves are for the most part applied uniformly. Strikingly, far from all Member States have made use of their right to accept market practices; further coordination may be needed in this respect should accepted market practices still exist under the new regulation.

93 Significant differences still exist regarding the rules and legal practice around sanctions. Not all Member States treat market manipulations as a crime and the maximum amount of administrative fine differs greatly. Forfeiture of profits is just as inconsistently applied throughout the European Union. The draft regulation and directive will mitigate this problem if adopted in its current form; however, the Commission could have gone a step further by directly harmonising administrative sanctions. For criminal sanctions on the financial markets, the directive was the only available method, because the TFEU does not allow for a regulation in this regard.

---

[228] ECJ of 20 September 2001, Case C-453/99 (*Courage*) (2001) ECR I-6314 (6324) and ECJ of 13 July 2006, joint Cases C-295/04 C-298/04 (*Manfredi*) (2006) I-6641 (6661).

[229] ECJ of 8 October 1996, joint Cases C-178/94, C-179/94, C-188/94, C-189/94, C-190/94, (1996) ECR I-4867 (4881–4883).

[230] A. Hellgardt, AG (2012), 154, 158.

[231] S. Kalss et al., *Kapitalmarktrecht I*, § 21 para. 48.

[232] OGH, 6 Ob 28/12d, 5.2 ff.

Lars Teigelack

§ 15 Short Selling

Bibliography

Avgouleas, Emilios, *A New Framework for the Global Regulation of Short Sales*, 15 Stan. J. L. Bus. & Fin. (2010), p. 376–425; Boehmer, Ekkehart and Wu, Juan (Julie), *Short Selling and the Informational Efficiency of Prices*, Working Paper (2012), available at: http://papers.ssrn.com/sol3/papers.cfm?abstract_id=972620; Boehmer, Ekkehart, Jones, Charles M. and Zhang, Xiaoyan, *Which Shorts Are Informed?*, 63 J. Fin. (2008), p. 491–527; Bris, Arturo, Goetzmann, William N. and Zhu, Short Ning, *Efficiency and the Bear: Short Sales and Markets Around the World*, 62 J. Fin. (2007), p. 1029–1079; Dörge, Andreas, *Rechtliche Aspekte der Wertpapierleihe* (1992); Gilson, Ronald J. and Kraakman, Reinier H., *The Mechanisms of Market Efficiency*, 70 Va. L. Rev. (1984), p. 549–644; Hull, John C., *Optionen, Futures und andere Derivate*, 6th ed. (2008); Laurer, Thomas, *Der Leerverkauf von Aktien—Abgrenzung, Formen und aufsichtsrechtliche Implikationen*, ZgesKredW (2008), p. 980–984; Lorenz, Manuel, *Regulierung von Leerverkäufen als Dauerbaustelle*, AG (2010), p. R 511–512; Lübke, Julia, *Kapitalverkehrsfreiheit in der Finanzkrise—Zur Renaissance staatlicher Sonderrechte an Unternehmen*, EWS (2010), p. 407–416; Miller, Edward M., *Risk, Uncertainty and Divergence of Opinion*, 32 J. Fin. (1977), p. 1151–1168; Mock, Sebastian, *Das Gesetz zur Vorbeugung gegen missbräuchliche Wertpapier- und Derivategeschäfte*, WM (2010), p. 2248–2256; Mittermeier, Martin, *Grundlagen und Regulierungsperspektiven von Leerverkäufen*, ZBB (2010), p. 139–149; Möllers, Thomas M.J., Christ, Dominique and Harrer, Andreas, *Nationale Alleingänge und die europäische Reaktion auf ein Verbot ungedeckter Leerverkäufe*, NZG (2010), p. 1167–1170; Mülbert, Peter and Sajnovits, Alexander, *Das künftige Regime für Leerverkäufe und Credit Default Swaps nach der VO (EU) Nr. 236/2012*, ZBB (2012), p. 266–285; Trüg, Gerson, *Ist der Leerverkauf von Wertpapieren strafbar?*, NJW (2009), p. 3202–3206; Tyrolt, Jochen and Bingel, Adrian, *Short Selling—Neue Vorschriften zur Regulierung von Leerverkäufen*, BB (2010), p. 1419–1426; Walla, Fabian, *Kapitalmarktrechtliche Normsetzung durch Allgemeinverfügung?—Hat die BaFin mit den Verboten für ungedeckte Leerverkäufe und bestimmte Kreditderivate vom 18. Mai 2010 ihre Kompetenzen überschritten?*, DÖV (2010), p. 853–857; Zimmer, Daniel and Beisken, Thomas, *Die Regulierung von Leerverkäufen de lege lata und de lege ferenda*, WM (2010), p. 485–491.

I. Introduction

1   A short sale is a transaction in which a party sells financial instruments for a fixed price while having an obligation to deliver the respective financial instruments to a third party at a later point in time without a fixed price.[1] Commonly, the definition is restricted to cases in which the seller does not yet own[2] or possess[3] the financial instruments at the time of entering into the agreement. This definition does not, however, include constellations in which the short sale is covered,[4] i.e. where the seller has borrowed the financial instrument, or made arrangements to ensure it can

---

[1] T. Laurer, ZgesKredW (2008), p. 980, 982; in line with this: G. Trüg, NJW (2009), p. 3202, 3203; J. Tyrolt and A. Bingel, BB (2010), p. 1419.

[2] Cf. A. Dörge, *Rechtliche Aspekte der Wertpapierleihe*, p. 28; J.C. Hull, *Optionen, Futures und andere Derivate*, p. 136.

[3] C. Kienle, in: H. Schimansky et al. (eds.), *Bankrechts-Handbuch*, § 105 para. 54; M. Lorenz, AG (2010), p. R 511.

[4] On this term see para. 4.

be borrowed before entering into the short sale agreement. In this respect, it falls short of the mark.[5]

2   Short sales can be divided into two types: (i) covered short selling where the seller has borrowed the security, or made arrangements to ensure it can be borrowed before the short sale, thereby ensuring that it will be able to fulfil his obligation; and (ii) "uncovered" or "naked" short selling where at the time of the short sale the seller has not yet borrowed the securities or ensured they can be borrowed.[6]

3   For the seller the economic intention behind short sales is to make profits by speculating on falling prices, enabling him to buy the financial instruments it owes at a lower price than the price it made with his sale. It will, however, suffer a loss if the price of the financial instruments rises higher than the price the buyer has the obligation to pay, before the seller has had the opportunity to acquire the financial instruments it owes. The possibility of making profits through short sales is often used for purposes such as hedging potential losses through other investments[7] and speculation on falling share prices.[8]

4   In cases of an uncovered or naked short sale, the seller must ensure that it obtains the financial instruments it owes within the performance period. It can do so either by acquiring or borrowing the shares.[9] Uncovered short sales can result in any number of transactions regarding the respective shares. In extreme cases, uncovered short sales may even result in more shares being traded than have actually been issued.[10]

II.   Potential Risks and Benefits of Short Sales

5   Short sales can contribute to the efficiency of the capital markets by allowing investors to act when they believe a security is overvalued, thereby leading to a more efficient pricing and increasing market liquidity.[11] Uncovered short sales are, however, accompanied by the risk of settlement failure.[12] Short selling can further lead to higher volatility and excessive downward spiral in prices.[13] This only becomes legally relevant when used as part of an abusive strategy, for example as a means to

---

[5] J. Tyrolt and A. Bingel, BB (2010), p. 1419.

[6] J. Ekkenga, in: K. Schmidt (ed.), *Münchener Kommentar HGB*, Effektengeschäft para. 66; G. Trüg, NJW (2009), p. 3202, 3203; D. Zimmer and T. Beisken, WM (2010), p. 485, 486; F. Walla, DÖV (2010), p. 853. The concept of uncovered short sellings was first described at the outset of the 17th century in the Netherlands, cf. H. de Graaf and E. Kalse, '*Naakt short gaan' iseenoud-Hollands kunstje*, Handelsblad of 25 July 2008; cf. further A. Bris et al., 62 J. Fin. (2007), p. 1029.

[7] Cf. IOSCO, *Regulation on Short Selling Final Report*, June 2009, p. 5.

[8] Short sellings are a common investment strategy of hedge funds. See on the regulatory framework for hedge funds § 9 para. 10.

[9] Cf. G. Trüg, NJW (2009), p. 3202, 3203.

[10] M. Lorenz, AG (2010), p. R 511. Cf. the effects of short selling in the case *Porsche/VW* at § 14 para. 41.

[11] Cf. E. Boehmer and J. Wu, *Short Selling and the informational efficiency of prices*, p. 1 ff.; E. Boehmer et al., 63 J. Fin. (2008), p. 491 ff.; M. Mittermeier, ZBB (2010), p. 139, 141; D. Zimmer and T. Beisken, WM (2010), p. 485, 486. Also R.J. Gilson and R. Kraakman, 70 Va. L. Rev. (1984), p. 549 ff.

[12] IOSCO, *Regulation on Short Selling Final Report*, June 2009, p. 22; M. Mittermeier, ZBB (2010), p. 139, 142.

[13] IOSCO, *Regulation on Short Selling Final Report*, June 2009, p. 21–22; cf. M. Mittermeier, ZBB (2010), p. 139, 141–142 on the dangers of short sellings for market integrity.

Fabian Walla

achieve market manipulation, or if the short sale results in a destabilization of the entire financial system.

1. Short Sales as a Means for Market Manipulation

6 Short sales can be used as a means for market manipulation in the sense of Article 5 MAD.[14] This particularly applies to so-called bear raids, i.e. the spreading of negative rumours in order to force down the share price.[15] Naked short sales must further be classed as market manipulations if they are abusive, i.e. the seller never intended to fulfil his obligation, aiming only to mislead the market.[16]

2. Short Sales as a Means for Destabilising the Financial System

7 In extreme market conditions with falling prices, short sellings can lead to further and excessive downward spirals in prices. During the global financial crisis EU Member States adopted a number of emergency measures to restrict or ban short sales of sovereign bonds of eurozone countries and shares of financial institutions due to concerns that price losses for these securities were particularly likely to destabilise the entire financial system.

III. National Regulatory Concepts

8 Prior to the enactment of the Short Selling Regulation the national approaches regarding the regulation of short sales varied significantly within the European Union.[17] Whilst Bulgaria, Estonia, Finland, Latvia, Poland, Romania, Sweden, Slovakia, Slovenia and the Czech Republic regarded the provisions on market abuse to be sufficient with regard to the regulation of short sales, other Member States followed different regulatory approaches, with the aim of reducing the potential risks arising from short sellings. For example, Denmark prohibited naked short sales entirely.[18] Austria, Belgium, Germany, France, Greece, Spain and Portugal all combined disclosure obligations for covered short sales and prohibitions of naked short selling. Luxembourg only prohibited naked short sellings of shares issued by financial institutions.[19] The United Kingdom merely adopted transparency obligations after a short ban on short sales.

[14] See § 14 para. 37 ff.
[15] G. Trüg, NJW (2009), p. 3202, 3206; D. Zimmer and T. Beisken, WM (2010), p. 485, 488.
[16] G. Trüg, NJW (2009), p. 3202, 3204; T.M.J. Möllers et al., NZG (2010), p. 1167, 1168.
[17] Cf. ESMA's continually updated overview, *Measures Adopted by Competent Authorities on Short Selling*, ESMA/2011/39a, May 2012.
[18] ESMA, *Measures Adopted by Competent Authorities on Short Selling*, ESMA/2011/39, January 2011.
[19] Ibid.

IV. The EU Short Selling Regulation

9   The Regulation on Short Selling,[20] enacted in March 2012, has rendered these national approaches regarding the regulation of short selling obsolete. The Regulation entered into force on 1 November 2012.[21] The Commission has endorsed two regulatory technical standards and one implementing technical standard by the ESMA[22] and enacted one delegated Regulation[23] that substantiate the rules of the short selling regulation. These delegated acts contain the details for the new European regulatory framework regarding short selling.

1.   Rules on Short Sales

10   The Regulation largely prohibits short sellings and contains specific transparency requirements. It is applicable (i) to all financial instruments that are admitted to trading on a trading venue in the European Union, including such instruments when traded outside a trading venue, (ii) to derivatives that relate to such a financial instrument, including such derivatives when traded outside a trading venue and (iii) to debt instruments issued by a Member State or the EU and derivatives thereof that relate to such debt instruments or to an obligation of a Member State or the EU. Articles 16 and 17 of the Regulation provide exemptions inter alia for principal trading venues outside the EU and for market making and primary market operations.

(a)   Prohibited Transactions

11   Pursuant to Article 12 of the Regulation, uncovered short sales in shares are generally prohibited.[24] A short sale is defined by Article 2(1)(b) of the Regulation. As a

---

[20] Regulation (EU) No. 236/2012 of the European Parliament and of the Council of 14 March 2012 on short selling and certain aspects of credit default swaps, OJ L86, p. 1. Cf. for a detailed analysis of the new regulation P.O. Mulbert and A. Sajnovits, ZBB (2012), p. 2 ff.

[21] Cf. Art. 48 Short Selling Regulation.

[22] Commission Delegated Regulation (EU) No. 826/2012 of 29 June 2012 supplementing Regulation (EU) No. 236/2012 of the European Parliament and of the Council with regard to regulatory technical standards on notification and disclosure requirements with regard to net short positions, the details of the information to be provided to the European Securities and Markets Authority in relation to net short positions and the method for calculating turnover to determine exempted shares, OJ L251, p. 1; Commission Delegated Regulation (EU) No. 919/2012 of 5 July 2012 supplementing Regulation (EU) No. 236/2012 of the European Parliament and of the Council on short selling and certain aspects of credit default swaps with regard to regulatory technical standards for the method of calculation of the fall in value for liquid shares and other financial instruments, OJ L274, p. 16; Commission Implementing Regulation (EU) No. 827/2012 of 29 June 2012 laying down implementing technical standards with regard to the means for public disclosure of net position in shares, the format of the information to be provided to the European Securities and Markets Authority in relation to net short positions, the types of agreements, arrangements and measures to adequately ensure that shares or sovereign debt instruments are available for settlement and the dates and period for the determination of the principal venue for a share according to Regulation (EU) No. 236/2012 of the European Parliament and of the Council on short selling and certain aspects of credit default swaps, OJ L251, p. 11.

[23] Commission Delegated Regulation (EU) No. 918/2012 of 5 July 2012 supplementing Regulation (EU) No. 236/2012 of the European Parliament and of the Council on short selling and certain aspects of credit default swaps with regard to definitions, the calculation of net short positions, covered sovereign credit default swaps, notification thresholds, liquidity thresholds for suspending restrictions, significant falls in the value of financial instruments and adverse events, OJ L274, p. 1.

[24] It remains unclear whether this also applies to intraday transactions. Consenting opinion M. Lorenz, AG (2010), p. R 511, R 512; dissenting opinion T.M.C. Möllers et al., NZG (2010), p. 1167, 1170.

consequence, short sales of shares are only allowed if the seller ensures that it is in possession of the shares at the time of the settlement of the transaction. Articles 5–8 of the implementing technical standard determine the types of agreements, arrangements and measures that adequately ensure that shares will be available for settlement. Article 13 of the Regulation prohibits uncovered short sales of sovereign bonds, subjecting this rule to the same exceptions as the short selling of shares and to the following additional exception: under Article 13(3) the restrictions do not apply if the transaction serves to hedge a long position in debt instruments of an issuer whose pricing has a high correlation with the pricing of the relevant bond. If the liquidity of a sovereign bond falls below a certain threshold,[25] the prohibitions may further be temporarily suspended by the competent national authorities, provided the competent authority notifies the ESMA and the other national authorities prior to the suspension.

(b)   Transparency Obligations

12   The Regulation also introduces transparency obligations for persons holding net short positions. A natural or legal person must notify the competent authority of any net short position that reaches, exceeds or falls below a percentage that equals 0.2% of the value of the issued share capital of the company concerned and any 0.1% above that.[26] If the net short position reaches, exceeds or falls below a threshold of 0.5% of the issued share capital of the company, Article 6 requires the public be notified of this fact. The Commission is empowered to modify the thresholds by means of delegated acts should the financial markets require such adjustments. Regarding significant net short positions in sovereign debt, the Commission specified the amounts and incremental levels of the notification thresholds in Article 21 of its Delegated Regulation No. 918.

13   It must further be noted that the Regulation does not require the trading venue to ensure that persons executing orders mark sell orders as short orders if the seller is entering into a short sale of the share. The Commission's initial proposal still contained this requirement.[27]

2.   Rules on Credit Default Swap Agreements

14   In addition to short sellings the Short Selling Regulation also addresses so-called sovereign CDS agreements,[28] i.e. derivative contracts in which one party pays a fee to another party in return for compensation or a payment in the event of a default of a sovereign issuer. The equation is justified by the fact that buying CDSs without having a long position in underlying sovereign debt can be used to secure a position economically equivalent to a short position in the underlying bonds. The buyer of an uncovered CDS benefits from the deterioration of the credit risk of the issuer in

---

[25] The calculation of threshold should be stipulated by the Commission via a delegated act, cf. Art. 14 (4) Regulation.
[26] Cf. Art. 5 Short Selling Regulation.
[27] Art. 13 Short Selling Regulation Draft.
[28] Cf. on the term credit default swap agreements see Art. 2(1)(c) Short Selling Regulation.

a very similar way as the seller of the bonds profits from this same deterioration decreasing the prices of the bonds.

15 Article 14 of the Regulation prohibits all transactions in uncovered CDSs. Article 4 defines the term "uncovered" as CDSs that do not serve to hedge against the risk of long positions to which the swap relates or the risk of a decline of the value of the sovereign debt for which the person holds assets or is subject to liabilities, such as financial contracts, a portfolio of assets or financial obligations whose value is correlated to the value of the sovereign debt. The restriction thus reaches farther than with regard to the short sale of shares.

16 The Commission substantiated these rules in its delegated Regulations. The competent national authorities can suspend the restrictions on transactions in uncovered CDSs temporarily, if, based on objective elements, they believe that their sovereign debt market is not functioning properly and that the restrictions might have a negative impact on the sovereign CDS market, especially by increasing the cost of borrowing for sovereign issuers or affecting the sovereign issuers' ability to issue new debt. Article 14(2)(a)–(e) of the Regulation contains a list of indicators for such a non-functioning market. If a national authority exercises its power to suspend the ban of CDSs, Article 8 additionally subjects these CDSs to the same notification obligations as short sales in sovereign bonds.[29]

3. Additional Powers of the National Authorities and the ESMA

17 The Short Selling Regulation grants the competent national authorities certain powers of intervention. Pursuant to Article 18, the national authorities can require market participants to reveal their net short positions in cases of adverse events or developments that constitute a serious threat to financial stability or to market confidence in the Member State, provided this is necessary in order to address such a threat and does not have a detrimental effect on the efficiency of financial markets that is disproportionate to its benefits. Article 19 empowers the national supervisory bodies to require market participants engaged in the lending of a specific financial instrument or class of financial instruments to notify any significant change in the fees requested for such lending. Articles 20 and 21 additionally empower the competent national authorities to ban transactions which are generally not prohibited by the Regulation. All measures imposed on the basis of Articles 18–21 are valid for an initial period not exceeding three months from the date of publication. They can be renewed for further three months after a review (Article 24). Article 23 further provides the national authorities with the power to temporarily restrict or prohibit short sales of financial instruments in case of a significant fall in price on a particular trading venue.

18 The ESMA has generally no direct supervisory powers over market participants. It should rather coordinate its national counterparts. However, Articles 28 and 29 convey the power to the ESMA to intervene vis-à-vis market participants in emergency situations in accordance with Article 9 of the ESMA Regulation.[30]

---

[29] On the regulation in Germany cf. S. Mock, WM (2010), p. 2248, 2252.
[30] See § 11 para. 60–61.

4. Sanctions

19   The Short Selling Regulation fails to provide detailed requirements regarding the sanctions to be imposed by the Member States for violations of its provisions. Article 41 merely stipulates that the Member States are to establish rules on administrative measures, sanctions and pecuniary penalties applicable to infringements of the Regulation and are required to take all measures necessary to ensure that they are implemented. Furthermore the Regulation only demands the measures, sanctions and penalties provided for to be effective, proportionate and dissuasive. The ESMA is expected to publish guidelines on the application of the sanctions imposed by the Member States and gather information on the sanctioning practices of the national authorities.

V.   Conclusion

20   Short sales have become a matter of public and political interest due to the current financial and sovereign debt crisis. Whilst short sales have positive impacts on the market, enhancing market efficiency by allowing investors to profit from decreasing prices and thereby increasing market liquidity, they may also be used for market manipulation. Excessive short sales can also create a risk for the overall stability of the financial system. Economists have tried to balance the benefits and the risks of short sales based on empirical data but have not yet been able to draw a final conclusion.[31]

21   The experiences made during the financial crisis, however, show that the development of regulatory means against short sellings and CDSs that endanger the stability of the financial markets is to be welcomed. Given the threat not only to Europe's economy but also its political stability it is justified to ban speculation on certain decreasing prices of financial instruments such as sovereign bonds or stocks of financial institutions. One must, however, keep in mind that speculation is generally an inherent element of capital markets and should not be banned solely for political reasons.

22   In evaluating the new European regulation on short sales one must appreciate in particular the unification of the national provisions on short selling, replacing the former legal fragmentation.[32] Europe's financial markets are meanwhile so closely intertwined that a Europe-wide answer to the risks of short sales was essential. In this context the involvement of the ESMA must also be welcomed. It subjects the young pan-European supervisory authority to another major challenge as a guardian for the stability of the financial system.

23   From a systematic point of view the European legislature's aim of protecting the stability of the financial system by regulating short sales introduces a relatively new

[31] See e.g. A. Bris et al., 62 J. Fin. (2007), p. 1029 ff.; cf. also E. Boehmer and J. Wu, *Short Selling and the Informational Efficiency of Prices*, p. 1 ff.
[32] Seen similarly by J. Lübke, EWS (2010), p. 407, 416.

aim to the current legal framework.[33] The Commission's most recent proposals for amendments to European capital markets law were also drafted with the intention of ensuring the stability of the financial system.[34] The Regulation on Short Selling can thus be seen as a precursor of the developments in capital markets law: in future, investor protection and ensuring the functioning of the capital markets will no longer be the sole aims of capital markets law. It will rather also be understood as a means to ensure the overall stability of the financial system.

---

[33] So far, only the rating agency regulation has a focus on the protection of the overall stability of the financial system.

[34] See § 4 para. 28.

4

Disclosure System

§ 16 Foundations

Bibliography

Akerlof, George A., *The Market for "Lemons": Quality Uncertainty and the Market Mechanism*, 84 Q. J. Econ. (1970), p. 488–500; Amihud, Yakov and Mendelson, Haim, *Liquidity, Volatility and Exchange Automation*, 3 J. Acc., Aud. Finance (1988), p. 369–395; Assmann, Heinz-Dieter, *Kapitalmarktrecht—Zur Formation eines Rechtsgebietes in der vierzigjährigen Rechtsentwicklung der Bundesrepublik Deutschland*, in: Nörr, Knut Wolfgang (ed.), *40 Jahre Bundesrepublik Deutschland—40 Jahre Rechtsentwicklung* (1989), p. 251–291; Beaver, William, *Financial Reporting*, 3rd ed. (1998); Brandeis, Louis D., *Other People's Money and How the Bankers Use It* (1914); Brellochs, Michael, *Publizität und Haftung von Aktiengesellschaften im System des Europäischen Kapitalmarktrechts* (2005); Brinckmann, Hendrik, *Kapitalmarktrechtliche Finanzberichterstattung* (2009); Dauses, Manfred A. (ed.), *Handbuch des EU-Wirtschaftsrechts*, loose-leaf (as of October 2008); Deckert, Martina and von Rüden, Jens, *Anlegerschutz durch Europäisches Kapitalmarktrecht*, EWS (1998), p. 46–54; Easterbrook, Frank H. and Fischel, Daniel R., *Mandatory Disclosure and the Protection of Investors*, 70 Va. L. Rev. (1984), p. 669–715; Commission, *The Development of a European Capital Market, Report of a Group of experts appointed by the EEC Commission* (Segré Report) (1966); Ewert, Ralf, *Bilanzielle Publizität im Lichte der Theorie vom gesellschaftlichen Wert öffentlich verfügbarer Information*, BFuP (1989), p. 245–263; Fama, Eugene F., *Efficient Capital Markets: A Review of Theory and Empirical Work*, 25 J. Fin. (1970), p. 383–417; Fama, Eugene F. and Laffer, Arthur B., *Information and Capital Markets*, 44 J. Bus. (1971), p. 289–298; Fleischer, Holger, *Informationsasymmetrie im Vertragsrecht* (2001); Fülbier, Rolf U., *Regulierung der Ad-hoc-Publizität* (1998); Gilson, Ronald J. and Kraakman, Reinier H., *The Mechanisms of Market Efficiency*, 70 Va. L. Rev. (1984), p. 549–641; Gonedes, Nicholas J., *The Capital Market, the Market for Information, and External Accounting*, 31 J. Fin. (1976), p. 611–630; Gonedes, Nicholas J. and Dopuch, Nicholas, *Capital Market Equilibrium, Information Production, and Selecting Accounting Techniques: Theoretical Framework and Review of Empirical Work*, Supplement to 12 J. Acc. Res. (1974), p. 48–129; Hirshleifer, Jack, *The Private and Social Value of Information and the Reward to Inventive Activity*, 61 Am. Econ. Rev. (1971), p. 561–574; Hopt, Klaus J., *Inwieweit empfiehlt sich eine allgemeine gesetzliche Regelung des Anlegerschutzes?*, Gutachten G für den 51. Deutschen Juristentag (1976); Hopt, Klaus J., *Vom Aktien- und Börsenrecht zum Kapitalmarktrecht?*, Teil 1: *Der international erreichte Stand des Kapitalmarktrechts*, 140 ZHR (1976), p. 201–235, Teil 2: *Die deutsche Entwicklung im internationalen Vergleich*, 141 ZHR (1977), p. 389–441; Köndgen, Johannes, *Die Relevanz der ökonomischen Theorie der Unternehmung für rechtswissenschaftliche Fragestellungen—ein Problemkatalog*, in: Ott, Claus and Schäfer, Hans-Bernd (eds.), *Ökonomische Analyse des Unternehmensrechts* (1993), p. 128–155; Kohl, Helmut et al., *Abschreibungsgesellschaften, Kapitalmarkteffizienz und Publizitätszwang—Plädoyer für ein Vermögensanlagegesetz*, 138 ZHR (1974), p. 1–49; Kress, Sabine L., *Effizienzorientierte Kapitalmarktregulierung* (1996); Meier-Schatz, Christian J., *Wirtschaftsrecht und Unternehmenspublizität* (1989); Merkt, Hanno, *Unternehmenspublizität* (2001); Möllers, Thomas M.J., *Anlegerschutz durch Aktien- und Kapitalmarktrecht—Harmonisierungsmöglichkeiten nach geltendem und künftigem Recht*, ZGR (1997), p. 334–367; Möllers, Thomas M.J., *Effizienz als Maßstab des Kapitalmarktrechts: Die Verwendung empirischer und ökonomischer Argumente zur Begründung zivil-, straf-, und öffentlich-rechtlicher Sanktionen*, 208 AcP (2008), p. 1–36; Mülbert, Peter O., *Konzeption des europäischen Kapitalmarktrechts für Wertpapierdienstleistungen*, WM (2001), p. 2085–2102; Rehberg, Markus, *Der staatliche Umgang mit Information: Das europäische Informationsmodell im Lichte von Behavioral Economics*, in: Eger, Thomas and Schäfer, Hans-Bernd (eds.), *Ökonomische Entwicklung der europäischen Zivilrechtsentwicklung* (2007), p. 314–354; Schmidt, Reinhard H., *Rechnungslegung als Informationsproduktion auf nahezu effizienten Kapitalmärkten*, 34 Zfbf (1982), p. 728–748; Stout, Lynn A., *The Unimportance of Being Efficient: An Economic Analysis of Stock Market Pricing and Securities Regulation*, 87 Mich. L. Rev. (1988), p. 613–709; Teigelack, Lars, *Finanzanalysen und Behavioral Finance* (2008); Veil, Rüdiger, *Die Ad-hoc-Publizitätshaftung im System kapitalmarktrechtlicher Informationshaftung*, 167 ZHR (2003), p. 365–402; Veil, Rüdiger, *Der Schutz des verständigen Anlegers durch Publizität und Haftung im europäischen und nationalen Kapitalmarktrecht*, ZBB (2006), p. 162–171; Verrecchia, Robert E., *Discretionary Disclosure*, 5 J. Acc. Econ. (1983), p. 179–194; Vokuhl, Nikolai, *Kapitalmarktrechtlicher Anlegerschutz und Kapitalerhaltung in der Aktiengesellschaft* (2007); West, Richard R., *On the Difference between Internal and External Market Efficiency*, 31 Fin. Analysts J. (1975), p. 30–34; Walz, Rainer, *Ökonomische Regulierungstheorien vor den Toren des Bilanzrechts*, ZfbF Sonderheft 32 (1993), p. 85–106; Wüstemann, Jens et al., *Regulierung durch Transparenz—Ökonomische Analysen, empirische Befunde und Empfehlungen für eine europäische Kapitalmarktregulierung*, in: Hopt, Klaus J. et al. (eds.), *Kapitalmarktgesetzgebung im Europäischen Binnenmarkt* (2008), p. 1–21.

I. Introduction

1   The legal framework for an efficient capital markets law essentially requires mandatory disclosure rules in order to supply the market with the necessary information on issuers. This was pointed out as early as 1966 by the Segré Committee in its Summary Report, thus preparing the ground for the development of a disclosure system in the European Member States. The Segré Committee underlined the fact that disclosure is a necessary prerequisite for the viability of a harmonised European capital market. It considered a Europe-wide minimal framework of mandatory disclosure rules to be a fundamental measure in improving investor information through capital-seeking issuers.[1] Subsequently, disclosure provisions became one of the central regulatory instruments of European capital markets law. This regulatory concept was inspired by the US Securities Regulation which has always followed a disclosure philosophy for regulating capital markets.[2]

2   Justice *Louis D. Brandeis* described the disclosure philosophy applied by the US Securities Regulation as follows: "Publicity is justly commended as a remedy for social and industrial diseases. Sunlight is said to be the best of disinfectants; electric light the most efficient policeman."[3] *Louis Loss* and *Joel Seligman* high-

[1] Commission, Segré Report, p. 225 ff.
[2] K.J. Hopt, 140 ZHR (1976), p. 201, 204 ff.; K.J. Hopt, 141 ZHR (1977), p. 389, 415.
[3] L.D. Brandeis, *Other People's Money and How the Bankers Use It*, p. 92.

lighted the importance of mandatory disclosure rules in capital markets law in a similarly simple way: "Then, too, there is the recurrent theme throughout these statutes of disclosure, again disclosure, and still more disclosure."[4]

3   The recognition that mandatory disclosure rules play an important role in the viability of capital markets as proclaimed by the Segré Committee is not an exclusively legal one. The necessity for a mandatory system of disclosure must rather be examined from an economic point of view. Theoretical studies on capital markets and economic models are of essential importance for the regulation of capital markets and are regarded as the justification for the disclosure philosophy in US capital markets law.[5] Therefore, the following short introduction into the underlying economic principles is necessary for understanding the disclosure system in European capital markets law.

II.   Transparency and Capital Market Efficiency

4   In economics the connection between disclosure and capital markets is examined under the benchmark of efficiency. In general, one distinguishes three different types of efficiency: allocational, institutional and operational.[6]

1.   Allocational Efficiency

5   Allocational efficiency describes the main function of capital markets as matching investment opportunities to investable financial capital.[7] Disclosure is regarded as having a positive influence on the reduction of information asymmetries between investors and issuers. Informational deficits of investors regarding important aspects of pricing and the quality of the issuers' investment offers can cause market failure or at least influence market efficiency decisively.[8] The "Market for Lemons" described by *Akerlof*, is a well-cited model in this context.[9]

6   Akerlof chose the market for used cars as an example of the problem of quality uncertainty. If the quality of the product is uncertain, the customer can no longer distinguish between good and bad quality by looking at the price. In this case the buyers' behaviour is determined by "adverse selection" and "moral hazard". In consequence sellers of good-quality products are at a disadvantage. They are unable to obtain a high enough price to make selling their products worthwhile. The higher costs of production cannot be passed on to the buyer as due to the uncertainty the buyer has to make deductions and will only be willing to pay an average price which therefore replaces the competitive price. These uncertainties are thus only advantageous for sellers of low-quality products, i.e.

---

[4] L. Loss and J. Seligman, *Securities Regulation*, p. 29.
[5] Cf. K.J. Hopt, 140 ZHR (1976), p. 201, 205; T.M.J. Möllers, 208 AcP (2008), p. 1, 5.
[6] Cf. H.-D. Assmann, in: K. Nörr (ed.), *Rechtsentwicklung*, p. 251, 263–264; H. Kohl et al., 138 ZHR (1974), p. 1, 16 ff.; M.K. Oulds, in: S. Kümpel and A. Wittig (eds.), *Bank- und Kapitalmarktrecht*, para. 14.147 ff.; N. Vokuhl, *Kapitalmarktrechtlicher Anlegerschutz*, p. 179 ff.
[7] T.M.J. Möllers, 208 AcP (2008), p. 1, 7; N. Vokuhl, *Kapitalmarktrechtlicher Anlegerschutz*, p. 182–183.
[8] Cf. N. Vokuhl, *Kapitalmarktrechtlicher Anlegerschutz*, p. 184.
[9] G.A. Akerlof, 84 Q. J. Econ. (1970), p. 488 ff.

"lemons". Therefore, more and more sellers of products of above-average quality are squeezed out of the market. This finally leads to a complete market collapse.[10]

7   In addition to Akerlof's "Market for Lemons" the "Theory of Informational Efficiency of Capital Markets"[11] proposed by *Fama* has also gained wide influence regarding the determination of the implications and effects of information on the markets. Originally this theory was developed for the analysis of investment papers. It soon, however, also found its way into general theories on capital markets. Nevertheless the theory's informative value regarding the allocational mechanism is only indirect, as the theory of informational efficiency does not refer to the actual market processes but rather to procedures prior to these. It explores the relationship between information and market prices, or, in other words, the messages communicated by certain prices.[12] The main assertion of the theory of informational efficiency is that a capital market is efficient if the stock prices immediately and fully reflect the available information.[13] The primary aim of the theory is to establish the actual degree of informational efficiency on the capital markets in order to be able to determine the amount of information already reflected in the prices. If the stock price already takes certain information into account and reflects it, investors will not profit from searching for said information. Excess returns can no longer be achieved as the investment paper was not mispriced.[14]

8   The stipulations made by the theory of informational efficiency can only be proven for the very restrictive condition of market equilibrium as it is imperative that the adjustment process takes place immediately, that there are zero transaction costs, the market participants have homogeneous investor expectations and that they behave strictly rationally regarding all new information.[15] If the theory of informational efficiency requires such restrictive conditions in order to have a significant explanatory power, it is as such very imprecise and useless for empirical analysis. For this reason Fama amended his theory with the efficient capital market hypothesis (ECMH).[16] This describes three versions of informational efficiency on capital markets depending on the degree to which the market price ideally reflects different information: a weak informational efficiency claims that the market price reflects historical information. In a semi-strong form of informational efficiency, the market prices reflect all publicly available information. Strong informational efficiency means that the market prices instantly reflect all price relevant information, i.e. not only all publicly available information, but also all hidden "inside information".[17]

9   There are dissenting opinions on the legal implications of the ECMH.[18] An essential observation that can be deduced from the semi-strong form of the ECMH is that if information is made public the capital markets are capable of reflecting this

---

[10] Cf. for this concept also H. Fleischer, *Informationsasymmetrie im Vertragsrecht*, p. 121 ff.
[11] E.F. Fama, 25 J. Fin. (1970), p. 383 ff.
[12] W. Beaver, *Financial Reporting*, p. 127, 134–135.
[13] E.F. Fama, 25 J. Fin. (1970), p. 383.
[14] S.L. Kress, *Effizienzorientierte Kapitalmarktregulierung*, p. 40.
[15] E.F. Fama, 25 J. Fin. (1970), p. 383, 387; R.R. West, 31 Fin. Analysts J. (1975), p. 30.
[16] Cf. E.F. Fama, 25 J. Fin. (1970), p. 383.
[17] Cf. also R. Veil, 167 ZHR (2003), p. 365, 377–378; N. Vokuhl, *Kapitalmarktrechtlicher Anlegerschutz*, p. 175.
[18] See H. Brinckmann, *Kapitalmarktrechtliche Finanzberichterstattung*, p. 61–62 in detail.

publication in the prices.[19] By disclosing the information informational efficiency is increased.

2.   Institutional Efficiency

10   Institutional efficiency outlines the criteria necessary for capital markets to function as markets. It is generally measured in terms of free market access for investors and traders, the range of products offered and the depth of financial capital available on the market.[20] Others consider investor confidence to be the main criteria for institutional efficiency. From this more politico-economic point of view, the main priority of capital markets law is to strengthen the level of investor confidence in the integrity and stability of the markets.[21] However, these diverging approaches only result in variations regarding terminology and reasoning while the specifications concerning the content of institutional efficiency are the same. Institutional efficiency is measured in liquidity and volatility.[22]

11   Disclosure can positively or negatively influence the decision regarding market participation and therefore have a direct impact on liquidity. If a market participant is uncertain about the accuracy of public information or is not able to compare investment possibilities sufficiently with the help of the disclosed information, this may restrain him from participating, thus resulting in a reduction of liquidity on the markets.[23] Disclosure can, if standardised and reliable, prevent this effect and thus have a positive effect on liquidity.[24] The influence of disclosure on the volatility of the market can be determined similarly. When new information is published, the market prices adapt accordingly, thus increasing volatility.[25] A certain volatility may even be seen as necessary with regard to informational efficiency in order for the prices to be able to adjust to the appearance of new information.[26] Similarly, when requesting an increase of liquidity one has to consider that in a situation of total liquidity, i.e. if an additional supply or demand will lead to no change in the equilibrium price, the price will not adjust to new information.[27] The market mechanisms can thus only function correctly if a certain level of volatility is accompanied by some degree of illiquidity.

3.   Operational Efficiency

12   Operational efficiency describes a process-orientated examination of capital markets

---

[19] M. Brellochs, *Publizität und Haftung*, p. 169–170.

[20] Cf. K.J. Hopt, *Gutachten G 51. Dt. Juristentag*, p. G 49; M.K. Oulds, in: S. Kümpel and A. Wittig (eds.), *Bank- und Kapitalmarktrecht*, para. 14.148; N. Vokuhl, *Kapitalmarktrechtlicher Anlegerschutz*, p. 180.

[21] S. Kümpel and A. Wittig, *Bank- und Kapitalmarktrecht*, para. 8.403; N. Vokuhl, *Kapitalmarktrechtlicher Anlegerschutz*, p. 180.

[22] Cf. S.L. Kress, *Effizienzorientierte Kapitalmarktregulierung*, p. 59 ff.

[23] R.H. Schmidt, 34 ZfbF (1982), p. 728, 741.

[24] C.J. Meier-Schatz, *Wirtschaftsrecht und Unternehmenspublizität*, p. 216–217; H. Merkt, *Unternehmenspublizität*, p. 345.

[25] S.L. Kress, *Effizienzorientierte Kapitalmarktregulierung*, p. 65.

[26] Y. Amihud and H. Mendelson, 3 J. Acc. Aud. Finance (1988), p. 369, 374; S.L. Kress, *Effizienzorientierte Kapitalmarktregulierung*, p. 66.

[27] S.L. Kress, *Effizienzorientierte Kapitalmarktregulierung*, p. 64.

involving aspects of time and transaction costs.[28] Insufficient disclosure may not necessarily lead to market migration, but will certainly lead to higher costs for an investor to make an informed investment decision. The informational efficiency of capital markets depends on the extent to which the information has spread. The circulation of information will in turn be higher the lower the informational costs are and vice versa.[29]

13   One can distinguish between three types of information costs: costs of acquisition, verification and processing.[30] Disclosure primarily reduces the costs for investors to acquire information that has been made publicly available. Additionally, requiring a specific content of the information to be disclosed and effective quality control can reduce the costs of verification and processing. The auditor's certificate attained through the audit of financial statements, for example, can be seen as an instrument ensuring the quality of the information, enabling investors to rely on it and thus reducing their costs of verification.[31] Operational efficiency can be increased if the effects of provisions on disclosure are seen as a whole: by burdening the issuers with mandatory disclosures instead of leaving the acquisition of information up to the investors the total transaction costs on the market are minimised.[32]

III.   Disclosure Provisions as Part of the Regulation of Capital Markets

1.   The Importance of Legal Disclosure Provisions from an Economic Point of View

14   Economics is often confronted with the task of having to find binding parameters for the development of legal disclosure provisions.[33] Only as binding regulatory requirements could such parameters ensure full market efficiency.[34] Economics does not, however, provide parameters that can be used to define and justify mandatory disclosure provisions. Rather, the findings can only be understood in a model theoretical context. The reference model is usually an allocationally efficient market and all deviations from this which occur in reality are immediately classed as market failure. Market failure thus becomes the criterion to describe a market that is unable to fulfil its allocational task.

15   In order to counteract market failure, regulatory intervention is regarded as necessary. Market failure may result from an asymmetrical distribution of information[35]

---

[28] Ibid., p. 44; N. Vokuhl, *Kapitalmarktrechtlicher Anlegerschutz*, p. 181.

[29] R.J. Gilson and R.H. Kraakman, 70 Va. L. Rev. (1984), p. 549, 593; R. Veil, 167 ZHR (2003), p. 365, 379.

[30] R.J. Gilson and R.H. Kraakman, 70 Va. L. Rev. (1984), p. 549, 593 ff.: "The lower the cost of particular information, the wider will be its distribution, the more effective will be the capital market mechanism operating to reflect it in prices, and the more efficient will be the market with respect to it."

[31] F.H. Easterbrook and D.R. Fischel, 70 Va. L. Rev. (1984), p. 669, 647–648; H. Merkt, *Unternehmenspublizität*, p. 470–471.

[32] Cf. R. Veil, 167 ZHR (2003), p. 365, 379–380.

[33] Cf. Meier-Schatz, *Wirtschaftsrecht und Unternehmenspublizität*, p. 161 ff.; H. Merkt, *Unternehmenspublizität*, p. 212 ff.

[34] Cf. J. Wüstemann et al., in: K.J. Hopt et al. (eds.), *Kapitalmarktgesetzgebung*, p. 11 and passim.

[35] In more detail H. Fleischer, *Informationsasymmetrie im Vertragsrecht*, p. 121 ff.; R.U. Fülbier, *Regulierung der Ad-hoc-Publizität*, p. 176 ff.

between market participants which can be prevented or reduced by legal disclosure provisions.[36]

16   The theory of the social value of public information, which can be traced back to *Fama/Laffer*[37] and *Hirshleifer*,[38] supports this concept, especially with regard to capital markets law. It shows that if information is merely obtained privately this can be disadvantageous for an allocationally efficient market mechanism. The costs of obtaining information constitute a use of resources by each market participant without any advantage for society as a whole. An excessive amount of information is produced as market participants generate the same information parallel to one another.[39] That is why the production of public information through a legal disclosure obligation is regarded as economically advantageous, substituting private procurement of information and reducing the loss of resources associated with an information surplus.[40] However, this cannot lead to the conclusion that mandatory legal regulation of disclosure is necessary. It must be noted that investors have collective means of forcing issuers to necessary disclosure measures. These means include risk surcharges, discounts[41] and influencing shareholder meetings.[42]

17   Others argue that economic incentives are sufficient to provide the necessary level of disclosure. The asymmetric distribution of information between issuers and investors results in so-called agency costs. These describe the costs for the investors to minimise the information advantages of the issuers.[43] The issuer's management has a large interest in keeping the agency costs low. The reduction in share price and manager remuneration as a result of the asymmetry of information lead directly to economic disadvantages for the management. Thus, the necessary information is voluntarily disclosed in order to reduce asymmetries of information.[44]

18   The signal theory generalises this idea by stating that anyone having better information will signal this, if he can gain economic advantages therefrom.[45] Similarly, there can be an incentive to disclose negative company data, as reluctance to do so will provoke scepticism in the investors. This scepticism may cause more of the investors to sell off their shares than would the disclosure of the negative information itself.[46] These incentives for voluntary disclosure resulting from agency costs and the signal theory are, however, put into perspective when compared to opposing incentive systems. In particular, *Verrecchia's* concept of "proprietary costs"[47] exemplifies how a company may be dissuaded from voluntary disclosure by the ensuing negative externalities.

---

[36] R.U. Fülbier, *Regulierung der Ad-hoc-Publizität*, p. 179.

[37] E.F. Fama and A.B. Laffer, 44 J. Bus. (1971), p. 289 ff.

[38] J. Hirshleifer, 61 Am. Econ. Rev. (1971), p. 561 ff.

[39] E.F. Fama and A.B. Laffer, 44 J. Bus. (1971), p. 289, 292; J. Hirshleifer, 61 Am. Econ. Rev. (1971), p. 573.

[40] R.U. Fülbier, *Regulierung der Ad-hoc-Publizität*, p. 177–178.

[41] Ibid., p. 178.

[42] R. Ewert, BFuP (1989), p. 245, 261.

[43] In more detail R. Richter and E.G. Furubotn, *Neue Institutionenökonomie*, p. 176–177.

[44] H. Merkt, *Unternehmenspublizität*, p. 212–213.

[45] C.J. Meier-Schatz, *Wirtschaftsrecht und Unternehmenspublizität*, p. 164; M. Rehberg, in: T. Eger and H.-B. Schäfer (eds.), *Ökonomische Entwicklung*, p. 314.

[46] H. Merkt, *Unternehmenspublizität*, p. 213; J. Köndgen, in: C. Ott and H.-B. Schäfer (eds.), *Ökonomische Analyse*, p. 128, 152, takes a more restrictive point of view by stating that disclosure provisions have to be at least partly mandatory.

[47] R. Verrecchia, 5 J. Acc. Econ. (1983), p. 179, 181.

19   A different line of argumentation focuses on the nature of information as a public good. Public goods can lead to market failure due to the so-called free-rider effect.[48] The free-rider effect describes a situation in which anybody can gain access to public goods without costs so that the market price of these public goods is reduced to zero. As a result, there is no longer any incentive to offer public goods on the market and a shortage may occur.[49] Yet whilst economic studies assume all information to be a public good,[50] thereby enabling disclosure to prevent market failure, this approach is too general: the nature of information changes, taking on the characteristics of a private good during the period of production and developing the character of a mixed good during distribution. Only when fully distributed can information then be classed as a public good.[51] There is proof of this understanding with regard to the capital markets: according to the ECMH, additional returns can be attained on semi-strong capital markets by making use of inside information. As a result share prices will adjust to the new level of information and no further returns will be attained by making use of the inside information—the information has been exhausted.[52] Information therefore must be classed as a hybrid good,[53] thus preventing a general statement on the necessity of disclosure obligations.

20   Market failure can further result from the monopoly which exists regarding information. Corporate information in particular is usually subject to the monopoly of the issuer who will mostly be the only one with access to internal company data—or at least the one whose access involves the lowest costs.[54] A disclosure obligation could prevent the issuer from exploiting his monopoly.[55] However, once again the above-mentioned incentives of voluntary disclosure militate against the understanding that a regulatory intervention is inevitable. They are said to ensure sufficiently that the issuer will not abuse his monopoly on corporate information.[56]

21   On the whole, various incentives can be found that may lead an issuer to disclose information voluntarily, thus reducing the lack of transparency. It has not been clearly determined to date whether voluntary disclosure is sufficient or whether legislative intervention remains necessary. Economic research findings remain unclear on this.

22   By contrast, the transaction cost theory promises considerable insight,[57] stipulating that disclosure provisions are not absolutely but only relatively mandatory from an

---

[48] A public good is defined by two aspects: firstly, that no rivalry exists regarding its consumption—even when one consumer makes use of public information it remains available for others; secondly, the fact that one cannot be excluded from the use of the good by not paying for it, R.U. Fülbier, *Regulierung der Ad-hoc-Publizität*, p. 172.

[49] C.J. Meier-Schatz, *Wirtschaftsrecht und Unternehmenspublizität*, p. 166–167; H. Merkt, *Unternehmenspublizität*, p. 219.

[50] The immaterial nature of information proves that the amount of existing information cannot be reduced by the fact that an individual makes use of it, N.J. Gonedes and N. Dopuch, Supplement to 12 J. Acc. Res. (1974), p. 48, 65, i.e. the use of information by one person does not exclude others from using it, N.J. Gonedes, 31 J. Fin. (1976), p. 611, 617.

[51] C.J. Meier-Schatz, *Wirtschaftsrecht und Unternehmenspublizität*, p. 170 ff.

[52] Ibid., p. 171; R.U. Fülbier, *Regulierung der Ad-hoc-Publizität*, p. 175.

[53] C.J. Meier-Schatz, *Wirtschaftsrecht und Unternehmenspublizität*, p. 172; H. Merkt, *Unternehmenspublizität*, p. 219.

[54] E.F. Fama and A.B. Laffer, 44 J. Bus. (1971), p. 289, 292; N.J. Gonedes, 31 J. Fin. (1976), p. 611, 618; T.M.J. Möllers, 208 AcP (2008), p. 1, 8.

[55] R.U. Fülbier, *Regulierung der Ad-hoc-Publizität*, p. 181.

[56] Cf. ibid., p. 182.

[57] For details see R. Richter and E.G. Furubotn, *Neue Institutionenökonomie*, p. 53 ff.

Hendrik Brinckmann

economic point of view, provided the legislative disclosure rules contribute to a reduction of transaction costs on the market. This can be determined by drawing up a balance in order to determine and compare the transaction costs with and without the respective disclosure provisions. A mandatory disclosure regime must be regarded as necessary if the overall level of the transaction costs improves under legislative disclosure provisions compared to without them.

23 In cases of information asymmetries regarding internal company data it must be kept in mind, that issuers have much easier and cheaper access to these than investors. The issuers can thus often be seen as the *cheapest cost avoiders*,[58] thus justifying placing them under the obligation of disclosure. Especially regarding capital markets, it has been suggested to lower transaction costs by introducing fixed standards that must be adhered to when providing information.[59] Legislative provisions which improve the content and quality of information and standardise the methods of disclosure hold many advantages over a concept relying on the market process. It is less cost-intensive, improves the possibilities of comparing the information provided and reduces the processing costs.[60] Yet one must bear in mind that standardising the disclosure mechanisms requires a consensus. In order to achieve this, opposing interests have to be assessed.[61] This usually results in a compromise which entails that mostly only minimum standards will be achieved.[62]

2. Disclosure Provisions as Part of Investor Protection

24 Academic theories have produced only a few parameters that can be applied to the disclosure systems of European capital markets. Therefore the development of a disclosure system can be seen more as a reaction to regulatory concerns that have occurred or been identified than as the implementation of economic theories guaranteeing ideal conditions for the functioning of the market. Legislative measures will usually be based on the justification that Europe-wide provisions are necessary to ensure investor protection.[63]

25 The extent to which investor protection is achieved through disclosure provisions has been subject to extensive legal discussions.[64] Some argue that disclosure provisions are crucial for an efficient capital market, are based on economic insights and thus only aim to achieve a supra-individual level of investor protection.[65] Others purport that the disclosure provisions are rather orientated towards the protection of the individual investor.[66] The European provisions do not provide a clear answer to this

---

[58] T.M.J. Möllers, 208 AcP (2008), p. 1, 10–11; L.A. Stout, 87 Mich. L. Rev (1988), p. 613, 705; R. Veil, 167 ZHR (2003) p. 365, 379–380; N. Vokuhl, *Kapitalmarktrechtlicher Anlegerschutz*, p. 181.

[59] See also, especially regarding the disclosure of accounting, J. Wüstemann et al., in: K.J. Hopt et al. (eds.), *Kapitalmarktgesetzgebung*, p. 11–12, 16.

[60] R. Walz, ZfbF Sonderheft 32 (1993), p. 85, 94–95; R.U. Fülbier, *Regulierung der Ad-hoc-Publizität*, p. 192; M. Rehberg, in: T. Eger and H.-B. Schäfer (eds.), *Ökonomische Entwicklung*, p. 314 ff.; N. Vokuhl, *Kapitalmarktrechtlicher Anlegerschutz*, p. 172.

[61] Cf. R. Walz, ZfbF Sonderheft 32 (1993), p. 85, 95.

[62] R.U. Fülbier, *Regulierung der Ad-hoc-Publizität*, p. 193.

[63] Cf. M. Deckert and J. v. Rüden, EWS (1998), p. 46, 49 ff.; P.O. Mülbert, WM (2001), p. 2085, 2092, 2100.

[64] For an overview on the German discussion cf. H. Brinckmann, *Kapitalmarktrechtliche Finanzberichterstattung*, p. 76 ff.; H. Merkt, *Unternehmenspublizität*, p. 301 ff.

[65] M. Deckert and J. v. Rüden, EWS (1998), p. 46, 49.

[66] Cf. T.M.J. Möllers, ZGR (1997), p. 334, 336 ff.

---

dispute. Most disclosure provisions are laid down in directives which require implementation into the national laws of the Member States, granting them discretion with regard to the exact wording of the provisions. Looking at the European provisions one can thus only determine with certainty that the provisions aim to ensure a supra-individual level of protection.[67] Whether individual investor protection is also achieved can only be determined by examining the national implementing laws of the individual Member State.

26   Disclosure provisions have the effect of controlling investors' decisions.[68] This entails the question as to what conception of investors is predominant in European capital markets law.[69] The disclosure provisions follow the concept of a reasonable investor who makes rational decisions on the capital market.[70] Recently, the idea of a rational investor has, however, been questioned due to new insights derived from *behavioral finance*.[71]

IV. Development of a Disclosure System in European Capital Markets Law

27   The development of a European disclosure system commenced in 1979, when the Securities Admission Directive was enacted. In the last 30 years it has been succeeded by various other legislative acts, all of which gradually helped to develop a disclosure system, the problem being that the European Community followed no overall concept. Thus, mandatory disclosure provisions only ever referred to limited aspects of capital markets law.[72] The first disclosure provisions in the Securities Admission Directive, the Securities Admission Prospectus Directive and the Half Yearly Report Directive, only contained provisions for issuers whose securities were admitted to the official listing of a stock exchange. Meanwhile the European Community has enlarged its regulatory activity from the primary markets to the secondary markets, enabling the development of an overall disclosure regime. This regime is open for a systematic examination.[73]

28   A company's disclosure obligations can be divided into three categories, depending on the company's stages of market participation.[74] The first disclosure obligations

---

[67] H. Brinckmann, *Kapitalmarktrechtliche Finanzberichterstattung*, p. 82 ff.

[68] For the idea of controlling people's decisions through disclosure provisions see C.J. Meier-Schatz, *Wirtschaftsrecht und Unternehmenspublizität*, p. 106–107; H. Merkt, *Unternehmenspublizität*, p. 338 ff.

[69] Cf. Art. 1(2) MAD. See also R. Veil, ZBB (2006), p. 162 ff.

[70] Cf. R. Veil, ZBB (2006), p. 162, 163.

[71] Regarding financial analysts see L. Teigelack, *Finanzanalysen und Behavioral Finance*, p. 269 ff. and passim.

[72] M. Brellochs, *Publizität und Haftung*, p. 26.

[73] S. Weber, in: M.A. Dauses (ed.), *Handbuch des EU-Wirtschaftsrechts*, F.III para. 17 ff. refers to the concept of a system of concentric circles on the markets regarding the disclosure provisions based mainly on European directives. Since regulated and non-regulated markets have been consolidated, cf. M. Brellochs, *Publizität und Haftung*, p. 50–51, the distinction between the different market areas which used to be laid out in the legislative regulation has been reduced. For a systematic presentation of European capital markets law see M. Brellochs, *Publizität und Haftung*, p. 26 ff.; H. Merkt, *Unternehmenspublizität*, p. 140 ff.; P.O. Mülbert, WM (2001), p. 2085, 2094–2095.

[74] Overview in: H. Brinckmann, *Kapitalmarktrechtliche Finanzberichterstattung*, p. 91 ff.; M. Brellochs, *Publizität und Haftung*, p. 30 ff.

Hendrik Brinckmann

arise when a company makes a public offering. According to the Prospectus Directive (PD) the issuer has then to publish a prospectus.[75] Activities on secondary
markets are accompanied by further periodic and ad hoc disclosure obligations.
Periodic disclosure ensures that the market is continually supplied with relevant
information about the company's accounts. The Transparency Directive (TD)
requires the regular publication of financial reports and interim management statements to these means.[76] Additionally there are various obligations on disclosure
for a company during market participation, the most important being the disclosure of inside information,[77] major holdings,[78] control over a target company[79] and
directors' dealings.[80] A mandatory disclosure upon market exit does not exist at a
European level.

29   In German legal literature there is intense discussion regarding the question of
whether an overall concept exists regarding the disclosure obligations in corporate,
capital markets and accounting law. In 2001 a fundamental study was published by
Merkt, developing criteria to systematise corporate disclosure.[81] He purports that
market participation correlates with disclosure, the disclosure obligations growing
the more capital the issuer raises on the market. The same applies with regard to the
mandatory disclosure on capital markets. From the perspective of capital markets
law, an issuer's relevance to the overall market increases with the amount of capital
it raises on the market.[82] The more capital the issuer raises, the more important
the issuer becomes regarding the protection of the investors and the institutional
efficiency of the capital markets as a whole. It also increases his impact on the
overall allocational efficiency of the markets, making an effective and correct pricing
mechanism for the issuer's securities more important. The correct pricing conveys
the allocational potential of an issuer. It becomes more important the more capital
is bound to him. Economically a misallocation of large amounts of capital entails
more ineffectual real investments of this issuer than would be the case for an issuer
with a lower market capitalisation. The amount of capital bound by an issuer thus
indicates his economic importance for the market.

[75] See § 17 para. 4,18.
[76] See § 18 para. 23 ff.
[77] See § 19 para. 25 ff.
[78] See § 20 para. 17 ff.
[79] See § 24 para. 35 ff.
[80] See § 21 para. 12 ff.
[81] H. Merkt, *Unternehmenspublizität*, p. 332 ff. and passim.
[82] H. Brinckmann, *Kapitalmarktrechtliche Finanzberichterstattung*, p. 139 ff.

§ 17   Prospectus Disclosure

Bibliography

Assmann, Heinz-Dieter, *Prospekthaftung als Haftung für die Verletzung kapitalmarktbezogener Informationsverkehrspflichten nach deutschem und US-amerikanischem Recht* (1985); Brandt, Christoph, *Prospekthaftung* (2005); Chvika, Eyal, *La responsabilité des intervenants dans le cadre d'une introduction en bourse*, RDBF (2008), p. 12–19; Crüwell, Christoph, *Die europäische Prospektrichtlinie*, AG (2003), p. 243–253; Deutsches Aktieninstitut (DAI), *Stellungnahme zu dem Vorschlag der Europäischen Kommission für eine Richtlinie des Europäischen Parlaments und des Rates über den Prospekt, der beim öffentlichen Angebot von Wertpapieren oder bei deren Zulassung zum Handel zu veröffentlichen ist*, NZG (2002), p. 1100–1101; Drinkuth, Henrik, *Die Kapitalrichtlinie—Mindest- oder Höchstnorm* (1998); Elsen, Jochen Robert and Jäger, Lars, *Revision der Prospektrichtlinie?—Ein erster Ausblick*, BKR (2008), p. 459–463; Elsen, Jochen Robert and Jäger, Lars, *Revision der Prospektrichtlinie—Überblick wesentlicher Neuerungen*, BKR (2010), p. 97–101; Ferran, Eilis, *Cross-border Offers of Securities in the EU: The Standard Life Flotation*, 4 ECFR (2007), p. 461–490; Fleischer, Holger, *Der Financial Services and Markets Act 2000: Neues Börsen- und Kapitalmarktrecht für das Vereinigte Königreich*, RIW (2001), p. 817–825; Fleischer, Holger, *Empfiehlt es sich, im Interesse des Anlegerschutzes und zur Förderung des Finanzplatzes Deutschland das Kapitalmarkt- und Börsenrecht neu zu regeln?*, Gutachten F für den 64. Deutschen Juristentag 2002; Franx, Jan Paul, *Disclosure Practices under the EU Prospectus Directive and the Role of CESR*, 2 CMLJ (2007), p. 295–305; Fuller, Geoffrey, *The Law and Practice of International Capital Markets*, (2009); Gebauer, Stefan, *Börsenprospekthaftung und Kapitalerhaltungsgrundsatz in der Aktiengesellschaft* (1999); Gerner-Beuerle, Carsten, *The Market for Securities and its Regulation through Gatekeepers*, 23 Temp. Int'l & Comp. L.J. (2009), p. 317–377; Grimaldos García, María I., *Algunos apuntes acerca del desarrollo reglamentario del régimen de la responsabilidad civil derivada del contenido del folleto*, 102 RDBB (2006), p. 271–278; Groß, Wolfgang, *Kapitalmarktrecht*, 4th ed. (2009); Holzborn, Timo and Schwarz-Gondek, Nicolai, *Die neue EU-Prospektrichtlinie*, BKR (2003), p. 927–935; Iribarren Blanco, Miguel, *Responsabilidad civil por la información divulgada por las sociedades cotizadas* (2008); Keunecke, Ulrich, *Prospekte im Kapitalmarkt*, 2nd ed. (2009); König, Kai-Michael, *Die neue europäische Prospektrichtlinie. Eine kritische Analyse und Überlegungen zur Umsetzung in das deutsche Kapitalmarktrecht*, ZEuS (2004), p. 251–288; Kullmann, Walburga and Metzger, Jürgen, *Der Bericht der Expertengruppe "Europäische Wertpapiermärkte" (ESME) zur Richtlinie 2003/71/EG ("Prospektrichtlinie")—Ausgewählte Aspekte des ESME-Berichts unter Berücksichtigung der Stellungnahme des Ausschusses der Europäischen Wertpapierregulierungsbehörden (CESR) zu "Retail Cascades" und der inhaltlichen Abgrenzung von Basisprospekt und endgültigen Bedingungen*, WM (2008), p. 1292–1298; Kullmann, Walburga and Sester, Peter, *Das Wertpapierprospektgesetz (WpPG)—Zentrale Punkte des neuen Regimes für Wertpapieremissionen*, WM (2005), p. 1068–1076; Kunold, Uta and Schlitt, Michael, *Die neue EU-Prospektrichtlinie, Inhalt und Auswirkungen auf das deutsche Kapitalmarktrecht*, BB (2004), p. 501–512; Rontchevsky, Nicolas, *Annotation on Sanct. AMF of 28 September 2006 and Annotation CA Paris* (31 March 2008), No. 2008/02370, RTDF 2008-1, p. 86–88; Rontchevsky, Nicolas, *Annotation on CA Paris* (26 June 2008), No. 07/14620, X c/Sté AB Arbitrage, RTD com. (2009), p. 182; Sandberger, Christoph, *Die EU-Prospektrichtlinie, Europäischer Pass für Emittenten*, EWS (2004), p. 297–303; Schäfer, Frank A., *Stand und Entwicklungstendenzen der spezialgesetzlichen Prospekthaftung*, ZGR (2006), p. 40–78; Schammo, Pierre, *A Prospectus Approval System*, 7 EBOR (2006), p. 501–523; Schammo, Pierre, *EU Prospectus Law—New Perspectives on Regulatory Competition in Securities Markets* (2011); Schlitt, Michael and Schäfer, Susanne, *Auswirkungen des Prospektrichtlinie-Umsetzungsgesetzes auf Aktien- und Equity-linked Emissionen*, AG (2005), p. 498–511; Schlitt, Michael, Singhof, Bernd and Schäfer, Susanne, *Aktuelle Rechtsfragen und neue Entwicklungen im Zusammenhang mit Börsengängen*, BKR (2005), p. 251–264; Seibt, Christoph H.,

Nikolai Vokuhl

von Bonin, Gregor and Isenberg, Gunnar, *Prospektfreie Zulassung von Aktien bei internationalen Aktientausch-Transaktionen mit gleichwertigen Dokumentenangaben (§ 4 Abs. 2 Nr. 3 WpPG)*, AG (2008), p. 565–577; Valmaña Ochaíta, María, *La responsabilidad civil derivada del folleto informativo en las ofertas públicas de suscripción y venta de acciones* (2006); Veil, Rüdiger and Wundenberg, Malte, *Prospektpflichtbefreiung nach § 4 Abs. 2 Nr. 3 WpPG bei Unternehmensübernahmen*, WM (2008), p. 1285–1292; Vokuhl, Nikolai, *Kapitalmarktrechtlicher Anlegerschutz und Kapitalerhaltung in der Aktiengesellschaft* (2007); Voß, Thorsten, *Die Überarbeitung der Prospektrichtlinie*, ZBB (2010), p. 194–211; Weber, Martin, *Unterwegs zu einer europäischen Prospektkultur, Vorgaben der neuen Wertpapierprospektrichtlinie vom 11.04.2003*, NZG (2004), p. 360–366; Wild, Eva-Maria, *Prospekthaftung einer Aktiengesellschaft unter deutschem und europäischem Kapitalschutz* (2007).

I.   Introduction

1   The aim of Directive 2003/71/EC (the PD) is to ensure investor protection and market efficiency.[1] Both regulatory aims are to be achieved by providing "full information concerning securities and issuers of those securities". The European legislature justified this by arguing that information is an effective means of increasing confidence in securities and thus of contributing to the proper functioning and development of securities markets. The appropriate way to make this information available is to publish a prospectus.[2]

2   The rules on prospectus disclosure are based on the recognition that securities are so-called credence products. Unlike with search goods, an investor cannot reduce uncertainties by obtaining information about the product prior to acquisition, or realistically assess securities at acceptable informational costs due to their complexity and the duration of capital investments. The investor must therefore rely upon the promised quality of the securities. This confidence can only be based on reliable information.[3]

3   Prospectus disclosure aims to reduce informational asymmetries.[4] European capital markets are not strictly efficient, resulting in an asymmetric distribution of information between issuers and investing market participants which are enhanced by the offer of such complex goods as securities.[5] These deficits are to be reduced with the help of prospectus disclosure.

4   The obligation to publish a prospectus applies when securities are offered to the public or admitted to trading on a regulated market,[6] as can be deduced from the aims and scope of application defined in Article 1 PD.[7] Article 3(1) PD further demands that the Member States prohibit any offer of securities to be made to the public within their territories without prior publication of a prospectus. Article 3(3)

---

[1] Recital 10 PD.
[2] Recital 18 PD.
[3] Cf. L. Burn, in: R. Panasar and P. Boeckmann (eds.), *European Securities Law*, para. 1.39; H. Fleischer, *Gutachten F 64. Dt. Juristentag*, p. F 23; N. Vokuhl, *Kapitalmarktrechtlicher Anlegerschutz*, p. 174 ff.; N. Moloney, *EC Securities Regulation*, p. 114.
[4] For more details on disclosure as a regulatory instrument see § 16 para. 14 ff.
[5] Cf. H.-D. Assmann, *Prospekthaftung*, p. 292 ff.; N. Vokuhl, *Kapitalmarktrechtlicher Anlegerschutz*, p. 176.
[6] Cf. on the offering process G. Fuller, *The Law and Practice of International Capital Markets*, para. 6.01–6.264.
[7] Cf. Art. 1 PD.

PD follows a similar aim, requiring that the Member States ensure that any admission of securities to trading on a regulated market is subject to the publication of a prospectus.

II. Regulatory Concepts

1. Requirements under European Law

5   The obligation to publish a prospectus was first introduced by the European legislature in 1979. Since then, it has been subject to a number of reforms.[8] For "reasons of consistency", the legislature regrouped the provisions in 2003, making extensive amendments. The PD constitutes an instrument essential to the achievement of the internal market.[9] It is complemented by the Prospectus Regulation, enacted by the European Commission on Level 2 of the Lamfalussy Process.[10] In November 2010, the PD was amended by Directive 2010/73/EU,[11] ensuring a more effective investor protection by introducing a summary in the prospectus, providing "key investor information".[12] All other the amendments mainly relate to technicalities.[13] Based on the recommendation of Directive 2010/73/EU to adopt further "delegated acts", the Prospectus Regulation was further supplemented by two amending regulations, as proposed by the European Securities and Markets Authority (ESMA).[14] The amendments do not only refer to the format and the content of the prospectus, but also relate to the disclosure requirements for certain offers of shares, such as (1) rights issues of companies admitted to trading on a regulated market, (2) offers of small and medium-sized enterprises and companies with reduced market capitalisation and (3) credit institutions, issuing securities referred to in Article 1(2)(j) PD that draw up a prospectus in accordance with Article 1(3) PD.

---

[8] See § 1 para. 5–6, 10 and 24; more details on historical aspects in N. Moloney, *EC Securities Regulation*, p. 103 ff.; A. Heidelbach, in: E. Schwark and D. Zimmer (eds.), *Kapitalmarktrechts-Kommentar*, Einl. WpPG para. 3 ff.; p. Schammo, *EU Prospectus Law*, p. 74 ff.

[9] Cf. Recital 4 PD.

[10] Commission Regulation (EC) No. 809/2004 of 29 April 2004 implementing Directive 2003/71/EC of the European Parliament and of the Council as regards information contained in prospectuses as well as the format, incorporation by reference and publication of such prospectuses and dissemination of advertisements, OJ L215, 16 June 2004, p. 1.

[11] Directive 2010/73/EU of the European Parliament and of the Council of 24 November 2010 amending Directives 2003/71/EC on the prospectus to be published when securities are offered to the public or admitted to trading and 2004/109/EC on the harmonisation of transparency requirements in relation to information about issuers whose securities are admitted to trading on a regulated market, OJ L327, 11 December 2010, p. 1.

[12] See para. 34–36.

[13] Overview in J.R. Elsen and L. Jäger, BKR (2010), p. 97; M.K. Oulds, in: S. Kümpel and A. Wittig (eds.), *Bank- und Kapitalmarktrecht*, para. 15.181 ff.; T. Voß, ZBB (2010), p. 194 ff.

[14] Commission Delegated Regulation (EU) No. 486/2012 of 30 March 2012 amending Regulation (EC) No. 809/2004 as regards the format and the content of the prospectus, the summary and the final terms and as regards the disclosure requirements, OJ L150, 9 June 2012, p. 1; Commission Delegated Regulation (EU) No. 862/2012 of 4.6.2012 amending Regulation (EC) No. 809/2004 as regards information on the consent to use of the prospectus, information on underlying indexes and the requirement for a report prepared by independent accountants or auditors, OJ L256, p. 4.

Nikolai Vokuhl

(a) Requirements under the Prospectus Directive and Prospectus Regulation

6   The PD defines the subject and scope of prospectus obligations as well as the procedure to be followed for the drawing up and approval of a prospectus. It further contains provisions concerning the prospectus for cross-border offers. The Prospectus Regulation primarily deals with the minimum content, the layout of the prospectus and possible forms of publication.

7   A prospectus may not be published until it has been approved by the competent authority of the home Member State.[15] "Approval" is defined in this context as "the positive act at the outcome of the scrutiny of the completeness of the prospectus by the home Member State's competent authority including the consistency of the information given and its comprehensibility".[16] It is thus not sufficient that the national authorities consider the completeness of the prospectus from a merely formal perspective.[17]

8   In order to avoid unnecessary costs and overlapping of responsibilities that may arise from a variety of competent authorities in the Member States,[18] the PD demands that only one central competent authority be designated in each Member State to approve prospectuses and to assume responsibility for supervising compliance with the directive for all prospectuses published by issuers of that Member State.[19] The authorities should be established as an administrative authority and in such a form that their independence from economic actors is guaranteed and conflicts of interest are avoided.[20]

9   Since the BaFin was founded in May 2002, it has been responsible for approving offer and admission prospectuses in Germany.[21] The stock exchange management is now only permitted to decide on the admission of securities to be traded on the stock exchange.[22] In the United Kingdom as of May 2002 the Financial Services Authority (FSA) and no longer the London Stock Exchange (LSE) is responsible for the approval of prospectuses.[23] Spain has declared the CNMV to be the responsible authority for approving prospectuses.[24] The managements of the stock exchanges now only have the power to decide on the admission of securities to the stock exchanges.[25] In France approvals of prospectuses are given by the AMF.[26] The admission to the regulated Eurolist market is decided by Euronext. In Italy Consob, founded in 1974, must approve of a prospectus before it may be published.[27] Sweden

---

[15] Art. 13(1) PD.

[16] Art. 2(1)(q) PD.

[17] Cf. C. Crüwell, AG (2003), p. 243, 250; U. Kunold and M. Schlitt, BB (2004), p. 501, 509; C. Sandberger, EWS (2004), p. 297, 300; in more detail A. Heidelbach, in: E. Schwark and D. Zimmer (eds.), *Kapitalmarktrechts-Kommentar*, § 13 WpHG para. 10 ff.; L. Burn, in: R. Panasar and P. Boeckmann (eds.), *European Securities Law*, para. 1.100–101.

[18] Recital 37 PD.

[19] See definition of home Member State in Art. 2(1)(m) PD.

[20] Art. 21(1) PD.

[21] Cf. §§ 3(1), 13(1), (2) No. 17 WpPG.

[22] Cf. § 32 para. 1 BörsG.

[23] Cf. sec. 87A, 72 and 417 FSMA.

[24] Cf. Art. 26.1 c LMV and Art. 24 RD 1310/2005.

[25] Cf. Art. 32.1 LMV.

[26] Art. L. 621-8 C. mon. fin. and Art. 212-2 RG AMF.

[27] Cf. Art. 113 I in conjunction with 94 I TUF.

has granted the power to approve of a prospectus to the FI;[28] the reform of the LHF abolished the possibility for the stock exchange management to decide whether a prospectus should be approved. In Austria prospectuses must be approved by the FMA.[29]

10   The respective authority must notify the issuer of its decision regarding the approval of the prospectus within 10 working days of the submission of the draft prospectus.[30] This time limit is extended to 20 working days if the public offer involves securities issued by an issuer that does not have any securities admitted to trading on a regulated market.[31] It only commences when the documents and the information provided by the issuer are complete.[32]

11   The exact duration of the time limit can thus be unpredictable for the issuer or offeror of securities.[33] In legal practice it is therefore not uncommon to agree on a time plan with a number of dates for the submission of documents with the supervisory authority. The supervisory authority can then comment on the documents that have been provided and notify the issuer as to what further information is required. The issuer will often submit multiple drafts of the prospectus to the authority.

12   Once approved, the prospectus is filed with the competent authority of the home Member State[34] and must be made available to the public in advance of, and at the latest at the beginning of, the offer to the public or the admission to trading of the securities involved.[35] The details of an electronic publication are described in the Prospectus Regulation.[36]

13   A prospectus is valid for 12 months after its publication for offers to the public or admissions to trading on a regulated market, provided that it is updated with any supplements required.[37] It may even be valid for the public offer or the admission to trading in any number of other Member States, provided that the competent authority of each host Member State is notified in accordance with Article 18 PD.[38] The notification must contain a copy of the prospectus and, if necessary, a translation of the summary produced by the issuer.[39] The competent authorities of the host Member States[40] may not undertake any approval or administrative procedures relating to prospectuses.[41] The concept of a single European passport enables an issuer to offer his securities in a number of Member States without having to obtain

---

[28] Cf. Kapitel 2, § 25 LHF; cf. N. Moloney, *EC Securities Regulation*, p. 166–167, on the concept of delegation under the Prospectus Directive.

[29] Cf. § 8a(1) KMG.

[30] Art. 13(2) PD.

[31] Art. 13(3) PD.

[32] Art. 13(4) PD.

[33] Cf. C. Crüwell, AG (2003), p. 243, 251; U. Kunold and M. Schlitt, BB (2004), p. 501, 509.

[34] Cf. Art. 14(1) PD.

[35] Cf. Art. 14(1) PD; see L. Burn, in: R. Panasar and P. Boeckmann (eds.), *European Securities Law*, para. 1.114; M.K. Oulds, in: S. Kümpel and A. Wittig (eds.), *Bank- und Kapitalmarktrecht*, para. 15.176.

[36] Cf. Art. 29 Prospectus Regulation.

[37] Cf. Art. 9(1) PD.

[38] Art. 17(1), Art. 18(1) PD. The competent authority of the home Member State must provide the competent authority of the host Member State with a certificate of approval within three working days following the request or, if the request is submitted together with the draft prospectus, within one working day after the approval of the prospectus, Art. 18(1) PD.

[39] Cf. Art. 18(1) PD.

[40] Art. 2(1)(n) PD.

[41] Art. 17(1) PD.

multiple approvals of the prospectus or demand admission to trading on each market individually.[42] The European legislature introduced the concept of a single European passport in order to facilitate the widest possible access to investment capital on a Community-wide basis,[43] thereby replacing the former partial and complex mutual recognition mechanism which was unable to achieve the European objectives.[44]

14   In order to promote common a supervisory approach and practice by the different competent authorities in the Member States, the Committee of European Securities Regulators (CESR), the ESMA's predecessor, published a questions and answers paper on the common position agreed upon by CESR members. This approach has been taken over by the ESMA, which also publishes questions and answers,[45] ensuring that the competent authorities under the PD are equipped with guidelines that enable them to act in accordance with the ESMA's conception of the provisions. The answers further aim to offer guidance for market participants.

(b)   Supporting Rules

15   The requirements listed in the PD and Prospectus Regulation only apply to information for investors on primary markets. The information required for secondary markets is ensured through other disclosure obligations: the Market Abuse Directive (MAD) demands that the Member States ensure that issuers of financial instruments inform the public of inside information directly affecting the respective issuer as soon as possible.[46] The TD requires the issuer to make public its annual financial report at the latest four months after the end of each financial year and additionally publish half-yearly, quarterly and interim financial reports.[47] It also contains the obligation to make public any changes in major shareholdings of the issuer.[48]

2.   Implementation in the Member States

16   The Member States have implemented the PD's requirements into their national laws,[49] mostly by adapting their existing rules on prospectus regulation rather than adopting the directive's rules one-to-one. The Prospectus Regulation is directly applicable in the Member States, and thus does not need to be implemented. The 2007 CESR Report on the Members' Powers under the PD and its Implementing Measures gives a good overview of implementation in national laws.[50]

17   In Germany, the respective provisions were adopted into the BörsG (German Stock Exchange Act) and the WpPG (Securities Prospectus Act) which were enacted in

---

[42] L. Burn, in: R. Panasar and P. Boeckmann (eds.), *European Securities Law*, para. 1.106–107.

[43] Cf. Recitals 1 and 4 PD.

[44] Cf. N. Moloney, *EC Securities Law*, p. 107 ff. for further details on the failure of the principle of mutual recognition.

[45] Cf. ESMA, *Questions and Answers, Prospectuses*, 15th updated version, ESMA/2012/417, July 2012.

[46] See § 19 para. 25–51.

[47] In more detail § 20 para. 23–56.

[48] In more detail § 20 para. 17–33.

[49] Directive 2010/73/EU of the European Parliament and of the Council is to be implemented into national law by the Member States by 1 July 2012.

[50] CESR, *Report on CESR Members' Powers under the PD and its Implementing Measures*, CESR/07-383, June 2007.

June 2005 in the course of the PD's implementation. The most important legal foundations in France can be found in Article L. 411-1 ff. Code monétaire et financier (C. mon. fin., French Monetary and Financial Code) and in the RG AMF (General Regulations of the French supervisory authority).[51] The Italian legislature adapted the existing provisions in the TUF (Italian Consolidated Laws on Finance) and RE (Italian Issuers' Regulation), rather than developing an entirely new set of rules. In Austria the capital markets law reforms in 2005 were used to amend the KMG (Austrian Capital Markets Act) and incorporate the new European requirements. The FMA also enacted an implementing regulation—the MVSV (Austrian Regulation on minimum content, disclosure and language requirements).[52] In Sweden the European requirements on prospectuses were implemented in the LVM (Swedish Securities Market Act).[53] The Spanish legislature implemented the PD with the Real Decreto Ley 5/2005 of 11 March 2005, which amended the LMV (Spanish Securities Market Act). In November 2005 these provisions were put into more concrete terms by the RD 1310/2005 (Royal Decree on Prospectuses). The United Kingdom provided a well-balanced prospectus regime long before the European legislature began developing rules thereon.[54] The PD could thus be implemented by slight amendments to the provisions in the Sixth Chapter of the Financial Services and Markets Act 2000 (FSMA).[55]

III. Drawing up a Prospectus

1. Scope of Application

18   Offers of securities to the public as well as the admission of securities to trading on a regulated market[56] that fall within the directive's scope of application are generally subject to the publication of a prospectus.[57] The scope of application of European prospectus law is thus defined through the terms "admission of securities to a regulated market"[58] and "offers of securities to the public".[59] In Article 2(1) (a), the PD defines "securities" as all transferrable securities with the exception of

---

[51] More details on the implementation in: R. Veil and P. Koch, *Französisches Kapitalmarktrecht*, p. 26.

[52] Cf. S. Kalss et al., *Kapitalmarktrecht*, § 10 para. 2.

[53] More details on the implementation in: R. Veil and F. Walla, *Schwedisches Kapitalmarktrecht*, p. 20 ff.

[54] Cf. G. Fuller, *The Law and Practice of International Capital Markets*, para. 6.42–6.4.3 and 6.88; P.C. Leyens and U. Magnus, in: K.J. Hopt and H.-C. Voigt (eds.), *Prospekt- und Kapitalmarktinformationshaftung*, p. 418, 427; R. Veil and M. Wundenberg, *Englisches Kapitalmarktrecht*, p. 18.

[55] The listing particulars under English law constitute an informational document unknown in European law (cf. sec. 79 ff. FSMA). The FSA Handbook defines listing particulars as "a document in such form and containing such information as may be specified in listing rules". The relationship between listing particulars and the prospectus is difficult to define for observers from other states. In simplified terms one may say that the obligation to publish listing particulars no longer applies once a prospectus becomes necessary under European law. Cf. LR 4.1.2 G FSA Handbook; G. Fuller, *The Law and Practice of International Capital Markets*, para. 6.88; R. Veil and M. Wundenberg, *Englisches Kapitalmarktrecht*, p. 20.

[56] Art. 3(3) PD.

[57] Art. 3(1) PD.

[58] The term regulated market is put into more concrete terms by reference to another directive (cf. Art. 4(1) (j) PD). In more detail § 7 para. 24–31.

[59] Cf. Art. 1(1) PD.

money market instruments having a maturity of less than 12 months.[60] The question whether a financial instrument should be classed as a security in this sense must thus be determined according to its tradability.[61]

19   The term "offer of securities to the public" means a communication to persons in any form and by any means, presenting sufficient information on the terms of the offer and the securities to be offered, in order to enable an investor to decide to purchase or subscribe to these securities.[62] This solves the problem that used to arise from the fact that the Member States had differing views on whether an offer requires a prospectus publication, resulting in a possible obligation to publish a prospectus in one Member State whilst the offer or the admission of the same security in a different Member State was possible without a prospectus.[63] Even with the new European rules, however, some interpretational questions are still answered differently amongst the Member States.[64] It remains particularly unclear what the requirements for an offer of securities to the public are. In Germany, even an offer to 100 or more people is not necessarily classed as such a public offer in the sense of the PD. Private placements are not regarded as public.[65] Determining a private placement must especially take into account the addressees of the offer and the method by which the information is distributed.[66]

20   The PD does not apply to all types of securities.[67] The securities to which it does not apply mainly include non-equity securities issued by a Member State, by one of a Member State's regional or local authorities or by the central banks or securities which have been unconditionally and irrevocably guaranteed by a Member State.[68] It further does not apply to securities issued in a continuous or repeated manner by credit institutions where the total consideration for the offer in the Union is less than €75 million EU and securities included in an offer where the total consideration for the offer in the Union is less than €5 million.[69]

2.   Exemptions from the Obligation to Publish a Prospectus

21   The PD does not apply to certain constellations.[70] These exemptions can be put into three categories. The first category makes an exception from the obligation to

---

[60] See § 8 para. 4–9.

[61] P. Schammo, *EU Prospectus Law*, p. 82–83; U. Kunold and M. Schlitt, BB (2004), p. 501, 502.

[62] Art. 2(1)(d) PD. This definition also applies to the placement of securities through financial intermediaries (Art. 2(1)(d) PD).

[63] P. Schammo, *EU Prospectus Law*, p. 80.

[64] Cf. ibid., p. 80–81; A. Heidelbach, in: E. Schwark and D. Zimmer (eds.), *Kapitalmarktrechts-Kommentar*, § 2 WpPG para. 14.

[65] Cf. A. Heidelbach, in: E. Schwark and D. Zimmer (eds.), *Kapitalmarktrechts-Kommentar*, § 2 WpPG para. 21.

[66] Publications via media packages pursuant to § 3 WpAIV are always public, cf. ibid.

[67] Art. 1(2) PD. The Member States may, however, provide an obligation to publish a prospectus for public offers thereof. Cf. T. Holzborn and N. Schwarz-Gondek, BKR (2003), p. 927, 928; U. Kunold and M. Schlitt, BB (2004), p. 501, 502; C. Crüwell, AG (2003), p. 243, 245.

[68] Art. 1(2) PD. The European legislature regarded the national possibilities on the regulation of bonds more suitable, cf. T. Holzborn and N. Schwarz-Gondek, BKR (2003), p. 927, 928–929.

[69] Art. 1(2)(h) and (j) PD as in Art. 1(1)(a) Directive 2010/73/EU; for details on these exemption cf. P. Schammo, *EU Prospectus Law*, p. 88 ff.

[70] Art. 3(2) and Art. 4 PD.

---

publish a prospectus for certain addressees, offers or securities.[71] The second and third categories exclude offers of securities to the public[72] and the admission of securities to the regulated market[73] from the obligation to compile a prospectus if the securities are issued under certain conditions.

(a) *Exceptions for Certain Addressees, Offers or Securities*

22   The PD exempts offers of securities addressed solely to qualified investors from the obligation to publish a prospectus.[74] The term "qualified investors" primarily refers to all professional investors such as credit institutions, investment firms, financial institutions and insurance companies.[75] These investors do not require protection due to their level of expertise and better access to information.[76]

23   The PD further contains an exception for an offer of securities addressed to fewer than 150 natural or legal persons per Member State, other than qualified investors,[77] which is aimed at facilitating private placements. It can, however, be difficult to determine how many investors were actually addressed with the respective offer.[78]

24   The obligation to publish a prospectus further does not apply to offers of securities addressed to investors who acquire securities for a total consideration of at least €100,000 per investor for each separate offer[79] or to offers of securities whose denomination per unit amounts to at least €100,000,[80] the European legislature thereby taking account of the different requirements for protection of the various categories of investors and their level of expertise.[81] A regulation is thus restricted to cases where this is necessary for protecting the investor.

(b) *Exemptions for Certain Issuances in Cases of Public Offers*

25   The obligation to publish a prospectus does not apply to offers to the public for certain types of securities.[82] The exemptions refer to constellations in which the securities are offered as substitutes for existing securities or in connection with certain transactions. In these cases investors have already been supplied with the necessary information at an earlier point.[83] Shares issued as substitutes for shares of the same class already issued need therefore not be accompanied by a prospectus if the issuing of such new shares does not involve any increase in the issued capital.[84] Similarly, securities offered in connection with a takeover or a merger by means of an exchange offer do not require a prospectus to be published provided that a

---

[71] Art. 3(2) PD.
[72] Art. 4(1) PD.
[73] Art. 4(2) PD.
[74] Art. 3(2)(a) PD.
[75] Cf. the extensive definition in Art. 2(1)(e) PD as in Art. 1(2)(a)(i) Directive 2010/73/EU.
[76] Cf. Recital 16 PD; cf. in more detail P. Schammo, *EU Prospectus Law*, p. 126 ff.
[77] Art. 3(2)(b) PD as in Art. 1(3)(a)(i) Directive 2010/73/EU.
[78] Cf. U. Kunold and M. Schlitt, BB (2004), p. 501, 504.
[79] Art. 3(2)(c) PD and Art. 1(3)(a)(i) Directive 2010/73/EU.
[80] Art. 3(2)(d) PD and Art. 1(3)(a)(i) Directive 2010/73/EU.
[81] Recital 16 PD.
[82] Art. 4(1) PD.
[83] In more detail C. Seibt et al., AG (2008), p. 565 ff.; R. Veil and M. Wundenberg, WM (2008), p. 1285 ff.
[84] Art. 4(1)(a) PD.

document is available containing information which is regarded as being equivalent to that of a prospectus by the competent authority.[85] This requirement will usually be fulfilled by the offer document in takeovers and the merger report.

(c)   Exemptions for Certain Issuances for the Admission to the Regulated Market

26   The obligation to publish a prospectus is also not applicable to certain types of securities and their admission to trading on a regulated market.[86] The constellations are similar to those mentioned above, with the addition of exemptions, such as that for securities already admitted to trading on another regulated market, provided certain conditions ensuring investor protection are fulfilled.[87] The admission of shares resulting from the conversion or exchange of other securities or from the exercise of the rights conferred by other securities to the regulated market is also not subject to the publication of a prospectus, provided that said shares are of the same class as the shares already admitted to trading on the same regulated market.[88]

(d)   Supplements

27   A prospectus is valid for 12 months after its publication, provided that the prospectus is complemented by the necessary supplements, as described in Article 16(1) PD:[89] every significant new factor, material mistake or inaccuracy relating to the information included in the prospectus must be added to the prospectus in a supplement if it is capable of affecting the assessment of the securities and arises or is noted between the time when the prospectus is approved and the final closing of the offer to the public or, as the case may be, the time when trading on a regulated market begins. The summary and any translations thereof must also be supplemented.[90]

28   Where the initiative for the supplement does not come from the issuer itself, the responsible supervisory authorities must ensure that the supplement is published correctly. The information requiring a supplement can be obtained through ad hoc notifications, enquiries, complaints or reports in the media.[91] A supplement must be approved by the supervisory authority and must be published within a maximum of seven working days.[92] The obligation to publish a supplement is accompanied by the investors' right to withdraw their acceptance if they agreed to purchase or subscribe for the securities before the supplement was published.[93]

29   This provision has been strongly criticised,[94] mainly with regard to the time frame within which the investor's acceptance may be withdrawn.[95] The European legisla-

---

[85] Art. 4(1)(b) and (c) PD.
[86] Art. 4(2) PD.
[87] Art. 4(2)(h) PD.
[88] Art. 4(2)(g) PD.
[89] Cf. Art. 9(1) PD.
[90] Art. 16(1) PD.
[91] CESR, *Report on CESR Members' Powers under the PD and its Implementing Measures*, CESR/ 07-383, June 2007, p. 12.
[92] Art. 16(1) PD.
[93] Art. 16(2) PD.
[94] Cf. U. Kunold and M. Schlitt, BB (2004), p. 501, 510; K.-M. König, ZEuS (2004), p. 251, 275; W. Kullmann and J. Metzger, WM (2008), p. 1292, 1297.
[95] Cf. P. Schammo, *EU Prospectus Law*, p. 105.

ture took this criticism into account in the PD's amendment by reducing this time frame to two days after the publication of the supplement. This period can only be extended by the issuer, the offeror or the person applying for the admission to trading on the regulated market. The European legislature did not, however, take into account the criticism regarding the fact that the investor's right to withdrawal is not limited to those cases in which the supplemented information had a negative influence on the investment decision.[96] As a result, the investor can withdraw from the agreement simply if it realises that it has made a "bad deal".[97]

3. Content, Format and Structure of a Prospectus

(a) General Rules

30 Pursuant to Article 5(1) PD, the prospectus must contain all information concerning the issuer and the securities to be offered to the public or to be admitted to trading on a regulated market, necessary for investors to make an informed assessment of the rights and obligations, the financial situation, profits and losses and the future of the issuer, and the rights connected to its securities. Such information, which needs to be sufficient and as objective as possible concerning the financial circumstances of the issuer and any guarantor as well as with regard to the rights attached to the securities, should be provided in a form that is easy to analyse and comprehend.

(b) Format of the Prospectus

(aa) Single or Separate Documents and Base Prospectus

31 The PD provides the possibility for the issuer, offeror or person asking for the admission to trading on a regulated market to draw up the prospectus as a single document or separate documents. Separate documents must divide the required information into a registration document (including information on the issuer), a securities note and a summary note.[98] In these cases, the registration document can be published in advance and remains valid for 12 months after its publication for innumerous offers to the public or admissions to trading on a regulated market (of course, a securities note and a summary note have to be published for each offer). It is especially suited to the needs of issuers that regularly place offers for the acquisition of securities to the public, such as banks.[99] As opposed to this, the single document appears more suited to the issuance of shares.[100]

32 The Prospectus Regulation contains details on the necessary content and the "composition of the prospectus".[101] A single document prospectus, for example, must be

---

[96] Cf. N. Moloney, *EC Securities Regulation*, p. 148; P. Schammo, *EU Prospectus Law*, p. 104.
[97] Cf. W. Kullmann and J. Metzger, WM (2008), p. 1292, 1297.
[98] Art. 5(3) PD.
[99] Cf. R. Panasar, L. de Carlos and J. Redonet, in: R. Panasar and P. Boeckmann (eds.), *European Securities Law*, para. 2.72; U. Kunold and M. Schlitt, BB (2004), p. 501, 505; K.-M. König, ZEuS (2004), p. 251, 272; N. Moloney, *EC Securities Regulation*, p. 147–148; C. Sandberger, EWS (2004), p. 298, 299.
[100] Cf. M. Schlitt et al., BKR (2005), p. 251, 251; U. Kunold and M. Schlitt, BB (2004), p. 501, 505. The Deutsche Bank, however, opted for separate documents, consisting of a registration form and securities description for its capital increase in 2010.
[101] Art. 25 Prospectus Regulation.

Nikolai Vokuhl

composed of a clear and detailed table of contents, a summary, the risk factors linked to the issuer and the type of security covered by the issue, and other information items included in the schedules and building blocks according to which the prospectus is drawn up[102] in this given order.[103] A prospectus composed of separate documents must comprise the following parts, so ordered: a clear and detailed table of contents, the risk factors linked to the issuer and the type of security covered by the issue, and the other information items.[104] Where the order of the items does not coincide with the required order of the information, the competent authority of the home Member State can ask the issuer, the offeror or the person asking for the admission to trading on a regulated market to provide a cross-reference list for the purpose of checking the prospectus before its approval.[105]

33 For offers of certain non-equity securities the prospectus can consist of a base prospectus[106] which must contain the same "relevant information" on the issuer and the securities as a single or separate document, with the exception of the final terms of the offer.[107] The information must further be supplemented where necessary. The base document provides the possibility to avoid making public the specific elements of an offer until directly before the commencement of the offer period. In practice, base prospectuses are therefore primarily applied for offering programmes such as medium-term notes and structured products such as certificates.[108] If the final terms of the offer are not included in either the base prospectus or a supplement, the final terms must be provided to investors and filed with the competent authority when each public offer is made as soon as practicable and if possible before commencement of the offer.[109] The final terms must then clearly indicate that the full information on the issuer and on the offer is only available on the basis of the combination of base prospectus and final terms.[110] The Prospectus Regulation contains rules on the structure required for a base prospectus[111] and allows the supervisory authorities to demand a cross-reference list, where the order of the items does not coincide with the order of the information provided for by the schedules and building blocks according to which the prospectus is drawn up.[112]

(bb) Summary

34 The prospectus must also include a summary that, in a concise manner and in non-technical language, provides key information in the language in which the prospectus was originally drawn up.[113] According to the European legislature, the

[102] See para. 37 ff.
[103] Art. 25(1) Prospectus Regulation.
[104] Art. 25(2) Prospectus Regulation.
[105] Art. 25(4) Prospectus Regulation.
[106] Cf. Art. 5(4) PD and Art. 22(6) Prospectus Regulation.
[107] Art. 2(1)(r) PD; Art. 22(7) Prospectus Regulation.
[108] Cf. R. Panasar, L. de Carlos and J. Redonet, in: R. Panasar and P. Boeckmann (eds.), *European Securities Law*, para. 2.73; W. Kullmann and J. Metzger, WM (2008), p. 1292, 1296; N. Moloney, *EC Securities Regulation*, p. 148; Schammo, *EU Prospectus Law*, p. 96 ff..
[109] Art. 5(4) PD.
[110] Art. 26(5) Prospectus Regulation.
[111] Art. 26(1) Prospectus Regulation.
[112] Art. 26(3) Prospectus Regulation.
[113] Art. 5(2) subsec. 1 PD as in Art. 1(5)(a)(i) Directive 2010/73/EU.

summary constitutes a key source of information for retail investors,[114] requiring a further specification of its necessary content: "It should focus on key information that investors need in order to be able to decide which offers and admissions of securities to consider further." The summary should be formatted in a way that allows comparison of the summaries of similar products by ensuring that equivalent information always appears in the same position in the summary. It must further contain a number of warnings informing the investors of the fact that the summary should be read as only the introduction to the prospectus and an investment decision should only be based on the entire prospectus. The investors must further be warned that claims relating to the content of the summary are subject to very specific conditions.[115] The directive contains precise details on the warnings that must be given.[116]

35   In the course of the reforms of prospectus law in 2010, the European legislature amended the provision on the summary, in order to guarantee a more effective investor protection, upgrading the summary to a form of key investor information.[117] Key investor information is defined as "essential and appropriately structured information which is to be provided to investors with a view to enabling them to understand the nature and the risks of the issuer, guarantor and the securities that are being offered to them or admitted to trading on a regulated market and to decide which offers of securities to consider further". Depending on the respective offer and security it includes the risks associated with and essential characteristics of the issuer (such as assets, liabilities and financial position), the risks associated with and essential characteristics of the investment in the relevant security, the general terms of the offer, including estimated expenses charged to the investor by the issuer or the offeror, details of the admission to trading, and reasons for the offer and use of proceeds.[118]

36   To ensure easy access to this information, the summary should not exceed 2,500 words in the language in which the prospectus was originally drawn up.[119] With regard to the detailed requirements concerning its content this will, however, rarely be achievable.[120] More complex securities, such as structured products, and base prospectuses will often require a more detailed summary in order to ensure investor protection.[121] The BaFin accepts longer summaries for the issuance of shares, but these should not exceed 5,000 words.[122] Similarly, the FSA also allows the summary to be longer than 2,500 words when, due to the particularly complex nature of the respective securities, the limit would make it difficult to explain the characteristics of and the risks associated with the issuer, potential guarantors and the securities.[123]

[114] Cf. Recital 15 Directive 2010/73/EU.
[115] See para. 44.
[116] Cf. Art. 5(2)(a)–(d) PD.
[117] Cf. J.R. Elsen and L. Jäger, BKR (2010), p. 97, 99.
[118] Art. 2(1)(s) PD as in Art. 1(2)(a)(ii) Directive 2010/73/EU.
[119] Recital 21 PD.
[120] Cf. T. Holzborn and N. Schwarz-Gondek, BKR (2003), p. 927, 932; C. Crüwell, AG (2003), p. 243, 247–248; U. Kunold and M. Schlitt, BB (2004), p. 501, 505.
[121] R. Panasar, L. de Carlos and J. Redonet, in: R. Panasar and P. Boeckmann (eds.), European Securities Law, para. 2.87–88; A. Heidelbach and G. Doleczik in: E. Schwark and D. Zimmer (eds.), Kapitalmarktrechts-Kommentar, § 5 WpPG para. 24; W. Kullmann and P. Sester, WM (2005), p. 1068, 1073.
[122] M. Schlitt and S. Schäfer, AG (2005), p. 498, 502.
[123] E. Ferran, 4 ECFR (2007), p. 461, 470.

(cc)   Incorporation by Reference

37   The PD allows the issuer to incorporate information in the prospectus by reference to other documents.[124] The investors must then be provided with a cross-reference list enabling them easily to identify specific items of information.[125] As opposed to this, the summary may not incorporate information by reference.[126] Additionally the cross-reference is restricted to previously or simultaneously published documents that have been approved by or filed with the competent authority of the home Member State.[127] The possibility to include cross-reference information mainly applies to information contained in annual and interim financial information, documents prepared on the occasion of a specific transaction such as a merger or demerger, audit reports and financial statements, memorandum and articles of association, earlier approved and published prospectuses and/or base prospectuses, regulated information or circulars to security holders.[128]

(c)   *Distinction between Different Security Constructions*

38   The minimum information to be included in the prospectus depends not only on the type of security offered, but also on the issuer.[129] The Prospectus Regulation follows a so-called building-block approach:[130] the numerous schedules and building blocks in the annex to the Prospectus Regulation contain lists of the information required. A "schedule" is defined as a list of minimum information requirements adapted to the particular nature of the different types of issuers and/or the different securities involved.[131] By combining the lists in the applicable annexes the information required for each specific security offered by the issuer can be determined.

39   The PD not only determines the scope of application for each individual schedule and building block,[132] but also which "combinations" of schedules and building blocks are possible.[133] The issuer of a security not listed in the regulation must add all the information required for comparable securities.[134] Where the issuer applies for approval of a prospectus or a base prospectus for a new type of security, the competent authority must decide, in consultation with the issuer, what information must be included in the prospectus.[135]

40   The minimum information required for certain types of securities is listed in the Prospectus Regulation's annexes: for shares, for example, Annex I on the Minimum Disclosure Requirements for the Share Registration Documents and Annex III on Minimum Disclosure Requirements for the Share Securities Notes apply,[136] requiring

---

[124] Art. 11(1) PD.
[125] Art. 11(2) PD.
[126] Art. 11(1) PD.
[127] Art. 11(1) PD.
[128] Cf. Art. 28(1) Prospectus Regulation.
[129] Cf. Art. 14, 18, 19 and 20 Prospectus Regulation.
[130] Cf. Art. 3(1) Prospectus Regulation.
[131] Cf. Art. 2(1) and (2) Prospectus Regulation.
[132] Art. 4–20a Prospectus Regulation.
[133] Art. 21(1) Prospectus Regulation; Annex XVIII Prospectus Regulation.
[134] Cf. Art. 23(2) Prospectus Regulation.
[135] Art. 23(3) Prospectus Regulation.
[136] According to Art. 4 Prospectus Regulation the schedule set out in Annex I is applicable and pursuant to Art. 6 Prospectus Regulation the schedule set out in Annex III.

information on the issuer, such as risk factors, a business overview, the operating results and financial condition, equity, management and supervisory bodies, major shareholders and financial information concerning the issuer's assets and liabilities, financial position, and profits and losses. The prospectus must further contain specific information on the securities to be offered, i.e. security-related risk factors, the issuer's capital, the terms and conditions of the offer and the admission to trading, and any dilution resulting from the offer.

(d) Language of the Prospectus

41   In the past, difficulties have arisen from the fact that the prospectus had to be translated into the language of the host Member State in order to be mutually recognised.[137] In order to facilitate the cross-border raising of capital, the European legislature amended this requirement in the PD. Article 19 PD distinguishes between four scenarios, the cross-border constellations being of particular practical relevance. Where an offer to the public is made or admission to trading on a regulated market is sought in one or more Member States excluding the home Member State, the prospectus may be drawn up "in a language customary in the sphere of international finance".[138] The competent authority of each host Member State may only require that the summary be translated into its official language.[139] Generally a prospectus will therefore be published in English.[140]

(e) Annual Document

42   The PD originally obliged issuers whose securities were admitted to trading on a regulated market to provide annually a document that contained or referred to all information that they had published or made available to the public over the preceding 12 months in one or more Member States and in third countries.[141] It was thus sufficient to provide a list containing all publications and where they could be found, if necessary indicating that some of the information was outdated. This provision constituted a foreign body in the PD's regulatory concept, and as such was strongly criticised.[142] The European legislature thus deleted the provision in the course of the reforms of the PD in 2010.[143] As a consequence, a registration document must now be updated by means of a supplement or securities note.[144]

---

[137] Cf. N. Moloney, *EC Securities Regulation*, p. 158; C. Crüwell, AG (2003), p. 243, 248; U. Kunold and M. Schlitt, BB (2004), p. 501, 508.
[138] For a list of the languages accepted for prospectus review and the translation of the summary in case of passporting, cf. R. Panasar, L. de Carlos and J. Redonet, in: R. Panasar and P. Boeckmann (eds.), *European Securities Law*, para. 2.123 ff.
[139] Art. 19(2) PD.
[140] R. Panasar, L. de Carlos and J. Redonet, in: R. Panasar and P. Boeckmann (eds.), *European Securities Law*, para. 2.121; Moloney, *EC Securities Regulation*, p. 158.
[141] Art. 10 PD.
[142] DAI, NZG (2002), p. 1100; J. R. Elsen and L. Jäger, BKR (2008), p. 459, 460–461.
[143] Cf. Art. 1(10) Directive 2010/73/EU.
[144] Recital 21 Directive 2010/73/EU.

IV. Sanctions

1. Requirements under European Law

43 The Member States must ensure that the appropriate administrative measures can be taken or administrative sanctions be imposed against the persons responsible, where the provisions adopted in the implementation of the PD have not been complied with. The measures must be effective, proportionate and dissuasive.[145] This wording gives the Member States much freedom in the construction of their national provisions,[146] in particular leaving it to their discretion whether to provide the right to impose criminal sanctions. The PD permits the competent authority to publicly disclose measures and sanctions that have been imposed for an infringement of the directive's provisions, unless the disclosure would seriously jeopardise the financial markets or cause disproportionate damage to the parties involved (so-called naming and shaming).[147] The directive does not oblige the supervisory authorities to use this sanctioning instrument or define more fully how the disclosure is to be made.[148]

44 The PD further requires the Member States to "ensure that responsibility for the information given in a prospectus attaches at least to the issuer or its administrative, management or supervisory bodies, the offeror, the person asking for the admission to trading on a regulated market or the guarantor, as the case may be. The persons responsible shall be clearly identified in the prospectus by their names and functions or, in the case of legal persons, their names and registered offices, as well as declarations by them that, to the best of their knowledge, the information contained in the prospectus is in accordance with the facts and that the prospectus makes no omission likely to affect its import." The provision does not attach the responsibility to a certain person, leaving the choice of the liable person and the construction of the respective provisions on liability to the Member States. As opposed to this, no civil liability is attached on the basis of an incorrect summary.[149]

45 Originally the PD aimed to avoid liability for incorrect summaries. This is now different, the summary being classed as "key investor information" since the 2010 reforms to the PD.[150] The Member States must now ensure that no civil liability is attached to any person solely on the basis of the summary, including any translation thereof, unless it is misleading, inaccurate or inconsistent, when read together with the other parts of the prospectus, or it does not provide key information in order to aid investors in their decision whether to invest in such securities.[151] The Member States must implement this controversial arrangement into their national laws by 1 July 2012.[152]

---

[145] Art. 25(1) PD.
[146] See § 12 para. 4 ff.
[147] Art. 25(2) PD.
[148] On the different legal practices in the European Member States see § 12 para. 10, 12, 16, 18 and 20.
[149] Art. 6(2) PD.
[150] See para. 34–36.
[151] Art. 6(2) subsec. 2 PD as in Art. 1(6) Directive 2010/73/EU.
[152] Cf. T. Voß, ZBB (2010), p. 194, 205.

2. Supervisory Measures

(a) Suspension or Prohibition of an Offer

46 Pursuant to Article 10(1) PD, a prospectus may not be published until it has been approved by the competent authority of the home Member State. This indicates the important role the supervisory authorities play in compiling a prospectus. The European legislature has equipped the supervisory authorities with a number of powers it regarded as necessary for carrying out the obligations laid down in the directive.[153] The competent authority has, for example, the right to require that the issuer include supplementary information in the prospectus, if it regards this as necessary for investor protection. It can further suspend a public offer or admission to trading for a maximum of 10 consecutive working days if it has reasonable grounds for suspecting that the provisions of this Directive have been infringed, or even prohibit a public offer if it finds that the provisions of the directive have been infringed or if it has reasonable grounds for suspecting that they would be infringed. The Member States have implemented these powers into their national laws; in some Member States the supervisory authorities have delegated the powers to the stock exchange management.[154]

(b) Fines

47 The administrative sanctions, mostly fines, differ considerably between the Member States.[155] The majority of the Member States have introduced either provisions regulating the maximum fines permitted or their competent authorities have set such a maximum fine. These vary between DKr30,000 (€4,050) in Denmark and €2.5 million in France. The United Kingdom does not regulate the maximum height of fines.[156] Some Member States further regulate the minimum fine to be imposed, which, as in the case of Italy (about €25,000), may even exceed the maximum fine in other Member States. The CESR Report contains no information on the practical effects of administrative fines. These can thus only be determined for each Member State individually through the respective, publicly accessible, sources.

48 In France sanctions may be imposed both against the issuer and against the management.[157] Between 18 March 2004 and 29 September 2008 the AMF's Commission des Sanctions imposed a total of 11 sanctions related to initial public offers.[158] Most fines were imposed for the publication of unrealistic prognoses.[159]

---

[153] Cf. Art. 21(3) and (4) PD.

[154] CESR, *Report on CESR Members' Powers under the PD and its Implementing Measures*, CESR/ 07-383, June 2007, p. 14 ff.; cf. N. Moloney, *EC Securities Regulation*, p. 166–167 on the concept of delegation under the Prospectus Directive.

[155] Cf. CESR, *Report on CESR Members' Powers under the PD and its Implementing Measures*, CESR/07-383, June 2007, p. 65 ff.

[156] Sec. 91(1A) FSMA; see R. Veil and M. Wundenberg, *Englisches Kapitalmarktrecht*, p. 37–38.

[157] E. Chvika, RDBF (2008), p. 12, 14.

[158] Cf. E. Chvika, RDBF (2008), p. 12, 13.

[159] Cf. AMF, Commission des sanctions, *M. Azoulay, société X, société Traditions Securities and Futures*, January 2006: €100,000 against the chairman; AMF, Commission des sanctions, *M. M. Andrieux* (8 July 2004): €500,000 personally (the turnover was predicted to be 34 times higher than it turned out to be).

3. Sanctions under Criminal Law

49   The enforcement of the PD's provisions is primarily ensured through administrative measures in the Member States, criminal sanction playing a subordinate role with only few Member States having actually introduced special provisions.[160] Most Member States have limited the protection under criminal law to the general rule,[161] which nevertheless plays an important role in legal practice.[162]

4. Sanctions under Civil Law

50   The civil liability for the publication of an incorrect prospectus could not differ more throughout the European Member States.[163] Whilst Germany,[164] the United Kingdom,[165] Spain,[166] Italy[167] and Austria,[168] for example, have introduced special provisions thereon, and may additionally apply the general civil law provisions, other Member States, such as France[169] and Sweden,[170] rely solely on their general civil law liability concepts.

51   The comparative legal literature has carefully scrutinised these different national legal concepts of civil law liability.[171] The underlying concepts[172] and details of the different provisions cannot be examined in detail here. Some central problems regarding prospectus liability in the Member States must, however, be examined more closely: which deficiencies result in prospectus liability? Which Member States require causation between the incorrect publication and the investment decision? What must be considered regarding the other requirements of a prospectus liability, such as responsibility, the capacity to sue and the legal consequences of prospectus liability?

(a) Deficiencies of the Prospectus

52   A prospectus is regarded as deficient if it contains incorrect or insufficient information. Information is incorrect if it does not relate to the facts. A prospectus contains insufficient information if it does not include all the information required by the Prospectus Regulation.

---

[160] Italy (Art. 173-bis TUF) and Austria (§ 15 KMG) provide a criminal provision specifically for sanctioning the publication of an incorrect prospectus.

[161] Cf. Germany § 399 AktG (incorrect information) and § 400 AktG (incorrect description) and also § 263 StGB (fraud) and § 266 StGB (embezzlement).

[162] Cf. for Sweden Högsta domstolen, NJA 1992, p. 691 ff. (Leasing Consult).

[163] Cf. N. Moloney, *EC Securities Regulation*, p. 164–165.

[164] Cf. §§ 21–25 WpPG (prior to June 2012, the provisions were contained in §§ 44, 45 BörsG).

[165] Cf. sec. 90 FSMA.

[166] Cf. Art. 28 LMV.

[167] Cf. Art. 97 VII TUF.

[168] Cf. § 11 KMG.

[169] Cf. Art. 1382 Cc.

[170] An issuer may be held liable on the legal basis of the Kapitel 29, § 1(1) 2, (2) 2 ABL and the general rules of tort law, cf. R. Veil and F. Walla, *Schwedisches Kapitalmarktrecht*, p. 25 ff.

[171] Cf. K.J. Hopt and H.-C. Voigt (eds.), *Prospekt- und Kapitalmarktinformationshaftung* (2004); R. Veil and M. Wundenberg, *Englisches Kapitalmarktrecht*, p. 24 ff.; R. Veil and P. Koch, *Französisches Kapitalmarktrecht*, p. 29 ff.; R. Veil and F. Walla, *Schwedisches Kapitalmarktrecht*, p. 20 ff.; C. Gerner-Beuerle, 23 Temp. Int'l & Comp. L.J. (2009), p. 317, 344–372.

[172] See H.-D. Assmann, *Prospekthaftung*, p. 213 ff.

53   Common examples are the reference to an incorrect or manipulated balance sheet in the prospectus or the omission of the fact that an action for annulment is pending against the capital increase resolution.

54   A prospectus can further be deficient if it reflects an unrealistic picture of the issuer or his financial situation or profit expectations.[173]

55   *Facts (abridged and simplified):*[174] The Beton- und Monierbau AG (BuM) was experiencing liquidity problems that could only be cleared with the help of a loan, guaranteed by the federal state of North Rhine-Westphalia. When new financial difficulties arose a short time later the company applied for a federal guarantee which was granted under the premise of a capital increase. After the prospectus was published, an investor acquired new shares from the capital increase. Less than six months later, bankruptcy proceedings were instituted against BuM. The Bundesgerichtshof (BGH, German Federal Court of Justice) ruled that when determining whether a prospectus contains incorrect or insufficient information it is not sufficient to examine the presented facts individually. One must rather also take into account the impression these facts give as a whole. In the case at hand, the general picture conveyed did not sufficiently indicate that the shares had to be classed as high-risk investments of a highly speculative nature. The prospectus rather attempted to give the impression that the difficulties were merely temporary and the capital increase was intended to consolidate the company's budget, indicating that the financial results would improve compared with those of previous year.

56   In Germany, Italy and Austria the rules on liability require that the prospectus has to be incorrect in an aspect material for the evaluation of the security.[175] This can be assumed, if the relevant aspect is taken into account for an investment decision of a reasonable investor. The prevalent understanding in Germany is that a reasonable investor must be able to read and understand a balance sheet without, however, having above-average expert knowledge.[176]

57   *Example:* In the case *Beton- und Monierbau AG (BuM)* the prospectus contained the information that the company's financial results would improve considerably in 1978, compared to 1977 when the company suffered severe losses. The BGH ruled that no reasonable investor would have got the overall impression that this improvement could still mean overall losses—albeit reduced compared to the year before. An average investor need not understand the terminology common to insiders.

58   It is particularly difficult to determine whether a prospectus is incorrect with regard to statements referring to future events and prognoses. In Germany, incorrect statements are also subject to prospectus liability. Statements on future events are

---

[173] BGH, NJW (1982), p. 2823 ff. (described in further detail in the example below); cf., however, OLG Frankfurt, ZIP (2012), p. 1240 ff., which held that a prospectus is not incorrect, if the valuation of the real estate owned by the issuer is overstated by 12%, as such deviation still ranges within the acceptable margin.

[174] BGH, NJW (1982), p. 2823 ff.

[175] In Germany, a prerequisite is that the aspect is sufficiently definite, which is deemed to be the case if the supervisory board has approved a transaction, cf. OLG Frankfurt ZIP 2012, p. 1236 ff.

[176] Cf. BGH, NJW (1982), p. 2823, 2824; OLG Frankfurt am Main, AG (2005), p. 851, 852; OLG Frankfurt am Main, WM (1994), p. 294, 295; OLG Stuttgart, WM (1984), p. 586, 592.

regarded as incorrect if they are not commercially justifiable or are not based on actual facts.[177]

59 *Example:* In *BuM* the BGH ruled that the wording of the provisions on prospectus liability did not include facts in the term "information" but also evaluative statements on the economic situation of the company and its future developments, as these could not always be clearly distinguished. An investor must therefore be able to rely on the evaluative statements to be conclusions deduced from the facts on the basis of a thorough analysis. Accordingly, the issuer of the prospectus could not be held liable for the incorrectness of the statements, his liability rather depending on whether the prognosis is commercially justifiable on the basis of the underlying facts.

60 France treats the problem of a liability for an incorrect prognosis similarly, all statements on future developments requiring a verifiable foundation.[178] If this is not the case and the prognosis is based on intentions or estimations, this must be made clear in the prospectus. A prognosis based on facts must be accompanied by information on how it was established. A number of examples put the content of prognoses into more concrete terms.[179] The United Kingdom offers a number of common law examples on this matter. The courts determine liability according to the question of whether the person to be held liable for the incorrect prospectus was convinced that his statement on future developments was correct[180] and whether it was assumed that his predictions would prove to be true.[181]

(b) Claimant and Opposing Party

61 In Germany, France and Austria it is not only investors holding securities who are entitled to assert claims, but also investors who have already disposed of the respective securities. Under German law this right exists for the acquisition of securities within 6 months of the prospectus publication, irrespective of whether the securities were acquired on the primary or secondary market.[182] Spain[183] and the United Kingdom[184] also provide for compensation claims for investors who have acquired respective securities on the secondary market within a certain time frame after the prospectus was published.

---

[177] BGH, NJW (1982), p. 2823, 2824; OLG Frankfurt am Main, WM (1994), p. 291, 295; LG Frankfurt am Main, WM (1998), p. 1181, 1184.

[178] Cf. Art. 212-14 to 212-16 RG AMF.

[179] Cf. H.-J. Puttfarken and A. Schrader, in: K.J. Hopt and H.-C. Voigt (eds.), *Prospekt- und Kapitalmarktinformationshaftung*, p. 600–601.

[180] A. Alcock, in: Lord Millett et al. (eds.), *Gore-Browne on Companies*, sec. 43-22 (Update 66); P.C. Leyens and U. Magnus, in: K.J. Hopt and H.-C. Voigt (eds.), *Prospekt- und Kapitalmarktinformationshaftung*, p. 417, 462–463.

[181] *Aaron's Reefs/Twiss* [1896] AC 273, 284; *In re Pacaya Rubber and Produce Company, Limited* [1914] 1 ChD 542, 549; A. Alcock, in: Lord Millett et al. (eds.), *Gore-Browne on Companies*, sec. 43-22 (Update 66); in more detail see R. Veil and M. Wundenberg, *Englisches Kapitalmarktrecht*, p. 37.

[182] Cf. § 21 (1) WpPG; see E. Schwark, in: E. Schwark and D. Zimmer (eds.), *Kapitalmarktrechts-Kommentar*, §§ 44, 45 BörsG para. 38.

[183] Cf. M. Iribarren Blanco, *Responsabilidad civil por la información divulgada por las sociedades cotizadas*, p. 47 f.; M.I. Grimaldos García, 102 RDBB (2006), p. 271, 278–279.

[184] Cf. P.L. Davies, *Gower and Davies' Principles of Modern Company Law*, para. 25–32; A. Alcock, in: Lord Millett et al. (eds.), *Gore-Browne on Companies*, sec. 43-8 (Update 66).

62   The PD does not specify against whom the claim is to be brought. It is thus hardly surprising that the Member States have not answered this question uniformly. In general it can be said that Germany, France, Italy, Austria, Spain and the United Kingdom all assume the issuer to be held liable, whilst Sweden does not provide a possibility for claims against the issuer.

63   In Germany, the action for prospectus liability can further be brought against any person responsible for the drawing up and publication of the prospectus,[185] i.e. the issuer[186] and the banks issuing the securities,[187] as well as against any person upon whose initiative the publication is based.[188] The latter is any person with an economic interest in the issuance, such as major shareholders or banks participating in the issuance of shares by a smaller and less solvent issuing company.[189] German legal literature does not assume any liability on the part of experts who only participate in drawing up parts of the prospectus without any personal economic interest in the issuance.[190]

64   In the United Kingdom, prospectus liability extends to the issuer, its directors, all prospective directors, and any person responsible for drawing up or approving the prospectus.[191] The risk of liability thus applies to both the bodies of the issuer and experts responsible for the prospectus. Professional advice on the content of the prospectus alone does not, however, entail liability.[192]

(c)   Causation

65   An essential element of prospectus liability is the question as to whether the claimant actually based his investment decision on the incorrect information. Germany and the United Kingdom have both eased the burden of proof of causation. In Austria[193] and Spain[194] legal literature recommends similar facilitations. France, Italy and Sweden do not provide any rules easing the burden of proof for the investor.

66   In Germany, the courts formerly ruled that a general disposition towards the acquisition of shares, initiated through publications in the media or investment consulting, was sufficient for the assumption of causation between the prospectus and

---

[185] § 21(1) No. 1 WpPG.
[186] § 5(3) WpPG.
[187] § 5(4) WpPG. All banks are held responsible in bank syndicates, independent of whether they actually participated in the drawing up of the prospectus, cf. E. Schwark, in: E. Schwark and D. Zimmer (eds.), *Kapitalmarktrechts-Kommentar*, §§ 44, 45 BörsG para. 10.
[188] § 21(1) No. 2 WpPG.
[189] E. Schwark, in: E. Schwark and D. Zimmer (eds.), *Kapitalmarktrechts-Kommentar*, §§ 44, 45 BörsG para. 9.
[190] W. Groß, *Kapitalmarktrecht*, §§ 44, 45 BörsG para. 36; E. Schwark, in: E. Schwark and D. Zimmer (eds.), *Kapitalmarktrechts-Kommentar*, §§ 44, 45 BörsG para. 12.
[191] English legal literature is actively discussing the question of who is to be held liable for deficiencies in a prospectus (cf. P.L. Davies, *Gower and Davies' Principles of Modern Company Law*, para. 25-34: "sensitive question"). Meanwhile PR 5.5. FSA Handbook contains detailed rules on liability. In more detail A. Alcock, in: Lord Millett et al. (eds.), *Gore-Browne on Companies*, sec. 43-9 (Update 66).
[192] PR 5.5.3(f) FSA Handbook.
[193] Cf. S. Kalss et al., *Kapitalmarktrecht*, § 11 para. 24.
[194] Cf. with different explanations M. Iribarren Blanco, *Responsabilidad civil por la información divulgada por las sociedades cotizadas*, p. 118; M. Valmaña Ochaíta, *La responsabilidad civil derivada del folleto informativo en las ofertas públicas de suscripción y venta de acciones*, p. 379.

the investor's decision to acquire the securities.[195] The investor was assumed to have indirectly gained knowledge of the content of the prospectus through information that was publicly available. The BGH ruled that the investor need not have read the prospectus or gained knowledge of it, ruling that it was sufficient if the report was decisive for the assessment of the security amongst experts and had thus helped to create a general disposition towards its acquisition.[196] The legislature finally adopted this understanding, implementing the concept of a general disposition towards acquisition in § 23(2) No. 1 WpPG, which now contains a legal assumption of causation: the claim is unsubstantiated if the decision to acquire the respective securities was not based on the information in the prospectus. The issuer must prove this missing causation by describing why there was no general disposition towards the acquisition of the respective shares, due to negative developments or reports or a sharp fall in the security's price, for example.

67   The United Kingdom also does not require the investor's actual knowledge of the content of the prospectus.[197] Causation in the sense of section 90(1)(b) FSMA can be assumed if the deficiency in the prospectus adversely affected the price of the security. The proof of causation in United Kingdom and in Germany is thus similarly facilitated.

(d)   Responsibility

68   All jurisdictions require responsibility for prospectus liability, negligence sufficing in the United Kingdom, Spain, France, Italy and Sweden, whilst in Austria the required standard of fault depends on the person who is to be held liable.[198] Germany has the most restrictive rules concerning responsibility.[199]

69   The legal foundation for prospectus liability in Germany is § 23(1) WpPG. Pursuant to this provision a person is exempt from liability if he can prove that he did not know that the prospectus contained incorrect or insufficient information and that his lack of knowledge was not based on gross negligence.[200] Proof of causation is thus reversed: the opposing party must prove that it was not responsible for the deficient prospectus. A person acts with gross negligence if he fails to exercise reasonable care in a particularly serious way,[201] i.e. if he failed to make the most obvious deliberations.[202] The standard can vary, as the personal and expert knowledge of a person must be taken into consideration when determining whether it acted with gross negligence.[203]

---

[195] Cf. RGZ 80, p. 196, 204; BGHZ 139, p. 225, 233; BGH, NJW (1982), p. 2823, 2826; BGH, NJW (1982), p. 2827, 2828; OLG Düsseldorf, ZIP (1984), p. 549, 558; OLG Frankfurt am Main, WM (1994), p. 291, 298; OLG Frankfurt am Main, WM (1996), p. 1216, 1219.

[196] BGHZ 139, p. 225, 233.

[197] A. Alcock, in: Lord Millett et al. (eds.), *Gore-Browne on Companies*, sec. 43-3 (Update 66); A. Hudson, in: G. Morse (ed.), *Palmer's Company Law*, para. 5.742.

[198] Cf. § 11(1) KMG.

[199] Cf. C. Gerner-Beuerle, 23 Temp. Int'l & Comp. L.J. (2009), p. 317, 374.

[200] § 23(1) WpPG.

[201] Cf. BGHZ 10, p. 14, 17; BGHZ 89, p. 153, 161.

[202] Cf. OLG Düsseldorf, WM (1984), p. 586, 595.

[203] Cf. W. Groß, *Kapitalmarktrecht*, §§ 44, 45 BörsG para. 75.

70   The United Kingdom has also introduced a provision (schedule 10 FSMA) according to which a person is exempt from liability:[204] a person does not incur any liability for loss caused by a statement if he satisfies the court that he reasonably believed the statement was true and not misleading, he could reasonably rely on the statement of an expert,[205] he published a correction in a manner calculated to bring it to the attention of persons likely to acquire the securities before the securities were acquired, or the investor acquired the securities in the knowledge that the published information was incorrect, misleading or incomplete. Schedule 10 FSMA thus assumes responsibility, even in cases of negligence, unless the defendant proves otherwise.[206]

(e)   Legal Consequences

71   The Member States attach different legal consequences to the liability for incorrect prospectus information which can be divided into two categories. In some jurisdictions, investors may claim the difference between the acquisition price and disposal price for the shares or the actual value of the security as damages. Other states additionally provide the possibility to rescind the contract or claim compensation by restoration of the previous situation.

72   In Germany, an investor can demand specific performance, i.e. the return of the securities against reimbursement of the acquisition price, pursuant to § 21(1) WpPG. If an investor has meanwhile disposed of the securities he can alternatively demand the difference in price between the acquisition and disposal, including all costs related thereto, such as the broker's commission paid to the issuing bank or a stockbroker and all costs attached to the exercise of subscription rights.[207]

73   The British FSMA does not contain any provisions on the calculation of damages. As no case law has as yet been spoken on section 90 FSMA, the legal effects of liability remain unclear.[208] According to the legal literature, the claimant is to be compensated for all detriments suffered due to the incorrect prospectus (out-of-pocket loss rule),[209] and is thus to be awarded the difference between the acquisition price and the actual value of the securities.[210] Section 90 FSMA does not, however, allow specific performance, i.e. the return of the securities against reimbursement of the acquisition price.[211]

74   It has yet to be decided whether payments the issuer must make to the investors based on the rules of prospectus liability comply with the capital maintenance

---

[204] Only selected exemptions can be described in more detail herein. For a more detailed presentation see R. Veil and M. Wundenberg, *Englisches Kapitalmarktrecht*, p. 28.

[205] Cf. C. Gerner-Beuerle, 23 Temp. Int'l & Comp. L.J. (2009), p. 317, 356–362.

[206] Cf. P.L. Davies, *Gower and Davies' Principles of Modern Company Law*, para. 25–32: "The purpose of Schedule 10 is to implement the policy of imposing liability on the basis of negligence but with a reversed burden of proof."

[207] E. Schwark, in: E. Schwark and D. Zimmer (eds.), *Kapitalmarktrechts-Kommentar*, §§ 44, 45 BörsG para. 66.

[208] Seen critically by A. Alcock, in: Lord Millett et al. (eds.), *Gore-Browne on Companies*, sec. 43-4 (Update 66).

[209] Cf. ibid.

[210] Cf. P.L. Davies, *Gower and Davies' Principles of Modern Company Law*, para. 25–31; see also E. Lomnicka and J.L. Powell, *Encyclopedia of Financial Services Law*, para. 2A-190 (as of R. 80, April 2007): "awarding him a sum representing the amount he overpaid for the securities"; A. Alcock, in: Lord Millett et al. (eds.), *Gore-Browne on Companies*, sec. 43-4 (Update 66): "mispricing loss from the error".

[211] Specific performance may, however, be possible under common law principles, cf. R. Veil and M. Wundenberg, *Englisches Kapitalmarktrecht*, p. 31 ff.

Nikolai Vokuhl

regime. German legal literature tends to purport that the German rules on prospectus liability comply with the principles on capital maintenance,[212] arguing that the respective stock exchange law provisions came into force after the rules on capital maintenance (*lex posterior* rule). The highest civil court in Austria (Oberste Gerichtshof) also ruled that the provisions on prospectus liability would override the rules on capital maintenance.[213] It appears doubtful, however, whether this interpretation complies with European law.[214] Whilst the PD requires an effective liability regime for incorrect prospectus publications, the Capital Directive requires that a certain amount of the company's assets may not be reduced by distributions to shareholders in order to protect the creditors of a company.[215]

V. Conclusion

75 With the enactment of the PD and the Prospectus Regulation, the European legislature aimed to ensure the largest possible access to investment capital at a European level. The aims of the provisions further include investor protection and market efficiency. These aims have largely been achieved. The detailed provisions of the PD leave the Member States with only little scope regarding their implementation. In connection with the provisions in the Prospectus Regulation, extensive harmonisation of the requirements for the drawing up and content of a prospectus for public offers and the admission of shares to trading is thus achieved. Whilst the density of regulation has not prevented the national supervisory authorities from following different approaches regarding their interpretation and application, the functioning of the markets does not currently appear to be impaired by this.

76 As opposed to this, the sanctioning level does not appear to be as well harmonised. The Member States provide a number of different sanctioning instruments under supervisory law and also varying sanctions under civil law. Prospectus liability is subject to very different prerequisites in the Member States. This sum of disparate regulatory concepts can cause uncertainty in the issuers[216] and investors concerning the exact risks of an offer or the admission of shares to trading in another Member State. The noticeable differences also have a negative effect on investor protection and market efficiency. It will therefore have to be examined closely in the next few years whether it is necessary to develop a more uniform level of protection for investors.

---

[212] Cf. A. Baumbach and K. J. Hopt, *HGB Kommentar*, § 44 BörsG para. 5; S. Gebauer, *Börsenprospekthaftung und Kapitalerhaltungsgrundsatz*, p. 190 ff.; distinguishing between acquisition on the primary markets (liability is restricted to free assets) and acquisitions on the secondary markets (no restriction on liability, cf. § 57 AktG); E. Schwark, in: E. Schwark and D. Zimmer (eds.), *Kapitalmarktrechts-Kommentar*, § 45 BörsG para. 13–14; cf. OLG Frankfurt am Main, AG (2000), p. 132, 134.

[213] Cf. OGH, GesRZ (2011), p. 193.

[214] This is the position of some authors in the German discussion; cf. N. Vokuhl, *Kapitalmarktrechtlicher Anlegerschutz*, p. 46 ff.; E.-M. Wild, *Prospekthaftung einer Aktiengesellschaft unter deutschem und europäischem Kapitalschutz*, p. 183 ff.

[215] According to Art. 15(1)(a) Capital Directive, "No distribution to shareholders may be made, except for cases of reduction of subscribed capital, when on the closing date of the last financial year the net assets as set out in the company's annual accounts are, or following such a distribution would become, lower than the amount of the subscribed capital plus those reserves which may not be distributed under the law or the statutes". See H. Drinkuth, *Die Kapitalrichtlinie—Mindest- oder Höchstnorm* (1998), p. 184.

[216] Cf. E. Ferran, 4 ECFR (2007), p. 461, 483 ff.

§ 18 Periodic Disclosure

Bibliography

Beaver, William H., *What Should Be the FASB's Objectives?*, 136 JOA (1973), p. 49–56; Beaver, William H. and Demski, Joel S., *The Nature of Financial Accounting Objectives: A Summary and Synthesis*, 12 J. Acc. Res. (1974), p. 170–187; Biard, Jean-François, *Transposition de la directive Transparence concernant les obligations d'information des sociétés cotées ou faisant appel public à l'épargne*, RDBF (2007), p. 36–38; Bouthinon-Dumas, Huges, comment on decision *CA Paris, 1ère chambre, section H, 20 mai 2008, No. 2007/14651, « Rhodia SA et X c/ AMF »*, Bull. Joly Bourse (2008), p. 492–504; Böcking, Hans-Joachim, *Zum Verhältnis von Rechnungslegung und Kapitalmarkt: Vom "financial accounting" zum "business reporting"*, ZfbF Sonderheft 40 (1998), p. 17–53; Bonneau, Thierry, *La réforme 2005 du prospectus*, RDBF (2005), p. 43–47; Boyle, Anthony J. et al. (eds.), *Gore-Browne on Companies*, loose-leaf (Update 76); Brellochs, Michael, *Publizität und Haftung von Aktiengesellschaften im System des Europäischen Kapitalmarktrechts* (2005); Brinckmann, Hendrik, *Periodische Kapitalmarktpublizität durch Finanzberichte* (2008), available at: www.iukr.de/downloads/1.arbeitspapieriukr.pdf; Brinckmann, Hendrik, *Kapitalmarktrechtliche Finanzberichterstattung* (2009); Busse von Colbe, Walther, *Die Entwicklung des Jahresabschlusses als Informationsinstrument*, ZfbF Sonderheft 32 (1993), p. 11–29; Campobasso, Gian Franco, *Diritto Commerciale*, Vol. 2, 6th ed. (2006); Chang, Hsihui, Chen, Jengfang, Liao, Woody M. and Mishra, Birendra K., *CEOs'/CFOs' Swearing by the Numbers: Does It Impact Share Price of the Firm?*, 81 TAR (2006), p. 1–27; Daigre, Jean-Jacques, *Qui devra assumer la responsabilité des rapports financiers annuels, semestriels et trimestriels dans les sociétés cotées à compter du 20 janvier 2007?*, RDBF (2006), p. 1–3; Dezeuze, Éric, comment on decision *TGI Paris, 11ème chambre correctionnelle, 1ère section, 12 septembre 2006, MM. O., D.V., et L. contre Ministère public, SIDEL et autres*, RTDF (2006–03), p. 162–167; Dezeuze, Éric, comment on decision *Cour d'appel de Paris, 9ème chambre, section B, 17 octobre 2008, MM. O., D.V. et L. contre Ministère public, Sidel et autres*, RTDF (2008), p. 137–141; Dezeuze, Éric, comment on decision *CA Paris, 9ème chambre, section B, 17 octobre 2008, No. 06/09036 ("Sidel")*, Bull. Joly Bourse (2009), p. 28–35; Dezeuze, Éric and Buge, Guillaume, comment on *Sanct. AMF, 5 juillet 2007 ("Marionnaud")*, Bull. Joly Bourse (2008), p. 46–60; Ekkenga, Jens, *Anlegerschutz, Rechnungslegung und Kapitalmarkt* (1998); Fleischer, Holger, *Prognoseberichterstattung im Kapitalmarktrecht und Haftung für fehlerhafte Prognosen*, AG (2006), p. 2–16; Fleischer, Holger, *Buchführungsverantwortung des Vorstands und Haftung der Vorstandsmitglieder für fehlerhafte Buchführung*, WM (2006), p. 2021–2029; Fleischer, Holger, *Der deutsche "Bilanzeid" nach § 264 Abs. 2 S. 3 HGB*, ZIP (2007), p. 97–106; Galgano, Francesco, *Diritto Commerciale, Le società*, 17th ed. (2009); Grignon Dumoulin, Hubert, *Commentaire de la directive "transparence" du 15 décembre 2004 et de la directive d'exécution du 8 mars 2007 sur les obligations d'information des sociétés cotées*, Rev. Soc. (2007), p. 281–314; Guerra Martín, Guillermo, *La reforma del régimen legal en materia de OPAs y transparencia informativa*, RMV (2007), p. 407; Hazen, Thomas Lee, *The Law of Securities Regulation*, 6th ed. (2009); Henn, Harry G. and Alexander, John R., *Laws of Corporations*, 3rd ed. (1983); Hertig, Gerard, Kraakman, Reinier and Rock, Edward, *Issuers and Investor Protection*, in: Kraakman, Reinier et al. (eds.), *The Anatomy of Corporate Law*, 2nd ed. (2009), p. 275–304; Iglesias, Juan-Luis and García de Enterría, Javier, *Las cuentas anuales de las sociedades anónima y limitada*, in: Aurelio Menéndez (ed.), *Lecciones de Derecho Mercantil*, 6th ed. (2008); Kumm, Nina, *Praxisfragen bei der Regelpublizität nach Inkrafttreten des TUG*, BB (2009), p. 1118–1122; Levy, Robert A., *Random Walks: Reality or Myth*, 32 Fin. Analysts J. (1967), p. 69–77; Lomnicka, Eva Z. and Powell, John L. (ed.), *Encyclopedia of Financial Services Law*, loose-leaf (R. 80 as of April 2007); Mattout, Jean-Pierre, *Information financière et responsabilité des dirigeants*, Droit des sociétés (2004), p. 11–14; Mackenzie, Bruce et al. (eds.), *Interpretation and Application of International Financial Reporting Standards* (2012); Merkt, Hanno and Göthel, Stephan R., *US-amerikanisches Gesellschaftsrecht*, 2nd ed. (2006); Möllers, Thomas M.J., *Effi-*

Hendrik Brinckmann

zienz als Maßstab des Kapitalmarktrechts: Die Verwendung empirischer und ökonomischer Argumente zur Begründung zivil-, straf- und öffentlich-rechtlicher Sanktionen, 208 AcP (2008), p. 1–36; Mülbert, Peter O. and Steup, Steffen, *Emittentenhaftung für fehlerhafte Kapitalmarktinformation am Beispiel der fehlerhaften Regelpublizität—das System der Kapitalmarktinformationshaftung nach AnSVG und WpPG mit Ausblick auf die Transparenzrichtlinie*, WM (2005), p. 1633–1655; Mülbert, Peter O. and Steup, Steffen, *Das zweispurige Regime der Regelpublizität nach Inkrafttreten des TUG—Nachbesserungsbedarf aus Sicht von EU- und nationalem Recht*, NZG (2007), p. 761–770; Palá Laguna, Reyes, *Proyecto de Ley de Reforma de la Ley 24/1988, de 28 de julio, del Mercado de Valores en materia de transparencia de los emisores*, RdS (2006), p. 179; Paolucci, Luigi F., *Manuale di diritto commerciale*, Vol. 1 (2008); Paredes, Troy A., *Blinded by the Light: Information Overload and its Consequences for Securities Regulation*, 81 Wash. U. L. Q. (2003), p. 229–242; Presti, Gaetano and Rescigno, Matteo, *Corso di diritto commerciale*, Vol. 2, 3rd ed. (2007); Ronen, Joshua, *The Dual Role of Accounting: A Financial Economic Perspective*, in: Bicksler, James L. (ed.), *Handbook of Financial Economics* (1979), p. 415; Rontchevsky, Nicolas, comment on decision *C.A. Paris, 9ème chambre, section B, 14 septembre 2007, No. 07/01477, X et Y c/ MP et autres*, RTDF (2007), p. 145–148; Sehgal, Sanjay and Gupta, Meenakshi, *Technical Analysis in the Indian Capital Market A Survey*, 32 Decision (2005), p. 91–122; Shutkever, Carol, *The Transparency Rules in Practice*, 7 JIBFL (2008), p. 346–348; Sottoriva, Claudio, *La nuova informazione regolamentata "continua" per la società quotate*, Le società (2008), p. 533–542; Strieder, Thomas and Ammedick, Oliver, *Der Zwischenlagebericht als neues Instrument der Zwischenberichterstattung*, DB (2007), p. 1368–1372; Tapia Hermida, Alberto J., *La transparencia de las sociedades cotizadas: el Real Decreto 1362/2007*, 108 RDBB (2007), p. 273; Torck, Stéphane, *Note sous arrêté du 8 janvier 2008*, RDBF (2008), p. 39–41; Tran Van, Lé Quang and Uzan, Carole, *Modification du règlement général de l'AMF: suite de la transposition de la directive Transparence*, Bull. Joly Bourse (2007), p. 107–113; Valuet, Jean-Paul, *L'information financière des sociétés cotées*, in: Barbièri, Jean-François et al. (Conseil scientifique), *Dictionnaire Joly Bourse et produits financiers*, Tome III, loose-leaf (as of 2 April 2009); Veil, Rüdiger, *Die Haftung des Emittenten für fehlerhafte Information des Kapitalmarkts nach dem geplanten KapInHaG*, BKR (2005), p. 91–98; Veil, Rüdiger, *Prognosen im Kapitalmarktrecht*, AG (2006), p. 690–698; Veil, Rüdiger, *Der Schutz des verständigen Anlegers durch Publizität und Haftung im europäischen und nationalen Kapitalmarktrecht*, ZBB (2006), p. 162–171; Viandier, Alain, *OPA, OPE et autres offres publiques*, 3rd ed. (2006); Wagner, Franz W., *Zur Informations- und Ausschüttungsbemessungsfunktion des Jahresabschlusses auf einem organisierten Kapitalmarkt*, 34 ZfbF (1982), p. 749–773; Walz, Rainer, *Ökonomische Regulierungstheorien vor den Toren des Bilanzrechts*, ZfbF Sonderheft 32 (1993), p. 85–106.

I.   Introduction

1.   Development of a System of Periodic Disclosure

1   Periodic disclosure is defined as the continual supply of the capital market with information on the issuer. The concept can first be found in the Securities Admission Directive of 1979.[1] It required companies and undertakings, whose shares and debt securities, respectively, were admitted to a stock exchange's official listing, to immediately make their annual accounts and annual report available to the public. The directive provided the possibility for group companies to publish additionally

---

[1] See § 1 para. 6.

or alternatively a consolidated account.[2] This marked the beginning of an annual mandatory disclosure under stock exchange law.

2   The disclosure obligation provided for by the European legislature with the Securities Admission Directive was restricted to annual accounts and annual reports which had already been harmonised with the Fourth Directive[3] and which were thus already subject to disclosure requirements.[4] The provisions of the Securities Admission Directive could thus build upon the already existing structures and only had to provide an additional disclosure obligation. This resulted in a dualistic regulatory concept, in which the obligation to disclose and the content thereof were regulated separately.

3   In 1982, the Securities Admission Directive was complemented by the Half-Yearly Report Directive[5] which required companies, whose shares were admitted to official listing on a stock exchange, to publish a half-yearly report on the activities, profits and losses of the company during the first six months of each financial year.[6] The directive constituted the European legislature's reaction to the recommendations in the Segré Report for the introduction of the requirement for a continuous flow of information for companies on capital markets.[7] Unlike the commonly known methods of annual accounts and annual reports that could be referred to in the Securities Admission Directive, the half-yearly reports described in the Half-Yearly Report Directive were until then an unknown reporting format. Therefore, the Half-Yearly Report Directive had to contain provisions on the content of the half-yearly report, in addition to laying down the disclosure obligation for it.[8]

4   In 1999, the Commission defined the measures necessary to fulfil the aim of a single market for financial services in its Financial Services Action Plan and underlined the importance of a directive to improve the rules on transparency.[9] In trying to comply with its time scale for the legislative reforms of the financial market, the Commission adhered to the Lamfalussy Report,[10] which recommended a more effective legislative process on four levels. Based on this, the TD was enacted as the fourth framework directive in 2004. It contains framework measures and general principles on the transparency requirements regarding information about issuers whose securities are admitted to trading on a regulated market. A Level 2 imple-

---

[2] Art. 4(2) in conjunction with Annex III Schedule C 4, Annex IV Schedule D A. 3 Council Directive 79/279/EEC of 5 March 1979 coordinating the conditions for the admission of securities to official stock exchange listing. These provisions were later adopted, without amendments in Art. 67, 80 Council Directive 82/148/EEC of 3 March 1982 amending Directive 79/279/EEC coordinating the conditions for the admission of securities to official stock exchange listing.

[3] Fourth Directive 78/660/EEC of the European Council of 25 June 1978, OJ L222, p. 11.

[4] Art. 47(1) Fourth Directive.

[5] Directive 82/121/EEC of the European Council of 15 February 1982, OJ L48 of 20 February 1982, p. 26. See § 1 para. 6.

[6] Art. 1(1), Art. 2 Council Directive 82/121/EEC of 15 February 1982 on information to be published on a regular basis by companies the shares of which have been admitted to official stock-exchange listing, later adopted without amendments in Art. 70 Directive 82/148/EEC.

[7] Commission, Segré Report, p. 228–229.

[8] Art. 5 Directive 82/121/EEC, later adopted without amendments in Art. 73 Directive 82/148/EEC.

[9] Cf. Recital 3 TD.

[10] The Committee of Wise Men, *Final Report of the Committee of Wise Men on Securities Markets Regulation*.

Hendrik Brinckmann

menting directive was enacted in 2007,[11] containing more detailed rules on the requirements described in the TD.

5   The TD essentially refined the system of periodic disclosure on the basis of financial reporting. It revoked existing provisions[12] and introduced a total of four new reporting formats: the annual financial report, the half-yearly financial report, the quarterly financial reports and the interim management statement. All financial reports, with the exception of the interim management statement, which is already terminologically excluded, are based on financial accounting information and subject the latter to a capital markets law disclosure obligation.

2.   Financial Accounting Information as the Basis of Financial Reporting

6   Periodic disclosure meets the capital market's continual need for information. Yet the determination of the exact need for information is difficult. An empirical study on all information required or used by investors for their investment decisions would probably bring to light a very complex picture: whilst professional investors mainly rely on economic data and indicators, such as sales figures, sales revenues and profits, as well as the analysis of charts and past share prices,[13] other investors will often only rely on the recommendations of supposed stock exchange gurus, investment advisors or, it appears, even on divination.[14] All these methods have in common that they give a basis for a prognosis[15] on future market developments,[16] which will, however, always be accompanied by a certain amount of uncertainty.[17]

7   Whilst no method can completely eliminate this uncertainty, it can nevertheless be assumed that some information will be more suitable than others as the basis for predicting future market developments. Financial accounting information is an established[18] and well-tried prognosis instrument and has been proven at least

---

[11] Commission Directive 2007/14/EC of 8 March 2007 laying down detailed rules for the implementation of certain provisions of Directive 2004/109/EC on the harmonisation of transparency requirements in relation to information about issuers whose securities are admitted to trading on a regulated market, OJ L69 of 9 March 2007, p. 27.

[12] Art. 32(5) TD.

[13] On the two different approaches of securities analysis—the fundamental and the technical one—and information processing through investors see S. Sehgal and M. Gupta, 32 Decision (2005), p. 91, 93; R. Levy, 23 FAJ (1967), p. 69; G. Franke and H. Hax, *Finanzwirtschaft des Unternehmens und Kapitalmarkt*, p. 402 ff. See also T. Hazen, *The Law of Securities Regulation*, § 3.8[1], p. 137–138.

[14] The high importance of future-oriented information for investors describes the US Court of Appeals in *Wielgos v. Commonwealth Edison Company*, 892 F.2d 509 (7th Cir. 1989): "Investors value securities because of beliefs about how firms will do tomorrow, not because of how they did yesterday. If enterprises cannot make predictions about themselves, then securities analysts, newspaper columnists, and charlatans have protected turf"; see also H. Fleischer, AG (2006), p. 2.

[15] On the importance of prognosis by management see T. Hazen, *The Law of Securities Regulation*, § 3.9[4], p. 144 ff.; G. Hertig et al., *Issuers and Investor Protection*, p. 275, 284; on prognosis in capital markets law in general see R. Veil, AG (2006), p. 690 ff.

[16] Cf. W. Beaver and J. Demski, 12 J. Acc. Res. (1974), p. 170, 171. Before an investor makes a decision regarding an investment or divestment it must make a prognosis as to which investments promise the highest returns in the future. If it decided correctly the price will adapt accordingly and thus correctly reflect where there is a scarcity of capital, cf. J. Ronen, *The Dual Role of Accounting*, p. 415, 431 ff.; G. Hertig et al., *Issuers and Investor Protection*, p. 275, 283 ff.; R. Walz, ZfbF Sonderheft 32 (1993), p. 85, 102.

[17] H. Brinckmann, *Kapitalmarktrechtliche Finanzberichterstattung*, p. 197.

[18] Cf. G. Hertig et al., *Issuers and Investor Protection*, p. 275, 284; W. Beaver, 136 JOA (1973), p. 49, 51; W. Busse von Colbe, ZfbF Sonderheft 32 (1993), p. 11, 15; J. Ronen, *The Dual Role of Accounting*, p. 415, 437 ff. On the problem of "information overload" see T.A. Paredes, 81 Wash. U. L. Q. (2003), p. 417, 448–449.

---

to reduce the uncertainties regarding future developments.[19] Although market reactions resulting from natural disasters or terrorist attacks cannot be taken into account, information on capital reserves, liabilities and pension provisions will give an insight into the future chances and risks of a company.[20] Therefore financial accounting information must be regarded as the best prognosis instrument business economics has so far developed.[21]

8   The European legislature's recourse to financial accounting information for a periodic disclosure to the capital markets can be justified by the fact that it is a common prognosis instrument and is, in general, price sensitive.[22] For this reason, financial accounting information holds a monopoly in financial reporting regarding periodic capital market information. Although investors may continually demand information not contained in the financial reports, the European legislature's aim is still to control the investors' market behaviour by supplying them with information gained from corporate accounting.

9   The fact that the information is to be used on the capital market influences the evaluation of the financial accounting information itself, as its primary aim is to inform investors.[23] This requires the most exact description possible of the issuer's economic situation. Thus the capital markets law provisions on disclosure of financial accounting information result in investor control based on real economic performance indicators. They ensure that share prices can periodically adjust to the company's real value, limiting the effects speculations had on the share price.

II.   Regulatory Concepts

1.   Requirements under European Law

(a)   Transparency Directive

10   Since the enactment of the TD the periodic supply of the capital market with information is ensured by an obligation for the issuer to publish financial reports. Apart from the interim management statement, all reporting formats are referred to as "financial reports", showing the European legislature's efforts to introduce a unified standard of reporting for periodic information about the capital market.

---

[19] Cf. W. Beaver, 136 JOA (1973), p. 49, 50 ff.; J. *Ekkenga, Anlegerschutz, Rechnungslegung und Kapitalmarkt*, p. 75–76; H. Brinckmann, *Kapitalmarktrechtliche Finanzberichterstattung*, p. 194 ff. On the relationship between capital markets and financial accounting information see also H.-J. Böcking, Zfbf Sonderheft 40 (1998), p. 17, 23 ff.

[20] Cf. J. Ronen, *The Dual Role of Accounting*, p. 415, 435 ff.

[21] On the reporting obligations of financial accounting information in the United States see T. Hazen, *The Law of Securities Regulation*, § 9.3, p. 315 ff.

[22] Empirical studies have proved that financial accounting information has influence on the share price, cf. W. Beaver, 136 JOA (1973), p. 49, 51; W. *Busse von Colbe*, ZfbF Sonderheft 32 (1993), p. 11, 16; F.W. Wagner, ZfbF 34 (1982), p. 749, 758 ff.; see also G. Hertig et al., *Issuers and Investor Protection*, p. 275, 279–280.

[23] Therefore, investors get better information under a reporting regime that consequently follows a "fair-value-approach" like the 'Anglo-Saxon' model or the IFRS, G. Hertig et al., *Issuers and Investor Protection*, p. 285 ff.; H. Brinckmann, *Kapitalmarktrechtliche Finanzberichterstattung*, p. 190 ff. and passim. On the development of the different financial reporting models see B. Mackenzie et al., *Wiley 2012: Interpretation and Application of Internationals Financial Reporting Standards*, p. 3 ff.

Hendrik Brinckmann

11 Financial reporting can be regarded as the disclosure of financial accounting under capital markets law. Periodic statements by the issuer are a central element of this—a financial statement is contained in the annual financial report and a condensed financial statement is included in the half-yearly financial report.[24] In addition, the TD introduced the quarterly financial report as an additional reporting format, without, however, stipulating any detail regarding its elements. Nevertheless, being a financial report, much can be said for subjecting the quarterly report to the same requirements as the annual and half-yearly financial reports, especially requiring it typically to have a structure characteristic of a (condensed) financial statement.[25]

12 The fact that the disclosure of financial accounting information is orientated towards capital markets law can be deduced from the functions connected to financial accounting.[26] It is based on the concept of control and accountability of a company's economic activity.[27] However, the disclosure of financial accounting information is addressed to the investors on the capital markets, aiming to bring their decisions regarding investments and divestment in line with the benchmark of allocational efficiency. The underlying legal and political objective is to control the companies on the capital markets with the help of market mechanisms and to attain transparency of, and thereby confidence in, the capital market.

(b) *Correlation with European Accounting Law as a Reflection of the Dualistic Regulatory Concept*

13 The dualistic regulatory concept first addressed in the Securities Admission Directive[28] has since intensified in the European legislature's rules on financial reports. Whilst originally elements of accounting law were only referred to regarding the annual disclosure obligations of annual accounts and reports, leaving the half-yearly report largely independent of these rules, the European legislature now refers to accounting law more extensively. Only interim management statements have no connection to the accounting provisions, whereas the content of all the financial reports is dominated by accounting law. Hence, the obligation to disclose is an element of capital markets law, whilst the content of the disclosure takes into consideration the objects of accounting law.

14 Similar can be said of the auditing obligation regarding financial statements. These are also subject to the provisions of the Fourth Directive and the Seventh Directive,[29] whilst the obligation to declare a balance sheet oath is an element related to the content developed by the European legislature exclusively for the area of financial reporting, based on the similar provision in the US *Sarbanes–Oxley Act*.[30] The instrumental character of the balance sheet oath also becomes apparent in the fact that the persons responsible within the issuer must submit a statement containing

---

[24] Art. 4(2)(a), 5(2)(a) TD.

[25] H. Brinckmann, *Kapitalmarktrechtliche Finanzberichterstattung*, p. 179–180.

[26] Cf. ibid, p. 181 ff.; J. Ronen, *The Dual Role of Accounting*, p. 415, 417 ff.

[27] Cf J. Ronen, *The Dual Role of Accounting*, p. 415, 417.

[28] See above para. 1.

[29] Seventh Council Directive 83/349/EEC of 13 June 1983 based on Article 54(3)(g) of the Treaty on consolidated accounts, OJ L193, p. 1. Cf. Art. 4(4) TD.

[30] Sec. 302(a) Sarbanes–Oxley Act 2002, cf. H. Chang et al., 81 TAR (2006), p. 1, 3–4; T. Hazen, *The Law of Securities Regulation*, § 9.3[2][A], p. 320–322; H. Fleischer, ZIP (2007), p. 97–98.

their name and function in which they declare that the financial statement and management report comply with the "true and fair view principle" as laid down in the applicable set of accounting standards.[31] A balance sheet oath must be made for all annual and half-yearly reports.[32]

(c) Addressee of the Disclosure Obligation

15　The annual financial report must be made public by all issuers,[33] the half-yearly report by all issuers of shares and debt securities,[34] and the interim management statement by all issuers whose shares are admitted to trading on a regulated market.[35] The TD defines the term "issuer" as a legal entity governed by private or public law, including a state, whose securities are admitted to trading on a regulated market.[36] The provisions thus exempt certain public bodies, especially states, regional or local authorities of a state, the ECB and the Member States' national central banks, from the rules on financial reporting.[37] Legal entities governed by public law are therefore only partly required to oblige with the rules on financial reporting.

16　The addressees of the provisions are further defined by the criteria "regulated market" and "securities". Both terms are defined in the Markets in Financial Instruments Directive (MiFID).[38] Put briefly, this entails that annual reports are required on all regulated securities markets, half-yearly reports are additionally necessary on all regulated markets for shares and debt securities, and interim management statements are required on all regulated shares markets.

2.　Implementation in the Member States

(a) France

17　In France, the TD was transposed with the "Breton Act" of 26 July 2005.[39] Further details were provided at a sub-legal level[40] through the enactment of numerous *arrêtés* (regulations).[41] France implemented the TD almost one-to-one, resulting in various provisions overlapping those of the previous disclosure system, especially regarding the optional annual reference document.[42] The reference document can substitute the annual report and—provided it is duly updated—the interim reports,

---

[31] Art. 4(2)(c), 5(2)(c) TD explicitly refers to the concept of true and fair view in its English version; see also C. Götze and N.-C. Wunderlich, in: M. Habersack et al., *Handbuch der Kapitalmarktinformation*, § 9 para. 52.

[32] Art. 4(2)(c), 5(2)(c) TD.

[33] Art. 4(1) TD.

[34] Art. 5(1) TD.

[35] Art. 6(1) TD.

[36] Art. 2(d) TD.

[37] Art. 8(1)(a) TD.

[38] For more details on the concept of a regulated market see § 7 para. 24–31 and on the term "security" § 8 para. 4–9.

[39] On the TD and its transposition in France see H. Grignon Dumoulin, Rev. Soc. (2007), p. 281 ff.

[40] Art. 222-1 ff. and Art. 221-1 ff. RG AMF.

[41] Especially the regulations of 4 January 2007, 7 December 2007 and 8 January 2008. The last regulation was not enacted until after Directive 2007/14/EC and a subsequent period of consultation. It contained questions on the content of half-yearly reports and cross-border constellations, cf. S. Torck, RDBF (2008), p. 39, 40.

[42] Cf. Art. 212-13 RG AMF.

　　　　　　　　　　　　　　　　　　　　　　　Hendrik Brinckmann

if it is compiled no later than four months after the end of the financial year. The question whether this is compatible with EU law does not as yet seem to have arisen in France. [43]

(b)   Germany

18   In Germany, the requirements on financial reporting laid down in the TD were implemented in §§ 37v–37z WpHG through the TUG (German Transparency Directive Implementation Act) which was enacted in January 2007. The German legislature restricted the applicability of the new provisions on financial reporting to domestic issuers, thus respecting the European "home Member State" principle.[44] An issuer in the sense of this provision is thus every issuer registered in Germany[45] (home Member State), whose securities are tradable on the German market or on the market of another state of the European Economic Area (EAA)[46] with insufficient rules on transparency under the TD. Issuers who are not registered in Germany but whose home Member State is also in the EEA are also to be regarded as domestic issuers if their securities are only admitted to trading on a regulated market in Germany.

(c)   Italy

19   In order to comply with the provisions on financial reporting in the TD, Italy amended the TUF (Italian consolidated laws on finance), the RE (Italian Issuers' Regulation) and the accounting provisions in the Codice Civile (Italian Civil Code).[47] Special attention must be paid to the newly introduced Article 154-ter TUF which contains framework provisions on financial accounting, complemented by Articles 77 e ff. RE.

(d)   Spain

20   In the course of the implementation of the TD the Spanish legislature amended the LMV (Spanish Securities Market Act) by Act 6/2007 of 12 April.[48] Implementing provisions are contained in the RD 1362/2007 (Royal Decree on Transparency on Capital Markets),[49] which summarises all information requirements for issuers addressed in regulations. Circular 1/2008 contains further provisions on the interim reports, including a model report.[50]

---

[43] Cf. L.Q. Tran Van and C. Uzan, Bull. Joly Bourse (2007), p. 107, 110, with reference to Art. 212-13 RG AMF; similarly J.-C. Biard, RDBF (2007), p. 36, 37. On the scepticism regarding the reference document concerning the duty to publish a prospectus see T. Bonneau, RDBF (2005), p. 43, 46–47.

[44] Cf. § 2(6), (7) WpHG.

[45] § 2(6) No. 1(a) WpHG.

[46] The European Economic Area encompasses the Member States of the European Union and the other contracting states of the European Economic Area Agreement, cf. § 2(14) WpPG.

[47] Cf. F. Galgano, Diritto Commerciale, p. 355.

[48] The obligations regarding financial reporting are now laid down in Art. 35 LMV.

[49] Cf. G. Guerra Martín, RMV (2007), p. 407, 408.

[50] Cf. Crónica Legislativa in RMV (2008), p. 324–325.

(e)   Sweden

21   Sweden implemented the provisions of the TD in the Lag om börs och clearingverk-samhet (Swedish Act on Stock Markets and Clearing)[51] which became effective in July 2007. Further provisions on the content of financial reports were implemented in the Årsredovisningslag (Swedish Accounts Act) which was amended to deal with this matter. Before the TD was implemented, periodic disclosure of information on the capital markets was mainly ensured through self-regulatory measures. The TD thus led to a stronger orientation on statutory rules in this area. The Stock Market and Clearing Act was substituted by the LVM (Swedish Securities Market Act) in the course of implementing the MiFID. Since November 2007 the provisions on financial reporting are therefore contained in Kapitel 16 LVM, whilst the provisions themselves have not been subject to any relevant changes.[52]

(f)   United Kingdom

22   In the United Kingdom, the implementation was originally based on the Companies Act 2006 which, in connection with the FSMA 2000, empowered the FSA to provide the necessary implementing measures.[53] The FSA made use of this possibility in January 2007 when it included provisions regarding financial reports in its Hand-book.[54]

III.   Annual Financial Report

1.   Overview

23   The TD requires the issuer to make public its annual financial report at the latest four months after the end of each financial year.[55] This constitutes the latest stage in the development of annual disclosure obligations, as first laid down in Directive 79/279/EEC coordinating the conditions for the admission of securities to official stock exchange listing, and later Directive 80/390/EEC coordinating the requirements for the drawing up, scrutiny and distribution of the listing particulars to be published for the admission of securities to official stock exchange listing. The annual financial report comprises the audited financial statement (lit. a) and management report (lit. b) as well as a statement made by the persons responsible within the issuer whose names and functions shall be clearly indicated to the effect that, to the best of their knowledge, the financial statements prepared in accordance with the applicable set of accounting standards give a true and fair view of the assets, liabilities, financial position and profit or loss of the issuer and the undertakings included in the

---

[51] SFS 1992:543.

[52] Cf. Prop. 2006/2007:115, p. 621–622.

[53] Part 43 Companies Act 2006, on financial reporting especially sec. 89C FSMA (inserted by sec. 1266(1) Companies Act 2006).

[54] FSA Handbook, ch. 4: Disclosure Rules and Transparency Rules (DTR). For more details on financial reporting in the United Kingdom see R. Veil and M. Wundenberg, *Englisches Kapitalmarktrecht*, p. 87 ff.

[55] Art. 4(1) TD.

consolidation taken as a whole. The management report must include a fair review of the development and performance of the business and the position of the issuer and the undertakings included in the consolidation taken as a whole, together with a description of the principal risks and uncertainties that they face (lit. c).[56]

24   This statement by the persons responsible within the issuer is termed the "balance sheet oath". The TD does not make sufficiently clear who the "persons responsible" are, this being a problem that has transferred itself to the Member States' implementations. Those Member States that adopted the directive's provisions one-to-one must therefore deal with this question in their national laws.

25   The United Kingdom has not finally decided on an understanding of the term "person responsible".[57] The FSA Handbook contains no interpretational help on this matter. The policy statement issued on the implementation of the TD declares that the issuer be responsible for determining the "person responsible".[58] The name of an individual managing director need only be published if that person acted on behalf of the person responsible. The FSA's statements in its non-binding newsletter *List!* can be similarly understood, providing that either the board as a whole or the individual director, acting on behalf of the board, is responsible.[59]

26   A particularity can be found in German law where the TD's provisions on the balance sheet oath are connected with the provisions in the HGB (German Commercial Code) on accounting law[60] by making reference to the latter.[61] As a consequence of this, the obligation to make the respective statement is addressed to the legal representatives of a corporation, in a German stock corporation (*Aktiengesellschaft*) this being the board members.

27   This only appears consistent when one considers that the accounting law in the German HGB generally calls upon all legal representatives regarding the obligation to compile annual accounts and annual reports,[62] thus expressing the principle of joint responsibility which underlies all German corporate law.[63] Dogmatically this connection between the balance sheet oath and the HGB accounting provisions, however, leads to problems with regard to foreign companies[64] if their home countries follow other principles regarding legal responsibility than that of joint responsibility.[65] Countries that follow the concept of a single-tier system for the board of a stock corporation will often provide for differing competencies

---

[56] Art. 4(2) TD.

[57] R. Veil and M. Wundenberg, *Englisches Kapitalmarktrecht*, p. 95.

[58] FSA, *Implementation of the Transparency Directive*, PS 06/11, October 2006, para. 2.50 (Audit Reports are required to be signed by the audit partner only).

[59] FSA, *List!*, No. 18, March 2008, para. 6.1.2 (on half-yearly reports).

[60] § 264(2), § 289(1), § 297(2) and § 315(1) HGB.

[61] For annual reports § 37v(2) No. 3 WpHG and for half-yearly reports § 37w(2) No. 3 WpHG, state that the reports must contain a statement as described in § 264(2) No. 3, § 289(1) HGB. For corporate group companies these provisions are referred to in § 37y No. 1 WpHG, where the legislature, however, accidentally referred to the third sentence of § 297(2) instead of the fourth sentence. This must be regarded as a merely editorial error.

[62] Cf. § 264(1) HGB.

[63] H. Fleischer, ZIP (2007), p. 97, 100 with further references.

[64] On the German concept of so-called domestic issuers which may also subject foreign issuers to the German rules on financial reporting see above para. 18.

[65] In more detail H. Brinckmann, *Kapitalmarktrechtliche Finanzberichterstattung*, p. 273 ff.

Hendrik Brinckmann

of the directors.[66] In the United States, for example, only the CEO and CFO are obliged to make a balance sheet oath.[67]

28   The elements of an annual financial report as described in the TD must be regarded as only minimum requirements. Member States are free to extend the content required in annual reports or to introduce further reporting duties, provided these do not distort the information required by the European legislature and the structure and nature of the financial report remain identifiable as such for the investor.

29   In the United Kingdom some of the reporting duties contained in the Listing Rules prior to the implementation of the TD still apply.[68] If the securities are mentioned in the "official list" the annual financial report must therefore fulfil the requirements of the Listing Rules in the FSA Handbook which exceed those of the TD.[69]

2.   Financial Accounting Information

(a)   Consolidated and Individual Accounts

30   The information to be made public in the annual financial report was not developed by the European legislature specifically for the TD. Rather, it refers to the harmonised provisions on accounting law which require a distinction between consolidated and individual accounts. Where the issuer is required to prepare consolidated accounts according to the Seventh Council Directive 83/349/EEC, the audited financial statements must comprise a consolidated account drawn up in accordance with the IAS/IFRS[70] Regulation as well as an annual account of the parent company drawn up in accordance with the national law of the Member State in which the parent company is incorporated.[71] Where the issuer is not required to prepare consolidated accounts, the audited financial statement must comprise the accounts prepared in accordance with the national law of the Member State in which the company is incorporated.[72]

31   The accounting standards regarding annual financial accounts differ greatly between the Member States. In the United Kingdom the issuer has the option to prepare not only the consolidated account but also the annual financial account in accordance with the IAS/IFRS.[73] However, after the first financial year in which the directors of a company prepare their annual accounts on the basis of IAS/IFRS, all subsequent annual accounts of the company must also be prepared in accordance with international accounting standards unless there is a relevant

---

[66] Cf. § 141(a) Delaware General Corporation Law (DGCL); on the legal situation in the United States see G. Henn and J. Alexander, *Laws of Corporations*, p. 564, 593 ff.; H. Merkt and S. Göthel, *US-amerikanisches Gesellschaftsrecht*, p. 327 ff.; G. Rehm, in: H. Eidenmüller (ed.), *Ausländische Kapitalgesellschaften im deutschen Recht*, § 11 para. 41.

[67] Sec. 302(a) Sarbanes–Oxley Act 2002. On the impact of the balance sheet oath in the United States see H. Chang et al., 81 TAR (2006), p. 1, 5 ff.

[68] Cf. LR 9.8.4 ff FSA Handbook.

[69] Cf. enumeration of A. Alcock and A. Hindmarch, in: A.J. Boyle et al. (eds.), *Gore-Browne on Companies*, para. 41-6 (Update 76). Cf. also LR 9.8.4 ff. FSA Handbook.

[70] On the process of IAS/IFRS stardard setting see B. Mackenzie et al., *Wiley 2012: Interpretation and Application of Internationals Financial Reporting Standards*, p. 7–8.

[71] Art. 4(2) TD.

[72] Art. 4(2) TD.

[73] Sec. 395(1) Companies Act 2006.

Hendrik Brinckmann

change in circumstances.[74] In France, Germany, Spain and Sweden, on the other hand, the annual financial account must be prepared in accordance with national accounting law. In Germany and Spain the national accounting law has, however, recently been approximated to international standards.[75] In contrast, Italy requires the annual account to be prepared in accordance with the IAS/IFRS if the SpA is listed or its shares and financial instruments are traded in a similar public way.[76] This generally applies to banks, investment and insurance companies and the financial intermediary company SIM.[77]

32   *Example:* The home Member State of issuer A is the United Kingdom. Issuer A is required to prepare consolidated accounts. Issuer B is also required to prepare consolidated accounts. Its home Member State is Germany. Issuer A has to prepare his consolidated account in accordance with IAS/IFRS and—to save costs—will probably also prepare his annual financial account in accordance with IAS/IFRS, which is permitted in the United Kingdom. Hence, the information made public by issuer A in his annual financial report is developed on a consistent accounting standard. Issuer B also has to prepare his consolidated account in accordance with IAS/IFRS, but will prepare his annual financial account in accordance with German accounting law, Germany not allowing annual financial accounts to be based solely on IAS/IFRS. Accounts compiled on this basis must rather simultaneously comply with German accounting law. As a consequence, the information disclosed by issuer B in his annual financial report will be based on two different accounting standards and will therefore not be consistent.

33   The European requirements regarding annual financial reports depend strongly on whether the report refers to an individual company or a group company, the respective provisions being from different legal fields. This dualistic regulatory concept depends strongly on accounting law. A uniform standard of accounting throughout Europe has so far only been achieved by the IAS/IFRS Regulation for consolidated accounts. The regulation is applicable to the consolidated accounts of publicly traded companies since the financial year starting 1 January 2005.[78] The annual accounts are still subject to the Member States' national provisions, a uniform level only being attained within the limits of the Fourth Directive. So far it is not foreseeable when and if the IAS/IFRS must also be made applicable to annual accounts Europe-wide. Annual accounts have farther-reaching functions in the Member States than solely informational purposes: they play an important role for determining the dividend

---

[74] Sec. 395(3) Companies Act 2006. There is a relevant change of circumstance if, at any time during or after the first IAS/IFRS year (a) the company becomes a subsidiary undertaking of another undertaking that does not prepare IAS/IFRS individual accounts, (b) the company ceases to be a company with securities admitted to trading on a regulated market in an EEA State, or (c) a parent undertaking of the company ceases to be an undertaking with securities admitted to trading on a regulated market in an EEA State, cf. sec. 395(4) Companies Act.

[75] In 2009 Germany adapted its accounting law in the HGB to the IAS/IFRS requirements. Spain undertook similar steps in 2007, cf. Introduction to RD 1514/2007. A.J. Tapia Hermida, 108 RDBB (2007), p. 273, 277; J.-L. Iglesias and J. García de Enterría, *Las cuentas anuales, de las sociedades anónima y limitada*, in: A. Menéndez (ed.), *Lecciones de Derecho Mercantil*, p. 432.

[76] G.F. Campobasso, *Diritto Commerciale*, p. 449; L.F. Paolucci, *Manuale di diritto commerciale*, p. 300; G. Presti and M. Rescigno, *Corso di diritto commerciale*, p. 302.

[77] L.F. Paolucci, *Manuale di diritto commerciale*, p. 300; G. Presti and M. Rescigno, *Corso di diritto commerciale*, p. 302.

[78] Art. 4 IAS/IFRS Regulation.

---

payout[79] and as the basis for tax assessment, thus preventing a stronger unification at a European level. In consequence, the provisions on annual financial reports contain different requirements for individual companies and group companies, resulting in difficulties when trying to compare the different annual financial reports.

(b)   Management Report

34   The management report contained in annual financial reports is also subject to the accounting laws. It is governed by Article 46 of the Fourth Directive 78/660/EEC and, should the issuer be required to prepare consolidated accounts, also by Article 36 of the Seventh Directive 83/349/EEC.[80]

IV.   Half-yearly Financial Reports

1.   Overview

35   In addition to the annual financial reports the European Commission introduced the half-yearly financial reports, covering the first six months of the financial year and replacing the provisions of the previous Half-Yearly Report Directive 82/121/EEC. The new provisions require an issuer of shares or debt securities to make public the half-yearly financial report covering the first six months of the financial year as soon as possible after the end of the relevant period, but at the latest two months thereafter.[81]

36   A special arrangement in this context can be found in Spain: if an issuer, who only issues shares, does not make public an annual financial report within two months after the end of the financial year, it must instead prepare a second half-yearly report for the whole twelve months of the financial year.[82]

37   The half-yearly financial report must comprise a condensed set of financial statements (lit. a), an interim management report (lit. b) and a balance sheet oath comparable to that of the annual financial report (lit. c).[83]

38   Whilst the half-yearly report required by the Half-Yearly Report Directive differed from the dualistic regulatory concept of the annual report by requiring independent content, the European legislature has meanwhile dismissed this individual approach and opted for an orientation on the annual financial report.

---

[79] When calculating the dividends the annual accounts are taken as the basis for determining the company's profits that can be distributed. A study published by KMPG on behalf of the European Union in 2008 showed that IAS/IFRS annual accounts are currently used as the basis for profit distribution in 17 of the 27 Member States in 10 of which the IFRS accounting profits are not modified for this, cf. KPMG, *Feasibility study on an alternative to the capital maintenance regime established by the Second Company Law Directive 77/91/EEC of 13 December 1976 and an examination of the impact on profit distribution of the new EU accounting regime*, p. 1.

[80] Art. 4(5) TD.
[81] Art. 5(1) TD.
[82] Art. 35.2 LMV, Art. 11.1 RD 1362/2007.
[83] Art. 5(2) TD.

Hendrik Brinckmann

2. Financial Accounting Information

(a) Consolidated and Individual Accounts

39 The condensed set of financial statements is not a question of harmonised accounting provisions. Rather, its content was first defined by the TD and follows the concept of the annual financial report. Once again one must distinguish between consolidated and individual accounts.

40 Where the issuer is required to prepare consolidated accounts, the TD requires that the condensed set of financial statements must be prepared in accordance with the IAS/IFRS applicable to interim financial reports.[84] The relevant standard for interim reports is described in IAS 34.[85] It defines an interim financial report as a financial report for an interim period, i.e. a financial reporting period shorter than a full financial year.[86] Whilst interim financial reports may contain either a complete set of financial statements or a set of condensed financial statements,[87] the TD only requires a set of condensed financial statements for the half-yearly financial report. According to IAS 34, a condensed set of financial statements must include, at a minimum, a balance sheet, income statement, statement showing all changes in equity, cash flow statement—all in condensed form—and selected explanatory notes.[88] For publicly traded companies the explanatory notes must contain segment information.[89]

41 Where the issuer is not required to prepare consolidated accounts, the condensed set of financial statements must at least contain a condensed balance sheet, a condensed profit and loss account and explanatory notes on these accounts.[90] In preparing these, the issuer must follow the same principles for recognising and measuring as when preparing annual accounts in accordance with the Fourth Directive. In preparing the condensed balance sheet and profit and loss account, the issuer must follow the same principles for recognising and measuring as when preparing annual financial reports.[91] Further minimum requirements regarding the content of the condensed set of financial statements can be found in the implementing directive to the TD. According to this, the condensed balance sheet and profit and loss account must show each of the headings and subtotals included in the most recent annual financial statements of the issuer.[92] Additional line items shall be included if, as a result of their omission, the half-yearly financial statements would give a misleading view of the assets, liabilities, financial position and profit or loss of the issuer.[93] In

---

[84] Art. 5(3) TD.
[85] On the objectives of interim financial reporting under IAS 34 see B. Mackenzie et al., *Wiley 2012: Interpretation and Application of Internationals Financial Reporting Standards*, p. 875.
[86] IAS 34.4; B. Mackenzie et al., *Wiley 2012: Interpretation and Application of Internationals Financial Reporting Standards*, p. 874.
[87] B. Mackenzie et al., *Wiley 2012: Interpretation and Application of Internationals Financial Reporting Standards*, p. 879.
[88] IAS 34.8; B. Mackenzie et al., *Wiley 2012: Interpretation and Application of Internationals Financial Reporting Standards*, p. 878 ff.
[89] IAS 34.16g.
[90] Art. 5(3) TD.
[91] Art. 5(3) TD.
[92] Art. 3(2) Directive 2007/14/EC.
[93] Art. 3(2) Directive 2007/14/EC.

addition, the condensed account must include a comparative balance sheet and a comparative profit and loss account of the preceding financial year.[94] The explanatory notes must include sufficient information to ensure the comparability of the condensed half-yearly financial statements with the annual financial statements and sufficient information and explanations to ensure a user's proper understanding of any material changes in amounts and of any developments in the half-year period concerned, which are reflected in the balance sheet and the profit and loss account.[95]

42   In Germany, companies that do not draw up their balance sheets in accordance with IAS/IFRS, can refer to the DRS 16 standards. In the United Kingdom the ASB provides rules on the half-yearly reports.[96] However, most companies rely on the IAS/IFRS provisions.[97] In Italy the condensed statements are to be made in accordance with IAS 34.[98]

(b)   Interim Management Report

43   The interim management report must include at least an indication of important events that have occurred during the first six months of the financial year, and their impact on the condensed set of financial statements, together with a description of the principal risks and uncertainties for the remaining six months of the financial year. For issuers of shares, the interim management report must also include major transactions of related parties.[99] This includes related parties' transactions that have taken place in the first six months of the current financial year and that have materially affected the financial position or the performance of the enterprise during that period and any changes in the related parties' transactions described in the last annual report that could have a material effect on the financial position or performance of the enterprise in the first six months of the current financial year.[100] Thus, the interim management report must—just as the balance sheet oath stipulates—be regarded as an independent part of the half-yearly financial report which was developed without any reference to accounting law.[101]

(c)   Auditing of the Half-yearly Financial Report

44   Unlike for the annual financial report, European law contains no provisions regarding the auditing of the half-yearly financial report. If the half-yearly financial report has been audited by choice, however, the audit report must be reproduced in full. The same must apply in the case of an auditors' review.[102] If the half-yearly financial report has not been audited or reviewed by auditors, the issuer must make

---

[94] Art. 3(2) Directive 2007/14/EC.

[95] Art. 3(3) Directive 2007/14/EC.

[96] Cf. FSA, List!, No. 14, April 2007, para. 2.18; FSA, Implementation of the Transparency Directive, PS 06/11, October 2006, para. 2.43.

[97] Cf. FSA, Implementation of the Transparency Directive, PS 06/11, October 2006, para. 2.43.

[98] Art. 2428 III Codice Civile in conjunction with 81 RE; Art. 154-ter II, III TUF.

[99] Art. 5(4) TD.

[100] Cf. Art. 4 Directive 2007/14/EC.

[101] For companies subject to the German accounting standards of the DRSC, DRS 16 contains further information on the interim report. Cf. T. Strieder and O. Ammedick, DB (2007), p. 1368 ff.

[102] Art. 5(5) TD.

Hendrik Brinckmann

a statement to that effect in its report.[103] The ensuing margin of appreciation left to the Member States has led to large differences between the national laws in this respect. Germany merely provides that the condensed set of financial statements and the interim management report *may* be reviewed by auditors.[104] Until 2010 Sweden had a similar recommendation in its Corporate Governance Codex, whilst as of 1 February 2010 the amended version contains no such rules on financial reporting. Spain also provides that the auditing of half-yearly reports is optional.[105]

45   German law furthermore defines the requirements of an auditor's review in more detail. It states that the auditor's review must be compiled in such a way that a conscientious auditor can exclude that the condensed set of financial statements and the interim management report are inconsistent with the applicable accounting standards in material aspects.[106] The auditor must therefore only guarantee that it overlooked no serious mistakes in the accounting.[107]

V.   Quarterly Financial Report and Interim Management Statement

1.   Overview

46   In the 2003 proposal for the TD the Commission followed the idea that the key data currently required under existing Community law for half-yearly reporting should in future be published as quarterly financial information.[108] The Commission's proposal therefore contained the provision that for issuers whose shares are admitted to trading on the regulated market quarterly financial information should be mandatory for the first and third quarter of a financial year.[109] As with the former half-yearly reports, the quarterly financial information was to contain the consolidated figures, presented in table form, indicating the net turnover and the profit or loss before or after deduction of tax as well as an explanatory statement relating to the issuer's activities and profits and losses during the relevant three-month period. Furthermore, the issuer was to choose whether it wanted to publish an indication of the likely future development for itself and its subsidiaries.

47   The Commission justified the shorter intervals with a comparison of the information standards in the Member States and the necessity to strengthen the European stock markets as compared with the US market where such quarterly financial reporting has been required since 1934.[110] In this context the Commission explained that quarterly financial information would provide more structured and reliable information thus enhancing the stock market performance and investor protection.[111]

---

[103] Art. 5(5) TD.
[104] § 37w(5) WpHG.
[105] Art. 14.1 RD 1362/2007.
[106] § 37w(5) WpHG.
[107] Cf. Begr. RegE TUG, BT-Drucks. 16/2498 (explanatory notes), p. 45; N. *Kumm*, BB (2009), p. 1118, 1121.
[108] Cf. Proposal for a Directive on the harmonisation of transparency requirements with regard to information about issuers whose securities are admitted to trading on a regulated market and amending Directive 2001/34/EC, COM(2003) 138 final, p. 16.
[109] Art. 6 TD Draft (COM(2003) 138 final).
[110] Cf. Commission, Proposal for a Transparency Directive, COM(2003) 138 final, p. 14.
[111] Cf. ibid.

48   Before the TD was enacted, only eight Member States, including Austria, France, Italy and Spain, required the publication of quarterly financial reports. In other Member States, such as Germany, quarterly financial reporting rules existed only on the basis of stock exchange rules.[112]

49   The Commission's suggestion on quarterly financial reporting as the new concept regarding periodic disclosure in Europe was not greeted warmly. After the report of the Committee on Economic and Monetary Affairs[113] the concept of quarterly financial reports threatened to be deleted altogether until a Council compromise proposal was accepted by the European Parliament. The negative attitude towards the requirement to disclose quarterly reports was mainly justified by the substantial additional costs for issuers and the danger of a focus on short-term earnings performance rather than on a company's longer-term strategy.[114] As a result the Commission's proposal was reduced to the format of interim management statements which have lower requirements regarding their content than the quarterly financial information.

2.   Content of Interim Management Statements

50   Issuers whose shares are admitted to trading on a regulated market must make public a statement by its management during the first six-month period of the financial year and another one during the second six-month period of the financial year.[115] The statement must be made within a period of ten weeks after the beginning and six weeks before the end of the relevant six-month period and must contain information covering the period between the beginning of the relevant six-month period and the date of publication of the statement.[116] It must contain (i) an explanation of material events and transactions that have taken place during the relevant period and their impact on the financial position of the issuer and its controlled undertakings; and (ii) a general description of the financial position and performance of the issuer and its controlled undertakings during the relevant period.[117] The interim management statements as such have no relation to the financial statements, rather constituting an independent reporting format in the TD. Their content is very similar to that of management reports.

51   The exact content of the interim management statements has still to be defined. In the United Kingdom[118] the FSA gives the issuers a large margin of discretion regarding the content of the interim management statements, reasoning that it is a question of the individual case that is important.[119] The FSA believes in a

---

[112] Cf. ibid.

[113] Cf. Report by the Committee on Economic and Monetary Affairs on the proposal for a European Parliament and Council directive on the harmonisation of transparency requirements, A5/2004/79 final, p. 38 ff.

[114] Explanatory Statement of the European Committee on Economic and Social Affairs on the Proposal for a Transparency Directive, OJ C80 of 30 March 2004, p. 87–88. Also seen critically by the European Central Bank, OJ C 242 of 9 October 2003, p. 8, that favours minimum disclosure obligations for issuers.

[115] Art. 6(1) TD.

[116] Art. 6(1) TD.

[117] Art. 6(1) TD.

[118] Some information on interim reports can be found in FSA, List!, No. 14, April 2007, para. 2.22 ff. See also R. Veil and M. Wundenberg, Englisches Kapitalmarktrecht, p. 99.

[119] This reflects the FSA's principle-based and risk-based approach, cf. FSA, List!, No. 14, April 2007, para. 2.29.

market-led solution in which the details of the interim management statements are developed by market practitioners and discussed between preparers and users of the information.[120] The FSA states that the interim management statements are less demanding than producing quarterly financial reports. The issuers will be able to meet the requirements based on the content of performance reports or trading statements. Numerical data is not required according to the FSA where the major events/transactions that have occurred during the relevant period become sufficiently clear through a meaningful narrative description.[121]

3.   Quarterly Financial Report

52   The TD introduced the non-binding format of a quarterly financial report by stating that issuers which, under either national legislation or the rules of the regulated market or of their own initiative, publish quarterly financial reports in accordance with such legislation or rules are not required to make public the aforementioned interim management statements.[122] The European legislature does not make any statements on the structure and content of the quarterly financial reports, rather referring to the fact that the requirements can be dictated and defined by national regulation or the rules of the regulated market. The quality requirements to be met are also not defined in the directive. It rather appears that the TD assumes the quarterly financial report to be a fixed standard without the need for further specifications. This, however, can only be regarded as correct in as far as systematically the quarterly financial reports are to substitute the interim management statements and must therefore at least fulfil their requirements to comply with the TD. The quarterly financial report was furthermore approximated to the annual and half-yearly financial report by the term "financial report", making it seem only logical that the quarterly financial report must contain the same periodic statement that is essential in the other two reports. [123]

53   The transposition of the TD confirms this point of view, showing similarities in the quarterly and half-yearly financial reports in many Member States.

54   Swedish accounting law contains general provisions for interim reports[124] that are applicable to both quarterly and half-yearly financial reports, making the reporting formats in these two cases identical.[125] In Germany the quarterly financial reports are to be prepared and published in accordance with the provisions on half-yearly financial reports if they are to comply with the provisions on interim management statements which they can substitute.[126] The quarterly financial report must therefore contain the same condensed set of financial statements and interim management report as the half-yearly financial report. Merely a balance sheet oath is not necessary according to the TD. Spanish law contains

---

[120] Cf. FSA, *Implementation of the Transparency Directive*, PS 06/11, para. 2.4 ff.; FSA, *List!*, No. 14, April 2007, para. 2.23.

[121] Cf. FSA, *Implementation of the Transparency Directive*, PS 06/11, October 2006, para. 2.4 ff.; FSA, *List!*, No. 14, April 2007, para. 2.22 ff.

[122] Art. 6(2) TD.

[123] H. Brinckmann, *Kapitalmarktrechtliche Finanzberichterstattung*, p. 127–128.

[124] Kapitel 9, § 3 ÅRL.

[125] Cf. Prop. 2006/2007:65, p. 344.

[126] Pursuant to § 37x(3) WpHG, § 37w(2) No. 1 and 2, (3) and (4) WpHG apply to quarterly financial reports.

only few details on the content of the quarterly financial reports, one of which being the requirement of a condensed set of financial statements.[127]

55   Legal obligations to make public quarterly financial reports are not common. The German legislature has merely defined the minimum requirements a quarterly financial report must fulfil if it is to substitute the interim management statement. Other than that an obligation to make public quarterly financial reports is only contained in some stock market rules.[128]

56   In other Member States even after the implementation of the TD no rules on quarterly financial reports exist. In the United Kingdom, for example, the FSA only implemented the provisions on the interim management statements in its Handbook.[129] However, the market rules may provide the possibility for quarterly financial reports.[130] Italy also refrained from adopting provisions on quarterly financial reports, although it is being discussed whether the interim management statement should be adapted to the requirements of a financial report by requiring an interim financial statement.[131]

VI. Disclosure Procedures

57   European law only stipulates two requirements regarding the disclosure of financial reports, the first being that the disclosure must take place through the media, the second being that the regulated information must be disseminated in a manner ensuring that it will reach as wide a public as possible.[132] These requirements can realistically only be met by use of the Internet, which is why the European legislature explicitly allows the information to be published on the issuer's website, provided this publication is then announced to the media.[133] The Internet is therefore the primary publication medium for financial reports. The Member States must supply an officially appointed mechanism for the central storage of regulated information, which complies with minimum quality standards of security and certainty as to the information source and guarantees easy access by end-users.[134]

58   These very general rules have led to a strong divergence in the disclosure procedures within the Member States. Prior to making the financial reports and the interim management statement publicly available for the first time, any company in Germany which issues securities as a domestic issuer must make a Europe-wide[135] publication

---

[127] Cf. third provision of Circular 1/2008.

[128] In Germany, issuers that list in the segment of so-called Prime Standards of the Frankfurt Stock Exchange are required to publish quarterly financial reports, cf. § 51 BörsO FWB as of 28 November 2011. In Sweden, an obligation to publish quarterly financial reports under IAS 34 arises for companies listed at NASDAQ OMX Stockholm, cf. NASDAQ OMX Stockholm, *Rule Book for Issuers* (11 January 2010), 3.2.

[129] DTR 4.3 FSA Handbook.

[130] C. Shutkever, 7 JIBFL (2008), p. 346. Also P.C. Leyens and U. Magnus, in: K.J. Hopt and H.-C. Voigt (eds.), *Prospekt- und Kapitalmarktinformationshaftung*, p. 526.

[131] C. Sottoriva, Le Società (2008), p. 533, 541.

[132] Art. 12(2) Directive 2007/14/EC.

[133] Art. 12(3) Directive 2007/14/EC.

[134] Art. 21(2) TD; see also § 28 para. 4–7.

[135] On the requirements regarding the media and the disclosure procedure see C. Götze and N.-C. Wunderlich, in: M. Habersack et al. (eds.), *Handbuch der Kapitalmarktinformation*, § 9 para. 43 ff.

concerning when and on which website the financial reports will be publicly available in addition to their availability in the company register. Simultaneously with the publication of such announcement, the company must notify the supervisory authority thereof.[136] Only after the publication of the announcement is the actual financial report disclosed—usually on the issuer's website[137]—and transmitted to the company register in order to be stored there.[138]

59   With regard to the quarterly financial report, German law merely clarifies that it must be transmitted to the company register without undue delay, but not before the publication of the announcement.[139] On the disclosure itself, German law contains no further details for quarterly financial report. Due to the fact that the quarterly financial report is based on the same underlying regulatory concept as the other financial reports, however, and in order to maintain the same standard as for the other financial reports, the disclosure of the quarterly financial report must be adapted to that of the annual and half-yearly financial reports.[140]

60   The information requested by the TD is so-called "regulated information", which, in the United Kingdom, must be published through a Regulated Information Service (RIS)— RISs constitute a system of information providers which are approved by the FSA if it is satisfied that the person can disclose regulated information in a manner ensuring fast output and access to such information on a non-discriminatory basis.[141] The FSA has therefore decided to continue its RIS system in order to comply with the TD's requirement of a central disclosure and storage system. There are currently seven providers acting as RIS providers from which companies making regulatory announcements can choose, all of these being set out in the FSA's list of RISs on its website.[142] In all other respects the applicable disclosure procedure is governed by the implementing directive of the TD.[143] At the same time, however, the financial reports must also be submitted to the FSA.[144] The FSA has announced that it will probably introduce an officially appointed mechanism in the future.[145] In Sweden, the FI's website gives access to a database in which all financial reports are stored.[146]

61   German law deviates from the TD's provisions. It contains an exemption from the obligation to disclose an annual financial report for issuers that are already subject to the obligation to disclose the respective accounting documents under commercial law.[147] This exemption only applies to German corporations,[148]

---

[136] § 37v(1), § 37w(1) WpHG, § 8b(3) No. 2 HGB.
[137] § 37v(1), § 37w(1), WpHG. This is not, however, mandatory, cf. N. *Kumm*, BB (2009), p. 1118, 1119.
[138] § 37v(1), § 37w(1), WpHG, § 8b(3) No. 2 HGB.
[139] § 37x(3) WpHG.
[140] S. Mock, in: H. Hirte and T.M.J. Möllers (eds.), *Kölner Kommentar zum WpHG*, § 37x para. 29; H. Hönsch, in: H.-D. Assmann and U.H. Schneider (eds.), *Kommentar zum WpHG*, § 37x para. 24. Dissenting opinion: N. Kumm, BB (2009), p. 1118, 1122; cf. also BaFin, *Emittentenleitfaden 2009* (issuer guideline), p. 238.
[141] Cf. FSA, *Criteria for Regulated Information Services*, May 2010.
[142] One of the most important informational systems is the London Stock Exchange's Regulatory News Service (RNS); see § 22 para. 6.
[143] Art. 12 Directive 2007/14/EC was adopted nearly one-to-one in the DTR 6.3.4–6.3.9. FSA Handbook.
[144] DTR 6.2.2. FSA Handbook.
[145] The FSA favours a solution in which an existing commercial storage medium is officially designated, cf. FSA, *Implementation of the Transparency Directive*, PS 06/11, October 2006, para. 5.6.
[146] The information is available at: https://fiappl.fi.se/FinansCentralen/search/Search.aspx.
[147] § 37v(1) WpHG.
[148] Cf. § 325 HGB.

whilst foreign companies must still make public an annual financial report.[149] The German legislature sought to relieve the German corporation from a double burden.[150] The result of this exemption is, however, that the disclosure procedure regarding annual financial reports differs for national and foreign issuers.[151]

VII. Sanctions

62   European law does not lay down a well-differentiated concept regarding the sanction for breaches of financial reporting duties. It is therefore in the power of the Member States to take the necessary measures. The TD merely requires these measures to be effective, proportionate and dissuasive.[152]

1.   Liability for Incorrect Financial Reporting

63   The TD requires Member States to ensure the necessary penalties for breaches in financial reporting duties. In this context the Member States must ensure that responsibility for drawing up the information and making this public lies at least with the issuer or its administrative, management or supervisory bodies, and that the national laws, regulations and administrative provisions on liability are applicable to the issuers, their bodies or the persons responsible within the issuers.[153] Whilst the European regulations remain vague and leave a large margin of appreciation to the Member States in the transposition of the directive,[154] it still becomes clear that a specific liability for incorrect financial reporting is required;[155] otherwise, the European legislature would not try to ensure that Member States take the necessary measures. General rules on liability will often be insufficient, as they do not achieve the specific level of protection required in financial reporting; in particular, the liability may not be restricted to cases of wilful action.[156] The European concept allows the liability rules to be addressed either solely to the issuer or also to the responsible bodies within the issuer.[157]

(a)   Specific Liability for Incorrect Financial Reporting

64   The transposition of Article 7 TD on the liability for incorrect financial reporting prompted some Member States to introduce specific additional sanctions. In Spain, for example, the issuer and the members of the administrative board (*administra-*

---

[149] H. Hönsch, in: H.-D. Assmann and U.H. Schneider (eds.), *Kommentar zum WpHG*, § 37v para. 14; M. Zimmermann, in: A. Fuchs (ed.), *Kommentar zum WpHG*, § 37v para. 7.

[150] Begr. RegE TUG, BT-Drucks. 16/2498 (explanatory notes), p. 43.

[151] For more details see H. Brinckmann, *Kapitalmarktrechtliche Finanzberichterstattung*, p. 283 ff. On possible conflicts resulting from this, see P.O. Mülbert and S. Steup, NZG (2007), p. 761, 763 ff.

[152] Art. 28(1) TD.

[153] Art. 7 TD.

[154] Cf. Recital 17 TD.

[155] Also see P.O. Mülbert and S. Steup, WM (2005), p. 1633, 1653; R. Veil, ZBB (2006), p. 162, 168–169.

[156] R. Veil, ZBB (2006), p. 162, 169.

[157] M. Brellochs, *Publizität und Haftung*, p. 95; H. Fleischer, WM (2006), p. 2021, 2027; R. Veil, ZBB (2006), p. 162, 168.

Hendrik Brinckmann

dores) are liable for damages if their annual or half-yearly financial reports do not reflect a "true and fair view" of the company, thus causing economic losses to a securities holder. [158]

65   In implementing the TD the United Kingdom introduced rules on a civil liability for incorrect financial reporting.[159] The scope of application of this provision was extended in October 2010. Section 90A FSMA now provides for a general informational liability on the capital market in Schedule 10, though this is restricted to cases of intent or recklessness.[160] The issuer thus is not held liable for cases of ordinary negligence. As opposed to prospectus liability, an investor can therefore not free himself from the requirement of a proof of causation simply by making reference to the fraud-on-the-market theory.[161]

(b)   Liability under the General Civil Law Rules

66   Most Member States, such as Germany and Sweden, have by no means integrated the financial reporting into their national rules on civil liability. In these cases, the question arises as to whether incorrect financial reporting is subject to the general rules on civil liability and whether these rules are sufficient with respect to the rules on liability for incorrect financial reporting as required by the TD.

67   Germany refrained from implementing the liability regulations contained in the TD,[162] although no specific liability rules regarding incorrect periodic disclosure exist in the national laws.[163] The liability for incorrect financial reports is thus widely discussed in Germany.[164] It is generally accepted as a fact that in cases of intentional damage contrary to public policy, a minimum protection is ensured by the general civil liability provided for in § 826 Bürgerliches Gesetzbuch (BGB, German Civil Code). In cases of criminal offences, especially incorrect balance sheet oaths, a liability may be provided under § 823(2) BGB in conjunction with § 331 HGB, § 400 Aktiengesetz (AktG, German Stock Corporation Act).[165] However, the liability remains fragmentary, leading the German legal literature to suggest applying the rules on liability regarding ad hoc disclosure analogously.[166] Yet this cannot hide

---

[158] Art. 35 LMV, Art. 10, 17 RD 1362/2007.

[159] Sec. 90A FSMA was inserted in the FSMA 2000 through sec. 1270 Companies Act 2006.

[160] The degree of liability depends on whether it refers to an act or an omission. "Recklessness" is only sufficient with regard to the publication of incorrect or misleading information (cf. sec. 90A Schedule 10A.3(2) FSMA). If the claim is based on the fact that relevant information is missing, the necessary degree of liability is higher and the issuer is required to have known the omission to be a dishonest concealment of a material fact (cf. sec. 90A Schedule 10A.3(3) FSMA).

[161] Seen critically by A. Alcock, in: A.J. Boyle et al. (eds.), *Gore-Browne on Companies*, para. 43-28A (Update 68).

[162] M. Brellochs, *Publizität und Haftung*, p. 141. The legislature's attempt to achieve a cohesive system of liability for incorrect financial reporting in the so-called KapInHaG (to be found in NZG (2004), p. 1042 ff.) went no further than the draft stage. Seen critically in R. Veil, BKR (2005), p. 91 ff.

[163] T.M.J. Möllers, 208 AcP (2008), p. 1, 29.

[164] For an overview see H. Brinckmann, *Kapitalmarktrechtliche Finanzberichterstattung*, p. 289 ff.

[165] § 331 No. 3a HGB.

[166] P.O. Mülbert and S. Steup, WM (2005), p. 1633, 1651–1652; H. Brinckmann, *Periodische Kapitalmarktpublizität durch Finanzberichte*, p. 22 ff. Dissenting opinion: T.M.J. Möllers and C. Leisch, in: H. Hirte and T.M.J. Möllers (eds.), *Kölner Kommentar zum WpHG*, § 37b, c para. 71.

the fact that the German legislature has as yet not fulfilled its transposition duties in this respect.[167]

68　The situation in Sweden is similar. The legal basis for shareholder and third-party claims under company law only applies to members of the administrative board that have intentionally or negligently breached their duties regarding the annual financial account.[168] Apart from this, i.e. for the financial reporting duties during the year, Sweden only provides provisions under tort law in conjunction with a breach of criminal provisions. These are, however, only addressed to members of the administration.[169] Furthermore only the rules on market manipulation apply for negligence, whilst all other provisions require intent.[170]

69　In France, civil liability for incorrect financial reporting is also mainly based on the general rules of liability.[171] However, compensation may also be awarded to the aggrieved person in a criminal proceeding for incorrect capital market information.

70　*Example:* In the case of *Flammarion* the court awarded former shareholders damages. The issuer had made public a negative half-yearly financial report without informing the shareholders that as a part of a change in control of the company in the following days a certain share price would be guaranteed. The shareholders' loss was due to the missed opportunity to dispose of the shares at that higher price a few days later. However, for lack of *faute détachable* the president of the issuer did not have to pay compensation.[172] In the case of *Regina Rubens*[173] a company had "cooked its books" in 1998 and 1990. Investors that had acquired rights immediately after the incorrect reports were entitled to damages to the value of the difference between the price they had paid and the shares' value when the fraud was discovered.

71　The case of *Sidel*[174] is also of particular importance. The Cour d'appel of Paris ruled that shareholders suffer personal losses (*préjudice direct et personnel*) when incorrect information is disseminated and incorrect accounts are published, provided they acquired or held on to shares due to being given an over-optimistic image of the company (*perspectives prometteuses manifestement surévaluées*).[175] Obviously, this cannot cover the whole difference between the (high) acquisition price and the (low) disposal price after the information was corrected, as risks

---

[167] Cf. also T.M.J. Möllers, 208 AcP (2008), p. 1, 29 ff.

[168] Kapitel 29, § 1 ABL.

[169] The relevant crimes are fraud pursuant to Kapitel 9, § 1 BrB, misdirection of the public (*svindleri*) under Kapitel 9, § 9 BrB and market manipulation pursuant to § 8 of the Market Abuse Act (Lag om straff för marknadsmissbruk vid handel med finansiella instrument).

[170] § 8 Lag om straff för marknadsmissbruk vid handel med finansiella instrument (Swedish Market Abuse Act), cf. R. Veil and F. Walla, *Schwedisches Kapitalmarktrecht*, p. 57–58.

[171] Art. 1382 f. Cc.

[172] Cf. J.-P. Mattout, Dr. soc. (2004), p. 11, 14; A. Viandier, *OPA, OPE et autres offres publiques*, p. 148 para. 856, with reference to *CA Paris 26 septembre 2003*; J.-P. Valuet, *L'information financière des sociétés cotées*, in: J.-F. Barbièri et al. (Conseil scientifique), *Dictionnaire Joly Bourse et produits financiers*, p. 104, with reference to *CA Paris, 25 chambre, section B, 26 septembre 2003*, Bull. Joly Bourse (2004), note É. Dezeuze.

[173] Cf. *CA Paris, 9ème chambre, section B, 14 septembre 2007, No. 07/01477, X et Y c/ MP et autres*, with extensive notes by R. Rontchevsky, RTDF (2007), p. 145 ff. (*Regina Rubens*).

[174] Cf. É. Dezeuze, RTDF (2008-4), p. 137 ff. In the lower instance it was mainly questions on criminal law that played a role (*TGI Paris, 11ème chambre correctionnelle, 1ère section, 12 septembre 2006, MM. O., D.V., et L. contre Ministère public, SIDEL et autres*), cf. É. Dezeuze, RTDF (2006), p. 162 ff.

[175] The fact that holding the instruments suffices contradicts former jurisprudence, cf. É. Dezeuze, Bull. Joly Bourse (2009), p. 28, 34 with further references.

　　　　　　　　　　　　　　　　　　　　　　　　Hendrik Brinckmann

and vicissitudes exist for any investment on the stock market (*en raison du risque et de l'aléa propre à tout investissement boursier*). The damage also cannot be seen as a non-material loss (*préjudice moral*). Rather, the damage consists of a loss of profit prospects (*perte d'une chance*).[176] The issuer and its managing director were jointly and severally liable for this damage.[177]

2. Sanctions under Criminal and Administrative Law

72 The TD provides additional rules on the implementation of a system of sanctions by obligating Member States to ensure that, without prejudice to the right for criminal penalties to be imposed, the appropriate administrative measures are to be taken or civil and/or administrative penalties imposed with respect to the persons responsible, where the provisions adopted in accordance with this Directive have not been complied with.[178]

73 In France the incorrect dissemination of information on the capital market, including incorrect financial reporting,[179] is covered by criminal law (*délit de fausse information*).[180]

74 In the case of *Rhodia* the issuer and its CEO were held liable for various over-optimistic statements on the financial situation of the issuer. The court ruled that the behaviour can be sanctioned even if the accounting rules in Article 632–1 RG AMF were abided by. In these cases the member of the administrative board who is responsible for the *comité des comptes* must be prosecuted.[181]

75 In the United Kingdom, if incorrect annual accounts are approved, any director of the company who knew that the annual accounts did not comply with the requirements, or was reckless as to whether they complied, and failed to take reasonable steps to secure compliance therewith or, as the case may be, to prevent the accounts from being approved, commits an offence.[182] On conviction, the director is, however, only liable to a fine, not to imprisonment.[183] Additionally the director must observe the criminal prohibition of making misleading, false or deceptive statements[184] which also applies to financial reports.[185]

76 Germany only introduced a specific criminal provision for financial reporting regarding sanctioning incorrect balance sheet oaths,[186] whilst the non-performance of the balance sheet oath remains unpunished. Additionally, there is an extensive catalogue of administrative offences regarding notification and disclosure obliga-

---

[176] *CA Paris, 9ème chambre, section B, 17 octobre 2008, No. 06/09036, Sidel*, note É. Dezeuze, Bull. Joly Bourse (2009), p. 28 ff.

[177] Cf. É. Dezeuze and G. Buge, Bull. Joly Bourse (Jan/Feb 2008), p. 46, 58.

[178] Art. 28(1) TD.

[179] Art. 632-1 RG AMF.

[180] Cf. Art. L. 465-2 al. 2 and L. 465-3 C. mon. fin.

[181] *CA Paris, 1ère chambre, section H, 20 mai 2008, No. 2007/14651, "Rhodia SA et X c/ AMF"*, note H. Bouthinon-Dumas, Bull. Joly Bourse (2008), p. 492 ff.

[182] Sec. 414(4) Companies Act 2006. The board's or director's duty to approve of the annual financial report result from sec. 414 Companies Act 2006 irrespective of whether the TD is applicable.

[183] Sec. 414(5) Companies Act 2006.

[184] Sec. 397(1) and (2) FSMA.

[185] A. Alcock, in: A.J. Boyle et al. (eds.), *Gore-Browne on Companies*, para. 43-28A (Update 68).

[186] § 331 No. 3a HGB.

tions with regard to financial reports and the respective administrative fines.[187] The liberating effect of the disclosure of accounting documents under commercial law for the obligation to prepare an annual financial report for companies that issue securities as domestic issuers[188] has resulted in differences between German and foreign issuers with regard to possible sanctions, the highest fine under accounting law being considerably lower than under the WpHG.[189]

77   The Swedish legislature has refrained from introducing specific criminal provisions for incorrect financial reporting, instead applying the general rules of criminal law.[190] A sanctioning possibility specifically for financial reporting is only to be found in supervisory law. The FI can impose special charges[191] or issue formal reprimands combined with a fine[192] if an issuer omits to prepare a financial report or does so incorrectly.

VIII. Conclusion

78   The capital markets must continually be supplied with information on the issuer in order to ensure an adequate price formation for securities. Capital market regulation must enable investors to compare different issuers and allow them to trust the information disclosed. The European legislature had this in mind when it enacted the TD. This Directive also takes into account that according to the current economic studies, only the company's accounts can provide a regular informational basis for investors. It therefore integrates the rules on company accounting into the regulatory concept of capital markets law.

79   Legal developments in this field of law are not yet complete. Improvement is necessary with regard to the fact that financial reports are not the only possible format for periodic disclosure. Interim management statements bear no reference to the company's accounts. Therefore, they constitute a disruptive factor within the system of European periodic disclosure. The Commission has meanwhile come to the same conclusion. In order to reduce the administrative burden linked to listing on regulated markets and to encourage long-term investments, the requirement to publish interim management statements is to be abolished for all listed companies.[193]

80   A solution must also be found for the fact that financial reports rely on accounting law which is still mainly in the hands of the Member States. The information in the financial reports is thus not subject to any uniform accounting standards, although

---

[187] § 39 WpHG, § 104a HGB.

[188] § 37v(1) WpHG.

[189] In more detail H. Brinckmann, *Kapitalmarktrechtliche Finanzberichterstattung*, p. 284–285.

[190] The relevant provisions under criminal law are those on misleading the public (*svindleri*) in Kapitel 9, § 9 BrB and fraud in Kapitel 9, § 1 BrB.

[191] Kapitel 25, § 18 LVM. The special charges lie between 50,000 and 10,000,000 SEK, Kapitel 28, § 19(2) LVM.

[192] Kapitel 25, § 22(1) LVM. The fine (*straffavgift*) can also lie between 50,000 and 10,000,000 SEK, Kapitel 25, § 23 LVM.

[193] Cf. Proposal for a Directive of the European Parliament and of the Council amending Directive 2004/109/EC on the harmonisation of transparency requirements in relation to information about issuers whose securities are admitted to trading on a regulated market and Commission Directive 2007/14/EC, COM(2011) 683/2, p. 7.

Hendrik Brinckmann

it is becoming increasingly apparent that the IAS/IFRS may become such internationally accepted standards.

81   Sanctions for incorrect financial reports are also very different amongst the Member States, raising the question as to whether the rules on sanctions and liability should be harmonised in future, in order to ensure an equally high quality of financial reports in all Member States.

§ 19 Disclosure of Inside Information

Bibliography
Abbadessa, Pietro, *La circolazione delle informazioni all'interno del gruppo*, in: Balzarini, Paola, *I gruppi di società: Atti del Convegno internazionale di studi* (1995), p. 567; af Sandeberg, Catarina, *Prospektansvaret—caveat emptor eller caveat venditor?* (2001); Annunziata, Filippo, *Abusi di mercato e tutela del risparmio, Nuove prospettive nella disciplina del mercato mobiliare* (2006); Annunziata, Filippo, *La Disziplina del Mercato Mobiliare*, 4th ed. (2008); Arsouze, Charles, *Annotation to CA Paris, 1re ch., sect. H, 9 October 2007, No. 2006/12937*, Bull. Joly Bourse (2008), p. 12; Bachmann, Gregor, *Kapitalmarktrechtliche Probleme bei der Zusammenführung von Unternehmen*, 172 ZHR (2008), p. 597–634; Baule, Rainer and Tallau, Christian, *Market Response to Ad Hoc Disclosures and Periodic Financial Statements: Evidence from Germany* (2010), available at: http://ssrn.com/abstract=1660679; Behn, Lars, *Ad-hoc-Publizität und Unternehmensverbindungen. Informationszugang des Emittenten im faktischen Aktienkonzern* (2012); Brandi, Tim Oliver and Süßmann, Rainer, *Neue Insiderregeln und Ad-hoc-Publizität—Folgen für Ablauf und Gestaltung von M&A-Transaktionen*, AG (2004), p. 642–658; Brellochs, Michael, *Publizität und Haftung von Aktiengesellschaften im System des Europäischen Kapitalmarktrechts* (2005); Bruno, Ferdinando and Ravasio, Nicoletta, *Ambito soggettivo ed oggettivo dell'informazione privilegiata post Market Abuse directive*, 8 Le società (2007), p. 1026–1033; Chvika, Eyal, *La responsabilité des intervenants dans le cadre d'une introduction en bourse*, RDBF (2008), p. 12–19; Conac, Pierre-Henri, *La pratique de la publicité des décisions de sanctions et d'absence de sanction par la commission des sanctions de l'AMF*, RTDF 1 (2006), p. 128–130; Ducouloux-Favard, Claude, *Infractions boursières*, in: Faugérolas, Laurent, *Dictionnaire Joly Bourse et produits financiers, Tome III*, looseleaf, as of 2 April 2009; Entrena Ruiz, Daniel, *El empleo de información privilegiada en el mercado de valores: un estudio de su régimen administrativo sancionador* (2006); Ferrarini, Guido, *I gruppi nella regolazione finanziaria*, in: Balzarini, Paola, *I gruppi di società: Atti del Convegno internazionale di studi* (1995), p. 1233; Ferrarrini, Guido and Leonardi, Marco, *Italien*, in: Hopt, Klaus J. and Voigt, Hans-Christoph (eds.), *Prospekt- und Kapitalmarktinformationshaftung* (2005), p. 713; Fleischer, Holger, *Ad-hoc-Publizität beim einvernehmlichen vorzeitigen Ausscheiden des Vorstandsvorsitzenden*, NZG (2007), p. 401–407; García Malsipica, Silvia, *Infracciones y sanciones*, in: Fernández, Francisco and Arranz, Gregorio, *Régimen jurídico de los mercados de valores y de las instituciones de inversión colectiva* (2007), p. 785; Gilotta, Sergio, *Disclosure in Securities Markets and the Firm's Need for Confidentiality: Theoretical Framework and Regulatory Analysis*, 13 EBOR (2012), p. 46–88; Gullifer, Louise and Payne, Jennifer, *Corporate Finance Law. Principles and Policy* (2011); Harbarth, Stephan, *Ad-hoc-Publizität beim Unternehmenskauf*, ZIP (2005), p. 1898–1909; Hellgardt, Alexander, *Kapitalmarktdeliktsrecht* (2008); Iribarren Blanco, Miguel, *Responsabilidad civil por la información divulgada por las sociedades cotizadas* (2008); Klöhn, Lars, *Die Regelung selektiver Informationsweitergabe gem. § 15 Abs. 1 Satz 4 u. 5 WpHG—eine Belastungsprobe*, WM (2010), p. 1869–1882; Koch, Philipp, *Die Ad-hoc-Publizität nach dem Kommissionsentwurf einer Marktmissbrauchsverordnung. Nicht ad-hoc-pflichtige Insiderinformationen und Aufschub der Veröffentlichung bei systemrelevanten Insiderinformationen*, BB (2012), p. 1365–1369; Martin Laprade, Frank, *Annotation to CA Paris, 1re ch., sect. H, 20 November 2007, No. 2007/00369, Sedia Développement SA c/ AMF*, Bull. Joly Bourse (2008), p. 19; McDonnell, Brian, *Handling and Disclosing Inside Information: A Guide to the Disclosure Rules*, 88 COB (2011), p. 1–33; Menéndez, Aurelio, *Lecciones de Derecho Mercantil*, 6th ed. (2008); Mennicke, Petra R., *Ad-hoc-Publizität bei gestreckten Entscheidungsprozessen und die Notwendigkeit einer Befreiungsentscheidung des Emittenten*, NZG (2009), p. 1059–1063; Lord Millett, Alcock, Alistair and Todd, Michael (eds.), *Gore-Browne on Companies*, looseleaf, as of 27 January 2009; Möllers, Thomas M.J., *Das europäische Kapitalmarktrecht im Umbruch*, ZBB (2003), p. 390–409; Möllers, Thomas M.J., *Der BGH, die BaFin und der EuGH: Ad-hoc-Publizität beim einvernehmlichen vorzeitigen Ausscheiden des Vorstandsvor-*

Philipp Koch

sitzenden Jürgen Schrempp, NZG (2008), p. 330–333; Möllers, Thomas M.J., *Insiderinformation und Befreiung von der Ad-hoc-Publizität nach § 15 Abs. 3 WpHG—Zur Neubeurteilung von mehrstufigen Entscheidungsprozessen durch das Anlegerschutzverbesserungsgesetz*, WM (2005), p. 1393–1400; Möllers, Thomas M.J., *The "Immediateness" of Ad Hoc Disclosure Statements in the Context of National and European Legal Doctrine*, 18 ICCLR (2007), p. 369–377; Möllers, Thomas M.J., *Zur "Unverzüglichkeit" einer Ad-hoc-Mitteilung im Kontext nationaler und europäischer Dogmatik*, in: Berger, Klaus P. et al. (eds.), *Festschrift für Norbert Horn* (2006), p. 473; Morse, Geoffrey, *Palmer's Company Law*, looseleaf, as of April 2011; Mucciarelli, Francesco, *L'informazione societaria: destini e limiti posti dalla normativa in materia di insider trading*, 1 Banca Borsa tit. Cred. (1999), p. 754; Nietsch, Michael, *Schadensersatzhaftung wegen Verstoßes gegen Ad-hoc-Publizitätspflichten nach dem Anlegerschutzverbesserungsgesetz*, BB (2005), p. 785–790; Palá Laguna, Reyes, *La obligación de información del consejo a los mercados: folletos y hechos relevantes (chapter 29)*, in: Artigas, Fernando R. et al. (eds.), *Derecho de Sociedades Anónimas Cotizadas, Tomo II* (2006), p. 1291; Pisani, Hervé, *L'information financière: les responsables*, 3 RTDF (2007), p. 18–20; Puttfarken, Hans-Jürgen and Schrader, Anne, *Frankreich*, in: Hopt, Klaus J. and Voigt, Hans-Christoph (eds.), *Prospekt- und Kapitalmarktinformationshaftung* (2005), p. 595; Rigotti, Marco, *Informativa societaria*, in: Griffi, Antonio et al. (eds.), *Intermediari finanziari, mercati e società quotate* (1999), p. 168; Roch, Géraldine, *Annotation to CA Paris, 1re ch., sect. H, 3 July 2007, No. 2006/19083, X. et autres c/ AMF*, Bull. Joly Bourse (2008), p. 204–209; Rontchevsky, Nicolas, *Annotation to AMF Commission des sanctions, 28.9.2006 and CA Paris, 3 July 2007*, 1 RTDF (2008), p. 86–88; Sastre Corchado, Galo J., *La Directiva de Abuso de Mercado—un nuevo marco en Europa*, 1 RMV (2007), p. 253–302; Sauer, Knut, *Haftung für Falschinformation des Sekundärmarktes* (2004); Scognamiglio, Guiliana, *L'acquisto di azioni della controllante nel d. leg. 1994, n. 315*, 2 Riv. Dir. Civ. (1995), p. 49; Schneider, Sven H., *Selbstbefreiung von der Pflicht zur Ad-hoc-Publizität*, BB (2005), p. 897–902; Schneider, Uwe H. and Gilfrich, Stephanie, *Die Entscheidung des Emittenten über die Befreiung von der Ad-hoc-Publizitätspflicht*, BB (2007), p. 53–56; Seminara, Sergio, *Disclose or abstain? La nozione di informazione privilegiata tra obblighi di comunicazione all pubblico e divieti di insider trading: Riflessioni sulla determinanza delle fattispecie sanzionatorie*, 3 Banca Borsa tit. Cred. (2008), p. 331; Seminara, Sergio, *Informazione finanziaria e mercato: alla ricerca di una strategia del controllo penale e amministrativo*, Analisi giur. Ec. (2006), p. 264; Sfameni, Paolo, *Art. 114. Comunicazioni al pubblico*, in: Marchetti, P. and Bianchi, Luigi A. (eds.), *La disciplina delle società quotate nel Testo Unico della finanza*, 1999, p. 518; Simon, Stefan, *Die neue Ad-hoc-Publizität*, Der Konzern (2005), p. 13–22; Storm, Philipp, *Alternative Freiverkehrssegmente im Kapitalmarktrecht* (2010); Tollkühn, Oliver, *Die Ad-hoc-Publizität nach dem Anlegerschutzverbesserungsgesetz*, ZIP (2004), p. 2215–2220; Tomasi, Martin, *L'imputation des manquements aux règles de l'Autorité des marchés financiers*, 109 Banque & Droit (2006), p. 35–43; Veil, Rüdiger, *Die Ad-hoc-Publizitätshaftung im System kapitalmarktrechtlicher Informationshaftung*, 167 ZHR (2003), p. 365–402; Veil, Rüdiger, *Die Haftung des Emittenten für fehlerhafte Information des Kapitalmarkts nach dem geplanten KapInHaG*, BKR (2005), p. 91–98; Veil, Rüdiger, *Marktregulierung durch privates Recht am Beispiel des Entry Standard der Frankfurter Wertpapierbörse*, in: Burgard, Ulrich et al. (eds.), *Festschrift für Uwe H. Schneider* (2011), p. 1312; Veil, Rüdiger and Koch, Philipp, *Towards a Uniform European Capital Markets Law: Proposals of the Commission to Reform Market Abuse* (2012), available at: http://ssrn.com/abstract=1998376; Vokuhl, Nikolai, *Kapitalmarktrechtlicher Anlegerschutz und Kapitalerhaltung in der Aktiengesellschaft* (2007); Ziemons, Hildegard, *Neuerungen im Insiderrecht und bei der Ad-hoc-Publizität durch die Marktmissbrauchsrichtlinie und das Gesetz zur Verbesserung des Anlegerschutzes*, NZG (2004), p. 537–543.

I. Introduction

1. Dual Function of Ad Hoc Disclosure Obligations

1   Once inside information has been made public, insiders lose their trading advantage. Disclosure obligations are therefore essential to curtailing insider dealings. The effectiveness of these measures has been proven in the United States over many years.[1] Additionally, the disclosure of price-sensitive information improves transparency and thereby ensures more equal chances for market participants. The combination of periodic disclosure obligations and the disclosure obligations for inside information enables the market to obtain the necessary information on an issuer. Ad hoc disclosure obligations must thus be seen as having a dual function— as a disclosure measure and a preventive measure.[2]

2   If one focuses on the preventive nature of disclosure obligations regarding insider dealings, it appears reasonable to require the same conditions when prohibiting insider trading[3] and when requiring disclosure. Both concepts can then apply the same notion of inside information. This was taken into account by the European legislator who understood the disclosure obligations as a complement to the prohibitions on insider trading;[4] this understanding is reflected in the MAD and its implementing measures.[5]

3   Yet transparency does not always require disclosure obligations and prohibitions of insider dealings to run parallel: not all information that may enable insider dealings must necessarily be disclosed. Disclosure might in some cases mislead the public, e.g. if the information refers to future events. In these cases disclosure obligations could be counterproductive, as the public might not be able to assess the information correctly, whilst prohibiting insider dealings may already be advisable at this time. Additionally, the issuer may have a legitimate interest in not immediately disclosing the inside information to the public.[6] The issuer may further not be informed from the outset about information by which it is only indirectly affected. When consid-

---

[1] Cf. H.-D. Assmann, in: H.-D. Assmann and U.H. Schneider (eds.), *Kommentar zum WpHG*, § 15 para. 32 with further references; for recent data on Germany see R. Baule and C. Tallau, *Market Response to Ad Hoc Disclosures and Periodic Financial Reports: Evidence from Germany*; cf. also R. Veil, 167 ZHR (2003), p. 365, 375 ff.

[2] Cf. H.-D. Assmann, in: H.-D. Assmann and U.H. Schneider (eds.), *Kommentar zum WpHG*, § 15 para. 2, 6; M. Pfüller, in: A. Fuchs (ed.), *Kommentar zum WpHG*, § 15 para. 34 ff.; T. Raiser and R. Veil, *Recht der Kapitalgesellschaften*, § 12 para. 29.

[3] See above § 13 para. 70–95.

[4] See below para. 11.

[5] Commission Directive 2003/124/EC of 22 December 2003 implementing Directive 2003/6/EC of the European Parliament and of the Council as regards the definition and public disclosure of inside information and the definition of market manipulation, OJ L339, 24 December 2003, p. 70; Commission Directive 2003/125/EC of 22 December 2003 implementing Directive 2003/6/EC of the European Parliament and of the Council as regards the fair presentation of investment recommendations and the disclosure of conflicts of interest, OJ L339, 24 December 2003, p. 73; Commission Directive 2004/72/EC of 29 April 2004 implementing Directive 2003/6/EC of the European Parliament and of the Council as regards accepted market practices, the definition of inside information in relation to derivatives on commodities, the drawing up of lists of insiders, the notification of managers' transactions and the notification of suspicious transactions, OJ L162, 30 April 2004, p. 70; Commission Regulation (EC) No. 2273/2003 of 22 December 2003 implementing Directive 2003/6/EC of the European Parliament and of the Council as regards exemptions for buy-back programmes and stabilisation of financial instruments, OJ L336, 23 December 2003, p. 33.

[6] See below para. 62 ff.

Philipp Koch

ering the disclosure of inside information under the concept of transparency, one must further determine its relationship to the other disclosure obligations on the secondary markets, especially the rules on periodic disclosure;[7] the obligation to make public inside information constitutes an essential element of the disclosure obligations on the secondary markets.[8]

4   Both functions of the disclosure obligations complement each other in their aim of achieving an efficient price structure on the capital markets. Nevertheless, the differences in the underlying concepts are still reflected in the Member States' individual implementations: in Germany, the rules on the disclosure of inside information directly follow the rules on the prohibition of insider dealings, whilst France has implemented the rules in conjunction with the rules on periodic disclosure. There is a general tendency towards understanding the disclosure obligations as an element of the transparency regime, which, however, simultaneously takes into account the aim of preventing insider trading.

5   The respective rules are therefore entitled *"information permanente"* in France and *"publicación de hechos relevantes"* in Spain. As opposed to this, the United Kingdom and Germany emphasise a combination of these rules with a number of further obligations, speaking of *"episodic or ad hoc reporting requirements"* and *"Ad-hoc-Publizität"*, respectively. Spain additionally distinguishes between inside information (*"información privilegiada"*) and (price-) sensitive information (*"hechos relevantes"*), only the latter being subject to the disclosure obligations. Sweden has implemented the rules prohibiting insider dealings in a separate statute on market abuse, whilst the disclosure obligations are integrated in the LVM (Swedish Securities Market Act).

6   In our opinion, the disclosure obligations for inside information must primarily be classified as rules on transparency for systematic reasons, requiring their incorporation in the further rules on transparency and disclosure. We therefore examine the disclosure of inside information in the context of the other disclosure obligations and not in the chapter on market integrity.

2. Practical Relevance

7   The obligation to disclose inside information plays an important role in legal practice. In most Member States, the number of disclosures published has been continually rising or at least stable over the last years: in Austria, for example, the highest number of disclosures was achieved in 2009, when 653 disclosures took place, compared to 569 disclosures of inside information in 2010 and 539 in 2011.[9] In Spain, the high total of 11,502 disclosures in 2011, and 11,033 in 2010,[10] is probably the result of the fact that the disclosure obligation was extended to further information.[11]

---

[7] See below para. 52–53.
[8] N. Moloney, *EC Securities Regulation*, p. 969; T. Raiser and R. Veil, *Recht der Kapitalgesellschaften*, § 12 para. 29.
[9] Cf. FMA, *Jahresbericht 2011* (annual report), p. 112.
[10] Cf. CNMV, *Annual Report 2011*, p. 144.
[11] See also para. 35.

8   Germany, however, has experienced a continued decrease in disclosures, only 2,002 disclosures taking place in 2011, after 2,207 in 2010 and 2,657 in 2009.[12] In the years before, the number of disclosures had risen to 5,421 in 2001.[13] This exorbitant number of disclosures made it difficult for investors to determine what information was actually relevant. This was mainly due to the fact that in many cases disclosure would not even have been required and companies appeared to be using ad hoc notification as a means of advertising and public relations.[14] The German legislator has finally reacted to this tendency by introducing § 15(2)1 WpHG (German Securities Trading Act)[15]. The decreased number of disclosures since 2002 is additionally assumed to be the result of the negative developments on the stock markets since 2001.

9   There is not yet much data on the use of the possibility of delaying disclosure.[16] With 202 cases in Germany in 2011, after 177 delayed disclosures in 2010 (2009: 240; 2008: 209), there does not yet exist a clear tendency.[17] In 2002 issuers only applied for a delay of disclosure in 26 cases, 18 of which were granted.[18] In Austria, there were only 12 delayed disclosures in 2011.[19]

10   It is further noteworthy how different informal agreements between issuers and the supervisory authorities are treated in the different Member States. Whilst this practice is relatively unknown to the BaFin, informal agreements on disclosure obligations are common practice in Italy, France and Spain.[20] In Sweden, informal agreements are common between the issuers and the stock management.[21] In ensuing legal disputes, the courts are obviously not bound by the supervisory authorities' prior judgments and decisions regarding a disclosure obligation.

II.   Regulatory Concepts

1.   Requirements under European Law

11   The obligation to disclose inside information is laid down in Article 6(1) MAD.[22] The European legislator thus primarily understands the obligation to disclose inside information as an instrument to prevent insider dealings,[23] the MAD's aim being to ensure the integrity of Community financial markets and to enhance investor con-

---

[12] Cf. BaFin, *Jahresbericht 2011* (annual report), p. 211.

[13] Cf. BaFin, *Jahresbericht 2002* (annual report), p. 75.

[14] Cf. M. Pfüller, in: A. Fuchs (ed.), *Kommentar zum WpHG*, § 15 para. 14.

[15] See below para. 61.

[16] See below para. 63 ff.

[17] Cf. BaFin, *Jahresbericht 2011* (annual report), p. 210, and BaFin, *Jahresbericht 2009* (annual report), p. 189.

[18] Cf. BaFin, *Jahresbericht 2002* (annual report), p. 75.

[19] Cf. FMA, *Jahresbericht 2011* (annual report), p. 112.

[20] These insights are based on a number of intense interviews the authors conducted with legal practitioners and academics in the respective Member States (see also § 12 para. 9).

[21] Cf. R. Veil and F. Walla, *Schwedisches Kapitalmarktrecht*, p. 14.

[22] On the preceding provisions see D. Zimmer and H. Kruse, in: E. Schwark and D. Zimmer (eds.), *Kapitalmarktrechts-Kommentar*, § 15 WpHG para. 1–2.

[23] L. Gullifer and J. Payne, *Corporate Finance Law*, p. 484. The regulatory approach taken by the European Unions is seen critically by M. Brellochs, *Publizität und Haftung*, p. 38; S. Grundmann, *European Company Law*, p. 470; N. Moloney, *EC Securities Regulation*, p. 970–971.

fidence in those markets by prohibiting market manipulation and insider dealings.[24] The obligation to disclose inside information should complement the prohibitions on insider dealings and prevent investor confidence in market integrity being impaired by a selective disclosure of information.[25]

12   Article 6(1) MAD requires the Member States to ensure that issuers of financial instruments inform the public of inside information which directly concerns the said issuers as soon as possible. The term "inside information" is defined in Article 1(1) MAD,[26] the definition applying both to the rules prohibiting insider dealings and to those requiring the disclosure of inside information. Article 6(2) MAD allows an issuer to delay the public disclosure of inside information at his own responsibility, provided that (i) the disclosure would prejudice his legitimate interests, (ii) the omission is not likely to mislead the public and (iii) the issuer is able to ensure the confidentiality of that information. Article 3(1) Implementing Directive 2003/124/EC contains two examples for an issuer's legitimate interest in a delay. Article 3(2) Implementing Directive 2003/124/EC puts the requirement of ensuring the confidentiality of the information into more concrete terms. Article 6(2) MAD further allows the Member States to require that an issuer informs the competent authority of the decision to delay the public disclosure of inside information without delay.

13   If confidential inside information is disclosed to a third party with no confidentiality obligation, Article 6(3) MAD obliges the Member States to require the issuer, or a person acting on his behalf or on his account, to make a complete and effective public disclosure of that information.

14   The disclosure procedure and the conditions under which disclosure may be delayed are described in detail in Articles 2 and 3 of the Commission's Implementing Directive 2003/124/EC. The TD has largely amended the disclosure procedure, developing a uniform procedure for the disclosure of all types of information listed in Article 2(1)(k) TD.

15   On 20 October 2011 the European Commission made public two proposals[27] regarding amendments to the rules on market abuse.[28] They contain only slight amendments concerning the disclosure of inside information, but develop an additional and entirely new category of inside information that is not to be subject to the disclosure obligations. If the information is of systemic importance the national supervisory authority is in future to be permitted to delay the disclosure. The discussion on these reforms has only just begun.[29]

---

[24] Cf. Recital 12 MAD.

[25] Cf. Recital 24 MAD.

[26] See § 13 para. 33.

[27] Proposal for a Regulation of the European Parliament and of the Council on Insider Dealing and Market Manipulation (Market Abuse), 20 October 2011, COM(2011) 651 final; Proposal for a Directive of the European Parliament and of the Council on Criminal Sanctions for Insider Dealing and Market Manipulation, 20 October 2011, COM(2011), 654 final. See also § 13 para. 11–13.

[28] Furthermore, the European Commission has published a Working Paper as an accompanying document to the two proposals (Commission Staff Working Paper Impact Assessment, 20 October 2011, SEC(2011) 1217 final).

[29] Cf. P. Koch, BB (2012), p. 1365 ff.; R. Veil and P. Koch, *Towards a Uniform European Capital Markets Law: Proposals of the Commission to Reform Market Abuse*, p. 1 ff.

2. Implementation in the Member States

16   All Member States have meanwhile implemented the MAD's provisions into their national laws.[30] Most of them opted for a one-to-one approach, others took their respective national particularities and traditions into account by deviating in certain aspects. It is widely disputed in German legal literature how far the MAD permits such deviations,[31] there no longer being a provision similar to the former Article 6 Insider Directive[32] allowing more stringent national provisions. The ECJ has left this question unanswered.[33]

(a)   Germany

17   Subsequent to the implementation of the MAD and Implementing Directive 2003/124/EC by the German AnSVG (German Improvement of Investor Protection Act),[34] disclosure obligations for inside information are primarily incorporated in the new § 15 WpHG.[35] Above all, the legislator thereby aimed to achieve market transparency.[36] §§ 37 b, 37 c WpHG contain special rules on the liability for incorrect or omitted publications of inside information. The new disclosure and notification regime laid down in Articles 19 ff. TD and Article 12 Implementing Directive 2007/14/EG[37] was implemented into German national law by the TUG (German Transparency Directive Implementation Act).[38] §§ 3 a ff. WpAIV (German Federal Ministry of Finance's Regulation on Security Trading Notification and Insider Lists), issued on the legal basis of § 17(7) WpHG, puts these provisions into more concrete terms.[39] Article 2(2) and (3) Implementing Directive 2003/124/EC were not implemented into German law, as the provisions did not exceed those of the MAD and

---

[30] On the implementation of the Market Abuse Directive in the Member States see § 13 para. 14–31.

[31] For a maximum harmonisation see T.M.J. Möllers, ICCLR (2007), p. 369, 374–375; T.M.J. Möllers, in: K. Berger et al. (eds.), *Festschrift für Norbert Horn*, p. 473, 484 ff.; T.M.J. Möllers, WM (2005), p. 1393, 1396; T.M.J. Möllers, NZG (2008), p. 330, 332; for a minimum harmonisation, at least with regard to Art. 6 MAD see L. Klöhn, WM (2010), p. 1869, 1879–1880.

[32] Council Directive 89/592/EEC of 13 November 1989 coordinating regulations on insider dealings, OJ L334, 18 November 1989, p. 30.

[33] ECJ of 23 December 2009, Case C-45/08 (*Spector*) [2009] ECR I-12073, para. 63–64; also OLG Stuttgart, ZIP (2009), p. 962, 970.

[34] Gesetz zur Verbesserung des Anlegerschutzes/Anlegerschutzverbesserungsgesetz (AnSVG; German Improvement of Investor Protection Act) of 28 October 2004, BGBl. I (2004), p. 2630.

[35] On the developments of ad hoc disclosure obligations in Germany and the inefficient outset in the former § 44a BörsG cf. M. Pfüller, in: A. Fuchs (ed.), *Kommentar zum WpHG*, § 15 para. 3 ff.

[36] Cf. Begr. RegE, BT-Drucks. 15/3174, p. 34 (explanatory notes); the BaFin also refers to transparency as the main regulatory aim, cf. BaFin, *Emittentenleitfaden 2009* (issuer guideline), p. 47. See also D. Zimmer and H. Kruse, in: E. Schwark and D. Zimmer (eds.), *Kapitalmarktrechts-Kommentar*, § 15 WpHG para. 7.

[37] Commission Directive 2007/14/EC of 8 March 2007 laying down detailed rules for the implementation of certain provisions of Directive 2004/109/EC on the harmonisation of transparency requirements in relation to information about issuers whose securities are admitted to trading on a regulated market, OJ L69, 9 March 2007, p. 27.

[38] German Implementing Act for Directive 2004/109/EC (Gesetz zur Umsetzung der Richtlinie 2004/109/EG des Europäischen Parlaments und des Rates vom 15.12.2004 zur Harmonisierung der Transparenzanforderungen in Bezug auf Informationen über Emittenten, deren Wertpapiere zum Handel auf einem geregelten Markt zugelassen sind, und zur Änderung der Richtlinie 2001/34/EG/ Transparenzrichtlinie-Umsetzungsgesetz—TUG) of 5 January 2007, BGBl. I (2007), p. 10.

[39] German Federal Ministry of Finance's Regulation on Security Trading Notification and Insider Lists (Wertpapierhandelsanzeige- und Insiderverzeichnisverordnung—WpAIV) of 13 December 2004, BGBl. I (2004), p. 3367.

Philipp Koch

the further provisions of the Implementing Directive 2003/124/EG according to the German legislator's—correct—interpretation.[40] The MAD's approach of a uniform definition of inside information was adopted into German national law, which now also applies the definition in § 13 WpHG to the prohibitions of insider dealings in § 14 WpHG.[41]

18 The BaFin has published an *Emittentenleitfaden* (issuer guideline)[42] which in chapter IV contains useful information on the application of the provisions on the disclosure of inside information in legal practice. The BaFin's interpretation is not legally binding on the courts. It nevertheless has a large practical relevance for the market participants, the BaFin being the supervisory authority and as such permitted to impose administrative sanctions.[43]

(b) Austria

19 Since the reforms of the BörseG (Austrian Stock Exchange Act) in 2004, the rules on the disclosure of inside information in Austria are contained in § 48d BörseG and VMV (the FMA's Implementing Regulation on Disclosure and Notification).[44] § 48a(1) No. 1 BörseG gives the Austrian definition of inside information. Under Austrian law the main aim of the disclosure is an efficient price formation, ensuring the functioning of the capital markets; additional aims are investor protection and—since the implementation of the MAD—protection against insider dealings.[45] Austrian law is orientated towards the structure and wording of the European provisions even more strictly than German law—the exact wording of Article 2(2) Implementing Directive 2003/124/EC, for example, having been copied into § 48d(1) No. 2 BörseG.[46]

(c) Sweden

20 In Sweden the rules on the disclosure of inside information were incorporated in Kapitel 15, § 6(1) No. 3 in conjunction with Kapitel 17, §§ 2–3 LVM in 2007. In legal practice, however, these provisions take second place after the disclosure obligations under No. 3.1.1 of the NASDAQ-OMX Stock Exchange Rules and are therefore rarely applied.[47] This is unique in Europe, the disclosure obligations contained in the stock exchange rules playing an important, but only complementary role in the other European Member States.[48]

---

[40] Cf. P. Versteegen, in: H. Hirte and T.M.J. Möllers (eds.), *Kölner Kommentar zum WpHG*, § 15 para. 32–33.
[41] Cf. ibid., § 15 para. 30.
[42] BaFin, *Emittentenleitfaden 2009* (issuer guideline); on the legal nature and practical relevance of the issuer guideline see § 5 para. 39–40.
[43] See § 11 para. 21.
[44] Cf. S. Kalss et al. (eds.), *Kapitalmarktrecht I*, § 14 para. 1.
[45] Cf. ibid., § 14 para. 2.
[46] Cf. P. Versteegen, in: H. Hirte and T.M.J. Möllers (eds.), *Kölner Kommentar zum WpHG*, § 15 para. 52.
[47] Cf. R. Veil and F. Walla, *Schwedisches Kapitalmarktrecht*, p. 83–84.
[48] See below para. 26–27.

(d) France and Spain

21   In France Articles 223–1-A ff. RG AMF (General Regulations of the French Supervisory Authority) provide rules on the disclosure of inside information. The Spanish rules contained in Article 82 LMV (Spanish Securities Market Act) are put into more concrete terms by Articles 6 ff. RD 1333/2005 (Royal Decree on Market Abuse), Orden Ministerio de Economía y Hacienda (EHA, Spanish Ministry of Economy and Finance) 1421/2009 and Circular 4/2009 of the Comisión Nacional del Mercado de Valores (CNMV, Spanish National Stock Market Commission). Orden EHA 1421/2009 offers criteria for distinguishing relevant from non-relevant information and determines how prognoses are to be treated, whilst the appendix to Circular 4/2009 contains an exemplary list of information not subject to disclosure obligations. The obligation for an issuer to name a contact for the CNMV is unprecedented. Both countries have adopted the European provisions almost entirely one-to-one.

(e) Italy

22   Italy first introduced an obligation to disclose inside information when implementing the MAD by Legge no. 62 of 18 April 2005. The provisions are now included in Article 114 TUF (Italian Consolidated Laws on Finance) and put into more concrete terms by Article 65-duodecies ff. RE (Italian Issuers' Regulation).

23   Italy is the only Member State to have partly introduced provisions for corporate groups, due to its experience in numerous scandals, such as the case of *Antonveneta*, which might have been prevented if the parent company's liability had been more extensive. Italian law now also requires the disclosure of information directly concerning subsidiaries, which is not required by Article 6(1) MAD. Furthermore, the disclosure obligation does not only apply to the issuer itself but also to the subsidiary, independent of whether it is itself a listed company.

(f) United Kingdom

24   The United Kingdom implemented the MAD and Implementing Directive 2003/124/EG through the Market Abuse Directive (Disclosure Rules) Instrument 2005, FSA 2005/16 of 23 February 2005. The provisions were incorporated into section 2 of the FSA Handbook's Disclosure and Transparency Rules (DTR). The wording of the directive was taken over almost one-to-one and complemented with notes on interpretation, which are labelled "guidance"[49] and are comparable to the BaFin's issuer guideline.[50] The legal literature does not as yet appear to be particularly interested in these provisions,[51] possibly a result of the fact that until recently incorrect or omitted ad hoc notifications did not result in civil law liability.[52]

---

[49] Cf. R. Veil and M. Wundenberg, *Englisches Kapitalmarktrecht*, p. 111–112, 114.
[50] On the legal nature of the BaFin's *Emittentenleitfaden 2009* (issuer guideline) and the guidance see § 5 para. 21.
[51] Cf., however, A. Alcock, in: Lord Millett et al. (eds.), *Gore-Browne on Companies*, para. 41-3; A. Hudson, in: G. Morse, *Palmer's Company Law*, para. 5.576 ff.; P.L. Davies, *Gower and Davies' Principles of Modern Company Law*, para. 26-6; B. McDonnell, 88 COB (2011), p. 1 ff.
[52] Cf. R. Veil and M. Wundenberg, *Englisches Kapitalmarktrecht*, p. 113–114.

Philipp Koch

III. Obligation to Disclose Inside Information

1. Addressees

(a) Issuers of Financial Instruments

25   The obligation to disclose inside information as laid down in Article 6(1) and (3) MAD is addressed primarily to the issuers of financial instruments. Financial instruments are defined in Article 1 No. 3 MAD, the term meaning all instruments admitted to trading on a regulated market in a Member State or for which a request for admission to trading on such a market has been made.[53]

26   The Member States have implemented this definition accordingly.[54] Issuers of financial instruments not traded on the regulated market but rather on the German open market[55] or the Austrian unregulated third market,[56] for example, are therefore not subject to the disclosure obligations. The respective stock exchange rules may, however, provide similar obligations.

27   § 19(2)(a) of the General Terms and Conditions of the Deutsche Börse AG, for example, contains similar rules for the open market at the Frankfurt Stock Exchange.[57] In Austria, penalties for breaches of the stock exchange rules play an important role in the Prime Standard segment of the Vienna Stock Exchange.[58] The fact that the Swedish stock exchange rules play an important role not only for the open market but also for issuers whose financial instruments are admitted to trading on the regulated market has already been discussed.[59]

28   The question as to in which Member State an issuer is subject to disclosure proves technical and difficult to answer but essential for legal practice. Pursuant to Article 21(1) in conjunction with Article 2(1)(i) TD, an issuer is subject to the disclosure provisions in its home Member State. Article 21(3) TD modifies this home Member State rule for cases in which securities are admitted to trading on a regulated market in only one host Member State and not in the home Member State. In Germany, for example, so-called *Inlandsemittenten* (domestic issuers) are therefore subject to the disclosure obligation pursuant to § 15(1) WpHG in conjunction with § 2(7) WpHG.[60]

(b) Persons Acting on Behalf or on Account of the Issuer

29   Article 6(3) MAD extends the disclosure obligation to persons acting on behalf or

---

[53] On the term "financial instrument" see § 8 para. 4–9 and § 13 para. 46–47.

[54] Cf. for example § 48a(1) No. 3 BörseG (Austria); § 15(1)1 and 2 WpHG (Germany).

[55] Cf. P. Versteegen, in: H. Hirte and T.M.J. Möllers (eds.), *Kölner Kommentar zum WpHG*, § 15 para. 69; seen critically by D. Zimmer and H. Kruse, in: E. Schwark and D. Zimmer (eds.), *Kapitalmarktrechts-Kommentar*, § 15 WpHG para. 27 ff.

[56] Cf. S. Kalss et al. (eds.), *Kapitalmarktrecht I*, § 14 para. 4.

[57] See P. Storm, *Alternative Freiverkehrssegmente im Kapitalmarktrecht*, p. 33; R. Veil, in: U. Burgard et al. (eds.), *Festschrift für Uwe H. Schneider*, p. 1313, 1316 ff.

[58] Cf. S. Kalss et al. (eds.), *Kapitalmarktrecht I*, § 14 para. 55.

[59] See para. 20.

[60] In more detail see D. Zimmer and H. Kruse, in: E. Schwark and D. Zimmer (eds.), *Kapitalmarktrechts-Kommentar*, § 15 WpHG para. 19 ff.

on account of the issuer and who disclose inside information to third parties in the normal exercise of their employment, profession or duties. In legal practice this provision is of little importance.[61] In general the issuer will in these cases also be subject to a disclosure obligation due to the fact that it can no longer ensure that the information remains confidential.[62]

(c)   Companies Controlled by the Issuer

30   Constellations in which subsidiaries of a company are involved lead to a number of problems with regard to the disclosure of inside information. The MAD and most national laws provide no solution to these problems. Companies in a corporate group can then only be subject to disclosure obligations individually, and the parent company, for example, cannot be obliged to disclose information on the listed financial instruments of a subsidiary.[63]

31   Only Italy has extended the disclosure obligation in Article 114(1) TUF to information concerning a parent company's subsidiaries, justifying this with the fact that information in the subsidiary's sphere can also be relevant for the price of the parent company's financial instruments.[64]

2.   Relevant Information

(a)   Foundations

32   Pursuant to Article 6(1) MAD, issuers must disclose all inside information directly concerning them. In both this context and in the prohibitions on insider dealings the same definition of the term "inside information" applies.[65] The application of this term causes difficulties with regard to disclosure obligations in protracted sets of facts such as multi-stage decision-making processes. When determining disclosure obligations of an issuer one must further evaluate which element of the existing inside information directly affects the issuer and is thus subject to the obligation.

33   As a result, the inside information subject to disclosure will always be less than the inside information resulting in prohibitions of insider dealings. Information that only refers to the financial instruments[66] and information only concerning the issuer indirectly[67] need not be made public. Where derivatives are concerned, the

---

[61] Cf. L. Klöhn, WM (2010), p. 1869 ff. on the aspects of the German implementation in § 15(1)4 and 5 WpHG that reach farther than the directive.

[62] See below para. 98.

[63] Cf. M. Pfüller, in: A. Fuchs (ed.), Kommentar zum WpHG, § 15 para. 69 with further examples; on German law see L. Behn, Ad-hoc-Publizität und Unternehmensverbindungen (2012).

[64] Cf. F. Annunziata, La Disziplina del Mercato Mobiliare, p. 393.

[65] On the term "inside information" see § 13 para. 33–48.

[66] For Germany see J. Stoppel, in: B. Grunewald and M. Schlitt (eds.), Einführung in das Kapitalmarktrecht, p. 262; M. Pfüller, in: A. Fuchs (ed.), Kommentar zum WpHG, § 15 para. 123 ff.; D. Zimmer and H. Kruse, in: E. Schwark and D. Zimmer (eds.), Kapitalmarktrechts-Kommentar, § 15 WpHG para. 34; dissenting opinion H.-D. Assmann, in: H.-D. Assmann and U.H. Schneider (eds.), Kommentar zum WpHG, § 15 para. 56; H. Ziemons, NZG (2004), p. 537, 541; S. Simon, Der Konzern (2005), p. 13, 15. Information that primarily refers to the issued financial instruments can also directly affect the issuer, for example in cases of takeover offers. Cf. S. Kalss et al. (eds.), Kapitalmarktrecht I, § 14 para. 6 for Austria and for Germany below, para. 43.

[67] Cf. BaFin, Emittentenleitfaden 2009 (issuer guideline), p. 53; S. Grundmann, European Company Law, p. 471; J. Stoppel, in: B. Grunewald and M. Schlitt (eds.), Einführung in das Kapitalmarktrecht, p. 262; M. Pfüller,

---

respective information cannot refer to the issuer of the underlying asset.[68] This rule has been implemented one-to-one into most national laws.[69]

34   An exception can be found in Sweden, where the disclosure obligation is not attached to the term "inside information", but rather to the broader term "price-sensitive information". This even applies to the disclosure obligation in No. 3.1.1 of the NASDAQ-OMX Stock Exchange Rules, which is of particular relevance in legal practice.[70] The definition of price-sensitive information can be found in the official commentary on the Stock Exchange Rule, the Rulebook for Issuers.[71]

35   Spain also does not require the disclosure of inside information (*información privilegiada*), Article 82.1 LMV rather attaching the disclosure obligation to (price-) relevant information (*información relevante*). Whether information is (price-) relevant depends solely on its potential to influence the instrument price. Article 7.1 RD 1333/2005, however, makes exemptions from the disclosure obligation for preparatory measures to decisions which will be subject to disclosure obligations, i.e. particularly for the circumstances listed in Article 3(1) Implementing Directive 2003/124/EC. Whether the disclosure obligation is not applicable in these cases, as the wording of the provision suggests, or whether, in accordance with Article 6(2) MAD, the disclosure obligation can simply be delayed, remains unclear.[72] Some even maintain that, in compliance with the directive, the term *información relevante* must be interpreted as meaning *información privilegiada*.[73]

36   Additionally, the LMV explicitly subjects certain types of information to the disclosure obligations applying to inside information: certain shareholder agreements, Article 112 LMV, the corporate governance report, Article 116 LMV and information on planned, price relevant, measures if the stock price or trading volume develops suspiciously, Article 83 bis (1)(f) LMV. The Annex to the CNMV's Circular 4/2009 contains a list of examples regarding information subject to the disclosure obligation.

---

in: A. Fuchs (ed.), *Kommentar zum WpHG*, § 15 para. 120; D. Zimmer and H. Kruse, in: E. Schwark and D. Zimmer (eds.), *Kapitalmarktrechts-Kommentar*, § 15 WpHG para. 34.

[68] Cf. BaFin, *Emittentenleitfaden 2009* (issuer guideline), p. 55; H.-D. Assmann, in: H.-D. Assmann and U.H. Schneider (eds.), *Kommentar zum WpHG*, § 15 para. 57.

[69] For Germany see §§ 15(1)1, 13 WpHG. See R. Veil and M. Wundenberg, *Englisches Kapitalmarktrecht*, p. 112–113 on the legal situation in the UK, where the term inside information is defined in sec. 118C FSMA. For France: Art. 223-2-I, 621-1 RG AMF. For Austria: § 48d BörseG and S. Kalss et al. (eds.), *Kapitalmarktrecht I*, § 14 para. 5. For Italy: Art. 114(1), 181 TUF which extends the term "inside information" to information directly affecting the issuer's subsidiaries.

[70] Cf. R. Veil and F. Walla, *Schwedisches Kapitalmarktrecht*, p. 83.

[71] NASDAQ-OMX, *Rulebook for Issuers*, as of 1 January 2009, p. 21 ff.

[72] See below para. 63 ff.

[73] Cf. D. Entrena Ruiz, *El empleo de información privilegiada en el mercado de valores: un estudio de su régimen administrativo sancionador*, p. 75–76; Madrazo, 2 RMV (2008), p. 471, 473 ff.; dissenting opinion: M. Iribarren Blanco, *Responsabilidad civil por la información divulgada por las sociedades cotizadas*, p. 90 ff., who recommends that insider prohibitions should be more extensive than the disclosure obligations.

```

Body:

*(b)* *Information Directly Concerning the Issuer*

37 The MAD does not offer a definition as to when information "directly concerns the issuer". This causes problems in legal practice, where the term needs to be put into more concrete terms in order to be applied correctly. Fulfilling its former role on Level 3 of the Lamfalussy Process,[74] the CESR published a positive list of circumstances which generally directly concern the issuer and a negative list of circumstances that will generally only concern an issuer indirectly.[75] The BaFin's issuer guideline contains a further, more detailed list, although none of these lists can be regarded as final. They must rather be understood as listing the most common constellations, the given examples having, however, to be interpreted in the light of the respective situation. Under certain circumstances a constellation may thus have to be regarded as concerning the issuer directly although it is listed as generally not doing so, and vice versa.[76]

38 Whilst these lists offer indispensable guidance to legal practice, they cannot replace a definition of the term. The level of discussion on this subject varies across Member States.[77]

39 General economic and market data do not fall within the direct concern of the issuer and are therefore not subject to the disclosure obligation. The distinction may, however, prove difficult in individual cases.[78] Similarly, the issuer generally need not disclose changes concerning competitors[79] and the development of commodity prices.[80]

40 As opposed to this, circumstances in the issuer's field of activity are always subject to disclosure. These constellations generally constitute the most important group of relevant information to be published and usually refer to measures taken by the management or other bodies of the issuer,[81] business-related activities undertaken by employees and any developments originating within the issuer's business.[82]

41 Article 7 Insider Directive, which was applicable before the MAD came into force, limited the disclosure obligations to this group of information. In Germany, the wording of § 15(1)3 WpHG still indicates this: the obligation to disclose this

---

[74] See § 4 para. 22.
[75] CESR, *Market Abuse Directive Level 3—second set of CESR guidance and information on the common operation of the Directive to the market*, CESR/06-562b, July 2007, p. 7 ff.; CESR, (amended version of) *CESR's Advice on Level 2 Implementing Measures for the proposed Market Abuse Directive*, CESR/02-089d, December 2002, p. 12 ff.
[76] H.-D. Assmann, in: H.-D. Assmann and U.H. Schneider (eds.), *Kommentar zum WpHG*, § 15 para. 62, 66–67; BaFin, *Emittentenleitfaden 2009* (issuer guideline), p. 55.
[77] On the practically non-existent discussion in the United Kingdom see R. Veil and M. Wundenberg, *Englisches Kapitalmarktrecht*, p. 112–113.
[78] For Germany: J. Stoppel, in: B. Grunewald and M. Schlitt (eds.), *Einführung in das Kapitalmarktrecht*, p. 263; H.-D. Assmann, in: H.-D. Assmann and U.H. Schneider (eds.), *Kommentar zum WpHG*, § 15 para. 64; M. Pfüller, in: A. Fuchs (ed.), *Kommentar zum WpHG*, § 15 para. 121, 126 ff. For Austria: S. Kalss et al. (eds.), *Kapitalmarktrecht I*, § 14 para. 9. For Italy: F. Annunziata, *La Disciplina del Mercato Mobiliare*, p. 396; S. Seminara, 3 Banca Borsa tit. Cred. (2008), p. 331, 348; F. Bruno and N. Ravasio, 8 Le Società (2007), p. 1026, 1029.
[79] For Germany: BaFin, *Emittentenleitfaden 2009* (issuer guideline), p. 54; J. Stoppel, in: B. Grunewald and M. Schlitt (eds.), *Einführung in das Kapitalmarktrecht*, p. 263. For Austria: S. Kalss et al. (eds.), *Kapitalmarktrecht I*, § 14 para. 9.
[80] H.-D. Assmann, in: H.-D. Assmann and U.H. Schneider (eds.), *Kommentar zum WpHG*, § 15 para. 64.
[81] Ibid., § 15 para. 59.
[82] Ibid., § 15 para. 61.

Philipp Koch
```

information is now listed as one of the "particular" cases in which information is to be classed as inside information.

42   Defining the disclosure obligations on the basis of whether the information has an effect on the issuer's financial situation is no longer a viable distinction: altering the dividend payments and changing the stock market segment or the legal form of the company does not influence the financial situation of the company but may still be subject to disclosure obligations.[83]

43   The disclosure obligation is not restricted to developments and activities in the issuer's sphere of activity.[84] Takeover offers made by another company, for example, also directly concern the issuer, control over the company not only having an effect on the financial instruments of the company but also on the decision-making process in the general meeting of the target company.[85] The same applies to squeeze-out procedures[86] or to changes in an agency's rating of the company.[87] In Italy it has been suggested that all information on developments or events that have their roots in the company itself and affect its income and financial situation or its future development chances, together with all information on other situations involving particular risks, should be subject to disclosure.[88]

44   Whether disclosure obligations exist can be particularly difficult to determine regarding external circumstances with an effect on the issuer. In general, it will have to be agreed with the BaFin that external circumstances only rarely concern the issuer directly.[89]

(c)   Future Circumstances

45   Information on future circumstances can also constitute inside information.[90] Whilst it appears justifiable to base the prohibition of insider dealings on such a wide definition of inside information, problems then arise with regard to disclosure. An early disclosure can prejudice an issuer's legitimate interest and will not always be helpful to the public, who may evaluate the information incorrectly and be misled.[91]

---

[83] For Austria: S. Kalss et al. (eds.), *Kapitalmarktrecht I*, § 14 para. 10. For Germany: T.M.J. Möllers, ZBB (2003), p. 390, 392; O. Tollkühn, ZIP (2004), p. 2215, 2217. For Italy: P. Sfameni, *Art. 114. Comunicazioni al pubblico*, in: P. Marchetti, and L.A. Bianchi, (eds.), *La disciplina delle società quotate*, p. 518 ff.; stricter CESR, *Market Abuse Directive Level 3—second set of CESR guidance and information on the common operation of the Directive to the market*, CESR/06–562b, July 2007, p. 7–8; BaFin, *Emittentenleitfaden 2009* (issuer guideline), p. 54.

[84] For Germany: H.-D. Assmann, in: H.-D. Assmann and U.H. Schneider (eds.), *Kommentar zum WpHG*, § 15 para. 10; D. Zimmer and H. Kruse, in: E. Schwark and D. Zimmer (eds.), *Kapitalmarktrechts-Kommentar*, § 15 WpHG para. 36.

[85] For Germany: J. Stoppel, in: B. Grunewald and M. Schlitt (eds.), *Einführung in das Kapitalmarktrecht*, p. 263; more extensively M. Pfüller, in: A. Fuchs (ed.), *Kommentar zum WpHG*, § 15 para. 128 ff.

[86] For Germany: BaFin, *Emittentenleitfaden 2009* (issuer guideline), p. 53; distinguishing: D. Zimmer and H. Kruse, in: E. Schwark and D. Zimmer (eds.), *Kapitalmarktrechts-Kommentar*, § 15 WpHG para. 44.

[87] O. Tollkühn, ZIP (2004), p. 2215, 2216; Begr. Regt, BT-Drucks. 15/3174, p. 35 (explanatory notes).

[88] P. Sfameni, *Art. 114. Comunicazioni al pubblico*, in: P. Marchetti and L.A. Bianchi, (eds.), *La disciplina delle società quotate*, p. 518 ff. Under the terminology of Italian legal literature only "corporate information" is subject to a disclosure obligation. This, however, does not only include information in the issuer's field of activity.

[89] BaFin, *Emittentenleitfaden 2009* (issuer guideline), p. 53.

[90] See § 13 para. 35–41.

[91] See above para. 3.

46   Nevertheless, future circumstances that directly concern the issuer must be disclosed pursuant to the MAD and its national implementations, most of which introduced a uniform definition of inside information for insider dealings and disclosure obligations. A reconciliation of interests is therefore only possible by granting the possibility of delayed disclosure. This is common ground in Germany and Austria.[92]

47   Italian law follows a different, and unique, approach: Article 66 RE limits the disclosure obligation to current or past events and circumstances (so-called "hard information"), and does not extend it to so-called "soft information", i.e. information based on conclusions or an assessment of uncertain future events.[93] Consob has explicitly stated that whilst information on future events may constitute inside information under Article 181 TUF, thus affecting the prohibitions on insider dealings, it cannot lead to disclosure obligations pursuant to Article 114(1) TUF.[94] Consob has thus confirmed that under Italian law intentions and strategic aims need not generally be disclosed as their outcome remains unclear.[95]

48   Consob's understanding is unique in Europe. Consob justifies its position on the basis that it is the result of having put the term "directly concerning the issuer" into more concrete terms, as permitted by European law. Consob further refers to the issuers' legitimate interests, which thus do not only become relevant with regard to a possible delay in disclosure (Article 114(3) TUF in conjunction with Article 66 bis RE) in Italy.[96] Following the Italian concept, a delay in disclosure until the respective decision has been made or the measure has been taken is not necessary, as no obligation to disclose the information exists, provided the issuer ensures the confidentiality of the information.[97] In accordance with the German and Austrian point of view, this approach is to be rejected as contrary to the directive.

(d)   Corporate Group Constellations

49   The particularly difficult constellations of corporate groups have only been included in the provisions on disclosure in Italy.[98] German legal literature follows a number of approaches.[99] Whilst only Italy subjects the corporate group and not only the individual companies to the disclosure obligations, information on subsidiaries can also cause disclosure obligations for the parent company in other Member States, especially with regard to consolidated financial statements.[100]

---

[92] For Germany: BaFin, *Emittentenleitfaden 2009* (issuer guideline), p. 60–61; BGH ZIP (2011), p. 72; BGH ZIP (2008), p. 639; OLG Stuttgart, ZIP (2009), p. 962, 965; in more detail: H. Fleischer, NZG (2007), p. 401, 403. For Austria: S. Kalss et al. (eds.), *Kapitalmarktrecht I*, § 14 para. 5.

[93] Cf. P. Sfameni, *Art. 114. Comunicazioni al pubblico*, in: P. Marchetti and L.A. Bianchi (eds.), *La disciplina delle società quotate*, p. 522 f; M. Rigotti, *Informativa societaria*, in: Griffi, Antonio et al. (eds.), *Intermediari finanziari, mercati e società quotate*, p. 168; S. Seminara, 3 Banca Borsa tit. Cred. (2008), p. 331, 349; F. Mucciarelli, Banca Borsa tit. Cred. I (1999), p. 754, 758 ff.

[94] Consob, *Comunicazione n. DME/6027054*, 28 March 2006, para. 5–6.

[95] Ibid., para. 19.

[96] Cf. F. Bruno and N. Ravasio, 8 Le Società (2007), p. 1026, 1028.

[97] Consob, *Comunicazione n. DME/6027054*, 28 March 2006, para. 11.

[98] See above para. 22.

[99] In more detail: J. Stoppel, in: B. Grunewald and M. Schlitt (eds.), *Einführung in das Kapitalmarktrecht*, p. 266–267 with further references.

[100] For Germany: M. Pfüller, in: A. Fuchs (ed.), *Kommentar zum WpHG*, § 15 para. 160 ff. For Austria: S. Kalss et al. (eds.), *Kapitalmarktrecht I*, § 14 para. 8.

Philipp Koch

50   If both the parent company and the subsidiary are subject to the disclosure obliga-
      tion, they must both fulfil this obligation individually.[101] Unlike in the disclosure
      regime for major shareholdings,[102] it is not possible for the parent company to
      fulfil the subsidiary's disclosure obligation, as sufficient information of the sub-
      sidiary's investors would not be ensured.[103] Nevertheless some maintain that joint
      declarations are permitted and are common in the legal practice of the Member
      States.[104] In particular the Italian Consob regards double-disclosure obligations as
      superfluous, although these are required by the wording of Article 114(1) TUF.
      Consob rather purports that it is sufficient for the market's interest in informa-
      tion if both companies make a joint disclosure or only one company publishes
      the respective ad hoc notification.[105]

51   Parts of the Italian legal literature further proclaim that an issuer's disclosure
      obligation should be limited to such information which subsidiaries are legally
      obligated to pass on to the issuer.[106] The issuer would otherwise be obligated to
      disclose information to which it has no legal way of gaining access, requiring him
      to do something legally impossible to fulfil his legal obligation as the subsidiary
      is not permitted to pass on this information as this would constitute a breach of
      insider law.

(e)   Relationship to Other Disclosure Rules

52   The MAD does not determine the relationship between the disclosure obligation
      for inside information and other disclosure obligations. This question has, however,
      been examined by the German legal literature.

53   The relationship between the rules on periodic disclosure and those on the disclo-
      sure of inside information plays a particularly important role. Generally speaking,
      both regimes are simultaneously applicable and independent from each another,
      the disclosure of inside information not only being an addition to the rules on
      periodic disclosure but also an independent instrument aimed at combating insider
      dealing.[107] Information subject to the rules on periodic disclosure may thus also
      have to be made public as inside information prior to its disclosure in the financial
      reports, if it is price sensitive. The upcoming publication of a financial report does
      not release the issuer from his duty to disclose inside information as soon as pos-

---

[101] Dissenting opinion for Austria: S. Kalss et al. (eds.), *Kapitalmarktrecht I*, § 14 para. 8 based on the fact that
the information becomes publicly known once one company discloses it and therefore loses its nature as inside
information; similarly for Germany: O. Tollkühn, ZIP (2004), p. 2215, 2217.

[102] See § 20 para. 31.

[103] Cf. M. Pfüller, in: A. Fuchs (ed.), *Kommentar zum WpHG*, § 15 para. 164 with further references; L. Behn,
Ad-hoc-Publizität und Unternehmensverbindungen, p. 90.

[104] For Austria: S. Kalss et al. (eds.), *Kapitalmarktrecht I*, § 14 para. 8.

[105] Consob, *Comunicazione n. DME/6027054*, 28 March 2006, para. 21–22; see also F. Annunziata, *La Disciplina del Mercato Mobiliare*, p. 394.

[106] Cf. P. Sfameni, *Art. 114. Comunicazioni al pubblico*, in: P. Marchetti, and L.A. Bianchi (eds.), *La disciplina delle società quotate*, p. 623; on the information obligations of a subsidiary towards the parent company:
G. Ferrarini, *I gruppi nella regolazione finanziaria*, in: *I gruppi di società: Atti del Convegno internazionale di studi*,
p. 1233, 1241 ff.; P. Abbadessa, *La circolazione delle informazioni all'interno del gruppo*, in: *I gruppi di società: Atti
del Convegno internazionale di studi*, p. 567, 571; G. Scognamiglio, 2 Riv. Dir. Civ (1995), p. 49, 66–67; partly
dissenting: L. Behn, *Ad-hoc-Publizität und Unternehmensverbindungen*, p. 116 ff.

[107] See above para. 2–3.

Philipp Koch

sible.[108] In some cases, it may, however, be possible to delay disclosure until the publication of the information takes place on the basis of the periodic disclosure duties.[109]

54   Not every financial report will contain inside information that would be subject to an additional disclosure obligation. When compiling the report, the issuer will often be faced with a protracted set of facts and will always have to check closely whether and when they will lead to a disclosure obligation on the basis of inside information.[110] In Germany, the supervisory board's participation in the adoption of the annual financial report pursuant to § 172 AktG (German Stock Corporation Act) will regularly justify a delay in disclosure, based on the rules for multi-stage decision-making processes.[111]

55   In general the obligation to disclose inside information is also independent from all other rules of transparency on the capital markets and the time limits for their disclosure.[112]

56   This especially refers to the rules on disclosure regarding major shareholdings, as laid down in Germany in §§ 21 ff. WpHG, for example.[113] Changes in the structure of shareholdings can have a direct effect on the issuer even before the thresholds regarding control have been reached, if the changes require the issuer to take certain measures.[114] The same applies with regard to the disclosure obligations for directors' dealings (cf. for Germany § 15a WpHG), although these will generally be of indirect concern to the issuer.[115]

57   The legal situation in German takeover law is different: § 10(6) WpÜG (German Securities Acquisiton and Takeover Act) explicitly states that § 15 WpHG should not apply in respect to "decisions to make an offer".[116] As opposed to this, the target company remains subject to the disclosure obligation in § 15 WpHG.[117] § 35(1) WpÜG makes reference to § 10(6) WpÜG for constellations in which control over a company is gained. Whether this conforms to the MAD's provisions appears doubtful.[118] Any exemption from the obligation to make inside information public beyond

---

[108] For Germany: BaFin, *Emittentenleitfaden 2009* (issuer guideline), p. 58–59; H.-D. Assmann, in: H.-D. Assmann and U.H. Schneider (eds.), *Kommentar zum WpHG*, § 15 para. 37; M. Pfüller, in: A. Fuchs (ed.), *Kommentar zum WpHG*, § 15 para. 171; P. Versteegen, in: H. Hirte and T.M.J. Möllers (eds.), *Kölner Kommentar zum WpHG*, § 15 para. 130. For Austria: FMA, *Jahresbericht 2009* (annual report), p. 111.

[109] For Germany: H.-D. Assmann, in: H.-D. Assmann and U.H. Schneider (eds.), *Kommentar zum WpHG*, § 15 para. 35.

[110] See § 13 para. 39–41.

[111] For Germany: M. Pfüller, in: A. Fuchs (ed.), *Kommentar zum WpHG*, § 15 para. 170.

[112] For Germany: BaFin, *Emittentenleitfaden 2009* (issuer guideline), p. 58–59; P. Versteegen, in: H. Hirte and T.M.J. Möllers (eds.), *Kölner Kommentar zum WpHG*, § 15 para. 135.

[113] See also § 20 para. 13.

[114] For Germany: M. Pfüller, in: A. Fuchs (ed.), *Kommentar zum WpHG*, § 15 para. 181; D. Zimmer and H. Kruse, in: E. Schwark and D. Zimmer (eds.), *Kapitalmarktrechts-Kommentar*, § 15 WpHG para. 15.

[115] For Germany: M. Pfüller, in: A. Fuchs (ed.), *Kommentar zum WpHG*, § 15 para. 230; P. Versteegen, in: H. Hirte and T.M.J. Möllers (eds.), *Kölner Kommentar zum WpHG*, § 15 para. 135.

[116] Cf. H.-D. Assmann, in: H.-D. Assmann and U.H. Schneider (eds.), *Kommentar zum WpHG*, § 15 para. 38.

[117] Cf. G. Bachmann, 172 ZHR (2008), p. 597, 616 with further references. See also § 24 para. 29.

[118] Cf. T.O. Brandi and R. Süßmann, AG (2004), p. 642, 651; P. Versteegen, in: H. Hirte and T.M.J. Möllers (eds.), *Kölner Kommentar zum WpHG*, § 15 para. 132.

these rules is most certainly illegal[119] and benchmark data of an envisaged offer will have to be published pursuant to § 15 WpHG, even if not pursuant to § 10 WpÜG.[120]

3. No Offsetting of Information

58   In the United Kingdom issuers have occasionally argued that negative information could be cancelled out by positive information. If the market expectations are not changed by the information as a whole, disclosure should not be necessary. The FSA ultimately refuted this approach in its ruling in the case of *Wolfson Microelectronics plc*:

59   *Facts (abridged):*[121] Wolfson Microelectronics plc was a listed company that produced semiconductors for consumer electronics. On 10 March 2008 a major customer, formerly generating approximately 18% of Wolfson's revenue, told Wolfson that they would not be ordering parts for future editions of products A and B, two of the major customer's products. For Wolfson this represented a loss of 8% of its forecast revenue for the year. At the same time Wolfson was informed that the same major customer would increase its demand for the supply of parts for product C, making Wolfson's overall revenues from the major customer in 2008 equivalent to those of the previous year. On the recommendation of external consultants, Wolfson disclosed the information on the loss of the order for products A and B on 27 March 2008, subsequently suffering an 18% fall in its share price.

60   The FSA ruled that the delay in disclosing information breached the obligation to disclose inside information as soon as possible to conform with DTR 2.2.1 and Listing Principle 4. Offsetting negative and positive news is not acceptable. Rather, companies should disclose both types of information and allow the market to determine whether, and to what degree, the positive information compensates for the negative information. Additionally, Wolfson's calculations failed to take the implications for revenues post 2008 into account although the previously anticipated level of 2008 revenues could be achieved. The information was significant for investors with regard to its implications for Wolfson's future status vis-à-vis the major customer.

4. Prohibition to Disclose Other Information

61   Transparency can be affected not only by price-sensitive information which remains undisclosed but also by a flood of information, impairing the processing of information important for investment decisions.[122] In Spain, the disclosure of future circumstances, which are not yet entirely certain, is understood as the most severe

---

[119] Cf. P. Versteegen, in: H. Hirte and T.M.J. Möllers (eds.), *Kölner Kommentar zum WpHG*, § 15 para. 134; D. Zimmer and H. Kruse, in: E. Schwark and D. Zimmer (eds.), *Kapitalmarktrechts-Kommentar*, § 15 WpHG para. 14.

[120] H.-D. Assmann, in: H.-D. Assmann and U.H. Schneider (eds.), *Kommentar zum WpHG*, § 15 para. 38; Pfüller, in: A. Fuchs (ed.), *Kommentar zum WpHG*, § 15 para. 195 ff.

[121] FSA, *Final Notice*, 19 January 2009; cf. B. McDonnell, 88 COB (2011), p. 1, 13–14; R. Veil and M. Wundenberg, *Englisches Kapitalmarktrecht*, p. 117–118.

[122] Cf. H.-D. Assmann, in: H.-D. Assmann and U.H. Schneider (eds.), *Kommentar zum WpHG*, § 15 para. 53.

risk to transparency regarding inside information.[123] Other issuers can use the disclosure as an instrument towards investor relations. The German legislator reacted to this by introducing § 15(2)1 WpHG, which prohibits the disclosure of information that "obviously fails to meet the [disclosure] requirement".[124] The provision is complemented by § 4(1)2 WpAIV which requires that the publication be kept short.[125] In Spain similar rules are being demanded,[126] whilst the Italian Consob tolerates issuers' far-reaching disclosures.[127]

5. Publication Procedure

62   The TD has amended the MAD's rules on the procedure according to which inside information must be made public.[128] According to Articles 19 and 21 TD, disclosure consists of two elements. Firstly, the issuer must file the information by electronic means via his website and such media as may reasonably be relied upon for the effective dissemination of information to the public throughout the Community. Secondly, it must submit the information to the central national storage system for regulated information.[129] In Germany, the issuer must additionally inform the BaFin and the stock exchange management pursuant to § 15(4)1 Nos. 1–3 WpHG.

IV. Delay in Disclosure

1.   Foundations

63   The far-reaching disclosure obligation laid down in Article 6(1)1 MAD, which also extends to future circumstances, requires correction.[130] In some cases, such as mergers or squeeze-outs, the early disclosure of this intent may endanger its success. Article 6(2)1 MAD therefore permits the issuer to delay the public disclosure of inside information under his own responsibility, if (i) the disclosure would prejudice his legitimate interests, (ii) the omission is not likely to mislead the public and (iii) the issuer is able to ensure the confidentiality of the information. Most Member States have remained close to this wording in their implementations,[131] an exception being Sweden, which allows the disclosure to be delayed if it is based on objec-

---

[123] As maintained by our Spanish interview partners (see fn. 20).

[124] Cf. H.-D. Assmann, in: H.-D. Assmann and U.H. Schneider (eds.), *Kommentar zum WpHG*, § 15 para. 199 ff.; M. Pfüller, in: A. Fuchs (ed.), *Kommentar zum WpHG*, § 15 para. 15–16; see also para. 8.

[125] Cf. further P. Versteegen, in: H. Hirte and T.M.J. Möllers (eds.), *Kölner Kommentar zum WpHG*, § 15 para. 255 ff.

[126] Cf. M. Iribarren Blanco, *Responsabilidad civil por la información divulgada por las sociedades cotizadas*, p. 22–23.

[127] As maintained by our Italian interview partners (see fn. 20).

[128] See above para. 14.

[129] See § 22 for further details.

[130] M. Pfüller, in: A. Fuchs (ed.), *Kommentar zum WpHG*, § 15 para. 355; S.H. Schneider, BB (2005), p. 897, 897, recommending a large scope of application for delay; similarly G. Bachmann, 172 ZHR (2008), p. 597, 608. See also S. Gilotta, 13 EBOR (2012), p. 45 ff. emphasising the issuer's need for secrecy.

[131] For Germany: § 15(3) WpHG. For Austria: § 48d(2) BörseG. For the United Kingdom: DTR 2.5 FSA Handbook; in more detail: R. Veil and M. Wundenberg, *Englisches Kapitalmarktrecht*, p. 113 ff. For Italy: Art. 114(3) TUF. For Spain: Art. 82.4 LMV. For France: Art. 223-2-II RG AMF, in more detail: R. Veil and P. Koch, *Französisches Kapitalmarktrecht*, p. 77–78.

tive criteria, the public is not misled and the confidentiality of the information is ensured.[132] The importance of this possibility of delay in the disclosure regime for inside information cannot be emphasised enough.[133]

64 Article 6(2)2 MAD enables the Member States to require that an issuer must immediately inform the competent authority of the decision to delay the public disclosure of inside information. Some Member States have made use of this possibility.[134] In legal practice, the issuers often do not only inform the supervisory authority but rather consult with it informally. In Spain this is so common that contrary to Article 82.4 LMV it is often assumed that the CNMV must grant the delay.[135] In Sweden, the FI is only rarely involved, but issuers consult with the stock exchange management, which is in effect the only authority responsible for the supervision of the disclosure of inside information.[136] The cooperation between the issuers and the authorities may be the reason why these Member States provide almost no material on the legal practice of the courts and supervisory authorities.

65 Germany and France do not require the issuer to inform the competent authority of the decision to delay the disclosure. In Germany, it is sufficient if the issuer informs the BaFin subsequently. The legislator's aim was to achieve a deregulation and reduce the BaFin's obligations. Otherwise the BaFin would have had to supervise the decision to delay disclosure pursuant to its general supervisory obligations under § 4 WpHG. This would have corresponded with the legal situation before the implementation of the MAD where, pursuant to § 15(1)5 WpHG in its former version, the issuer had to apply for an administrative act granting him the delay.[137] This form of indirect control now exists in Austria, which formerly also required an application for the delay.[138] In the legislative procedures concerning the MAD Germany took the former legal situation and the risk of a liability of the authorities for damages into consideration and explicitly recommended a conception of Article 6(2) MAD according to which the issuer alone is responsible for the delay.[139] For the issuer this deregulation results in a great risk: a delay that does not comply with the requirements is now no longer authorised by the authority's binding decision which even protected the issuer from liability before the civil law courts.[140]

66 The—short—period necessary for determining whether a disclosure obligation exists is not regarded as a delay as in these cases the disclosure takes place "as

---

[132] Cf. Kapitel 15, § 7 LVM which also the practically relevant stock exchange rules refer to.

[133] Cf. D. Zimmer and H. Kruse, in: E. Schwark and D. Zimmer (eds.), *Kapitalmarktrechts-Kommentar*, § 15 WpHG para. 52.

[134] For Italy: Art. 66-bis (4) RE. For Spain cf. Art. 82.4 2 LMV. For Austria: § 48d(2) BörseG.

[135] Cf. R. Palá Laguna, in: Artigas et al. (eds.), *Derecho de Sociedades Anónimas Cotizadas*, p. 1291, 1311, 1313; L. Cortés, in: A. Menéndez, *Lecciones de Derecho Mercantil*, p. 755.

[136] R. Veil and F. Walla, *Schwedisches Kapitalmarktrecht*, p. 87.

[137] Cf. M. Pfüller, in: A. Fuchs (ed.), *Kommentar zum WpHG*, § 15 para. 342, 347; H.-D. Assmann, in: H.-D. Assmann and U.H. Schneider (eds.), *Kommentar zum WpHG*, § 15 para. 131–132.

[138] Cf. S. Kalss et al. (eds.), *Kapitalmarktrecht I*, § 14 para. 31.

[139] S.H. Schneider, BB (2005), p. 897, 897; H.-D. Assmann, in: H.-D. Assmann and U.H. Schneider (eds.), *Kommentar zum WpHG*, § 15 para. 131; cf. T.M.J. Möllers, WM (2005), p. 1393, 1395; D. Zimmer and H. Kruse, in: E. Schwark and D. Zimmer (eds.), *Kapitalmarktrechts-Kommentar*, § 15 WpHG para. 52.

[140] For Germany: M. Pfüller, in: A. Fuchs (ed.), *Kommentar zum WpHG*, § 15 para. 348. For Austria: S. Kalss et al. (eds.), *Kapitalmarktrecht I*, § 14 para. 45.

Philipp Koch

soon as possible".[141] After this period a delay is only possible provided the above-mentioned prerequisites are given; in the case that a requirement ceases to exist, the information must be disclosed immediately. The issuer must therefore check continually whether all the requirements for the delay are still given.[142] This means that disclosure may in some cases be delayed indefinitely, as the MAD contains no maximum duration for the delay.

67   The issuer will then have to disclose the information without undue delay. The relevant date for assessing which information must be disclosed is the time at which the requirements for the delay cease to exist. If by this time the information has lost its character as inside information it need not be disclosed. This is, for example, conceivable, if the issuer has meanwhile abandoned his plans to take certain measures.[143]

2.   Legitimate Interests

68   The issuer's "legitimate interests" that may justify a delay in disclosure are a key element of the disclosure regime. It is therefore essential to put this abstract concept into more concrete terms.

(a)   Requirements under European Law

69   Whilst the European legislator does not define the term "legitimate interests", Article 3(1) of Directive 2003/124/EC lists two "non-exhaustive circumstances" to which the legitimate interests may relate. These are:

70   (i)   negotiations in course, or related elements, where the outcome or normal pattern of those negotiations would be likely to be affected by public disclosure. In particular, in the event that the financial viability of the issuer is in grave and imminent danger;

71   (ii)   decisions taken or contracts made by the management body of an issuer which need the approval of another body of the issuer in order to become effective, where the organisation of such an issuer requires the separation between these bodies, provided that a public disclosure of the information before such approval together with the simultaneous announcement that this approval is still pending would jeopardise the correct assessment of the information by the public ("multi-stage decision-making processes").

72   The CESR has put both constellations into more concrete terms and given examples which mainly include the acquisition or disposal of shares, product development and patents. The CESR refrained from providing a list of further circumstances, in order to prevent this from counteracting the delay's nature as an exception. Nevertheless

---

[141] Cf. on the German implementation BaFin, *Emittentenleitfaden 2009* (issuer guideline), p. 66; S.H. Schneider, BB (2005), p. 897, 901.

[142] Cf. CESR, *Market Abuse Directive Level 3—second set of CESR guidance and information on the common operation of the Directive to the market*, CESR/06–562b, July 2007, p. 11.

[143] For Germany: § 15(3)2 WpHG and BaFin, *Emittentenleitfaden 2009* (issuer guideline), p. 65; H.-D. Assmann, in: H.-D. Assmann and U.H. Schneider (eds.), *Kommentar zum WpHG*, § 15 para. 173; J. Stoppel, in: B. Grunewald and M. Schlitt (eds.), *Einführung in das Kapitalmarktrecht*, p. 265–266 with further references on dissenting opinions.

this does not mean that either the cases listed in Article 3(1) Directive 2003/124/EC or the CESR's examples are exhaustive.[144]

(b)   Legal Practice in the Member States

73   Most Member States have adopted the exact wording of Article 3(1) Directive 2003/124/EC.[145] In particular, the second constellation referring to multi-stage decision-making processes is being discussed intensively. Some Member States have added further circumstances, whilst others have attempted a dogmatic approach to the legal issues arising from the term "legitimate interests of the issuer".

74   In this context the different national legal traditions become particularly apparent. The United Kingdom puts the emphasis on disclosure, placing less importance on the issuer's interests.[146] According to the FSA, a delay is only possible in the constellations listed in its Handbook, accepting no further constellations that may justify a delay.[147] Spain has largely avoided developing any national specifications, orientating itself entirely towards the European level, based on the argument that on Level 4 of the Lamfalussy Process the CESR is entrusted to put the legislative acts into more concrete terms. The CESR's recommendations on the application and interpretation of the MAD are therefore taken especially seriously in Spain.[148] As opposed to this and on the recommendation of the legal literature, the BaFin in Germany interprets the constellations in which a delay is permitted very generously, and does not adhere to the given constellations.[149] In Italy, the strict understanding of the term "inside information" in the context of disclosure obligations, with the result that many constellations already do not fall within the scope of the disclosure obligation,[150] has the effect that the question whether a delay should be permitted only rarely arises.

(aa)   Attempts at a Dogmatic Approach

75   Especially in Germany, attempts have been made not only to develop further constellations but also to find a dogmatic approach to the question when legitimate interests of the issuer justify a delay in disclosure. § 6 sentence 1 WpAIV assumes that a legitimate interest in delaying publication exists if the issuer's interest in keeping the information secret outweighs the interest of the capital market in complete and prompt publication.

---

[144] Cf. CESR, *Market Abuse Directive Level 3—second set of CESR guidance and information on the common operation of the Directive to the market*, CESR/06–562b, July 2007, p. 9–10.

[145] For the United Kingsdom: DTR 2.5.4 FSA Handbook and the ensuing restrictions, R. Veil and M. Wundenberg, *Englisches Kapitalmarktrecht*, p. 115. For Spain: Art. 7.1 RD 1333/2005. For France: Art. 223-2-III RG AMF. For Austria: § 48d(2) No. 1(a) and (b) BörseG. For Italy: Art. 66-bis(2) RE. For Germany: § 6 sentence 2 WpAIV and on the requirement of an interpretation in accordance with the Market Abuse Directive, H.-D. Assmann, in: H.-D. Assmann and U.H. Schneider (eds.), *Kommentar zum WpHG*, § 15 para. 138.

[146] P.L. Davies, *Gower and Davies' Principles of Modern Company Law*, para. 26-6; R. Veil and M. Wundenberg, *Englisches Kapitalmarktrecht*, p. 115; see also N. Moloney, *EC Securities Regulation*, p. 973 for the "limited delay mechanism".

[147] Cf. DTR 2.5.5 FSA Handbook.

[148] Cf. M. Iribarren Blanco, *Responsabilidad civil por la información divulgada por las sociedades cotizadas*, p. 93, 101 ff.

[149] Cf. BaFin, *Emittentenleitfaden 2009* (issuer guideline), p. 67; P. Versteegen, in: H. Hirte and T.M.J. Möllers (eds.), *Kölner Kommentar zum WpHG*, § 15 Anh.—§ 6 WpAIV para. 20.

[150] See above para. 47–48.

---

76   The issuer has an interest in keeping the information secret if a disclosure of the information may be detrimental to him. The detriment need not necessarily refer to the same circumstances as the respective inside information but may, for example, affect the autonomy of a company's bodies; neither the wording nor the aim of Article 6(1)1 MAD and § 6 sentence 1 WpAIV require a restrictive interpretation in this sense.[151] Third-party interests are generally irrelevant. Especially in corporate group constellations, however, the interests of a third company can sometimes become interests of the issuer.[152] The detriment need not be a certainty—a mere probability that the detriment will occur already being sufficient to justify the issuer's interest in the delay. This approach coincides with the wording of Article 6(2) MAD[153] and is also taken in France.[154]

77   § 6 sentence 1 WpAIV requires that the issuer's interests outweigh those of the capital market. This must be determined by examining and evaluating the conflicting interests,[155] an approach that reflects the understanding of the former § 15(1)5 WpHG.[156] Weighing up the different interests is in part regarded as contrary to Article 6(2) MAD which does not explicitly allow such a procedure and thus supposedly prohibits stricter national rules, as Article 6(2)2 MAD would otherwise be superfluous.[157] A clearer definition of the "legitimate" interests of the issuer could help to defuse this discussion. As yet, all interests of a certain relevance are classed as legitimate,[158] and interests concerning the issuer's reputation or stock price, both of which will certainly suffer from a disclosure of negative information, are therefore not regarded as sufficient.[159] The wording of Article 6(1)1 MAD would, however, also allow the determination of legitimate interests to depend on an evaluation of the conflicting interests and make it dependent on whether the issuer's interests outweigh those of the capital market. In German legal practice, this question does not play an important role, delaying disclosure generally being permitted for any legitimate interests of a certain relevance.[160]

---

[151] Cf. P. Versteegen, in: H. Hirte and T.M.J. Möllers (eds.), *Kölner Kommentar zum WpHG*, § 15 Anh.—§ 6 WpAIV para. 9 ff.; dissenting opinion: H.-D. Assmann, in: H.-D. Assmann and U.H. Schneider (eds.), *Kommentar zum WpHG*, § 15 para. 150.

[152] Cf. P. Versteegen, in: H. Hirte and T.M.J. Möllers (eds.), *Kölner Kommentar zum WpHG*, § 15 Anh.—§ 6 WpAIV para. 12; M. Pfüller, in: A. Fuchs (ed.), *Kommentar zum WpHG*, § 15 para. 165, 352; H.-D. Assmann, in: H.-D. Assmann and U.H. Schneider (eds.), *Kommentar zum WpHG*, § 15 para. 157; in more detail L. Behn, *Ad-hoc-Publizität und Unternehmensverbindungen*, p. 91 ff.

[153] Cf. P. Versteegen, in: H. Hirte and T.M.J. Möllers (eds.), *Kölner Kommentar zum WpHG*, § 15 Anh.—§ 6 WpAIV para. 13; M. Pfüller, in: A. Fuchs (ed.), *Kommentar zum WpHG*, § 15 para. 358; H.-D. Assmann, in: H.-D. Assmann and U.H. Schneider (eds.), *Kommentar zum WpHG*, § 15 para. 138, 150; D. Zimmer and H. Kruse, in: E. Schwark and D. Zimmer (eds.), *Kapitalmarktrechts-Kommentar*, § 15 WpHG para. 56.

[154] Cf. A. Couret et al. (eds.), *Droit financier*, para. 1464.

[155] Cf. BaFin, *Emittentenleitfaden 2009* (issuer guideline), p. 66.

[156] Cf. O. Tollkühn, ZIP (2004), p. 2215, 2218.

[157] Cf. P. Versteegen, in: H. Hirte and T.M.J. Möllers (eds.), *Kölner Kommentar zum WpHG*, § 15 Anh.—§ 6 WpAIV para. 16; on the Member States' margin of appreciation regarding the implementation see above, para. 16.

[158] Cf. O. Tollkühn, ZIP (2004), p. 2215, 2218; J. Stoppel, in: B. Grunewald and M. Schlitt (eds.), *Einführung in das Kapitalmarktrecht*, p. 264; H.-D. Assmann, in: H.-D. Assmann and U.H. Schneider (eds.), *Kommentar zum WpHG*, § 15 para. 150; M. Nietsch, BB (2005), p. 785, 788; P. Versteegen, in: H. Hirte and T.M.J. Möllers (eds.), *Kölner Kommentar zum WpHG*, § 15 Anh.—§ 6 WpAIV para. 19.

[159] Cf. P. Versteegen, in: H. Hirte and T.M.J. Möllers (eds.), *Kölner Kommentar zum WpHG*, § 15 Anh.—§ 6 WpAIV para. 22.

[160] Cf. ibid., § 15 Anh.—§ 6 WpAIV para. 16.

Philipp Koch

78   Issuers do not have a "large margin of appreciation" for determining whether they have a legitimate interest in the delay.[161] The decision does not constitute an economic decision in the sense of the business judgment rule. Only then would such a large margin of appreciation be acceptable. Additionally, such extensive possibilities to delay disclosure would effectively result in disclosure "as soon as possible" becoming the exception.

79   French courts have developed a different approach in the case of *Metaleurop SA*,[162] which concerned a restructuring agreement between Metaleurop, its major shareholder and the banks involved. The AMF and the Cour d'Appel in Paris allowed Metaleurop to delay the disclosure of the details of the agreement, whilst requiring an immediate disclosure of the fact that Metaleurop's financial situation had deteriorated considerably as no justification existed for delaying the disclosure of this general information.

(bb)   Further Constellations

80   Some Member States have put the concept of an issuer's legitimate interest into more concrete terms by developing additional constellations to those listed in Article 3(1) Directive 2003/124/EC. English law, for example, lists two further constellations in which delaying disclosure may be justified.

81   The most important constellation has its origin before the enactment of the MAD and refers to "impending developments" that may be jeopardised by premature disclosure as described in DTR 2.5.5 FSA Handbook. The rule is intended for guidance and thus constitutes a non-binding interpretational help. Similarly, France allows a delay in disclosure for financial measures that may be jeopardised by premature disclosure in Article 223–6 RG AMF and Italy permits delaying disclosure for all such measures in Article 66 bis (2) RE.

82   In the course of the financial crisis, when the case of Northern Rock Bank turned the attention to public liquidity support facilities, DTR 2.5.5 A FSA Handbook was introduced in the United Kingdom. It now states that an issuer may have a legitimate interest in delaying disclosure of inside information concerning the provision of liquidity support by the Bank of England or by another central bank to it or to a member of the same group as the issuer.[163]

83   The Italian provision Article 66 bis (2) RE further assumes a legitimate interest in delaying disclosure if for inherent reasons the circumstances could not be disclosed in a way that would enable a correct assessment of the information by the public.

84   This results in extensive possibilities to delay disclosure in Italy—a fact that is often seen critically by the legal literature given that full transparency, as envisaged by the MAD, can no longer be achieved.[164] It is further unclear whether

---

[161] D. Zimmer and H. Kruse, in: E. Schwark and D. Zimmer (eds.), *Kapitalmarktrechts-Kommentar*, § 15 WpHG para. 74; dissenting opinion: OLG Frankfurt am Main, WM (2009), p. 647, 648; S.H. Schneider, BB (2005), p. 897, 900.

[162] Cf. CA Paris of 13 December 2005, *Metaleurop SA*, and the decision in first instance AMF of 14 April 2005 (as cited by A. Couret et al. (eds.), *Droit financier*, para. 1464). On the parallels in the United Kingdom see R. Veil and M. Wundenberg, *Englisches Kapitalmarktrecht*, p. 115.

[163] Cf. R. Veil and M. Wundenberg, *Englisches Kapitalmarktrecht*, p. 116–117.

[164] S. Seminara, 3 Banca Borsa tit. Cred. (2008), p. 331, 350; S. Seminara, *Informazione finanziaria e mercato*, p. 264; F. Mucciarelli, 1 Banca Borsa tit. Cred. I (1999), p. 754, 759–760.

the cases listed in Article 66 bis (2) RE are to be understood as exhaustive. This would not be convincing as the issuer may also have a considerable interest in a delay in further constellations.[165]

85   In Germany, an additional constellation discussed in legal literature and the courts is that of personnel decisions. In the case of *Daimler/Geltl*[166] the Oberlandesgericht (OLG, Higher Regional Court) Stuttgart ruled that the issuer had a legitimate interest in not disclosing the CEO's intention to resign from his post. It must be possible to appoint a successor without damaging the potential candidate's reputation by a public discussion beforehand.[167] This constellation is also discussed in the Italian legal literature.[168]

(cc)   Multi-Stage Decision-Making Processes

86   The problem of how to treat multi-stage decision-making processes as described in Article 3(1)(b) Directive 2003/124/EC particularly arises in companies with a two-tier-system such as the German *Aktiengesellschaft* (stock corporation), in which certain measures require the consent of the supervisory board. It therefore comes as no surprise that the discussion on this possibility of delaying disclosure is particularly intense in Germany, whilst the English FSA sees this topic as one of very limited relevance.[169]

87   Delaying disclosure in these cases is necessary as it is often the case that the disclosure obligation will arise before the supervisory board has made its decision. Generally the planned measure leads to sufficiently precise information on a future circumstance, thus requiring disclosure.[170] In Italy the smaller range of information subject to disclosure obligation usually prevents this constellation from becoming relevant.[171]

88   Delaying disclosure in these cases is justified by two different lines of argumentation. The BaFin, for example, fears that a premature disclosure could influence the supervisory board in its decision which would indirectly harm the investors.[172] Others fear that the public may be misled and only accept a delay if a public disclosure of the information prior to the supervisory board's approval and the simultaneous announcement that this approval is still pending would jeopardise the correct assessment of the information by the public.[173] Others emphasise the similarities between the capital market's interest in information and the issuer's interest in a

---

[165] F. Annunziata, *Abusi di mercato e tutela del risparmio*, p. 24.
[166] OLG Stuttgart, ZIP (2009), p. 962 ff. See § 13 para. 57.
[167] Cf. OLG Stuttgart, ZIP (2009), p. 962, 970.
[168] Cf. F. Annunziata, *Abusi di mercato e tutela del risparmio*, p. 24.
[169] Cf. R. Veil and M. Wundenberg, *Englisches Kapitalmarktrecht*, p. 115.
[170] For Germany: T. Raiser and R. Veil, *Recht der Kapitalgesellschaften*, § 12 para. 31; H.-D. Assmann, in: H.-D. Assmann and U.H. Schneider (eds.), *Kommentar zum WpHG*, § 15 para. 60; T.O. Brandi and R. Süßmann, AG (2004), p. 642, 649; OLG Stuttgart, ZIP (2007), p. 481, 484; OLG Frankfurt am Main, WM (2009), p. 647, 648; T.M.J. Möllers, WM (2005), p. 1393, 1394–1395. For Austria: S. Kalss et al. (eds.), *Kapitalmarktrecht I*, § 14 para. 33.
[171] See para. 47.
[172] BaFin, *Emittentenleitfaden 2009* (issuer guideline), p. 58; OLG Stuttgart, ZIP (2009), p. 962, 969 with further references.
[173] H.-D. Assmann, in: H.-D. Assmann and U.H. Schneider (eds.), *Kommentar zum WpHG*, § 15 para. 142; M. Pfüller, in: A. Fuchs (ed.), *Kommentar zum WpHG*, § 15 para. 370, justifying a delay in disclosure also with the concept of respect towards the supervisory board, as known in the law on stock corporations.

delay.[174] Article 6(2)1 MAD only allows a delay if the issuer has a legitimate interest therein. It is therefore not sufficient to determine solely whether there is a risk of the public being misled, although Article 3(1)(b) Directive 2003/124/EC appears to follow exactly the opposite understanding.

89   Ensuring that the supervisory board comes to an independent decision can justify delaying disclosure irrespective of the constellation described in Article 3(1)(b) Directive 2003/124/EC, e.g. in cases in which the measure only requires a resolution by the supervisory board. These cases may still concern protracted sets of facts although the decision-making process does not take place in multiple stages, an example being the appointment and removal of the management board pursuant to § 84 AktG, as was the case in *Daimler/Geltl*, on which the OLG Stuttgart had to rule.[175]

90   In German legal practice, delaying disclosure in cases in which the supervisory board's decision is still pending is meanwhile more or less automatic, especially as the BaFin generally agrees.[176] Some require the management to make a prognosis on the probability of the supervisory board's consent in order to determine whether a delay is possible.[177] This approach is also favoured in Austria.[178]

91   If the decision of the general shareholder's meeting is still pending, the situation must be seen differently. Secrecy is no longer possible once the invitations to the general meeting are sent out.[179] In Italy the pending decision of the general shareholders' meeting therefore does not justify delaying disclosure.[180]

3.   No Misleading the Public

92   Whether the public may be misled by the delay in disclosure is difficult to determine. Generally speaking, any delay leads to a pricing that does not reflect all the relevant information, the price-sensitive nature of the information being a defining element of the concept of information and therefore a necessary prerequisite for any disclosure obligation. Applying this understanding of the term "misleading the public" would, however, be absurd.[181] Misleading the public is therefore only to be assumed if the information available to the market gives an impression that is contrary to the actual situation under consideration of the inside information and the issuer's behaviour.[182]

---

[174] OLG Stuttgart, ZIP (2009), p. 962, 970.

[175] OLG Stuttgart, ZIP (2009), p. 962, 966, 969; H. Fleischer, NZG (2007), p. 401, 404; see § 13 para. 58–59 for more details.

[176] BaFin, *Emittentenleitfaden 2009* (issuer guideline), p. 67; H.-D. Assmann, in: H.-D. Assmann and U.H. Schneider (eds.), *Kommentar zum WpHG*, § 15 para. 26.

[177] Cf. M. Pfüller, in: A. Fuchs (ed.), *Kommentar zum WpHG*, § 15 para. 371 ff.

[178] Cf. S. Kalss et al. (eds.), *Kapitalmarktrecht I*, § 14 para. 36.

[179] Cf. H.-D. Assmann, in: H.-D. Assmann and U.H. Schneider (eds.), *Kommentar zum WpHG*, § 15 para. 146; M. Pfüller, in: A. Fuchs (ed.), *Kommentar zum WpHG*, § 15 para. 379.

[180] S. Seminara, 3 Banca Borsa tit. Cred. (2008), p. 331, 350; S. Seminara, *Informazione finanziaria e mercato*, p. 264; Mucciarelli, 1 Banca Borsa tit. Cred. I (1999), p. 754, 759–760.

[181] Cf. CESR, *Market Abuse Directive Level 3—second set of CESR guidance and information on the common operation of the Directive to the market*, CESR/06-562b, July 2007, p. 11. For Germany: OLG Stuttgart, ZIP (2009), p. 962, 970; M. Pfüller, in: A. Fuchs (ed.), *Kommentar zum WpHG*, § 15 para. 385.

[182] For Germany: OLG Stuttgart, ZIP (2009), p. 962, 970; H.-D. Assmann, in: H.-D. Assmann and U.H. Schneider (eds.), *Kommentar zum WpHG*, § 15 para. 160; M. Pfüller, in: A. Fuchs (ed.), *Kommentar zum WpHG*, § 15 para. 387 ff.

93   In legal practice an issuer will regularly have to decide how to treat rumours. According to the CESR the issuer can follow a "no comment policy".[183] As opposed to this, Italy requires a disclosure pursuant to Article 66(4) RE if the share price deviates considerably from the market price on the previous day. In Spain, the CNMV also generally recommends a "no comment policy", making an exception only for cases in which the rumour is actually based on true inside information and requiring disclosure in these cases.[184] In Germany the BaFin merely prohibits the issuer from giving active signals that would contradict the non-disclosed inside information, such as denying the inside information or giving an opposing statement.[185] A "no comment policy" is, however, regarded as legitimate.[186] Some German legal literature distinguishes between positive and negative rumours, an approach that is not supported by the statutory wording.[187]

94   Only if a rumour is the result of an information leak within the issuer, and it must therefore be assumed that the issuer is no longer able to ensure the confidentiality of the information, must disclosure take place immediately.[188]

4.   Ensuring Confidentiality

95   In order to ensure the confidentiality of inside information, Article 3(2) Directive 2003/124/EC requires the Member States to ensure that: (i) the issuer has established effective arrangements to deny access to such information to persons other than those who require it for their functions within the issuer; (ii) the issuer has taken the necessary measures to ensure that any person with access to such information acknowledges the legal and regulatory duties entailed and is aware of the sanctions attached to the misuse or improper circulation of such information; (iii) the issuer has measures in place which allow immediate public disclosure in case the issuer was not able to ensure the confidentiality of the relevant inside information.

96   Most Member States have implemented this provision using practically the same wording.[189] The very general approach has led to a discussion in Germany as to which obligations actually result for the issuer. Whilst it may be recommendable in practice, the provision does not appear to require the development or use of organised compliance structures.[190] The issuer is further not obliged to document the

---

[183] See § 13 para. 69.
[184] CNMV, *Criterios para la gestión de noticias y rumores difundidos sobre valores cotizados*, December 2008.
[185] H.-D. Assmann, in: H.-D. Assmann and U.H. Schneider (eds.), *Kommentar zum WpHG*, § 15 para. 170.
[186] BaFin, *Emittentenleitfaden 2009* (issuer guideline), p. 67.
[187] Cf. H. Ziemons, NZG (2004), p. 537, 543; dissenting opinion (as herein): T.M.J. Möllers, WM (2005), p. 1393, 1396; J. Stoppel, in: B. Grunewald and M. Schlitt (eds.), *Einführung in das Kapitalmarktrecht*, p. 264–265.
[188] H.-D. Assmann, in: H.-D. Assmann and U.H. Schneider (eds.), *Kommentar zum WpHG*, § 15 para. 168; BaFin, *Emittentenleitfaden 2009* (issuer guideline), p. 67–68; stricter: T.O. Brandi and R. Süßmann, AG (2004), p. 642, 652–653 and 657.
[189] For Austria: § 48d(2) No. 2 BörseG. For France: Art. 223-2 II RG AMF. For Germany: § 7 WpAIV, § 15b(1)3 WpHG and D. Zimmer and H. Kruse, in: E. Schwark and D. Zimmer (eds.), *Kapitalmarktrechts-Kommentar*, § 15 WpHG para. 69. For the United Kingdom: DTR 2.6.1 and 2.6.2 FSA Handbook. For Sweden: Kapitel 10, § 4 FFFS 2007:17.
[190] OLG Stuttgart, ZIP (2009), p. 962, 971 with further references; P. Versteegen, in: H. Hirte and T.M.J. Möllers (eds.), *Kölner Kommentar zum WpHG*, § 15 para. 164; H.-D. Assmann, in: H.-D. Assmann and U.H. Schneider (eds.), *Kommentar zum WpHG*, § 15 para. 297; dissenting opinion: T.O. Brandi and R. Süßmann, AG (2004), p. 642, 650; O. Tollkühn, ZIP (2004), p. 2215, 2216. Similarly BaFin, *Emittentenleitfaden 2009* (issuer guideline), p. 67: "organisational measures" necessary.

measures taken in order to preserve confidentiality. Documentation may, however, be recommendable in order to avoid liability under civil or administrative law.[191]

97 The OLG Stuttgart had to examine the obligation to take measures to ensure that the duties ensuing from inside information are acknowledged by any person involved in the case of *Daimler/Gett.*[192] The court ruled that this obligation also existed towards members of the board, even though these were bound to confidentiality through their position. It argued that only persons with a general obligation to confidentiality are allowed access to inside information. The instruction required by Article 3(2) Directive 2003/124/EC takes this into account and aims at further information in order to ensure that the insider is reminded of his obligations as an insider and the sanctions for breaches of these obligations.[193] A further important statement of the court was that a breach of this obligation by the issuer does not entail any civil liability. The reason for this is that the issuer can always refer to the fact that even if it had acted correctly, it would only have instructed the respective person, but would not have disclosed the respective information sooner.

98 If inside information is leaked to the public and confidentiality is therefore no longer ensured, the issuer must promptly make a complete disclosure of that information, a good indication being whether rumours have arisen.[194] Unusual developments of the stock exchange price or trade volume can also indicate that the information has been leaked. Whilst the BaFin[195] allows issuers in Germany to delay disclosure further, if certain that the information has not been leaked, Spain automatically requires immediate disclosure in these cases pursuant to Article 83 bis 1(f) LMV. In order to enable immediate disclosure, it is recommendable to prepare a fully formulated ad hoc announcement.[196]

5. Conscious Decision by the Issuer?

99 There is a heated discussion in the German legal literature on the question of whether it is sufficient pursuant to § 15(3)1 WpHG if the requirements for a delay are given,[197] or whether the issuer must additionally make a conscious decision to this end.[198] The issuer may in particular fail to make a conscious decision in a pro-

[191] OLG Stuttgart, ZIP (2009), p. 962, 971 with further references; H.-D. Assmann, in: H.-D. Assmann and U.H. Schneider (eds.), *Kommentar zum WpHG*, § 15 para. 165; P. Versteegen, in: H. Hirte and T.M.J. Möllers (eds.), *Kölner Kommentar zum WpHG*, § 15 para. 164; dissenting opinion: T.O. Brandi and R. Süßmann, AG (2004), p. 642, 650.
[192] OLG Stuttgart, ZIP (2009), p. 962, 969, 972.
[193] OLG Stuttgart, ZIP (2009), p. 962, 972.
[194] On dealing with rumours see para. 93.
[195] Cf. BaFin, *Emittentenleitfaden 2009* (issuer guideline), p. 68.
[196] The OLG Stuttgart, ZIP (2009), p. 962, 973 left the question whether an obligation to this respect exists, unanswered.
[197] OLG Stuttgart, ZIP (2009), p. 962, 973; P. Versteegen, in: H. Hirte and T.M.J. Möllers (eds.), *Kölner Kommentar zum WpHG*, § 15 para. 171; H.-D. Assmann, in: H.-D. Assmann and U.H. Schneider (eds.), *Kommentar zum WpHG*, § 15 para. 165d; D. Zimmer and H. Kruse, in: E. Schwark and D. Zimmer (eds.), *Kapitalmarkt-rechts-Kommentar*, § 15 WpHG para. 54; G. Bachmann, 172 ZHR (2008), p. 597, 610; unclear in: OLG Frankfurt am Main, WM (2009), p. 647, 648.
[198] BaFin, *Emittentenleitfaden 2009* (issuer guideline), p. 65; M. Pfüller, in: A. Fuchs (ed.), *Kommentar zum WpHG*, § 15 para. 345; S. Harbarth, ZIP (2005), p. 1898, 1906; U.H. Schneider and S. Gilfrich, BB (2007), p. 53, 54 ff.; P.R. Mennicke, NZG (2009), p. 1059, 1061; and CESR, *Market Abuse Directive Level 3—second set of CESR*

tracted set of facts if it realises too late that certain information qualifies as inside information.

100 In the civil proceedings in *Daimler/Geltl* the OLG Stuttgart ruled[199] that a delay in disclosure under § 15(3)1 WpHG does not necessarily require the issuer's conscious decision. The OLG Frankfurt, entrusted with the supervisory proceedings in the same case, left the question unanswered.[200]

101 The discussion has lost importance since the OLG Stuttgart decided that the issuer cannot be held liable pursuant to § 37 b WpHG based on the delayed disclosure, the reason for this being that even if the issuer had made a conscious decision, the information would not have been disclosed immediately as disclosure would then have been delayed. The question remains relevant for the supervisory consequences, the BaFin explicitly requiring a conscious decision.[201] If delaying disclosure requires a decision the issuer breaches his obligation to make inside information public immediately if it does not make the conscious decision to delay this publication.

102 In fact, it remains unclear why a delay should require more than the objective requirements listed in the respective provision. These are sufficient to ensure that the capital market is informed in due time.[202] At the same time, the wording of Article 6(2)1 MAD indicates that European law requires a conscious decision: If "an issuer *may* ... delay" disclosure this constitutes an action which necessitates an underlying decision.

103 In conformity with the directive, German law must therefore also require a conscious decision.[203] This approach is also supported by the wording of Article 6(2)2 MAD which explicitly refers to the issuer's decision when allowing the Member States to require that an issuer must inform the competent authority. The fact that Germany has not made use of this possibility does not affect the underlying concept of Article 6(2) MAD as a whole. Furthermore, the German legislator's aim was only to substitute the formerly necessary decision of the supervisory authority with a decision by the issuer himself.[204] The wording of § 15(3)1 and 4 WpHG, § 8(5) WpAIV also indicates that a conscious decision is required. This approach is necessary in order to achieve an interpretation that conforms to the directive. The BaFin therefore rightly assumes that disclosure must be delayed actively by way of a decision of the management.[205]

104 The requirements this decision must meet remain unclear, some regarding global authorisations to this effect or a delegation to other bodies, such as a disclosure committee or the department for compliance, as sufficient, whilst others emphasise the existence of a documentation obligation.[206]

---

guidance and information on the common operation of the Directive to the market, CESR/06-562b, July 2007, p. 10–11, recommending documentation of the delay.

[199] OLG Stuttgart, ZIP (2009), p. 962 ff.
[200] OLG Frankfurt am Main, WM (2009), p. 647 ff.
[201] See fn. 198.
[202] H.-D. Assmann, in: H.-D. Assmann and U.H. Schneider (eds.), *Kommentar zum WpHG*, § 15 para. 165–166.
[203] M. Pfüller, in: A. Fuchs (ed.), *Kommentar zum WpHG*, § 15 para. 345.
[204] Ibid., § 15 para. 346.
[205] BaFin, *Emittentenleitfaden 2009* (issuer guideline), p. 65.
[206] Cf. U.H. Schneider and S. Gilfrich, BB (2007), p. 53 ff.; H.-D. Assmann, in: H.-D. Assmann and U.H. Schneider (eds.), *Kommentar zum WpHG*, § 15 para. 165b; S.H. Schneider, BB (2005), p. 897, 902; P.R. Mennicke, NZG (2009), p. 1059, 1062.

Philipp Koch

V. Sanctions

1. Importance of National Legal Traditions

105 Sanctioning breaches of disclosure obligations for inside information is largely a matter of national law, Article 14(1) MAD merely requiring that the Member States "ensure, in conformity with their national law, that the appropriate administrative measures can be taken or administrative sanctions be imposed against the persons responsible where the provisions adopted in the implementation of this Directive have not been complied with", without prejudice to the Member States' right "to impose criminal sanctions". The measures must be "effective, proportionate and dissuasive". The provision does not contain any rules on civil law liability as the EU would not have had the competence[207] in this respect and the civil law liability contained in Article 7 TD also does not apply to the disclosure of inside information.

106 The Member States therefore are free to develop a system that is integrated into their national traditions.[208] This is reflected in the wide variety of approaches to enforcement taken in the different Member States, which make use of and combine various sanctions under civil, administrative and criminal law in very different ways. In Germany, legal literature and practice focus mainly on claims for damages which are favoured as an effective means of indemnification for the individual and of private enforcement for the regime in general, in a way that neither criminal law nor supervisory law could achieve.[209]

107 In France, behavioural control is traditionally ensured through provisions on white-collar crime. Nevertheless the AMF was conferred the power to impose sanctions under Article L. 621–15 ff. C. mon. fin., which have proved to be very effective. Legal enforcement in Spain also focuses on the administrative sanctions that the CNMV can impose, as damages are commonly regarded as difficult to determine in capital markets law.[210]

2. Civil Liability

(a) Germany

108 As there will generally be no contractual relationship between the investor and the issuer or his management, liability for breaches of the obligation to disclose inside information will usually be based on tort law or the special provisions in §§ 37b,

---

[207] Cf. Explanatory Memorandum on Art. 14 of the draft proposal for a MAD of 30 May 2001, COM(2001) 281 final., OJ E240, 28 August 2001, p. 265; T.M.J. Möllers and F.C. Leisch, in: H. Hirte and T.M.J. Möllers (eds.), *Kölner Kommentar zum WpHG*, §§ 37b, 37c para. 17 ff.

[208] Cf. on the European requirements regarding sanctions for breaches of the disclosure obligations M. Brellochs, *Publizität und Haftung*, p. 80 ff., especially p. 92 ff.

[209] Cf. T.M.J. Möllers and F.C. Leisch, in: H. Hirte and T.M.J. Möllers (eds.), *Kölner Kommentar zum WpHG*, §§ 37b, 37c para. 4.

[210] As maintained by our Spanish interview partners (see fn. 20).

37c WpHG.[211] The draft proposal for a KapInHaG (German Improvement of the Liability for Incorrect Information on the Capital Market Act) has been dismissed.[212]

109   In tort law, liability is attached either to the violation of a protected right or interest in § 823(1) BGB, the infringement of a protective law in § 823(2) BGB or an intentional damage contrary to public policy in § 826 BGB. As breaches of the disclosure obligation result in pure economic losses and § 15(6)1 WpHG excludes the applicability of § 823(2) BGB, tortious liability for incorrect or omitted publications of inside information is usually restricted to § 826 BGB.[213]

110   A liability pursuant to § 823(2) BGB can usually not be constructed with reference to other provisions: breaches of the disclosure obligation will only rarely constitute a market manipulation (§ 20a WpHG), a misrepresentation of the issuer's financial situation (§ 400(1) No. 1 AktG), fraud (§ 263 StGB (German Criminal Code)) or capital investment fraud (§ 264a StGB).[214] If a quarterly financial report is made public as inside information, this may, however, result in a liability pursuant to § 823(2) BGB in conjunction with § 400(1) No. 1 AktG.[215]

111   The case of *Infomatec* is one of the BGH's leading cases on § 826 BGB in which the court set out the basic requirements for a tortious liability for incorrect information.

112   *Facts (abridged)*:[216] Infomatec AG published the information that a mobile telephone network provider had placed an order for wifi hubs and their licences with a total order volume of more than DM55 million as inside information. In fact, the binding order the customer had placed only had an order volume of DM9.8 million. Immediately after the publication the share price rose by 20%. Two months later an investor acquired shares at this high share price, which dropped considerably in value after it became public that the information was incorrect.

113   The BGH held the members of the management board liable for the damage suffered, arguing that the conscious publication of incorrect information was contrary to public policy and immoral. The BGH was of the opinion that management had published the information intentionally in order to induce investors to acquire shares at an extortionate price. The acquisition of shares was causally linked to the disclosure of the information. This required full proof of causation by the claimants who could not base their claims on the prima facie proof that there was a general tendency of the public to acquire the respective shares (*Anlagestimmung*). The defendants were sentenced to reimburse the purchase price and take back the shares the claimant had acquired.

---

[211] Certain voices in legal literature maintain that §§ 37b, 37c WpHG have the nature of tort law, cf. T.M.J. Möllers and F.C. Leisch, in: H. Hirte and T.M.J. Möllers (eds.), *Kölner Kommentar zum WpHG*, §§ 37b, 37c para. 12 ff. with further references.

[212] Cf. NZG (2004), p. 1042 ff.; on this R. Veil, BKR (2005), p. 91 ff.

[213] Cf. A. Hellgardt, *Kapitalmarktdeliktsrecht*; M. Brellochs, *Publizität und Haftung*, p. 109 ff., 144 ff.; K. Sauer, *Haftung für Falschinformation des Sekundärmarktes*.

[214] Cf. M. Pfüller, in: A. Fuchs (ed.), *Kommentar zum WpHG*, § 15 para. 440 ff.; BGHZ 160, p. 134 ff. (*Infomatec I*).

[215] Cf. BGH, NZG (2005), p. 672 ff. (*EM.TV*).

[216] BGHZ 160, p. 134 ff. (*Infomatec I*); BGHZ 160, p. 149 ff. (*Infomatec II*); on this T. Raiser and R. Veil, *Recht der Kapitalgesellschaften*, § 12 para. 42. T.M.J. Möllers and F.C. Leisch, in: H. Hirte and T.M.J. Möllers (eds.), *Kölner Kommentar zum WpHG*, §§ 37b, 37c para. 411 ff.; R. Sethe, in: H.-D. Assmann, in: H.-D. Assmann and U.H. Schneider (eds.), *Kommentar zum WpHG*, §§ 37b, 37c para. 115 ff.

114 The BGH developed this line of argumentation towards a tort liability for the publication of incorrect information further in *EM.TV*[217] and *Comroad*.[218] Both the issuer
(§§ 826, 31 BGB) and the members of the management board responsible for the
disclosure (§ 826 BGB) can be held liable. In legal practice, the personal liability of
the members of the management will be more relevant for investors, as the issuer
himself will often be insolvent—as in *Infomatec*.

115 Requiring full proof of causation between the incorrect information and the investor's decision to acquire the shares is seen particularly critically, as this is usually
nearly impossible for the investor. The BGH nonetheless grants no alleviation of
the burden of proof, and does not allow a prima facie proof of a general tendency
of the public towards an acquisition, arguing that the decision to acquire shares
requires the decision of an individual person and cannot be generalised.[219] The BGH
further does not accept the US "fraud on the market theory", according to which the
general deception of investor confidence in the integrity of market prices constitutes
liability, purporting that this would lead to an interminable applicability of § 826
BGB.[220] As opposed to this, the issuer may be held liable if an investor has abstained
from disposing of his shares on the basis of incorrect information resulting from a
breach of the disclosure obligation.[221]

116 The nature of claimable damages was also unclear. Specific performance pursuant
to § 249 BGB, i.e. the reimbursement of the acquisition price and the return of
the shares or—should the shares meanwhile have been disposed of—payment of
the difference between the acquisition and disposal price, subjects the defendant
to the risk of all price fluctuations. It would therefore appear more reasonable to
restrict the damages to the difference between the acquisition price and the price
that would have developed if the information had been disclosed correctly.[222] The
BGH, however, sees the damage in any detriment to a legitimate interest or exposure
to an undesired legal obligation, allowing restitution (*Naturalrestitution*) and therefore not restricting the investor's claims to the difference between the actual and the
hypothetical acquisition price (*Kursdifferenzschaden*). If the investor only claims the
latter, the exact amount of damages must be determined according to the methods
of modern finance. In this procedure the damages are determined on the basis of
the difference in price after the true facts have become known. According to the
BGH, the judge will in certain cases have to estimate the damages on the legal basis
of § 287 Zivilprozessordnung (ZPO, German Civil Procedure Code).[223]

117 Restitution must further be seen critically with regard to the provisions on capital
maintenance in §§ 57 ff. AktG and the restricted possibilities of an issuer to acquire
his own shares, pursuant to § 71 AktG. Yet the BGH has given restitution priority
over the special rules on company law in cases of intentional damage contrary to

---

[217] BGH, NZG (2005), p. 672 ff. (*EM.TV*).
[218] BGH, NZG (2007), p. 345–346; BGH, NZG (2007), p. 346–347; BGH, NZG (2007), p. 269 ff.; BGH, NZG (2007), p. 708 ff.; BGH, NZG (2007), p. 711 ff.; BGH, NZG (2008), p. 382 ff.; BGH, NZG (2008), p. 385–386; BGH, NZG (2008), p. 386 ff. (*Comroad I-VIII*).
[219] Cf. BGHZ 160, p. 134, 144 ff. (*Infomatec I*).
[220] T. Raiser and R. Veil, *Recht der Kapitalgesellschaften*, § 12 para. 43; BGH, NZG (2007), p. 269 (*Comroad III*).
[221] BGH, NZG (2005), p. 672, 675 (*EM.TV*).
[222] Cf. A. Fuchs, in: A. Fuchs (ed.), *Kommentar zum WpHG*, §§ 37b, 37c para. 54.
[223] BGH, NZG (2005), p. 672 ff. (*EM.TV*); BGHZ 160, p. 134 ff. (*Infomatec I*).

public policy, arguing that the investor may not be treated differently from a third-party creditor of the issuer if it acquired the shares on the secondary market. The issuer's liability could therefore not be restricted to the issuer's free assets. The acquisition of the shares by the issuer only takes place more or less by chance, if the issuer decides not to dispose of the shares to a third party and claim the difference in price from the issuer, but rather to claim the full amount from the issuer.[224]

118   In 2002 the German legislator further introduced special rules on the liability for incorrect or omitted information in §§ 37b, 37c WpHG, which have meanwhile led to a number of proceedings.[225] § 37b WpHG constitutes a liability for the omission to disclose inside information, whilst § 37c WpHG applies to the publication of incorrect inside information. The provisions only concern the issuers of financial instruments that have been admitted to trading on a domestic stock exchange. The management can be held responsible by the company pursuant to § 93 AktG.

119   According to § 37b WpHG the issuer is to be held liable if the investor bought the financial instruments after the omission and still owns the financial instruments upon disclosure of the information, i.e. paid too high a price due to the omission to disclose the negative information. The issuer is further to be held liable if the investor bought the financial instruments before the existence of the relevant inside information and sells them after the omission at too low a price due to the omission to disclose the positive information. § 37c WpHG declares the issuer to be held liable if the investor made the investment decision because it relied on the false information, if the issuer acted with intent or gross negligence and the investor has incurred damages. This can be the case if the investor bought the financial instruments after publication due to the overly positive impression given and still owns the financial instruments at the point in time at which it becomes publicly known that the information was inaccurate. Such is also the case if it bought the financial instruments before publication and sold them at too low a price before it became clear that the information was inaccurate because of the unduly negative impression the information gives.

120   §§ 37b(2), 37c(2) WpHG exempt the issuer from liability if it can prove that it acted neither with intent nor with gross negligence. A similar reversal of the burden of proof concerning causation[226] between the breach of the disclosure obligation and the investment decision does not, however, exist.[227] As in § 826 BGB, the BGH allows the investor to claim restitution and does not restrict claims to the difference between the actual and the hypothetical acquisition price.[228] It has not as yet been

---

[224] BGH, NZG (2005), p. 672, 674 (*EM.TV*); BGH, NZG (2007), p. 269, 270 (*Comroad III*); dissenting opinion based on the non-conformity with the Capital Maintenance Directive: N. Vokuhl, *Anlegerschutz und Kapitalerhaltung*, p. 42 ff., 106 ff.

[225] Cf. BGH, ZIP (2012), p. 318 ff. (*IKB*) and the foregoing ruling of the OLG Düsseldorf, 27 January 2010—I 15 U 230/09 (*IKB*) (available at: www.juris.de); OLG Düsseldorf, 7 April 2011—I 6 U 7/10; OLG Schleswig, WM (2005), p. 696 ff.

[226] Cf. on this discussion R. Veil, ZHR 167 (2003), p. 365, 370 with further references.

[227] BGH, ZIP (2012), p. 318 ff. (*IKB*); seen critically therefore by R. Veil, 167 ZHR (2003), p. 365, 370 ff. with further references.

[228] BGH, ZIP (2012), p. 318 ff. (*IKB*); dissenting opinion: R. Sethe, in: H.-D. Assmann and U.H. Schneider (eds.), *Kommentar zum WpHG*, §§ 37b, 37c para. 75, 123 with further references; differentiating: R. Veil, 167 ZHR (2003), p. 365, 390–391.

determined whether the liability is further restricted to the issuer's free assets or may attach to the nominal capital or reserves.[229]

121   During the subprime crisis investors argued that the issuer's involvement in certain securities—directly or via special-purpose vehicles—should have been disclosed as inside information. The BGH[230] shared this view and ruled that the issuer had to reimburse the acquisition price if the investors could prove that they would not have purchased the shares if the issuer had disclosed his involvement in the usual way. If the investors could not prove causation, they could still claim the difference between the actual and the hypothetical acquisition price. At the same time, the BGH argued that §§ 37b, 37c WpHG could not be applied analogously to simple press releases as no gap in the law in this respect existed.

(b)   Other Member States

122   In all other Member States civil liability towards investors appears to play a less important role. With the exception of the United Kingdom, none of the other Member States provides a special legal foundation for damages based on a breach of disclosure obligations or has published decisions on this matter. The legal literature gives little attention to this question, although in general the possibility to claim damages under tort law appears to be accepted.

123   In Spain a liability under tort law is possible pursuant to Article 1902 CC (Spanish Civil Code), although in legal practice the claim will be met by strict requirements and the outcome will usually be uncertain.[231] Whilst the general rule on a liability for torts in France, Article 1382 C. civ. (French Civil Code), would also be applicable to these constellations, it has not as yet played any role in legal practice.[232] In both states the discussion is mostly combined with that on a liability for breaches of the periodic disclosure obligations, i.e. under the generic term of a liability for incorrect information on the secondary market.[233] Whilst Italian legal literature also discusses the tort liability of issuers and the management, no legal practice to this regard is apparent.[234] Similarly, Swedish legal literature acknowledges the applicability of the general provisions of tort law, although legal practice has not yet adopted this approach.[235]

124   In the United Kingdom, a legal foundation for investor's claims for damages was introduced into the FSMA on 1 October 2010.[236] Section 90A in conjunction with Schedule 10A now establishes a liability of the issuer for any incorrect, misleading or

---

[229] With reference to the Capital Maintenance Directive R. Veil, 167 ZHR (2003), p. 365, 393 ff.; N. Vokuhl, *Anlegerschutz und Kapitalerhaltung*, passim.

[230] BGH, ZIP (2012), p. 318 ff. (*IKB*).

[231] Cf. G.J. Sastre Corchado, 1 RMV (2007), p. 253, 254.

[232] Cf. H.-J. Puttfarken and A. Schrader, in: K.J. Hopt and H.-C. Voigt (eds.), *Prospekt- und Kapitalmarktinformationshaftung*, p. 615.

[233] Cf. M. Iribarren Blanco, *Responsabilidad civil por la información divulgada por las sociedades cotizadas*, passim.

[234] Cf. G. Ferrarini and M. Leonardi, in: K.J. Hopt and H.-C. Voigt (eds.), *Prospekt- und Kapitalmarktinformationshaftung*, p. 720.

[235] Cf. R. Veil and F. Walla, *Schwedisches Kapitalmarktrecht*, p. 87.

[236] The amendments were implemented by the Financial Services and Markets Act 2000 (Liability of Issuers) Regulations 2010; for more detail see L. Gullifer and J. Payne, *Corporate Finance Law*, p. 496–504.

delayed information or the omission to publish the information. Liability is attached to the question whether the information was made public "by recognised means". Inside information is made public by such means.[237] Any person, who possesses, acquired or disposed of shares based on the belief that the published information was complete and correct is entitled to claim damages pursuant to this provision.[238] The burden of proof has not been facilitated for investors—in particular the US "fraud on the market theory" is not applicable. A further requirement in cases of incorrect or incomplete information is that the issuer intentionally or recklessly failed to disclose the information correctly. If the publication was omitted entirely, the issuer is only held liable for intent.[239]

125 Austrian legal literature orientates itself towards the German discussion, yet partly develops its own conclusions. The obligation to disclose inside information is—unlike the situation in Germany—regarded as a protective rule, aimed directly at the protection of investors, thereby enabling claims based on § 1311 ABGB (Austrian General Civil Code) in conjunction with § 48d BörseG in cases of negligence. Damages for the intentional publication of incorrect information can be claimed on the basis of § 1300 ABGB and § 1295(2) ABGB, the latter applying to intentional behaviour contrary to public policy. The Austrian approach further understands the obligation to disclose inside information as a special legal relationship between issuer and investor that may lead to a liability for negligent breaches of this obligation on the basis of the concept of *culpa in contrahendo*. Austrian law also accepts the possibility of damages pursuant to § 2 öUWG (Austrian Act against Unfair Practices). Generally, damages cannot be claimed from the issuer's bodies directly;[240] rather the issuer himself is held liable for their behaviour pursuant to § 26 ABGB.[241]

126 Damages may be claimed not only by investors who have acquired of disposed of shares to their detriment, but in some cases also by investors who simply still hold the respective shares.[242] Potential investors that abstained from acquiring the shares due to an incorrect or omitted ad hoc notification only lose the opportunity to make profits. This opportunity is not recoverable.[243]

127 Unlike in Germany, the proof of causation between the breach of the obligation and the investor's disposition is facilitated for the investor: it is sufficient for him to prove that the information the issuer omitted was subject to a disclosure obligation at the time of his investment decision or that the incorrect or incomplete notification was known to the market at this time. The ensuing general inclination towards investments constitutes sufficient legal grounds for liability. If this inclination cannot, however, be substantiated, the claimant will once again be subjected to the full burden of proof.[244] Generally breaches of the modalities of disclosure

---

[237] Cf. L. Gullifer and J. Payne, *Corporate Finance Law*, p. 499; R. Veil and M. Wundenberg, *Englisches Kapitalmarktrecht*, p. 112.

[238] Sec. 90A schedule 10A(3) and (5) FSMA.

[239] Sec. 90A schedule 10A(3) FSMA states: "The issuer is liable in respect of the omission of any matter required to be included in published information only if a person discharging managerial responsibilities within the issuer knew the omission to be a dishonest concealment of a material fact."

[240] S. Kalss et al. (eds.), *Kapitalmarktrecht I*, § 19 para. 17 ff.

[241] Ibid., § 19 para. 11.

[242] Ibid., § 19 para. 24–25.

[243] Ibid., § 19 para. 27.

[244] Ibid., § 19 para. 6–7, 28.

can also entitle the investor to damages. In these cases causation will, however, be particularly difficult to prove.[245]

128 The extent of the issuer's liability is viewed more strictly in Austria than in Germany: the investor can generally only claim the difference in the market price, unless it proves that it would under no circumstances have acquired the financial instruments on the basis of the correct information. In these cases it is to be awarded the entire acquisition price, including the costs of the acquisition, lost dividends and interest, together with any damages incurred due to the fact that it omitted to make an alternative acquisition.[246] These claims are not regarded as being contrary to the principle of equal treatment (§ 47a öAktG (Austrian Stock Corporation Act), § 83 BörseG), the prohibition to retransfer capital contributions (§ 52 öAktG) or the prohibition for the issuer to buy back his own shares (§ 65 öAktG). Damages will generally be restricted by the rules on capital maintenance, only being payable from the accumulated profits, free capital reserves and possibly appropriated reserves.[247]

3. Administrative Sanctions

(a) Fines

129 Pursuant to Article 14 MAD almost all Member States have provided their national supervisory authority with the power to impose administrative sanctions for breaches of the obligation to disclose inside information. Generally breaches will be sanctioned with fines that may be imposed against the issuer or the management. All but one of the 29 CESR Member States have introduced fines for breaches of the obligation laid down in Article 6(1) MAD. Yet the conceptual and practical differences should not be underestimated, maximum sanctions ranging from €100 in Bulgaria and Finland to €2.5 million in Ireland, Portugal and Belgium, whilst the United Kingdom[248] does not restrict the level of fines.[249]

(aa) Germany

130 In Germany, intentional or grossly negligent breaches of the obligations listed in § 15 WpHG are subject to administrative fines pursuant to § 39(2) No. 2(c), Nos. 5–7 WpHG. § 39(4) WpHG determines that administrative offences are punishable by a fine not exceeding €1 million for breaches of the obligations listed in Article 6(1) MAD, whilst the fine for breaches of the less important obligations may not exceed €200,000. § 17(2) OWiG (German Administrative Offences Act) reduces the maximum fine by half in cases of negligence.[250] The possibility to impose fines as high as €1 million was introduced in order to compensate for the non-applicability

---

[245] Ibid., § 19 para. 3.
[246] Ibid., § 19 para. 4–5.
[247] Ibid., § 19 para. 15–16.
[248] For examples of FSA enforcement action see B. McDonnell, 88 COB (2011), p. 1, 15 ff.
[249] Cf. CESR, *Executive Summary to the Report on Administrative Measures and Sanctions and the Criminal Sanctions available in Member States under the Market Abuse Directive (MAD)*, CESR/08-099, February 2008, p. 5, 10; see also the individual descriptions on p. 34 ff.
[250] M. Pfüller, in: A. Fuchs (ed.), *Kommentar zum WpHG*, § 15 para. 450.

of the civil law liability in § 823(2) BGB and ensures that the sanction fulfils its aim towards listed companies and their management.[251]

131   The level of the sanction imposed in each individual case depends largely on the degree of liability. Gross negligence can be assumed when a person fails to exercise reasonable care to an unusually large extent.[252] Due to the fact that the issuers are companies and cannot as such be held liable, the sanctions will generally be imposed against the members of the management board, who are held liable pursuant to § 130 OWiG for the disclosure of inside information.[253] The issuer can further be sanctioned on the basis of § 30 OWiG, as a consequence of the management's liability, the sanctions in § 39(4) WpHG applying.[254]

132   In *Daimler* the BaFin imposed particularly noteworthy sanctions against DaimlerChrysler AG for a grossly negligent breach of the disclosure obligations in §§ 13, 15, 39(2) No. 5(a) WpHG in their version applicable from 28 October 2004 to 31 October 2007. Based on §§ 9(1) No. 1, (2) No. 1, 30(1) No. 4, (4) OWiG it imposed a fine of €200,000.[255]

(bb)   France

133   In France, the AMF's Commissions des sanctions have been able to impose fines of up to €10 million for legal entities and €1.5 million for persons pursuant to Article L. 621–15-III C. mon. fin. since 2008. Alternatively, the Commissions des sanctions can determine that the sanction be ten times the realised profits.[256] The AMF rarely explains the level of the fines it imposes, usually only referring to the particular seriousness and extent of the offence (*à raison de leur particulière gravité et de leur ampleur*).[257] Unlike under criminal law, the sanctions are not limited to cases in which the issuer acted with intent or negligence, although intent will have an effect on the height of the fines imposed.[258]

134   One must distinguish between cases in which the issuer himself is held liable and cases in which the sanctions are to be imposed against the management. As the law does not contain any provision on whom to sanction and taking account of the constitutional principle that violations are to be attributed to the offender only (*principe de personnalité des poursuites et peines*) the AMF has developed different criteria to this means. The issuer is, for example, to be held responsible for a lack of organisation.[259] Some maintain that the issuer could always be held liable for breaches of the obligations committed by the management.[260] The AMF's approach is, as yet, not entirely clear, both concepts being legally justifiable. The management

---

[251] H.-D. Assmann, in: H.-D. Assmann and U.H. Schneider (eds.), *Kommentar zum WpHG*, § 15 para. 290.

[252] Ibid., § 15 para. 289.

[253] Ibid., § 15 para. 291–292.

[254] Ibid., § 15 para. 299 ff.

[255] Cf. the OLG Frankfurt am Main in its appeal decision, WM (2009), p. 647 ff. It denied the existence of an unavoidable mistake as to the wrongful nature of the act on the basis of the unclear legal situation; BaFin, *Jahresbericht 2009* (annual report), p. 191.

[256] CA Paris, 1re ch., section H, 20 Nov. 2007, No. 200/00369, *Sedia Développement SA c/ AMF*, Bull. Joly Bourse (2008), p. 19 ff. annotated by F. Martin Laprade with a dissenting opinion.

[257] Cf. C. Arsouze, Bull. Joly Bourse (2008), p. 12, 17.

[258] Cf. F. Martin Laprade, Bull. Joly Bourse (2008), p. 19, 26.

[259] Cf. further M. Tomasi, 109 Banque & Droit (2006), p. 35 ff.

[260] Cf. Cass. com. of 19 December 2006 with annotation by Garrigues, 1 RTDF (2007), p. 122, 123.

is not protected by a doctrine of *faute détachable* under supervisory law.[261] There are, however, a few court decisions according to which the company is always to be held liable for the management's communication.[262]

(b) Naming and Shaming

135 Article 14(4) MAD further requires that the Member States ensure that the competent authorities can disclose any measure or sanction imposed for infringement of the directive's provisions to the public, unless such disclosure would seriously jeopardise the financial markets or cause disproportionate damage to the parties involved. Whilst this instruction has generally been followed, naming and shaming has only proved an effective measure in a few Member States.

136 The concept is particularly well developed in France, where all sanctions were made public on the AMF's website pursuant to Article L. 621–15-V C. mon. fin., even before the MAD was enacted. This legal practice is also recommended with regard to the directives based on the Financial Services Action Plan.[263,264] In 2007 the Conseil d'État ruled that the disclosure of imposed sanctions constitutes a sanction in itself. It does not require the decision to have full legal effect before it is made public in order to comply with the presumption of innocence.[265] The publication must, however, follow the principles of legality and proportionality.[266] The AMF regards naming and shaming as particularly effective, not only due to its disciplinary effects but also as a deterrent to others.

137 Spain publishes all sanctions in a register kept by the CNMV pursuant to Article 98.3 LMV. Certain sanctions are further noted in the commercial register on the basis of Articles 102 and 103 LMV, particularly severe breaches of the provisions also being published in the Spanish law gazette. In the United Kingdom publication pursuant to section 123(3) FSMA plays a very important role in legal practice.

138 In Germany Article 14(4) MAD was implemented in § 40b WpHG which leaves it within the BaFin's discretion to publish incontestable measures it has taken. The BaFin has not made use of the possibility as yet, thereby protecting the issuers' fundamental rights.[267]

(c) Further Administrative Sanctions

139 Further administrative sanctions are possible. In France these include reprimands, warnings or bans (Article L. 621–15-III C. mon. fin.). In Spain, Articles 102 f. LMV

---

[261] Cf. Cass. com. of 31 March 2004, No. 03-14991, 65 Bull. civ. IV, cited according to A. Couret et al. (eds.), *Droit financier*, p. 896 para. 1484 ; E. Chvika, RDBF (2008), p. 12, 14; more details on *faute détachable* in French capital markets law in R. Veil and P. Koch, *Französisches Kapitalmarktrecht*, p. 22.

[262] Seen critically by H. Pisani, 3 RTDF (2007), p. 18, 19 with reference to Cass. com. of 19 December 2006 "Vivendi".

[263] See § 1 para. 13.

[264] Cf. P.-H. Conac, 1 RTDF (2006), p. 128 ff.

[265] Cf. G. Roch, Bull. Joly Bourse (2008), p. 204, 207. Seen critically by N. Rontchevsky, 1 RTDF (2008), p. 86 ff.

[266] Cf. C. Ducouloux-Favard, *Infractions boursières*, p. 32.

[267] Cf. K. Altenhain, in: H. Hirte and T.M.J. Möllers (eds.), *Kölner Kommentar zum WpHG*, § 40b para. 5; J. Vogel, in: H.-D. Assmann and U.H. Schneider (eds.), Kommentar zum WpHG, § 40b para. 1.

contains not only fines and public reprimands, but also further sanctions, such as the suspension or restriction of the trade in the respective securities and the revocation of market authorisations. The management can be sanctioned under Articles 95, 105 f. LMV by suspending their activities with the issuer for one to three years or by banning them from their profession for up to five years. The supervisory authority has a free choice between the different sanctions, fines being most common in legal practice.[268] Bans and suspensions on management activity are, however, greatly feared in Spain and appear to have a particularly strong preventive effect.[269]

140   In France the AMF, as the successor of the self-regulatory CMF, not only imposes the standard administrative measures but also the so-called *sanctions disciplinaires* for breaches of the rules of conduct and internal rules of the securities trading professions in separate proceedings.

4.   Criminal Law

141   Criminal sanctions for breaches of the disclosure obligations for inside information play a subordinated role in Europe. Breaches of Article 6(1) MAD are only sanctioned under criminal law in 9 out of 29 CESR Member States, possible penalties reaching from fines of €5,000 in Ireland to a maximum prison sentence of eight years in Italy.[270] Whilst criminal liability does not require special provision but can rather be based on the general provisions for pecuniary offences, it appears of little importance in legal practice.

VI.   Supervision

142   Article 11 MAD states that the national supervisory authorities are responsible for ensuring that the directive's provisions are applied correctly. They must follow the same rules as for insider trading.[271]

143   Data on the supervisory authorities' legal practice are scarce. In Germany, the BaFin commenced 23 new proceedings for breaches of the disclosure obligations in 2011. In four cases it imposed fines of up to €95,000, after nine similar decisions in 2010. Seven proceedings were terminated without the BaFin taking any measures, as opposed to 10 dropped procedures in 2010.[272] In Austria only 18 proceedings were initiated in 2011 for the entire area of market abuse and trading rules.[273] France imposed administrative sanctions to 23 persons for incorrect information of the

---

[268] Cf. S. García Malsipica, in: F. Fernández and G. Arranz, *Régimen jurídico de los mercados de valores y de las instituciones de inversión colectiva*, p. 831.

[269] As maintained by our Spanish interview partners (see fn. 20).

[270] Cf. CESR, *Executive Summary to the Report on Administrative Measures and Sanctions and the Criminal Sanctions available in Member States under the Market Abuse Directive (MAD)*, CESR/08-099, February 2008, p. 5, 10; see also the individual descriptions on p. 34 ff.

[271] See § 13 para. 99–108.

[272] Cf. BaFin, *Jahresbericht 2011* (annual report), p. 211.

[273] Cf. FMA, *Jahresbericht 2011* (annual report), p. 109.

capital market in 2010.[274] In Spain, the CNMV initiated no proceedings in 2011, after two new proceedings in 2010.[275]

VII. Conclusion

144   The European regime on the disclosure of inside information is largely complete with regard to the behavioural rules and proves to follow a clear and coherent concept. It is all the more surprising that these detailed rules at a European level have not managed to achieve a larger unification in the Member States, where large differences continue to exist.

145   Conceptually, the unified approach for the prohibitions on insider trading and the disclosure of inside information, orientated towards the term "inside information", remains critical, not all information relevant for insider trading necessarily requiring disclosure obligations. By extending the list of information requiring disclosure, the main focus of the regime has shifted to the possibilities of delaying disclosure. The Commission's proposal for reforms constitutes a first small but still insufficient step in the right direction, developing a new category of inside information that is exempt from the disclosure obligation.

146   The legal situation in the Member States remains highly inconsistent with regard to the sanctions imposed for breaches of the disclosure obligations. The Commission's aim of achieving a much stronger unification of the laws with its reform proposals must therefore be viewed in a positive light.

---

[274] Cf. AMF, *Annual Report 2010*, p. 199.
[275] Cf. CNMV, *Annual Report 2011*, p. 184.

§ 20 Transparency of Major Shareholdings and Financial Instruments

Bibliography

Baj, Claude, *Action de concert et dépôt d'une offre publique obligatoire: réflexions à la lumière de l'affaire Gecina*, RDBF (2008), p. 57–66; Baums, Theodor and Sauter, Maike, *Anschleichen an Übernahmeziele mit Hilfe von Aktienderivaten*, ZHR 173 (2009), p. 454–503; Biard, Jean-François, *Comment on Consultations publiques*, RDBF (2009), p. 70–73; Bethel, Jennifer E., Liebeskind, Julia Porter and Opler, Tim, *Block Share Purchases and Coporate Performance*, 53 J. Fin. (1998), p. 605–634; Brandt, Ulrich, *Meldepflichten für aktienbasierte Instrumente: Anmerkungen zum Diskussionsentwurf des Bundesfinanzministeriums (AnlegerStärkungsG)*, BKR (2010), p. 270–275; Brav, Alon, Jiang, Wie, Partnoy, Frank and Thomas, Randall, *Hedge Fund Activism, Corporate Governance, and Firm Performance*, 63 J. Fin. (2008), p. 1729–1775; von Bülow, Christoph, *Acting in Concert: Anwendungsprobleme des neuen Zurechnungstatbestands*, in: Veil, Rüdiger, *Übernahmerecht in Praxis und Wissenschaft* (2009), p. 137–162; von Bülow, Christoph and Petersen, Sven, *Stimmrechtszurechnung zum Treuhänder?*, NZG (2009), p. 1373–1378; von Bülow, Christoph and Stephanblome, Markus, *Acting in Concert und neue Offenlegungspflichten nach dem Risikobegrenzungsgesetz*, ZIP (2008), p. 1797–1806; Burgard, Ulrich, *Die Berechnung des Stimmrechtsanteils nach §§ 21–23 Wertpapierhandelsgesetz*, BB (1995), p. 2069–2078; Carbonetti, Francesco, *I patti parasociale nelle società non quotate alla luce del Testo Unico della Finanza*, Riv soc. (1998), p. 909; Choi, Dosoung, *Toehold Acquisitions, Shareholder Wealth, and the Market for Corporate Control*, 26 J. Fin. Quant. Analysis (1991), p. 391–407; Conac, Pierre-Henri, *Le nouveau régime des franchissements de seuils issu de l'ordonnance no 2009–105 du 30 janvier 2009 et du Règlement général de l'AMF*, Revue des sociétés (2009), p. 477–501; Dwyer, William, *Committee of European Securities Regulators Consults on Pan-European Long Disclosure Code*, 25 JIBLR (2010), p. 577–578; Dwyer, William, *Final Rules on Information about Major Shareholdings*, 24 JIBLR (2009), p-. 435–438; Engert, Andreas, *Unanwendbarkeit von § 30 Abs. 2 WpÜG auf die Wahl des Aufsichtsratsvorsitzenden*, JZ (2007), p. 314–316; Elster, Nico, *Europäisches Kapitalmarktrecht. Recht des Sekundärmarktes* (2002); Ferrarini, Guido, *Equity Derivatives and Transparency: When Should Substance Prevail*, in: Grundmann, Stefan et al. (eds.), *Festschrift für Klaus J. Hopt zum 70. Geburtstag* (2010), p. 1803–1822; Fleischer, Holger, *Finanzinvestoren im ordnungspolitischen Gesamtgefüge von Aktien-, Bankaufsichts- und Kapitalmarktrecht*, ZGR (2008), p. 185–224; Fleischer, Holger, *Mitteilungspflichten für Inhaber wesontlicher Beteiligungen (§ 27a WpHG)*, AG (2008), p. 873–883; Fleischer, Holger and Bedkowski, Dorothea, *Stimmrechtszurechnung zum Treuhänder gemäß § 22 I 1 Nr. 2 WpHG: Ein zivilgerichtlicher Fehlgriff und seine kapitalmarktrechtlichen Folgen*, DStR (2010), p. 933–938; Fleischer, Holger and Schmolke, Klaus Ulrich, *Das Anschleichen an eine börsennotierte Aktiengesellschaft*, NZG (2009), p. 401–409; Fleischer, Holger and Schmolke, Klaus Ulrich, *Kapitalmarktrechtliche Beteiligungstransparenz nach §§ 21 ff. WpHG und "Hidden Ownership"*, ZIP (2008), p. 1501–1512; Fleischer, Holger and Schmolke, Klaus Ulrich, *Zum beabsichtigten Ausbau der kapitalmarktrechtlichen Beteiligungstransparenz bei modernen Finanzinstrumenten (§§ 25, 25a DiskE-WpHG)*, NZG (2010), p. 846–854; Fleischer, Holger and Schmolke, Klaus Ulrich, *Die Reform der Transparenzrichtlinie: Mindest- oder Vollharmonisierung der kapitalmarktrechtlichen Beteiligungspublizität?*, NZG (2010), p. 1241–1248; Funck-Brentano, François and Mason, Alan, *La dérive des produits dérivés. Considérations pratiques sur les produits dérivés et les franchissements de seuils*, RTDF (2009), p. 31–36; Fusi, Alessandra, *I patti parasociali alla luce della nuova disciplina societaria e le possibili applicazioni dei voting trust*, 6 Le Società (2007), p. 689–694; Goyet, Charles, *Action de concert*, in: *Dictionnaire Joly Bourse et produits financiers*, Vol. I, looseleaf booklet, as of 30 November 2008; Grillier, Frédéric and Segain, Hubert, *Franchissements de seuils: Réglementation applicable et évolutions souhaitables*, RTDF (2007), p. 20–44; König, Wolfgang, *Das Risikobegrenzungsgesetz—offene und gelöste Fragen*, BB (2008),

p. 1910–1914, Kunz, Peter V., *Die Stimmrechtssuspendierungsklage im revidierten Börsenrecht—Eine neue Sanktion bei Meldepflichtsverletzungen mit grossem Drohpotential*, SZW 80 (2008), p. 280–298; Le Cannu, Paul, *Les silences d'un concert espagnol, note sous Cour d'appel de Paris, 1re ch., sect. H, 2 avril 2008, SA Sacyr Vallehermoso et autre c/ SA Eiffage*, Revue des sociétés (2008), p. 394–404; Maison-Blanche, Catherine and Lecat, Dimitri, *Essai de synthèse sur les sanctions en cas de violation de l'obligation de declarations des franchissements de seuils dans le capital et les droits de vote des sociétés dont les actions sont admises sur un marché réglementé*, RTDF (2007), p. 146–151; Merkner, Andreas and Sustmann, Marco, *Vorbei mit dem unbemerkten Anschleichen an börsennotierte Unternehmen?*, NZG (2010), p. 681–688; Meo, Giorgo, in: Bessone, Mario, *Trattato di diritto privato*, Vol. XVII, *Le Società di capitali* (2008); Mikkelson, Wayne H. and Ruback, Richard S., *An Empirical Analysis of the Interfirm Equity Investment Process*, 14 J. Fin. Econ. (1985), p. 523–553; Möllers, Thomas M.J. and Holzner, Florian, *Die Offenlegungspflichten des Risikobegrenzungsgesetzes (§ 27 II WpHG-E)*, NZG (2008), p. 166–172; Muñoz Pérez, Ana Felicitas, *El concierto como presupuesto de la OPA obligatoria*, La Ley, (2007); Neye, Hans-Werner, *Gemeinschaftsrecht und Recht der verbundenen Unternehmen*, ZGR (1995), p. 191–207; Omaggio, Alexandre, *Ordonnance du 30 janvier 2009: regard critique sur la reforme relative aux declarations de franchissement de seuils et aux declarations d'intentions*, Dr. sociétés April (2009), p. 49–53; Piselli, Diego, *La validità e l'efficacia dei patti parasociali dopo la riforma societaria*, 2 Le Società (2009), p. 197–204; Prechtl, Felix, *Kapitalmarktrechtliche Beteiligungspublizität* (2010); Querfurth, Jan, *§ 27a WpHG und die Folgen eines Verstoßes*, WM (2008), p. 1957–1963; Reburn, James Patrick, *A Note on Firm Size, Information Availability and Market Reactions to US Stock Ownership Reporting Announcements*, 21 J. Bus. Fin. & Account (1994), p. 445–455; Rechtschaffen, Alan N., *Capital Markets, Derivatives and the Law* (2009); Ringe, Wolf-Georg, *Die Neuregelung des Internationalen Kapitalmarktpublizitätsrechts durch die Neufassung der Transparenz-RL*, AG (2007), p. 809–815; Schanz, Kay-Michael, *Schaeffler/Continental: Umgehung von Meldepflichten bei öffentlichen Übernahmen durch Einsatz von derivativen Finanzinstrumenten*, DB (2008), p. 1899–1905; Scherr, Frederick C., Abbott, Ashok and Dillon, Upinder, *Returns to Target Shareholders from Initial Purchases of Common Shares: A Multivariate Analysis*, 32 Q. J. Bus. & Econ. (1993), p. 66, 72–73; Schiessl, Maximilian, *Beteiligungsaufbau mittels Cash-settled Total Return Equity Swaps—Neue Modelle und Einführung von Meldepflichten*, Der Konzern (2009), p. 291–299; Schmidt, Dominique, *Action de concert et dépôt d'une offre publique obligatoire*, RDBF (2008), p. 56–70; Schneider, Uwe H., *Der kapitalmarktrechtliche Strategie- und Mittelherkunftsbericht—oder: wem dient das Kapitalmarktrecht?*, in: Habersack, Mathias et al. (eds.), *Festschrift für Gerd Nobbe zum 65. Geburtstag* (2009), p. 741–754; Schneider, Uwe H. and Anzinger, Heribert M., *Umgehung und missbräuchliche Gestaltungen im Kapitalmarktrecht oder: Brauchen wir eine § 42 AO entsprechende Vorschrift im Kapitalmarktrecht?*, ZIP (2009), p. 1–10; Schockenhoff, Martin and Schumann, Alexander, *Acting in Concert—Geklärte und ungeklärte Fragen*, ZGR (2005), p. 568–610; Schockenhoff, Martin and Wagner, Eric, *Zum Begriff des "acting in concert"*, NZG (2008), p. 361–368; Schouten, Michael C., *The Case for Mandatory Ownership Disclosure*, 15 Stan. J. L. Bus. & Fin. (2009), p. 127–182; Segain, Hubert, *Les franchissements de seuil: évolutions récentes*, RTDF (2008), p. 7; Seligman, Joel, *The Historical Need for a Mandatory Corporate Disclosure System*, 9 J. Corp. Law (1983), p. 1–61; Teichmann, Christoph and Epe, Daniel, *Neuer Regelungsansatz in der kapitalmarktrechtlichen Beteiligungstransparenz: Generalklausel statt Fallgruppen-Lösung*, WM (2010), p. 1477–1483; Uzan, Carole, *Des projets de réforme en matière de franchissement de seuils, de déclarations d'intention et d'offre obligatoire*, Bull. Joly Bourse (2008), p. 530–536; Veil, Rüdiger, *Der Schutz des verständigen Anlegers durch Publizität und Haftung im europäischen und nationalen Kapitalmarktrecht*, ZBB (2006), p. 162–171; Veil, Rüdiger, *Stimmrechtszurechnungen aufgrund von Abstimmungsvereinbarungen gemäß § 22 Abs. 2 WpHG und § 30 Abs. 2 WpÜG*, in: Bitter, Georg et al. (eds.), *Festschrift für Karsten Schmidt zum 70. Geburtstag* (2009), p. 1645–1664; Veil, Rüdiger and Dolff, Christian, *Kapitalmarktrechtliche Mitteilungspflichten des Treuhänders. Grundsätze und Grenzen der Zurechnung von Stimmrechtsanteilen nach § 22 WpHG*, AG (2010), p. 385–391; Veil, Rüdiger, *Enforcement of Capital Markets Law in Europe—Observations from a Civil Law Country*, 11 EBOR (2010), p. 409–422; Veil,

Rüdiger, *Wie viel "Enforcement" ist notwendig? Zur Reform des Instrumentenmix bei der Sanktionierung kapitalmarktrechtlicher Mitteilungspflichten gemäß §§ 21 ff.* WpHG, ZHR 175 (2011), p. 83–109; Witt, Carl-Heinz, *Übernahmen von Aktiengesellschaften und Transparenz der Beteiligungsverhältnisse* (1998); Zabala, Erasun, *Urteilsanmerkung zu CA Paris, 1re ch., sect. H, 24 juin 2008, no 2007/21048, Gecina SA,* Bull. Joly Bourse (2008), p. 389; Zetzsche, Dirk A., *Hidden Ownership in Europe: BAFin's Decision in Schaeffler v. Continental,* 10 EBOR (2009), p. 115–147; Zetzsche, Dirk A., *Against Mandatory Disclosure of Economic—Only Positions Referenced to Shares of European Issuers—Twenty Arguments against CESR Proposal,* 11 EBOR (2010), p. 231–252; Zimmermann, Martin, *Die kapitalmarktrechtliche Beteiligungstransparenz nach dem Risikobegrenzungsgesetz,* ZIP (2009), p. 57–64.

I. Introduction

1   The transparency regarding major holdings was high on the agenda of the European legislature from a very early point in time. It was regarded as necessary in order to ensure an equal level of investor protection throughout the Community and to make for greater interpenetration of the Member States' transferrable securities markets, thus helping to establish a true European capital market.[1] The TD from 1988 therefore obliged Member States to develop rules on disclosure and information to be published when a major holding in a listed company is acquired or disposed of.[2] However, it only contained a non-cohesive collection of thresholds, obliging the Member States to ensure that a person or legal entity notifies the company and the competent authority if, following the acquisition or disposal of a holding in a company, the proportion of voting rights held by them reaches, exceeds or falls below the thresholds of 10%, 20%, 1/3, 50% and 2/3.

2   Most of the Member States at that time did not regard this level of information as sufficient and provided additional thresholds in their national laws.[3] It was therefore not surprising that the European legislature saw the need to amend the former European provisions by adopting Directive 2004/106/EC[4] and establishing a "more securities market directed transparency regime".[5] The directive obliged Member

---

[1] Cf. Recitals of Council Directive 88/627/EEC of 12 December 1988 (Transparency Directive I); on its historical background see § 1 para. 9.

[2] The first directive to contain provisions on this was the Council Directive 79/279/EEC of 5 March 1979 coordinating the conditions for the admission of securities to an official stock exchange listing (cf. § 1 para. 6), obligating companies to inform the public by including information in the prospectus on changes in the structure of major holdings (ownership and shares) of its capital compared to former publications.

[3] Cf. Commission, Proposal for a Directive of the European Parliament and of the Council of 26 March 2003 on the harmonisation of transparency requirements with regard to information about issuers whose securities are admitted to trading on a regulated market and amending Directive 2001/34/EC, COM(2003) 138 final, p. 18. (only three out of 15 Member States limited themselves to the level of transparency provided for by the Transparency Directive I).

[4] Directive 2004/109/EC of the European Parliament and of the Council of 15 December 2004 on the harmonisation of transparency requirements in relation to information about issuers whose securities are admitted to trading in a regulated market and amending Directive 2001/34/EC (Transparency Directive II), hereafter simply referred to as Transparency Directive (TD) most recently amended by Directive 2010/78/EU of the European Parliament and of the Council of 24 November 2010, OJ L331, 15 December 2010, p. 120.

[5] Cf. Commission, Proposal for a Directive of the European Parliament and of the Council of 26 March 2003 on the harmonisation of transparency requirements with regard to information about issuers whose securities are admitted to trading on a regulated market and amending Directive 2001/34/EC, COM(2003) 138 final, p. 18.

States to introduce additional thresholds and to provide transparency rules for financial instruments resulting in an entitlement to acquire shares to which voting rights are attached. These rules were intended to enhance investor protection and market efficiency by enabling shareholders to have full knowledge of changes in the voting structure when acquiring or disposing of shares.[6] Furthermore, this was to "ensure an effective control of share issuers".[7]

3　The regulatory aims of the directive are only described in an abstract way and are therefore unsuitable as an interpretational help.[8] The considerations of the German legislature when it implemented the TD into German law are more helpful in this respect.[9] It underlined the importance of the criteria of shareholder composition and the changes regarding major holdings for the investors' decisions, especially for domestic and foreign institutional investors, and the large influence these criteria have on the price of shares.[10] Knowing the identity of major shareholders provides investors with important information such as allowing them to assess the possibility of conflicts of interest.[11] A high level of transparency regarding major holdings also prevents investors from creeping in on issuers.[12] These considerations show that the main aim of notification and disclosure obligations is to inform investors of shareholders acquiring larger stakes and imminent takeovers.[13]

4　Additionally, offering market participants, and especially investors, the latest and the most extensive information provides a transparency that counteracts the abuse of inside information. The general knowledge of the volume of shares freely nego-tiable and the identity of major shareholders reduces information asymmetries.[14] Thus, the system of disclosure of major shareholdings—similar to the obligation of disclosure of inside information[15]—reinforces the provisions on market abuse.[16]

5　The TD only dictates a minimum harmonisation[17] regarding the disclosure of major shareholdings.[18] The Member States may therefore enact provisions that are more

---

[6] Cf. Recital 1 TD.

[7] Cf. Recital 18 TD.

[8] Cf. F. Prechtl, *Kapitalmarktrechtliche Beteiligungspublizität*, p. 27.

[9] Cf. Begr. RegE 2. Finanzmarktförderungsgesetz, BT-Drucks. 12/6679, p. 52 (explanatory notes).

[10] The price relevance of information on changes in major shareholdings has been proven in empirical studies. On US-American capital markets law see W.H. Mikkelson and R. Ruback, 14 J. Fin. Econ. (1985), p. 523, 532–543: price increase of 2.88% after the disclosure of Schedule 13D; J.P. Reburn, 21(3) J. Bus. Fin. & Account (1994), p. 445: 2.46%; F.C. Scherr et al., 32(4) Quarterly J. Bus. & Econ. (1993), p. 66, 72–73: 2.49%; D. Choi, 26(3) J. Fin. Quant. Analysis (1991), p. 391, 396: 2.2%; J. Brav et al., 63 J. Fin. (2008), p. 1729, 1755: 2%.

[11] Commission, Proposal for a Directive of the European Parliament and of the Council of 26 March 2003 on the harmonisation of transparency requirements with regard to information about issuers whose securities are admitted to trading on a regulated market and amending Directive 2001/34/EC, COM(2003) 138 final, p. 21; also F. Prechtl, *Kapitalmarktrechtliche Beteiligungspublizität, p. 31.*

[12] Cf. Begr. RegE TUG, BT-Drucks. 16/2498, p. 28 (explanatory notes).

[13] Cf. L. Burn, in: R. Panasar and P. Boeckman (eds.), *European Securities Law*, para. 1.274; F. Prechtl, *Kapitalmarktrechtliche Beteiligungspublizität*, p. 33; C.-H. Witt, *Übernahmen von Aktiengesellschaften und Transparenz der Beteiligungsverhältnisse*, p. 69 ff.

[14] Begr. RegE 2. Finanzmarktförderungsgesetz, BT-Drucks. 12/6679, p. 52 (explanatory notes).

[15] See § 19 para. 1–6.

[16] S. Kalss et al., *Kapitalmarktrecht I*, § 17 para. 5; F. Prechtl, *Kapitalmarktrechtliche Beteiligungspublizität*, p. 32; R. Veil, in: K. Schmidt and M. Lutter (eds.), *Kommentar zum AktG*, Vor §§ 21 ff. WpHG para. 5.

[17] On the concept of minimum harmonisation see § 4 para. 38–44.

[18] Cf. F. Prechtl, *Kapitalmarktrechtliche Beteiligungspublizität*, p. 22; R. Veil, in: *Festschrift für Karsten Schmidt*, p. 1645, 1664.

---

stricter than those provided for in the directive.[19] Some Member States have taken advantage of this possibility, introducing thresholds as low as 2% and reducing the intervals between the thresholds provided for by the TD. They have also developed stricter provisions on the attribution of voting rights attached to shares belonging to a third party. Some of these measures, such as the introduction of stricter national provisions on acting in concert, are aimed in particular at disclosing the influence of financial investors. These measures have been criticised by some as they raise the price of takeovers, thus allegedly restricting the market for corporate control.[20]

6   A further element of capital markets law concerning transparency of major holdings is the regime on the obligation to disclose the aims underlying the purchase of voting rights. Some EU Member States, such as Germany and France, followed the example of the United States[21] and introduced a respective obligation. The issuer then has to publish this information. European law so far does not oblige the Member States to introduce such provisions.

II.   European Concepts of Regulation

1.   Requirements under European Law

(a)   Foundations

7   The TD—one of the four framework directives in capital markets law[22]—defines the general principles underlying the harmonisation of transparency obligations. The European Commission enacted an implementing directive on Level 2 of the Lamfalussy Process in order to ensure a uniform application of these provisions, mainly containing procedural rules.[23] So far, neither the CESR nor the ESMA has published "Guidelines" that could be used as a necessary interpretational help regarding abstract legal concepts, as was the case in those that the CESR published regarding the MAD.[24] In particular, the provisions on the attribution of voting rights attached to shares belonging to a third party contain various problems regarding their interpretation. As several Member States have adopted some of the attribution rules one-to-one in their national laws, recommendations on the interpretation would prove very helpful. The CESR has, however, only published a document on

---

[19] Cf. Art. 3(1) TD. H. Fleischer and K.U. Schmolke NZG (2010), p. 1241, 1244 ff. recommend a maximum harmonisation of the disclosure regime de lege ferenda.

[20] Cf. N. Elster, *Europäisches Kapitalmarktrecht*, p. 22.

[21] In US-American law the investor's obligation to disclose and make public his intents play a central role. The legal foundation for an investors' disclosure obligation regarding major shareholdings are contained in sec. 13(d) SEA. The provisions were introduced in the Williams Act of 1968 (Act of July 29, 1968, Pub. L. No. 90-439, 82 Stat. 454). The SEC further developed Rules 13d-1 to 13d-7 and facilitated disclosure by supplying a form (Schedule 13D). Item 4 requires the reporting person to state the purpose of his transaction and describe any plans or proposals it has with regard to changes in the company. For more details on the US-American law see T. Hazen, *The Law of Securities Regulation*, p. 381 ff.

[22] Cf. § 1 para. 26.

[23] Commission Directive 2007/14/EC of 8 March 2007 laying down detailed rules for the implementation of certain provisions of Directive 2004/109/EC on the harmonisation of transparency requirements in relation to information about issuers whose securities are admitted to trading on a regulated market.

[24] Cf. § 13 para. 7.

frequently asked questions regarding the TD which does not contain standards, guidelines or recommendations.[25]

(b) Scope of Application and Regulatory Powers

8   The TD "establishes requirements in relation to the disclosure of periodic and ongoing information about issuers whose securities are already admitted to trading on a regulated market situated or operating within a Member State".[26] It follows that the directive's scope of application is restricted to securities trading on *regulated markets*.[27] The Member States need not apply these provisions to their non-regulated markets, an example being the open market (*Freiverkehr*) in Germany or the Alternative Investment Market in the United Kingdom.[28]

9   The TD is addressed to the "home Member States". These must ensure that a notification on the acquisition or disposal of major holdings takes place and the information contained in the notification is then published. The term "home Member State" is defined in the directive. For issuers of shares incorporated in the Community the term refers to the Member State where the issuer has its registered office.[29] The location of the head office is irrelevant.[30] The notification obligations regarding changes in major holdings also apply to third-country investors as the TD makes no restrictions regarding the origin of the person acquiring or disposing of shares with voting rights.[31] An investor from China or the United States must therefore notify the issuer as must an investor from an EU Member State.

10   *Example:* For a French public limited company (*Société Anonyme*) that has its registered office in France the home Member State is therefore France. Any shareholder thus has to fulfil the French provisions on disclosure when acquiring or disposing of shares—irrespective of from where it may come. These will even apply if the issuer has transferred its administrative head office to Belgium—provided this is permissible under French company law.

11   Where the issuer is incorporated in a third country, the home Member State is the country in which the company is required to file the annual information[32] with the competent authority.[33]

(c) Disclosure Obligations

12   The TD requires "information about major holdings", such as the provision on the "notification of the acquisition or disposal of major holdings" in Article 9 which can be regarded as the core of the disclosure system for major holdings. The provi-

---

[25] CESR, *Frequently Asked Questions Regarding the TD: Common Positions Agreed by CESR members*, CESR/09-168, May 2009.

[26] Cf. Art. 1(1) TD.

[27] The term "regulated market" is defined in Art. 2(1)(c) TD. For more details see § 7 para. 24–31.

[28] See § 7 para. 20.

[29] Cf. Art. 2(1)(i) first indent TD.

[30] Cf. W.-G. Ringe, AG (2007), p. 810–811; F. Prechtl, *Kapitalmarktrechtliche Beteiligungspublizität*, p. 20–21.

[31] Cf. F. Prechtl, *Kapitalmarktrechtliche Beteiligungspublizität*, p. 19.

[32] Cf. Art. 10 PD.

[33] Cf. Art. 2(1)(i) second indent TD; seen critically by L. Burn, in: R. Panasar and P. Boeckman (eds.), *European Securities Law*, para. 1.171.

sion defines to whom the notification obligation applies and which procedures are subject to notification. Article 10 TD extends the notification obligations of Article 9 to further cases in which the obligation "shall apply", i.e. cases in which someone is not owner of the shares but is nonetheless entitled to acquire or to dispose of the shares or may exercise voting rights belonging to a third party. Without this addition the general rules on notification could easily be avoided. Hereafter the provisions in Articles 9 and 10 will therefore be regarded as an entity. Both articles aim to ensure transparency regarding any changes in major holdings. A further notification obligation introduced by the TD concerns situations in which a person has the possibility of influencing voting rights. According to Article 13 TD, however, this obligation only applies to such financial instruments that result in an entitlement to acquire, on such holder's initiative alone, shares to which voting rights are attached. According to the European Commission, a rule like this is necessary as influence in a company can be indirectly exercised through financial instruments when these reach the extent of major holdings.[34]

(d)   Further Disclosure Requirements

13   The underlying understanding for the rules regarding the major shareholding notifications is that changes in the voting rights are of relevance for the shareholders' decisions to invest or divest. Therefore, the issuer must be notified of this information in order that it can make it public. This can also be required by other provisions, such as the provisions of the MAD which oblige the issuers of financial instruments to inform the public as soon as possible of inside information which directly concerns them.[35] Whether this ad hoc disclosure obligation also applies to changes in major holdings was not decided by the European legislature. The TD does not define its relationship to the MAD. This question can therefore only be answered by an interpretation of the respective provisions and is much discussed in Germany. With respect to their divergent purposes, it is assumed that neither the regime on transparency of major holdings nor the regime on ad hoc disclosure generally has priority over the other.[36] An issuer can therefore be obliged to publish immediately the acquisition or disposal of major shareholdings if this fact should be regarded as price sensitive and therefore has to be considered as inside information.[37]

(e)   Reform

14   On 25 October 2011 the European Commission published a proposal for a directive amending the TD.[38] The primary aim is to introduce extended disclosure obligations

[34] Cf. Commission, Proposal for a Directive of the European Parliament and of the Council of 26 March 2003 on the harmonisation of transparency requirements with regard to information about issuers whose securities are admitted to trading on a regulated market and amending Directive 2001/34/EC, COM(2003) 138 final, p. 19.
[35] See § 19 para. 25–51.
[36] Cf. for example H. Hirte, in: H. Hirte and C. von Bülow (eds.), in *Kölner Kommentar zum WpHG*, § 21 para. 56 f.; K.-D. Dehlinger and M. Zimmermann, in: A. Fuchs (ed.), *Kommentar zum WpHG*, Vor §§ 21 bis 30 WpHG para. 33.
[37] This can only be determined for the individual case, in particular by examining whether the acquisition or disposal of a major shareholding may considerably influence the price of the shares. On this aspect of inside information see § 13 para. 42–43.
[38] Proposal for a Directive of the European Parliament and of the Council amending Directive 2004/109/EC

for the holders of financial instruments. According to the proposal, the Member States are no longer to be permitted to "make a holder of shares, or a natural person or legal entity referred to in Articles 10 or 13, subject to requirements more stringent than those laid down in this Directive".[39] The Commission justifies this maximum harmonisation with three arguments: it is to ensure legal certainty, increase transparency and reduce administrative burdens for cross-border investors.[40]

15   The Commission further aims to enhance the sanctioning powers of the competent authorities, making the system more effective.[41] The draft therefore contains detailed rules on the sanctions to be introduced into the national laws of the Member States. The Member States are further to be obliged to empower the competent authorities to suspend the exercise of voting rights for holders of shares and financial instruments who do not comply with the notification requirements. It is further to be possible to impose additional pecuniary sanctions. According to the proposal, administrative pecuniary sanctions against legal persons of up to 10% of the total annual turnover in the preceding business year may be imposed; administrative pecuniary sanctions in the case of a natural person are limited to €5,000,000.[42] The proposed amendments also include precise criteria for the national supervisory authorities to take into account when imposing sanctions. This is supposed to ensure a more uniform sanctioning practice than was common in the past.

2.   Implementation in the Member States

16   The transposition of the TD's provisions in the Member States was achieved in various ways. The German,[43] French,[44] Austrian[45] and Swedish[46] legislatures chose not to copy the provisions one-to-one but rather to develop their own provisions meeting the directive's purposes. In this respect, Germany and France in particular have exceeded the level of information required by European law. Both states have more extensive rules on the attribution of voting rights. Italian law[47] also contains features

---

on the harmonization of transparency requirements in relation to information about issuers whose securities are admitted to trading on a regulated market and Commission Directive 2007/14/EC, 25.10.2011, COM(2011) 683/2. For further information see Commission Staff Working Paper, Impact Assesment, SEC(2011) 1279 final, Brussels, 25 October 2011.

[39] Cf. Art. 3(1)2 TD Draft.
[40] Cf. Recital 10 TD Draft (COM(2011) 683 final).
[41] Cf. Recital 14 TD Draft; see also Commission Staff Working Paper, Impact Assesment, SEC(2011) 1279 final, Brussels, 25 October 2011, p. 84–85.
[42] Cf. Art. 28a(2)(d) and (e) TD Draft.
[43] The German legislature implemented the Transparency Directive's provisions into the §§ 21 ff. WpHG and the WpAIV.
[44] The provisions on transparency of major holdings (*franchissements de seuils*) are contained in Art. L. 233-7 ff. C. com. and in Art. 223-11 ff. RG AMF. Cf. R. Veil and P. Koch, *Französisches Kapitalmarktrecht*, p. 79, 146 ff.
[45] In Austria, the obligation to disclose changes in major holdings is defined in §§ 91–94 BörseG. Cf. S. Kalss et al., *Kapitalmarktrecht I*, § 17 para. 3.
[46] The Swedish provisions on the transparency of major holdings can be found in Kapitel 4 LHF. Cf. R. Veil and F. Walla, *Schwedisches Kapitalmarktrecht*, p. 89.
[47] Italy introduced the first provisions on the transparency of major holdings in 1974 in Art. 120 ff. TUF and the Regolamento Emittenti (RE).

that were not as such laid down by the TD. Spain[48] and the United Kingdom,[49] on the other hand, have implemented most of the provisions one-to-one, especially those on the attribution of voting rights.[50]

III. Notification Obligations on Changes in Voting Rights

1. Prerequisites

17   The TD prescribes the introduction of notification obligations toward the issuer on changes in voting rights. The home Member States[51] must ensure that a shareholder notifies the issuer of the proportion of voting rights it holds as a result of an acquisition or disposal where that proportion reaches, exceeds or falls below the thresholds of 5, 10, 15, 20, 25, 30, 50 and 75% (cf. Article 9(1)). These thresholds are binding for the Member States. A Member State can, however, refrain from applying the 30%, respectively the 75% threshold, if a threshold of one-third, respectively two-thirds, of all voting rights is applied in lieu (cf. Article 9(3) TD).

(a) Procedures Subject to Notification

18   As a general rule, it can be stated that a notification obligation not only ensues from the acquisition but also from the disposal of shares. The spirit and purpose of the TD, however, restrict the obligation to transactions that are effective, i.e. where the ownership has been transferred.[52] As to when this is the case is not defined in the TD and must therefore be determined in accordance with the civil law of the respective Member State. The acquisition of shares of a German or Austrian issuer, for example, is only completed when ownership of the shares has actually been transferred and not already on the conclusion of the contract.[53]

19   Shareholders are also required to "notify the issuer of the proportion of voting rights, where that proportion reaches, exceeds or falls below the thresholds provided for … as a result of events changing the breakdown of voting rights" (Article 9(2)). This provision refers in particular to preference shares without voting rights. Under German law, for example, shares which carry the benefit of a cumulative preference right with respect to the distribution of profits may be issued without voting rights (§ 139(1) AktG). If the preference dividend is not paid or not paid in full in any given year and the shortfall is not made up within the following year, the prefer-

---

[48] Spain's regime on the disclosure of major holdings (*communicación de participaciones*) is laid out in Art. 53 LMV and Art. 23 ff. RD 1362/2007.

[49] As of 20 January 2007 DTR 5 of the FSA Handbook contains provisions on the transparency of major holdings. Cf. R. Veil and M. Wundenberg, *Englisches Kapitalmarktrecht*, p. 123–124. On its relation to the LSE's Admission and Disclosure Standards cf. R. Panasar and S. Glasper, in: R. Panasar and P. Boeckman (eds.), *European Securities Law*, 21.83.

[50] Cf. R. Veil and M. Wundenberg, *Englisches Kapitalmarktrecht*, p. 129–130.

[51] On the concept of "home Member States" see above para. 9–11.

[52] S. Kalss et al., *Kapitalmarktrecht I*, § 17 para. 19; regarding Transparency Directive I Cf. N. Elster, *Europäisches Kapitalmarkrecht*, p. 21.

[53] Cf. on German law K.-D. Dehlinger and M. Zimmermann, in: A. Fuchs (ed.), *Kommentar zum WpHG*, § 21 para. 28; R. Veil, in: K. Schmidt and M. Lutter (eds.), *Kommentar zum AktG*, § 21 WpHG para. 16; on Austrian law S. Kalss et al., *Kapitalmarktrecht I*, § 17 para. 19.

Rüdiger Veil

ence shareholders are given a voting right until payment of the shortfall (§ 140(2) AktG). If the preference shareholder reaches or exceeds one of the thresholds of the directive due to this exceptional voting right it must also notify the issuer thereof.

(b)   Thresholds

20   Since the reform in 2004 the European law provides a non-cohesive system of notification obligations. The first notification threshold only begins at 5% of the voting rights, thereafter rising at 5% intervals up to 30% of the voting rights. The interval between 30% and 50% was further broken down by many Member States as this was considered too large an interval.

21   Several Member States, whose national company laws allow for corporate restructuring with a two-thirds majority vote, have made use of the possibility to provide alternative thresholds as described in Article 9(3) TD. This is, for example, the case in Sweden.

22   Additionally, some Member States—notably Germany,[54] Spain[55] and the United Kingdom,[56] but not, however, Austria and Sweden—have introduced an initial threshold at 3% of all voting rights. The German legislature justified this with the fact that shareholders can already have a strong influence on the issuer with less than 5% of the voting rights.[57] Italy has even introduced a threshold as low as 2% of the voting rights, allowing Consob temporarily to reduce this threshold even further should this be necessary for protection of the investor and the market for corporate control.[58]

23   Yet most Member States have not only reduced the lowest threshold level, but also provided for additional thresholds in their national capital markets laws. The most stringent rules can be found in the United Kingdom where any changes in voting rights of more than 1% (acquisition or disposal) must be disclosed from a level of 3% upwards.[59] Italy, Austria and Spain have also developed a cohesive system of notification thresholds. The notification obligations in these states begin at 5% and continue in 5% steps up to the threshold of 50%. Furthermore, most Member States—amongst others France, Italy, Austria, Sweden and Spain, though not, however, Germany—require notification should 90% or 95% of all voting rights or shares be held. This results from the fact that in these states such shareholdings enable a squeeze-out of small shareholders and these should be notified thereof.

24   Additionally, it is noteworthy that France and Sweden, with other Member States, refer not only to changes in the voting rights but also to the proportion of capital,[60] since the stock corporation laws in these countries permit multiple voting rights.[61]

---

[54] Cf. § 21 WpHG.
[55] Cf. Art. 23.1 RD 1362/2007.
[56] Cf. DTR 5.1.2 FSA Handbook.
[57] Cf. Begr. RegE Transparenzrichtlinie-Umsetzungsgesetz (TUG), BT-Drucks. 16/2498, p. 34 (explanatory notes).
[58] Cf. Art. 120 II TUF. However, this only applies to companies with a high market value and a wide circle of investors.
[59] The notification duty in DTR 5.1.2. FSA Handbook only applies to "UK Issuers". Cf. R. Veil and M. Wundenberg, *Englisches Kapitalmarktrecht*, p. 125.
[60] Cf. for France Art. 233-7.1 C. com. and for Sweden Kapitel 4, § 5(1)1 LHF.
[61] Cf. R. Veil and F. Walla, *Schwedisches Kapitalmarktrecht*, p. 90.

25 As the TD only requires a minimum harmonisation regarding the notification obligations on acquisition or disposal of major holdings, so-called "gold plating" is legally permissible and widespread throughout the European Union. France[62] follows the concept that an issuer must have the possibility to define further thresholds regarding voting rights or the proportion of capital in its articles of association. This concept is also consistent with the TD which gives Member States freedom regarding the implementation. In France, this possibility of providing thresholds in the articles of association plays an important role: 95% of all companies listed in the CAC 40, i.e. the French stock market index, have provided specific thresholds in their articles of associations, the lowest of which start at 0.5%.[63] And even beyond the 5% threshold defined by European law several French issuers have set down further thresholds in their articles of association.[64] Should these additional thresholds defined in the articles of association be exceeded, only the company itself need be notified, not, however, the capital market. [65]

26 Determining the exact proportion of the voting rights may be difficult due to various technical questions in this context. The most important of these has been decided upon by the European legislature in the TD: the voting rights shall be calculated on the basis of all the shares to which voting rights are attached[66] even if the exercise thereof is suspended.[67] Thus even a suspension of voting rights will not prevent them from being taken into consideration when determining the total amount of voting rights.[68]

(c) Exemptions from the Notification Obligation

27 The notification on changes in major holdings is not always necessary. In cases in which the acquirer or the transferor does not exercise his voting rights such notification is superfluous. For this reason the obligations described in the TD are not applicable (i) to shares acquired for the sole purpose of clearing and settling within the usual short settlement cycle of a maximum length of three trading days,[69] and (ii) to custodians holding shares in their custodian capacity provided such custodians can only exercise the voting rights attached to such shares under instructions given in writing or by electronic means.[70]

28 A further exemption has been provided for so-called market makers, i.e. persons "holding themselves out on the financial markets on a continuous basis as being willing to deal on own account by buying and selling financial instruments against their proprietary capital at prices defined by them".[71] Market makers ensure the

---

[62] Cf. Art. 233-7.3 C. com.
[63] Cf. F. Grillier and H. Segain, RTDF (2007), p. 20, 24.
[64] Cf. R. Veil and P. Koch, *Französisches Kapitalmarktrecht*, p. 81–82.
[65] Seen critically by P.-H. Conac, Rev. soc. (2009), p. 477, 485, 499–500.
[66] At the end of each calendar month during which an increase or decrease of the total number of voting rights has occurred the issuer is required to disclose to the public the total number of voting rights and capital (cf. Art. 15 TD).
[67] Art. 9(1) TD.
[68] The reasons for this can be multiple, for example a shareholding losing the rights attributed to his shares due to the failure to comply with his notification duties. On this sanction see below para. 91–95.
[69] Cf. Art. 5 Directive 2007/14/EC.
[70] Art. 9(4) TD.
[71] Cf. Art. 2(1)(n) TD. On this see also § 4 para. 15.

markets' liquidity and in general are not interested in exercising their voting rights, thus justifying their in many ways privileged position: a market maker's acquisition or disposal of a major holding which reaches or crosses the 5% threshold is not subject to the notification obligation of Article 9 TD provided the market maker is authorised by his home Member State.[72] Furthermore, the exemption only applies if the market maker does not intervene in the management of the issuer concerned or exert influence on the issuer to buy such shares or back the share price.[73]

29   *Example:* A market maker acquires 6% of an issuer's voting rights. If the conditions of the exempting provision are fulfilled it is not obliged to notify the issuer about the fact that it has exceeded the 5% threshold. It must, however, immediately inform the supervisory authority that regarding the respective shares it is acting as a market maker. If it acquires another 5% of the voting rights it must notify the issuer, as it then exceeds the 10% threshold.

2.   Legal Consequences

(a)   Notification

30   The notification to the issuer must be effected as soon as possible, but not later than within four trading days.[74] Germany and Spain adopted this time limit, whilst other Member States reduced it to only one or two days.[75] The notification must contain the resulting situation in terms of voting rights, the date on which the threshold was reached or crossed and the identity of the shareholder.[76] If the voting rights attributed are attached to shares held by another member of the same corporate group[77] the notification must also contain the chain of controlled undertakings through which voting rights are effectively held.[78]

31   In practice, it is especially important that the TD allows the notification to be made by the parent undertaking (P). In these cases an undertaking is exempt from making the required notification.[79] If, for example, the subsidiary company (S) holds 5% of the voting rights, P can make the notification, thus releasing S from its legal obligation.

(b)   Publication

32   Upon receipt of the notification, but no later than three trading days thereafter, the issuer is obligated to make public all the information contained in the notification.[80]

---

[72] Those Member States that have introduced lower thresholds (of 2% or 3%) have extended these exceptions to these initial thresholds. Cf. for German law § 23(4) WpHG.

[73] Art. 9(5) TD and Art. 6 Directive 2007/14/EC.

[74] Art. 12(2) TD. Transparency Directive I of 12 December 1988 still prescribed the notification to take place within seven calendar days.

[75] In the UK the notification to the issuer must be effected as soon as possible, but not later than two trading days (cf. DTR 5.8.3 FSA Handbooks). This two-day rule only applies to "UK Issuers", cf. R. Veil and M. Wundenberg, *Englisches Kapitalmarktrecht*, p. 125–126. The same time frame is laid down in Austria (cf. § 91(1) BörseG).

[76] Art. 12(1)(a), (b) and (d) TD.

[77] On this see below para. 69–73.

[78] Art. 12(1)(c) TD.

[79] Art. 12(3) TD.

[80] Art. 12(6) TD.

The home Member State may exempt issuers from this requirement if the information contained in the notification is made public by its competent supervisory authority.[81] France has exercised this possibility, now requiring that the information on changes of major holdings be filed with the AMF no later than four days after the shareholding threshold has been crossed.[82] The AMF must ensure that the information is made public within an additional three trading days.[83]

33   The disclosure must take place in a manner that guarantees easy access to the regulatory information on a non-discriminatory basis. In particular, the home Member State must ensure that the issuer uses such media as may reasonably be relied upon for the effective dissemination of information to the public throughout the Community,[84] such as news agencies, print media and Internet pages regarding the financial market.[85]

3.   Attribution of Voting Rights

(a)   Regulatory Concepts

34   In accordance with Article 10 TD the notification requirements defined in Article 9 also apply to a natural person or legal entity to the extent it is entitled to acquire, to dispose of, or to exercise voting rights in any of the constellations laid out in lit. (a)–(h). These constellations are described relatively precisely.[86] They are not all based on common ground but rather constitute borderline cases, such as voting rights attached to shares in which that person or entity has the life interest (usufruct), where it is unclear who holds the voting rights and who is thus required to notify the issuer. Other constellations described refer to cases in which a person has a legally secured influence on the voting rights.

35   Most of the constellations described in Article 10 TD refer to cases in which a person is attributed the voting rights attached to shares belonging to a third party.[87]

36   *Example:* If a person holds 5% of the shares with voting rights attached to them and is additionally entitled to exercise voting rights as described in Article 10(a) TD to the extent of 5%, both voting rights have to be totalled, thus obliging the person to notify the issuer that his proportion of the voting rights has reached the 10% threshold. The German legislature clarified this by making the notification requirement dependant on whether a shareholder reaches, exceeds or falls below the thresholds by purchase, sale or *"by any other means"*. The threshold is affected *"by any other means"* if voting rights of third party shares are attributed

---

[81] Art. 12(7) TD.

[82] Cf. Art. R. 233-1 C. com. and Art. 223-14.1 RG AMF.

[83] Cf. Art. 223-14.3 RG AMF.

[84] Art. 21(1) TD.

[85] See in more detail § 22 para. 4–7.

[86] The TD does not contain a general clause, comparable to the US-American Rule 13d-3(b) SEA on "the determination of beneficial ownership", preventing forms of circumvention of the provisions. Yet as the directive only aims to achieve minimum harmonisation, the Member States are free to develop their own general clauses preventing circumvention. Should the amendments to the TD, however, be enacted (see para. 14) this would no longer remain possible.

[87] This was laid down more explicitly in the former TD of 1988 in Art. 7, which declared that "the following voting rights shall be regarded as voting rights held by that person or entity". Cf. N. Elster, *Europäisches Kapitalmarktrecht*, p. 26–27.

        Rüdiger Veil

to the shareholder.[88] Therefore a person can also be required to notify the issuer if he holds nothing but voting rights attributed to him through third-party shares.

37   According to the concept of the TD the attribution of voting rights leads to a multiple notification and disclosure of voting rights. The third party remains obligated to notify the issuer on the voting rights of his shares. There is no provision according to which voting rights attributed to someone else do not have to be taken into account for the shareholder himself.[89] The capital markets are not likely to be misled, as in the case of an attribution of voting rights in a corporate group the notification must contain the chain of controlled companies.[90]

(b)   Cases of an Attribution of Voting Rights

38   The TD lists eight cases in which notification requirements regarding the attribution of voting rights attached to third-party shares exist. The European Commission adopted most of these from the first TD in 1988 and the Directive 2001/34/EC,[91] taking only a few of the consultations regarding the reform into account.[92] This already indicates that it is probably now necessary to revise some of the provisions.

39   In the following the various cases of an attribution of voting rights will be examined in terms of the legal practice in the different Member States, who may extend the provision and provide further cases of an attribution of voting rights.[93] Some Member States have made extensive use of these regulatory powers.

(aa)   "Acting in Concert"

40   Notification is required for voting rights held by a third party with whom a person or entity has concluded an agreement, which obliges them to adopt, by concerted exercise of their voting rights, a lasting common policy towards the management of the issuer in question.[94]

41   The Commission's original proposal for a new TD from 2003 still required the parties to conclude an *effective* agreement, obliging them to adopt, by concerted exercise of the voting rights they hold, a lasting common policy towards the management of the issuer in question.[95] However, the case of "acting in concert" was nevertheless adopted as in the former TD and Directive 2001/34/EC. An effective agreement is therefore not explicitly required.

42   It needs first to be clarified which types of agreements fulfil the definition of acting in concert. The starting point for this is the wording of the provisions according to which the concerted exercise of the voting rights has to have the aim of ensuring

---

[88] The attribution of voting rights in Germany takes place on the legal basis of § 22 WpHG.

[89] Cf. N. Elster, *Europäisches Kapitalmarktrecht* p. 27 on TD I.

[90] See above para. 30.

[91] On this directive see § 1 para. 19.

[92] Cf. Commission, Proposal for a Directive of the European Parliament and of the Council of 26 March 2003 on the harmonisation of transparency requirements with regard to information about issuers whose securities are admitted to trading on a regulated market and amending Directive 2001/34/EC, COM(2003) 138 final, p. 25.

[93] On the minimum harmonisation provided for by the Transparency Directive see above para. 5.

[94] Art. 10(a) TD.

[95] Cf. Commission, Proposal for a Directive of the European Parliament and of the Council of 26 March 2003 on the harmonisation of transparency requirements with regard to information about issuers whose securities are admitted to trading on a regulated market and amending Directive 2001/34/EC, COM(2003) 138 final, p. 25.

a lasting common policy regarding the management of the issuer. Shareholders of stock companies incorporated in the Member States usually have no power to issue instructions addressed to the directors. However, acting in concert in the sense of the TD does not presuppose such means of influence.[96] The definition reaches further, encompassing all questions on which the shareholder has influence—albeit indirectly—e.g. the election of the supervisory board.[97] The requirement of a "lasting" common policy expresses that an ad hoc coalition does not suffice.[98]

43   Furthermore, acting in concert with respect to the TD can only be assumed if the respective parties reach a contractual agreement. For this a minimum of two persons is required, i.e. an attribution of voting rights can also take place regarding an agreement between more than two people. The agreement has to refer to the concerted exercise of the voting rights. Whilst the TD does not explicitly require the agreement to be legally effective, it is to be assumed that only legally binding agreements can be intended.

44   An attribution of voting rights due to acting in concert results in a reciprocal attribution of voting rights. If, for example, A (5% of the shares) and B (10% of the shares) act in concert, A is attributed the voting rights attached to B's shares in accordance with Article 10(a) TD. At the same time, however, B is also subject to Article 10(a) TD and is attributed the voting rights attached to A's shares, thus obliging both A and B to notify the issuer that they hold voting rights of 15%.

45   The legal ground for this attribution is the influence the contracting party has over the pooled voting rights. Whilst neither of the two contracting parties will be able to prevail over the other, both have the legally ensured possibility to influence the other party's voting. This community of interest justifies the attribution of voting rights to the respective other party.[99]

(1) Legal Practice in France

46   In French law acting in concert is defined as any agreement (*accord*) on the acquisition, transfer or exercise of voting rights with the aim of a common policy regarding the management of the issuer.[100] Acting in concert has gained great attention in France on account of a few spectacular cases, the most famous being *Sacyr/Eiffage* and *Gecina*. These contain questions of takeover law and will therefore be examined in the section on disclosure when acquiring corporate control.[101] It is especially noteworthy that even a person who holds no shares himself must fulfil the disclosure requirements for voting rights attributed to him, as it can potentially influence the exercising of these voting rights.[102]

47   This leads to two aspects of the French rules which will be examined in more detail. The discussion centres on the question whether an agreement necessarily has to

---

[96] Cf. U. Burgard, BB (1995), p. 2069, 2075; N. Elster, *Europäisches Kapitalmarktrecht*, p. 33.

[97] Cf. N. Elster, *Europäisches Kapitalmarktrecht*, p. 33.

[98] Cf. U. Burgard, BB (1995), p. 2069, 2075; N. Elster, *Europäisches Kapitalmarktrecht*, p. 33.

[99] Cf. N. Elster, *Europäisches Kapitalmarktrecht*, p. 32; R. Veil, in: *Festschrift für Karsten Schmidt*, p. 1645, 1648 ff.

[100] Cf. Art. L. 233-10 C. com. and Art. L. 233-9.1.3 C. com. The provisions were most recently amended in October 2010.

[101] See § 24 para. 47.

[102] Cf. F. Grillier and H. Segain, RTDF (2007), p. 20, 29.

have the nature of a contract under civil law or whether other types of agreements are also sufficient for assuming acting in concert.[103] In *Eiffage*[104] the court appears to adopt a wide understanding of the term "agreement" (cf. "*les dispositions de l'article L. 233–10 du code de commerce n'exigent pas que l'accord résulte d'un écrit, ni qu'il revête un caractère contraignant*"). The French legal literature on this question, however, states that this statement cannot be regarded as a renunciation of the requirement of a contract.[105]

48   A further characteristic of French law is the wide understanding of a common company policy, including not only the company policy which the shareholders aim at influencing by making use of their voting rights in the shareholders meeting and which is defined in the TD, but also the strategy which the shareholders acting in concert pursue with the acquisition and exercise of their voting rights. The French understanding is thus that the concepts of a "common policy" and "control" merge.[106] Therefore, it comes as no surprise that the term "acting in concert" is described in French as *flou*, i.e. vague.[107] Thus, it can only be welcomed that French law clearly defines a few cases in which an *accord* is statutorily presumed.[108]

(2) Legal Practice in Germany

49   The concept of acting in concert has attracted a lot of attention in Germany due to the fact that shareholder agreements are widespread and Germany has exceeded the European legislature's provisions, introducing much stricter rules regarding the notification requirements for acting in concert.

50   One of the main issues with respect to acting in concert is the attribution of voting rights in cases of pooling agreements in which certain parties of the agreement prevail over others. This can occur if the parties of the pooling agreement adopt resolutions concerning the exercise of the pooled voting rights in the issuer's general meeting by majority vote. This form of agreement raises the question whether voting rights may have to be attributed reciprocally.

51   *Facts:*[109] A, B, C and D conclude a pooling agreement. A holds 9.0% and B 4.0% of the voting rights, C is attributed 0.5% of the voting rights attached to shares held by a subsidiary company and D has no voting rights. The BaFin is of the opinion that the voting rights must be attributed reciprocally in this case, i.e. all four persons must notify the company that they hold 13.5% of the voting rights, A being attributed 4.5%, B 9.5%, C 13.0% and D 13.5% of the voting rights. This understanding is unconvincing.[110] The spirit and purpose of the provisions on the transparency of major holdings require an attribution of voting rights if the

---

[103] Cf. E. Zabala, Bull. Joly Bourse (2008), p. 389, 395; C. Baj, RDBF (2008), p. 57, 59.

[104] CA Paris, 1re ch., sect. H, 18 décembre 2008, no. 2008/07645, *Adam c/ société Sacyr Vallehermoso SA*, Bull. Joly Bourse (2009), p. 185 ff.

[105] Cf. p. Le Cannu, Rev. soc. (2008), p. 394, 403–404.

[106] Cf. D. Schmidt, RDBF (2008), p. 56.

[107] Cf. C. Goyet, *Action de concert*, p. 9.

[108] Cf. Art. L233-10 C. com. The text of the provision can be found in R. Veil and P. Koch, *Französisches Kapitalmarktrecht*, p. 154. The CA Paris ch. 5–7, 15 septembre 2011, no. 2011/00690, *Adam et al. c/ SARL Émile Hermès et al.*, concluded from the behaviour of family members that they acted in concert ("family concerted action").

[109] Cf. BaFin, *Emittentenleitfaden 2009* (issuer guideline), p. 144–145.

[110] In more detail R. Veil, in: *Festschrift für Karsten Schmidt*, p. 1645 ff.

person may influence the voting rights attached to the shares. This is generally the case if all of the shareholders involved in the pooling agreement have the same legal possibility to influence the voting rights of the other participating shareholders. However, if one or more of the shareholders of the pooling agreement can prevail over the others, the latter need not be attributed its voting rights as they do not have the legal possibility of influencing the exercise of the voting rights.

52　The provision regarding the attribution of voting rights in cases of acting in concert reaches even farther in Germany: voting rights of a third party are not only attributed to a person or legal entity with a notification obligation on the grounds of a binding voting or pooling agreement but also if the parties coordinate their behaviour with regard to the issuer, based on an agreement or in another manner, with the exception of an agreements in individual cases.[111] A person or a legal entity is also attributed the voting rights of a third party if the parties coordinate their behaviour with regard to the issuer "*in another manner*".

53　By extending the provision to "coordinations *in another manner*" the German legislature aimed to achieve transparency regarding the influence of financial investors on issuers. Supervisory practice has shown that it is not always easy to prove that financial investors have coordinated their behaviour. The term "coordination *in another manner*", however, leads to difficulties, especially regarding the question as to how much contact between the shareholders is necessary in order to be able to assume such coordination. Legal practice generally requires a wilful cooperation with the aim of continually exercising and coordinating the rights attached to the shares. Simply following parallel business strategies, such as the restructuring of the company through a certain concept, does not suffice.[112]

54　The person with the notification obligation must coordinate his behaviour with that of the third party. This is defined in § 22(2) WpHG: coordinated conduct requires that the notifying party or its subsidiary and the third party reach a consensus on the exercise of voting rights or collaborate in another manner with the aim of bringing about a permanent and material change in the issuer's business strategy.[113]

55　The reform of the provision in 2008 has caused many discussions.[114] Even non binding agreements *outside* the *general shareholder meeting* can be classed as acting in concert under the new rule. However, the agreement must have the aim of bringing about a permanent and material change in the issuer's business strategy and the shareholders must follow a joint strategy such as is the case in one-on-one consultations.[115] These describe constellations in which the shareholders collaborate with the aim of exerting pressure on the management of the company to change the company's strategy.[116]

---

[111] Cf. § 22(2) WpHG.
[112] OLG Frankfurt/Main ZIP (2004), p. 1309.
[113] Cf. § 22(2) WpHG.
[114] Cf. H. Fleischer ZGR (2008), p. 185, 196; *König*, BB (2008), p. 1910; T.M.J. Möllers and F. Holzner, NZG (2008), p. 166; M. Schockenhoff and E. Wagner, NZG (2008), p. 361.
[115] Bericht Finanzausschuss Risikobegrenzungsgesetz, BT-Drucks. 16/9821, p. 16.
[116] Cf. C. von Bülow, in: R. Veil (ed.), *Übernahmerecht in Praxis und Wissenschaft*, p. 141, 164.

56   Other forms of collaboration outside the general meeting do not lead to an attribution of voting rights in Germany. A collaborative acquisition of shares does not suffice.[117]

(3) Legal Practice in Italy

57   The Italian provisions on acting in concert differ greatly from those in the TD. Shareholder agreements are defined as agreements whose object is the exercise of voting rights in a company with listed shares or in a company that controls it.[118] Italian law provides that any person with a shareholding of less than 2% partaking in a shareholder agreement is attributed the voting rights of the other parties to the agreement at thresholds of 5, 10, 15, 20, 25, 30, 50 and 70%.[119] The notification must contain information on the total amount of shares to which the agreement refers and also on the shares held by that person but not included in the shareholder agreement.

58   In practice, shareholder agreements are of great importance in Italy due to the fact that most listed companies are companies with a long tradition and still family owned, the most famous example being Fiat. For the families a shareholder agreement can be a means of ensuring their influence on the company and will thus mostly deal with questions of company policy and pre-emption rights for shares.[120]

59   The decisive element of the provisions on notification and publication is the concept of the shareholder agreement, which under Italian law is understood in a wide sense. Article 120 RE (Regulation for Issuers) on the attribution of voting rights refers to Article 122 I, V(a) and (d) TUF with regard to the meaning of a shareholder agreement. It must therefore be an agreement whose object is the exercise of voting rights.[121] Additionally, Article 122 TUF also applies to an agreement that creates obligations of consultation prior to the exercise of voting rights[122] or that has as its object or effect the exercise, jointly or otherwise, of a dominant influence on the company.[123]

60   Consob must be notified of any agreement regarding the exercise of voting rights within five days of its conclusion. In addition the agreement must be published in abridged form in the daily press within ten days of the date of its conclusion and entered in the Company Register where the company has its registered office within fifteen days from the date of their conclusion.[124] These measures are intended to improve the transparency of the markets.[125]

61   Italy's sanctions in the case of non-compliance with these provisions are harsh. If the shareholder agreement is not made public it is null and void. Breaches of disclosure

---

[117] Cf. E. Schockenhoff and A. Schumann, ZGR (2005), p. 568, 582; R. Veil, in: K. Schmidt and M. Lutter (eds.), *Kommentar zum AktG*, § 22 WpHG para. 41. Dissenting opinion: A. Engert, JZ (2007), p. 314.

[118] Art. 122 TUF.

[119] Art. 120 RE.

[120] Cf. G. Meo, in: M. Bessone (ed.), *Trattato di diritto privato*, p. 81 ff.; A. Fusi, 6 Le Società (2007), p. 689.

[121] Cf. Art. 122 I TUF.

[122] Cf. Art. 122 V(a) TUF.

[123] Cf. Art. 122 V(d) TUF.

[124] Cf. Art. 122 I TUF.

[125] Cf. F. Carbonetti, Riv. soc. (1998), p. 909, 911; D. Piselli, 2 Le Società (2009), p. 199, 200.

oblications may also lead to a loss of voting rights. [126] If the voting rights are exercised, Consob can challenge any resolution made in the shareholder meeting. The challenge will, however, only be successful if the required majority would not have been reached without the votes attached to the challenged agreement.[127] In practice this possibility of appeal does not appear to have played an important role so far.

(4) Legal Practice in Spain

62   Spanish law defines acting in concert similarly to the TD, requiring the conclusion of an agreement between a person or legal entity and a third party obligating them to adopt a lasting common policy towards the management of the issuer or with the aim of influencing the management through a concerted exercise of voting rights.[128] This definition is more restrictive than that of Spanish takeover law,[129] which also applies to agreements that refer to the exercise of voting rights in the company's administrative board or executive committee (*comisión ejecutiva o delegada de la sociedad*).[130] The notification requirement is addressed to all parties of the contract together and can only be fulfilled by a joint notification.

63   Shareholder agreements that affect the exercise of voting rights in the shareholder's meeting or restrict the free transferability of shares immediately have to be communicated to the company and the Spanish national supervisory authority, the CNMV. The respective document has to be deposited at the trade register. The shareholder agreement also has to be published as an ad hoc notification,[131] otherwise it does not become effective.

(bb) Temporary Transfer of Voting Rights

64   A person or legal entity is also required to notify the company of voting rights held by them due to an agreement providing for the temporary transfer of voting rights as consideration.[132] In the TD from 1988 and the Directive 2001/34/EC this obligation still required a written agreement.[133] This is no longer necessary. The wording of the German version of the directive was also amended, now stating more clearly than before that the voting rights are only held by the person or entity temporarily, i.e. will eventually be transferred back to the original owner. This was achieved by supplementing the term *vorläufige Übertragung* (provisional transfer) with the term *zeitweilige Übertragung* (temporary transfer).

65   The provision refers to those constellations to which Article 10(g) TD is not applicable as the voting rights are not held "on behalf of" the other person or entity. Its objective is to prevent a shareholder from "parking" his funds with a third party whilst secretly increasing his holding,[134] thus justifying the attribution of the third-

---

[126] Cf. Art. 122 IV TUF.
[127] Cf. Art. 122 IV TUF in conjunction with Art. 14 VI TUF.
[128] Cf. Art. 24 1.a. RD 1362/2007.
[129] Cf. Art. 5.1.b RD 1066/2007.
[130] Cf. A.F. Muñoz Pérez, *El concierto como presupuesto de la OPA obligatoria*, p. 267–268.
[131] Cf. Art. 112.2 LMV.
[132] Art. 10(b) TD.
[133] Seen critically by N. Elster, *Europäisches Kapitalmarktrecht*, p. 35.
[134] Cf. ibid.

party's voting rights. In contrast to the constellation described by Article 10(g) TD, the shareholder holds the voting rights on his own behalf in these cases.[135]

(cc) Notification Obligations of the Secured Party

66   The TD also requires notification for voting rights attached to shares which are lodged as collateral with a person or entity provided that person or entity controls the voting rights and declares its intention of exercising them.[136] A notification requirement in such cases stands to reason as voting rights will automatically ensue if the shares are transferred by way of security. However, regarding the internal relationship with the collateral provider the secured party will usually not exercise these voting rights. The provision creates legal certainty by laying down a notification obligation in the event that the secured party plans on exercising its voting rights.

67   It is questionable whether the collateral provider must notify the company in these cases. When answering this it must be taken into account that the collateral provider may be entitled to instruct the secured party on how to exercise the voting right. In this case the voting rights may be attributed pursuant to Article 10(g) TD.[137] The question whether the secured party should also notify the company about voting rights attributed to it if the collateral provider has not made specific instructions on the exercise of the voting rights is answered by Article 10(f) TD.[138]

(dd) Life Interest

68   A life interest awards the beneficiary with the benefits of the shares. In particular, it receives the dividend. It is, however, unclear whether the beneficiary is also permitted to exercise the voting rights, this question being answered inconsistently in the different Member States' civil laws. The TD appears to attribute the voting right to the beneficial owner, at least regarding the notification requirements: for voting rights attached to shares in which a person or an entity has the life interest this person or entity is subject to the notification requirement described in Article 9 TD.[139]

(ee) Voting Rights Held or Exercised by a Controlled Undertaking

69   Further notification requirements are laid down for a person or a legal entity with voting rights held or exercised within the meaning of Art. 10 points (a)–(d), by an undertaking controlled by that person or entity.[140] The voting rights attached to shares held by the subsidiary company are therefore attributed to the parent undertaking. Furthermore, voting rights that are attributed to the subsidiary company must also in a chain of attribution be attributed to the parent undertaking. The practical relevance has grown enormously compared to the precursory provision due to its wider scope of application.[141]

[135] Cf. ibid., p. 35.
[136] Art. 10(c) TD.
[137] See below para. 76.
[138] See below para. 74.
[139] Art. 10(d) TD.
[140] Art. 10(e) TD.
[141] "Following numerous requests" the European Commission developed a "determination of situations in which voting rights which may be exercised on behalf of controlled undertakings [that] is much wider" than in

70   Examining the attribution of voting rights in a corporate group requires definition
      of a "controlled undertaking". According to the TD this is

> "any undertaking (i) in which a natural person or legal entity has a majority of
> the voting rights; or (ii) of which a natural person or legal entity has the right
> to appoint or remove a majority of the members of the administrative, manage-
> ment or supervisory body and is at the same time a shareholder in, or member
> of, the undertaking in question; or (iii) of which a natural person or legal entity
> is a shareholder or member and alone controls a majority of the shareholders'
> or members' voting rights, respectively, pursuant to an agreement entered into
> with other shareholders or members of the undertaking in question; or (iv) over
> which a natural person or legal entity has the power to exercise, or actually exer-
> cises, dominant influence or control".[142]

71   As opposed to this, the TD does not provide a definition of when a person or a
      legal entity has the power to exercise, or actually exercises, dominant influence or
      control over an issuer. Whilst these terms were also contained in Directive 83/349/
      EEC, they served a different aim, which was to extend the obligation to consolidate
      accounts to a wide range of subsidiaries.[143]

72   The question becomes relevant when a shareholder only has a minority stake but
      the usual attendance at the shareholders' general meeting may allow this to suffice
      for resolutions to be made. The Member States do not appear to have answered
      this question of interpretation in their national capital markets laws, rather
      adopting the legal definition contained in the TD into their national laws one-
      to-one. The FSA Handbook refers to the national company law in this context,[144]
      and defines the concepts of "parent undertaking" and "controlled undertaking" in
      accordance with the provisions of the Directive 83/349/EEC on annual accounts
      of corporate groups.[145] In contrast, German capital markets law refers to the
      accounting provisions for the definition of a controlled undertaking[146] and to the
      stock corporation provisions regarding the definition of a controlling influence.[147]
      The latter is given a broad meaning by the BGH. If a minority shareholding can
      have the same influence on the general meeting as a major holding, the holder
      of the minority shareholding must be regarded as a controlling enterprise.[148]

73   The present legal situation is unsatisfactory. The problems of interpretation described
      here are not mere trivialities but must be regarded as topics of a very general nature
      which should ideally be treated uniformly by the capital markets laws of all Member
      States. This need not necessarily mean an amendment of the TD by the European
      legislature, rather being a possible task for the new European supervisory authority

---

the former provisions. "This [was] possible due to a wider definition laid down in the proposed Article 2(f)."
Cf. Commission, Proposal for a Directive of the European Parliament and of the Council of 26 March 2003 on
the harmonisation of transparency requirements with regard to information about issuers whose securities are
admitted to trading on a regulated market and amending Directive 2001/34/EC, COM(2003) 138 final, p. 25.

[142] Art. 2(1)(f) TD.
[143] Cf. H.-W. Neye, ZGR (1995), p. 191, 197.
[144] Sec. 1162 Companies Act 2006.
[145] Cf. R. Veil and M. Wundenberg, *Englisches Kapitalmarktrecht*, p. 130–131.
[146] Cf. § 22(3) WpHG in conjunction with § 290 HGB.
[147] Cf. § 22(3) WpHG in conjunction with § 17 AktG.
[148] Cf. for German law BGHZ 69, 334; BGHZ 135, 107.

(i.e. the ESMA) which could define the concept of a controlled undertaking more clearly.

(ff) Deposited Shares

74 A person or legal entity must furthermore notify the company of voting rights attached to shares which have been deposited with them and which they can exercise at their discretion in the absence of specific instructions from the shareholders.[149] The person with whom the shares are deposited is not the owner of the shares, thus necessitating a rule on the attribution of the voting rights attached to third-party shares.

75 A deposition of the shares does not require the respective person physically to hold the shares, rather allowing any management of the shares for a third party to suffice.[150] For the application of the provision the important question is whether the depositary can exercise the voting rights at its own discretion.[151] This is still the case even if the depositary has to take into account the shareholder's interest. Article 10(d) TD can become relevant for credit institutions and other persons that have been empowered to exercise voting rights of the shareholders. Voting rights exercised by proxy are, however, also covered by Article 10(h) TD.[152]

(gg) Shares Held on Behalf of Another Person

76 A person or legal entity must also notify the company if it is entitled to acquire, to dispose of, or to exercise voting rights held by a third party in its own name but on behalf of that person or entity.[153] This provision especially envisages the trust in the United Kingdom and the *Treuhand* in Germany[154] in which a trustor, respectively *Treugeber*, is attributed the voting rights attached to shares which are held for him by a trustee/*Treuhänder*. In Germany, the legal literature supports the point of view that the *Treugeber* (trustor) must be permitted to instruct the *Treuhänder* (trustee), otherwise there is no guarantee that the trustor can influence the trustee's vote. If the trustee is only subject to the trustor's instructions de facto and not in a legally binding way an attribution of voting rights is not justified.[155]

77 *Example (abridged and simplified):* Three shareholders, L (5%), T (5%) and S (5%), acted in concert regarding the issuer, resulting in a reciprocal attribution of the voting rights attached to their shares. L had further transferred an additional 5% of its shares to a trustee (*Treuhänder*). The OLG Munich[156] decided that all voting rights attributed to trustor (*Treugeber*) L, due to acting in concert, would also have to be attributed to *Treuhänder* H. The court justified its decision by

---

[149] Art. 10(f) TD.
[150] Cf. U. Burgard, BB (1995), p. 2069, 2076; N. Elster, *Europäisches Kapitalmarktrecht*, p. 40.
[151] Cf. N. Elster, *Europäisches Kapitalmarktrecht*, p. 40.
[152] See below para. 81.
[153] Art. 10(g) TD.
[154] Cf. European Parliament, Report on the proposal for a European Parliament and Council directive on the harmonisation of transparency requirements with regard to information about issuers whose securities are admitted to trading on a regulated market and amending Directive 2001/34/EC, 26 March 2003, Amendment 85.
[155] Cf. C. von Bülow, in: H. Hirte and T.M.J. Möllers (eds.), *Kölner Kommentar zum WpHG*, § 22 para. 71; K.-D. Dehlinger and M. Zimmermann, in: A. Fuchs (ed.), *Kommentar zum WpHG*, § 22 para. 50; R. Veil, in: K. Schmidt and M. Lutter (eds.), *Kommentar zum AktG*, § 22 WpHG para. 16.
[156] OLG München, AG (2009), p. 793.

describing the need to prevent investors from avoiding the provision and emphasising the fact that the *Treugeber* who was entitled to instruct the *Treuhänder* was
bound by the acting in concert. This explanation is not convincing when one
considers that the *Treuhänder* had no influence whatsoever on how the *Treugeber*
exercises its voting rights in the pool with the other shareholders.[157] The BGH
therefore ruled in favour of the appellant and against the OLG Munich, stating
that voting rights held by a third party acting in concert with the *Treugeber*
(trustor) could not being attributed to the *Treuhänder* (trustee).[158]

78   Article 10(g) TD further gains practical relevance for stock lending agreements.
These exist for multiple reasons and play an especially important role regarding
short sellings. The following case concerns a shareholder who had increased its
shareholdings to 95% of the shares with the help of stock lending agreements. Its
aim was to squeeze out the remaining minority shareholders, this being possible in
Germany from this proportion upwards.[159]

79   *Example (abridged and simplified):*[160] A shareholder (A) had transferred shares
with voting rights of 12% to a different shareholder (B). The contract was concluded for an indefinite period and contained the provision that for the duration
of the loan the cash dividends relating to the loan would belong to A. On ter-
mination of the contract B was to transfer shares of the same type and number
back to A. The BGH saw B as the owner of the shares since a "second-class"
shareholding does not exist. Thus shareholder B was held responsible for the
notification. B was required to notify the issuer that it had exceeded the threshold
of 10%. Furthermore the BGH ruled that the voting rights attached to the shares
referred to in the stock lending agreement could not be attributed to the lender
(A) pursuant to § 22(1) sentence 1 No. 2 WpHG which constitutes the German
implementation of Article 10(g) TD. Therefore, lender A had to notify the issuer
that it had fallen below the threshold of 10%.[161]

80   The attribution of voting rights is also discussed controversially with regard to so-
called *cash-settled equity swaps,*[162] a type of contract where a bank promises to pay
an investor the difference between the price of certain shares at the beginning and
the end of the contractual period plus dividends, that may have been paid by the
issuer, in exchange for interest and fees payable by the investor. Under the TD it has
been argued that shares acquired by the bank as collateral may not be attributed to
the investor because it typically has no influence on the voting rights attached to
these shares.[163] Some Member States have reacted to the TD's deficit in transparency
by providing additional disclosure rules in their national capital markets laws.[164]

---

[157] Cf. C. von Bülow and S. Petersen, NZG (2009), p. 1373; H. Fleischer and D. Bedkowski, DStR (2010),
p. 933; R. Veil and C. Dolff, AG (2010), p. 385.

[158] BGH ZIP (2011), 1862.

[159] The legal basis for squeeze-outs are the § 327a ff. AktG.

[160] BGHZ 180, 154.

[161] In this case lender A may be subject to a notification obligation pursuant to Art. 13 TD.

[162] Cf. on this type of derivatives A. N. Rechtschaffen, *Capital Markets, Derivatives and the Law*, p. 178–180.

[163] Cf. T. Baums and M. Sauter, 173 ZHR (2009), p. 454, 467; H. Fleischer and K.U. Schmolke, ZIP (2008),
p. 1501, 1506. Dissenting opinion: *Zetzsche*, 10 EBOR (2009), p. 115, 132.

[164] See below para. 108–124.

(hh) Voting Rights Exercised by Proxy

81   Voting rights that a person or a legal entity may exercise by proxy, at its discretion and without specific instructions, are also subject to the notification requirements.[165]

82   The TD from 1988 and Directive 2001/34/EC did not contain such a provision. The European Commission's justification for the new disclosure obligation was that since proxy participation across Member States is usually allowed in general meetings, a company should be duly informed about major shareholdings for which a proxy received common instructions from a number of shareholders.[166] The TD adopting this provision, does not, however, require a common instruction of the proxy by the shareholders.

83   It is unclear if voting rights exercised by a credit institution as a proxy are also covered by Article 10(h) TD. In Germany a financial institution may, with the exception of explicit instructions received from the shareholder, only exercise its proxy voting rights in accordance with its own proposal or the proposal of the management or supervisory board for the exercising of the voting rights.[167] It has no discretion in this. Therefore, voting rights exercised by a credit institution as a proxy are not attributed.

(c)   Exceptions

84   The TD allows the Member States to make exemptions from its provisions regarding securities trading for its credit institutes and investment firms. Home Member States may provide that voting rights held by credit institutes and investment firms shall not be counted for the purpose of determining whether notification requirements exist.[168] Shares provided for or by the members of the ESCB are also exempt from these provisions.[169]

4.   Supervision

85   Each Member State must designate a central competent administrative authority[170] responsible for ensuring that the provisions adopted pursuant to the TD are carried out. This administrative authority must be provided all the powers necessary for the performance of this function.[171] It must be empowered to require holders of shares or other financial instruments to submit information and documents[172] and to notify it on changes in major holdings.[173] It must also be empowered to take appropriate action should the issuer not disclose in a timely fashion the required

---

[165] Art. 10(h) TD.
[166] Cf. Commission, Proposal for a Directive of the European Parliament and of the Council of 26 March 2003 on the harmonisation of transparency requirements with regard to information about issuers whose securities are admitted to trading on a regulated market and amending Directive 2001/34/EC, COM(2003) 138 final, p. 28.
[167] Cf. § 135 AktG; explained by T. Raiser and R. Veil, *Recht der Kapitalgesellschaften*, § 16 para. 95 ff.
[168] Cf. Art. 9(6) TD.
[169] Cf. Art. 11 TD.
[170] Art. 24(1) TD.
[171] Art. 24(4) TD.
[172] Art. 24(4)(a) TD.
[173] Art. 24(4)(c) TD.

information in order to ensure that the public has effective and equal access to this information in all Member States.[174]

86   In Germany the BaFin is entitled to prescribe when a person must make a notification, correct a former notification or refrain from making a notification in order to fulfil his notification duties.[175] The BaFin may even notify the respective company itself,[176] although it has not yet exercised this possibility.

87   Member States must ensure that their respective authorities have the power to make public that an issuer, or a holder of shares or other financial instruments, or a person or entity who is attributed voting rights attached to shares of a third party is failing to comply with its obligations.[177] In Germany, this "naming and shaming" is not treated as a repressive sanction of a criminal or administrative nature but rather as a preventive measure.[178] The practical relevance of these publications varies between Member States. Although all Member States have implemented the directive's provisions on publishing any failure to comply with the obligations, not all national authorities actually apply this possibility. In Germany, the BaFin has so far not made public any measures taken to sanction the failure to comply with the notification requirements.[179] In contrast, in the United Kingdom and France, the respective authorities, i.e. the FSA[180] and the AMF,[181] regularly make public which sanctions they have imposed.

5.   Sanctions

88   The TD only vaguely describes what sanctions are to be introduced by the Member States. It does not include any instructions on criminal penalties, merely stipulating that Member States must ensure that the appropriate administrative measures are taken or civil and/or administrative penalties are imposed.[182] It is thus for the each Member State to decide whether it introduces administrative fines or sanctions under civil law,[183] provided it ensures that the chosen measures are effective, proportionate and dissuasive.[184]

89   As Member States have much room for discretion it is hardly surprising that their sanctioning regimes differ greatly.[185] Whilst some Member States rely on a combina-

---

[174] Art. 24(4)(f) TD.

[175] This results from the obligation to prevent situations that could impair the trading with financial instruments, as defined in § 4(1)2 WpHG.

[176] Cf. § 4(6) WpHG.

[177] Art. 24(4)(g) TD; cf. also Art. 28(2) TD.

[178] Cf. K. Altenhain, in: H. Hirte and T.M.J. Möllers (eds.), *Kölner Kommentar zum WpHG*, § 40b para. 4; J. Vogel, in: H.D. Assmann and U.H. Schneider (eds.), *Kommentar zum WpHG*, § 40b para. 4.

[179] The legal foundation for the publication is § 40b WpHG. No publications are available on the BaFin's website. Whilst the BaFin claims in its annual report that it has imposed fines for the failure to comply with notification and publication duties, it does not explain against whom and for what reasons these were imposed.

[180] The FSA publishes the sanctions it imposes on its website under "Enforcement Notices and Application refusals". See www.fsa.gov.uk/pages/library/communication/notices/index.shtml.

[181] The AMF publishes the sanctions it imposes on its website under "Sanctions/Décisions de la Commission des sanctions". See www.amf-france.org.

[182] Art. 28(1) TD.

[183] Cf. R. Veil, ZBB (2006), p. 162.

[184] Art. 28(1) TD.

[185] The European Commission therefore plans to amend the TD and supply the Member States with more precise rules for an effective enforcement. See above para. 14.

tion of administrative sanctions, etc., under civil law, others have adopted a regime of criminal penalties. The following overview focuses on administrative fines and the sanctions under civil law, such as a loss of voting rights and liability for damages towards the investors.

(a)   Administrative Fines

90   All EU Member States except for Denmark provide the possibility of imposing administrative fines for breaches of the notification requirements.[186] There is no convergence among the Member States with regard to the severity of the administrative fines imposed, Germany, for example providing for fines of up to €1 million[187] with the possibility of exceeding this amount pursuant to § 17 OWiG for a disgorgement of illicit profits.[188] The BaFin has, however, so far not applied this provision.[189] The legal situation in France is stricter. The AMF may impose fines of up to €10 million,[190] although in practice the imposed fines are typically far lower, not yet having exceeded €30,000 EUR.[191] In the United Kingdom the FSA has the ability to impose unlimited fines and to disgorge illicit profits.[192] These powers are the farthest reaching throughout the European Union. The maximum administrative fines in Italy, Belgium, Ireland and Portugal are between €1 million and €10 million.[193]

(b)   Loss of Rights

91   Germany, France, Italy, Luxembourg, Austria, Portugal and the Czech Republic attach a loss of rights under civil law to the failure of a shareholder to comply with the notification requirements. Germany's regime[194] is the harshest, affecting all shareholder rights—especially the rights on participation in a general shareholders' meeting, information, voting and dividend.[195]

92   The loss of rights occurs by act of law in Germany and thus need not be ordered by the BaFin. All rights are lost, including those attached to shares held by subsidiaries or a trustee (*Treuhänder*) that have been attributed to the person or legal entity in breach of the notification requirement. The failure of a parent company or a trustor (*Treugeber*) to comply with the notification requirements will thus be to the detriment of a third party, i.e. the subsidiary company or the trustee. The prevailing opinion is that a loss of rights requires at least a negligent breach of the

---

[186] CESR, *Report on the mapping of supervisory powers, administrative and criminal sanctioning regimes of Member States in relation to the Transparency Directive (TD)*, CESR/09-058, July 2009, p. 8; some Member States also impose criminal sanctions for the failure to comply with notification obligations, a recent example for this being Switzerland. Cf. P.V. Kunz, SZW 80 (2008), p. 280, 281–282.

[187] § 39(4) WpHG as amended by the Anlegerschutz- und Funktionsverbesserungsgesetz (Act on the improvement of investor protection and the functioning of the capital markets) of 5 April 2011 (BGBl. I, 538).

[188] Cf. § 17(4) OWiG.

[189] Cf. R. Veil, in: K. Schmidt and M. Lutter (eds.), *Kommentar zum AktG*, § 28 WpHG para. 26.

[190] Cf. Art. L. 621-15 C. mon. fin.

[191] Cf. AMF, *Jousse Morillon Investissements*, Bull. Joly Bourse, numéro 2 (2007), p. 191.

[192] R. Veil and M. Wundenberg, *Englisches Kapitalmarktrecht*, p. 8, 134.

[193] Cf. CESR, *Report on the mapping of supervisory powers, administrative and criminal sanctioning regimes of Member States in relation to the Transparency Directive (TD)*, CESR/09-058, July 2009, p. 8.

[194] Cf. § 28 WpHG.

[195] Cf. OLG Stuttgart, AG 2005, p. 125, 128; R. Veil, in: K. Schmidt and M. Lutter (eds.), *Kommentar zum AktG*, § 28 WpHG para. 10.

Rüdiger Veil

notification duties.[196] The loss of rights ends with fulfilment of the notification requirements, unless the shareholder acted grossly negligent or with intent, in which case the loss continues for another six months after notification pursuant to § 28(2) WpHG. The German legislature introduced this provision in 2008 in order to provide for the possibility of shareholders creeping in before a general meeting without disclosing their stake.[197]

93   All of the above-mentioned Member States only provide for a loss of voting rights.[198] The sanction is of civil law nature and affects the shareholder when resolutions are passed in the general meeting. If a shareholder exercises its voting rights in the general meeting, despite losing them due to the failure to comply with the notification requirements, the resolution can be set aside. The Member States' national laws determine who has the authority to set aside the resolution, this mostly being the shareholders, whilst in Italy the supervisory authority Consob is also permitted to file the action.

94   The duration of the loss of rights also varies between Member States. In France,[199] a shareholder loses all voting rights for which it has not fulfilled the notification requirements for two years, and this period does not begin until the notification has been corrected. A court may additionally fix a loss of voting rights for up to five years.[200]

95   A loss of voting rights is regarded as a very effective sanction both in Germany[201] and in France[202] due to its preventative nature. The legal practice in Italy also realises the effectiveness of this sanction, however, in judicial practice it has not so far been widely applied and Consob also has not yet set aside any resolution of a general meeting upon the grounds of it being based on lost voting rights.

(c)   Investor Protection by Means of Civil Liability

96   A further means of enforcing the provisions on notification is the possibility of a civil law liability for damages caused to the investors. This possibility does not, however, appear to be at the top of the legislatures' agendas in Europe. Whilst in all Member States the general provisions on civil law liability—especially of the law of torts—are applicable to the failure to comply with notification and disclosure, so far no investors have applied these rules to claim damages from shareholders or issuers for non-compliance.

97   Investor protection through rules on civil liability has also not attracted much interest in the legal literature. In Germany, some maintain that an investor can demand damages under tort law, reasoning that the capital markets law provisions on the

---

[196] Cf K.-D. Dehlinger and M. Zimmermann, in: A. Fuchs (ed.), *Kommentar zum WpHG*, § 28 para. 16; G. Kremer and H. Oesterhaus, in: H. Hirte and T.M.J. Möllers (eds.), *Kölner Kommentar zum WpHG*, § 28 para. 31; P. Opitz, in: F.A. Schäfer and U. Hamann (eds.), *Kapitalmarktgesetze, Kommentar*, § 28 WpHG para. 7; U.H. Schneider, in: H.D. Assmann and U.H. Schneider, *Kommentar zum WpHG*, § 28 para. 20.

[197] Begr. RegE Risikobegrenzungsgesetz, BT-Drucks. 16/7438, p. 13 (explanatory notes).

[198] Cf. R. Veil, 11 EBOR (2010), p. 409, 419 ff.

[199] Cf. Art. L. 233-14 C. com.

[200] Cf. H. Segain, RTDF (2008), p. 7, 10; R. Veil and P. Koch, *Französisches Kapitalmarktrecht*, p. 97 ff.

[201] Cf. R. Veil, 175 ZHR (2011), p. 83, 86.

[202] Cf. C. Maison-Blanche and D. Lecat, RTDF (2007), p. 146, 151.

transparency regarding major holdings are protective laws in terms of tort law.[203] An argument against this is, however, that the aim of the notification and publication requirements is primarily to ensure the functioning of the capital markets. The legislature did not specifically aim to ensure individual investor protection.[204]

98   The situation in the other EU Member States is similar. In the laws of the United Kingdom, France, Italy and Sweden there are no specific regulations regarding claims for investors against shareholders or issuers not fulfilling their notification or publication duties. Once again, only the general civil law provisions, especially those under the law of torts, may apply, although it remains unclear whether their requirements can be met if a shareholder breaches its notification requirements.

IV.   Notification Requirements when Holding Financial Instruments

1.   Prerequisites

99   The TD demands the inclusion of financial instruments from the Member States into their transparency systems, as can be deduced from the TD's goal of "moving towards more capital market-oriented thinking".[205] This ensures that investors are informed if a holder of financial instruments acquires shares and exercises the voting rights resulting therefrom. The obligation concerns a natural person or legal entity that holds financial instruments that result in an entitlement to acquire, on such holder's own initiative alone, under a formal agreement, shares to which voting rights are attached, already issued, of an issuer whose shares are admitted to trading on a regulated market.[206]

100   The reference to Article 9 indicates that the notification requirement only exists if through the acquisition or disposal of financial instruments a person reaches, exceeds or falls below a threshold of 5, 10, 15, 20, 25, 30, 50 or 75% of the voting rights. Whilst the Member States are entitled to provide a lower threshold, here too they have not made use of this possibility, unlike in the case of notifications regarding major holdings. The German legislature justified this by wanting to reduce the obligations for the parties involved to the extent necessary for transparency. [207]

101   Implementing Directive 2007/14/EC lists the types of financial instruments that result in a notification obligation. These are transferrable securities, options, futures, swaps, forward rate agreements and any other derivative contracts, provided that they result in an entitlement to acquire under a formal agreement shares to which

---

[203] Cf. W. Bayer, in: W. Goette and M. Habersack (eds.), *Münchener Kommentar zum AktG*, § 21 WpHG para. 2; H. Hirte, in: H. Hirte and T.M.J. Möllers (eds.), *Kölner Kommentar zum WpHG*, § 21 para. 4; H.-G. Kopensteiner, in: C.P. Claussen et al. (eds.), *Kölner Kommentar zum AktG*, Anh. §§ 21 ff. WpHG para. 46; G. Kremer and H. Oesterhaus, in: H. Hirte and T.M.J. Möllers (eds.), *Kölner Kommentar zum WpHG*, § 28 para. 86; U.H. Schneider (eds.), in: H.D. Assmann and U.H. Schneider, *Kommentar zum WpHG*, § 28 para. 79.

[204] Cf. R. Veil, 175 ZHR (2011), p. 83, 88–89.

[205] Cf. Commission, Proposal for a Directive of the European Parliament and of the Council of 26 March 2003 on the harmonisation of transparency requirements with regard to information about issuers whose securities are admitted to trading on a regulated market and amending Directive 2001/34/EC, COM(2003) 138 final, p. 19.

[206] Art. 13(1) TD.

[207] Cf. Begr. RegE Transparenzrichtlinie-Umsetzungsgesetz (TUG), BT-Drucks. 16/2498, p. 37 (explanatory notes).

voting rights are attached, on the holder's own initiative alone. The shares must furthermore already have been issued by an issuer whose shares are admitted to trading on a regulated market.[208] Additionally, the instrument holder must enjoy, on maturity, either the unconditional right to acquire the underlying shares or the discretion whether or not to exercise its right to acquire such shares.[209]

102   This is, for example, the case for so-called call-options, provided they do not only include the right to receive a cash settlement but also the delivery of the stocks. The sole possibility of an acquisition of shares, therefore, does not suffice. Cash-settled equity swaps[210] are thus not to be qualified as financial instruments subject to notification requirements due to the fact that the holder of such instruments cannot demand delivery of the shares, this being solely at the discretion of the counterparty.[211]

103   A central question is in what way the potential influence on voting rights resulting from financial instruments has to be communicated to the market. The European legislature opted for an aggregation of voting rights,[212] thus leading to the initial threshold of 5% being reached sooner and increasing the number of notifications.

2.   Legal Consequences

104   The holder of an instrument must make a notification to the issuer that includes a number of data, such as "the resulting situation in terms of voting rights" and the date on which the threshold was reached or crossed. For instruments with an exercise period, the notification must contain an indication of the date or time period when the shares will or can be acquired. The instrument holder must also inform the issuer on date of maturity or expiration of the instrument and the identity of the holder together with the name of the underlying issuer.[213]

105   The notification should be made as soon as possible, within a maximum period of four trading days,[214] to the competent authority of the home Member State of the issuer and the issuer of the underlying shares itself.[215] The latter must then disclose the information contained in the notification.[216]

3.   Sanctions

106   The TD contains no specific rules on the introduction of sanctions for a breach of notifications duties by the holders of financial instruments. The Member States are therefore free to establish their own sanctions. Contrary to the sanctions in the case of the notification requirements regarding changes in major holdings, the Member

---

[208] Art. 11(1) Directive 2007/14/EC.

[209] Art. 11(1) Directive 2007/14/EC.

[210] See above para. 80.

[211] Cf. H. Fleischer and K.U. Schmolke, ZIP (2008), p. 1501, 1504; C. von Bülow and M. Stephanblome, ZIP (2008), p. 1797, 1800.

[212] Art. 11(2) Directive 2007/14/EC.

[213] Art. 11(3)(a)–(g) Directive 2007/14/EC.

[214] Art. 11(4) Directive 2007/14/EC in conjunction with Art. 12(2) TD.

[215] Art. 11(5) Directive 2007/14/EC.

[216] Cf. Art. 21 TD. For more details see above para. 32.

States have adopted an exclusively administrative sanctioning regime,[217] allowing any breach of notification duties regarding financial instruments to be sanctioned with a fine.[218] The range of the administrative fines differs greatly across the European Union: some Member States allow fines of up to €20,000, whilst in most the maximum fine ranges between €100,000 and €1 million. The FSA has the ability to impose unlimited fines in the United Kingdom.[219]

4.   Reform

107   In recent years investors have been able to use financial instruments with no notification requirements, in particular cash-settled equity swaps,[220] in order to creep in on a listed company and achieve a takeover.[221] Some national legislatures reacted to the problem and developed notification requirements for these financial instruments in their national capital markets laws.

(a)   United Kingdom

108   The United Kingdom established notification requirements for so-called contracts for difference as early as 1 June 2009.[222] Which financial instruments with "similar economic effects" are affected by this is specified in detail.[223] However, the instruments are not listed explicitly, the FSA rather having defined clearly when "similar economic effects" to the financial instruments already subject to notification duties can be assumed. In doing so, the FSA adopted a principles-based approach.[224] The notification duty does not require that an instrument holder influences the exercising of voting rights or aims to achieve such an influence.[225] The thresholds correspond with those applying to the acquisition or disposal of shares.

(b)   Germany

109   The German legislature also saw the necessity for additional rules in this area. The cause for these reforms were two spectacular cases in which an investor managed to creep in on a company with the help of financial instruments about which it had not had to notify the company.

---

[217] France plans to extend the rules on loss of voting rights to breaches of the notification obligations regarding financial instruments, cf. draft law of 29 June 2011.

[218] The European Commission aims to enhance the sanctions and has submitted a number of regulatory proposals with this aim (see above para. 14). The Member States are, for example, to be obliged to grant their national supervisory authorities the right to declare a loss of voting rights for breaches of the provisions.

[219] Cf. CESR, *Report on the mapping of supervisory powers, administrative and criminal sanctioning regimes of Member States in relation to the Transparency Directive (TD)*, CESR/09-058, July 2009, p. 47.

[220] See above para. 80.

[221] The cases are described briefly in CESR's Consultation Paper, *CESR Proposal to extend major shareholding notifications to instruments of similar economic effect to holding shares and entitlements to acquire shares*, CESR/09-1215b, January 2010. Cf. also T. Baums and M. Sauter, 173 ZHR (2009), p. 454; H. Fleischer and K.U. Schmolke, ZIP (2008), p. 1501.

[222] The notification duties for contracts for difference are described in DTR 5.1 and DTR 5.3 of the FSA Handbook.

[223] On this see R. Veil and M. Wundenberg, *Englisches Kapitalmarktrecht*, p. 127.

[224] On principles-based regulation see § 4 para. 51.

[225] Cf. R. Veil and M. Wundenberg, *Englisches Kapitalmarktrecht*, p. 127–128.

110   *Example:* When announcing its takeover offer regarding shares of Continental AG, the Schaeffler-Group held 2.97% shares with voting rights. It also held financial instruments which entitled it to acquire a further 4.95% of Continental's shares. The Schaeffler-Group concluded contracts for difference with various banks, providing them with another 28% of the shares. A notification was necessary neither based on proportion of the shares owned directly by it, nor based on the financial instruments due to the fact that the initial threshold for notification requirements in Germany is 3% for shares[226] and 5% for financial instruments[227]. Contracts for difference were not subject to any notification requirements, according to the BaFin's point of view, as generally they will not give an investor any influence on voting rights.[228]

111   The *Continental/Schaeffler* and *Porsche/VW*[229] cases triggered an intense discussion on the question of whether the provisions on notification requirements should be amended. Eventually, the legislature enacted a law to enhance investor protection and improve the functioning of the capital markets[230] which introduced new rules regarding the notification requirements for holders of financial and other instruments in § 25a WpHG. The aim was to prevent further major holdings being built up unknown to the company and to ensure market integrity.[231] German legal literature mostly welcomed these amendments,[232] reasoning that the abuse of loopholes in the law by individual investors undermines the confidence in the functionality of the markets.[233] However, care should be taken that this does not result in an *information overload*.[234]

112   The new provisions establish notification duties for persons directly or indirectly holding financial instruments or other instruments that enable their owner to acquire shares already issued and with voting rights attached to them.[235] The obligations only apply if the holder reaches, exceeds or falls below one of the thresholds listed in § 21(1)1 WpHG, with the exception of the 3% threshold, the initial threshold thus lying at 5%. The legislature justifies this with the fact that the provision should refer to transactions that may lead to a takeover or be associated with dangers for market integrity.

113   Unlike in the original draft, the provision now requires the addition of the voting rights with those attached to shares of which the company has to be notified

---

[226] See above para. 23.

[227] See above para. 100.

[228] Cf. BaFin, press release, 21 August 2008; T. Baums and M. Sauter, 173 ZHR (2009), p. 454, 467; M. Schiessl, Der Konzern (2009), p. 291, 295; H. Fleischer and K.U. Schmolke, ZIP (2008), p. 1501, 1506; dissenting opinion: K.-M. Schanz, DB (2008), p. 1899, 1903.

[229] This case also affected aspects of market manipulation, cf. § 14 para. 17.

[230] Gesetz zur Stärkung des Anlegerschutzes und Verbesserung der Funktionsfähigkeit des Kapitalmarkts vom 7.4.2011, BGBl. I S. 538 (German Investor Protection Enhancement and Improvement of the Functioning of the Capital Markets Act).

[231] In *Porsche/VW* the use of financial instruments lead to a low free float. This led to significant losses for short sellers (see § 14 para. 41).

[232] Cf. H. Fleischer and K.U. Schmolke, NZG (2010), p. 846, 852; A. Merkner and M. Sustmann, NZG (2010), p. 681, 683 ff.; C. Teichmann and D. Epe, WM (2010), p. 1477, 1480 ff.

[233] Cf. H. Fleischer and K.U. Schmolke, NZG (2010), p. 846, 852.

[234] Cf. C. Teichmann and D. Epe, WM (2010), p. 1477, 1480 ff.

[235] Cf. § 25a(1) WpHG.

pursuant to §§ 21, 22 and 25 WpHG.[236] In other words the voting rights that may possibly be acquired through the instruments as in § 25a WpHG have to be taken into account in addition to the voting rights defined in §§ 21, 22 WpHG and the instruments as defined in § 25 WpHG.[237] The aim of this rule is to achieve more transparency regarding existing and possible future voting rights.

114   The provision is kept as broad as possible in order to ensure that the notification requirement includes the widest possible range of evasive actions. Legal certainty, on the other hand, is ensured by § 25a(1)2 WpHG, which defines the two practically most important constellations more precisely and describes the situations in which financial or other instruments enable the acquisition of shares to which voting rights are attached.

115   An instrument "enables" an investor to acquire shares if the other party to the instrument could avoid or lower (hedge out) the risks resulting from its contractual obligations by buying shares (§ 25a(1)2 No. 1 WpHG). It is irrelevant if the other party actually does acquire shares or refrains from hedging.

116   This constellation refers in particular to instruments with cash settlements such as those acquired in *Continental/Schaeffler* and *Porsche/VW*, i.e. contracts for difference and swap deals.

117   An investor is further "enabled" to acquire shares when financial instruments or other instruments convey the right or the obligation to acquire shares on an investor (§ 25a(1)2 No. 2 WpHG). This refers to cases in which the acquisition is possible directly due to the nature of the instrument. The most important examples are put options with physical settlement which require the seller to notify the issuer of its potential voting rights attached to the underlying instruments, as well as call options with physical settlement that are not covered by § 25 WpHG, i.e. call options that provide for a condition which cannot be effected by the buyer alone.

118   The wording of § 25a WpHG appears to subject share acquisitions in the context of M&A transactions and resulting from shareholder agreements to the rules on notification obligations.[238] However, the fact that these do not constitute financial instruments or other instruments must be seen as an argument against this interpretation.

119   The application of the new provision is to be facilitated by the BaFin, which is compiling and publishing a list of all financial instruments that can possibly require notification.[239] The Federal Ministry of Finances is also empowered to provide exceptions from the notification duty by way of regulations, for instruments held by investment firms for trading (held-for-trading securities) or to execute customer transactions.[240] The Ministry can also by way of regulation empower the BaFin to develop such exceptions. However, the legislature will not enact such a regulation

---

[236] Cf. § 25a(1) WpHG.
[237] These are financial instruments that must be disclosed pursuant to Art. 13 TD. See para. 100.
[238] Seen critically by A. Merkner and M. Sustmann, NZG (2010), p. 681, 685.
[239] Cf. Begr. RegE Anlegerschutz- und Funktionsverbesserungsgesetz, BT-Drucks. 17/3628, p. 20.
[240] Cf. § 25a(4)2 WpHG.

until new insights on the effects of these notification requirements and the practical relevance of possible exemptions exist.[241]

120 The proportion of voting rights to which the notification duty refers can be deduced from the number of shares that the financial instrument enables the holder to acquire.[242] If the contractual agreement on the instrument refers to a specific number of shares, this shall generally be relevant, in all other cases the number of shares that would have to be obtained in order for the instrument to be fully secured shall determine the proportion of voting rights to which notification obligations are attached.

121 Financial instruments that the holder has to notify the company of are not to be taken into account when determining whether an investor has acquired control over a company and must therefore make a mandatory offer.[243] The financial instruments and other instruments do not convey any influence on the corporation so that the hypothetical voting rights do not have to be attributed to the investor pursuant to the rules of the German takeover law.

122 A breach of these duties is treated as an administrative offence with a maximum fine of €1 million.[244] The legislature has not provided the possibility for an additional loss of rights.[245]

(c) France

123 Derivates are a common instrument in France for investors to creep in on issuers.[246] The AMF appointed a committee responsible for developing proposals for a reform,[247] but the legislature ultimately opted for an approach that amends the existing regime as little as possible.[248]

124 According to Article 13 TD, Article L. 233–7 C. com. (French Commercial Code) and Articles 223–11 ff. RG AMF (General Regulations of the French Stock Market Authority) only list specific financial instruments to which voting rights are attributed. These are options which confer the owner with the unconditional right to acquire shares. In contrast to the recommendations submitted by the AMF's working group, the options that do not lead to a physical acquisition of shares (*instruments financiers dérivés sans dénouement physique*), such as cash-settled equity swaps (*contrats d'échange d'actions dénoués en numéraire*) and contracts for difference (*contrats pour différence*), are not attributed. These financial instruments are only to be disclosed if the holder of the financial instruments reaches or exceeds one of the legal thresholds,[249] whilst the sole acquisition of derivatives does not lead to any statutory

---

[241] Cf. Begr. RegE Anlegerschutz- und Funktionsverbesserungsgesetz, BT-Drucks. 17/3628, p. 21 (explanatory notes).

[242] The basis for the calculation of the voting rights subject to notification is laid out in § 25a(2) WpHG.

[243] The legal basis for mandatory offers are §§ 35(2), 29 WpÜG.

[244] Cf. § 39(4) WpHG.

[245] On this sanction for breaches of notification obligations regarding changes in major shareholdings under § 21 WpHG see above para. 91–95.

[246] Cf. E. Zabala, Bull. Joly Bourse (2008), p. 389, 397.

[247] The report is available at: www.amf-france.org/documents/general/8479_1.pdf. On this see J.-F. Biard, RDBF (2009), p. 70.

[248] More details on the reform in P.-H. Conac, Rev. soc. (2009), p. 477 ff.

[249] Cf. F. Funck-Brentano and A. Mason, RTDF (2009), p. 31, 36.

obligations.[250] This, however, did not prevent the AMF from imposing a fine of €1.5 million in one particular case in which an investor gained considerable influence over the company, exceeding the 20% threshold with the help of derivative financial instruments.[251]

(d) Europe

125 The introduction of provisions on transparency regarding financial instruments that are so far not subject to any notification requirements is meanwhile also being discussed at European level. At the beginning of January 2010 the CESR submitted a recommendation to introduce notification requirements regarding financial instruments conveying an economic interest,[252] as it must be assumed that the investor in these cases will try and influence the issuer. This recommendation was not with universal approval.[253] The main argument against notification requirements was the considerable costs for investors.[254] Furthermore, the obligations would increase the price of company takeovers, thus interferring with the market for corporate control. Nevertheless, the European Commission was right to attend to this question.[255] It cannot be regarded as desirable for the European capital markets if strong variations in notification requirements exist between the Member States. The Commission's proposal in October 2011 for an amended TD that will enhance and unify the notification and disclosure obligations is thus a step in the right direction.[256]

126 Article 10 TD is, for example, to be complemented by two general clauses. The notification obligation is in future also to apply to financial instruments that, on maturity, give the holder discretion regarding its right to acquire the respective shares[257] or have a similar economic effect, irrespective of the right to a physical settlement.[258] The amendment further lists which financial instruments result in disclosure obligations.[259] In order to ensure legal certainty, the ESMA is to compile an exemplary list of financial instruments subject to notification obligations.[260]

---

[250] Seen critically by P.-H. Conac, Rev. sociétés (2009), p. 477, 486; F. Funck-Brentano and A. Mason, RTDF (2009), p. 31, 36; A. Omaggio, Dr. sociétés (2009), p. 49, 50. A draft law made public in June 2011 suggests that other derivatives should also be subject to a disclosure obligation if, under consideration of voting rights, they correspond with a shareholding of at least 10% of the company's shares.

[251] Cf. AMF, *Decision de la Commission des Sanctions à l'egard de la société Wendel SA, de M. Jean Bernard Lafonta et de la société Deutsche Bank Paris*, 13 December 2010.

[252] Cf. CESR, *Proposal to extent major shareholding notifications to instruments of similar economic effect to holding shares and entitlements to acquire shares*, CESR/09-1215b, January 2010.

[253] Seen critically by U. Brandt, BKR (2010), p. 270 ff.; D.A. Zetzsche, 11 EBOR (2010), p. 231 ff.

[254] Cf. C. Teichmann and D. Epe, WM (2010) p. 1477, 1481.

[255] Cf. Report from the Commission to the Council, the European Parliament, The European Economic and Social Committee and the Committee of the Regions, COM(2010)243 final, 27 May 2010.

[256] See above para. 14.

[257] Cf. Art. 13(1)(a) TD Draft.

[258] Cf. Art. 13(1)(b) TD Draft.

[259] Cf. Art. 13(1b)1 TD Draft: transferrable securities, and options, futures, swaps, forward rate agreements, contracts for differences and any other derivative contracts which may be settled physically or in cash.

[260] Cf. Art. 13(1b)2 TD Draft.

V. Notification of Intent

127 US capital markets law introduced provisions requiring a person to disclose his purposes regarding the future developments of the issuer in 1968.[261] The obligation applies to all investors acquiring at least 5% of the company's shares and constitutes the centrepiece of the rules on investor transparency. The notification of intent is regarded as having a high informational value. Empirical studies have proven that the reaction of investors depends not only on the disclosure of an acquisition of a major shareholding but rather also on the aims the respective issuer pursued with the acquisition.[262]

128 Neither the TD nor the other directives on capital markets law request that EU Member States introduce provisions that would obligate investors to disclose their intent regarding the acquisition or disposal of shares. France and Germany, however, introduced such provisions nonetheless. These shall be described below, taking into account the possibility of addressing this question at EU level.

1. France

129 France has far-reaching rules on the investor's notification of intent,[263] which were originally based on section 13d of the US Securities Exchange Act. The French provision was enacted in 1988 and contains a notification obligation for exactly these cases. However, the provision did not prove very successful in France, the notifications submitted often being formulaic and of little informative value.

130 Examples of the investor notifications were: "We retain the option of acquiring or disposing of further shares in the future, depending on the opportunities on the market." Or: "We declare that we momentarily do not have the intention of appointing one or more members to the board. However, we retain the option of doing so in the future."[264]

131 These problems were the reason for the reforms of the French rules in 2009.[265] The amendments ensured that investors must now give precise information about their strategy, their methods of financing the acquisition of shares and the measures planned regarding the issuer—i.e. mergers, restructuring, the assignment of assets and changes in the dividend policy, the company structure, the capitalisation, the area of business, the articles of association and any agreements on regarding shares and voting rights. The investor must further notify the company whether it intends to acquire control of the company.[266]

132 The notification is restricted to aims in the next six months. The investor is not bound by this declaration; it can change its intentions any time, provided it notifies the company of this. The thresholds at which the notification must be made are 10,

---

[261] See above para. 6.
[262] Cf. W.H. Mikkelson and R.S. Ruback, 14 J. Fin. Econ. (1985), p. 532, 536; J. E. Bethel et al., 53 J. Fin. (1998), p. 605, 628; F. Scherr et al., 32(4) Quarterly J. Bus & Econ. (1993), p. 66. 70, 73.
[263] Defined in Art. L233-7 C. com. and Art. 223-14 RG AMF.
[264] C. Uzan, Bull. Joly Bourse, (2008), p. 530, 533.
[265] Cf. P.-H. Conac, Rev. Soc. (2009), p. 477, 495 ff.
[266] In detail J.-F. Biard, RDBF (2009), p. 70 ff.

Rüdiger Veil

15, 20 and 25% of the voting rights. Since the reform, the notification must be made within ten trading days. Failure to comply with the obligation results in a loss of voting rights for two years after the notification is completed.[267] Additionally, appropriate regulatory measures may be taken by the AMF, which tends to impose fines.

2.   Germany

133   In 2008 Germany introduced provisions on the notification duties for major holdings, reasoning that German capital markets law provisions fell short of rules on notification provided for in France and the USA.[268] Therefore, § 27a WpHG now determines that a shareholder must notify the issuer of the aims underlying the purchase of the voting rights when it reaches or exceeds a threshold of 10% or one of the further thresholds.[269] The company must also be informed about any changes to the aims.[270]

134   The word "aim" is ambiguous. Therefore, § 27a(1)3 WpHG defines more closely which aims the issuer has to notify the company of: these are whether (1) the investment is aimed at implementing strategic objectives or at generating a trading profit; (2) it plans to acquire further voting rights within the next twelve months by means of a purchase or by any other means; (3) it intends to exert an influence on the appointment or removal of members of the issuer's administrative, managing and supervisory bodies and (4) it intends to achieve a material change in the company's capital structure, in particular as regards the ratio between own funds and external funds and the dividend policy.[271]

135   The notification obligations have been criticised.[272] The information content of some of the data required in a notification of intent remains unclear. This especially refers to the fact that the investor has to reveal the origin of the funds, i.e. whether these are own funds or external funds raised by the notifying party in order to finance the purchase of the voting rights. It has also been criticised that no notification requirement applies for the question as to whether the investor intends to acquire control of the company. The fact that the articles of association of an issuer may exempt the company from the notifictaion requirements[273] is also seen critically, as it is in the public interest that the investor notifies the issuer of his intents.

136   Legal practice in Germany shows that the investors' notifications of intent often contain reservations or are formulated restrictively. Others contain explanatory details, in which an investor may, for example, describe itself as a "long-term investor".[274]

---

[267] Cf. on this R. Veil and P. Koch, *Französisches Kapitalmarktrecht*, p. 102–103.

[268] Begr. RegE Risikobegrenzungsgesetz, BT-Drucks. 16/7438, p. 8 (explanatory notes).

[269] The thresholds are laid out in § 21(1) WpHG which is referred to in § 27a(1) WpHG with the result that a notification under § 27a WpHG is necessary at the thresholds of 10, 15, 20, 25, 30, 50 and 75% of the voting rights.

[270] Cf. § 27a(1) WpHG.

[271] Cf. § 27a(1) WpHG.

[272] H. Fleischer, AG (2008), p. 873; J. Querfurth, WM (2008), p. 1957; U.H. Schneider, in: *Festschrift für Gerd Nobbe*, p. 741; M. Zimmermann, ZIP (2009), p. 57.

[273] Cf. § 27a(3) WpHG.

[274] Cf. R. Veil, in: K. Schmidt and M. Lutter (eds.), *Kommentar zum AktG*, § 27a WpHG para. 7.

137   The notification must follow within 20 trading days of reaching or exceeding the threshold (§ 27a(1) WpHG). This rule is not convincing. There is no reason why an investor should be granted such a long period of time to disclose its aims. The publication of the information is up to the issuer and must take place within three trading days of receiving the notification or discovering the failure to comply with the requirements.

138   Failure to comply with § 27a WpHG does not—unlike in France—entail any sanctions. The BaFin is not entitled to impose fines on the investor who breached his notification duties and the investor is not subject to a loss of rights. The question whether a civil liability of the investor towards shareholders must be assumed in these cases remains unclear.[275]

3.   Reforms at European level

139   The European legislature has not yet reached a conclusion in the discussion[276] about whether the Member States should be obligated at a European level to introduce provisions on a notification of intent. The proposals for an amendment of the TD published in October 2011[277] do not contain any notification or disclosure obligations for investors. The topic does not appear to be at the top of the European Commission's agenda.

VI. Conclusion

140   The European legislature attributes great importance to the transparency of major holdings for the functioning of the capital markets. This leads to the question whether these high aims have been achieved. Has this field of capital markets law really been harmonised and a functional regime installed?

141   One may have doubts about this, taking into account how many cases of creeping in with the help of cash-settled equity swaps have occurred during the last few years throughout the Member States. It appears that in practice new loopholes can always be found. A further problem is the freedom the TD leaves the Member States regarding notification requirements for which the directive only provides a number of non-cohesive thresholds. Whilst some Member States restricted themselves to implementing these provisions into their national capital markets laws, the majority opted for the introduction of additional thresholds or for provision allowing the issuers to stipulate additional thresholds in their articles of association. In France the latter has, however, proved not to provide market efficiency but rather to be employed when trying to prevent hostile takeovers.

142   Another cause for concern are the provisions on the attribution of voting rights attached to third-party shares which vary greatly between the Member States, some

---

[275] Cf. ibid, § 27a WpHG para. 24.
[276] Cf. Statement of the European Corporate Governance Forum on Proportionality, June 2007 (available at: http://ec.europa.eu/internal_market/company/docs/ecgforum/workinggroup_proportionality_en.pdf).
[277] See para. 14.

Rüdiger Veil

Member States once again having adopted stricter provisions. Acting in concert, for example, is defined very differently in France, Germany, Italy and Spain. Furthermore a unified European level of information cannot be assumed when one considers how far some Member States have gone in their requirements for a notification of intent.

143 Possible sanctions are only defined in a non-cohesive way in the TD. Thus, it is not surprising that the Member States operate with very diverse instruments. However, up to a certain extent this is acceptable and can be traced back to the specific legal cultures in the Member States, making certain supervisory or civil instruments more suited to the particularities. A further harmonisation is not necessary, provided the rules can be effectively enforced with the existing measures. This, again, can be doubted. Those Member States that have subjected a failure to comply with notification requirements to a loss of rights place a greater emphasis on transparency of major holdings und capital markets law than those that mainly rely on supervisory sanctions. The Commission's amendments to the TD, enhancing and unifying sanctions at a European level, can thus only be welcomed.

§ 21 Directors' Dealings

Bibliography

Bednarz, Liane, *Pflichten des Emittenten bei einer unterlassenen Mitteilung von Directors' Dealings*, AG (2005), p. 835–842; Cox, James D. and Hazen, Thomas Lee, *Corporations* (2003), § 12.08; Dymke, Björn M., *Directors' Dealings am deutschen Kapitalmarkt—eine empirische Bestandsaufnahme*, Finanz-Betrieb (2007), p. 450–460; Fey, Gerrit, *Kosten und Nutzen der Regulierung börsennotierter Unternehmen: Ergebnisse einer Umfrage, Studien des Deutschen Aktieninstituts* (2007); Fischer zu Cramburg, Ralf and Hannich, Fabian, *Directors' Dealings. Eine juristische und empirische Analyse des Handels von Organmitgliedern mit Aktien des eigenen Unternehmens, Studien des Deutschen Aktieninstituts* (2002); Fleischer, Holger, *Directors' Dealings*, ZIP (2002), p. 1217–1218; Friederich, Sylvain, Gregory, Alan, Matatko, John and Tonks, Ian, *Short-run Returns around the Trades of Corporate Insiders on the London Stock Exchange*, 8 European Financial Management (2002), p. 7–30; Gregory, Alan, Matatko, John, Tonks, Ian and Purkis, Richard, *UK Directors' Trading—The Impact of Dealings in Smaller Firms*, 104 The Economic Journal (1994), p. 37–53; Heidorn, Thomas, Meyer, Bernd and Pietrowiak, Alexander, *Performance-Effekte nach Directors' Dealings in Deutschland, Italien und den Niederlanden*, in: Hochschule für Bankwirtschaft (ed.), *Arbeitsberichte* 57 (2004); Hillier, David and Marshall, Andrew P., *The Market Evaluation of Information in Directors' Trades*, 29 JBFA (2002), p. 77–110; Hower-Knobloch, Christian, *Directors' Dealings gem. § 15a WpHG. Eine ökonomische Analyse einer Mitteilungspflicht über Wertpapiergeschäfte von Personen mit Führungsaufgaben* (2007); Jacobs, Arnold S., *An Analysis of Section 16 of the Securities Exchange Act of 1934*, 32 N.Y.L. Sch. L. Rev. (1987), p. 209; Osterloh, Falk, *Directors' Dealings* (2007); Rau, Michael, *Directors' Dealings am deutschen Aktienmarkt. Empirische Analyse meldepflichtiger Wertpapiergeschäfte* (2004); Riedl, Albert M., *Transparenz- und Anlegerschutz am deutschen Kapitalmarkt. Eine empirische Analyse am Beispiel meldepflichtiger Wertpapiergeschäfte nach § 15a WpHG (Directors' Dealings)* (2008); Rüttenauer, Frank, *Directors' Dealings. Untersuchung von Performanceeffekten nach meldepflichtigen Aktiengeschäften* (2007); Schmidt, Martin H., *Directors' Dealings am deutschen Kapitalmarkt. Performance-Effekte von offenlegungspflichtigen Wertpapiergeschäften nach § 15a WpHG* (2010); Schneider, Uwe H., *Der pflichtauslösende Sachverhalt bei "Directors' Dealings". Der sachliche Anwendungsbereich des § 15 a WpHG*, BB (2002), p. 1817–1821; Schuster, Gunnar, *Kapitalmarktrechtliche Verhaltenspflichten von Organmitgliedern am Beispiel des § 15a WpHG*, 167 ZHR (2003), p. 193–215; Steinberg, Marc I. and Landsdale, Daryl L., *The Judicial and Regulatory Constriction of Section 16 (b) of the Securities Exchange Act of 1934*, 68 Notre Dame L. Rev. (1992), p. 33; Taylor, Ellen, *Teaching an Old Law New Tricks: Rethinking Section 16*, 39 Ariz. L. Rev. (1997), p. 1315; Veil, Rüdiger, *Gewinnabschöpfung im Kapitalmarktrecht*, ZGR (2005), p. 155–199; Wang, William and Steinberg, Marc, *Insider Trading* (2010); Wastl, Ulrich, *Directors' Dealings und aktienrechtliche Treuepflicht*, NZG (2005), p. 17–23.

I. Introduction

1 The necessity for transparency regarding dealings executed by the management of a company was not discovered by the European legislature until surprisingly late. The first directives on capital markets law[1] did not yet contain provisions thereon. It was not until the MAD was enacted in 2003 that notification and disclosure obligations for directors' dealings were required to be introduced into the Member States' national laws. The provisions followed the example of the US capital markets law

[1] See § 1 para. 5–6.

obligations for directors, officers, and principal stockholders regarding the disclosure of certain securities transactions.[2]

2   The notification and disclosure obligations are intended as preventive measures against market abuse.[3] The German legislature, which implemented the respective transparency requirements as soon as 2002, further justified an immediate notification obligation with the fact that this would prevent the suspicion of the directors taking advantage of their insider knowledge—such may arise if the dealing only becomes publicly known at a later time.[4] The notification of transactions conducted by persons discharging managerial responsibilities on their own account within an issuer also constitutes an additional means for competent authorities to supervise markets.[5] The European legislature further believed that the disclosure of directors' dealings would provide a better informational basis for investment decisions. The publication of individual transactions could be a highly valuable source of information for investors.[6] The notification and publication obligations should therefore be regarded as an additional instrument for ensuring the functioning of the capital markets. This and not the director's duty of loyalty towards the company should be the justification for the obligations.[7]

3   Whether directors' dealings that have been made public can be an indication of the future prospects of the company is doubtful. The reasons why the directors performed the specific transaction need not be made public in the statements and will therefore usually remain unknown. The underlying motives for the share transaction will often be entirely irrelevant for the assessment of the profit expectations of the company. The publication of transactions for the directors' own accounts can also be deceiving and bears the additional risk of a so-called noise trading, i.e. investors basing their investment decisions on unfounded, alleged information.[8] A further problem is the flood of information on the capital markets that results from such binding obligations: in Germany, for example, an average of 5,000 publications of directors' dealings are submitted to the market annually.[9]

4   These disadvantages have not prevented the majority of the economic and legal literature from viewing the notification and disclosure obligations for directors' dealings positively. Various empirical studies on German,[10] English[11] and other

---

[2] Sec. 16(a) Securities Exchange Act. A detailed analysis of the obligations can be found in A.S. Jacobs, 32 N.Y.L. Sch. L. Rev. (1987), p. 209.

[3] Cf. Recital 26 MAD.

[4] Cf. Begr. RegE, 4. Finanzmarktförderungsgesetz, BT-Drucks. 14/8017, p. 87 (explanatory notes).

[5] Cf. Recital 7 Directive 2004/72/EC.

[6] Cf. Recital 26 MAD.

[7] In German legal literature there is, however, a discussion on whether a disclosure obligation can be deduced from the duty of loyalty towards the company in stock corporation law. Cf. U. Wastl, NZG (2005), p. 17; L. Bednarz, AG (2005), p. 835, 840.

[8] Cf. G. Schuster, 167 ZHR (2003), p. 193, 200.

[9] Cf. BaFin, *Jahresbericht 2009* (annual report), p. 191: 2005 (5.118), 2006 (4.687), 2007 (4.603), 2008 (4.978) and 2009 (2.673); BaFin, *Jahresbericht 2011* (annual report), p. 212: 2010 (2258), 2011 (2869). The reduced number of publications in 2009 was supposedly caused by the general market situation and the introduction of a withholding tax on dividends and capital gains (so-called *Abgeltungssteuer*) on 1 January 2009.

[10] Cf. B.M. Dymke, Finanz-Betrieb (2007), p. 450, 452 ff.; M. Rau, *Directors' Dealings am deutschen Aktienmarkt*, p. 153 ff.; A.M. Riedl, *Transparenz und Anlegerschutz am deutschen Kapitalmarkt*, p. 123 ff.; for a summary of the emperical studies on US-American and German stock markets see F. Rüttenauer, *Directors' Dealings*, p. 37 ff.

[11] Cf. S. Friederich et al., 8 European Financial Management (2002), p. 7, 16 ff.; A. Gregory et al., 104 The Economic Journal (1994), p. 37, 46 ff.

European[12] capital markets have confirmed the legislature's reasons for their introduction, confirming that members of the management of the supervisory board generally achieve excess return from up to 5% with their transactions,[13] thus justifying the provisions on the transparency of directors' dealings.[14]

II. Regulatory Concepts

1. Requirements under European Law

(a) Legal Foundation

5   The MAD demands from the Member States that they introduce provisions obligating persons discharging managerial responsibilities within an issuer to notify the competent authority of the existence of transactions conducted on their own account. Only changes in their holdings are subject to this obligation, whilst a general notification obligation regarding shareholdings does not exist. The Member States must further ensure that public access to information concerning such transactions is available.[15] These vague obligations were rendered more precise in the European Commission's Implementing Directive 2004/72/EC which was enacted on Level 2 of the Lamfalussy process. It contains details on the persons to whom the notification obligations are addressed and on the necessary content of a notification.[16]

6   The directive aims at achieving a minimum harmonisation of this field of capital markets law in the Member States, allowing them to provide stricter rules. This was explicitly confirmed by the European Commission in the implementing directive.[17] The practical relevance of the possibility is, however, relatively slight compared with that regarding other areas of capital markets law, such as the rules on insider dealings[18] and the transparency of major shareholdings in listed companies.[19]

7   The Commission has recently presented a proposal for a Market Abuse Regulation.[20] It foresees much more detailed provisions than the MAD,[21] but the changes are relatively moderate. The most important new provision would affect the disclosure

---

[12] On Germany, Italy and the Netherlands see T. Heidorn et al., *Performance-Effekte nach Directors' Dealings in Deutschland, Italien und den Niederlanden*, in: Hochschule für Bankwirtschaft (ed.), *Arbeitsberichte 57*, p. 15 ff.

[13] Cf. M. Rau, *Directors' Dealings am deutschen Aktienmarkt*, p. 219 ff.; A.M. Riedl, *Transparenz und Anlegerschutz am deutschen Kapitalmarkt*, p. 233 ff.; seen more restrictively by A. Gregory et al., 104 The Economic Journal (1994), p. 37, 52 (above-average returns can especially occur in small and medium-sized firms); seen sceptically by B.M Dymke, Finanz-Betrieb (2007), p. 450, 460.

[14] Cf. F. Osterloh, *Directors' Dealings*, p. 68–69; seen critically on the basis of a legal economic analysis C. Hower-Knobloch, *Directors' Dealings gem. § 15a WpHG*, passim.

[15] Cf. Art. 6(4) MAD.

[16] Cf. Art. 1 and 6 Directive 2004/72/EC.

[17] Cf. Art. 6(1) Directive 2004/72/EC: "... and without prejudice to the right of Member States to provide for other notification obligations than those covered by that Article ...".

[18] See § 13 para. 14–31.

[19] See § 20 para. 17–33.

[20] Proposal for a Regulation of the European Parliament and of the Council on Insider Dealing and Market Manipulation (Market Abuse), 20 October 2011, COM(2011) 651 final; Proposal for a Directive of the European Parliament and of the Council on Criminal Sanctions for Insider Dealing and Market Manipulation, 20 October 2011, COM(2011) 654 final; cf. for the legislative background § 1 para 41.

[21] Art. 14 MAR Draft.

itself: directors would no longer have to inform the relevant competent authorities within five working days,[22] but would have to ensure disclosure of the information within two working days.[23]

(b) Additional Disclosure Rules

8   The notification obligations for directors conducting transactions on their own account coexist with the ad hoc disclosure obligations for inside information[24] and for changes in major shareholdings.[25,26] Therefore, the obligation to disclose the acquisition of shares by a director may be accompanied by the obligation to notify the issuer that a certain threshold[27] has been reached or exceeded. This will, however, only rarely happen, the first threshold lying at 3% of the voting rights.

9   The notification obligations apply to all transactions concerning shares or financial instruments of the issuer. The MAD does not require the disclosure of the shareholdings as such. A prospectus, however, must contain information thereon.[28] A disclosure can additionally be necessary pursuant to the national company laws of the Member States.

2. Implementation in the Member States

10   In the United Kingdom the rules on the disclosure of directors' dealings were originally laid down in company law. Meanwhile the provisions are part of capital markets law.[29] The German legislature first introduced the obligation to disclose directors' dealings in 2002 with the enactment of the Viertes Finanzmarktförderungsgesetz (Fourth Financial Market Development).[30] These provisions had to be amended only two years later in order to comply with the requirements of the MAD.

11   In legal practice a number of problems have arisen regarding the rules on disclosure and publication, some of which are very specific. The national supervisory authorities aim to solve these in order to achieve legal certainty. In Germany, for example, the BaFin's *Emittentenleitfaden* (issuer guideline) contains detailed statements on those to whom the obligations apply, the dealings subject to notification and the requirements for correct notification.[31] The FSA has also published a statement regarding the question of who, in its opinion, has to notify an issuer of transactions made in the issuer's shares.[32] Whilst the BaFin's and the FSA's guidelines are not legally binding, a person discharging managerial responsibilities will usually be able to absolve himself from liability if he acted in accordance with the administrative practice.

---

[22] Art. 6(1) Directive 2004/72/EC.
[23] See Art. 14(1) MAR Draft.
[24] See above § 19 para. 56.
[25] See above § 20 para. 13.
[26] R. Sethe, in: H.-D. Assmann and U.H. Schneider (eds.), *Kommentar zum WpHG*, § 15a para. 146–147.
[27] On the numerous different thresholds see § 20 para. 20–26.
[28] Cf. Art. 3 and 4 in conjunction with Annex I No. 18.1 Regulation (EC) No. 809/2004.
[29] Cf. sec. 96A(1)(f) FSMA and DTR 3.1 FSA Handbook.
[30] Cf. § 15a WpHG.
[31] Cf. BaFin, *Emittentenleitfaden 2009* (issuer guideline), p. 83 ff.
[32] Cf. Market Watch, *Newsletter on Market Conduct Issues*, Issue 12 (June 2005), p. 8–9.

III. Notification Requirements

1. Prerequisites

(a) Persons Subject to the Notification Obligation

12 The obligation to disclose directors' dealings as defined in the MAD is addressed to persons discharging managerial responsibilities within an issuer. Directive 2004/72/EC puts this concept into more concrete terms, defining such a person as a member of the administrative, management or supervisory bodies of the issuer. Additionally any senior executive, who is not a member of one of these bodies but has regular access to inside information relating directly or indirectly to the issuer, and the power to make managerial decisions affecting the future developments and business prospects of the issuer, is also subject to this obligation.[33] It can only be determined in each individual case who belongs to this second management level. According to the CESR this especially refers to so-called "Top Executives".[34] In a German stock corporation (*Aktiengesellschaft*) these will, however, only rarely be found below the level of the management or supervisory body. They include chief representatives and members of the so-called extended executive committee.[35]

13 A further practically relevant question is whether the bodies of a subsidiary that deal in the issuing parent company's financial instruments must be defined as such a "senior executive". Generally this is assumed if the subsidiary is the only operationally active subsidiary of a holding company.[36] It also remains unclear whether the bodies of the parent company are subject to the notification requirements if they deal in the issuing subsidiary's shares. Whilst the European legislative acts contain no provisions hereon, German legal literature confirms a notification obligation if the parent company had access to the subsidiary's information.[37]

14 The MAD further provides that the notification obligation may "where applicable" also refer to persons closely associated with persons discharging managerial responsibilities. The Member States must ensure that a notification obligation for share transactions by these persons is also introduced. The extension of the obligation to these cases is necessary in order to prevent the rule from being circumvented. The European legislative acts especially refer to spouses or any partners considered by national law as equivalent to a spouse, dependent children and other relatives of the person discharging managerial responsibilities.[38] The directive further subjects any legal person, trust or partnership to these obligations, if their managerial responsibilities are discharged by a person who is regarded as discharging managerial responsibilities with the issuer.[39]

---

[33] Cf. Art. 1(1)(a) and (b) Directive 2004/72/EC.
[34] Cf. CESR, *Advice on the Second Set of Level 2 Implementing Measures for a Market Abuse Directive*, CESR/03/212c, August 2003, No. 42.
[35] Cf. BaFin, *Emittentenleitfaden 2009* (issuer guideline), p. 85.
[36] Cf. *Pfüller*, in: Fuchs (ed.), *Kommentar zum WpHG*, § 15a para. 76.
[37] Cf. ibid, § 15a para. 77 for cases in which the subsidiary's board of directors is contractually obligated to act in accordance with the parent company's directions pursuant to § 308 AktG.
[38] Cf. Art. 1(2)(a)–(c) Directive 2004/72/EC.
[39] Cf. Art. 1(2)(d) Directive 2004/72/EC.

Rüdiger Veil

(b) Transactions Subject to the Notification Requirements

15   The MAD defines "all transactions conducted on [a persons'] own account relating to shares of the ... issuer, or to derivatives or other financial instruments linked to them" as subject to the notification requirement.[40] The Member States may provide that no notification is required or notification may be delayed until 31 January of the following year until the total amount of transactions has reached €5,000 at the end of a calendar year.[41] This exemption is to prevent a flood of notifications and an "information overload" regarding irrelevant transactions. Germany, for example, made use of the option clause. In practice, the exemption causes difficulties when the threshold of €5,000 is exceeded in the course of the year. In these cases all prior transactions must subsequently be reported to the competent authorities.[42]

16   The definition of a transaction depends on the civil law of the respective Member State. In Germany, the BaFin defines a transaction subject to the notification requirements as any contractual and legal disposition.[43] The type of transaction is usually irrelevant and can include exchange deals as well as sales contracts.[44] If the sales contract is subject to a condition precedent and the occurrence of the condition depends solely on the person subject to the rules on directors' dealings, the notification obligation will arise upon conclusion of the contract.[45]

17   In certain cases the acquisition of shares does not give rise to market abuse. In these cases a notification obligation would not fulfil any purpose, an example for this being an executive acquiring financial instruments solely as a part of his/her contractually agreed remuneration package. Given the over-the-counter nature of the (usually long-term) agreement entered into between the issuer and the executive, these cases must not be reported to the market.[46] The same applies to the acquisition of shares through gifts/donations or inheritances.[47]

2.   Legal Consequences

(a) European Requirements on Notification and Publication

18   The MAD demands Member States to ensure that public access to information concerning directors' dealings "on at least an individual basis, is readily available as soon as possible".[48] This vague instruction is put into more concrete terms by Implementing Directive 2004/72/EC: the notification must be made within five

---

[40] Cf. Art. 6(4) MAD.

[41] Cf. Art. 6(2) Directive 2004/72/EC.

[42] Cf. BaFin, *Emittentenleitfaden 2009* (issuer guideline), p. 89.

[43] Cf. ibid.

[44] In these cases the notification must contain information on the shares given as consideration. Cf. ibid., p. 102.

[45] Cf. ibid, p. 102; in more detail R. Sethe, in: H.-D. Assmann and U.H-Schneider (eds.), *Kommentar zum WpHG*, § 15a para. 73: generally for the conclusion of a contract. Dissenting opinion: U.H. Schneider, BB (2002), p. 1817, 1819: on occurrence of the condition.

[46] Cf. BaFin, *Emittentenleitfaden 2009* (issuer guideline), p. 89.

[47] Cf. ibid.; *Pluskat*, BB 2003, p. 2133, 2137. Dissenting opinion on exchange deals: R. Sethe, in: H.-D. Assmann and U.H-Schneider (eds.), *Kommentar zum WpHG*, § 15a para. 79.

[48] Cf. Art. 6(4) MAD.

working days of the transaction date[49] and must contain information on the name of the person discharging managerial responsibilities, the reason for the obligation to notify, the name of the relevant issuer, a description of the financial instrument, the nature of the transaction (e.g. acquisition or disposal), the date and place as well as the price and volume of the transaction.[50]

19   The MAD contains no precise requirements regarding the publication, merely demanding that the Member States ensure that the persons "at least notify to the competent authority the existence of transaction on their own behalf". In what way the public should be informed is not defined in the MAD. It rather leaves the choice of measures to be taken in order "to ensure that the public is correctly informed" to the supervisory authorities in the Member States.[51] It is obvious that these abstract requirements regarding the information of the public are not able to ensure a rapid dissemination of the information throughout the whole of Europe. The European legislature therefore developed a uniform and effective regime for the disclosure of "regulated information" in the TD of 15 December 2004. The term "regulated information" includes information on directors' dealings.[52]

20   The TD aims to achieve rapid access to information:[53] the information is to be disclosed "in a manner ensuring fast access to such information on a non-discriminatory basis".[54] The home Member State must further ensure that the issuer uses such media "as may reasonably be relied upon for the effective dissemination of information to the public throughout the Community".[55]

(b)   Legal Practice in the Member States

21   Despite the numerous provisions in European law, Member States have developed different rules on the details of the notification and publication requirements. In Germany, for example, persons discharging managerial responsibilities are obliged to notify the issuer and the BaFin of their own transactions in shares within five business days. The issuer must then, without undue delay, publish the information and simultaneously notify the BaFin of the publication.[56] Whilst the notification period of five days is often exceeded in practice, it is criticised by legal literature as being too long a period.[57] The United Kingdom, however, also provides for a notification period of four days.[58]

22   The individual Member State must determine whether a dissemination of the information in daily newspapers or via the Internet is sufficient.[59] In Germany the issuer must use a combination of different media which are able to actively disseminate

---

[49] Cf. Art. 6(1) Directive 2004/72/EC.
[50] Cf. Art. 6(3) Directive 2004/72/EC.
[51] Cf. Art. 6(7) MAD.
[52] The term "regulated information" is defined in Art. 2(1)(k) TD.
[53] Cf. Art. 21(1) TD.
[54] Cf. Art. 12(2) Directive 2007/14/EC.
[55] Cf. Art. 21(1) TD.
[56] Cf. § 15a(4) WpHG.
[57] Cf. F. Osterloh, *Directors' Dealings*, p. 188; R. Sethe, in: H.-D. Assmann and U.H-Schneider (eds.), *Kommentar zum WpHG*, § 15a para. 105.
[58] Cf. DTR 3.1.2 FSA Handbook.
[59] In more detail § 22 para. 4–7.

the information as rapidly and as promptly as possible in all EU Member States.[60] According to the BaFin, possible media are an electronic information dissemination system, news providers and agencies, important national and European journals and financial websites.[61] A publication on the issuer's website is no longer required in Germany. It is, however, permitted and many issuers make use of this possibility. The BaFin also publishes "Notifications pursuant to § 15a WpHG (Directors' Dealings)" for a period of one year.[62] In the United Kingdom the notification obligations of persons discharging managerial responsibilities in respect of transactions conducted on their own account in shares of the issuer are set out in DTR 3.1 FSA Handbook. The dissemination procedure is laid down in DTR 6.3. FSA Handbook.[63] An issuer must entrust an RIS with the disclosure of regulated information to the public.[64]

IV. Supervision and Sanctions

1. Requirements Laid Down by the Market Abuse Directive

23   The compliance with the Member States' provisions on directors' dealings is supervised by the national supervisory authorities[65] which have the supervisory and investigatory powers laid down in Article 12(1) and (2) MAD.[66] The general rules of the MAD also apply with regard to the sanctions that can be imposed for breaches of these notification and publication duties: the Member States must provide effective, proportionate and dissuasive sanctions.[67] These must not only apply to persons discharging managerial responsibilities and persons associated with them who must submit a notification to the supervisory authority on the transactions conducted on their own account, but also to the issuer with regard to his obligation to publish this information.

2. Fines and Criminal Sanctions

24   The Member States have met the demand to introduce sanctions in a number of ways.[68] Most have empowered their supervisory authorities with the possibility of imposing fines for the breach of the notification obligations; only in three jurisdictions—Bulgaria, Denmark and Norway—is this possibility non-existent.[69] The severity of the sanctions varies greatly, the maximum sanction being €1.5 million in France and €2.5 million in Belgium whilst the United Kingdom has no limit, thus

---

[60] Cf. § 3a(2)1 WpAIV.
[61] Cf. BaFin, *Emittentenleitfaden 2009* (issuer guideline), p. 94.
[62] Cf. http://ww2.bafin.de/database/DealingsInfo/.
[63] Cf. R. Panasar and S. Glasper, in: R. Panasar and P. Boeckman (eds.), *European Securities Law*, para. 21.118–21.123.
[64] DTR 6.3.3 FSA Handbook.
[65] Cf. Art. 11(1) MAD.
[66] See above § 13 para. 99–101, 109–113.
[67] For more details see § 9 para. 9 and 114 and § 12 para. 4.
[68] Cf. CESR, *Report on Administrative Measures and Sanctions as well as the Criminal Sanctions available in Member States under the Market Abuse Directive (MAD)*, CESR/07-693, February 2008.
[69] Denmark and Norway provide the possibility of imposing sanctions under criminal law. Cf. ibid. on "Art. 6 (4) Manager Transactions".

making the sanctions in Germany (€100,000), the Netherlands (€24,000), Austria (€30,000) and Finland (€1,000 for persons, €10,000 for legal entities) appear comparatively low.[70] In five jurisdictions—Denmark, Iceland, Ireland, the Netherlands and Norway—breaches of the notification obligation can result in sanctions under criminal law, even imprisonment in Iceland and Ireland.

25   Yet the legal practice of sanctioning the non-compliance with notification duties appears to be very restrictive. The BaFin commenced proceedings concerning administrative penalties in seven cases in 2008, in four cases in 2009, in three cases in 2010 and in two cases in 2011, with only six cases resulting in fines of €2,000–12,000 in 2009–2011.[71]

3.   Forfeiture of Profits

26   In the United States, the cradle of capital markets law, the phenomenon of directors having an informational advantage and using this unfairly is countered by strict rules on the recovery of profit by the issuer. The issuer, and under certain conditions also the shareholders, are in these cases permitted to recover so-called "short swing trading profits".[72] The forfeiture of profits does not require that the director breached his notification obligation regarding security tradings on his own account.[73] It rather encompasses all profits that were attained by the acquisition or disposal of the issuer's shares during a six-month-period ("short-swing trading profits"). These profits can be recovered by the issuer irrespective of whether the offender had access to inside information, had possession thereof, intended to make use of the information or to make profits.[74] It is irrefutably assumed that the respective person possessed inside information during the six-month-period.[75] The length of the period was chosen due to the fact that insider dealings usually take place during a relatively short time.[76] The strict liability was already described as a "crude rule of thumb" during the legislative procedure.[77]

27   In Europe, a similarly strict sanction does not exist. Whether the general provisions on a forfeiture of profits are applicable must be determined for each Member State individually. The general provisions on forfeiting profits under German law for administrative offences are not applicable. The director does not obtain the economic advantage through the administrative offence, i.e. the failure to notify the authority on the security transaction, as would be required for a liability under § 17(4) OWiG (Administrative Offences Act), but rather through the transaction itself.[78] As opposed to this, a forfeiture of profits in Spain is possible. Should the

---

[70] Cf. C. Hower-Knobloch, *Directors' Dealings gem. § 15a WpHG*, p. 178–179, with the recommendation of "drastically increasing" the fines.

[71] Cf. BaFin, *Jahresbericht 2009* (annual report), p. 192; BaFin, *Jahresbericht 2011* (annual report), p. 212.

[72] Cf. sec. 16(b) SEA.

[73] This notification obligation is laid down in sec. 16(a) SEA.

[74] Cf. W. Wang and M. Steinberg, *Insider Trading*, § 15.1.

[75] J.D. Cox and T.L. Hazen, *Corporations*, § 12.08; M.I. Steinberg and D.L. Landsdale, 68 Notre Dame L. Rev. (1992), p. 33, 35.

[76] Cf. *Blau v. Max Factor & Co.*, 342 F.2d 304, 308 (9th Cir.), cert. denied, 382 U.p. 892 (1965).

[77] Thomas Corcoran (principal spokesman of the Congress), as cited in A.S. Jacobs, 32 N.Y.L. Sch. L. Rev. (1987), p. 209, 345 fn. 1533.

[78] Cf. R. Veil, ZGR (2005), p. 155, 168.

Rüdiger Veil

profit not be determinable, up to 2% of the offender's assets or 2% of the capital it made use of for the transaction can be recovered.[79]

4. Civil Liability

28   The question as to whether individual investors may claim damages from members of the company's bodies or other persons obligated to notification for a breach of their duties regarding directors' dealings remains as yet largely unclear. This question can arise especially if a member of the administrative or supervisory board makes an incorrect notification and the issuer publishes this information.

29   The predominant opinion in Germany is that the provisions on directors' dealings do not constitute "protective rules" in the sense of the law of torts, granting the right to claim damages.[80] The legislature's aim was, however, not the protection of the individual investor's financial interests but rather ensuring the functioning of the capital markets.[81] Therefore, the only applicable legal basis for damage claims is § 826 BGB which is, however, hardly likely to be of practical relevance due to its strict prerequisite of an intentional damage contrary to public policy. Investors would further have to prove that their transaction was based on incorrect notification—a requirement that is already difficult to prove in cases of incorrect ad hoc notifications.[82]

V.   Conclusion

30   The MAD only contains key elements of the introduction of a disclosure regime for directors' dealings. The implementing directive enacted by the European Commission puts these into more concrete terms and contains numerous relevant additions, such as the additional rules applying to top executives and persons in a close relationship to the directors, preventing an evasion of the provisions. Nevertheless a number of interpretational questions remain unanswered by the national supervisory authorities. So far it appears highly unlikely that the ESMA will make any statements thereon.

31   When examining the annual reports and other publications of the national supervisory authorities it becomes apparent that the notification obligation regarding directors' dealings is a central element of European capital markets law. Whilst the information intermediaries and market participants may not be able to draw reliable conclusions regarding the future profits of an issuer from every transaction, empirical studies show that directors' dealings do allow certain conclusions to be drawn. The notification obligations additionally constitute a help for the national supervisory authorities in uncovering insider dealings.

---

[79] Cf. CESR, *Report on Administrative Measures and Sanctions as well as the Criminal Sanctions available in Member States under the Market Abuse Directive (MAD)*, CESR/07-693, February 2008 on "Art. 6(4) Manager Transactions".

[80] Cf. R. Sethe, in: H.-D. Assmann and U.H-Schneider (eds.), *Kommentar zum WpHG*, § 15a para. 140; Schuster, ZHR 167 (2003), p. 193, 215; F. Osterloh, *Directors' Dealings*, p. 202–203.

[81] On the regulatory aims see above para. 2.

[82] See § 19 para. 113.

§ 22 Access to Information

Bibliography
Moloney, Niamh, *EC Securities Regulation*, 2nd ed. (2008), p. 202–210, 971–973; Nießen, Tobias, *Die Harmonisierung der kapitalmarktrechtlichen Transparenzregeln durch das TUG*, NZG (2007), p. 41–46; Panasar, Raj and Boeckman, Philipp (eds.), *European Securities Law* (2010), p. 1273–1274 and 1290–1291.

I. Requirements under European Law

1 Capital market participants are to have prompt access to the relevant information, without carrying any significant costs. The European legislature realised the importance of access to information for the functioning of the capital markets[1] and introduced specific requirements regarding the disclosure and storage of "regulated information" in the TD and Implementing Directive 2007/14/EG[2]. The term "regulated information" refers to all information which the issuer is required to disclose under the TD and under Article 6 MAD,[3] i.e. notifications on major shareholdings,[4] on financial instruments,[5] financial reports,[6] inside information[7] and directors' dealings.[8]

2 The Member States must ensure that an issuer discloses regulated information in a manner ensuring prompt access to such information on a non-discriminatory basis.[9] It must be disseminated in a manner ensuring that it is capable of being disseminated to as wide a public as possible.[10] The issuer must refer to such media as may reasonably be relied upon for the effective dissemination of information to the public throughout the Community.[11] The Member States must further ensure that the issuer makes the regulated information available to the "officially appointed mechanism",[12] i.e. to a database responsible for the storage of the regulated information.[13]

---

[1] Originally the requirements regarding disclosure were outlined in the respective directives. Cf. N. Moloney, *EC Securities Regulation*, p. 971–973. The enactment of the TD enabled a unification of the rules on the access to information.

[2] Commission Directive 2007/14/EC of 8 March 2007 laying down detailed rules for the implementation of certain provisions of Directive 2004/109/EC on the harmonisation of transparency requirements in relation to information about issuers whose securities are admitted to trading on a regulated market.

[3] Cf. Art. 2(k) TD.

[4] See § 20 para. 32–33

[5] See § 20 para. 104–105.

[6] See § 18 para. 57–61.

[7] See § 19 para. 62.

[8] See § 21 para. 18–22.

[9] Cf. Art. 22(1) 1 TD.

[10] Cf. Art. 12(2) Directive 2007/14/EC.

[11] Cf. Art. 22(1)3 TD.

[12] Cf. Art. 22(1)1 TD.

[13] Cf. Art. 22(2) TD.

Rüdiger Veil

II.   Implementation in the Member States

3   The European requirements are limited to the general foundations of disclosure and storage of information; each Member State is responsible for the details thereof, such as the exact media to be employed. The individual Member State must determine whether a dissemination of the information in daily newspapers or via the Internet is sufficient. This will be illustrated on the basis of the examples of Germany and the United Kingdom.[14]

1.   Germany

4   Germany has not enacted any legislation determining the permitted media for the disclosure of capital market information. The WpAIV (German Federal Ministry of Finance's Regulation on Security Trading Notification and Insider Lists) only contains information on the form and language of the disclosure.[15] The BaFin, however, lists the following publication channels in its *Emittentenleitfaden* (issuer guidelines): electronic information systems,[16] news providers, news agencies, printed media and Internet pages for the financial market.[17] The BaFin states that the issuer must comply with certain minimum standards and make use of all five channels for disclosure.[18] At least one of the channels must enable an active, Europe-wide dissemination and every channel must further disseminate the information to those countries in which the shares are permitted to trading on the stock exchange.

5   The information must further be submitted to the business register—an "officially appointed mechanism" in the sense of the TD—for storage. The Federal Ministry of Justice administrates the register electronically.[19] It is accessible online.[20]

2.   United Kingdom

6   In the United Kingdom the dissemination procedure is laid down in DTR 6.3. FSA Handbook.[21] An issuer must entrust an RIS with the disclosure of regulated information to the public.[22] Furthermore an issuer must, for a period of one year following publication, post on its Internet sites all inside information that it is required to disclose by means of an RIS.[23] An RIS must fulfil certain criteria, determined by the FSA, with regard to the dissemination of information, data protection and

---

[14] Cf. on the legal situation in France A. Couret et al., *Droit financier*, para. 1436–1437.

[15] Cf. § 3a and § 3b WpAIV.

[16] In Germany the most common service provider is the Deutsche Gesellschaft für Ad-hoc-Publizität (www. dgap.de).

[17] Cf. BaFin, *Emittentenleitfaden 2009* (issuer guideline), 173; T. Nießen, NZG 2007, p. 41, 46.

[18] BaFin, *Emittentenleitfaden 2009* (issuer guideline), p. 173.

[19] Cf. § 8b HGB.

[20] Cf. www.unternehmensregister.de/ureg.

[21] Cf. R. Panasar and S. Glasper, in: R. Panasar and P. Boeckman (eds.), *European Securities Law*, para. 21.118–21.123.

[22] DTR 6.3.3 FSA Handbook.

[23] Cf. DTR 2.3.5 FSA Handbook.

Rüdiger Veil

accessibility.[24] Currently, seven RISs have been authorised by the FSA,[25] one of the best-known being the LSE's Regulatory News Service (RNS).

7   In order to fulfil the TD's requirement of a central storage mechanism, the FSA has listed the contact information of all authorised RISs on its homepage.[26]

III. Reform

8   The European Commission is planning reforms with regard to access to financial information, the current concept of 27 national databases which are insufficiently connected, being regarded as too complex.[27] The proposals for amendments to the TD published in October 2011[28] aim to grant the Commission and the ESMA further powers in order to harmonise the national provisions.[29] In the long run the only viable solution will be an information database at a European level.[30]

[24] Cf. FSA, *Criteria for Regulated Information Services*, May 2010.
[25] Cf. the list on containing Regulated Information Services on the website of the FSA, www.fsa.gov.uk/pages/doing/ukla/ris/contact/index.shtml.
[26] Cf. FSA, *Policy Statement 06/11, Implementation of the Transparency Directive*, October 2006, para. 5.2, available at: www.fsa.gov.uk/pubs/policy/ps06_11.pdf.
[27] Cf. Explanatory Statement Proposal (fn. 28), p. 9.
[28] Proposal for a Directive of the European Parliament and of the Council amending Directive 2004/109/EC on the harmonization of transparency requirements in relation to information about issuers whose securities are admitted to trading on a regulated market and Commission Directive 2007/14/EC, 25 October 2011, COM(2011) 683/2.
[29] Cf. Art. 21 and 22 TD Draft.
[30] Cf. Actica, *Feasibility Study for a pan-European storage system for information disclosed by issuers of securities—Final Report*, 18 October 2011.

§ 23   Disclosure of Information Necessary for Shareholders to Exercise their Rights

Bibliography

Dauner-Lieb, Barbara, *Siegeszug der Technokraten?—Der Kampf der Bits und Bytes gegen das Papier bei Börseninformationen am Beispiel von Art. 17 des Entwurfs der Transparenzrichtlinie*, DStR (2004), p. 361–366; Moloney, Niamh, *EC Securities Regulation*, 2nd ed. (2008), p. 202–203.

I.   Introduction

1   When the European legislature enacted the TD in 2004, its aim was to ensure that the holders of shares traded on the regulated market could exercise their rights. This presents a particular problem for investors not situated in the issuer's home Member State[1] as obtaining information on the general meeting and the procedures for exercising voting rights is more difficult from abroad. The TD aims at ensuring access to information about the investor and facilitating the use of proxies.[2] It merely establishes requirements concerning the information necessary for shareholders to be able to exercise their rights. All aspects of company law are covered by the directive on the exercise of certain rights of shareholders in listed companies,[3] the latter especially containing provisions on proxy voting: every shareholder has the right to appoint any other natural or legal person as a proxy holder to attend and vote at a general meeting in his name.[4]

II.   Regulatory Concepts

2   The TD centres around two different concepts regarding the information of shareholders: firstly, it requires issuers to make public without delay any change in the rights attaching to the various classes of shares;[5] secondly, it requires that issuers of shares[6] and debt securities[7] admitted to trading on a regulated market ensure that all information necessary to enable the holders to exercise their rights is publicly available. In both cases the requirements are thus addressed to the issuer.[8] The

---

[1] Cf. Recital 25 TD.

[2] Cf. Commission of the European Communities, Proposal for a Directive of the European Parliament and of the Council on the harmonisation of transparency requirements with regard to information about issuers whose securities are admitted to trading on a regulated market and amending Directive 2001/34/EC, COM(2003) 138 final, p. 22.

[3] Directive 2007/36/EC of the European Parliament and of the Council of 11 July 2007, OJ L184, 14 July 2007, p. 17.

[4] Cf. Art. 10(1) Directive on the exercise of certain rights of shareholders in listed companies.

[5] Cf. Art. 16 TD.

[6] Cf. Art. 17 TD.

[7] Cf. Art. 18 TD.

[8] Defined in Art. 2(1)(d) TD.

Rüdiger Veil

provisions are therefore to be classed as regulatory disclosure obligations.[9] The TD does not only contain disclosure obligations but also demands that all shareholders in the same position be treated as equal.[10] A corresponding right of equal treatment exists for the holders of debt securities.[11]

3 The TD empowers the Commission to adopt implementing measures in order to take into account technical developments in financial markets, e.g. developments in information and communication technology, in order to ensure the uniform application of its provisions.[12] Regarding the obligations laid down in Articles 17 and 18 TD, the Commission has not as yet made use of this possibility.[13]

III. Disclosure of Changes in the Rights Attached to Shares

4 According to Article 16 TD, the Member States must introduce three different disclosure obligations. The first applies to issuers whose shares are admitted to trading on a regulated market. They must disclose all changes in the rights attaching to the various classes of shares, including changes in the rights attaching to derivative securities issued by the issuer itself and giving access to the shares of that issuer. The rights referred to will mostly be voting and dividend rights.

5 The second disclosure obligation applies to issuers of securities other than shares admitted to trading on a regulated market, such as loans,[14] especially convertible bonds and warrant bonds.[15] Issuers of such financial instruments are also required to make public without delay any changes in the rights of holders which could indirectly affect the rights, resulting in particular from a change in loan terms or in interest rates.[16]

6 The third disclosure obligation also applies to issuers of securities admitted to trading on a regulated market. They are obliged to make public without delay the issuance of new loans and in particular any guarantee or security in respect thereof.[17] This information can be of interest for shareholders as issuing new securities increases the issuer's level of debt and can interfere with his capability to pay back the original loans.[18] Public international bodies of which at least one Member State is a member are exempted from this disclosure obligation.[19]

---

[9] Cf. P. Mülbert, in: H.-D. Assmann and U.H. Schneider (eds.), *Kommentar zum WpHG*, vor § 30a para. 11.
[10] Cf. Art. 17(1) TD.
[11] Cf. Art. 18(1) TD.
[12] Cf. Art. 17(4) and Art. 18(5) TD.
[13] Directive 2007/14/EC of 8 March 2007 does not provide for implementing provisions.
[14] Cf. the definition of the term securities in Art. 2(1)(a) TD; in more detail see § 5 para. 4 ff.
[15] Cf. P. Mülbert, in: H.-D. Assmann and U.H. Schneider (eds.), *Kommentar zum WpHG*, § 30e para. 9.
[16] Cf. Art. 16(2) TD.
[17] Cf. Art. 16(3) TD.
[18] Cf. P. Mülbert, in: H.-D. Assmann and U.H. Schneider (eds.), *Kommentar zum WpHG*, § 30e para. 14.
[19] Cf. Art. 16(3) TD.

Rüdiger Veil

IV. Disclosure of Information Necessary for Exercising Rights

1. Information Necessary for Shareholders

7   An issuer of shares admitted to trading on the regulated market must ensure that all the facilities and information necessary to enable holders of shares to exercise their rights are available in the home Member State and that the integrity of data is preserved.[20] The directive divides this general requirement into four more specific obligations for the issuer.

8   The issuer must provide information on the place, time and agenda of meetings, the total number of shares and voting rights and the rights of holders to participate in meetings in order to facilitate the correct participation in the general meetings for the investors.[21] This information is particularly helpful to foreign investors.

9   The issuer must further make a proxy form available to each person entitled to vote at a shareholders' meeting, either on paper or, where applicable, by electronic means, together with the notice concerning the meeting or, on request, after an announcement of the meeting.[22] This provision aims to facilitate the use of proxies for the general meeting.

10   The provision according to which the issuer must designate a financial institution through which shareholders may exercise their financial rights as its agent[23] has the same aim. The legal foundations for proxy voting through agents of financial institutions can be found in the company laws of the Member States.

11   An issuer must further publish notices or distribute circulars concerning the allocation and payment of dividends and the issue of new shares, including information on any arrangements for allotment, subscription, cancellation or conversion.[24]

2. Information Necessary for the Holders of Debt Securities

12   Issuers of debt securities admitted to trading on a regulated market are also subject to extensive disclosure requirements. 'Debt securities' include bonds or other forms of transferable securitised debts, with the exception of securities which are equivalent to shares in companies or which, if converted or if the rights conferred by them are exercised, give rise to a right to acquire shares or securities equivalent to shares.[25]

13   Issuers of debt securities must also ensure that all the facilities and information necessary to enable debt securities holders to exercise their rights are publicly available in the home Member State and that the integrity of data is preserved.[26] This general obligation is defined more precisely by numerous more detailed disclosure require-

[20] Cf. Art. 17(2) TD.
[21] Cf. Art. 17(2)(a) TD.
[22] Cf. Art. 17(2)(b) TD.
[23] Cf. Art. 17(2)(c) TD.
[24] Cf. Art. 17(2)(d) TD.
[25] Cf. Art. 2(1)(b) TD.
[26] Cf. Art. 18(2) TD.

ments which largely coincide with those binding for issuers of shares admitted to trading on a regulated market.

14   The issuer of debt securities must, for example, publish notices, or distribute circulars, concerning the place, time and agenda of meetings of debt securities holders, the payment of interest, the exercise of any conversion, exchange, subscription or cancellation rights, and repayment, as well as the right of those holders to participate therein.[27] It must further make a proxy form available either on paper or, where applicable, by electronic means, to each person entitled to vote at a meeting of debt securities holders, together with the notice concerning the meeting or, on request, after an announcement of the meeting.[28] Finally, the issuer is required to designate a financial institution as its agent through which debt securities holders may exercise their financial rights.[29]

V.   Conclusion

15   Issuers of shares and debt securities can fulfil their disclosure obligations with the help of electronic devices, ensuring that the costs are manageable for the issuers.[30] The obligation to provide certain information is flanked by the requirements of the "Directive on the exercise of certain rights of shareholders in listed companies" which ensures that voting by proxy is not subject to unnecessary administrative requirements and cannot be restricted without reason. This enables shareholders to participate in general meetings and votes irrespective of their permanent residence. Shareholders can also participate by electronic means. It remains to be seen whether these improved possibilities to participate in general meetings and exercise voting rights do actually increase participation in general meetings. Either way, the disclosure requirements provided for by the TD are necessary in order to enable shareholders from abroad to exercise their rights more efficiently and effectively than to date.

[27] Cf. Art. 18(2)(a) TD.
[28] Cf. Art. 18(2)(b) TD.
[29] Cf. Art. 18(2)(c) TD.
[30] Seen critically by B. Dauner-Lieb, DStR (2004), p. 61 ff.

Rüdiger Veil

§ 24   Disclosure Obligations in Takeover Law

Bibliography

Baj, Claude, *Action de concert et dépôt obligatoire d'une offre publique d'achat : deux réflexions à la lumière de l'affaire Eiffage*, RDBF (2008), p. 8; Baj, Claude, *L'action de concert dans l'affaire Eiffage: les aspects débattus*, RDBF (2008), p. 10; Baums, Theodor, *Low Balling, Creeping in und deutsches Übernahmerecht*, ZIP (2010), p. 2374–2390; Baums, Theodor and Thoma, Georg F., *Takeover Laws in Europe*, (2003); Biard, Jean-François, *Action de concert et non-conformité d'une offre publique*, RDBF (2008), p. 67; Bolle, Caroline, *A Comparative Overview of the Mandatory Bid Rule in Belgium, France, Germany and the United Kingdom* (2008); Button, Maurice and Bolton, Sarah, *A Practitioner's Guide to the City Code on Takeovers and Mergers* (2000/2001); Claussen, Carsten Peter and Scherrer, Gerhard (eds.), *Kölner Kommentar zum Rechnungslegungsrecht* (2011); Cramer, Carsten, *Change of Control-Klauseln im deutschen Unternehmensrecht* (2009); Crawshay, Charles M., *Mandatory Bids in UK*, in: Veil, Rüdiger (ed.), *Übernahmerecht in Praxis und Wissenschaft* (2009), p. 83–92; Dolff, Christian, *Der Rechtsverlust gem. § 28 WpHG aus der Perspektive eines Emittenten* (2011); Edwards, Vanessa, *The Directive on Takeover Bids—Not Worth the Paper it's Written on?*, 1 ECFR (2004), p. 416–439; Enriques, Luca, *European Takeover Law: The Case for a Neutral Approach*, 22 EBLR (2011), p. 623–639; Fleischer, Holger and Kalss, Susanne, *Das neue Wertpapiererwerbs- und Übernahmegesetz* (2002); Fleischer, Holger, *Finanzinvestoren im ordnungspolitischen Gesamtgefüge von Aktien-, Bankaufsichts- und Kapitalmarktrecht*, ZGR (2008), p. 185–224; Hamann, Uwe, *Die Angebotsunterlage nach dem WpÜG—Ein praxisorientierter Überblick*, ZIP (2001), p. 2249–2257; Hirte, Heribert, *The Takeover Directive—A Mini-Directive on the Structure of the Corporation: Is it a Trojan Horse?*, 2 ECFR (2005), p. 1–19; Kalss, Susanne, *The Austrian Law on Public Offers and Takeovers*, 1 EBOR (2000), p. 479–506; Kirsch, Hans-Jürgen and Köhrmann, Hannes, *Inhalt des Lageberichts*, in: Castan, Edgar et al. (eds.), *Beck'sches Handbuch der Rechnungslegung* (2007); Le Nabasque, Hervé, *Annotation to CA Paris, 1re ch., sect. H., 2 April 2008, Sté Sacyr Vallehermoso c/ Sté Eiffage*, RDBF (2008), p. 54; Maul, Silja and Kouloridas, Athanasios, *The Takeover Bids Directive*, 5 GLJ (2004), p. 355–366; Maul, Silja and Muffat-Jeandet, Danièle, *Die EU-Übernahmerichtlinie— Inhalt und Umsetzung in nationales Recht*, AG (2004), p. 221–234 and 306–318; McCahery, Joseph A. and Vermeulen, Erik P.M., *The Case Against Reform of the Takeover Bids Directive*, 22 EBLR (2011), p. 541–557; Montalenti, Paolo, in: Cottino, Gastone, *Trattato di diritto commerciale* (2011), p. 146 ff.; Mülbert, Peter O., *Umsetzungsfragen der Übernahmerichtlinie—erheblicher Änderungsbedarf bei den heutigen Vorschriften des WpÜG*, NZG (2004), p. 633–642; Nussbaum, Matthias, *Abfindungen und Anerkennungsprämien für Vorstandsmitglieder deutscher Aktiengesellschaften. "Goldene Handschläge" und "Fallschirme"* (2009); Sailer, Viola, *Offenlegung von Change of Control-Klauseln im Jahresabschluss*, AG (2006), p. 913–927; Seibt, Christoph H. and Heiser, Kristian J., *Analyse des Übernahmerichtlinie-Umsetzungsgesetzes (Regierungsentwurf)*, AG (2006), p. 301–320; Stephan, Klaus Dieter, *Angebotsaktualisierung*, AG (2003), p. 551–561; Stohlmeier, Thomas, *German Public Takeover Law*, Bilingual Edition with an Introduction to the Law, 2nd ed. (2007); Strunk, Klaus-Jürgen, Holst, Raven and Salomon, Heike, *Aktuelle Entwicklungen im Übernahmerecht*, in: Veil, Rüdiger (ed.), *Übernahmerecht in Praxis und Wissenschaft* (2009), p. 1–42; Veil, Rüdiger, *Die Übernahmerichtlinie und ihre Auswirkungen auf das nationale Übernahmerecht*, in: Veil, Rüdiger and Drinkuth, Henrik (eds.), *Reformbedarf im Übernahmerecht* (2005), p. 95–111; Venturozzo, Marco, *Takeover Regulation as a Wolf in Sheep's Clothing: Taking UK Rules to Continental Europe*, 11 U. Pa. J. Bus. L. (2008–2009), p. 135–174; Wooldridge, Frank, *The Recent Directive on Takeover-Bids*, 15 EBLR (2000), p. 147–158.

I.   Introduction

1   The Takeover Directive (TOD) coordinates the laws, regulations, administrative provisions, codes of practice and other arrangements of the Member States on takeover
bids.[1] Its scope of application is restricted to offers for securities of companies whose
securities are admitted to trading on a regulated market in one or more Member
States and which are governed by the laws of a Member State.[2] The TOD does not
apply to offers for the acquisition of securities on open markets.[3]

2   The TOD is a framework directive,[4] merely laying down the central elements of
takeover proceedings, but permitting the Member States to develop their own, more
specific rules on certain aspects. This can, for example, be seen with regard to mandatory bids: the TOD contains no rules on how an offeree gains control over the
target company, leaving the Member States to decide.[5] Other aspects, however, such
as the procedure[6] and its supervision by the national authorities,[7] are described in
great detail in the directive. The TOD also contains specific provisions for the board
of the offeree company[8] and exceptions from restrictions on takeover bids,[9] leaving
the Member States little room for deviation in the implementation.

3   This section gives an overview of those provisions of the TOD that are relevant with
regard to the transparency of capital market information. These are firstly provisions
on the disclosure of defensive structures and mechanisms in listed companies.[10]
The TOD obliges the Member States to ensure that the companies provide detailed
information concerning restrictions on voting rights and the transfer of securities.
The provisions on the publication of bids are a second essential element in the transparency regime of the directive:[11] the Member States must ensure that a decision to
make a bid is made public without delay. They must also require offerors to draw up
and make public in good time an offer document containing the information necessary to enable the holders of the offeree company's securities to reach a properly
informed decision on the bid.

4   Finally reference must be made to the fact that an investor can gain control over
the target company without having made a takeover bid. In these cases, the Member
States are also required to maintain shareholder protection under the directive—for

---

[1] The TOD was enacted after decades of legal and political discussions. For more details on legal history see
§ 1 para. 28–29.

[2] Cf. Art. 1(1) Takeover Directive.

[3] On the term open market see § 7 para. 20.

[4] The proposals for a directive submitted in 1989 and 1990 aimed to fully regulate all aspects. Not until
1996 did the European Commission follow the doubts of some Member States and restrict its proposal to some
framework provisions. Cf. H. Fleischer, in: H. Fleischer and S. Kalss (eds.), *Das neue Wertpapiererwerbs- und
Übernahmegesetz*, p. 50.

[5] See para. 38–42.

[6] Cf. S. Maul and D. Muffat-Jeandet, AG (2004), p. 221, 231 ff.

[7] Any association or private body empowered by national law or the national authorities can act as supervisory body. Cf. Art. 4(1)2 Takeover Directive.

[8] Cf. Art. 9 Takeover Directive; on this see R. Veil, in: R. Veil and H. Drinkuth (eds.), *Reformbedarf im
Übernahmerecht*, p. 83 ff.

[9] Cf. Art. 11 and 12 Takeover Directive and S. Maul and D. Muffat-Jeandet, AG (2004), p. 306, 310 ff.; R. Veil,
in: R. Veil and H. Drinkuth (eds.), *Reformbedarf im Übernahmerecht*, p. 83, 95 ff, 100 ff.

[10] Cf. Art. 10 Takeover Directive.

[11] Cf. Art. 6 and 8 Takeover Directive.

example, by ensuring that the offeror is required to make a bid addressed to all minority shareholders for all their holdings at an equitable price as a means of protection.[12] This mandatory bid also serves a capital markets law function, and must therefore be treated in more detail in the following.

II. Transparency Regarding Defensive Structures and Mechanisms

1. Regulatory Aims

5   One of the key aims of the European legislature was to reinforce the freedom to deal in the securities of companies and the freedom to exercise voting rights. Following the recommendations of the High Level Group of Company Law Experts,[13] the TOD requires that the Member States introduce provisions obliging companies to make their defensive structures and mechanisms transparent.[14] This obligation is to enable potential offerees to assess the target and possible barriers to takeover bids.[15]

6   The rules on transparency only apply to companies[16] whose securities are all or partly admitted to trading on the regulated market[17] of one or more Member States.[18] Unlike the framework directives under capital markets law,[19] the TOD restricts its understanding of securities to transferrable securities carrying voting rights in a company,[20] i.e. shares. The TOD does not distinguish between small and larger companies, this being seen critically considering the costs involved. It cannot be determined as yet, however, whether the TOD will be amended to exclude small and medium-sized enterprises (SME) from its scope of application.[21]

2. Transparency Requirements

7   When giving an overview of the information a company must disclose, it is not necessary to mention the national implementing laws separately, as the directive's provisions are so precise that they cover all possible cases in which a public takeover may be affected. No noteworthy leeway is given to the Member States for gold plating. The TOD also defines exactly which medium must be used for publication and which additional information is required: the information must be published in the company's annual reports.[22] Furthermore, the board of directors must present

---

[12] Cf. Art. 5 Takeover Directive.

[13] Cf. *Report of the High Level Group of Company Law Experts on Issues Related to Takeover Bids* (so-called Winter Group), of 10 January 2002, p. 6 and 25–26.

[14] Cf. Recital 18 Takeover Directive.

[15] Cf. K.W. Lange, in: K. Schmidt (ed.), *Münchener Kommentar zum HGB*, § 289 para. 129.

[16] The company must be subject to the law of a Member State. Cf. Art. 1(1) Takeover Directive and Recital 1.

[17] On the concept of a regulated market see § 3 para. 21 ff.

[18] Cf. Art. 10(1) in conjunction with Art. 1(1) Takeover Directive.

[19] See § 1 para. 19–27.

[20] Cf. Art. 2(1)(e) Takeover Directive.

[21] Cf. European Commission, Consultation document on the modernisation of the Directive 2004/109/EC on the harmonisation of transparency requirements in relation to information about issuers whose securities are admitted to trading on a regulated market, 27 May 2010, p. 5.

[22] Cf. Art. 10(2) Takeover Directive; on the management report see § 18 para. 34.

an explanatory report on the information published to the annual general meeting of shareholders.[23]

(a) Structure of the Capital

8   The annual report must contain information on the structure of the capital, including securities which are not admitted to trading on a regulated market. An offeror must be capable of gaining insight into the company's financing.[24] Companies that offer different classes of shares—e.g. non-voting shares or shares with a priority over common stock in the payment of dividends—must also include an indication of the different classes of shares and, for each class of shares, the rights and obligations attaching to it and the percentage of total share capital that it represents.

(b) Restrictions Regarding the Transfer of Shares

9   Companies must further provide information regarding the restrictions on the transfer of their securities. The TOD lists a number of examples for this, such as limitations on the holding of securities or the need to obtain the approval of the company or other holders of securities. Not all Member States have the same types of restrictions. Some, such as Germany, permit no limitations on the holding of securities under company law. Italy and the Netherlands, on the other hand, provide the possibility to introduce limitations on the percentage of shares that may be held in the company's articles of association.[25] Where such limitations exist the company must provide information thereon in its annual report.

10 Limitations requiring the approval of the company for the transfer of securities are of the greatest relevance in legal practice. In Germany this primarily affects registered shares (*Namensaktien*).[26] Such limitations can impede takeovers[27] and must therefore be disclosed. The aim of the disclosure obligation is to require the company to disclose the conditions that must be met in order for approval to be declared and whether the management or the general shareholders' meeting is responsible for the approval.

(c) Significant Shareholdings

11 Companies must further publish information on all significant direct or indirect shareholdings, for example in the form of pyramid financial schemes and cross-shareholdings. To put the concept of a significant shareholding into more concrete terms, the TOD makes reference to Article 85 of Directive 2001/34/EC, which laid

---

[23] Cf. Art. 10(3) Takeover Directive.
[24] Cf. S. Maul and D. Muffat-Jeandet, AG (2004), p. 306, 308.
[25] Cf ibid.
[26] Cf. § 68(2) AktG; on the requirements for the transferral of such shares see T. Raiser and R. Veil, *Recht der Kapitalgesellschaften*, § 11 para. 82 ff.
[27] Whether the management or supervisory board may make use of provisions requiring approval in order to prevent a takeover is an entirely different question. This question must be answered under consideration of the management and administrative board's obligation not to take any measures that may prevent a takeover bid (cf. Art. 9 Takeover Directive). Preventing a pending takeover will only rarely be in the interest of the company, thus generally prohibiting a refusal to consent. Cf. T. Raiser and R. Veil, *Recht der Kapitalgesellschaften*, § 44 para. 25.

down disclosure requirements regarding major shareholding prior to the enactment of the TD in 2004.[28] According to this former provision, notification obligations ensued if an investor's voting rights reached or exceeded 10%.[29] The annual report of a listed company must therefore only contain information on shareholdings exceeding 10% of the company's capital;[30] indirect holdings must be added to direct holdings in accordance with the provisions on the disclosure of major shareholdings.[31]

12   *Example:* A shareholder has 5% of a company's shares; a subsidiary holds another 3% and further 3% are held by a trustee of the shareholder. In such a scenario the company must publish the total of 11% of the company's shares held by this shareholder in its annual report. It can do so due to the fact that on exceeding a threshold of 10% of the company's shares the shareholder must notify the company of this fact.[32]

13   With the enactment of the TD in 2004 the European legislature undertook fundamental reforms to the regime of disclosure of major shareholdings. It reduced the lowest threshold from 10% to 5%, in order to increase market efficiency. A holding of 5% can be sufficient for exerting considerable influence on a listed company if the shares are mainly free floating. It would be advisable to apply these amendments in securities law to takeover law *de lege ferenda* and also introduce disclosure obligations for major shareholdings from a threshold of 5% onwards in the TD.

(d)   Holders of Special Rights

14   In its annual report a company must further publish information on holders of any securities with special control rights by name and a description of those rights. Special rights usually refer to the power to name members of the management, administrative or supervisory board. Whether such special rights exist must be determined according to the national law of the respective Member State. In Germany, for example, rights to appoint may only be granted with respect to a certain percentage of the shareholder representatives in the supervisory board.[33] Other special rights cannot be granted due to the fact that the German Stock Corporation Act is conclusive in this respect.[34] Other Member States have introduced different forms of special rights, such a right to veto,[35] multiple voting rights, common especially in France, England and Sweden.[36]

---

[28] See § 1 para. 19.

[29] Cf. Art. 85(1) in conjunction with Art. 89(1) Directive 2001/34/EC.

[30] The German legislature has included this in § 289(4) No. 3 HGB.

[31] Cf. H.-J. Kirsch and H. Köhrmann, in: E. Castan et al. (eds.), *Beck'sches Handbuch der Rechnungslegung*, Abschnitt B 510 Inhalt des Lageberichts, para. 238.

[32] See § 20 para. 17 and 20.

[33] A maximum of one third of the members of the supervisory board may be appointed from the pool of shareholders. Cf. § 101(2) AktG.

[34] See § 23(5) AktG. Cf. T. Raiser and R. Veil, *Recht der Kapitalgesellschaften*, § 11 para. 1 ff.

[35] Cf. S. Maul and D. Muffat-Jeandet, AG (2004), p. 306, 308; C.P. Claussen, in: G. Scherer and C.P. Claussen (eds.), *Kölner Kommentar zum Rechnungslegungsrecht*, § 289 HGB para. 60.

[36] Cf. T. Raiser and R. Veil, *Recht der Kapitalgesellschaften*, § 8 para. 38–39.

Rüdiger Veil

(e)   System of Control for Employee Share Schemes

15   A company must further make public which system of control exists for any employee share scheme where the control rights are not exercised directly by the employees. Such an indirect influence is usually only possible if the voting rights can be separated from the shares under company law.[37] In Germany this is not permitted. Other possible constellations are that the employees hold shares through investment companies[38] or if they jointly hold shares and their voting rights are exercised by a shared proxy.[39]

(f)   Restrictions on Voting Rights

16   The obligation to publish information on all restrictions on voting rights is a centrepiece of transparency regarding defensive structures and mechanisms envisaged by the companies. The TOD lists examples of restrictions, such as "limitations of the voting rights of holders of a given percentage or number of votes, deadlines for exercising voting rights, or systems whereby, with the company's cooperation, the financial rights attaching to securities are separated from the holding of securities".[40] Limitations depending on the percentage of number of voting rights held are of varying popularity in the Member States,[41] being prohibited, for example, for listed companies in Germany.[42]

17   "Systems whereby, with the company's cooperation, the financial rights attaching to securities are separated from the holding of securities" must also be made public. This particularly applies to the Dutch certification system.[43]

(g)   Agreements between Shareholders

18   Any agreements between shareholders which are known to the company and may result in restrictions on the transfer of securities and/or voting rights must also be made public. This includes agreements between the shareholders on how voting rights are to be exercised,[44] a form of agreement particularly common in companies in which one or more families hold shares.[45]

19   Numerous jurisdictions do not allow the company to have knowledge of these agreements, most shareholders aiming to keep them secret—an interest that is respected in most European jurisdictions. In Germany, for example, the issuer has the right

---

[37] Cf. H.-J. Kirsch and H. Köhrmann, in: E. Castan et al. (eds.), *Beck'sches Handbuch der Rechnungslegung*, Abschnitt B 510 Inhalt des Lageberichts, para. 241.

[38] Cf. C.H. Seibt and K.J. Heiser, AG (2006), p. 301, 316.

[39] Cf. H.-J. Kirsch and H. Köhrmann, in: E. Castan et al. (eds.), *Beck'sches Handbuch der Rechnungslegung*, Abschnitt B 510 Inhalt des Lageberichts, para. 241.

[40] Cf. Art. 10(1)(f) Takeover Directive.

[41] Cf. S. Maul and D. Muffat-Jeandet, AG (2004), p. 306, 309.

[42] Cf. § 134(1)2 AktG.

[43] On this see S. Maul and D. Muffat-Jeandet, AG (2004), p. 306, 309.

[44] Cf. C.P. Claussen, in: G. Scherer and C.P. Claussen (eds.), *Kölner Kommentar zum Rechnungslegungsrecht*, § 289 HGB para. 58; K.W. Lange, in: K. Schmidt (ed.), *Münchener Kommentar zum HGB*, § 289 para. 132.

[45] Cf. H.-J. Kirsch and H. Köhrmann, in: E. Castan et al. (eds.), *Beck'sches Handbuch der Rechnungslegung*, Abschnitt B 510 Inhalt des Lageberichts, para. 235.

to demand proof of a shareholder's holding in the company,[46] not, however, the right to demand submission of the agreement.[47] If the company does not have any knowledge of the agreement the shareholder need not inform it thereof, unlike in Italy[48] and Spain,[49] where a legal obligation to make public agreements between shareholders exists and the agreement will not become effective until it has been made public.[50]

(h) Provisions on the Appointment and Replacement of Board Members

20   The annual report must further contain information on the company rules governing the appointment and replacement of board members and the amendment of the articles of association. The reason for this is that an investor may have an interest in replacing the management after a successful takeover, for example, if it follows different strategic aims from the former management. Especially in companies with a two-tier system (board of directors and supervisory board) it can be very difficult for an offeror to replace the management, making it essential to be informed of the legal basis for this in the respective company before the takeover.[51]

21   Generally it is sufficient if the annual report makes reference to the respective legal provisions. However, the articles of association may contain special provisions on their amendment, for example requiring a higher rate of approval for resolutions (such as 9/10 instead of 3/4 of the represented share capital). In these cases, the articles of association must also be listed in the annual report.[52]

(i) Powers of Board Members to Issue and Buy Back Shares

22   A company is also obliged to make public information on the powers of board members to issue and buy back shares. Whilst it need not provide information on the general rights and obligations of the board members, it must describe the powers conveyed to the management or the administrative board by the articles of association or in resolutions of the general meeting.[53]

23   It must further inform the public whether the board members are permitted to use authorised capital, issue convertible or participating bonds or acquire the company's shares. Any of these measures could cause the takeover to become more expensive for the offeror, the issue of new shares causing a dilution of the offeror's stocks.

---

[46] The issuer's right to be informed of major shareholdings as described in § 27 WpHG refers to "notified shares". Cf. R. Veil, in: K. Schmidt and M. Lutter (eds.), *Kommentar zum AktG*, § 27 WpHG para. 2.

[47] Cf. C. Dolff, *Der Rechtsverlust gem. § 28 WpHG aus der Perspektive eines Emittenten* (2011).

[48] Cf. Art. 122 I TUF; cf. P. Montalenti, in: G. Cottino (ed.), *Trattato di diritto commerciale*, p. 146 ff.

[49] Cf. Art. 112.2 LMV.

[50] In Spain, the CNMV can free the affected shareholders from their obligation to disclose the agreement under certain conditions, cf. Art. 112.5 LMV.

[51] Cf. S. Maul and D. Muffat-Jeandet, AG (2009), p. 306, 309.

[52] Cf. H.-J. Kirsch and H. Köhrmann, in: E. Castan et al. (eds.), *Beck'sches Handbuch der Rechnungslegung*, Abschnitt B 510 Inhalt des Lageberichts, para. 243; K.W. Lange, in: K. Schmidt (ed.), *Münchener Kommentar zum HGB*, § 289 para. 136; S. Maul and D. Muffat-Jeandet, AG (2009), p. 306, 309.

[53] Cf. H.-J. Kirsch and H. Köhrmann, in: E. Castan et al. (eds.), *Beck'sches Handbuch der Rechnungslegung*, Abschnitt B 510 Inhalt des Lageberichts, para. 245.

(j)   Change of Control Clauses

24   European takeover law also requires that the company makes public any significant agreements to which the company is a party and which take effect, alter or terminate upon a change of control of the company following a takeover bid, and the effects thereof. Such change-of-control clauses can impede or even prevent a company takeover.[54] It is especially important for an offeror to receive information on the possible economic effects resulting from an agreement.[55] The disclosure obligation refers to loan agreements and employment contracts,[56] but exempts any agreements the disclosure of which would be seriously prejudicial to the company.[57] This exception does not, however, apply to cases in which the company is specifically obliged to disclose such information on the basis of other legal requirements.

25   This provision refers to agreements to which the company is party, and therefore does not involve any transparency regarding the contracts that terminate or may be rescinded in subsidiaries due to the takeover.[58] A further problem is the fact that an offeror will not receive any information on agreements with change of control clauses newly concluded during the current fiscal year, as the TOD contains no obligation to keep the information in the annual report up to date.[59]

(k)   Compensation Agreements

26   The annual report must finally also contain information on the agreements between the company and its board members (*golden parachutes*) or employees (*tin parachutes*) providing compensation if they resign or are made redundant without valid reason or if their employment ceases due to a takeover bid.[60] Such agreements can also hinder a takeover and must therefore be disclosed. The company must further publish the height of the compensation and the persons benefiting from it, including their position in the company.[61] Otherwise the aim of the provision would not be fulfilled.

III.   Obligation to Disclose Bids

1.   Types of Bids

27   The TOD classes different types of bids. "Takeover bid" or "bid" refers to a public offer (other than by the offeree company itself) made to the holders of the securities

---

[54] Cf. C. Cramer, *Change of Control-Klauseln im deutschen Unternehmensrecht*, p. 110 ff.

[55] Cf. H.-J. Kirsch and H. Köhrmann, in: E. Castan et al. (eds.), *Beck'sches Handbuch der Rechnungslegung*, Abschnitt B 510 Inhalt des Lageberichts, para. 252.

[56] Cf. S. Maul and D. Muffat-Jeandet, AG (2004), p. 306, 309.

[57] Examples in: C. Cramer, *Change of Control-Klauseln im deutschen Unternehmensrecht*, p. 289 ff.

[58] Cf. ibid, p. 294–295.

[59] Seen critically by ibid., p. 295.

[60] See M. Nussbaum, *Abfindungen and Anerkennungsprämien für Vorstandsmitglieder deutscher Aktiengesellschaften*, p. 31 ff. and 150 ff. on the admissablilty of such clauses under takeover law.

[61] Cf. H.-J. Kirsch and H. Köhrmann, in: E. Castan et al. (eds.), *Beck'sches Handbuch der Rechnungslegung*, Abschnitt B 510 Inhalt des Lageberichts, para. 257; V. Sailer, AG (2006), p. 913, 921; C.H. Seibt and K.J. Heiser, AG (2006), p. 301, 316.

Rüdiger Veil

of a company to acquire all or some of those securities, whether mandatory or voluntary, which follows or has as its objective the acquisition of control of the offeree company.[62] "Securities" in the sense of the directive are only transferrable securities carrying voting rights in a company,[63] i.e. shares. Shares to which no voting rights are attached do not fall within the scope of the directive.[64] The Member States are, however, not prevented from extending the scope of application of the directive in their national implementing takeover laws.[65]

28   The TOD applies to bids that refer to a certain percentage of shares (i.e. 10%) and to bids referring to all shares, the latter being called a takeover bid. Should the offeror have gained control of the company following a voluntary bid, i.e. by enlarging his percentage of shares from 15% to 40% by way of a public offer, the TOD requires him to make a bid to all holders of the offeree company's securities,[66] the only exception being for cases in which control was acquired following a voluntary bid made to all the holders of securities for all their holdings.[67]

2.   Decision to Launch a Bid

29   The takeover procedure cannot be described in detail in this book. However, a further central element of the European obligations concerning the information of the capital markets must be noted: Member States have to ensure that a decision to make a bid is made public without delay and that the supervisory authority is informed of the bid.[68] This requirement is based on the European legislature's aim to reduce the possibilities for insider dealings.[69] The concept of this disclosure obligation is thus part of the obligation to disclose inside information as laid down in the MAD.

30   The directive does not define when a decision to make a bid has actually been made, although there would have been a strong necessity for such a definition: different bodies in a stock corporation can be entrusted with takeover proceedings. In a company with a two-tier system, the board of directors will usually be entrusted with the matter before the supervisory board examines the possible takeover and gives its consent.[70] It is also possible that the matter is brought before the companies' general shareholder meeting. The decision to make a takeover bid will therefore always be a multilevel procedure.

31   The question when an offeror has made his decision to bid must thus be determined through interpretation. It is helpful that according to the European legislature's concept, the offeror must always announce his decision to launch a bid as soon as possible.[71] Taking into account the aim of reducing the possibilities of insider

---

[62] Cf. Art. 2(1)(a) Takeover Directive.
[63] Cf. Art. 2(1)(e) Takeover Directive.
[64] Cf. S. Maul and D. Muffat-Jeandet, AG (2004), p. 221, 225–226.
[65] Cf. Recital 11 Takeover Directive.
[66] Cf. S. Maul and D. Muffat-Jeandet, AG (2004), p. 221, 225.
[67] Cf. Art. 5(2) Takeover Directive.
[68] Cf. Art. 6(1) Takeover Directive.
[69] Cf. Recital 12 Takeover Directive.
[70] In a German stock corporation the decision to make a takeover bid may be subject to the supervisory authority's consent, cf. § 111(4) AktG.
[71] Cf. Recital 12 Takeover Directive.

dealings, it also appears possible to refer to the concepts of the MAD and the Implementing Directive 2003/124/EC, according to which information on future events can also be classed as inside information.[72] A decision to make a bid in the sense of the TOD has thus been made as soon as there is a sufficient probability that the supervisory board will agree to the management's decision to make a takeover bid.

32   The German legislature foresaw this problem in interpretation and thus introduced the provision that the obligation to make public a decision also applies if the decision itself still depends on a resolution of the general shareholder meeting of the offeror.[73] Whether an obligation to make the decision public can already arise before the supervisory board of a stock corporation has agreed to the takeover pursuant to § 111(4) AktG (German Stock Corporation Act) remains unclear. It appears recommendable to treat this similarly to cases of an obligation to disclose inside information:[74] a decision must be made public as soon as the supervisory board's consent seems sufficiently probable. This must be determined from case to case.[75] The management may, however, be permitted to postpone publication if it has a legitimate interest in keeping the information secret.[76] A different question, and one that was not addressed by the TOD, is whether the target company can be required to make public the fact that a takeover bid is going to be made. This question will most certainly arise once the target company obtains knowledge of the fact that an offeror has made such a decision. The question must be affirmed, as § 10(6) WpÜG (German Securities Acquisition and Takeover Act) does not prevent § 15(1) WpHG (German Securities Trading Act) from being applicable.[77]

3.   Offer Document

33   Member States must ensure that an offeror draws up and makes public in good time an offer document containing the information necessary to enable the holders of the offeree company's securities—including shares—to reach a properly informed decision on the bid.[78] The offer document constitutes the offer to acquire securities as required under civil law.[79] Its necessary content is described in the TOD in detail[80] and includes the terms of the offer and the identity of the offeror.

34   Whilst the details of the offer document need not be examined any closer,[81] it is important to know that the offeror must also give information on his intentions with regard to the future business of the offeree company. This obligation is similar to an investor's obligation towards the capital market in France and Germany if it acquires

---

[72] See § 13 para. 35–41.
[73] Cf. § 10(1) WpÜG.
[74] Cf. S. Walz, in: W. Haarmann and M. Schüppen (eds.), *Frankfurter Kommentar zum WpÜG*, § 10 para. 24.
[75] Dissenting opinion: H.D. Assmann, in: H.D. Assmann et al. (eds.), *Kommentar zum WpÜG*, § 10 para. 19 ff.
[76] Disclosure may be postponed pursuant to § 15(3) WpHG, applied analogously. See § 19 para. 63–104.
[77] Cf. H. Drinkuth, in: R. Marsch-Barner and F.A. Schäfer (eds.), *Handbuch börsennotierte AG*, § 60 para. 67.
[78] Cf. Art. 6(2) Takeover Directive.
[79] Cf. W. Renner, in: W. Haarmann and M. Schüppen (eds.), *Frankfurter Kommentar zum WpÜG*, § 11 para. 13; G.F. Thoma, in: T. Baums and G.F. Thoma (eds.), *Kommentar zum WpÜG*, § 11 para. 6.
[80] Cf. Art. 6(3) Takeover Directive.
[81] On this see U. Hamann, ZIP (2001), p. 2249; K.D. Stephan, AG (2003), p. 551.

more than 10% of a company's shares.[82] The TOD puts the offeror's obligation to make his intentions regarding the future business of the offeree company public into more concrete terms, requiring that the offeror also provide information on his strategic plans for the company and the likely repercussions for employment and companies' places of business.[83]

IV. Mandatory Bid

1. Legal Foundations and Aims

35 The TOD requires the Member States to introduce provisions on a mandatory bid. The mandatory bid must be addressed to all holders of securities in the target company. Securities are to be understood as shares in the company. When, as a result of an acquisition of shares, a natural or legal person holds securities of the company which, added to any existing holdings of those securities, directly or indirectly give him a specified percentage of voting rights in that company and thus control of that company, the person must make a mandatory bid to all shareholders for their shares.[84]

36 *Example:* A shareholder is in possession of 10% of a company's shares and acquires a further 25%. Assuming the threshold for control lies at 30%,[85] this shareholder has then obtained a percentage of voting rights giving it control of the company, and is therefore obliged to make a mandatory bid for the additional 65%.

37 The mandatory bid's primary function is one under company law: the TOD assumes that it is necessary to protect minority shareholders.[86] The mandatory bid can thus be understood as a special concept of group law, protecting shareholders in cases in which the company is to become part of a group.[87] This preventative measure is not seen as unnecessary solely on account that the target company is protected from detrimental influence by the controlling company under the national company laws of the Member States.[88] The mandatory offer can also be understood as an element of capital markets law: the target company's shareholders based their decision to invest in the company on the fact that the company had no major shareholder who could considerably influence the future of the company's.[89] The mandatory offer thus improves the functioning of the capital markets by increasing investor confidence

---

[82] See § 20 para. 129–138.
[83] Cf. Art. 6(3)(i) Takeover Directive.
[84] Cf. Art. 5(1) Takeover Directive.
[85] See para. 39.
[86] Cf. Art. 5(1) Takeover Directive.
[87] Cf. K. Hasselbach, in: H. Hirte and C. von Bülow (eds.), *Kölner Kommentar zum WpÜG*, § 35 para. 1; U. Noack, in: E. Schwark, and D. Zimmer (eds.), *Kapitalmarktrechts-Kommentar*, § 35 WpÜG para. 2.
[88] In Germany, subsidiaries are protected from a disadvantageous decision of the parent company under §§ 311 ff. AktG. See T. Raiser and R. Veil, *Recht der Kapitalgesellschaften*, § 53 para. 24 ff.
[89] Cf. U. Noack, in: E. Schwark, and D. Zimmer (eds.), *Kapitalmarktrechts-Kommentar*, § 35 WpÜG para. 2.

in the fact that the company had no controlling shareholder at the time of their decision and thus was independent.[90]

2. Control

38   It is relevant to determine where "control" of a company begins. The European legislature left this question open: the percentage of voting rights required for control of a company and the calculation of this percentage must be determined under the national laws of the Member State in which the company has its seat.[91]

39   The Member States have introduced very different thresholds regarding the concept of control.[92] Some Member States introduced thresholds as high as 40% (Lithuania and the Czech Republic), 50% (Latvia and Malta) or even 66% (Poland). In most Member States, such as Austria, Belgium, Cyprus, Finland, France, Germany, Ireland, Italy, the Netherlands, Spain and the United Kingdom, the threshold lies at 30% of all voting rights. Other Member States, such as Luxembourg and Slovakia as well as Switzerland have opted for a threshold of 33.33%. Hungary and Slovenia only require 25% of the voting rights for control of the company. Some jurisdictions have introduced second thresholds at 50% of all voting rights. The United Kingdom has exceeded this, introducing a so-called "creeper rule" that requires offerors to make mandatory bids for every additional acquisition of shares after the 30% threshold.[93] A similar rule can be found in Austria and France. In Germany the introduction of a "creeper rule" has been a controversial topic.[94]

40   The TOD does not state whether the term "control" is to be defined in a formal or material way by the Member States. The German and the Austrian legislature[95] both opted for a so-called formal definition of control which does not require an actual controlling influence of voting rights for the assumption of control.[96] Whilst this concept has the advantage of legal certainty, its results are not always convincing.

41   *Example:* Shareholder A has acquired 32% of a company's shares. If the company has a further major shareholder, holding 55% of all shares and all other shares are in free float, shareholder A will not be able to take any control at the general shareholder meeting.

42   In these cases the obligation to make a mandatory bid is not really justified. The share package of 32% does not give the holder any possibility to exercise control. The provision must therefore provide the possibility for a shareholder to be exempted from the obligation to give a bid. The TOD has determined that this is a matter for the national laws of the Member States who can now decide independently whether

---

[90] H. Krause and T. Pötzsch, in: H. D. Assmann et al. (eds.), *Kommentar zum WpÜG*, § 35 para. 32; P. Hommelhoff and C.-H. Witt, in: W. Haarmann and M. Schüppen (eds.), *Frankfurter Kommentar zum WpÜG*, vor §§ 35 bis 39 para. 35; K. Hasselbach, in: H. Hirte and C. von Bülow (eds.), *Kölner Kommentar zum WpÜG*, § 35 para. 10.

[91] Cf. Art. 5(3) Takeover Directive.

[92] Cf. European Commission, Report on the implementation of the Directive on Takeover Bids, Commission Staff Working Document, Annex 2, p. 13–14.

[93] Cf. C.M. Crawshay, in: R. Veil (ed.), *Übernahmerecht in Praxis und Wissenschaft*, p. 83, 85.

[94] On the legal and political discussion concerning the introduction of similar provisions into German takeover law see T. Baums, ZIP (2010), p. 2374.

[95] Cf. C. von Bülow, in: H. Hirte and C. von Bülow (eds.), *Kölner Kommentar zum WpÜG*, § 29 para. 11.

[96] Cf. ibid, § 29 para. 71.

Rüdiger Veil

and under which conditions an offeror can be exempted from making a mandatory bid.[97] The differing national provisions play an important role in the legal practice of takeovers.[98] Member States following a formal concept of control have had to introduce farther-reaching exemptions than those Member States adopting a material approach to the concept of control.

3. Gaining Control by Acting in Concert

(a) Legal Foundations

43 The TOD contains detailed provisions concerning the attribution of voting rights to an offeror in order to determine his notification obligations.[99] It contains particularly detailed rules on the attribution of voting rights in corporate groups or attached to shares held in trust—both of particular relevance in legal practice. The TOD, however, leaves these questions to the discretion of the Member States,[100] only requiring that a mandatory offer must be made as soon as the acquisition of shares—by the person himself or by persons acting in concert with him—leads to a total sum of voting rights sufficient for him to take control of the company.[101] In this context, "persons acting in concert" are defined by the TOD as any natural or legal person who cooperates with the offeror or the offeree company on the basis of an agreement, either express or tacit, either oral or written, aimed either at acquiring control of the offeree company or at frustrating the successful outcome of a bid.[102]

44 The Member States are thus not entirely free in their understanding of the term "acting in concert": a mandatory bid must be made even when control has only been gained through an "acting in concert",[103] and an agreement on the acquisition of shares may also lead to the obligation to make a mandatory bid.[104] Whilst England,[105] France,[106] Austria[107] and Switzerland[108] adhere strictly to this understanding, Germany has introduced its own definition of "acting in concert".[109]

---

[97] Cf. Art. 4(5)2 in conjunction with Art. 4(2)(e) Takeover Directive; P.O. Mülbert, NZG (2004), p. 633, 641.

[98] Cf. on the legal practice of takeovers in Germany K.-J. Strunk, R. Holst and H. Salomon, in: R. Veil (ed.), *Übernahmerecht in Praxis and Wissenschaft*, p. 1, 23 ff.; on the legal practice in England C.M. Crawshay, in: R. Veil (ed.), *Übernahmerecht in Praxis and Wissenschaft*, p. 83, 89 ff.

[99] See § 20 para. 34–84.

[100] Cf. Art. 5(3) Takeover Directive.

[101] Cf. Art. 5(1) Takeover Directive.

[102] Cf. Art. 2(1) Takeover Directive.

[103] Cf. P.O. Mülbert, NZG (2004), p. 633, 642.

[104] Cf. P.O. Mülbert, NZG (2004), p. 633, 642; H. Fleischer, ZGR (2008), p. 185, 198–199.

[105] Cf. Rule 9.1 Takeover Code.

[106] Cf. R. Veil and P. Koch, *Französisches Kapitalmarktrecht*, p. 85–86. See also the famous case *Gecina*: CA Paris, 1re ch., 24 Juin 2008, no. 07-21.048, *Société Gecina*, with annotations by T. Bonneau, Dr. soc. Oct. 2008, p. 39 ff.; F. Martin Laprade, Rev. soc. (2008), p. 644 ff.; H. Le Nabasque, Bull. Joly Soc. (2008), p. 135 ff.; published in J.-F. Biard, RDBF (2008), p. 67, 70 ff.

[107] Cf. § 1 Nr. 6 ÜbG; on this C. Diregger et al., in: W. Goette and M. Habersack (eds.), *Münchener Kommentar zum AktG*, Österreichisches Übernahmerecht (ÜbG) para. 179 ff.

[108] Cf. Art. 27 BEHV–EBK.

[109] Cf. § 30(2) WpÜG.

(b)   Legal Practice in the Member States

45   The Member States have widely varying experiences with acting in concert. This is mainly due to the fact that neither the TD nor the TOD gives a precise definition of the concept, only minimum requirements regarding implementation, thus permitting Member States to exceed these and introduce stricter rules

46   It therefore comes as no surprise that national concepts of acting in concert differ greatly. A description of all the national rules on takeover law would go beyond the scope of this book.[110] We shall rather depict the problems encountered by the supervisory authorities and courts in legal practice on the basis of two cases, when determining whether shareholders are acting in concert. Both also show the difficulties of regulating the concept of acting in concert at a European level.

(aa)   *Sacyr/Eiffage* (France)

47   The case of *Sacyr/Eiffage* shows how difficult it is in legal practice to determine reliably when shareholders are acting in concert and must therefore be obliged to make a mandatory bid.

48   *Facts (abridged):*[111] The Spanish company Sacyr had first acquired shares in the French company Eiffage in December 2005 and had subsequently attempted to merge the two companies. At Eiffage's general meeting in April 2007, the chair of the general meeting denied Sacyr's voting rights and those of 88 other Spanish shareholders due to the fact that they had failed to disclose that they had exceeded one of the thresholds by acting in concert. On 19 April 2007 Sacyr made an exchange offer for shares of Eiffage. At this time Sacyr held 33.32% of Eiffage's nominal capital and 29.61% of all voting rights. The AMF declared the public exchange offer to be illegal and required Sacyr to make a mandatory bid for Eiffage and another mandatory bid for the Eiffage-subsidiary Autoroutes Paris-Rhin-Rhône (APRR) which constituted one of the main assets of Eiffage.

49   The AMF reasoned that Sacyr, acting in concert with at least six other shareholders, had exceeded the threshold of holding one-third of Eiffage's capital and had acquired more than 5% of its nominal capital within the last 12 months. This resulted in an obligation to make a mandatory bid with an optional cash offer, the minimum price corresponding at least with the highest share price paid by Sacyr and the other persons acting in concert within the last 12 months.[112]

50   The court subsequently entrusted with the case also came to the conclusion that the shareholders had made an agreement to act in concert at the extraordinary general meeting in April 2007 with the aim of achieving a reorganisation of the administrative board that would allow Sacyr to merge the two companies.[113] Neither the AMF nor the court could prove that such an agreement had actually been reached. They

---

[110] Cf. C. Bolle, *A Comparative Overview of the Mandatory Bid Rule* (2008).

[111] CA Paris, 1re ch., sect. H, 2 Avril 2008, no. 2007/11675, *Sacyr Vallehermoso SA et autres c/ Eiffage SA*, Dr. soc. Oct. 2008, 35 ff. Summarised by J. Baj, RDBF (2008), p. 8–9.

[112] A mandatory bid would have been double as expensive for *Sacyr*.

[113] The court agreed with the AMF that the exchange offer was illegal, however, reversing the obligation to make a mandatory bid on the basis of a procedural error, as the AMF had omitted to hear the other parties acting in concert. The court avoided using the term *action de concert*, rather speaking of a *démarche collective organisée*. Seen critically by H. Le Nabasque, RDBF (2008), p. 54–55.

based their decision solely on circumstantial evidence, the most relevant elements being:

51 — Sacyr's request to appoint its own representatives to the administrative board was dismissed at the general meeting on 19 April 2006. Sacyr had not yet achieved this aim by April 2007.

— According to its declaration of intent of 5 April 2006[114] based on Article L. 233-7 C. com., Sacyr intended neither to take control of Eiffage nor to make a public offer. This was repeated only a few days before the draft exchange offer was submitted.

— Between 19 April 2006 and 23 March 2007 Sacyr acquired about 2.2 million shares of Eiffage (a quarter of these within the last four days), thereby increasing its shareholding to 33.32%.

— Sacyr wanted to be introduced to the shareholders that were to support Sacyr's request to nominate five representatives of the administrative board at the general meeting on 19 April 2006. Sacyr asked its bank for the necessary contact information.

— The six other persons acting in concert all acquired shares in Eiffage between June 2006 and March 2007, all remaining below the 1% threshold. If they had reached this threshold, they would have been legally obliged to disclose their shareholdings under Eiffage's articles of association.

— Two of these companies temporarily exceeded the 1% threshold without complying with their notification obligations, before quickly reducing their shares to below 1% once again.

— The management and/or shareholders of five of the companies acting in concert with Sacyr had a personal, financial or business interest in Sacyr. Their company purposes were entirely different to Sacyr's.

52 Even in countries where acting in concert does not require an actual agreement between the shareholders, it can be difficult to prove concerted action. In 2005,[115] for example, the German BaFin was not able to prove that several investment companies around the British TCI The Children's Investment Fund Management were acting in concert in the German sense of the term. They could therefore not be required to make a mandatory bid to the other shareholders of Deutsche Börse AG.[116]

(bb) *WMF (Germany)*

53 The case of *WMF* depicts clearly how difficult it is to draw the line between influence on the management and supervisory board that is not relevant under takeover law and actual control over the company.

---

[114] On this disclosure obligation see § 20 para. 129–132.

[115] German takeover law defines acting in concert as any behaviour of the offeror concerning the target company that has been adjusted on the basis of an agreement or in any other way (cf. § 30(2) WpÜG). A concerted action "in another way" is defined as any legally non-binding agreement or concerted behaviour without the intention to thereby be legally bound. Cf. C. von Bülow, in: H. Hirte and C. von Bülow (eds.), *Kölner Kommentar zum WpÜG*, § 30 para. 214.

[116] Cf. BaFin, press release, 19 October 2005: "However, the statements provided by the parties involved did not provide sufficient proof that the fund companies coordinated their efforts to exert influence on Deutsche Börse's management and supervisory boards."

54   *Facts (abridged):*[117] In 1993, a former major shareholder (G) of a listed stock corporation sold some of his shares to three financial investors. Ten years later G and the financial investors agreed to vote unanimously at the upcoming general meeting for certain candidates at the election of the shareholder representatives for the supervisory board. Despite this agreement they could not agree on a chairman for the board of directors: G wanted to elect his representative M, whilst the financial investors wanted to vote for A. Shortly before the general meeting, the financial investors informed G that they expected him to vote for A and would not accept an abstention from the vote. G, as requested by the investors, succumbed and the shareholder representatives for the supervisory board were elected in the general meeting according to the plan. The supervisory board then nominated A as its chairman and M as second deputy chairman. G later claimed interest payments from one of the financial investors based on § 38 WpÜG. He argued the voting rights of the other financial investors had to be attributed to this investor due to concerted action, subsequent to which the defendant had gained control of the company.

55   In a principle-establishing judgement the BGH ruled on a number of interpretational aspects.[118] Firstly, the court ruled that the motivation behind an agreement played no role for the question as to whether the parties had acted in concert. Concerted action can therefore also be assumed if the behaviour is the result of a struggle for power between two or more major shareholders. In the case at hand, it was therefore not only the financial investors who had acted in concert but also the financial investors with the former major shareholder (G). According to the wording of the provision, this rule of German takeover law, however, only applies to agreements that refer to the exercise of voting rights attached to shares of the target company, i.e. only to voting rights at the general meeting.[119]

56   Supervisory board votes are therefore not subject to the rules on acting in concert. The BGH justified this interpretation with the wording of the statute. The provision could also not be applied analogously to this case. Capital markets law provisions are generally not applicable by analogy. The violation of the provisions on mandatory offers is subject to fines. They are thus to be understood as a part of criminal law, which under the German constitution is subject to a strict prohibition of analogies to the detriment of the respective person.[120] The BGH also did not see the necessity to class agreements regarding the vote for a chair and deputy chair of the supervisory board as concerted acts: all members of the supervisory board are bound by the company's best interests. They are free from taking any orders and it would therefore be inappropriate to treat them as shareholder representatives.[121]

57   This interpretation of the German provisions proves how difficult it is to define the concept of acting in concert at a European level. Strict rules may even be counterproductive as effective corporate governance has an interest in having active shareholders that clearly describe their interest to the management. The notion of

---

[117] BGHZ 169, p. 98.
[118] The attribution of voting rights on the basis of an *acting in concert* is based on § 30(2) WpÜG.
[119] Cf. BGHZ 169, p. 98, 105 para. 17.
[120] Cf. BGHZ 169, p. 98, 106 para. 17.
[121] Cf. BGHZ 169, p. 98, 106 para. 18.

acting in concert must also take into account the underlying concepts of company law. The provisions under company law regarding the rights and duties of board members and members of the administrative board have not been harmonised at a European level.[122] It is therefore essential to determine the rights and obligations of these persons according to the respective Member State's law before any conclusions can be drawn regarding the concept of acting in concert.

V. Conclusion

58   The TOD contains a number of essential elements for a European regime on capital market information. It lays down various disclosure obligations that help to give a potential offeror an idea of the defensive structures and mechanisms in listed companies. These obligations are based on the aim of achieving a functioning market for corporate control, an aim that has been largely achieved. It must be conceded, however, that numerous aspects are in need of reform. One could, for example, discuss whether it has become necessary to require a general disclosure of all agreements between shareholders, following the example of Italy and Spain. Need for action most certainly exists with regard to transparency of change of control clauses. The European provisions allow far too much leeway, enabling disclosure evasion.

59   It must further be pointed out that the TOD makes additions to the general disclosure obligations contained in the MAD for public takeovers, defining an investor's decision to make a takeover bid as inside information. It is only right that the TOD thus requires this decision to be made public as soon as possible.

60   The TOD also aims to protect the minority shareholders of the target company when an investor takes control of the company. It therefore requires the Member States to introduce an obligation to make a mandatory bid. Whether this protection is really legitimate can clearly be disputed—especially in cases where a Member State, as is the case in Germany, already protects investors very effectively through company law. Nevertheless a mandatory offer is still justified in these jurisdictions too, fulfilling an essential function under capital markets law. It seems acceptable that the TOD does not contain a precise threshold at which control of the company is taken—the national provisions to this respect only differ marginally. As opposed to this, the fact that the TOD does not define precisely how the voting rights held by the respective person are to be calculated must be viewed critically.[123] It would be recommendable to determine this at a European level, whilst at the same time possibly even amending the respective provisions in the TOD. The so-called *creeping-in* phenomenon is also subject to very different rules in the Member States. It remains to be seen whether Europe can achieve a uniform solution in this respect.

---

[122] The draft proposal for a fifth directive on the structure of stock corporations from 1991 was unsuccessful. Cf. T. Raiser and R. Veil, *Recht der Kapitalgesellschaften*, § 60 para. 28.

[123] See on the provisions of the TOD about the attribution of voting rights § 20 para. 34–37.

5

Intermediaries

§ 25 Investment Firms

Bibliography

Balzer, Peter, *Vermögensverwaltung durch Kreditinstitute* (1999); Kalss, Susanne, *Civil Law Protection of Investors in Austria—A Situation Report from Amidst a Wave of Investor Lawsuits*, 13 EBOR (2012), p. 211–236; Kumpan, Christoph and Hellgardt, Alexander, DB (2006), p. 1714–1720; Moloney, Niamh, *EC Securities Regulation*, 2nd ed. (2008), p. 591–636; Möllers, Thomas M.J., *Effizienz als Maßstab des Kapitalmarktrechts*, 208 AcP (2008), p. 1–36; Moloney, Niamh, *The Investor Model Underlying the EU's Investor Protection Regime: Consumers or Investors?*, 13 EBOR (2012), p. 169–193; Mülbert, Peter, *Auswirkungen der MiFID-Rechtsakte für Vertriebsvergütungen im Effektengeschäft der Kreditinstitute*, 172 ZHR (2008), p. 170–209; Nelson, Paul, *Capital Markets Law and Compliance—The Implications of MiFID* (2008); Perrone, Andrea and Valente, Stefano, *Against All Odds: Investor Protection in Italy and the Role of Courts*, 13 EBOR (2012), p. 31–44; Veil, Rüdiger, *Anlageberatung im Zeitalter der MiFiD—Inhalt und Konzeption der Pflichten und Grundlagen einer zivilrechtlichen Haftung*, WM (2007), p. 1821–1827; Veil, Rüdiger and Lerch, Marcus P., *Auf dem Weg zu einem Europäischen Finanzmarktrecht: die Vorschläge der Kommission zur Neuregelung der Märkte für Finanzinstrumente*, WM (2012), p. 1557–1565 (part I) and 1605–1613 (part II); Walla, Fabian, *The Swedish Capital Markets Law from a European Perspective*, 22 EBLR (2011), p. 211–221.

I.   Introduction

1   Investors usually carry out the acquisition and sale of shares with the assistance of banks,[1] which generally acquire the shares in their own name on behalf of another (commission). It is also possible for a bank to acquire the shares for its own account (proprietary trading) and then resell the shares to its clients. Banks also offer a number of further securities-related services, investment advisory services constituting a very important aspect of their work. Investors only rarely have an overview of all the financial products and do not possess the expertise to correctly assess the

---

[1] Investors cannot carry out security transactions without the participation of persons licensed to trade on the stock exchange. The details can be found in the stock exchange and capital market statutes of the Member States and in the respective stock exchange rules (Rules of the London Stock Exchange and Börsenordnung Frankfurter Wertpapierbörse).

suitability of these.[2] Investors also have an entirely different readiness to assume risks and are thus, in the eyes of the European legislature, increasingly dependent on personal recommendations.[3]

2   The Markets in Financial Instruments Directive (MiFID) and its implementing directive[4] therefore contain provisions on investment advisory services.[5] The provisions fall into the category of banking law, which is not part of this book. Nevertheless it appears necessary to give a short overview of the legal requirements regarding investment services as banks in their function as investment advisory service providers fulfil an important regulatory function in European capital markets law. They are responsible for processing the information that is disclosed (ad hoc) by the issuers in prospectuses[6] and financial reports,[7] and use this to produce investment recommendations for their clients. Investment firms can thus be classified as financial intermediaries. The MiFID requires Member States to ensure investor protection in order to achieve a high level of protection.[8] This chapter focuses on the European requirements for investment advisory services, without going into detail with regard to the implementation in the Member States.[9]

II.   Investment Advisory Services

1.   Definition

3   The MiFID defines investment advisory services as "personal recommendations to a client, either upon his request or at the initiative of the investment firm, in respect of one or more transactions relating to financial instruments".[10] Advice about financial instruments given in newspapers, journals, magazines, on the Internet or in any television or radio broadcast does not, however, constitute investment advice in the sense of the MiFID.[11] Advice to be found in stock market information services and stock exchange newsletters also generally does not constitute investment advice.

---

[2] Cf. P. Balzer, *Vermögensverwaltung durch Kreditinstitute*, p. 14.

[3] Cf. Recital 3 MiFID.

[4] Commission Directive 2006/73/EC of 10 August 2006 implementing Directive 2004/39/EC of the European Parliament and of the Council as regards organisational requirements and operating conditions for investment firms and defined terms for the purposes of that Directive, OJ L241, 2 September 2006, p. 26–58.

[5] The term is defined in Art. 4(1)2 in conjunction with Annex 1(A) MiFID as the reception and transmission of orders in relation to one or more financial instruments, the execution of orders on behalf of clients, dealing on own account, portfolio management, investment advice, underwriting of financial instruments and/or placing of financial instruments on a firm commitment basis, placing of financial instruments without a firm commitment basis, operation of multilateral trading facilities.

[6] See § 17 para. 30–41.

[7] See § 18 para. 23–56.

[8] Cf. Recital 2 MiFID and Recital 5 Directive 2006/73/EC.

[9] In Germany the requirements were implemented in §§ 31 ff. WpHG and in the implementing regulation WpDVerOV. In the United Kingdom they can be found in the Conduct of Business Sourcebook (COBS), which is part of the FSA's Handbook.

[10] Cf. Art. 4(1)4 MiFID and Art. 52 Directive 2006/73/EG.

[11] Cf. Recital 79 Directive 2006/73/EG.

2. Obligations of Investment Firms

4 The MiFID aims to put clients in a position to make substantiated investment decisions that adequately reflect their interests. In order to achieve this aim it lists a number of obligations by which investment firms must abide when providing their services. The MiFID distinguishes between professional and retail clients, depending on the clients' business experience.[12] The investment firm is subject to different obligations, depending on the category into which each client falls.[13] The description below refers to the obligations with regard to retail clients and shows that the aim of the provisions is also to protect entirely inexperienced and risk-averse investors.[14]

(a) Exploration and Assessment of the Suitability of an Investment

5 An investment firm is expected to obtain the necessary information regarding a client's or potential client's knowledge of and experience in investment in order to ascertain the type of product best suited to his financial situation and his investment objectives in order to enable the firm to recommend suitable financial instruments (exploration).[15] This is also described by the catchphrase *"know your customer"*.[16]

6 The general requirements contained in the MiFID are put into more concrete terms by Directive 2006/73/EC.[17] The information on the client's financial situation must, for example, include information on the source and extent of his regular income, his assets, including liquid assets, investments and real property, and his regular financial commitments.[18] The information regarding the investment objectives of the client is to include information on the length of time for which the client wishes to hold the investment, his preferences regarding risk taking, his risk profile and the purposes of the investment.[19]

7 An investment firm must be able to assume that (i) the investment that is to be recommended to the client complies with his investment objectives, (ii) the client is able financially to bear any related investment risks consistent with his investment objectives and (iii) the client has the necessary experience and knowledge in order to understand the risks involved in the transaction or in the management of his portfolio (*suitability test*).[20] These requirements show that the advice which an investment firm must give a customer depends entirely on the customer: whilst option contracts may be the ideal solution for a commercially experienced lawyer,

---

[12] Cf. Art. 4(1)10–12 MiFID.
[13] N. Moloney, *EC Securities Regulation*, p. 595–599.
[14] Cf. on the "eclipse of the empowered investor and the emergence of the consumer" N. Moloney, 13 EBOR (2012), p. 169, 179–185.
[15] Cf. Art. 19(4) MiFID.
[16] Cf. P. Nelson, *Capital Markets Law and Compliance*, para. 14.52.
[17] Furthermore the ESMA has developed guidelines on certain aspects of the MiFID suitability requirements. The guidelines apply to investment firms, including credit institutions that provide investment services, UCITS management companies, and competent authorities. Cf. ESMA, *Guidelines on Certain Aspects of the MiFID Suitability Requirements, Final Report*, ESMA/2012/387, July 2012, Annex II (pp. 25–38).
[18] Cf. Art. 35(3) Directive 2006/73/EG.
[19] Cf. Art. 35(4) Directive 2006/73/EG; cf. P. Nelson, *Capital Markets Law and Compliance*, para. 11.2.2.2 and 11.4.
[20] Cf. Art. 35(1) Directive 2006/73/EG.

the ideal solution for a risk-averse retired person who is interested in long-term investment possibilities for his life savings will be entirely different.

(b)   Information Obligations

8   An investment firm must further provide the clients with appropriate information in a comprehensible form. This is to enable the client to understand the nature and risks of the investment service and of the specific type of financial instrument that is being offered and, consequently, to take investment decisions on an informed basis.[21] The possibility to provide the information in a standardised form[22] is regularly made use of in practice.

9   The exact requirements regarding the information to be given to the clients are listed in detail in Articles 29–33 of Directive 2006/73/EC. It is particularly important that investment firms provide the clients with a general description of the nature and risks of financial instruments, especially taking into account the client's categorisation as either a retail client or a professional client.[23] The description of the risks must consider the type of financial instruments and must, for example, include an explanation of leverage and its effects and the risk of losing the entire investment with regard to derivatives.[24] Investment firms are further obliged to inform their clients about the price volatility of the respective instrument.[25]

3.   Supervision

10   The national supervisory authorities are responsible for ensuring that the investment firms abide by the conduct of business rules, which are therefore regarded as supervisory law. Thus the MiFID requires the Member States to grant the supervisory authorities certain powers, such as the right to demand access to any document, to demand information from any person and to carry out on-site inspections.[26] Other than these requirements, the rules on supervision are a national matter of the Member States and beyond the scope of this book.

4.   Sanctions

11   The MiFID requires the Member States to ensure that the appropriate administrative measures can be taken or administrative sanctions be imposed against the persons responsible where the provisions adopted in the implementation of this directive have not been fulfilled. The Member States must ensure that these measures are effective, proportionate and dissuasive.[27] The directive does not contain any specific requirements with regard to the sanction to be imposed and in particular does not

---

[21] Cf. Art. 19(3)1 MiFID.
[22] Cf. Art. 19(3)2 MiFID.
[23] Cf. Art. 31(1)1 Directive 2006/73/EG.
[24] Cf. Art. 31(2)(a) Directive 2006/73/EG.
[25] Cf. Art. 31(2)(b) Directive 2006/73/EG.
[26] Cf. Art. 50(2)(a)–(c) MiFID.
[27] Cf. Art. 51 Abs. 1 MiFiD.

contain provisions on a possible civil liability of an investment firm for incorrect investment advice.[28]

12   In numerous Member States damage claims of investors against banks and other companies offering investment advice play an important role.[29] These claims are based on the understanding that the investment advice providers, such as banks and other consultants, have breached their contractual obligations. As a result investors will usually be compensated for the entire sum of the damages they have suffered.[30] The phenomenon of rational apathy based on the fact that investors usually only suffer a small amount of damages does not exist in these cases, making *private enforcement* a far more effective sanction than the rules on *public enforcement* contained in the MiFID.

13   The financial crisis has led to a renewed interest in investor claims based on incorrect investment advice. The insolvency of the US investment bank Lehman Brothers led to considerable damages for those who had acquired Lehman certificates, causing investors to claim damages for incorrect investment advice in Europe and the United States, arguing that they had not been sufficiently informed of the risks. The legal questions which arise must be answered according to the national contract laws and thus exceed the scope of this book.[31]

III.   Conclusion

14   The task of regulating investment advice services is immense. The European legislature placed particular emphasis on investor protection and has developed detailed clarification and information obligations. On closer inspection it becomes apparent that the extent of these rules corresponds with a level of protection that is provided in consumer protection laws.[32] The problem that banks still follow their own monetary interests when providing investment advice remains unsolved. Whilst the advice is free of charge for the clients, this being expected, banks receive monetary benefits such as sales commissions from third parties. This is generally not known to the clients and is often financed through increased prices for the investments. The current provisions react to the resulting conflicts of interests with transparency requirements and prohibitions to accept benefits by third parties.

---

[28] Cf. N. Moloney, *EC Securities Regulation*, p. 641; R. Veil, WM (2007), p. 1821, 1824–1825.

[29] Cf. for Germany C. Kumpan and A. Hellgardt, DB (2006), p. 1714; for Italy A. Perrone and S. Valente, 13 EBOR (2012), p. 31, 33.

[30] The damage consists of the fact that the investor would not have made the particular investment had it been advised correctly. Investors can therefore rescind the investment contract.

[31] Germany does not have any express rules on civil liability for incorrect investment advice. The BGH, however, nevertheless assumed the existence of a civil liability in the famous Bond decision (BGHZ 123, p. 126) and confirmed it more recently with regard to the Lehman case (BGH ZIP 2011, p. 2237). Sweden has introduced a separate law on investor claims for damages in cases of incorrect investment advice. Cf. F. Walla, 22 EBLR (2011), p. 211, 218–219.

[32] Cf. C. Vogel, *Vom Anlegerschutz zum Verbraucherschutz: Informationspflichten im europäischen Kapitalmarkt-, Anlegerschutz- und Verbraucherschutzrecht* (2005).

15   The European Commission does not regard this approach as sufficient and presented a proposal for amendments to the MiFID in October 2011,[33] one of the main aims being an improved investor protection.[34] The Commission plans, in particular, to introduce a new concept for investment advisory services, in future allowing both independent and dependent advisory services. Investment firms that offer their clients independent advice shall be subject to particularly strict obligations.[35] They shall further be prohibited from accepting a commission for the advice or any other consideration from a third party or a person acting in the name of a third party. This reflects the current situation in legal practice, where clients receive advice free of charge and the banks receive a commission from the company whose products were recommended, without the clients being informed of this fact.[36] Independent advice would in future require the client to pay for the advisory services. The planned EU regulation will allow clients to choose between the different forms of investment advice. This approach can only be welcomed, ideally leading to a competition between the two forms and thereby resulting in an improved quality of both. However, it remains to be seen whether the Commission's proposal is enacted.

---

[33] Proposal for a Directive of the European Parliament and of the Council on Markets in Financial Instruments repealing Directive 2004/39/EC of the European Parliament and of the Council, 20 October 2011, COM(2011) 656 final.

[34] Cf. Recital 56 MiFID II Draft.

[35] Vgl. Art. 24(5) MiFID II Draft.

[36] Cf. R. Veil and M.P. Lerch, WM (2012), p. 1605, 1608–1612.

Rüdiger Veil

§ 26   Financial Analysts

Bibliography

Achleitner, Ann-Kristin and Bassen, Alexander (eds.), *Investor Relations am Neuen Markt* (2001); Akerlof, George A., *The Market for "Lemons": Quality Uncertainty and the Market Mechanism*, 84 Q. J. Econ. (1970), p. 488–500; Agrawal, Anup and Chen, Mark A., *Do Analyst Conflicts Matter? Evidence from Stock Recommendations*, 51 JLE (2008), p. 503–553; Barber, Brad M. and Odean, Terrance, *All That Glitters: The Effect of Attention and News on the Buying Behavior of Individual and Institutional Investors*, 21 Rev. Fin. Studies (2008), p. 785–818; Bernhardt, Dan, Campello, Murillo and Kutsoati, Edward, *"Who herds?"*, 80 J. Fin. Econ. (2006), p. 657–675; Chen, Qi and Jiang, Wei, *Analysts' Weighing of Public and Private Information*, 19 Rev. Fin. Studies (2006), p. 319–355; Choi, Stephen J., *A Framework for the Regulation of Securities Markets Intermediaries*, 45 BBLJ (2003), p. 45–82; Choi, Stephen J. and Fisch, Jill E., *How to Fix Wall Street: A Voucher Financing Proposal for Securities Intermediaries*, 113 Yale Law J. (2003), p. 269–346; Coffee, John C., *Gatekeepers, The Professions and Corporate Governance* (2006); Coffee, John C., *Market Failure and the Case for a Mandatory Disclosure System*, 70 Virginia L. Rev. (1984), p. 717–753; Dechow, Patricia M., Hutton, Amy P. and Sloan, Richard G., *The Relation between Analysts' Forecasts of Long-Term Earnings Growth and Stock Price Performance Following Equity Offerings*, 17 CAR (2000), p. 1–32; Fisch, Jill E., *Regulatory Responses to Investor Irrationality: The Case of the Research Analyst*, 10 Lewis & Clark L. Rev. (2006), p. 57; Fisch, Jill E., *Does Analysts Independence Sell Investors Short?*, 55 UCLA L. Rev. (2007), p. 39–96; Fisch, Jill E. and Sale, Hillary A., *Securities Analyst as Agent: Rethinking the Regulation of Analysts*, 88 Iowa Law Review (2003), p. 1035–1098; Forum Group on Financial Analysts, *Best practices in an integrated European financial market* (2003), available at: http://ec.europa.eu/internal_market/securities/docs/analysts/bestpractices/report_en.pdf; Kämmerer, Jörn A. and Veil, Rüdiger, *Analyse von Finanzinstrumenten (§ 34b WpHG) und journalistische Selbstregulierung*, BKR (2005), p. 379–387; Knauth, Oliver and Käsler, Corina, *§ 20a WpHG und die Verordnung zur Konkretisierung des Marktmanipulationsverbotes (MaKonV)*, WM (2006), p. 1041–1052; Malmendier, Ulrike and Shanthikumar, Devin M., *Are Small Investors Naive about Incentives?*, 85 J. Fin. Econ. (2007), p. 457–489; Meyer, Andreas, *Haftung für Research Reports und Wohlverhaltensregeln für Analysten*, AG (2003), p. 610–622; Michaely, Roni and Womack, Kent L., *Conflict of Interest and the Credibility of Underwriter Analyst Recommendations*, 12 Rev. Fin. Studies (1999), p. 653–686; Mülbert, Peter O., *Empfiehlt es sich, im Interesse des Anlegerschutzes und zur Förderung des Finanzplatzes Deutschland das Kapitalmarkt- und Börsenrecht neu zu regeln?*, JZ (2002), p. 826–837; Naffziger, Fred and Fox, Mark, *A need for balance in the regulation of analysts' conflicts*, 15 International Company and Commercial Law Review (2004), p. 320–324; Porak, Victor, *Kapitalmarktkommunikation* (2002); van Rooij, Maarten, Lusardi, Annamaria and Alessie, Rob, *Financial Literacy and Stock Market Participation*, 101 J. Fin. Econ. (2011), p. 449–472; Schilder, Jörg, *Die Verhaltenspflichten von Finanzanalysten nach dem Wertpapierhandelsgesetz* (2005); Seibt, Christoph, *Finanzanalysten im Blickfeld von Aktien- und Kapitalmarktrecht*, ZGR (2006), p. 501–539; Spindler, Gerald, *Finanzanalyse vs. Finanzberichterstattung: Journalisten und das AnSVG*, NZG (2004), p. 1138–1147; Stout, Lynn A., *Are Stock Markets Costly Casinos? Disagreement, Market Failure, and Securities Regulation*, 81 Va. L. Rev. (1995), p. 611–712; Teigelack, Lars, *Finanzanalysen und Behavioral Finance* (2009).

I.   Introduction

1   Financial analysts are information intermediaries charged with the task of helping to overcome negative effects resulting from an asymmetric distribution of information

on the capital markets.[1] Not only investors and issuers, but also the market as a whole and thus the public as a whole ultimately benefit from this. Financial analysts help investors to filter relevant information from the flood of information available on the market and to translate the available information into an investment decision (transformation).[2] Financial analysts obtain information from a number of sources, such as press releases, company reports, ad hoc notifications and other publications. Additionally they gain important insights through their contact with the issuers' management and attendance of financial analysts' conferences. Whilst financial analysts must not obtain inside information from management,[3] meetings with an issuer's top personnel can nevertheless help analysts to assess management's credibility. Surveyed about principal information sources, analysts have declared personal contact with management to be the most important source of information.[4] Financial analysts further monitor an issuer's profits, thereby helping to prevent unlawful transfers of profits from the issuer to management (principal–agent conflict).[5]

2   Issuers also benefit from financial analysts, because the supply of information to investors reduces the issuers' costs of capital: the better investors are informed about an issuer, the higher the price they will pay for an investment; uncertainty, on the other hand, has a negative effect on investment decisions (discount). Additionally, financial analysts can distribute information to a large number of investors.[6] It is therefore more effective for an issuer to inform a limited number of analysts than attempt to distribute information to all investors.[7]

3   Financial analysts further help to improve the functioning of capital markets. Lower transaction costs enhance operational efficiency, and a clearer distinction between "good and bad" companies improves the markets' allocative efficiency. Financial analysts also increase informational efficiency of the markets by ensuring that new information is reflected in the prices of securities as soon as possible.[8] The functioning of the markets is in the public interest, as companies and states require financing and citizens increasingly rely on publicly traded securities in saving for retirement.

4   The activities of financial analysts require regulation due to the severe consequences resulting from incorrect research. If analysts fulfil their task as information intermediaries poorly, investors run the risk of (partly) losing their invested capital. Whilst the capital is merely redistributed, the investor who has lost his entire financial means will be dependent on the social security system.[9]

[1] J.E. Fisch, 55 UCLA L. Rev. (2007), p. 39, 46; A.-K. Achleitner and A. Bassen, *Investor Relations am Neuen Markt*, p. 47–48.
[2] J.E. Fisch, 55 UCLA L. Rev. (2007), p. 39, 47.
[3] On the prohibition on the disclosure of information under the rules on insider dealings see § 13 para. 84–93.
[4] Cf. V. Porak, *Kapitalmarktkommunikation*, p. 139 ff., 147 ff.
[5] A.-K. Achleitner and A. Bassen, *Investor Relations am Neuen Markt*, p. 48 ff.; T.M.J. Möllers, in: H. Hirte and T.M.J. Möllers (eds.), *Kölner Kommentar zum WpHG*, § 34b para. 3.
[6] J.E. Fisch, 55 UCLA L. Rev. (2007), p. 39, 45; Forum Group, *Best Practices in an Integrated European Financial Market*, p. 13; on a similar phenomenon with regard to private investors see B.M. Barber and T. Odean, 21 Rev. Fin. Studies (2008), p. 785.
[7] J.C. Coffee, 70 Virginia L. Rev. (1984), p. 717, 724.
[8] J.E. Fisch, 55 UCLA L. Rev. (2007), p. 39, 48; on informational efficiency see § 16 para. 7–9.
[9] L.A. Stout, 81 Va. L. Rev. (1995), p. 619, 620 ff.

Lars Teigelack

5   Flawed research may furthermore severely undermine investor confidence. Capital markets trade in expectancies, not in tangible goods, and this is only possible if market participants can rely on fair procedures.[10] Financial analysts are regarded as reliable and fair appraisers of the financial markets (so-called gatekeepers). If investors can no longer rely on information being processed correctly by financial analysts, investors will withdraw from the market, reducing liquidity and possibly causing market failure in the long run.

6   A negative assessment of a financial instrument by an analyst can raise an issuer's cost of capital and thus even considerably affect the share price.[11] A report containing an incorrect negative assessment of an issuer can cause considerable damage to the company.

7   In 2008, for example, Air Berlin plc strongly objected to the negative assessment published by financial analysts from Dresdner Kleinwort Wasserstein and blamed them for the continuing substantial decline in their securities price.[12] Prior to this case, LVMH aroused attention when the company went to court against an allegedly incorrect negative assessment published by a financial analyst.[13]

8   Incorrect research can harm the markets' allocative efficiency and thus dampen investment activities of "good" companies as their financing will also be impaired.[14] Private pension plans also rely heavily on the correct functioning of the capital markets. This poses a risk for social security systems that would not be able to cover fully capital requirements of investors after their retirement. States also depend on fully functional capital markets in order to be able to finance public obligations.

II.   Types of Financial Analysts

9   Financial analysts are typically divided into three categories. *Buy-side analysts* primarily work for investors. They are usually employees of institutional investors such as funds, insurances or investment consulting firms and analyse their employers' portfolios to enhance performance. Reports will generally not be made public as the institutional investor will only want to use the results for its own means.[15]

10   *Sell-side analysts* work for the sellers of securities, usually banks providing services to institutional investors. In addition to other services (e.g. corporate finance), these institutions offer financial analysis to improve customer satisfaction. In practice, *sell-side analysts* will typically first provide reports to their own clients, before informing the bank's general business unit of the results. In a third step, research results are made public via the Internet, newspapers or financial journals.[16]

[10] Recital 2 MAD; Recital 1 Implementing Directive 2003/125/EC.
[11] Cf. references in J.E. Fisch, 10 Lewis & Clark L. Rev. (2006), p. 57, 65.
[12] FTD of 25 July 2008.
[13] See J.E. Fisch, 55 UCLA L. Rev. (2007), p. 39, 58; F. Naffziger and M. Fox, 15 (10) ICCLR (2004), p. 322.
[14] T.M.J. Möllers, in: H. Hirte and T.M.J. Möllers (eds.), *Kölner Kommentar zumWpHG*, § 34b para. 8.
[15] J.C. Coffee, *Gatekeepers*, p. 247, 249; Forum Group, *Best Practices in an Integrated European Financial Market*, p. 18; IOSCO, *Report on Securities Analyst Conflicts of Interest*, September 2003, p. 3.
[16] J.C. Coffee, *Gatekeepers*, p. 248.

11   *Independent financial analysts* maintain no ongoing relationship with any market participants. They sell their reports individually or as a subscription to any interested person.

III. Regulatory Concepts

12   The compilation and dissemination of financial research is regulated on three different levels: (i) the rules in Article 6(5) Market Abuse Directive (MAD) and Implementing Directive 2003/125/EC[17] with reference to financial analysts; (ii) the general rules of conduct on insider trading and market manipulation which also play a role for financial analysts; and (iii) MiFID, which defines investment research and financial analysis as ancillary securities services,[18] together with Implementing Directive 2006/73/EC.[19]

1.   Requirements under European Law

13   The MAD aims to strengthen the integrity of the European capital markets[20] and is the European legislature's response to the discovery of numerous cases of misconduct by financial analysts from the 1990s to the beginning of the twenty-first century: banks had published incorrect research results to the benefit of their clients in order to receive more investment banking business (i.e. capital increases, initial public offerings, M&A transactions). In other cases the incentive for the publication of incorrect reports resulted from analysts' salaries being linked to the turnover of the investment banking division.[21] The lack of objectiveness of the reports reduced market participants' confidence in financial analysts.

14   Artice 6(5) MAD therefore obligates Member States to ensure that there is appropriate regulation in place to ensure that persons who produce or disseminate research concerning financial instruments, issuers of financial instruments or other information recommending or suggesting investment strategies "take reasonable care to ensure that such information is fairly presented and disclose their interests or indicate conflicts of interest concerning the financial instruments to which that information relates". This is the only regulatory requirement laid down in the MAD, leaving it to Implementing Directive 2003/125/EC to put the individual elements, such as "analysis" and "other information recommending or suggesting investment strategy", into more concrete terms. The Implementing Directive further contains

---

[17] Commission Directive 2003/125/EC of 22 December 2003 implementing Directive 2003/6/EC of the European Parliament and of the Council as regards the fair presentation of investment recommendations and the disclosure of conflicts of interest, OJ L339, p. 73.

[18] Annex I Section B No. 5 MiFID.

[19] Commission Directive 2006/73/EC of 10 August 2006 implementing Directive 2004/39/EC of the European Parliament and of the Council as regards organisational requirements and operating conditions for investment firms and defined terms for the purposes of that Directive, OJ L241, 2 September 2006, p. 26.

[20] Recital 2 MAD; cf. § 1 para. 22.

[21] For a comprehensive account of the so-called "analyst scandals" see J.E. Fisch, 10 Lewis & Clark L. Rev. (2006) p. 57, 60 ff.; conflicts of interest are decribed at IOSCO, *Report on Securities Analyst Conflicts of Interest*, September 2003, p. 8 ff.

Lars Teigelack

the definitions of "fairly presented" research and lays down the circumstances that may lead to disclosure obligations.

15 The Commission has recently presented a draft proposal for a Market Abuse Regulation.[22] In line with the MAD's approach, the proposal only establishes abstract requirements such as the general rule that financial analyses should be presented fairly and that conflicts of interests must be disclosed. The ESMA is expected to draft technical standards developing more detailed rules.[23]

2. Implementation in the Member States

16 The German legislature has implemented MAD's requirements in § 34b WpHG (German Securities Trading Act) and the FinAnV (German Regulation on Research in Financial Instruments). Whilst other Member States have adopted the Directive's wording one-to-one, the wording of the German provisions differs from the European requirements. The United Kingdom has implemented the provisions into the Financial Services and Markets Act 2000 (FSMA) and the FSA Handbook.[24] Spain introduced a royal decree to this matter[25] and included financial analysts in the LMV's list of addressees for the rules of conduct.[26] Sweden had not subjected financial analysts to any governmental regulation before the European provisions came into force and therefore had to develop new provisions, which were implemented into the LHF. The *Finansinspektionen* (FI) also enacted an implementing regulation.[27] Italy introduced rules on financial analysts in the TUF (Italian Consolidated Laws on Finance) and the RE (Italians Issuers' Regulation).[28] In France, where the provisions of Implementing Directive 2003/125/EC only apply to investment firms,[29] additional provisions had to be introduced regarding individual and independent financial analysts.[30]

IV. Specific Regulation of Financial Analysts

1. Definition of Research Concerning Financial Instruments

17 Member States' regulation must address all "research concerning financial instruments or of issuers of financial instruments and [any] information recommending or suggesting investment strategy, intended for distribution channels or for the public".

---

[22] Proposal for a Regulation of the European Parliament and of the Council on Insider Dealing and Market Manipulation (Market Abuse) of 20 October 2011 COM(2011) 651 final; Proposal for a Directive of the European Parliament and of the Council on Criminal Sanctions for Insider Dealing and Market Manipulation of 20 October 2011, COM(2011), 654 final; cf. for the legislative background § 1 para. 41.
[23] Art. 15 Market Abuse Regulation Draft.
[24] FSA Handbook, New Conduct of Business Sourcebook (COBS), para. 12.1–12.4.
[25] Chapter IV RD 1333/2005.
[26] Art. 78 in conjunction with Art. 63.2.e LMV.
[27] Kapitel 5a §§ 1, 2 LHF; Regulation FFFS 2005:9; the power was conferred to the FI in Kapitel 7, § 1 Nr. 7 LHF.
[28] Art. 114(8) TUF and Art. 69 ff. RE.
[29] Art. 315-1 ff. RG AMF.
[30] Art. 313-25 ff. RG AMF and Art. 327-1 ff. RG AMF.

The MAD primarily defines financial instruments as shares and other securities.[31] The provisions are to apply to any person, whether natural or legal, who produces or disseminates any such information.[32]

(a) Recommending an Investment Strategy

18   Implementing Directive 2003/125/EC puts the terms "research" and "other information recommending or suggesting investment strategy" into more concrete terms. In a first step it defines "recommendation" in Article 1(3) as "research or other information recommending or suggesting an investment strategy, explicitly or implicitly, concerning one or several financial instruments or the issuers of financial instruments, including any opinion as to the present or future value or price of such instruments". The information must, however, be intended for distribution channels or for the public. In a second step, Article 1(4) defines the term "research or other information recommending or suggesting an investment strategy" as information that "directly or indirectly, expresses a particular investment recommendation in respect of a financial instrument or an issuer of financial instruments". The two essential elements to be considered are therefore "information" and "recommendation".

19   The recommendation of a certain investment strategy can be explicit (e.g. "buy", "hold" or "sell" recommendations) or implicit (by reference to a price target or otherwise).[33] No written report is needed; oral recommendations, e.g. on television or on the radio, can also meet the criteria. [34]

20   The required intensity of regulation depends on the person issuing the recommendation. Recommendations by "an independent analyst, an investment firm, a credit institution, any other person whose main business is to produce recommendations or a natural person working for them under a contract of employment or otherwise" are subject to the provisions of Implementing Directive 2003/125/EC, whether expressed directly or indirectly.[35] However, the Implementing Directive is only applicable to direct recommendations if the information is produced by any other person.[36] The directive makes this distinction because the first group enjoys a certain reputation on the market and the legislature assumes that investors place greater confidence in their recommendations, even when only given indirectly.

21   In Germany, there is an ongoing discussion on how substantial the information must be before it can be considered a financial analysis. BaFin has determined that based on consideration of all material circumstances, the research must give the impression of having examined the financial instrument or its issuer closely. An actual examination of the financial instrument or the issuer, i.e. an evaluation of corporate finance and trading data, is not necessary. It is sufficient that the

---

[31] Art. 1(3) MAD; on details see § 8 para. 4–9.
[32] Art. 1(6) MAD.
[33] Recital 2 Implementing Directive 2003/125/EC.
[34] Cf. CESR, *CESR's Advice on Possible Level 2 Implementing Measures for the Proposed Market Abuse Directive*, CESR/02-89d, December 2002, p. 26.
[35] Art. 1(4)(a) Implementing Directive 2003/125/EC; on the terms *credit institution* and *investment firm* see Art. 1(1), (2) Implementing Directive 2003/125/EC.
[36] Art. 1(4)(b) Implementing Directive 2003/125/EC.

facts, opinions and comments given in the context of the recommendation or the form and context in which the recommendation itself is given, convey the impression that such an actual examination took place.[37] Other authors require a certain weight to the information in order for the term "research" to be fulfilled.[38] Yet this approach is not practical as it will usually not be apparent to an investor how much research the financial analyst actual carried out before publishing his results. The BaFin's approach is therefore preferable.[39]

22   The distinction becomes relevant for the question which statements by financial analysts are subject to the directive's provisions. Recommendations can often be found in spam e-mails that advertise certain securities in order to influence their price. Television appearances and newspaper interviews by financial analysts must, however, also be examined closely in order to determine whether they comply with the directive's provisions.

(b)   Relevant Person

23   Article 1(5) Implementing Directive 2003/125/EC limits the applicability of the rules of conduct to *relevant persons*, i.e. any "natural or legal person producing or disseminating recommendations in the exercise of his profession or the conduct of his business". As a result, Member States are not required to introduce provisions for private individuals offering investment advice in Internet chat rooms.[40]

24   Special rules apply to journalists. The European legislature took the freedom of press into account by requiring that the Commission consider all rules governing the profession of journalism when implementing technical arrangements.[41] The respective provisions therefore do not apply to journalists, provided they are subject to equivalent regulation in the Member States, including equivalent appropriate self-regulation, if this regulation achieves similar effects as those achieved by the Implementing Directive 2003/125/EC.[42]

25   Germany has implemented this concept in § 34b(4) WpHG and exempts journalists, subject to a comparable self-regulation. The German Press Council has published a code of conduct for financial reporting which, however, does not yet fully comply with the requirements of the directive.[43]

26   The United Kingdom has developed a similar mechanism. Journalists are subject to the Investment Recommendation (Media) Regulations 2005, unless the respective journalist is subject to a code of self-regulation or a similarly suitable self-regulatory mechanism. The Press Complaints Commission's Code of

---

[37] BaFin, *Rundschreiben* (Circular) 4/2010 (WA)—Minimum Requirements for the Compliance Function and Additional Requirements Governing Rules of Conduct, Organisation and Transparency pursuant to Sections 31 et seq. of the Securities Trading Act (Wertpapierhandelsgesetz—WpHG) for Investment Services Enterprises (MaComp), BT 5.2 No. 2, June 2011.

[38] A. Fuchs, in: A. Fuchs (ed.), *Kommentar zum WpHG*, § 34b para. 22; I. Koller, in: H.-D. Assmann and U.H. Schneider (eds.), *Kommentar zum WpHG*, § 34b para. 5.

[39] T.M.J. Möllers, in: H. Hirte and T.M.J. Möllers (eds.), *Kölner Kommentar zum WpHG*, § 34b para. 80.

[40] The behaviour may, however, constitute market manipulation, cf. § 14 para. 13 and 39–48.

[41] Art. 6(10) MAD.

[42] Art. 2(4), 3(4), 5(5) Implementing Directive 2003/125/EC.

[43] T.M.J. Möllers, in: H. Hirte and T.M.J. Möllers (eds.), *Kölner Kommentar zum WpHG*, § 34b para. 234, cf. J.A. Kämmerer and R. Veil, BKR (2005), p. 379 ff.

Practice, the BBC's Producers' Guidelines and any codes published by the Office of Communication on the basis of section 324 Communications Act 2003 are accepted by the FSA as ensuring a sufficient standard.[44]

27   Austrian law exempts journalists from the directive's provisions provided they are subject to an equivalent self-regulation, yet omits to list which codes fulfil this requirement.[45] In Sweden none of the existing self-regulatory codes for journalists are regarded as sufficient to fulfil the requirements of Implementing Directive 2003/125/EC.[46] Italy adopted the implementing directive's approach one-to-one, permitting Consob to determine when self-regulation is sufficient. Consob may further modify and complement the existing rules.[47] The self-regulation of journalists is carried out by the Consiglio Nazionale degli Ordini dei Giornalisti (The Italian National Council's Regulation of Journalists).

2.   Fair Presentation of Investment Recommendations

(a)   General Requirements

28   Member States are obliged to introduce appropriate regulation to ensure that all relevant persons take reasonable care to ensure a fair presentation of investment recommendations.[48] The aim is to make the research results comprehensible for investors in order to prevent them from being misled. The relevant persons must take reasonable care to ensure that

— facts are clearly distinguished from interpretations, estimates, opinions and other forms of non-factual information;

— all sources are reliable or, where there is any doubt as to whether a source is reliable, this is clearly indicated;

— all projections, forecasts and price targets are clearly labelled as such and the material assumptions made in producing or using them are indicated.[49]

29   The national supervisory authority can further request the relevant person to prove that their recommendation can be substantiated as reasonable.[50] In other words, the supervisory authority can demand an explanation for a certain recommendation if it retrospectively proves to be "incorrect". This provision is not without criticism, because it encourages typical "herd behaviour" among financial analysts. The more an individual analyst deviates from the recommendations of other analysts, the higher the need to justify his recommendation as "reasonable". This could encourage financial analysts to lean towards the recommendations of others rather than presenting a diverging prognosis.[51]

[44] FSA, *Implementation of the Market Abuse Directive*, PS 05/3, para. 4.2 ff.; FSA, *Market Watch*, No. 12, June 2005, p. 10 ff.

[45] Cf. § 48f Abs. 2 BörseG; also S. Kalss et al., *Kapitalmarktrecht I*, § 8 para. 11, 14.

[46] In more detail R. Veil and F. Walla, *Schwedisches Kapitalmarktrecht*, p. 119.

[47] Art. 114(10) TUF in conjunction with Art. 69-octies RE.

[48] Art. 3 Implementing Directive 2003/125/EC.

[49] Art. 3(1)(a)–(c) Implementing Directive 2003/125/EC.

[50] Art. 3(3) Implementing Directive 2003/125/EC.

[51] On this "herd behaviour" in financial analysts see D. Bernhardt et al., 80 J. Fin. Econ. (2006), p. 657 ff.; Q. Chen and W. Jiang, 19 Rev. Fin. Stud. (2006), p. 319 ff.; J.C. Coffee, *Gatekeepers*, p. 252 ff .

(b)   Special Requirements for Certain Persons

30   Additional obligations exist where "the relevant person is an independent analyst, an investment firm, a credit institution, any related legal person, any other relevant person whose main business is to produce recommendations, or a natural person working for them under a contract of employment or otherwise".[52] Member States must ensure that a higher standard of care applies to these persons.[53] Two specific regulatory requirements in this respect must be examined more closely.

31   These persons must indicate all substantially material sources, including the relevant issuer and whether the recommendation has been disclosed to the issuer and amended following this disclosure before its dissemination.[54] It is to be ensured that investors are informed if the issuer had the possibility to influence the wording of the research results as this can be an indication that the issuer's interests played too important a role in the financial analyst's decision making process.

32   Member States must further require that "any basis of valuation or methodology used to evaluate a financial instrument or an issuer of a financial instrument, or to set a price target for a financial instrument, is adequately summarised".[55] Analysts must in these cases also be obliged to disclose the meaning of any recommendation made, such as buy, sell or hold, which may include the time horizon of the investment, to which the recommendation relates and any appropriate risk warning, including a sensitivity analysis of the relevant assumptions.[56] Investors are to make their own assessment, without having to have to rely solely on the financial analyst's recommendation, although only institutional investors will usually have the necessary expertise.[57] The significance of the recommendation is also to be made clear to the investors. During the New Economy boom in the late 1990s, some analysts issued "hold" recommendations, which in informed circles were correctly understood as "sell" recommendations. To prevent retail investors from being at a disadvantage, recommendations must now be presented in detail, for example by describing which expectations can be deduced from certain price developments of a certain security (e.g. *strong buy* in cases of +15% within six months).

3.   Disclosure Obligations

33   The disclosure obligations refer to the identity of the issuer of the recommendation and to information on the interests and possible conflicts of interest. They express the MAD's underlying concept of not attempting to prohibit certain behaviour but rather informing market participants thereof, leaving them to decide freely whether the recommendation was influenced by certain interests or conflicts of interest.

---

[52] Art. 4 Implementing Directive 2003/125/EC.
[53] Cf. Art. 4(1)(a)–(f) Implementing Directive 2003/125/EC.
[54] Art. 4(1)(a) Implementing Directive 2003/125/EC.
[55] Art. 4(1)(b) Implementing Directive 2003/125/EC.
[56] Art. 4(1)(c) Implementing Directive 2003/125/EC.
[57] On the total lack of financial knowledge of private investors see M. van Rooij et al., *Financial Literacy and Stock Market Participation*, p. 11 ff.; IOSCO, *Report on Securities Analyst Conflicts of Interest*, September 2003, p. 17 also mentions investor education as a tool for understanding and discounting for analyst conflicts of interest.

(a)   Identity of the Producer of Investment Recommendations

34   The identity of the producer of investment recommendations, his conduct of business rules and the identity of his competent authority are considered valuable
information for investors.[58] Member States must therefore ensure "that there is
appropriate regulation in place to ensure that any recommendation discloses clearly
and prominently the identity of the person responsible for its production, in particular, the name and job title of the individual who prepared the recommendation
and the name of the legal person responsible for its production".[59]

35   Investment firms and credit institutions[60] must additionally disclose the identity of
the relevant competent authority.[61] Where the relevant person is neither an investment firm nor a credit institution, but is subject to self-regulatory standards or
codes of conduct, the financial analyst must disclose those standards or codes.[62]
The aim of these provisions is to enable financial analysts to develop a reputation
by making the results of their prior recommendations public.

(b)   Actual and Potential Conflicts of Interest

(aa)   General Provisions

36   The Member States must ensure "that relevant persons disclose all relationships
and circumstances that may reasonably be expected to impair the objectivity of the
recommendation, in particular where relevant persons have a significant financial
interest in one or more of the financial instruments which are the subject of the recommendation, or a significant conflict of interest with respect to an issuer to which
the recommendation relates".[63] In other words, recommendations in which the
financial analysts have a significant interest are not prohibited; market participants
are, however, to be informed of this fact in order for them to be able to decide on the
objectivity of the recommendation themselves. Implementing Directive 2003/125/
EC contains minimum disclosure requirements.[64] It omits, however, to define the
terms "interest" and "conflict of interests".

(bb)   Special Requirements for Certain Persons

(1)   Obligation to Disclose Certain Conflicts of Interest

37   Recommendations produced by an independent analyst, an investment firm, a
credit institution, any related legal person, or any other relevant person whose main
business is to produce recommendations, must contain certain information on their
interests and conflicts of interest,[65] which the European legislature deemed particularly likely to influence the objectiveness of the recommendation.

---

[58] Recital 5 Implementing Directive 2003/125/EC; Forum Group, *Best Practices in an Integrated European Financial Market*, p. 7.
 [59] Art. 2(1) Implementing Directive 2003/125/EC.
 [60] Art. 1(1), (2) Implementing Directive 2003/125/EC.
 [61] Art. 2(2) Implementing Directive 2003/125/EC.
 [62] Art. 2(2)2 Implementing Directive 2003/125/EC.
 [63] Art. 5(1)1 Implementing Directive 2003/125/EC.
 [64] Art. 5(2)(a), (b) Implementing Directive 2003/125/EC.
 [65] Art. 6 Implementing Directive 2003/125/EC.

38   The recipient of the recommendation must be informed about major shareholdings between the relevant person or any related legal person on the one hand and the issuer on the other hand. This encompasses all cases in which the relevant person or any related legal person holds more than 5% of the total issued share capital of the issuer or vice versa.[66]

39   Member States may provide for thresholds lower than 5%.[67] Italy has introduced a threshold of 2%, aiming to achieve a parallel with the notification obligations regarding major shareholdings.[68] Sweden, France, Austria, the United Kingdom and Spain adopted the directive's provisions one-to-one, although it remains unclear whether the shareholding of a credit institution is to be calculated on the basis of the shares held for trading or those held for long-term investment. BaFin has deliberately abstained from answering this question.[69] German legal literature refers to the shares held for investment.[70] Contrary to this approach, the FSA has made numerous clarifying remarks on this matter, especially regarding the attribution of shares in groups of companies.[71]

40   In addition, Member States must ensure the disclosure of any other "significant financial interests held by the relevant person or any related legal person in relation to the issuer".[72] The Implementing Directive does not specify which interests are affected. German legal literature follows the understanding that neither financial instruments held for trading or trading activities with regard to these, nor net short positions or credit and account relationships with the issuer, are subject to disclosure obligations in this respect.[73] The German supervisory authority has not yet commented on this approach to interpretation.[74]

41   Member States must further ensure that analysts disclose their position (or that of any related legal person) as market maker or liquidity provider in the financial instruments of the issuer.[75] Similarly, they must require disclosure, if, over the previous 12 months, the analyst or any related legal person has acted as lead manager or co-lead manager of any public offer of the issuer's financial instruments.[76] Empirical studies have shown that analysts of an underwriter tend to assess new stock issues more positively than analysts entirely uninvolved in the transaction.[77] Underwriters will always aim to place newly issued financial instruments in their entirety and negative research is likely to impede this aim.[78]

---

[66] Art. 6(1)(a) Implementing Directive 2003/125/EC; on an individual level, holdings under 5% may very well also constitute a conflict, but are not addressed in the Directive; cf. J.C. Coffee, *Gatekeepers*, p. 250. Many firms prohibit their analysts from holding shares in the issuers they cover; also see IOSCO, *Statement of Principles for Addressing Sell-Side Securities Analyst Conflicts of Interest*, September 2003, p. 4.

[67] Art. 6(1)(a) Implementing Directive 2003/125/EC.

[68] CESR, *Review Panel Report—MAD Options and Discretions*, CESR/09-1120, March 2010, p. 134.

[69] BaFin, *MaComp* (fn. 37), BT 5.6 No. 2.

[70] U. Göres, in: M. Habersack et al. (eds.), *Handbuch Kapitalmarktinformation*, § 24 para. 107.

[71] FSA, *Implementation of the Market Abuse Directive*, PS 05/3, March 2005, para. 4.8.

[72] Art. 6(1)(b) Implementing Directive 2003/125/EC.

[73] U. Göres, in: M. Habersack et al. (eds.), *Handbuch Kapitalmarktinformation*, § 24 para. 117 ff.

[74] BaFin, *MaComp* (fn. 37), BT 5.6 No. 2.

[75] Art. 6(1)(c) Implementing Directive 2003/125/EC.

[76] Art. 6(1)(d) Implementing Directive 2003/125/EC.

[77] P.M. Dechow et al., 17 CAR (2000), p. 1 ff.; R. Michaely and K.L. Womack, 12 Rev. Fin. Studies (1999), p. 653; evidence is mixed, however, cf. J.E. Fisch, 55 UCLA L. Rev. (2007), p. 39, 62.

[78] Cf. J.E. Fisch, 55 UCLA L. Rev. (2007), p. 39, 57; U. Göres, in: M. Habersack et al. (eds.), *Handbuch Kapitalmarktinformation*, § 24 para. 111.

42   Member States must also require disclosure if the financial analyst or any related legal person is "party to any other agreement with the issuer relating to the provision of investment banking services, provided that this would not entail the disclosure of any confidential commercial information and that the agreement has been in effect over the previous 12 months or has given rise during the same period to the payment of a compensation or to the promise to get a compensation paid".[79] Reports on preferential treatment of clients of an analyst's own investment banking division are numerous. An analyst of Lehman Brothers, for example, is said to have been instructed in a number of e-mails by his superior that the stock price target of US$50 was to be upheld out of consideration for the investment banking department, in spite of the share price having dropped from US$32 to US$4.[80]

43   Analysts must further disclose any agreements with the issuer relating to the production of the recommendation.[81] Smaller companies usually pay analysts for coverage, wanting to draw attention to themselves, as institutional investors in particular will usually place their investments according to the number of analysts monitoring the respective financial instruments.[82]

44   The disclosure obligations aim to make transparent actual or potential personal interests of the parties involved, so that the market can discount them when assessing the value and neutrality of the recommendation.[83] At the same time, it appears questionable whether all market participants are equally able to determine and assess the existence of possible conflicts of interest adequately. Behavioural economic studies have indicated that private investors in particular cannot assess possible conflicts of interest correctly, whilst institutional investors usually evaluate the risks appropriately. This is, however, a very generalised approach.[84]

(2) Further Disclosure Obligations

45   The link of financial analysts' remuneration to investment banking results has been strongly criticised since 2002. Implementing Directive 2003/125/EC does not prohibit the remuneration from being tied to investment banking transactions, but requires disclosure of any such connections.[85] In addition, "where those natural persons receive or purchase the shares of the issuers prior to a public offering of such shares, the price at which the shares were acquired and the date of acquisition [must] also be disclosed".[86] The directive itself does not prohibit trading in the covered instruments,[87] though most firms will have a prohibition to this effect in their internal rules of conduct.

46   The directive further assumes that issuers to whom the relevant person offers investment banking services will usually be assessed more positively. Hence, investment

---

[79] Art. 6(1)(e) Implementing Directive 2003/125/EC.

[80] J.E. Fisch, 10 Lewis & Clark L. Rev. (2006), p. 57, 63.

[81] Art. 6(1)(f) Implementing Directive 2003/125/EC.

[82] B.M. Barber and T. Odean, 21 Rev. Fin. Studies (2008), p. 785 ff. and J.E. Fisch, 55 UCLA L. Rev. (2007), p. 39, 46.

[83] Recital 7 Implementing Directive 2003/125/EC.

[84] Cf. A. Agrawal and M.A. Chen, 51 JLE (2008), p. 503 ff.; U. Malmendier and D.E. Shanthikumar, 85 J. Fin. Econ. (2007), p. 457–458; overview in L. Teigelack, *Finanzanalysen und Behavioral Finance*, p. 125–126.

[85] Art. 6(3)1 Implementing Directive 2003/125/EC.

[86] Art. 6(3)2 Implementing Directive 2003/125/EC.

[87] But Art. 25(2)(a) Implementing Directive 2006/73/EC establishes such a prohibition.

Lars Teigelack

firms and credit institutions are to disclose, "on a quarterly basis, the proportion of all recommendations that are 'buy', 'hold', 'sell' or equivalent terms, as well as the proportion of issuers corresponding to each of these categories to which the investment firm or the credit institution has supplied material investment banking services over the previous 12 months".[88] This transparency is a two-edged sword: investors are likely to assume that all clients, for which the analysing company issues recommendations, also receive material investment banking services. The European legislature has, in other words, deemed the situation a risk to transparency, although in some cases the disclosure obligation may lead to more confusion than helpful advice and investors may have been able to make a more valid assessment themselves.

4.   Dissemination of Investment Recommendations Produced by Third Parties

47   The distribution of a financial analyst's recommendations to third parties entails the risk that the recipient may evaluate the recommendation incorrectly and be misled. The European legislature therefore adopted a regulatory approach similar to the one pursued regarding the provisions on the compilation of financial analyses and recommendations. The disclosure requirements are, however, less strict for the dissemination of a recommendation, because the disseminator cannot have influenced the results due to a conflict of interests. Only if the disseminator made considerable changes to the recommendation prior to the dissemination are additional disclosure obligations required, in order to enable market participants to assess the nature of the alterations.[89]

(a)   General Requirements

48   Pursuant to Article 7 Implementing Directive 2003/125/EC, Member States must introduce "appropriate regulation … to ensure that, whenever a relevant person under his own responsibility disseminates a recommendation produced by a third party, the recommendation indicates clearly and prominently the identity of that relevant person".[90] The directive further contains provisions ensuring that whenever a recommendation produced by a third party is substantially altered within disseminated information, that information clearly indicates the substantial alteration in detail.[91] Germany has implemented this provision in § 7(2)1 FinAnV, which requires any alteration to be clearly indicated. The FSA has introduced a similar provision in COBS 12.4.16(1)(a) of its Handbook; Austria has adopted the provision in § 48f Abs. 8 BörseG (Austrian Stock Exchange Act).

49   Provided the substantial alteration consists of a change in the direction of the recommendation (e.g. changing a "buy" recommendation into a "hold" or "sell" recommendation or vice versa), the same disclosure obligations apply to the person disseminating the recommendation as to a person compiling a financial analysis.[92]

---

[88] Art. 6(4) Implementing Directive 2003/125/EC.
[89] Recital 8 Implementing Directive 2003/125/EC.
[90] Art. 7 Implementing Directive 2003/125/EC.
[91] Art. 8(1)1 Implementing Directive 2003/125/EC.
[92] Art. 8(1)2 Implementing Directive 2003/125/EC; on the transposition in Germany see § 7(2)2 FinAnV; in the United Kingdom: COBS 12.4.16 (1); in Austria: § 48f (8) BörseG.

50   These requirements are intended to give the recipient of the substantially altered information access to the identity of the person producing it, to the recommendation itself and to the disclosure of the producer's interests or conflicts of interest, because substantial alterations could be based on the personal interests of the disseminator. The investor must be informed of this possibility in order to be able to evaluate and assess the existence of possible conflicts of interests and to be able to adapt his investment decision accordingly.

51   In some cases, the recommendation may not be disseminated in an unabridged form, but rather summarised prior to dissemination. This regularly happens on websites when the host of the site provides a summarised overview of recommendations sorted by issuer or producer. Member States must take the necessary measures that "the relevant persons disseminating such summaries ensure that the summary is clear and not misleading, mentioning the source document and where the disclosures related to the source document can be directly and easily accessed by the public provided that they are publicly available".[93] The reader must be able to draw his own conclusions on the original analysis and possible conflicts of interest.

(b)   Additional Obligations for Certain Persons

52   If the relevant person is an investment firm, a credit institution or a natural person working for such a company under a contract of employment or otherwise disseminates recommendations produced by a third party, Member States must ensure that the following additional requirements are fulfilled:

— The name of the competent authority of the investment firm or credit institution must be clearly and prominently indicated.[94]

— If the producer of the recommendation has not already disseminated the recommendation through a distribution channel, the requirements laid down for producers of recommendations must be met by the disseminator.[95]

— If the investment firm or credit institution has substantially altered the recommendation, the requirements for producers of recommendations[96] must also be fulfilled.[97]

5.   Principle of Proportionality

53   Measures affecting an individual's rights must always be in proportion to their aim.[98] This principle of proportionality can be found in numerous places in the European legislative acts, especially with regard to the provisions on the sanctions that the Member States are to introduce into their national laws.[99] Member States

---

[93] Art. 8(4) Implementing Directive 2003/125/EC.
[94] Art. 9(a) Implementing Directive 2003/125/EC.
[95] Art. 9(b) Implementing Directive 2003/125/EC.
[96] Art. 2–6 Implementing Directive 2003/125/EC.
[97] Art. 9(c) Implementing Directive 2003/125/EC.
[98] ECJ of 3 December 1998, Case C-368/96 (*Generics*) [1998] ECR I-7967, para. 66–67.
[99] Cf. para. 56–57.

must further ensure that there is appropriate regulation in place ensuring that the requirements of a provision can be adapted in order not to be disproportionate.[100]

54 In Germany, this is ensured by § 6(2), (3) FinAnV. Pursuant to § 6(2) FinAnV the requirements to be fulfilled according to Article 4 Implementing Directive 2003/125/EC and the provisions on conflicts of interest (Articles 5 and 6 Implementing Directive 2003/125/EC) may be substituted by a reference to a website or a place, easily accessible to the public, insofar as the application of the provisions would be disproportionate with regard to the total volume of the financial analysis. § 6(3) FinAnV allows the producer of a recommendation to substitute the publication of this information, the identity of the producer and the information required by Article 3(1) Implementing Directive 2003/125/EC entirely by a reference to a website or similarly accessible place if the financial recommendation was not compiled in writing, as defined in § 126b Bürgerliches Gesetzbuch (BGB, German Civil Code).

55 Austria has adopted similar provisions in the BörseG (Austrian Stock Exchange Act). Unlike the German approach, however, Austria does not restrict the substitution to the disproportionate elements, rather allowing the reference to the alternative place of publication to refer to the entire financial recommendation. The wording of the Austrian provisions is largely identical to that of the directive.[101] France has introduced the principle of proportionality in Article 315–10f. RG AMF (General Regulations of the French Supervisory Authority). The provisions place particular emphasis on the proportionality of the required information in cases of non-written recommendations, introducing a self-regulatory approach to disclosure in these cases. France has further abstained from describing fixed obligations, rather only requiring the best possible efforts to be made. Spain has adopted the provisions of the directive.[102] In Sweden no explicit legislative requirements regarding the principle of proportionality exist. The FI has, however, introduced an explanatory directive, permitting the producer of non-written recommendations to restrict the publication of mandatory information to a website. The explanatory memorandum on Kapitel 5a LHF (Swedish Act on the Trading with Financial Instruments) further provides less stringent requirements for non-written recommendations.[103] Italy has also not introduced specific rules on proportionality. The requirements for non-written recommendations are, however, few.[104] The United Kingdom has closely followed the wording of the directive, stating in numerous places of the FSA Handbook that the provisions are only applicable to non-written recommendations if the application is proportionate.

---

[100] Art. 2(3), 3(2), 4(3), 5(4), 6(6) Implementing Directive 2003/125/EC.
[101] § 48f (4) No. 6 BörseG.
[102] RD 1333/2005.
[103] Cf. R. Veil and F. Walla, *Schwedisches Kapitalmarktrecht*, p. 118.
[104] Art. 69-bis (2) RE refers to Art. 69-bis (1) RE, which is a one-to-one implementation of Art. 3(1) Implementing Directive 2003/125/EC.

6.   Sanctions

(a)   Requirements under European Law

56   Neither the MAD nor Implementing Directive 2003/125/EC contains precise requirements concerning the conception or severity of the sanctions for the provisions on financial analysts. Member States are merely obliged to ensure that the appropriate administrative measures can be taken or administrative sanctions can be imposed against the persons responsible for the non-compliance with the provisions. Administrative measures can thus be regarded as minimum requirements. Member States must further ensure that the measures are "effective, proportionate and dissuasive".[105] In addition, they must enact provisions according to which the competent authority is required to make public "every measure or sanction that will be imposed for infringement of the provisions adopted in the implementation of this Directive, unless such disclosure would seriously jeopardise the financial markets or cause disproportionate damage to the parties involved".[106]

57   Member States have used greatly different approaches to the implementation of these European provisions. This difference is illustrated by the examples of Germany and the United Kingdom, especially regarding the additional possibility of a civil law liability of financial analysts.[107]

(b)   Germany

58   Breaches of the rules for financial analysts laid down in § 34b WpHG are sanctioned by administrative law.[108] The administrative authority is authorised to impose sanctions of up to €200,000. This limit can be exceeded if necessary in order to disgorge economic profits.[109] The BaFin has not made use of this power as yet and has similarly so far refrained from making the imposed sanctions public.[110]

59   Whether German law permits investors to recover damages caused by incorrect recommendations from financial analysts remains unclear. A contractual liability can only be assumed towards investors who entered into a contract regarding the compilation of a report. The MAD, however, primarily refers to reports that are distributed publicly. The rules on prospectus liability (§§ 22 ff. WpPG (Prospectus Act)) are also not applicable. Whilst research reports may have a certain similarity to a prospectus, aiming to help market participants come to an investment decision, they do not have to contain *all* relevant information. Unlike a prospectus,[111] a research report is further strongly subjective, reflecting the personal opinion of the producing financial analyst and not merely supplying the objective facts.[112]

---

[105] Art. 14(1) MAD.
[106] Art. 14(4) MAD.
[107] In France the question of a civil law liability arose in the case *LVMH/Morgan Stanley*. The claim was based on Art. 1382 Code civil.
[108] Cf. § 39(1) Nos 5 and 6 (4) WpHG.
[109] Cf. § 17(4) OWiG.
[110] Cf. § 40b WpHG; cf. § 12 para. 10.
[111] Cf. § 17 para. 30.
[112] U. Göres, in: M. Habersack et al. (eds.), *Handbuch Kapitalmarktinformation*, § 31 para. 39; A. Meyer, AG (2003), p. 610, 618; suggesting an analogy to the prospectus liability rules in § 44 BörsG (now § 22 WpPG); C.H. Seibt, ZGR (2006), p. 501, 532.

60   Civil law liability would thus only be possible under tort law.[113] This possibility must, however, be declined. The obligations resulting from the MAD are aimed at the protection of all market participants as a group. That explains why, for example, the provisions are only applicable to financial analysts who publish recommendations for an indefinite number of recipients. Individual investors are only protected as a reflex of this general protection and are thus not entitled to any claims under tort law.[114] Extreme cases, however, may give rise to a claim for damages under § 826 BGB.[115] The mere fact that certain events do not occur as expected, is not sufficient to cause liability.[116]

(c)   United Kingdom

61   The FSA can impose unlimited fines for any breaches of the rules of conduct and make public the sanctions imposed.[117] The FSA has, however, so far only made very restricted use of its far-reaching power to impose fines.[118]

62   Private investors can also claim damages from financial analysts for incorrect recommendations. Although neither the FSA Handbook nor the FSMA contain specific provisions on such a liability, the general liability provision—section 150 FSMA—is also applicable to financial analysts. Claims can be brought by private investors if the analyst is an authorised person. Journalists who do meet the criteria of authorised persons can be held liable pursuant to section 13 Investment Recommendation (Media) Regulations 2005 which largely contains identical requirements.[119]

V.   Relevance of the General Rules of Conduct for Financial Analysts

1.   Market Manipulation

(a)   Information-Based Manipulation

63   Information-based manipulation is the "dissemination of information that gives, or is likely to give, false or misleading signals as to financial instruments, including the dissemination of rumours and false or misleading news, where the person who made the dissemination knew, or ought to have known, that the information was false or misleading".[120] This prohibition is of great practical relevance for financial analysts who can only fulfil their function as information intermediaries by dissemi-

---

[113] Confirmed by G. Spindler, NZG (2004), p. 1138, 1147; for the duties of care laid down in § 34b WpHG P.O. Mülbert, JZ (2002), p. 826, 836–837.

[114] A. Fuchs, in: A. Fuchs (ed.), *Kommentar zum WpHG*, § 34b para. 3; I. Koller, in: H.-D. Assmann and U.H. Schneider (eds.), *Kommentar zum WpHG*, § 34b para. 103; T.M.J. Möllers, in: H. Hirte and T.M.J. Möllers (eds.), *Kölner Kommentar zum WpHG*, § 34b para. 284.

[115] T.M.J. Möllers, in: H. Hirte and T.M.J. Möllers (eds.), *Kölner Kommentar zum WpHG*, § 34b para. 303.

[116] BGH, NJW (1982), p. 2823 ff. on prospectus liability; see also § 17 para. 55–60.

[117] These powers are laid down in sec. 66 FSMA (for misconduct of approved persons) and sec. 205, 206 FSMA (for misconduct of firms). The details of sanctions are laid down in DEPP (Decision Procedure and Penalties) of the FSA Handbook.

[118] See § 12 para. 19.

[119] Sec. 13 Investment Recommendation (Media) Regulations (2005).

[120] Art. 5 in conjunction with Art. 1(2)(c) MAD; in more detail § 14 para. 13 ff.

nating the information they have acquired.[121] If their recommendation gives false or misleading signals regarding the analysed financial instrument, the financial analyst breaches the prohibition of market manipulation.

64   Incorrect facts in the reporting part of the analysis, i.e. information on actual circumstances that does not reflect reality, are the most obvious instances of a "false signal". The analyst must, for example, ensure that the information provided on the company's trading volume and debts is correct.

65   The question whether the recommendation to "hold", "buy" or "sell" can itself constitute a "false signal" remains unanswered in the directive.

66   In Germany this question is being discussed intensively. Legal literature is predominantly of the opinion that a recommendation constitutes a value judgement that is false if it is based on facts but cannot be plausibly deduced from these.[122] If the recommendation does not contain any factual elements, a false signal is given, if the recommendation is evidentially unsubstantiated.[123] Based on this understanding and assuming the responsible persons acted intentionally, the recommendations to acquire Enron shares, even after Enron had to restate its financial statements in October 2001,[124] must (retrospectively) be regarded as evidentially unjustifiable. Legal literature in the other Member States does not appear to discuss this problem.

67   Identifying misleading signals proves more difficult. Any approach to a definition must be based on the premise that this can only mean a correct statement of facts, because the presentation of incorrect facts is already covered by the term "false". Misleading signals must therefore be defined as true circumstances that nevertheless give a wrong impression of reality. If the descriptive part of the recommendation, for example, provides extensive information that presents the issuer positively, whilst the existence of negative information is only indicated vaguely, this is likely to mislead the investor. Incomplete information can also give a wrong impression and must therefore be regarded as misleading.[125] The analysis must therefore also contain information on an issuer's overwhelming debt and not merely imply otherwise by making reference to a substantial order backlog.

(b)   Fictitious Devices or Any Other Form of Deception or Contrivance

68   The MAD further defines "transactions or orders to trade which employ fictitious devices or any other form of deception or contrivance" as market manipulation.[126] The provision is to prevent any transactions that affect price stability and therefore cannot be accepted if the functioning of the markets is to be ensured.

69   Article 5 Implementing Directive 2003/125/EC lists circumstances that may indicate a market manipulation and are therefore prohibited. An indication of manipulative

---

[121] See para. 1 ff.

[122] H. Fleischer, in: A. Fuchs (ed.), *Kommentar zum WpHG*, § 20a para. 20; S. Mock et al., in: H. Hirte and T.M.J. Möllers (eds.), *Kölner Kommentar zum WpHG*, § 20a para. 162; J. Vogel, in: H.-D. Assmann and U.H. Schneider (eds.), *Kommentar zum WpHG*, § 20a para. 60.

[123] S. Mock et al., in: H. Hirte and T.M.J. Möllers (eds.), *Kölner Kommentar zum WpHG*, § 20a para. 162.

[124] For a description of the Enron recommendations see J.C. Coffee, *Gatekeepers*, p. 30.

[125] S. Mock et al., in: H. Hirte and T.M.J. Möllers (eds.), *Kölner Kommentar zum WpHG*, § 20a para. 163.

[126] Art. 1(2)(b) MAD.

behaviour included in the list especially for analysts, are "orders to trade ... given or transactions ... undertaken by persons before or after the same persons or persons linked to them produce or disseminate research or investment recommendations which are erroneous or biased or demonstrably influenced by material interest".[127] The provision is thus only applicable with regard to specific transactions and to the behaviour of persons who personally produce research or investment recommendations or are linked to such persons.

70   *Erroneous* in the sense of Article 5(b) Implementing Directive 2003/125/EC refers to any recommendation that cannot be justified or is based on incorrect facts without causing false or misleading signals regarding the financial instrument. The recommendation would otherwise have to be treated as an information-based manipulation.[128] Any financial recommendation that has not been compiled with the necessary expertise, care and diligence, or is incomplete for other reasons, must be considered erroneous under this definition.[129] The meaning of the term "biased" is equally difficult to determine, because the directive is silent as to the cause of the bias. German legal literature generally interprets the term as referring to financial recommendations that are neither incorrect nor erroneous but still mislead investors as to the real situation.[130]

71   The directive does not define when a recommendation is demonstrably influenced by material interest. The question can only be answered on a case-by-case basis.[131] The provision applies to situations in which the analyst holds shares of the respective company. This constellation, however, can also be seen as a form of *scalping*. If the rules on scalping are not applicable due to correct disclosure of the financial instruments the analyst holds, the behaviour may still fall under the scope of this provision.

(c)   Scalping

72   Market manipulation also includes "taking advantage of occasional or regular access to the traditional or electronic media by voicing an opinion about a financial instrument (or indirectly about its issuer) while having previously taken a position on that financial instrument and profiting subsequently from the impact of the opinions voiced on the price of that instrument, without having simultaneously disclosed that conflict of interest to the public in a proper and effective way".[132]

73   This behaviour, called *scalping*, is particularly relevant with regard to financial analysts. A scalper must ensure that as many investors as possible take his opinion into account and must possess sufficient authority for his opinion to be regarded as well-founded and truthful. Financial analysts usually meet both requirements.

[127] Art. 5(b) Implementing Directive 2003/124/EC.
[128] Art. 5 in conjunction with Art. 1(2)(c) MAD; on the following see also S. Mock et al., in: H. Hirte and T.M.J. Möllers (eds.), *Kölner Kommentar zum WpHG*, § 20 Anh. I § 4 MaKonV para. 15.
[129] On these requirements see para. 28 ff.
[130] J. Vogel, in: H.-D. Assmann and U.H. Schneider (eds.), *Kommentar zum WpHG*, § 20a para. 229.
[131] S. Mock et al., in: H. Hirte and T.M.J. Möllers (eds.), *Kommentar zum WpHG*, § 20 Anh. I § 4 MaKonV para. 15.
[132] Art. 1(2)(c) al. 3 MAD; see also § 10 para. 43 ff.

74　During the New Economy boom in Germany, a number of television programmes offered investment advice to potential investors. An anchorman advertised shares that he had personally acquired and convinced investors to follow suit by predicting high profits. His aim was to subsequently sell the security himself at a profit following the rise in the market price due to his recommendation.[133] The case was presented to the BGH and the court held that scalping constitutes a form of market manipulation, reasoning that inside facts, such as the acquisition of shares and a recommendation based on the intention of achieving a better sale price, did not fall under the definition of "precise information", as required by the former Insider Directive. This approach was confirmed by the MAD and the German legislature, both of which also considered scalping a form of market manipulation.[134]

(d) Effects of Implementing Directive 2003/125/EC on the Definition of Market Manipulation

75　Recommendations made public in conformity with the provisions of Implementing Directive 2003/125/EC on the compilation and fair presentation of a financial recommendation cannot be false or misleading information[135] with regard to the fair presentation of investment recommendations and the disclosure of conflicts of interest.[136] The aim of Implementing Directive 2003/125/EC is to prevent investors from being misled.[137] If a market participant abides by these rules, it cannot be accused of having misled the public. If, however, a market participant is found to have breached the Implementing Directive's provisions, this can also constitute a breach of the rules against market manipulation.

2.　Prohibition of Insider Dealings

76　A financial analyst must ensure it conforms to the rules on insider dealings when compiling or distributing research. Recommendations presented by financial analysts can only be considered inside information, however, if they are not based on publicly known information.[138] If confidential information was also taken into account in the financial analysis, it must be determined for each case individually whether the report itself also constitutes inside information.[139]

77　Making use of inside information by acquiring or disposing of shares[140] is also prohibited for financial analysts. If they collect inside information when compiling a recommendation they become primary insiders. Financial analysts are therefore

---

[133] Cf. BGHSt 48, p. 375.
[134] See § 4(3)2 MaKonV.
[135] Art. 1(2)(c) MAD.
[136] On the relationship between the different German implementing provisions S. Mock et al., in: H. Hirte and T.M.J. Möllers (eds.), *Kölner Kommentar zum WpHG*, § 20a Anh. I § 4 MaKonV para. 15; J. Vogel, in: H.-D. Assmann and U.H. Schneider (eds.), *Kommentar zum WpHG*, § 20a para. 229.
[137] Recital 4 Implementing Directive 2003/125/EC.
[138] Recital 31 MAD.
[139] Cf. H.-D. Assmann, in: H.-D. Assmann and U.H. Schneider (eds.), *Kommentar zum WpHG*, § 13 para. 75–76; T.M.J. Möllers, in: H. Hirte and T.M.J. Möllers (eds.), *Kölner Kommentar zum WpHG*, § 34b para. 34.
[140] Art. 2(1) MAD.

prohibited from using that information to acquire or dispose of financial instruments. The decision to "hold" a financial instrument is thus not affected by this prohibition, pursuant to the wording of the directive. Should the financial analyst have planned to dispose of the shares and then abstained from doing so due to the inside information it acquired when compiling the recommendation, this behaviour does not constitute a breach of the provisions on insider dealings.[141]

78   The prohibition regarding the disclosure of inside information can also become relevant with regard to financial analysts. A financial analyst may not disclose inside information that has become known to him in his recommendation.[142] By doing so, the analyst would pass on the information to a third party, i.e. the recipient of the financial analysis. It must further take into account the rules prohibiting the recommendation of the financial instruments or the inducement of others.[143] According to the directive this only affects recommendations to acquire or sell shares, hold-recommendations are not covered, even if they are based on knowledge of inside information.

3.   Organisational Requirements

79   The MiFID lists financial analyses as a form of ancillary financial service.[144] It contains no specific provisions on financial analyses, rather relying on Articles 24 and 25 Implementing Directive 2006/73/EC. These provisions are limited to introducing organisational obligations.

80   Member States are required to introduce organisational requirements for investment firms. The applicability of the directive is thus limited to a certain group of financial analysts active on the financial market. The MiFID understands the term "financial recommendation" as any "investment research that is intended or likely to be subsequently disseminated to clients of the firm or to the public",[145] thus also applying to clients that have explicitly been exempt from the scope of application of Implementing Directive 2003/125/EC.[146]

(a)   General Organisational Requirements

81   Investment firms must abide by the general requirements regarding possible conflicts of interest.[147] This is to ensure the independence of the financial analysts involved in the compilation of a recommendation. The Member States must introduce provisions that ensure that procedures to be followed and measures to be adopted in order to manage conflicts of interest "are designed to ensure that relevant persons engaged in different business activities involving a conflict of interest carry on those activities at a level of independence appropriate to the size and activities of the

---

[141] Cancelling or amending an order may also violate the prohibition according to the Commission's draft proposal for a Market Abuse Regulation, Article 7(1) MAR-Draft (COM(2011) 651 final)); cf. para. 15.
[142] On the disclosure obligations for companies pursuant to Art. 6(3) MAD see § 15 para. 25 ff.
[143] Cf. § 13 para. 94–98.
[144] Appendix I(B)5.
[145] Art. 25(1) Implementing Directive 2006/73/EC.
[146] Recital 3 Implementing Directive 2003/125/EC.
[147] Art. 22(1)–(3) Implementing Directive 2006/73/EC.

investment firm and of the group to which it belongs, and to the materiality of the risk of damage to the interests of clients".[148] Investment firms are thus obligated to take certain measures, listed in the directive "as necessary and appropriate for the firm to ensure the requisite degree of independence".[149] The investment firm itself may decide which measures are necessary and appropriate in the individual case, taking into consideration its organisational structure.

82   This choice does not, however, apply with regard to financial analysts. Member States must ensure that investment firms ensure the implementation of all the measures set out in Article 22(3) in relation to the financial analysts.[150] These measures include effective procedures to prevent or control the exchange of information between relevant persons engaged in activities involving a risk of conflict of interest where the exchange of that information may harm the interests of one or more clients.[151] The investment firms must therefore build Chinese walls that ensure that confidential information remains at its source.[152] This confidentiality was formerly regularly impaired, for example, when the research department passed on information to the trading desk or departments responsible for initial public offerings or M&A transactions. Such an extensive exchange of information is no longer legitimate; the distribution of information to other departments is now in practice restricted to essential information for which confidentiality is ensured.

83   Investment firms must further ensure that there is no direct connection between the remuneration of financial analysts and the remuneration of other relevant persons principally engaged in an activity, where a conflict of interest may arise in relation to those activities.[153] The provision aims to prevent financial analysts' revenues from being dependent on the success of the investment banking department, in order to prevent financial analysts from having a personal incentive for supplying the investment banking department with (overly) positive financial analyses. Whilst the MAD regarded it as sufficient to require disclosure of any dependencies, MiFID lays down stricter requirements with regard to investment firms. Bonuses that the financial analysts receive dependent on the transaction volume of the company as a whole remain admissible, yet must be disclosed.[154]

84   Investment firms must further take measures "to prevent or control the simultaneous or sequential involvement of a relevant person in separate investment or ancillary services or activities where such involvement may impair the proper management of conflicts of interest".[155] Member States are thus not obliged to introduce a general prohibition, but rather a control mechanism to determine when the involvement of a certain person must be prevented. The directive does not list any examples for situations that will generally lead to such a prohibition, making a case-by-case assessment necessary in legal practice. The participation of financial analysts in pitches, i.e. presentations or events organised in order to acquire new clients, e.g. for

---

[148] Art. 22(3) Implementing Directive 2006/73/EC.
[149] Art. 22(3)2 Implementing Directive 2006/73/EC.
[150] Art. 25(1) Implementing Directive 2006/73/EC.
[151] Art. 22(3)(a) Implementing Directive 2006/73/EC.
[152] In more detail see § 29 para. 64 ff.
[153] Art. 22(3)(c) Implementing Directive 2006/73/EC.
[154] U. Göres, in: M. Habersack et al. (eds.), *Handbuch Kapitalmarktinformation*, § 24 para. 122.
[155] Art. 22(3)2(e) Implementing Directive 2006/73/EC.

initial public offerings, will usually be problematic. In Germany the joint participation of investment bankers and financial analysts in pitches is seen as illegal,[156] the attendance of financial analysts only being permitted under stricter requirements, at so-called deal-related road shows, following the example of the respective US provisions.[157]

(b)   Special Organisational Requirements

85   The Member States must ensure that the investment firms prohibit financial analysts and other relevant persons from undertaking personal transactions or transactions on behalf of the investment firm in financial instruments to which the investment research relates.[158] This provision is to prevent investment firms from front-running, i.e. making use of the content of an analysis for their own means and generating profits before the recipients of the investment research have had a reasonable opportunity to act thereon. In practice, analysts will only rarely also be responsible for customer orders or be active as market makers. Nevertheless this problem is not uncommon, especially within smaller firms.

86   Member States must further prohibit investment firms, financial analysts and other relevant persons involved in the production of the investment research from accepting inducements from those with a material interest in the subject-matter of the investment research.[159] Especially issuers are assumed to have such a material interest in the research. The internal rules of conduct of the investment firms must further contain provisions on the treatment of inducements offered to the financial analysts.

87   Additionally the directive requires Member States to determine under what circumstances investment firms, financial analysts and other relevant persons involved in the production of the investment research are prohibited from promising issuers "favourable research coverage".[160] This should go without saying for any financial market, yet was not taken too seriously in the past. Additionally, Member States must ensure that investment firms have arrangements designed to ensure that, if the draft includes a recommendation or a target price, issuers, relevant persons other than financial analysts (this especially refers to the investment banking unit), and any other persons do not review a draft of the investment research for the purpose of verifying the accuracy of factual statements made in that research, or for any other purpose than to verify compliance with the firm's legal obligations before the dissemination of investment research is permitted.[161] The provision thus does not prevent the compliance function from reviewing a financial analysis.[162] The issuer will only rarely have the need to verify the figures as larger houses usually provide sufficient databases for their financial analysts.

---

[156] U. Göres, in: M. Habersack et al. (eds.), *Handbuch Kapitalmarktinformation*, § 24 para. 165.
[157] Ibid., § 24 para. 167.
[158] Art. 25(2)(a) Implementing Directive 2006/73/EC.
[159] Art. 25(2)(c) Implementing Directive 2006/73/EC.
[160] Art. 25(2)(d) Implementing Directive 2006/73/EC.
[161] Art. 25(2)(e) Implementing Directive 2006/73/EC.
[162] For more details see § 29 para. 30 ff.

VI. Conclusion

88   Financial analysts are subject to detailed regulation. The differences between the national concepts are negligible, as all Member States have largely adopted the European provisions one-to-one. The European legislature introduced the MAD in order to win back market confidence in financial analysts. Whilst this was largely successful, some elements of the directive show too clearly that the European legislature merely reacted to past forms of misconduct. The sanctions for breaches of the provisions on financial analysts vary between Member States, the possibility of a civil law liability remaining largely unexplored. The exact scope of amendments that are planned at a European level in the near future cannot yet be foreseen.

Lars Teigelack

§ 27 Rating Agencies

Bibliography

Becker, Florian, *Die Regulierung von Ratingagenturen*, DB (2010), p. 941–945; Blaurock, Uwe, *Verantwortlichkeit von Ratingagenturen—Steuerung durch Privat- oder Aufsichtsrecht?*, ZGR (2007), p. 603–653; Deipenbrock, Gudula, *Was ihr wollt oder der Widerspenstigen Zähmung? Aktuelle Entwicklungen der Regulierung von Ratingagenturen im Wertpapierbereich*, BB (2005), p. 2085–2090; Deipenbrock, Gudula, *Aktuelle Rechtsfragen zur Regulierung des Ratingwesens*, WM (2005), p. 261– 268; Deipenbrock, Gudula, *"Mehr Licht!"?—Der Vorschlag einer europäischen Verordnung über Ratingagenturen*, WM (2009), p. 1165–1174; Deipenbrock, Gudula, *Das europäische Modell einer Regulierung von Ratingagenturen—aktuelle praxisrelevante Rechtsfragen und Entwicklungen*, RIW (2010), p. 612–618; Gerke, Wolfgang and Mager, Ferdinand, *Die Macht der Ratingagenturen? Der Fall der ThyssenKrupp AG*, BFuP (2005), p. 203–214; Haar, Brigitte, *Das deutsche Ausführungsgesetz zur EU-Rating-Verordnung—Zwischenetappe auf dem Weg zu einer europäischen Finanzmarktarchitektur*, ZBB (2010), p. 185–193; Haar, Brigitte, *Haftung für fehlerhafte Ratings von Lehman-Zertifikaten—Ein neuer Baustein für ein verbessertes Regulierungsdesign im Ratingsektor?*, NZG (2010), p. 1281–1285; Dichev, Ilia D. and Piotroski, Joseph D., *The Long-Run Stock Returns Following Bond Ratings Changes*, 56 J. Fin. (2001), p. 173; Eilers, Stephan et al., *Unternehmensfinanzierung* (2008); Habersack, Matthias, *Rechtsfragen des Emittenten-Ratings*, ZHR 169 (2005), p. 185–211; Hunt, John Patrick, *Credit Rating Agencies and the "Worldwide Credit Crisis": The Limits of Reputation, the Insufficiency of Reform, and a Proposal for Improvement*, Colum. Bus. L. Rev. (2009), p. 109–209; IOSCO Report on Analyst Conflicts of Interest (Sept. 2003) and *Statement of Principles for Addressing Sell-side Securities Analyst Conflicts of Interest* (Sept. 2003); Johnston, Andrew, *Corporate Governance Is the Problem not the Solution: A Critical Appraisal of the European Regulation of Credit Rating Agencies*, 11 J. Corp. L. Stud. (2011) p. 395–441; Krimphove, Dieter and Kruse, Oliver, *Regulierung und Haftung von Ratingagenturen: Status quo und Perspektiven*, Kreditwesen (2005), p. 413–416; Lerch, Marcus P., *Ratingagenturen im Visier des europäischen Gesetzgebers*, BKR (2010), p. 402–408; Leyens, Patrick C., *Intermediary Independence: Auditors, Financial Analysts and Rating Agencys*, 11 J. Corp. L. Stud. (2011), p. 33–66; Linciano, Nadia, *The Reaction of Stock Prices to Rating Changes*, available at: http:// ssrn.com/abstract=572365; Möllers, Thomas M.J., *Regulierung von Ratingagenturen*, JZ (2009), p. 861–871; Partnoy, Frank, *How and Why Credit Rating Agencies Are Not Like Other Gatekeepers*, in: Fuchita, Yasuyuki and Litan, Robert E. (eds.), *Financial Gatekeepers: Can They Protect Investors?* (2006), pp. 59–99; Partnoy, Frank, *The Siskel and Ebert of Financial Markets: Two Thumbs Down for the Credit Rating Agencies*, 77 Wash. U. L. Q. (1999), p. 619; von Schweinitz, Oliver, *Die Haftung von Ratingagenturen*, WM (2008), p. 953–959; Seibt, Christoph H., *Regulierung und Haftung von Ratingagenturen*, in: Bachmann, Gregor et al. (eds.), *Steuerungsfunktionen des Haftungsrechts im Gesellschafts- und Kapitalmarktrecht* (2007), p. 191–213; Teigelack, Lars, *Finanzanalysen und Behavioral Finance* (2009); Vasella, David, *Die Haftung von Ratingagenturen* (2011); Vassalou, Maria and Xing, Yuhang, *Default Risks in Equity Returns*, 59 J. Fin. (2004), p. 831–868; Wildmoser, Gerhard, Schiffer, Jan and Langoth, Bernd, *Haftung von Ratingagenturen gegenüber Anlegern?*, RIW (2009), p. 657–668.

I. Introduction

1   It is not only since the recent financial crisis that rating agencies have been the focus of criticism for investors, issuers and politicians alike. Even prior to the crisis, the crash of Enron, WorldCom and Parmalat led to the criticism that the ratings for

these companies had not adapted quickly enough to the changes in the market situation.[1] During the financial crisis the focus changed, the excellent ratings for certain financial products and the slow speed at which ratings were adapted to changes in the markets becoming the centre of attention for the critics when it became apparent that these had been two of the causes of the financial crisis.[2] Issuers further purported that the ratings assigned by the agencies were often too negative, attributing this to the lack of transparency with regard to the criteria of the rating procedure. The regulation on rating agencies is one of the reactions to this criticism.

1. Aims of Rating

2   Ratings have three functions. Primarily, they provide intermediary services between a company and investors. Rating agencies assess the creditworthiness of companies or debt instruments. Ideally, this enables investors to make a well-founded investment decision by eliminating or at least reducing the informational asymmetries between the investor and the company or issuer of debt instruments.[3] The assessment usually consists of a certain combination of letters, such as AAA, AA+ (Standard & Poor's) or Aaa, Aa1 (Moody's).[4]

3   Rating agencies further act as so-called *gatekeepers* for the companies or issuers of debt instruments.[5] They give issuers access to the capital market and regulate market access. In some market segments stock exchange rules or statutes explicitly require a rating,[6] whereas in other segments market participants take ratings for granted. A positive rating reduces the issuer's costs of capital,[7] whereas an issuer with a negative rating will have to pay considerable interest in order to be able to place bonds[8] on the market.

4   The costs of capital for ThyssenKrupp AG, for example, rose by nearly €20 million, after a downgrade by Standard & Poor's. The agency had begun taking into account the company's pension obligations in its credit rating.[9]

5   Ratings also fulfil a regulatory function. Some jurisdictions employ ratings as a means to directly or indirectly regulate financial products or market participants. According to the second Basel Accord (Basel II), for example, a bank may rely on an external rating when assessing whether it has sufficient capital reserves for its lending activities.[10] Whilst the assessment of credit risk formerly depended on the

---

[1] Cf. G. Deipenbrock, WM (2005), p. 261, 263; summarising the Enron and Parmalat cases U. Blaurock, ZGR (2007), p. 603, 613.

[2] Cf. G. Deipenbrock, RIW (2010), p. 612; T.M.J. Möllers, JZ (2009), p. 861; see also Commission Proposal for a Rating Regulation COM(2008) 704 final, p. 2.

[3] On the comparable functions of financial analysts see § 26 para. 2.

[4] Fitch and Standard & Poor's employ the same letter designations; an overview of the different rating scales can be found in L.R. Krämer, in: S. Eilers et al. (eds.), *Unternehmensfinanzierung*, para. 404; under the Commission proposal, the ESMA may set technical standards harmonising the rating scale, COM(2011) 747 final, p. 10.

[5] Cf. U. Blaurock, ZGR (2007), p. 603, 608; M.P. Lerch, BKR (2010), p. 402, 403; on the comparable functions of financial analysts see § 26 para. 6.

[6] For example sec. 36(3)3 of the Terms and Conditions for the open market of the Stuttgart Stock Exchange.

[7] Cf. U. Blaurock, ZGR (2007), p. 603, 609; M.P. Lerch, BKR (2010), p. 402, 403.

[8] On the term "bond" see § 8 para. 15–17.

[9] Cf. W. Gerke and F. Mager, BFuP 57 (2005), p. 204; L.R. Krämer, in: S. Eilers et al. (eds.), *Unternehmensfinanzierung*, C para. 408.

[10] Cf. U. Blaurock, ZGR (2007), p. 603, 619.

risk class of the debtor, Basel II now provides a risk calculation for each debtor individually on the basis of external or internal ratings.[11] Additionally, some Member States, such as Germany, only allow insurance companies, pension funds and home loan banks to invest in financial instruments with an investment-grade rating.[12]

2. Effects of a Rating

6 An essential difference exists on rating markets between instruments with a so-called investment-grade rating and papers with a non-investment-grade rating.[13] The latter are often named junk bonds or high-yield bonds. The distinction between both forms is not gradual, but rather abrupt, so that the development from a lower-investment-grade rating to a "good" junk rating will usually not cause merely slight changes to the costs of capital. Rather, there is a "cliff"[14] between an investment-grade rating and a non-investment-grade rating, the costs of borrowed capital being disproportionately high in the latter case. For the issuer, a junk rating also has the effect that the *covenants*, i.e. the figures and rules of conduct it must fulfil when borrowing funds, are far stricter. Economic studies have shown that even downgrades of debt instruments also negatively influence the issuer's equity returns. The studies have not as yet been able to determine, however, whether this is a result of the rating itself or rather of the underlying information.[15]

7 The day it became publicly known that the ThyssenKrupp AG had been rated down, for example, not only the bond price but also the share price dropped by 6%.[16]

8 In practice, many loan agreements or the terms of high-yield-bonds contain provisions to the effect that changes in the rating have certain effects, such as changes in the interest rate or stricter covenants.[17] A further possibility is that a due diligence process prior to an equity transaction may be less intense for an issuer who has received an investment-grade rating than for an issuer who has received a non-investment-grade rating.[18]

3. Market Structure and Development of Regulation in Europe

9 The market for rating agencies is characterised by oligopolistic structures. The three largest rating agencies active worldwide—Standard & Poor's, Moody's and Fitch—

---

[11] Art. 80, 81 Directive 2006/48/EC of the European Parliament and of the Council of 14 June 2006 relating to the taking up and pursuit of the business of credit institutions, OJ L177, 30 June 2006, p. 1; Basel Committee on Banking Supervision, *International Convergence of Capital Measurement and Capital Standards (Basel II)*, November 2005, p. 15.

[12] Cf. § 54(1) VAG; see also para. 6 and BaFin, *Rundschreiben* (circular) R 15/2005 (VA), August 2005, p. 2; J. Baur, in: H.-D. Assmann and R.A. Schütze (eds.), *Handbuch des Kapitalanlagerechts*, § 20 para. 167.

[13] The first rating below investment-grade level is BB+ on the Standard & Poor's and Fitch scale and Ba1 on Moody's scale.

[14] The European legislature meanwhile also uses the term "cliff effect", cf. COM(2011)747 final, p. 4.

[15] Cf. I.D. Dichev and J.D. Piotroski, 56 J. Fin. (2001) p. 173–203; overview in N. Linciano, p. 3–4 and M. Vassalou and Y. Xing, 59 J. Fin. (2004), p. 831, 833.

[16] Manager-Magazin of 21 February 2003.

[17] Cf. U. Blaurock, ZGR (2007), p. 603, 611 (rating triggers); L.R. Krämer, in: S. Eilers et al. (eds.), *Unternehmensfinanzierung*, C para. 412.

[18] L.R. Krämer, in: R. Marsch-Barner and F.A. Schäfer (eds.), *Handbuch börsennotierte AG*, § 10 para. 71.

have a total market share of 95%.[19] To date it has not been possible to establish a competitive European rating agency.[20]

10   For a long time, rating agencies were not subject to specific regulation, the IOSCO Code[21] being a voluntary[22] but, in the eyes of many, sufficient regulatory measure.[23] The MAD therefore was not applicable to rating agencies and even the spectacular case of the ThyssenKrupp AG and the Asian crisis did not lead the European legislature to make any regulatory changes. It was not until the recent financial crisis broke out that Europe reconsidered the possibility that rating agencies may have been one of the causes of the crisis.[24]

11   The Rating Regulation,[25] enacted by the European Parliament and Council in September 2009, is largely based on the Commission's draft proposal of November 2008.[26] It was amended in May 2011 as recommended by the Commission,[27] in order to adapt the supervisory structures to the newly founded ESMA. The national implementing laws only need to regulate a few aspects. The Member States are now no longer responsible for the supervision of rating agencies, the latest amendments to the Rating Regulation now conferring the right to supervision and to impose sanctions on the ESMA.

12   The Rating Regulation is divided into four parts: (1) Subject matter, scope and definitions; (2) Issuing of credit ratings; (3) Surveillance of credit rating activities; (4) Penalties, committee procedure, reporting and transitional and final provisions. For the sake of clarity the Rating Regulation further contains two annexes, both of which are part of the regulation and as such directly applicable in the Member States. Appendix I on "Independence and avoidance of conflicts of interest", divided into five parts (A–E), is the most important.

II.   Regulatory Concepts

13   The Rating Regulation constitutes the first specific regulation for rating agencies in Europe. It is directly applicable in the Member States[28] and need therefore not be implemented into national law. Subsequently, the central provisions of the Rating Regulation will be described in more detail, whilst the general provisions of capital

[19] Further references in B. Haar, NZG (2010), p. 1281, 1282.
[20] On the attempts to break up the oligopolistic structures and the limits of reputational mechanisms see T.M.J. Möllers, JZ (2009), p. 861, 863; M.P. Lerch, BKR (2010), p. 402, 407.
[21] Cf. IOSCO, *Statement of Principles Regarding the Activities of Credit Rating Agencies*, September 2003 and IOSCO, *Code of Conduct Fundaments for Credit Rating Agencies*, December 2004.
[22] More details on the IOSCO principles in G. Deipenbrock, BB (2005), p. 2085 ff.
[23] Cf. C.H. Seibt, in: G. Bachmann et al. (eds.), *Steuerungsfunktionen des Haftungsrechts*, p. 191, 198. M. Habersack, ZHR 169 (2005), p. 185, 190 ff. holds the opposite opinion.
[24] Cf. Recital 10 Rating Regulation EC 1006/2009 of 16 September 2009; see in more detail at para. 23.
[25] Regulation (EC) No. 1060/2009 of the European Parliament and of the Council of 16 September 2009 on credit rating agencies, OJ L302, 17 November 2009, p. 1. The Rating Regulation entered into force on 7 December 2009.
[26] COM(2008) 704 final.
[27] Regulation (EU) No. 513/2011 of the European Parliament and of the Council of 11 May 2011 amending Regulation (EC) No. 1060/2009 on credit rating agencies, OJ L145, 31 May 2011, p. 30.
[28] On the legal nature of regulations see § 3 para. 13–14.

Rüdiger Veil/Lars Teigelack

markets law, which are also applicable, will not be presented in detail, as they do not play any important role with regard to rating agencies. Suffice it to make clear that the distribution of information—especially from the issuer to the rating agency— may constitute an insider dealing and be prohibited as such. [29] The rating itself may also be classed as inside information. The issuer will then be confronted with the question whether it is obliged to disclose the rating without delay, as required by Article 6(1) MAD. [30]

14   Rating agencies must further comply with the general rules of civil law. Whilst they merely present their opinion on the issuer's creditworthiness and the rating must thus be regarded as a prognosis, [31] this does not hinder the application of Member States' national tort laws to a rating. [32]

15   Very recently, the European Commission has addressed several other problems in a draft amendment to the regulation on rating agencies. [33] These include overreliance on ratings by investors and regulators on external ratings, problems with sovereign ratings and the lack of redress for investors who have suffered losses. In order to combat these problems the European Commission has proposed a civil liability framework. [34]

III. Scope of Application

1. Subject Matter of Regulation

16   The underlying aim of the regulation is to enhance the integrity, transparency, responsibility, good governance and reliability of rating activities, thereby contributing to the improvement in quality of ratings. This is to further the smooth functioning of the internal market whilst achieving a high level of consumer and investor protection. [35] The fact that the European legislature defines a "subject matter" of the regulation is remarkable, this being characteristic of a principles-based approach to legislation, which only provides market participants with an (abstract or concrete) regulatory aim, leaving free the choice of the means by which this aim is achieved. [36]

17   The Rating Regulation does not only list investor protection, but also consumer protection as its regulatory aim. [37] This comes as a surprise considering that, unlike banks, rating agencies do not normally communicate directly with individual investors, but rather operate for the capital market as a whole. Whether the approach

---

[29] On the prohibitions under insider law see § 13 para. 84–98.

[30] On the term "inside information" see § 13 para. 33–48 and on the legal nature of a rating as inside information subject to disclosure obligations see § 19 para. 43.

[31] Cf. M. Habersack, ZHR 169 (2005), p. 185, 200.

[32] See below para. 63.

[33] Proposal for a Regulation of the European Parliament and the Council amending Regulation (EC) No. 1060/2009 on credit rating agencies, COM(2011) 747 final.

[34] See below para. 66.

[35] Art. 1 Rating Regulation.

[36] See § 4 para. 51–58 and § 29 para. 4–11.

[37] One of the reasons for this may be that UK supervisory law and the FSA treat investor protection and consumer protection as equivalents. Cf. sec. 2 Abs. 2 FSMA 2000 ("protection of consumers"); on the "statutory objectives" see www.fsa.gov.uk/Pages/about/aims/statutory/index.shtml.

taken in Article 1 Rating Regulation, especially the mention of investor and consumer protection, implies that the regulatory aim is the protection of individual financial interests remains unclear.[38]

2. Scope

18   The Rating Regulation only applies to rating agencies registered in the European Union. This does not necessarily require the company's headquarters to be in the European Union. It is sufficient for the rating agency to have established a branch in the Community.[39] Any rating which has been disclosed publicly or distributed by subscription falls within the scope of the regulation.[40] The Rating Regulation has exempted a number of cases from its scope of application. These primarily include private credit ratings that are provided exclusively to the person who ordered them, credit scoring systems, credit ratings produced by export credit rating agencies and certain credit ratings produced by central banks.[41]

19   The Commission proposal of November 2011 extends some of the Rating Regulation's provisions on conflicts of interest, accuracy and transparency to rating outlooks, i.e. the agency's opinion on the likely future of a rating. The Commission considers outlooks to be just as relevant as the ratings themselves.[42]

3. Definitions

20   The rules of conduct contain various terms that require clarification. Similar to the other European legislative acts, the Rating Regulation provides a number of definitions, such as for the terms "credit rating", "credit rating activities" and "structured finance instrument".

21   A "credit rating" is defined as an "opinion regarding the creditworthiness of an entity, a debt or financial obligation, debt security, preferred share or other financial instrument, or of an issuer of such an [instrument], issued using an established and defined ranking system of rating categories".[43] The definition explicitly does not apply to recommendations and financial analyses,[44] both of which are dealt with in the MAD and its implementing directives.[45] The term "credit rating activities" in the sense of the Rating Regulation refers to "data and information analysis and the evaluation, approval, issuing and review of credit ratings".[46] As most provisions of the regulation only apply to agencies, the term "credit rating agencies" is also defined in this context, as "a legal person whose occupation includes the issuing of credit ratings on a professional basis".[47]

22   The fact that the Rating Regulation places particular emphasis on "structured

---

[38] See below para. 65.
[39] The Rating Regulation is further relevant with regard to agencies from third countries, see below para. 46.
[40] Art. 2(1) Rating Regulation.
[41] Art. 2(2) Rating Regulation.
[42] Cf. Recital 4 COM(2011) 747 final.
[43] Art. 3(1)(a) Rating Regulation.
[44] Art. 3(2)(a), (b) Rating Regulation.
[45] See § 26 para. 28 ff.
[46] Cf. Art. 3(1)(o) Rating Regulation.
[47] Cf. Art. 3(1)(b) Rating Regulation.

finance instruments" is probably due to the fact that these were regarded as one of the causes of the financial crisis. A "structured finance instrument" means "a financial instrument or other assets resulting from a securitisation transaction or scheme referred to in Article 4(36) of Directive 2006/48/EC".[48] Some of the Rating Regulation's provisions distinguish between ratings for structured financial instruments and other types of financial instruments. The reason for this is that the rating of structured financial instruments causes specific problems, for example with regard to the rating methods employed, but also with regard to the interests of the market participants involved in the rating procedure.[49]

IV. Regulatory Approach and Obligations

23 Rating agencies generate turnover by receiving consideration from an issuer for the rating they provide. It is therefore issuers and not investors that pay for ratings. The European legislature accepted this concept[50] and introduced a number of obligations rather than a prohibition in order to achieve the regulatory aims mentioned above. The obligations can be divided into four categories. Firstly, the Rating Regulation subjects credit ratings to certain conditions and introduces rules on the organisation and conduct of credit rating agencies which promote their independence and prevent conflicts of interest.[51] The Rating Regulation further aims to achieve an improved quality of the ratings available on the market. Additionally, it establishes new transparency requirements and finally it introduces a policy of compulsory registration for all credit rating agencies.

1. Avoidance of Conflicts of Interest

(a) Independence of Credit Rating Agencies

24 Conflicts of interest of intermediaries are one of the most pressing problems of capital market regulation.[52] The European legislature has addressed this problem by developing a closely knit net of rules of conduct. The provisions are built around a provision of a principles-based nature, requiring rating agencies to "take all necessary steps to ensure that the issuing of a credit rating is not affected by any existing or potential conflict of interest or business relationship involving the credit rating agency issuing the credit rating, its managers, rating analysts, employees, any other natural person whose services are placed at the disposal or under the control of the credit rating agency, or any person directly or indirectly linked to it by control".[53]

---

[48] Art. 3(1)(l) Rating Regulation. The Directive relating to the taking up and pursuit of the business of credit institutions which the definition in the Rating Regulation refers to defines securitisation as "a transaction or scheme, whereby the credit risk associated with an exposure or pool of exposures is tranched, having the following characteristics: (a) payments in the transaction or scheme are dependent upon the performance of the exposure or pool of exposures; and (b) the subordination of tranches determines the distribution of losses during the ongoing life of the transaction or scheme."
[49] See also below para. 40.
[50] Cf. M.P. Lerch, BKR (2010), p. 402, 406.
[51] Art. 1 Rating Regulation.
[52] Cf. P.C. Leyens, 11 J. Corp. L. Stud. (2011), p. 33, 59–63.
[53] Art. 6(1) Rating Regulation.

Compliance with this rule is ensured by the organisational and operational requirements rating agencies must fulfil, which are listed in Appendix I sections A and B.[54]
This approach is the result of the occurrences during the financial crisis, when rating
agencies orientated themselves towards the issuers instead of fulfilling their function
as a neutral third party.[55]

25 Section A lists numerous organisational requirements, the most detailed being those
on compliance. A rating agency is obliged to establish and maintain a permanent
and effective compliance function which operates independently. The compliance
function is required to monitor and report on compliance of the credit rating agency
and its employees with the credit rating agency's obligations.

26 In order to enable the compliance function to discharge its responsibilities properly and independently, the respective credit rating agency must ensure that the
compliance function has the necessary authority, resources, expertise and access
to all relevant information. The rating agency must further appoint a compliance officer responsible for the compliance function. The compliance officer must
ensure that any conflicts of interest relating to the persons placed at the disposal
of the compliance function are properly identified and eliminated. It must make
regular reports to senior management and the independent members of the
administrative or supervisory board on his work.[56] The compliance requirements
listed in the Rating Regulation correspond with those contained in the MiFID
and its implementing directives.[57]

27 The regulation further contains requirements on the internal control of a credit
rating agency: at least one-third, but no less than two, of the members of the
administrative or supervisory board of a credit rating agency must, for example, be
independent and may not be involved in credit rating activities.[58]

28 The operational requirements laid down in section B deal with conflicts of interest
by requiring rating agencies to keep records and prohibiting credit ratings and
consultancy or advisory services under certain conditions. Section B also stipulates
requirements as to the reporting and communication channels within an agency as
well as documentation obligations.

29 In particular, the prohibition to provide certain consultancy or advisory services[59]
must be understood as a reaction to certain events prior to the financial crisis.
Rating agencies had advised companies how to structure complex financial instruments. In order to prevent a loss of business the rating agencies had then supplied
the financial products with ratings or had issued an AAA rating, although this rating
was not objectively justifiable as the products did not provide the necessary security
against credit default risks.[60]

---

[54] Art. 6(2) Rating Regulation.
[55] CESR, *CESR's Second Report to the European Commission on the compliance of credit rating agencies with
the IOSCO Code and the role of credit rating agencies in structured finance*, CESR/08-277, May 2008, para. 96.
[56] Cf. Annex I.A para. 6 Rating Regulation.
[57] See in more detail § 29 para. 29 ff.
[58] Annex I Section A para. 5, 6 Rating-Regulation.
[59] Annex I Section B para. 4, 5 Ratings-Regulation.
[60] This conflict of interests is also mentioned in CESR, *CESR's Second Report to the European Commission on
the compliance of credit rating agencies with the IOSCO Code and the role of credit rating agencies in structured
finance*, CESR/08–277, May 2008, para. 96.

Rüdiger Veil/Lars Teigelack

30   An instant-messenger communication by Standard & Poor's, for example, contained the following announcement: "We rate every deal. It could be structured by cows and we would rate it."[61]

31   The regulation now prohibits ratings entirely under certain circumstances, i.e. if the agency stands in a structural connection to the rated company. Such a connection is to be assumed, for example, if the credit rating agency or an employee directly or indirectly owns financial instruments of the rated entity or if a member of the credit rating agency simultaneously holds a seat on the administrative or supervisory board of the rated entity. If a credit rating already exists, these circumstances obligate the credit rating agency to disclose immediately that the credit rating is potentially affected by this fact.[62]

32   To enable the supervisory authority to verify a rating, the rating agencies are required to keep records on the identity of the rating analysts participating in the determination of the credit rating and the methods employed for the rating information as to whether the credit rating was solicited or unsolicited, and the date on which the credit rating action was taken. The records must be stored on the premises of the registered credit rating agency for at least five years.[63]

33   The Commission proposal of November 2011 introduces a rotation rule for all rating agencies engaged by the issuer, except for unsolicited and sovereign ratings. No agency may rate an issuer or its debt instruments for more than a total of six years. After the maximum rating duration, a cooling-off period will be required and the outgoing agency will have to provide handover files to the incoming agency.[64]

(b)   *Persons Involved in the Rating Procedure*

34   The Rating Regulation aims to prevent persons involved in the rating procedures from being misguided by monetary incentives. The compensation and evaluation of performance of these individuals may not therefore be contingent on the amount of revenue that the credit rating agency derives from the rated entities or related third parties.[65] These persons are therefore also prohibited from being allowed to initiate or participate in negotiations regarding fees or payments with any rated entity.[66] The large variety of structured financial instruments entails the problem that issuers will have a number of subsequent transactions to offer to the rating agencies. Unlike a regular rating, this can give the credit rating agency the incentive to award a positive rating in order to be awarded the subsequent rating deals.[67]

35   This pressure on the rating agencies to submit positive ratings becomes apparent in an e-mail of August 2004 by Standard & Poor's: "We just lost a huge Mizuho RMBS deal to Moody's due to a huge difference in the required credit support

---

[61] Exhibit 30a United States Senate Hearing on the role of rating agencies in the financial crisis, p. 132.
[62] Annex I.B para. 3 Rating-Regulation.
[63] Annex I.B para. 7 Rating-Regulation.
[64] Art. 6b COM(2011) 747 final.
[65] Art. 7(5) Rating Regulation.
[66] Art. 7(2) Rating Regulation.
[67] CESR, *CESR's Second Report to the European Commission on the compliance of credit rating agencies with the IOSCO Code and the role of credit rating agencies in structured finance*, CESR/08-277, May 2008, para. 99.

level. … Losing one or even several deals due to criteria issues … is so significant it may have an impact in the future deals."[68]

36　Rating agencies are further required to establish an appropriate so-called "gradual rotation mechanism" with regard to the rating analysts and persons approving credit ratings, in order to prevent any close personal ties developing between the individual rating analysts and the rated entity.[69] The latest Commission proposal combines this mechanism to the agency rotation mechanism in order to prevent a lead analyst from taking client files when switching to another agency.[70]

37　Behavioural finance[71] additionally purports that a rotation mechanism can also prevent rating from being distorted without intent, simply because the analyst has gained a so-called *inside view*. An *inside view* is the tendency no longer to place problems into general categories, being fixated on the specific case. Insiders run the risk of overestimating the chances of success of the project by ignoring the statistical success rate.[72] According to this theory, a rating analyst may therefore be in the danger of overrating a company simply because it has spent so much time assessing it. It is not necessary, however, to determine whether this theory is always correct. The risk of monetary incentives is by itself sufficient to justify a gradual rotation mechanism.

2. Improvement of the Quality of Ratings

38　After the financial crisis, critics of rating agencies particularly pointed out the deficiencies in the rating methods, i.e. ratings not being adjusted to the altered market situation soon enough.[73] Additionally, the models applied for the compositions of ratings were said not to adequately reflect the risks of newly structured financial products.

39　The Rating Regulation took this criticism into account and introduced new provisions on the methods, models and general assumptions on which a rating is based, aiming to improve the quality of ratings available on the market. As investors often rely solely on ratings, it must be ensured that these provide as much information as possible.[74] A credit rating agency must therefore use "rating methodologies that are rigorous, systematic, continuous and subject to validation based on historical experience, including back-testing".[75] The Rating Regulation thereby wants to prevent rating methods being applied for products to which they are not suited due to a lack of experience with such products in the past.[76]

40　Credit rating agencies are further obliged to disclose the methodologies, models and key rating assumptions used and to monitor and review their credit ratings and methodologies on an ongoing basis and at least annually.[77] If the methods, models

---

[68] Exhibit 2 US Senate Hearing, p. 44.
[69] Art. 7(4) Rating Regulation.
[70] COM(2011) 747 final, p. 9.
[71] See § 6 para. 21–32.
[72] Further references in L. Teigelack, *Finanzanalysen und Behavioral Finance*, p. 96–97.
[73] Cf. Recital 10 Rating Regulation.
[74] Commission Proposal for a Rating Regulation, COM(2008) 704 final, p. 9.
[75] Art. 8(3) Rating Regulation.
[76] Cf. US Senate Hearing, p. 7.
[77] Art. 8(1), (5) Rating Regulation. Pursuant to Recital 23 Rating Regulation credit rating agencies must review credit ratings at least annually.

or general assumptions change, the agency must take certain actions in order to ensure that the rating is adapted as soon as possible. The credit rating agency must therefore immediately disclose the likely scope of credit ratings to be affected, review the affected credit ratings as soon as possible and, no later than six months after the change, place the ratings on the watch list in the meantime[78] and re-rate all credit ratings affected by such changes.[79]

41   In the past, delays in adapting the rating were primarily caused by lack of staff and resources and the fear of displeasing investment banks and investors by downgrading their products.[80] Moody's explicitly admitted to re-rating only selectively: "Moody's does not re-evaluate every outstanding affected rating. ... This decision to selectively review certain ratings is made due to resource constraints." Standard & Poor's adopted a similar approach: "[W]e don't have the model or resource capacity to do so, nor do we all believe that even if we did have the capability, it would be the responsible thing to do to the market."[81]

42   The Commission proposal of November 2011 tightens the rules regarding the disclosure of rating methods, extending the obligation to explain the methods from structured finance products to all asset classes.[82] All new or altered methods must now be presented to the ESMA and may only be used after the ESMA has approved them.

3.   Transparency Obligations

(a)   Disclosure and Presentation of Credit Ratings

43   The new provisions on the disclosure and presentation of credit ratings aim to protect investors from misunderstanding the aim and relevance of a rating.[83] Investors have tended to rely blindly on the results of ratings, especially where the complexity of structured finance instruments allowed them no assessment of their own.[84] Rating agencies are now obliged to adhere to the requirements listed in Appendix I section D Rating Regulation, which sets out general and specific rules for ratings of structured finance instruments.[85] A credit rating must, for example, now name all material sources and describe the principal methodology or version of methodology that was used in determining the rating in detail.[86] When a credit rating agency issues a credit rating for a structured finance instrument, it must ensure with an additional symbol that the rating category attributed to the structured finance instrument can be clearly distinguished from rating categories used for any other entities, financial instruments or financial obligations.[87] The credit rating agency is

[78] On the instrument see § 29 para. 74.
[79] Art. 8(6) Rating Regulation.
[80] US Senate Hearing, p. 8–9.
[81] Exhibit 1e US Senate Hearing, p. 33–34.
[82] COM(2011) 747 final, p. 9.
[83] Seen critically by M.P. Lerch, BKR (2010), p. 402, 406.
[84] CESR, *CESR's Second Report to the European Commission on the compliance of credit rating agencies with the IOSCO Code and the role of credit rating agencies in structured finance*, CESR/08-277, May 2008, para. 103, 105.
[85] Art. 10(2) Rating Regulation.
[86] Annex I.D No. 1 para. 1, 2.
[87] Art. 10(3) Rating Regulation; cf. T.M.J. Möllers, JZ (2009), p. 861, 868–869.

further obliged to disclose all credit ratings, as well as any decision to discontinue a credit rating in a timely manner.[88] The Rating Regulation further contains additional information obligations for unsolicited credit ratings.[89]

(b) Transparency Report

44   A credit rating agency is obliged to publish certain information on an annual basis, no later than three months after the end of each financial year by way of a transparency report as described in Appendix I section E(III). This report must, for example, contain information on the agency's rotation policy, statistics on the internal allocation of its staff to ratings and financial information on the revenue of the credit rating agency. The report must remain available on the website of the agency for at least five years.[90]

4.   Registration

45   If the credit rating agency is a legal person established in the EU, Article 14(1) Rating Regulation requires it to apply for registration for the purposes of Article 2(1). Registration is thus a prerequisite for rating agencies to be permitted to issue ratings in the Community, disclose them publicly or distribute them by subscription.[91]

46   Agencies from third countries are not subject to the registration obligation. The European legislature does not have the power to introduce such a general registration obligation for agencies incorporated outside the European Union, although a general applicability of the Rating Regulation's provisions appears desirable. In order to achieve this, a regulatory "trick" was necessary: credit institutes (and the other firms listed) are only permitted to use credit ratings for supervisory purposes if they are issued by credit rating agencies with their legal seat in the EU and registered in accordance with the regulation.[92] Agencies from third countries are therefore indirectly "forced" to register in the European Union if they wish to offer their services on the internal market.[93] The regulation further imposes the obligation on an issuer to include information in a securities prospectus on whether or not a credit rating was issued by a credit rating agency established in the Community and registered under the regulation.[94]

47   The application for registration must be submitted to the ESMA in any of the official languages of the institutions of the Union.[95] The ESMA then has 20 working days to

---

[88] Art. 10(1) Rating Regulation.

[89] Art. 10(4), (5) Rating Regulation.

[90] Art. 12 Rating Regulation; requirements are tightened under the Commission proposal, cf. COM(2011) 747 final, p. 9.

[91] Art. 14(2) Rating Regulation.

[92] Art. 4(1) Rating Regulation.

[93] However, ratings from third countries can be used for supervisory means, provided they were compiled under similarly strict conditions as laid down in the Rating Regulation. Cf. Recital 13 and Art. 4(3) Rating Regulation. See in more detail G. Deipenbrock, RIW (2010), p. 612, 614–615.

[94] Recital 5 and Art. 4(1)2 Rating Regulation; on securities prospectuses in general see § 17 para. 30–40.

[95] Art. 15 Abs. (1), (3) Rating Regulation.

assess whether the application is complete.[96] Within a further 45 working days, the ESMA must then examine the application for registration of the credit rating agency. The examination period may be extended by 15 working days.[97] At the end of the (extended) examination period the ESMA must adopt a fully reasoned decision to register or refuse registration which takes effect on the fifth working day following its decision.[98] A regularly updated list of all the credit rating agencies registered in accordance with the regulation can be found on the ESMA's website.[99] In February 2013 the list comprised 33 rating agencies.

48   Once a rating agency is registered, it can only lose this registration if the ESMA withdraws it. The ESMA can take this action if the credit rating agency waives the registration, has provided no credit ratings for the preceding six months, has obtained the registration by making false statements or by any other irregular means, no longer meets the conditions under which it was registered, or has continually and seriously infringed upon the regulation's provisions on rating activities.[100] A competent authority of a Member State that finds one of these cases to be fulfilled may request that the ESMA examines whether the conditions for the withdrawal of the registration of the credit rating agency concerned are given, provided the credit ratings issued by the credit rating agency concerned were used in the respective Member State.[101]

49   A revocation by the ESMA enters into force immediately. The credit rating may, however, continue to be used during a transitional period of ten working days from the date of the ESMA's decision if there are credit ratings of the same financial instrument or entity issued by other credit rating agencies or three months if no other ratings of the financial instrument or entity exist.[102] The two different transitional periods are to ensure that the market is not without access to information.[103] If other ratings exist, investors can refer to other sources and a long transitional period is not necessary.

5.   The Commission Proposals of November 2011

50   The Commission proposal of November 2011 further addresses the overreliance on ratings and problems related to "so-called" sovereign ratings, i.e. ratings of a state, a regional or local authority of a state or of a debt instrument of one of these issuers.[104] It identifies overreliance—or "mechanistical" reliance—by certain financial institutions as a substantial problem and therefore prescribes that these institutions must make their own assessment of the "creditworthiness of an entity or financial instrument".[105] European supervisory authorities are not to refer to ratings in their

---

[96] Art. 15(4) Rating Regulation.
[97] Art. 16(1), (2) Rating Regulation.
[98] Art. 16(3), (4) Rating Regulation.
[99] Art. 18(3) Rating Regulation.
[100] Art. 20(1)(a)–(c) and Art. 24(1)(a) Rating Regulation.
[101] Art. 20(2) Rating Regulation.
[102] Art. 20(3), 24(4)(a), (b) Rating Regulation.
[103] Commission Proposal for a Rating Regulation, COM(2008) 704 final, p. 3.
[104] COM(2011) 746 and 747 final.
[105] Art. 5a COM(2011) 747 final.

"guidelines, recommendations and technical standards where such references have the potential to trigger mechanistic reliance".[106]

51   Sovereign ratings have been and still are at the heart of the recent debt crisis throughout Europe. The proposal states that "insufficient objectiveness, completeness and transparency on the sovereign rating process" can lead to "cliff and contagion effects of sovereign rating changes".[107] It does not, however, prohibit sovereign ratings, rather stipulating enhanced disclosure requirements: underlying information would have to be verified, the full rating report published and sovereign ratings would have to be reassessed every six instead of twelve months.[108]

V.   Supervision

1.   Foundations

52   It was not until the outset of the financial crisis that the European legislature replaced the IOSCO Codes' self-regulatory approach with state supervision of rating agencies. The competent national authorities are now responsible for supervising that the credit institutions only make use of ratings by registered agencies for regulatory purposes,[109] whilst the ESMA is responsible for all other aspects of the supervision of rating agencies—granting it more general and extensive powers than in most other areas of capital markets law.[110]

53   The ESMA is, however, not permitted to influence the content of a rating.[111] Measures taken by the ESMA may be addressed to rating agencies, any persons involved in rating activities, third parties to whom the credit rating agencies have outsourced certain functions or activities, the rated issuers and any third parties related to them, or any person related or connected to credit rating agencies or credit rating activities. The ESMA may require any of these persons to provide all information necessary in order for the authority to carry out its duties.[112] Officials and other persons authorised by the ESMA are further empowered to (a) examine any records, data, procedures and any other material relevant to the execution of their tasks; (b) take or obtain certified copies of or extracts from such records, data, procedures and other material; (c) request oral or written explanations on facts or documents related to the subject matter and purpose of the inspection; (d) interview any other natural or legal person; (e) request records of telephone and data traffic.[113]

54   The ESMA is also permitted to conduct all necessary onsite inspections on the business premises.[114] The individuals conducting the inspections act on the basis of a

---

[106] Art. 5b COM(2011) 747 final.
[107] COM(2011) 747 final, p. 4.
[108] For details: COM(2011) 747 final, p. 10.
[109] Art. 25a(1) Rating Regulation.
[110] This "trial run" is seen positively by G. Deipenbrock, RIW (2010), p. 612, 618.
[111] Art. 23 Rating Regulation.
[112] Art. 23b(1) Rating Regulation.
[113] Art. 23c(1) Rating Regulation.
[114] Art. 23d(1) Rating Regulation.

special power of attorney issued by the ESMA after notifying the competent national authority of the affected Member State.[115] The ESMA may impose penalties in order to compel a person to submit to an onsite inspection.[116]

2. Procedure

55   The supervisory measures laid down in the Rating Regulation are subject to detailed procedural rules which also require the ESMA's Board of Supervisors to give the persons subject to the proceedings the opportunity to be heard.[117]

56   If the ESMA finds that there are serious indications of the possible existence of facts liable to constitute an infringement of the Rating Regulation it is obliged to appoint an independent investigating officer.[118] The investigating officer must then investigate the alleged infringements and submit a complete file with his findings to the ESMA's Board of Supervisors,[119] notifying the persons subject to investigation of this fact.[120]

57   The Board of Supervisors must then determine whether the respective person actually committed an infringement of the provisions of the Rating Regulation on the basis of the information submitted by the investigating officer. Should this be the case the Board of Supervisors will impose a supervisory measure.[121] The wording of Article 24(1) Rating Regulation indicates that the Board of Supervisors is not permitted to abstain from imposing a supervisory measure. It is rather obliged to impose at least one of the measures listed and is also permitted to take more than one decision.[122] If the rating agency has breached one of the regulation's provisions intentionally or negligently, the Board of Supervisors will impose a fine.[123] This decision is also not at the discretion of the authority but rather the inevitable consequence of an infringement.

VI.   Measures and Sanctions

1.   Administrative Instruments

58   The amendments to the Rating Regulation in June 2011 entail that the ESMA, and no longer the national supervisory authorities, is now responsible for imposing administrative measures and sanctions. Appendix III Rating Regulation takes account of the constitutional principle common in some Member States that prohibits provisions interfering with fundamental rights from being formulated vaguely. These amendments explicitly list certain obligations, the infringement of which allows the ESMA to impose certain administrative measures and fines. The list distinguishes

---

[115] Art. 23c(2), (4) Rating Regulation.
[116] Art. 36b Rating Regulation.
[117] Art. 25 Rating Regulation.
[118] Art. 23e(1) Rating Regulation.
[119] Art. 23e(2) Rating Regulation.
[120] Art. 23e(4) Rating Regulation.
[121] Art. 23e(5) Rating Regulation.
[122] Art. 24(1) Rating Regulation.
[123] Art. 36a(1) Rating Regulation.

between 54 different infringements related to conflicts of interest, organisational or operational requirements, 8 infringements related to obstacles to the supervisory activities and 11 infringements related to disclosure provisions.

59   If the ESMA finds that a rating agency has committed an infringement of an obligation listed in Annex III, it can take one or more of the following decisions:

(a) withdraw the registration of the credit rating agency;

(b) temporarily prohibit the credit rating agency from issuing credit ratings with effect throughout the European Union, until the infringement has been brought to an end;

(c) suspend the use for regulatory purposes of the credit ratings issued by the credit rating agency with effect throughout the Union, until the infringement has been brought to an end;

(d) require the credit rating agency to bring the infringement to an end;

(e) issue public notices.[124]

60   Pursuant to Article 36a Rating Regulation the ESMA may further impose a maximum fine of of €750,000 for infringements of the obligations listed in Annex III. The fines must be proportionate to the seriousness of the infringement. The fines are divided into different categories with specific limits applying to each category. The ESMA applies a two-stage procedure in order to determine the height of a fine, firstly determining a basic amount at which the fine should be set before adapting this with the help of certain aggravating or mitigating factors. The basic amount is determined on the basis of the annual turnover in the preceding business year.

2.   Criminal Measures

61   The Rating Regulation does not contain any criminal law measures for breaches of the regulation's provisions. The Member States may therefore decide independently whether they want to provide criminal sanctions. The prosecution of these crimes is then a matter for the respective Member State, the ESMA not having any powers in this respect.[125]

3.   Civil Law Liability

62   The Rating Regulation further does not contain any rules on a possible civil law liability for rating agencies towards issuers or investors. Whether investors can claim damages thus depends on the national law of the respective Member State.[126] This is similar to the rules of conduct contained in the framework directives. As opposed to this, the Commission's Consultation Paper of November 2010 examined the question whether a specific provision on the civil liability of credit rating agencies should be introduced at a European level.[127]

---

[124] Art. 24(1)(a)–(e) Rating Regulation.
[125] Art. 23e(8) Rating Regulation.
[126] Recital 69 Rating Regulation.
[127] Public Consultation on Credit Rating Agencies of 5 November 2010, p. 24.

(a) Legal Situation in the Member States

63 The civil liability of credit rating agencies is not discussed in depth in the Member States. Jurisprudence on damage claims by investors hardly exists.[128] In Germany, a distinction is made between solicited and unsolicited ratings. If a contract exists (solicited rating), breaches of the supervisory provisions are likely also to constitute a breach of contractual obligations entitling the issuer to damages under § 280 BGB. Unsolicited ratings can only lead to damage claims under tort law, primarily on the basis of § 824 BGB. A right of prohibition may be claimed pursuant to § 1004 BGB.[129]

64 Civil law investor protection for incorrect ratings continues to be a subject of controversy in Germany. As yet no undisputed approach has been found. There is, however, a consensus that investors may claim damages on the basis of § 826 BGB for damages caused intentionally and contrary to public policy. If the issuer solicited the rating, it may further be entitled to contractual damages.[130] A further suggestion is to apply the underlying concept of damages for breaches of trust as can be found in §§ 37b, 37c WpHG (German Securities Trading Act), § 21 WpPG (German Securities Prospectus) and § 12 WpÜG (Securities Acquisition and Takeover Act) analogously, giving the investor damage claims if a rating agency published an incorrect rating.[131]

65 The enactment of the Rating Regulation has additionally sparked discussion as to whether the European rules of conduct can be classed as protective provisions in the sense of § 823(2) BGB. This understanding is confirmed by the fact that the Rating Regulation explicitly aims at achieving investor protection.[132,133] At the same time, this general aim does not exonerate the European legislature from making the aims of the provision clear for each rule of conduct individually. Especially the organisational obligations do not appear to have been enacted in order to protect the investors' financial interests, whilst the rules aiming to improve the quality of a rating[134] and the provisions on the publication and presentation of a rating[135] do not appear to have any other aim. The ensuing problems regarding the damages that may be claimed have not yet been solved.[136]

---

[128] A ruling of the OLG Frankfurt (BB 2012, p. 215) on an investor claim against a foreign credit rating agency is pending.

[129] See KG, WM 2006, p. 1432.

[130] § 280 BGB in conjunction with the German principle of a contract with protective effect to the benefit of a third party. See O. von Schweinitz, WM (2008), p. 953, 956; dissenting: B. Haar, NZG (2010), p. 1281, 1283; M. Habersack, 169 ZHR (2005), p. 185, 205–206.

[131] C.H. Seibt, in: G. Bachmann et al. (eds.), *Steuerungsfunktionen des Haftungsrechts*, p. 191, 206 restricting the legitimate expectations resulting from rating reports to the cardinal obligations such as expertise, objectiveness, neutrality and independence.

[132] Cf. Art. 1 Rating Regulation.

[133] Seen sceptically due to the supervisory nature of the Rating Regulation by B. Haar, NZG (2010), p. 1281, 1285.

[134] See above para. 38 ff.

[135] See above para. 43 ff.

[136] U. Blaurock, ZGR (2007), p. 603, 635–636.

Rüdiger Veil/Lars Teigelack

(b) Proposal for a European Civil Liability

66 The Commission proposal of November 2011 contains a civil liability framework based on the reasoning that ratings can have a substantial effect on investment decisions. Agencies can be held liable by individual investors for intentional or grossly negligent breaches of the obligations contained in the Rating Regulation. The investor can only recover losses suffered from reliance on the rating if these losses are caused by the infringement and if the infringement has affected the rating. The burden of proof is partially reversed. The investor must make a reasonable case for an infringement, thus forcing the agency to prove that there either was no infringement or that the infringement did not affect the rating. The actual damage and the causality of the infringement for the damage remain for the investor to prove.[137] The Commission's Proposal does not, however, examine other aspects of liability, such as the liability towards the issuer in cases of a solicited rating.

VII. Conclusion

67 For the first time rating agencies are now subject to a uniform and comprehensive regulation. The regulatory process is, however, still ongoing, the next step being the Council's decision on the Commission's proposal of November 2011. The existing rules are particularly noticeable due to their approach of developing a uniform supervisory and sanctioning system, contrary to almost all other areas of capital markets law in Europe. Whether the current framework ultimately proves to be ideal remains to be seen. Further emphasis must be placed on the fact that the Commission proposal has lifted the unsolved problem of investor protection through civil liability to the European level. It is now necessary to discuss whether a European system of liability is really necessary, what standard of liability should be required and whether unsolicited ratings should also be subject to these provisions.

---

[137] On the liability framework cf. Recitals 24–28 and the new Article 35a in COM(2011) 747 final.

6

Compliance in Investment Firms

§ 28   Foundations

Bibliography

Bazley, Stuart and Haynes, Andrew, *Financial Services Authority and Risk-based Compliance*, 2nd ed. (2009); Buff, Herbert G., *Compliance: Führungsrolle durch den Verwaltungsrat* (2000); Casper, Matthias, *Rechtliche Grundlagen und aktuelle Entwicklungen der Compliance am Beispiel des Kapitalmarktrechts*, in: Hadding, Walther et al. (eds.), *Verbraucherschutz im Kreditgeschäft, Compliance in der Kreditwirtschaft, Bankrechtstag 2008*, p. 139–177; Dreher, Meinrad, *Ausstrahlungen des Aufsichtsrechts auf das Aktienrecht*, ZGR (2010), p. 496–542; Edwards, Jonathan and Wolfe, Simon, *The Compliance Function in Banks*, 12 J. Fin. Reg. & Comp. (2004), p. 216–224; Eisele, Dieter, *Insiderrecht und Compliance*, WM (1993), p. 1021–1026; Kalss, Susanne, *Amtshaftung und Compliance als Instrumente zur Durchsetzung kapitalmarktrechtlicher Regelungen—Diskutiert am Beispiel Österreich*, in: Möllers, Thomas M.J., *Vielfalt und Einheit: wirtschaftliche und rechtliche Rahmenbedingungen von Standardbildung* (2008), p. 81–105; Klein, Peter, *Anwendbarkeit und Umsetzung von Risikomanagementsystemen auf Compliance-Risiken im Unternehmen* (2008); Küting, Karlheinz and Busch, Julia, *Zum Wirrwarr der Überwachungsbegriffe*, DB (2009), p. 1361–1367; Lösler, Thomas, *Compliance im Wertpapierdienstleistungskonzern* (2003); Lucius, Otto et al. (eds.), *Compliance im Finanzdienstleistungsbereich* (2010); Marekfia, Wolfgang and Nissen, Volker, *Strategisches GRC-Management*, in: Nissen, Volker, *Forschungsberichte zur Unternehmensberatung*, Working Paper (2009); Menzies, Christof, *Sarbanes–Oxley und Corporate Compliance* (2006); Mills, Annie, *Essential Strategies for Financial Services Compliance* (2008); Morton, Jeffrey C., *The Development of a Compliance Culture*, 6 J. Invest. Comp. (2005), p. 59–66; Racz, Nicolas, Weippl, Edgar and Seufert, Andreas, *A Frame of Reference for Research of Integrated Governance, Risk & Compliance (GRC)*, in: Decker, Bart De, Schaumüller-Bichl, Ingrid (eds.), *Communications and Multimedia Security*, p. 106–117, available at: http://grc-resource.com/resources/racz_al_frame_reference_grc_cms2010.pdf; Schneider, Uwe H., *Compliance als Aufgabe der Unternehmensleitung*, ZIP (2003), p. 645–650; Securities Industry Association, *The Role of Compliance*, 6 J. Invest. Comp. (2005), p. 4–22; Spindler, Gerald, *Compliance in der multinationalen Bankengruppe*, WM (2008), p. 905–918; Taylor, Chris, *The evolution of compliance*, 6 J. Invest. Comp. (2005), p. 54–58; Walker, Rebecca, *International corporate compliance programmes*, 3 Int'l J. Discl. & Gov. (2006), p. 70–81; Weiss, Ulrich, *Compliance-Funktion in einer deutschen Universalbank*, Die Bank (1993), p. 136–139; Wild, Robert J., *Designing an Effective Securities Compliance Program, Corporate Compliance Series*, Volume 10, Looseleaf (2010–2011).

I. Compliance

1   "Compliance" is one of today's most controversially discussed legal concepts,[1] and a uniform understanding of the term has not yet been achieved.[2] Based on the general meaning of the word, compliance (to comply with) means conforming to a rule.[3] It has, however, been acknowledged by legal practitioners and academics alike that the concept reaches farther than merely describing the obligation to act in accordance with the law, also encompassing the organisational provisions, policies and procedures that aim to prevent or expose breaches of law.[4] Elements of this so-called compliance organisation include, inter alia: (i) internal compliance policies that contain basic principles to be followed by management and staff; (ii) Chinese walls which regulate the flow of confidential information within a company; (iii) whistleblowing and reporting systems for exposing and reporting violations of law; (iv) compliance-training programmes; and (v) compliance-monitoring and surveillance systems that monitor whether the laws and the internal rules of the company are applied correctly.[5] In addition to this functional meaning of compliance, the concept is also used in an organisational sense, describing an independent department of a company's organisation, responsible for any compliance-related tasks.[6] This "compliance department" thus fulfils executive functions within the compliance organisation.[7]

II. Relationship between Compliance and Risk Management

2   The relationship between compliance and the other internal control functions of a company, such as risk management, has not yet been fully examined. At first, the distinction appears straightforward: while compliance aims to ensure conformity with legal requirements, risk management systematically identifies, assesses, monitors, controls and mitigates material risks that are likely to affect the company. Both areas, however, overlap to the extent that the risk of non-compliance with legal requirements always also constitutes an operational risk that is covered by risk management. Compliance must therefore be regarded as an element of qualitative risk

---

[1] Cf. S. Kalss, in: T.M.J. Möllers (ed.), *Vielfalt und Einheit*, p. 81, 98 (one of the most important terms of company law).

[2] Countless attempts have been made to define the term. For an overview of the approaches taken in Anglo-American and Continental-European law see A. Mills, *Financial Services Compliance*, p. 16–18; H.G. Buff, *Compliance: Führungsrolle durch den Verwaltungsrat*, p. 10 ff.

[3] A. Mills, *Financial Services Compliance*, p. 16–18; C. Hauschka, in: C. Hauschka (ed.), *Corporate Compliance*, § 1 para. 2; U.H. Schneider, ZIP (2003), p. 645, 646.

[4] Cf. A. Mills, *Financial Services Compliance*, p. 16–18; R. Walker, 3 Int'l J. Discl. & Gov. (2006), p. 70, 71; M. Casper, in: W. Hadding et al. (eds.), *Bankrechtliche Vereinigung, Bankrechtstag 2008*, p. 139, 141–142.

[5] Cf. R.J. Wild, in: *Corporate Compliance Series*, § 3.1 ff.; D. Eisele, in: H. Schimanski et al. (eds.), *Bankrechts-Handbuch*, § 109 para. 125 ff.; C. Hauschka, in: C. Hauschka (ed.), *Corporate Compliance*, § 1 para. 24 ff.

[6] K. Küting and J. Busch, DB (2009), p. 1361, 1364.

[7] Securities Industry Association, 6 J. Invest. Comp. (2005), p. 4 ff. ("compliance departement"); C. Casper, in: W. Hadding et al. (eds.), *Bankrechtliche Vereinigung, Bankrechtstag 2008*, p. 139, 145. See also G. Spindler, WM (2008), p. 905, 907 (horizontal control bodies in companies). US-American legal literature in particular understands compliance in a very broad sense, which also includes the ethical dimension of business. Compliance is therefore understood as the "moral DNA" of a company. Cf. J. Morton, 6 J. Invest. Comp (2005), p. 59; R. Walker, 3 Int'l J. Discl. & Gov. (2006), p. 70.

Malte Wundenberg

management.[8] Conversely, the fact that the requirements for the organisation of the company's risk management have become subject to supervisory law makes them relevant to the compliance department of the supervised company, which is in turn responsible for ensuring compliance with the risk-management provisions.[9] The relationship between compliance and risk management can therefore be described as follows: compliance constitutes an element of qualitative risk management, which must control and mitigate compliance risks. At the same time, however, compliance also constitutes an indispensable prerequisite for risk management, as the compliance function monitors the effectiveness of the risk management systems and ensures abidance with the regulatory requirements.[10]

3   The close functional and conceptual relationship between both elements of internal control has led to the understanding that compliance and risk management constitute one uniform organisational task for the company: based on the governance, risk and compliance (GRC) model developed in business practice, the areas concerning governance, risk management and compliance are increasingly implemented in the organisation of firms in an integrated way.[11] The supervisory authorities confirm this close connection between compliance and risk management,[12] the latter also termed as "compliance in a broader sense".[13]

III. Developments and Legal Foundations

4   In Anglo-American countries, banks began developing compliance organisations in the 1960s.[14] In continental Europe investment firms have also been setting up compliance programmes for decades.[15] The implementation of compliance pro-

---

[8] Basel Committee on Banking Supervision, *Compliance and the Compliance Function in Banks*, April 2005, Principle 11 (*"core risk management function"*). This coincides with the understanding of numerous national supervisory authorities. Cf. BaFin, *Rundschreiben* (circular) 4/2010 (WA)—*Mindestanforderungen an die Compliance-Funktion und die weiteren Verhaltens-, Organisations- und Transparenzpflichten nach §§ 31 ff. WpHG für Wertpapierdienstleistungsunternehmen (MaComp)*, July 2010, AT 7 para. 2 (Germany); CSSF Circular 04/155, *The Compliance Function*, September 2004, para. 9 (Luxemburg); Board of Governors of the Federal Reserve System, *Compliance Risk Management Programs*, October 2008 (USA); FSA, *Managing Compliance Risk in Major Investment Banks—Good Practices*, July 2007 (UK); Rundschreiben der eidg. Bankenkommission, *Überwachung und interne Kontrolle* (circular), September 2006, para. 100 ff. (Switzerland). The MiFID also follows a risk-orientated approach to compliance, see below § 29 para. 23–26.

[9] M. Dreher, ZGR (2010), p. 496, 537.

[10] Compliance and risk management stand in a symbiotic relationship to one another: an effective risk management is not possible without an effective compliance organisation, whilst compliance at the same time requires a fully operational risk management. Cf. P. Klein, *Risikomanagementsysteme*, p. 102.

[11] Cf. N. Racz et al., *Integrated Governance, Risk & Compliance*, p. 106–117; C. Menzies (ed.), *Corporate Compliance*, p. 63–77; W. Marekfia and V. Nissen, *Strategisches GRC-Management*, p. 9 ff. Technically this can be achieved through standardised IT systems, such as those offered by SAP (business objects GRC solutions).

[12] Cf. Banca d'Italia, *Supervisory Regulations, The Compliance Function*, July 2007, p. 6 (interaction with other corporate functions). See now also ESMA, *Guidelines on Certain Aspects of the MiFID Compliance Function Requirements, Final Report*, ESMA/2012/388, July 2012, general guideline 9, para. 71.

[13] BaFin, *Rundschreiben* (circular) *4/2010 (MaComp)*, June 2011, BT 1.1.1 para. 5. At an organisational level, one must generally draw a distinction between compliance and risk management. See below § 29 para. 38.

[14] On the development of the compliance concept in the USA see Securities Industry Association, 6 J. Invest. Comp. (2005), p. 4 ff.; on the UK see C. Taylor, 6 J. Invest. Comp. (2005), p. 54 ff.

[15] On the origin of compliance in Germany see D. Eisele, WM (1993), p. 1021; U. Weiss, *Die Bank*, p. 136; on the developments in Austria see B. Bauer and K. Muther-Pradler, in: O. Lucius et al. (eds.), *Compliance im Finanzdienstleistungsbereich*, p. 36 ff.

grammes was generally optional and based on self-regulation initiatives, aimed at preventing insider dealings.[16] Only gradually did compliance become affected by the European Union's efforts to harmonise the law. This development began with the legally non-binding Commission Recommendations of 25 July 1977 concerning a European code of conduct relating to transactions in transferrable securities which contained general principles on investment advice, the management of conflicts of interest, and controlling the flow of information in a company.[17] The Investment Services Directive,[18] enacted on 10 May 1993, was the first European legislative act to contain minimum binding organisational requirements for investment firms in order to ensure investor protection. Subsequently, the recommendations and supervisory principles of the Basel Committee on Banking Supervision (hereafter the "Basel Committee") triggered further developments. The ten organisational principles published in the Basel Committee's policy paper *Compliance and the Compliance Function in Banks*,[19] based on Principle 14 of the "Core Principles for Effective Supervision"[20] of September 1997, lay down the most relevant aspects that banks and banking groups must take into account when setting up a compliance organisation.[21] The final version of these principles was enacted in April 2005 and has enlarged the focus of compliance in a crucial way: the Basel Committee does not only regard compliance as essential for preventing insider dealings and reacting to conflicts of interest but also as an element of general legal risk management.[22] Although not legally binding, the recommendations of the Basel Committee have effectively become the primary standards of banking practice and as such have had a decisive influence on European legal developments.[23]

5   Recently the Markets in Financial Instruments Directive (MiFID), 2004/39/EC, has achieved a comprehensive harmonisation of the organisational requirements that have to be taken into account by investment firms. This framework directive, however, only contains general principles, which are put into more concrete terms on the second level of the Lamfalussy Process[24] by Directive 2006/73/EC[25] (denoted "Organisational Requirements Directive" or "implementing directive" hereafter).[26] These legislative acts introduced compliance, risk management and internal audit functions at a European level for the first time. The European provisions reflect a regulatory trend that has also become apparent in other areas of supervisory law: to require the supervised firms to develop comprehensive systems of internal control

---

[16] Cf. Securities Industry Association, 6 J. Invest. Comp. (2005), p 4; T. Lösler, *Compliance im Wertpapierdienstleistungskonzern*, p. 15 ff.

[17] Commission Recommendation No. 77/534/EEC, OJ L212, 20 August 1977, p. 37 ff.

[18] Council Directive 93/22/EEC of 10 May 1993 on investment services in the securities field, OJ L141, 11 June 1993, p. 27 ff. See § 1 para. 13.

[19] Basel Committee on Banking Supervision, *Compliance and the Compliance Function in Banks*, October 2003 (consultation paper) and April 2005 (final).

[20] Equivalent to Principle 17 of the "Core Principles" as of 2006.

[21] For details see J. Edwards and S. Wolfe, 12 J. Fin. Reg. & Comp. (2004), p. 216 ff.

[22] On these legal developments see S. Bazley and A. Haynes, *Risk-based Compliance*, p. 173–174 and T. Fett, in: E. Schwark and D. Zimmer (eds.), *Kapitalmarktrechts-Kommentar*, § 33 WpHG para. 1.

[23] D. Gebauer and S. Niermann, in: C. Hauschka (ed.), *Corporate Compliance*, § 36 para. 5–6.

[24] See § 4 para. 16–21 and 29–35 ff.

[25] Commission Directive 2006/73/EC of 10 August 2006 implementing Directive 2004/39/EC of the European Parliament and of the Council as regards organisational requirements and operating conditions for investment firms and defined terms for the purposes of that Directive, OJ L241, 2 September 2006, p. 26.

[26] The implementing directive was preceded by "technical standards" published by CESR in January 2005.

in order to ensure investor protection and increase the supervisory requirements for the management and control of the firms.[27]

6 Compliance has grown even more important in the course of the financial crisis, during which serious shortcomings regarding internal control systems and governance arrangements became apparent.[28] The reports on the causes of the financial crisis indicate that these deficits and weak points in corporate governance, led to a loss of investor confidence, thus weakening the stability of the financial system. These findings have prompted calls for more stringent supervisory requirements for financial service providers and for an increased significance of compliance and risk management.[29] As a result, the European Securities and Markets Authority (ESMA) has recently published guidelines that aim to increase the effectiveness of the compliance function.[30] The European Commission has also indicated that it intends to place greater importance on the compliance function as an essential element of the internal control system in the future and aims to ensure its independence from senior management.[31] The loss of millions of euros suffered by the Société Général due to the speculative transactions of the trader Jérome Kerviel are a good example of the risks of insufficient internal control structures. Compliance failings and weak corporate governance arrangements have also contributed to the recent manipulation of Libor and Euribor rates.[32]

---

[27] Similar developments took place in insurance supervision, Art. 41 ff. of the Solvency-II Directive (2009/138/EC) list requirements (consisting of risk management, compliance, internal audit and actuarial functions) for governance systems of (re-)insurance companies.
[28] Cf. de Larosière Report, para. 13 ff., 23 ff., 122 ff. and 236; Green Paper of the European Commission on Corporate governance in financial institutions and remuneration policies, COM(2010) 284 final, p. 2.
[29] Green Paper of the European Commission on corporate governance in financial institutions and remuneration policies, COM(2010) 284 final. On risk management see also the declaration of the Summit of Financial Markets and the World Economy of the Group of Twenty meeting of 15 November 2008, para. 2 and 8.
[30] ESMA, *Guidelines on Certain Aspects of the MiFID Compliance Function Requirements, Final Report*, ESMA/2012/388, July 2012, general guideline 9, para. 71.
[31] European Commission, Public Consultation: Review of the Markets in Financial Instruments Directive (MiFiD), December 2010, p. 67–68. The Commission suggests that all three functions, i.e. compliance, risk management and internal audit, should be able to report directly to the board of directors and that the removal of the officers responsible for the internal control functions should be subject to prior approval by the board. This basically ensures the officer's independence from the management. See § 29 para. 50–52. Similar provisions can now be found in the ESMA guidelines.
[32] See § 29 para 84.

§ 29 Organisational Requirements

Bibliography

Abegglen, Sandro, *Wissenszurechnung bei der juristischen Person und im Konzern, bei Banken und Versicherungen* (2004); Alexander, Kern, *Principles v. Rules in Financial Regulation*, 10 EBOR (2009), p. 163–173; Andrés, Anna M., *La regulación de las "murallas chinas": una técnica de prevención de conflictos de interés en el mercado de valores español*, 81 RDBB (2001), p. 49–86; Baglieri, Maria R., *Conflicts of Interest and Duty: A Persistent Threat—The Italian Legislation*, 31 Company Lawyer (2010), p. 186–189; Bauer, Barbara and Muther-Prader, Katharina, *Gesetzliche und aufsichtsrechtliche Anforderungen an Compliance*, in: Lucius, Otto et al. (eds.), *Compliance im Finanzdienstleistungsbereich* (2010), p. 36–66; Bazley, Stuart and Haynes, Andrew, *Financial Services Authority Regulation and Risk-Based Compliance* (2006); Benicke, Christoph, *Wertpapiervermögensverwaltung* (2006); Black, Julia, *Forms and Paradoxes of Principles-Based Regulation*, 3 CMLJ (2008), p. 425–457; Black, Julia, *The Rise, Fall and Fate of Principles Based Regulation* (2010), available at: http://papers.ssrn.com/sol3/papers.cfm?abstract_id=1267722; Biegelman, Martin T., *Building a World-Class Compliance-Program* (2008); Boardman, Nigel and Crosthwait, John, *A Practitioners Guide to FSA Regulation of Investment Banking* (2002); Buck-Heeb, Petra, *Insiderwissen, Interessenkonflikte und Chinese Walls bei Banken*, in: Grundmann, Stefan et al. (eds.), *Festschrift für Klaus J. Hopt*, Vol. I (2010), p. 1647–1670; Buisson, Françoise, *La transposition de la directive européenne Marchés d'Instruments Financiers (MIF) en droit français*, RTDF (2007), p. 6; Casper, Matthias, *Der Compliancebeauftragte*, in: Georg Bitter et al. (eds.), *Festschrift für Karsten Schmidt* (2009), p. 199–216; Coglianese, Cary and Lazer, David, *Management-Based Regulation*, 37 Law & Soc'y Rev. (2003), p. 691–730; Coglianese, Cary and Mendelson, Evan, *Meta-Regulation and Self-Regulation*, in: Baldwin, Robert, Cave, Martin and Lodge, Martin (eds.), *The Oxford Handbook of Regulation* (2010), p. 146–168; Cortés, Luis J., *El mercado de valores (I): organización. La inversión colectiva*, in: Menéndez, Aurelio (ed.), *Lecciones de Derecho Mercantil*, 6th ed. (2008), p. 739; Ford, Cristie L., *New Governance, Compliance, and Principles-Based Securities Regulation*, 45 Am. Bus. Law J. (2008), p. 1–60; Fulconis-Tielens, Adréane, *Responsable conformité, une nouvelle fonction devenue clé*, Revue Banque (November 2008), p. 28; Früh, Andreas, *Legal & Compliance—Abgrenzung oder Annäherung (am Beispiel einer Bank)*, CCZ (2010), p. 121–126; Gabbi, Giampaolo, Tanzi, Paola Musile, Previati, Daniele and Schwizer, Poala, *Managing Compliance Risk after MiFID* (2012), available at: http://papers.ssrn.com/sol3/papers.cfm?abstract_id=2028860; Gallo, Manuela, *The Compliance Function and the Evolution of Internal Structure of Italian Banking Intermediaries*, Studi e Note di Economia (2009), p. 325; Gray, Joanna, *Is it Time to Highlight the Limits of Risk-Based Financial Regulation?*, 4 CMLJ (2009), p. 50–62; Harm, Julian A., *Compliance in Wertpapierdienstleistungsunternehmen und Emittenten von Finanzinstrumenten* (2008); Hollander, Charles and Salzedo, Simon, *Conflicts of Interest & Chinese Walls*, 2nd ed. (2004); Hopt, Klaus J., *Prävention und Repression von Interessenkonflikten*, in: Susanne Kalss et al. (eds.), *Festschrift für Peter Doralt* (2004), p. 213–234; Illing, Diana and Umnuß, Karsten, *Die arbeitsrechtliche Stellung des Compliance Managers—insbesondere Weisungsunterworfenheit und Reportingpflichten*, CCZ (2009), p. 1–8; Jarvis, Kit, *Does the Fiduciary Bell Toll?*, 3 J. Financ. Crime (2007), p. 192–195; Jochnick, Kerstin and Jansson, Per, *MiFID—ettsteg påvägenmot en europeiskvärdepappersmarknad*, ERT (2007), p. 741–757; Jost, Oliver, *Compliance in Banken* (2010); Kittelberger, Ralf, *Einführung einer neuen Berichtspflicht für Wertpapierdienstleistungsunternehmen und deren Folgen* (2005); Kloepfer Pelèse, Martine, *Analyse financière produite et diffusée par un PSI: les précisions apportées par l'AMF. (Sanct. AMF, 1re sect., 8 janv. 2009, Société Euroland finance)*, Bull. Joly Bourse (2009), p. 204–210; Great Britain Law Commission, *Fiduciary Duties and Regulatory Duties (Consultation Paper)* (1992); Lippe, Donovan, *Compliance in Banken und Bankkonzernen* (2011); Lipton, Martin and Mazur, Robert B., *The Chinese Wall Solution of the Conflict Problem of Securities Firms*, 50 NYU L. Rev. (1975), p. 459–511; Lösler, Thomas, *Das mod-*

Malte Wundenberg

erne Verständnis von Compliance im Finanzmarktrecht, NZG (2005), p. 104–108; Lösler, Thomas, *Spannungen zwischen der Effizienz der internen Compliance und möglichen Reporting-Pflichten des Compliance Officers*, WM (2007), p. 676–683; Lösler, Thomas, *Zur Rolle und Stellung des Compliance-Beauftragten*, WM (2008), p. 1098–1104; Lösler, Thomas, *Die Mindestanforderungen an Compliance und die weiteren Verhaltens-, Organisations- und Transparenzpflichten nach §§ 31 et seq. WpHG (MaComp)*, WM (2010), p. 1917–1923; McVea, Harry, *Financial Conglomerates and the Chinese Wall* (1993); Moloney, Niamh, *Financial Services and Markets*, in: Baldwin, Robert et al. (eds.), The Oxford Handbook of Regulation (2010), p. 437–461; Mwenda, Kenneth K., *Banking Supervision and Systemic Bank Restructuring* (2000); Nelson, Paul, *Capital markets law and compliance* (2008); Newton, Andrew, *The Handbook of Compliance* (1998); Niermann, Stephan, *Die Compliance-Organisation im Zeitalter der MaComp*, ZBB (2010), p. 400–427; Oelkers, Janine, *Compliance in Banken*, in: Lucius, Otto et al. (eds.), *Compliance im Finanzdienstleistungsbereich*, p. 36–66; Poser, Norman, *Chinese Wall or Emperor's New Clothes? Regulating Conflicts of Interest of Securities Firms in the US and the UK*, 9 Mich. YBI Legal Stud. (1988), p. 91–103; Renz, Hartmut and Stahlke, Karsten, *Wird die Watch-List bei Kreditinstituten durch das Insiderverzeichnis abgelöst?*, ZfgK (2006), p. 353–355; Rodewald, Jörg and Unger, Ulrike, *Kommunikation und Krisenmanagement im Gefüge der Corporate Compliance-Organisation*, BB (2007), p. 1629–1635; Röh, Lars, *Compliance nach der MiFID—zwischen höherer Effizienz und mehr Bürokratie*, BB (2008), p. 398–410; Rönnau, Thomas and Schneider, Frédéric, *Der Compliance-Beauftragte als strafrechtlicher Garant*, ZIP (2010), p. 53–61; Sandmann, Daniel, *Der Compliance-Bericht im Wertpapierdienstleistungsunternehmen*, CCZ (2008), p. 104–107; Scharpf, Marcus A., *Corporate Governance Compliance und Chinese Walls* (2000); Schlicht, Manuela, *Compliance nach Umsetzung der MiFID-Richtlinie*, BKR (2006), p. 469–475; SDA Bocconi, *The Evolution of Compliance Function and Compliance Risk in Investement Services* (June 2009), available at: http://papers.ssrn.com/sol3/papers.cfm?abstract_id=1446759; Skinner, Chris, *The Future of Investing* (2007); Spindler, Gerald, *Compliance in der multinationalen Bankengruppe*, WM (2008), p. 905–918; Taylor, Chris, *The Evolution of Compliance*, 6 J. Invest. Comp. (2005), p. 54–58; Veil, Rüdiger, *Compliance-Organisation in Wertpapierdienstleistungsunternehmen im Zeitalter der MiFID*, WM (2008), p. 1093–1098; Walsh, John H., *Right the First Time: Regulation, Quality, and Preventive Compliance in the Securities Industry*, Colum. Bus. L. Rev. (1997), p. 165–240; Wolf, Stefan, *Der Wandel der spanischen Finanzmärkte durch neue europarechtliche Entwicklungen* (2008); Wundenberg, Malte, *Compliance und die prinzipiengeleitete Aufsicht über Bankengruppen* (2012). Cf. further the bibliography in § 28.

I. Regulatory Concepts in European Law

1. Overview

1   The MiFID requires Member States to ensure that investment firms comply with the fundamental organisational requirements set out in Article 13[1] MiFID.[2] The European provisions are, however, drafted in a rather abstract fashion: Article 13(2), for example, merely requires investment firms to "establish adequate policies

---

[1] Art. 13 corresponds with Art. 16 of the proposal for a Directive on markets in financial instruments repealing Directive 2004/39/EC of the European Parliament and of the Council, COM(2011) 656 final (published 20 October 2011). The regulatory provisions concerning compliance have yet not been subject to (significant) reforms.

[2] The MiFID defines the term "investment firm" as any legal person—and under certain conditions undertakings which are not legal persons—whose regular occupation or business is the provision of one or more investment services to third parties and/or the performance of one or more investment activities on a professional basis; cf. Art. 4(1) No. 1 MiFID.

and procedures sufficient to ensure compliance of the firm including its managers, employees and tied agents with its obligations under the provisions of this Directive as well as appropriate rules governing personal transactions by such persons". Article 13(3) proves to be equally vague, demanding that investment firms maintain and operate effective organisational and administrative arrangements with a view to taking all reasonable steps designed to prevent conflicts of interest as defined in Article 18 from adversely affecting the interests of its clients.

2   The organisational requirements to be met by investment firms are more concretely defined in Articles 5 ff. of the Organisational Requirements Directive,[3] which was enacted as an implementing directive to the MiFID. The implementing directive puts the general organisational principles of the MiFID into more concrete terms as follows: Article 5 defines the term "general organisational requirements". Articles 6–8 set forth the requirements regarding internal control structures, Article 6 referring to compliance, Article 7 dealing with risk management and Article 8 pertaining to internal audit. All three of these organisational provisions must be seen in connection with the requirements regarding a conflict of interest management as laid down in Articles 21 ff. According to these provisions, Member States must, for example, ensure that the respective investment firms "establish, implement and maintain an effective conflicts of interest policy set out in writing and appropriate to the size and organisation of the firm and the nature, scale and complexity of its business".[4] This section will place particular emphasis on the examination of the organisational requirements for compliance in investment firms, as described in Article 13(2) MiFID in conjunction with Article 6 of the Organisational Requirements Directive.

3   The regulatory provisions regarding the compliance function have recently been more clearly defined in detailed guidelines published by the ESMA.[5] The purpose of these guidelines (issued under Article 16 ESMA regulations) is to promote greater convergence in the interpretation of the European compliance requirements by both market participants and national supervisory authorities. Even though the guidelines published by the ESMA are technically not binding, it is likely that market participants and supervisory authorities will follow the Authority's interpretation and the guidelines will therefore be of great importance for legal practice.[6]

2. Principles-based Approach to Regulation

4   The requirements contained in the MiFID and the Organisational Requirements Directive are based on very vague legal criteria, as is typical of an approach to regulation that is commonly described as *principles-based regulation* in Anglo-American

[3] Commission Directive 2006/73/EC of 10 August 2006 implementing Directive 2004/39/EC of the European Parliament and of the Council as regards organisational requirements and operating conditions for investment firms and defined terms for the purposes of that Directive, OJ L241, 2 September 2006, p. 26.
[4] Art. 22(1) Organisational Requirements Directive.
[5] ESMA, *Guidelines on Certain Aspects of the MiFID Compliance Function Requirements, Final Report*, ESMA/2012/388, July 2012.
[6] See for details § 11 para. 64–65.

law.[7] While this concept has its origins in the United Kingdom's capital markets law,[8] elements of principles-based regulation can also be found in EU law. According to the European Commission, the reliance on "clear principles" constitutes one of the main political considerations that guided the drafting of the Organisational Requirements Directive.[9] This approach to regulation can be described as follows:

5   "The Level 1 Directive and its implementing directive introduce a modern and comprehensive regime governing organisational and operating requirements for investment firms. The implementing directive covers all facets of an investment firm's organisation and introduces a high level of investor protection in the areas concerned with the relationship between investment firms and their clients. It has relied mainly on a *principles-based approach establishing clear standards and objectives that investment firms need to attain rather than prescribing specific and detailed rules.* The advantage of this approach is that it provides the flexibility needed when regulating a diverse universe of entities and activities while also imposing a significant degree of responsibility on all the actors concerned."[10]

6   The principles-based approach to regulation taken by the European Commission has two main characteristics. Firstly, the regulation is primarily based on high-level regulatory *objectives*[11] that are formulated in a very general way, and do not provide any detailed and prescriptive rules. The second characteristic is visible in the flexibility inherent in the regulation such that the regulatory objectives can be achieved by investment firms through the means they consider most appropriate regarding the size and the nature of their business, provided a sufficient level of investor protection is achieved.[12]

7   The Commission's regulatory approach has two aims. The regulatory regime is supposed to be flexible enough to take into account the wide variety of investment firms with regard to their size, structure and the nature of their business.[13] Regulatory solutions following a "one-size-fits-all" approach are deemed inadequate for catering to different needs resulting from a heterogeneous corporate landscape. The Organisational Requirements Directive has therefore incorporated the principle of proportionality in a number of clauses in order to allow an adaptation of the organisational requirements to the nature of the individual company.[14] Furthermore, the focus on the regulatory outcomes is to ensure a high level of investor protection.

---

[7] See on this in the context of the MiFID C. Skinner, *The Future of Investing*, p. 85; N. Moloney, *EC Securities Regulation*, p. 372 ff., 470–471, 507–508 and passim; N. Moloney, in: R. Baldwin et al., *Oxford Handbook of Regulation*, p. 437, 447–449. In general on principles-based regulation see § 4 para. 51–61 and in detail M. Wundenberg, *Compliance und die prinzipiengeleitete Aufsicht über Bankengruppen*, p. 34–116 (examining the characteristics of principles-based regulation and the theoretical distinction between rules and principles in banking supervisory law).

[8] See R. Veil and M. Wundenberg, *Englisches Kapitalmarktrecht*, p. 9–13.

[9] Cf. Commission, *Working Document ESC/18/2005 (Explanatory Note)* (May 2005).

[10] Commission, *Background Note Draft Commission Directive implementing Directive 2004/39/EC (Background Note)*, sec. 2.1. (emphasis added).

[11] Cf. ibid.; Commission, *Working document ESC/18/2005 (Explanatory Note)* (May 2005), No. 3.1 ("*general compliance objectives*", "*regulatory objectives*").

[12] Cf. Commission, *Working document ESC/18/2005 (Explanatory Note)* (May 2005), No. 3.1: "Our decision reflects our view that, where possible and where it does not compromise investor protection, regulation should be sufficiently flexible to allow the investment firms to achieve the regulatory objectives through the means they consider most appropriate to their size and structure and the nature of their business."

[13] Recital 11 Organisational Requirements Directive. See also R. Veil, WM (2008), p. 1093, 1095.

[14] Art. 6(1) subsec. 2 and (3) subsec. 2 (Compliance); Art. 7(2) (Risk management); Art. 8 (Internal audit)

8   The principles-based approach becomes visible both at the level of rule-making and the level of rule enforcement.[15] On the level of *rule-making* the principles-based approach is characterised by a regulatory regime that relies mainly on outcome-based standards with a high level of generality. As opposed to detailed and prescriptive behavioural-based rules, principles generally focus on the regulatory aim and only vaguely outline the behavioural and organisational requirements necessary to achieve this aim. The provisions on compliance management of investment firms examined in this chapter can be seen as a typical example of principles-based rule-making, being drafted as qualitative regulatory objectives, complemented by a general organisational requirement: Article 13(2) MiFID, for example, requires that investment firms establish "adequate policies and procedures" (organisational requirement) sufficient to ensure compliance of the firm, including its managers, employees and tied agents, with its obligations under the provisions of this Directive as well as appropriate rules governing personal transactions by such persons (regulatory objective). The regulatory objectives are put in more concrete terms by the supervisory authorities in cooperation with market participants, enabling a continual adaptation of the organisational principles to the latest market developments. On the level of *rule enforcement* principles-based regulation can thus be seen as a regulatory regime in which the market rules are not unilaterally dictated by the legislator but are developed step-by-step in cooperation with supervisory authorities and market participants.[16]

9   According to the Commission, the principles-based approach to regulation has a considerable impact on the responsibilities of national supervisory authorities as well as investment firms: it imposes the responsibility on the investment firm and its senior management to monitor the firm's own activities and to determine whether these comply with the principles set out in the MiFID and the implementing directive. The national supervisory authorities will need to acquire the operational expertise required in order to guide the industry and to enforce the new provisions effectively.[17] The Commission therefore expects the national supervisory authorities to issue guidance pertaining to the applicability and interpretation of the general organisational requirements, thus mitigating any legal uncertainty associated with the principles-based approach.[18]

10   Most Member States have responded to the Commission's request. In Germany the Bundesanstalt für Finanzdienstleistungsaufsicht (BaFin, German Federal Financial Supervisor) published a Circular on the "Minimum Requirements

Organisational Requirements Directive. The importance of the principle of proportionality has been stressed by ESMA, *Guidelines on Certain Aspects of the MiFID Compliance Function Requirements, Final Report*, ESMA/2012/388, July 2012, para. 12.

[15] For more details on the characteristics of principles-based regulation and the theoretical distinction between rules and principles in banking supervisory law see M. Wundenberg, *Compliance und die prinzipiengeleitete Aufsicht über Bankengruppen*, p. 35–116.

[16] Cf. J. Black, 3 CMLJ (2008), p. 425, 434 ff.; C.L. Ford, 45 Am. Bus. Law J. (2008), p. 1 ff. (principles-based regulation as a form of new governance); M. Wundenberg, *Compliance und die prinzipiengeleitete Aufsicht über Bankengruppen*, p. 34–72. See below para. 9–10 and 17.

[17] Cf. Commission, *Background Note*, sec. 2.1.

[18] Recital 12 Organisational Requirements Directive.

for the Compliance Function and Additional Requirements Governing Rules of Conduct, Organisation and Transparency pursuant to Section 31 et seq. of Securities Trading Act (WpHG) for Investment Services Enterprises (MaComp)" on 7 June 2010, after extensive consultations with representatives of investment practice. The MaComp puts the directive's compliance requirements for investment firms into more concrete terms.[19] The French supervisory authority (Autorité des Marchés Financiers (AMF)) has also published instructions (no. 2008–01 of 8 February 2008), rendering the compliance obligations more precise.[20] In Italy the Banca d'Italia has laid down its expectations towards the construction of a compliance organisation in a Disposizioni di Vigilanza (supervisory regulation).[21] The Austrian approach to specifying the principles is especially noteworthy: the Standard Compliance Code published by the Austrian credit industry plays an important role and has even been described as a "dominant commercial practice" on the homepage of the Austrian supervisory authority (FMA). The guidelines are available on the FMA's website and are also applied to the FMA's "on-site inspection" audits.[22] The FMA has further made public a circular on the organisational requirements of compliance, risk management and internal audit, which defines the provisions of the WAG 2007 (Austrian Securities Supervision Act) more concretely.[23] In the United Kingdom the Financial Services Authority (FSA) deliberately abstained from publishing comprehensive guidance on compliance requirements,[24] and only offers "good practices" on the management of compliance risks in large investment firms.[25] Interpretational guidelines have also been published by the supervisory authorities in Luxembourg,[26] Switzerland[27] and Spain.[28] As noted above, the ESMA has recently published "Guidelines on Certain Aspects of the MiFID Compliance Function Requirements", which aim to clarify the application of the MiFID compliance requirements and to promote greater convergence in the interpretation of these rules.[29]

11   In legal literature, the principles-based approach to regulation has proved controversial. A disadvantage of this approach is the fact that it leads to increased legal uncertainty and unpredictability for market participants. Principles-based regulation further places high demands on the competent national authorities which must supervise the investment firms and ensure abidance with the principles. The experience gained during the financial crisis has further raised doubts regarding the effectiveness of this regulatory approach.[30] The ensuing discussion on the merits

---

[19] BaFin, *Rundschreiben* (circular) *4/2010* (WA), June 2011.

[20] Available at: www.amf-france.org/documents/general/8199_1.pdf.

[21] Banca d'Italia, *The Compliance Function*, July 2007.

[22] B. Bauer and K. Muther-Prader, *Gesetzliche und aufsichtsrechtliche Anforderungen an Compliance*, in: O. Lucius et al. (eds.), *Compliance im Finanzdienstleistungsbereich*, p. 38.

[23] FMA, *Rundschreiben* (circular) *betreffend die organisatorischen Anforderungen des Wertpapieraufsichtsgesetzes 2007 im Hinblick auf Compliance, Risikomanagement und interne Revision*.

[24] Cf. FSA, *PS 06/13: Organisational Systems and Controls*, November 2006, para. 1.9. and 1.10.

[25] FSA, *Managing Compliance Risk in Major Investment Banks—Good Practices*, July 2007.

[26] CSSF, *Circular 04/155, The Compliance Function*, September 2004.

[27] Eidg. Bankenkommission, *Rundschreiben* (circular) *06/6, Überwachung und interne Kontrolle*, September 2007.

[28] CNMV, *Iniciativa contra abuso de mercado*, January 2007.

[29] ESMA, *Guidelines on Certain Aspects of the MiFID Compliance Function Requirements, Final Report*, ESMA/2012/388, July 2012, para. 12.

[30] Seen critically by J. Gray, 4 CMLJ (2009), p. 50 ff.; K. Alexander, 10 EBOR (2009), p. 163 ff. See also J. Black, *The Rise, Fall and Fate of Principles Based Regulation* (2010).

and the perils of principles-based regulation has shown that an effective enforcement of the principles can only be ensured if the principles are accompanied by adequate sanctioning powers for the supervisory authorities. Neither the MiFID nor its implementing directive, however, contains provisions in this regard. An effective supervision cannot therefore be guaranteed, especially in Member States with no experience with the principles-based approach to regulation.[31] The Commission's request for national interpretational guidelines for the directives' general principles must also be seen critically, as it increases the risk of different national approaches to interpretation and legal fragmentation.[32] Against this backdrop, the recent attempts made by the ESMA to promote greater convergence in the interpretation of the organisational principles laid down in the MiFID as well as the supervisions of these principles by the competent national authorities must be welcomed.[33]

3. Regulatory Aim

12 The compliance obligations laid down in Article 13(2) MiFID in conjunction with Article 6 Organisational Requirements Directive have two regulatory aims. On the one hand they aim to protect investment firms from potential civil and administrative sanctions as well as reputational damages that result from a violation of MiFID rules. On the other hand the compliance obligations also aim to ensure investor protection and the efficient functioning of the capital markets:[34] the compliance requirements are supposed to ensure that the rules designed to protect investors are effectively applied and do not remain "law in the books".[35] By harmonising the behavioural and organisational requirements in the European Union, illegal practices are supposed to be prevented, thereby increasing investor confidence and market efficiency.[36] Both regulatory aims (protection of the investment firm and investor protection) must be kept in mind when interpreting the directives' provisions.[37]

13 Regulating and supervising the internal organisation of investment firms is a typical characteristic of the regulatory concept described as *"management-based-regulation"* (sometimes also referred to as a form of *"meta-based regulation"*) in Anglo-American law.[38] It typically combines internal control mechanisms with instruments of public supervision. The investment firms are required to organise

---

[31] As pointed out by N. Moloney, *EC Securities Regulation*, p. 374.

[32] Cf. N. Moloney, *EC Securities Regulation*, p. 374.

[33] ESMA, *Guidelines on Certain Aspects of the MiFID Compliance Function Requirements, Final Report*, ESMA/2012/388, July 2012. See also ESMA, *Guidelines on Certain Aspects of the MiFID Suitability Requirements, final Report*, ESMA/2012/387, July 2012.

[34] Improving investor protection is one of the MiFID's key aims. See Recitals 2, 31, 44 and 71 Directive 2004/39/EC and Recital 5 Organisational Requirements Directive. Cf. Commission, *Working Document ESC/18/2005 (Explanatory Note)*, No. 3.

[35] Securities and Markets Stakeholder Group, *Advice on Guidelines on Certain Aspects of the MiFID Compliance Function Requirements*, February 2012, p. 1. See also FSA, *CP 06/9: Organisational Systems and Controls*, May 2006, para. 1.1: "Confidence in the … financial markets depends on firms organising and controlling their affairs responsibly and effectively."

[36] Cf. A. Fuchs, in: A. Fuchs (ed.), *Kommentar zum WpHG*, § 33 para. 3.

[37] The dual regulatory objective of the compliance obligations can give rise to interpretational difficulties regarding the responsibilities of the compliance staff and senior management. See in the context of the legal status of the compliance officer below para. 49 ff.

[38] Cf. C. Coglianese and D. Lazer, 37 Law & Soc'y Rev. (2003), p. 691 ff. On meta-based regulation see C. Coglianese and E. Mendelson, in: R. Baldwin et. al (eds.), *Oxford Handbook of Regulation*, p. 146 ff.

Malte Wundenberg

and monitor their company in a way that fulfils certain regulatory requirements of supervisory legislation—such as the provisions of European capital markets law. The control system is thereby used for supervisory means (i.e. preventing breaches of the law), in order to increase investor protection and market efficiency. The European requirements regarding compliance and risk management can thus be understood as an internal enforcement strategy[39] that complements the traditional mechanisms of private and public enforcement.[40]

II.   Implementation in the Member States

14   All Member States have implemented the provisions of the MiFID and the Organisational Requirements Directive into their national laws on a one-to-one basis.[41] Instead of enacting parliamentary statutes, several Member States have introduced regulations that have been defined more concretely by interpretational guidelines of the supervisory authorities.[42] The extent to which the Member States considered it necessary to render the abstract behavioural and organisational obligations more precisely differs greatly.

1.   France

15   The European requirements for compliance (*dispositif conformité*) were introduced into Articles 313–1 ff. RG AMF (General Regulations of the French Supervisory Authority) by Article L. 533–10 Code monétaire et financier (C. mon. fin., French Monetary and Financial Code)[43] and are put into more concrete terms with the help of instruction no. 2008–01 of 8 February 2008.[44] Nevertheless the requirements remain vague and hardly differ from the directive's wording. It therefore appears noteworthy that French law contains very strict requirements regarding the approval and qualification of the compliance officer (*responsable de la conformité*).[45]

2.   Germany

16   In Germany Article 13 MiFID and the implementing provisions of the Organisational Requirements Directive were gradually transposed into national law. First the

---

[39] On compliance as a concept of internal law enforcement J.H. Walsh, 165 Colum. Bus. L. Rev. (1997), p. 165 ff.

[40] On this aspect in the concept of "qualitative banking supervision" see M. Wundenberg, *Compliance und die prinzipiengeleitete Aufsicht über Bankengruppen*, p. 82–83.

[41] Cf. Begr. RegE FRUG, BT-Drucks. 16/4028 (explanatory notes), p. 52 (Germany); FSA, *PS 06/13: Organisational Systems and Controls*, November 2006, para. 1.8: "*copy-out approach*" (United Kingdom). Critically on the one-to-one implementation R. Veil, WM (2008), p. 1093, 1094–1095. See also § 4 para. 46–48

[42] See above para. 10.

[43] Cf. Art. 313-3 RG AMF. For more details on the implementation of the MiFID in France see R. Veil and P. Koch, *Französisches Kapitalmarktrecht*, p. 107 ff. and F. Buisson, RTDF (2007-2), p. 6 ff.

[44] While the legal status of this instruction remains unclear, it is treated by market participants as legally binding. See R. Veil and P. Koch, *Französisches Kapitalmarktrecht*, p. 9.

[45] Art. 313-4 RG AMF. See below para. 46–47.

Malte Wundenberg

FRUG (German Financial Instruments Directive Implementation Act)[46] of July 2007 amended the organisational requirements contained in § 33 WpHG. Nevertheless the WpHG only contains "organisational principles".[47] These were further specified in a second step by §§ 12 and 13 of the WpDVerOV (German Regulation on the Rules of Conduct and Organisational Requirements for Investment Firms).[48] It was not until the BaFin published MaComp, however, that clear and definite outlines for the organisational requirements came into effect.[49] The MaComp constitute administrative provisions published by the BaFin, following comprehensive discussion with investment firms and representatives of different interest groups, as a reaction to the financial crisis. It contains detailed requirements regarding the supervisory obligations of the management and the structure of the compliance organisation.[50]

17   The MaComp are a typical example of a principles-based approach to legislation and an attempt to render the general principles more precisely, as described above.[51] They are an essential instrument of German capital markets supervision, by which the compliance obligations are—in cooperation with market participants—continuously revised and adjusted to the latest developments.

3.   Italy

18   The MiFID was implemented into Italian law by the TUF (Italian Consolidated Laws on Finance)[52] and rendered more precisely by the Regolamento Congiunto (Italian Compliance Regulation) enacted by the Banca d'Italia and Consob.[53] Prior to the publication of the regulation, banking supervisory law was already subject to *Disposizioni di Vigilanza* (supervisory regulations) which contain detailed requirements regarding the compliance organisation and the tasks of the compliance officer. The legal requirements for compliance in investment firms are primarily laid down in Articles 12 and 16 Regolamento Congiunto.

4.   Spain

19   For the Spanish legislator, the MiFID was the incentive to include all organisational obligations for investment firms in one statute.[54] The implementing statute for the

---

[46] Gesetz zur Umsetzung der Richtlinie über Märkte für Finanzinstrumente und der Durchführungsrichtlinie der Kommission (Finanzmarktrichtlinie-Umsetzungsgesetz—Act on the implementation of the MiFID and the Commission's implementing directive) of 16 July 2007, BGBl. I 2007, p. 1330.

[47] Begr. RegE FRUG, BT-Drucks. 16/4028 (explanatory notes), p. 70. Legislation now evolves around § 33(1)2 No. 1 WpHG, according to which investment firms are obliged to develop appropriate principles, provide funds and introduce procedures that ensure that neither the investment firm nor its employees can avoid fulfilling their obligations under this statute, in particular by introducing a permanent and effective compliance function that can fulfil its responsibilities independently. § 33(1)2 No. 3 WpHG refers to conflicts of interest.

[48] Verordnung (regulation) of 20 July 2007, BGBl. I 2007, p. 1432.

[49] BaFin, *Rundschreiben* (circular) 4/2010 (WA), June 2011.

[50] The legal nature and binding effects of the MaComp remain unclear, cf. S. Niermann, ZBB (2010), p. 400, 404 ff. and (on banking supervision) M. Wundenberg, *Compliance und die prinzipiengeleitete Aufsicht über Bankengruppen*, p. 92–97.

[51] See para. 8.

[52] Cf. Art. 21 I(d) TUF.

[53] Cf. D.Lgs. 17 September 2007, n. 164; D.Lgs. 6 November 2007, n. 195 and D.Lgs. 19 November 2007, n. 229. On the implementation of the MiFID see M.R. Baglieri, 31 Company Lawyer (2010), p. 186.

[54] On the importance of the MiFID for further developments of the organisational obligations in Spain see S. Wolf, *Der Wandel der spanischen Finanzmärkte*, p. 49.

MiFID is the LMV (Spanish Securities Market Act),[55] while the Organisational Requirements Directive was implemented into national law by the regulation Real Decreto 217/2008 (Royal Decree on Investment Firms). Article 13(2) MiFID and Article 6 of the implementing directive can now be found in Article 70 ter.1.b LMV and Article 28 RD 217/2008.

5. Sweden

20   In Sweden no legal obligations regarding compliance existed prior to the implementation of the MiFID.[56] The organisational obligations are now incorporated in Kapitel 8, §§ 3–11 LVM (Swedish Securities Market Act)[57] and are put into more concrete terms in Kapitel 6, § 9 of the Finansinspektionen's regulation FFFS 2007:16, the wording of which is comparable to the Organisational Requirements Directive.[58]

6. United Kingdom

21   The United Kingdom adopted the European organisational requirements on a one-to-one basis in the section "Senior Management Arrangements, Systems and Controls" (SYSC) of the FSA Handbook.[59] This section already contained a large number of provisions regarding senior management controls as well as internal governance arrangements.[60] This comes as no surprise, as the United Kingdom has long recognised the need to regulate and to supervise internal governance mechanisms and senior management controls.[61] The implementation of the MiFID led to amendments in the SYSC section of the Handbook without making any changes to the existing organisational requirements.[62] The most relevant provisions on compliance can now be found in SYSC 6.1 FSA Handbook.[63] However, it must be noted that the obligation to establish effective internal control arrangements and compliance structures can already be deduced from Principle 3 of the FSA Handbook, which requires firms to take reasonable care to organise and control their affairs responsibly and effectively, with adequate risk management systems. With regard to so-called

---

[55] Implemented by the law 47/2007.

[56] Investment firms started introducing a compliance function even prior to the enactment of the MiFID. Cf. K. Jochnick and P. Jansson, ERT (2007), p. 741, 755.

[57] SFS 2007:528.

[58] R. Veil and F. Walla, *Schwedisches Kapitalmarktrecht*, p. 103 ff.

[59] FSA, *Senior Management Arrangements, Systems and Controls (Markets in Financial Instruments and Capital Requirements Directives) Instrument 2006/50*, November 2006.

[60] See Webbon, in: N. Boardman and J. Crosthwait, *A Practitioners Guide to FSA Regulation of Investment Banking* (2002), p. 49: "As is apparent from the title of the module, the new regulations combine senior management arrangements with systems and control requirements, making an account of one incomplete without consideration of the other." In the UK supervisory law therefore has considerable influence on the general corporate governance structure of a company. Cf. ibid.: "It seems that today it is the changing regulatory environment which is driving corporate governance decisions and the responsibilities of the boards of financial services institutions" (p. 55).

[61] A starting point in this development has been the collapse of the Barings Bank. Cf. P. Nelson, *Compliance*, para. 5.1.

[62] Cf. FSA, *PS 06/13: Organisational Systems and Controls*, November 2006, para. 5.1. ("broadly in line without existing Handbook provisions").

[63] The rules on general organisational requirements in SYSC 4, on risk management systems in SYSC 7, on outsourcing in SYSC 8 and on conflicts of interest in SYSC 10 FSA Handbook must also be taken into account when setting up the compliance organisation.

Malte Wundenberg

"approved persons" who exert significant influence within the firm, Principle 7 of the Principles for Approved Persons requires those persons to take reasonable steps to ensure that the business of the firm for which they are responsible complies with regulatory requirements.[64] As the case law reveals, the FSA continues to rely on the high-level principles of the FSA Handbook to sanction compliance failings.[65]

22   Unlike Germany and Austria,[66] the United Kingdom supplies only few interpretational guidelines and explanations in the FSA Handbook.[67] The legislator intentionally refrained from including more concrete provisions, following the FSA's principles-based approach to legislation[68] and relying on informal cooperation and coordination between investment firms and the supervisory authority.[69] The legal framework for compliance is therefore based in the United Kingdom on a number of high-level rules.

III. Regulatory Objectives and Scope of Compliance Obligations

1.   Mitigation of Compliance Risk

23   The regulatory objective laid down in Article 13(2) MiFID to ensure compliance of investment firms with their obligations under the provision of the MiFID is put into more concrete terms by Article 6(1) Organisational Requirements Directive in three ways. Firstly, Member States shall ensure that "investment firms establish, implement and maintain adequate policies and procedures designed to detect any risk of failure by the firm to comply with its obligations under [the MiFID], as well as the associated risks". Secondly, investment firms shall further be able to provide adequate "measures and procedures" designed to minimise such risks. Finally, Member States shall "enable the competent authorities to exercise their powers effectively" which requires the documentation of the measures and precautions that have been taken.

24   Article 6(1) Organisational Requirements Directive reflects the risk-based approach to compliance[70] taken by European law: the overall aim is to minimise the risk of legislative violations by identifying, evaluating and monitoring compliance risks and

---

[64] See also below para. 47.

[65] See para. 84 and 87. This could lead to potential conflicts with the fact that the MiFID is widely regarded as a maximum harmonisation directive. This has been recognised by the FSA, as PRIN 3.1.6 of the FSA Handbook states that a firm will not be subject to a Principle to the extent that it would be contrary to the UK's obligations under an EU instrument. See also the Guidance issued in PRIN 4.1. of the FSA Handbook.

[66] See above para. 10.

[67] See R. Veil and M. Wundenberg, *Englisches Kapitalmarktrecht*, p. 141 ff.

[68] Cf. FSA, *PS 06/13: Organisational Systems and Controls*, November 2006, para. 1.10: "In line with principles-based regulation, it is for a firm's management to decide how best their firm might meet our requirements and it is more appropriate for a firm to discuss issues or concerns bilaterally with its supervisors."

[69] Cf. ibid. This was the case until the FSA, as a reaction to the outbreak of the financial crises corrected the concept of supervision. Cf. R. Veil and M. Wundenberg, *Englisches Kapitalmarktrecht*, p. 12–13 and J. Black, *The Rise, Fall and Fate of Principles Based Regulation* (2010), p. 13 ff. (especially p. 15).

[70] This approach is based on the work of the Basel Committee on Banking Supervision. For more details on the development of a "risk-based compliance" see S. Bazley and A. Haynes, *Financial Services Authority Regulation and Risk-Based Compliance*, p. 173 ff. and passim.

Malte Wundenberg

taking suitable measures in order to manage these risks.[71] The responsibility for this obligation lies with senior management.[72]

25   The risk-orientated approach to regulation has far-reaching consequences for the structure of the compliance organisation: the investment firm and its senior management must identify the areas of risk that are particularly relevant for the specific business of the firm by way of self-assessment.[73] In line with this risk-based approach the ESMA argues that a "compliance risk assessment" should be used to determine the focus of the monitoring and advisory activities of the compliance function.[74] As a result of the MiFID's risk-orientated approach the organisational requirements to be adhered to are not the same for all investment firms but depend on the respective risk situation. This is stated explicitly in Article 6(1)2 Organisational Requirements Directive, which states that Member States must ensure that investment firms take into account the nature, scale and complexity of the business of the firm, and the nature and range of investment services and activities undertaken in the course of that business. This provision must therefore be understood as a manifestation of the principle of proportionality, which is central to the MiFID.

26   The principle of proportionality is a common feature in today's international financial markets regulation. It can be also found in similar forms in insurance and banking supervision.[75] With regard to the development of a compliance organisation the principle of proportionality entails that the procedures and instruments applied by investment firms to manage the legal risk can differ greatly. As a general rule, larger investment firms with a more complex product portfolio will be subject to stricter organisational requirements than smaller financial institutes with a standardised choice of financial instruments.[76] European law thus provides flexible organisational requirements depending on the risk structure in each individual case.[77] It is the task of the investment firm's senior management to determine the suitable structure of the compliance organisation, taking into consideration the specific compliance risks faced by the

---

[71] According to the Basel Committee on Banking Supervision, *Compliance and Compliance Function in Banks*, April 2005, para. 3 the compliance risk can be defined as the "risk of legal or regulatory sanctions, material financial loss, or loss to reputation a bank may suffer as a result of its failure to comply with laws, regulations, rules, related self-regulatory organisation standards, and codes of conduct applicable to its banking activities".

[72] Art. 9 Organisational Requirements Directive. The overall responsibility of the senior management for compliance is internationally accepted. Cf. Basel Committee on Banking Supervision, *Compliance and Compliance Function in Banks*, April 2005, principle 2. See also A. Mills, *Financial Services Compliance*, p. 18 ff.

[73] For details see S. Gebauer and S. Niermann, in: C.E. Hauschka (ed.), *Corporate Compliance*, § 36 para. 41 ff.; M. Schlicht, BKR (2006), p. 469, 470 (with examples from legal practice). On risk assessment see R.J. Wild, in: *Corporate Compliance Series*, § 2.13 ff.

[74] ESMA, *Guidelines on Certain Aspects of the MiFID Compliance Function Requirements, Final Report*, ESMA/2012/388, July 2012, general guideline 1, para. 14.

[75] Cf. Art. 22(2), 123(2) and 124(4) Banking Directive; Art. 29(3) Solvency II Directive. For more details on the "double proportionality" principle in banking supervision see M. Wundenberg, *Compliance und die prinzipiengeleitete Aufsicht über Bankengruppen*, p. 83–91.

[76] CESR, *Advice on Possible Implementing Measures of the Directive 2004/39/EC on Markets in Financial Instruments, Consultation Paper*, CESR/04-261b, June 2004, p. 11. For an overview of the factors that can be taken into account in deciding which organisational measures are proportionate see ESMA, *Guidelines on Certain Aspects of the MiFID Compliance Function Requirements, Final Report*, ESMA/2012/388, July 2012, general guideline 8, para. 61.

[77] See above para. 8.

---

investment firm.[78] The principle of proportionality is visible in the numerous opening clauses of the MiFID: an investment firm is, for example, not required to comply with Article 6(3)(c) or (d) if in view of the nature, scale and complexity of its business, and the nature and range of investment services and activities, it is able to demonstrate that the organisational requirements are disproportionate and its compliance function is effective without these additional requirements.[79] Even in these cases, however, the appointment of a compliance officer and the development of a compliance function must be ensured.

2. Scope of the Compliance Obligation

27 According to the wording of the directive, the supervisory obligations of management only refer to the compliance of the firm with its obligations under the provisions of the MiFID.[80] Yet systematically the obligation must reach farther, also including the supervision of possible insider dealings by employees of the investment firm in the scope of the compliance obligation.[81] An organisational obligation aimed at preventing any possible legal risk cannot, however, be deduced from the European provisions.

28 Some Member States follow a far more comprehensive approach regarding the concept of compliance. The United Kingdom's capital markets law, for example, extends the compliance obligations much farther: according to SYSC 6.1.1. FSA Handbook the obligation of the investment firm to ensure compliance is not restricted to the MiFID, but rather refers to the entire "regulatory system".[82] German,[83] French,[84] Italian,[85] Swedish,[86] and Spanish[87] law also have a more extensive understanding of compliance than the MiFID. The regulatory approach of the Luxembourg Commission de Surveillance du Secteur Financier (CSSF) is particularly noteworthy in this context: while the supervisory authority generally requires investment firms to ensure compliance comprehensively, it exempts them from a compliance obligation with regard to provisions that do not refer

---

[78] See Cf. ESMA, *Guidelines on Certain Aspects of the MiFID Compliance Function Requirements, Final Report*, ESMA/2012/388, July 2012, general guideline 8, para. 61: "Investment firms should decide which measures, including organizational measures and the level of resources, are best suited to ensuring the effectiveness of the compliance function in the firm's particular circumstances."

[79] See for details ibid., general guideline 8, para. 60–66.

[80] Art. 13(2) MiFID, Art. 6(1) and 9(1) Organisational Requirements Directive.

[81] Art. 12 Organisational Requirements Directive. More details on the supervision of employee transactions D. Eisele, in: H. Schimansky et al. (eds.), *Bankrechts-Handbuch*, § 109 para. 130 ff.

[82] Cf. FSA, *PS 06/13: Organisational Systems and Controls*, November 2006, para. 3.4. and 4.6.

[83] Pursuant to § 33(1) No. 1 WpHG the compliance obligation refers to all obligations under the WpHG.

[84] Cf. Art. 313-2 RG AMF, which refers to Art. L. 621-15 II C. mon. fin. The obligations listed herein are far more extensive than those contained in the MiFID.

[85] According to the Banca d'Italia the compliance function does not only ensure adherence to legal provisions but also to legally non-binding self-regulatory rules. As a consequence, compliance risk is defines as the "risk of incurring judicial or administrative sanctions, material financial losses or reputational harm as a result of violations of statutory provisions (laws or regulations) or self-regulatory codes (e.g. by laws, codes of ethics, corporate governance codes)". Cf. Banca d'Italia, *The Compliance Function*, July 2007, p. 1–2.

[86] Cf. Kapitel 6, § 8 Regulation FFFS 2007:16. According to this provision, it is necessary to monitor not only the adherence to the LVM provisions enacted in the course of the implementation of the MiFID, but also to all rules regulating the business activities of investment firms.

[87] Cf. Art. 28.1 RD 217/2008 which refers to the applicable provisions in general (*las normas que resulten de aplicación*). See also Art. 70 ter.1 LMV (la normativa del Mercado de Valores—capital markets law provisions).

Malte Wundenberg

to banking or financial service activities.[88] The Basel Committee's recommendations and supervisory standards also understand compliance as referring to all applicable laws and regulations.[89] The guidelines issued by the ESMA offer a potentially more narrow interpretation of the scope of compliance obligations, stating that the compliance risk assessment should take into account the applicable obligations "under MiFID and the national implementing regulation".[90]

IV. Elements of a Compliance Organisation

29   Based on CESR recommendations[91] the Organisational Requirements Directive distinguishes between "principles, measures and procedures" designed to detect and minimise compliance risk and the establishment of a permanent and effective "compliance function" by investment firms operating independently (see below 1). The Organisational Requirements Directive requires investment firms to appoint a compliance officer, who is responsible for the compliance function and compliance reports (see below 2). Another essential element of any compliance organisation are "Chinese walls" that restrict the flow of information within the investment firm (see below 3).

1.   Compliance Function

30   In conformity with the Basel Committee's recommendations,[92] Article 6(2) Organisational Requirements Directive requires investment firms to establish and maintain a permanent and effective compliance function which operates independently. As to be expected from a principles-based approach to regulation, the term "compliance function" is not further defined in the directive.[93] European law thus does not prescribe a certain form of organisation; the Organisational Requirements Directive only formulates three abstract regulatory objectives of the compliance function (independence, effectiveness, permanence) and only gives rough outlines of its responsibilities.[94]

---

[88] CSSF, *Circular 04/155, The Compliance Function*, September 2004, para. 12.

[89] Basel Committee on Banking Supervision, *Core Principles for Effective Banking Supervision*, October 2006, principle 17; Basel Committee on Banking Supervision, *Compliance and the Compliance Function in Banks*, April 2005, para. 3–5.

[90] ESMA, *Guidelines on Certain Aspects of the MiFID Compliance Function Requirements, Final Report*, ESMA/2012/388, July 2012, general guideline 1, para. 16.

[91] CESR, *Technical Advice on Possible Implementing Measures of the Directive 2004/39/EC on Markets in Financial Instruments, 1st Set of Mandates*, CESR/05-024c, January 2005, p. 13 ff. (Box 2).

[92] Basel Committee on Banking Supervision, *Compliance and the Compliance Function in Banks*, April 2005, Principles 5 ff.

[93] Commission, *Background Note*, Sec. 3.2. See also Basel Committee on Banking Supervision, *Compliance and the Compliance Function in Banks*, April 2005, para. 6; IOSCO, *Compliance Function at Market Intermediaries*, March 2006, p. 2. A more general definition can be found in recital 31 Solvency II Directive (2009/138/EC), which refers to the compliance function as the administrative capacity undertaking particular governance tasks.

[94] Cf. ESMA, *Guidelines on Certain Aspects of the MiFID Compliance Function Requirements, Final Report*, ESMA/2012/388, July 2012, general guideline 8, para. 61. See also above para. 24–25.

(a)   Requirements

(aa)   Independence

31   In order to enable the compliance function to discharge its responsibilities effectively, it is a necessary prerequisite that the compliance staff is independent of the business units that it monitors. [95] This legal principle of independence involves a number of different aspects: as a general rule, persons involved in the compliance must perform their monitoring and advisory functions objectively and free from any conflicts of interest. The provisions of the Organisational Requirements Directive highlight two constellations in which the principle of independence assumes particular relevance. Firstly, the relevant persons in the compliance function are not permitted to be involved in the performance of the services or activities they monitor.[96] This rule refers to the general prohibition of self-monitoring under the concept of operational independence. Secondly, the Organisational Requirements Directive purports financial independence. The method of determining the remuneration of the relevant persons involved in the compliance function must therefore not compromise their objectivity and must not be likely to do so.[97]

(1) Operational and Financial Independence

32   The prohibition of self-monitoring entails that the compliance function must be held separate from the operational business units in order to prevent influence from being exercised on the compliance staff.[98] This does not, however, mean that the compliance function cannot be involved in any of the business processes of the investment firm, as an effective management of legal risks requires active cooperation between the monitoring instances and the operative business units.[99] This becomes particularly clear with regard to the development of new financial products, for which it can be helpful, and often even advisable, to include compliance staff in the product approval process in order to identify legal risks at an early stage in the distribution process.[100]

33   Financial independence restricts the possibilities of a performance-based remuneration for compliance staff. The remuneration structure must ensure that the compliance staff's salary does not depend on the results of the monitored business units, thereby prohibiting any remuneration concepts that provide financial incentives to cover up breaches of law in order to increase the operative profits

---

[95] Ibid., general guideline 7, para. 57–59. The importance of the principle of independence is emphasised in nearly all statements and has meanwhile been internationally recognised as an essential criterion of an effective compliance organisation. Cf. Basel Committee on Banking Supervision, *Compliance and the Compliance Function in Banks*, April 2005, Principle 5; IOSCO, *Compliance Function at Market Intermediaries*, March 2006, topic 3; Board of Governors of the Federal Reserve System, *Compliance Risk Management*, October 2008, sec. 2.

[96] Art. 6(3)(c) Organisational Requirements Directive.

[97] Art. 6(3)(d) Organisational Requirements Directive. On the compliance officer's independence from the management and in disciplinarian questions see below para. 49–53.

[98] Cf. ESMA, *Guidelines on Certain Aspects of the MiFID Compliance Function Requirements, Final Report*, ESMA/2012/388, July 2012, general guideline 7, para. 57–59.

[99] T. Lösler, NZG (2005), p. 104, 107–108.

[100] See ESMA, *Guidelines on Certain Aspects of the MiFID Compliance Function Requirements, Final Report*, ESMA/2012/388, July 2012, general guideline 4, para. 41; Basel Committee on Banking Supervision, *Compliance and the Compliance Function in Banks*, April 2005, Principle 7, para. 37; BaFin, *Rundschreiben* (circular) *4/2010 (MaComp)*, June 2011, BT 1.2. para. 3.

Malte Wundenberg

and thereby the compliance staff's own salary.[101] Performance-based remuneration is therefore only permitted if it is constructed as a long-term incentive and focuses on the company's profits as a whole.[102]

34   Both the CESR and national supervisory authorities address this problem regarding the remuneration of compliance staff. The CESR states that "the independence of compliance function personnel may be undermined if their remuneration is related to the financial performance of the business line for which they exercise compliance responsibilities. However, it should generally be acceptable to relate their remuneration to the financial performance of the investment firm as a whole."[103] The British FSA[104] and the German BaFin[105] come to the same conclusion. The Austrian FMA recommends a performance-orientated remuneration following qualitative and not quantitative criteria.[106]

35   The principles of operational and financial independence cannot be applied without exception. According to the Organisational Requirements Directive investment firms are not obliged to comply with the obligations laid down in Article 6(3)(c) and (d) if they are able to demonstrate that, in view of the nature, scale and complexity of their business, and the nature and range of investment services and activities, the requirement under that point is not proportionate. This exemption is, however, only applicable if the senior management has been able to confirm that the company's compliance function continues to be effective.[107]

(2) Organisational Independence

36   The principle of independence further entails that the compliance function's structural arrangements must be independent from the operative business units, constituting an independent part of the corporate structure. This follows from the principle of a separation of functions, inherent in the entire field of company supervision. Investment firms, however, have a large margin of appreciation with regard to the organisational approach they take in order to fulfil this requirement[108] and therefore do not necessarily need to introduce a separate compliance department.[109] The degree to which the compliance function must be organised independently depends on the nature, scale and complexity of the company's business. National supervisory practice generally regards an independent organisational unit as necessary provided the staff has regular access to inside and other confidential information.[110]

---

[101] M. Casper, in: Bankrechtliche Vereinigung (ed.), *Bankrechtstag 2008*, p. 139, 149.

[102] Cf. ibid. Similarly Basel Committee on Banking Supervision, *Compliance and the Compliance Function in Banks*, April 2005, Principle 5, para. 29 ("remuneration related to the financial performance of the bank as a whole should generally be acceptable"). In more detail G. Spindler, WM (2008), p. 905, 910.

[103] CESR, *Technical Advice on Possible Implementing Measures of the Directive 2004/39/EC on Markets in Financial Instruments*, 1st Set of Mandates, CESR/05-024c, January 2005, p. 12.

[104] FSA, *PS 06/13: Organisational Systems and Controls*, November 2006, para. 4.8.

[105] BaFin, *Rundschreiben* (circular) *4/2010 (MaComp)*, June 2011, BT 1.1.1 para. 8.

[106] FMA, *Rundschreiben* (circular) *betreffend die organisatorischen Anforderungen des Wertpapieraufsichtsgesetzes*, May 2007, p. 7.

[107] See above para. 23 ff.

[108] See above para. 4 ff.

[109] Commission, *Background Note*, Sec. 3.2: "[T]hese functions [Compliance, risk management and internal audit] may be embedded in the organisation of the firm in different ways. These differences reflect the nature of these functions as well as the need for proportionality."

[110] BaFin, *Rundschreiben* (circular) *4/2010 (MaComp)*, June 2011, BT 1.1.1 para. 3.

37   In this context the question if (and under which circumstances) the compliance function can be combined with other internal control functions, such as risk management or internal audit, assumes particular importance.[111] The Organisational Requirements Directive only contains explicit rules on the relationship between the compliance function and the internal audit function. Pursuant to Article 8 investment firms must establish and maintain an internal audit function which is separate and independent from the other functions and activities of the investment firm and fulfils the responsibilities listed in Article 8(a)–(d). The internal audit must thus not only be independent from the other supervisory functions of the investment firms but must rather also be organised separately as an independent department. The reason for this is that the internal audit is charged with the oversight of the adequacy and effectiveness of the investment firm's compliance function.[112] This requires the internal audit to have a separate organisation from the other business units.[113]

38   Whether compliance and risk management also require strict organisational separation is under dispute.[114] The legislative records indicate that European law takes a rather flexible and principles-based approach to this issue: while the principle of independence includes the general rule that the compliance function should generally not be an organisational component of risk management, this distinction is less clear with regard to the internal audit function. It is necessary to keep in mind that the responsibility of the compliance function also includes the task of monitoring compliance with the rules on risk management and that effective oversight always requires sufficient organisational independence of the controlling body from the controlled instances. At the same time, recital 15 of the Organisational Requirements Directive does not necessarily see the independent functioning of compliance as jeopardised if risk management and compliance functions are performed by the same person. Only for larger firms does the directive assume that a clear organisational distinction between both units is generally necessary. Organisational independence is thus subject to and restricted by the principle of proportionality.[115] This interpretation is in line with the guidelines issued by the ESMA.[116]

---

[111] Cf. ESMA, *Guidelines on Certain Aspects of the MiFID Compliance Function Requirements, Final Report*, ESMA/2012/388, July 2012, general guideline 9, para. 67–71. Business practice offers a number of possible structures. Cf. Gabbi et al., *Managing Compliance Risk after MiFiD*, p. 5–10; J. Oelkers, *Compliance in Banken*, in: O. Lucius et al. (eds.), *Compliance im Finanzdienstleistungsbereich*, p. 131, 152 ff. (Austria); M. Gallo, *Compliance Function*, p. 325 ff. (Italy); M.T. Biegelman, *Compliance Program*, p. 178 (USA).

[112] Art. 8(a) Organisational Requirements Directive. Cf. ESMA, *Guidelines on Certain Aspects of the MiFID Compliance Function Requirements, Final Report*, ESMA/2012/388, July 2012, general guideline 9, para. 69.

[113] According to the ESMA guidelines the separation of compliance and internal audit may, however, be disproportionate for very small investment firms.

[114] The connection of the compliance function to the risk management function is particularly common in Anglo-American banks and investment firms. Cf. C. Taylor, 6 J. Invest. Comp. (2005), p. 54, 58. On the functional relationship between both functions see § 28 para. 2–3.

[115] For more details see the Swedish report on implementation, *One Year with MiFID*, April 2009, p. 8–9. On the relationship of the compliance function with the legal department see A. Früh, CCZ (2010), p. 121 ff.; T. Lösler, WM (2010), p. 1917, 1920; S. Niermann, ZBB (2010), p. 400, 422.

[116] According to the ESMA the combination of the compliance function with other control functions (such as risk management) may be acceptable if this does not compromise the effectiveness and independence of the compliance function and if this is appropriately documented. See ESMA, *Guidelines on Certain Aspects of the MiFID Compliance Function Requirements, Final Report*, ESMA/2012/388, July 2012, general guideline 9, para. 67.

Malte Wundenberg

39   The German BaFin decrees that the compliance function may be combined with other control units, such as departments responsible for money-laundering prevention or risk control, but that internal audit must remain separate at all times.[117] In Italy the Banca d'Italia made the following statement: "[T]he compliance function's activities may be performed by different organizational structures already established within the bank (for example, legal, organizational, operational risk management), provided that the risk management process and operations of the function are centralized through the appointment of a compliance officer."[118] The Austrian FMA underlines the fact that the compliance staff must be restricted to fulfilling compliance duties and should at no time be permitted to take over other duties or advise clients. The simultaneous assignment of an employee to the risk management function and the legal department is generally accepted.[119]

(bb)   Permanence and Effectiveness

40   The compliance function must be established permanently and must be institutionalised in the company's organisation by appropriate measures.[120] Although the wording of the directive does not explicitly require a written documentation of the status and authority of the compliance function, this requirement can be deduced from the requirement of permanence.[121]

41   Article 6(3)(a) of the Organisational Requirements Directive describes the elements of an effective compliance function: it must have the necessary authority, resources, expertise and access to all relevant information.[122] National supervisory practice further demands that the compliance staff is to be supplied with all relevant information and documents, and has unrestricted access to the premises, records and data-processing systems as well as to any further information necessary for determining the relevant facts.[123] According to the Austrian Standard Compliance Code, withholding information constitutes a serious offence for company employees and calls for disciplinary action.[124]

(b)   Responsibilities

42   Legal literature traditionally distinguished between advisory and informational responsibilities of the compliance function and responsibilities regarding quality

---

[117] BaFin, *Rundschreiben* (circular) *4/2010 (MaComp)*, June 2011, BT 1.1.1 para. 4.

[118] Banca d'Italia, *The Compliance Function*, July 2007, p. 3.

[119] FMA, *Rundschreiben* (circular) *betreffend die organisatorischen Anforderungen des Wertpapieraufsichtsgesetzes*, May 2007, p. 8.

[120] Cf. ESMA, *Guidelines on Certain Aspects of the MiFID Compliance Function Requirements, Final Report*, ESMA/2012/388, July 2012, general guideline 6, para. 53; L. Röh, BB (2008), p. 398, 403.

[121] ESMA, *Guidelines on Certain Aspects of the MiFID Compliance Function Requirements, Final Report*, ESMA/2012/388, July 2012, general guideline 6, para. 53; Basel Committee on Banking Supervision, *Compliance and the Compliance Function in Banks*, April 2005, Principle 5, para. 22 ff.; Banca d'Italia, *Compliance Function*, July 2007, p. 5 ("formalize the function's status and authority").

[122] See for details ESMA, *Guidelines on Certain Aspects of the MiFID Compliance Function Requirements, Final Report*, ESMA/2012/388, July 2012, general guideline 5, para. 43.

[123] BaFin, *Rundschreiben* (circular) *4/2010 (MaComp)*, June 2011, BT 1.1.2 para. 1. See also Basel Committee on Banking Supervision, *Compliance and the Compliance Function in Banks*, April 2005, Principle 5, para. 30 ff. For details on the compliance officer's informational rights and right to issue instructions see below para. 54–56.

[124] Standard Compliance Code, *Grundsätze ordnungsgemäßer Compliance*, No. 6.

Malte Wundenberg

control and marketing.[125] Since the enactment of the MiFID the responsibility towards investor protection must also be considered a priority.[126] The Organisational Requirements Directive places particular emphasis on two responsibilities of the compliance function: (i) the more repressive measures of monitoring and assessing the adequacy and effectiveness of the procedures designed to mitigate compliance risk;[127] and (ii) advisory and assisting responsibilities with more preventive effects.[128]

(aa) Monitoring and Assessment

43   The compliance function monitors and assesses the principles and procedures developed by the investment firm in order to minimise legal risks.[129] These monitoring and assessment responsibilities are to ensure that, with the help of senior management, all relevant legal risks can be identified and any shortcomings of the compliance function can be determined. According to the implementing directive, the monitoring responsibility is comprehensive: it applies both to the organisational measures and procedures taken by senior management in order to prevent legal risks, as well as to the day-to-day business carried out by the operative staff, although the latter cannot be deduced from the provision's wording.[130] However, this does not prevent the compliance function (following a risk-based approach) from establishing priorities determined by the compliance risk assessment ensuring that compliance risks are adequately monitored. The aim of compliance monitoring is to ensure that company employees abide by the internal organisational principles and internal rules. If the compliance function identifies weaknesses in the principles and procedures developed by the investment firm, it must make suggestions on how to improve the compliance organisation and submit a report to the senior management thereon.[131] The compliance function must further determine and manage conflicts of interest and monitor the flow of inside information.[132]

(bb) Advice and Assistance

44   Article 6(2)(b) of the implementing directive defines a further responsibility of the compliance function: it must "advise and assist the relevant persons responsible for carrying out investment services and activities to comply with the firm's obligations under Directive 2004/39/EC". The advice and assistance given by the compliance function is becoming increasingly important in legal practice and should prevent offences and conflicts of interest from occurring.[133] It reflects the MiFID's understanding of the compliance function as an essential element of the investment firm's

---

[125] Cf. Standard Compliance Code, *Grundsätze ordnungsgemäßer Compliance*, No. 2. In detail T. Lösler, NZG (2005), p. 104 ff.

[126] See above para. 12.

[127] Art. 6(2)(a) Organisational Requirements Directive.

[128] Art. 6(2)(b) Organisational Requirements Directive.

[129] On the compliance function's responsibilities concerning monitoring and control see ESMA, *Guidelines on Certain Aspects of the MiFID Compliance Function Requirements, Final Report*, ESMA/2012/388, July 2012 general guideline 2, para. 18–26. A. Newton, *Compliance*, p. 143 ff.; S. Gebauer and S. Niermann, in: C.E. Hauschka (ed.), *Corporate Compliance*, § 36 para. 22 ff.

[130] J.A. Harm, *Compliance*, p. 44.

[131] See below para. 60.

[132] See below (in the context of the establishment of Chinese walls) para. 64–81.

[133] K. Rothenhöfer, in: S. Kümpel and A. Wittig (eds.), *Bank- und Kapitalmarktrecht*, para. 3.375. The compliance function's responsibility for the management of conflicts of interest does not result directly from Art. 6

value chain.[134] The compliance function can give advice and assistance in three ways.[135] It advises senior management and staff on individual aspects of the interpretation and application of statutes and internal guidelines. It further trains staff to recognise and understand regulatory requirements, thereby reducing the risk of "accidental" offences due to a lack of legal knowledge.[136] Finally, it compiles compliance handbooks and codes of conduct that give guidance to the operative units in their day-to-day business.

2.   Compliance Officer

45   A novel concept introduced by the implementing directive is the obligation to appoint a compliance officer, responsible for the compliance function and compliance reports.[137] The legal status, responsibilities and powers of the compliance officer are only outlined roughly in the directive. It thus comes as no surprise that with regard to the status of the compliance officer significant differences in the legal practice of the Member States exist.

(a)   Appointment

(aa)   Registration and Qualification Requirements

46   Pursuant to Article 6(3)(b) Organisational Requirements Directive the compliance officer must be appointed by the investment firm.[138] The directive does not require registration or a supervisory assessment of the potential officer's qualifications, the directive merely stating that the "relevant persons for the compliance function"—a term that also includes the compliance officer—must have the necessary expertise.[139]

Organisational Requirements Directive, but rather from an interpretation of Art. 13(2), (3) MiFID in conjunction with Art. 22(2), (3) Organisational Requirements Directive.

[134] On the development of the compliance function from an internal control body, acting repressively, to a central management function essential to the value chain see C. Taylor, 6 J. Invest. Comp. (2005), p. 54, 58 ("genuinely strategic, forward facing management function that rightly has the ear of the board and the senior management"); A. Newton, *Compliance*, p. 72 ff.; SDA Bocconi, *Evolution of Compliance Function* (June 2009), p. 5 (empirical evidence). See also T. Fett, in: E. Schwark and D. Zimmer, *Kapitalmarktrechts-Kommentar*, § 33 WpHG para. 20.

[135] Cf. D. Lippe, *Compliance*, p. 176 ff.; A. Fuchs, in: A. Fuchs (ed.), *Kommentar zum WpHG*, § 33 para. 72–73; K. Rothenhöfer, in: S. Kümpel and A. Wittig (eds.), *Bank- und Kapitalmarktrecht*, para. 3.371 ff. See now also ESMA, *Guidelines on Certain Aspects of the MiFID Compliance Function Requirements, Final Report*, ESMA/2012/388, July 2012, general guideline 4, para. 33–42.

[136] For details on "compliance training" see A. Newton, *Compliance*, p. 113 ff. and ESMA, *Guidelines on Certain Aspects of the MiFID Compliance Function Requirements, Final Report*, ESMA/2012/388, July 2012, general guideline 4, para. 35.

[137] The compliance requirements under capital markets law are more extensive than those under insurance and banking supervision. Neither the Banking Directive nor the Solvency II framework directive contain the legal obligation to introduce the concept of compliance officers. Only the Basel Committee on Banking Supervision, *Compliance and the Compliance Function in Banks*, April 2005, Principle 5, para. 24 ff. recommends the appointment of a so-called "head of compliance"—a concept that has recently also been introduced for rating agencies. See § 27 para. 26.

[138] This organisational requirement is binding and not subject to the principle of proportionality, cf. Art. 6(3)2 Organisational Requirements Directive which only refers to Art. 6(3)(c) and (d) *e contrario*.

[139] See above para. 41.

Compliance in Investment Firms

47   Based on recommendations of the CESR[140] and the Basel Committee[141] the supervisory practice in the Member States usually requires investment firms to inform the supervisory authorities of any change in the person of the compliance officer. This procedure is recommendable as the compliance officer generally coordinates the exchange of information between the senior management, the staff and the supervisory authorities, and therefore functions as a contact person for the supervisory authorities.[142] The details of the notification, registration and approval obligations regarding compliance officers vary between the Member States. The BaFin, for example, requires investment firms in Germany to inform the BaFin of the appointment or dismissal of a compliance officer[143] and to state in writing the reasons for a dismissal.[144] The German Bundestag has further decided on a legal obligation to register compliance officers.[145] Italian supervisory law provides similar notification obligations,[146] whilst the supervisory authority's powers in France are far more extensive: Compliance officers (*responsable de la conformité*) must be registered with the AMF and must obtain administrative permission to exercise their profession (*carte professionnelle*) which will only be granted if they first pass an oral suitability test.[147] In the United Kingdom, it is an established principle of financial supervision that so-called approved persons with special responsibilities within a company must acquire separate permission before they are permitted to exercise so-called "controlled functions",[148] i.e. particularly important functions within an investment firm.[149] This additional requirement also applies to the position of the compliance officer.[150] The permission is granted if the person passes the *fit and proper test*, i.e. if the compliance officer is regarded as being able to exercise his responsibilities with honesty and integrity as well as with competence and capability. Both in the United Kingdom and in France the appointment of a compliance officer is thus subject to a prior and comprehensive administrative examination. There is a tendency in all Member States not only to subject the investment firm itself and its senior management to capital market supervision, but also the members of the second management tier.[151]

---

[140] CESR, *Technical Advice on Possible Implementing Measures of the Directive 2004/39/EC on Markets in Financial Instruments, 1st Set of Mandates*, CESR/05-024c, January 2005, p. 15, Box 2 No. 9c).

[141] Basel Committee on Banking Supervision, *Compliance and the Compliance Function in Banks*, April 2005, Principle 5, para. 27.

[142] Cf. ESMA, *Guidelines on Certain Aspects of the MiFID Compliance Function Requirements, Final Report*, ESMA/2012/388, July 2012, general guideline 4, para. 42.

[143] BaFin, *Rundschreiben* (circular) *4/2010 (MaComp)*, June 2011, BT 1.3. The notification must contain the employee's CV and documents providing sufficient proof of the applicant's qualifications.

[144] BaFin, *Rundschreiben* (circular) *4/2010 (MaComp)*, June 2011, BT 1.3.

[145] Art. 1 No. 9 AnSVG, BGBl. I 2011, p. 583.

[146] Banca d'Italia, *The Compliance Function*, July 2007, p. 3.

[147] Art. 313-4 in conjunction with Art. 313-38 ff. RG AMF. See A. Fulconis-Tielens, *Revue Banque* (November 2008), p. 28–29 and R. Veil and P. Koch, *Französisches Kapitalmarktrecht*, p. 109.

[148] A list of "controlled functions" can be found in SUP 10.4.5 FSA Handbook.

[149] Sec. 59 FSMA and SUP 10 FSA Handbook. Cf. S. Bazley and A. Haynes, *Financial Services Authority Regulation and Risk-Based Compliance*, para. 1.7.; P. Nelson, *Compliance*, para. 5.3.1 ff.

[150] S. Bazley and A. Haynes, *Financial Services Authority Regulation and Risk-Based Compliance*, para. 1.7. Cf. SUP 10.7.8 FSA Handbook ("compliance oversight person").

[151] On the underlying regulatory concept of "management-based regulation" see above para. 13.

 Malte Wundenberg

(bb) Appointment of Members of Senior Management as Compliance Officers

48   The European provisions do not state explicitly whether a member of the senior management can be appointed as a compliance officer. The CESR's technical advice, which was published to help carry out the organisational requirements set up by the MiFID, allows members of senior management to simultaneously be appointed as compliance officers.[152] The BaFin also assumes that members of senior management can also become compliance officers, provided the specific risk situation of the company does not require a full-time compliance officer.[153] In the light of the prohibition of self-monitoring this combination of positions must, however, be seen critically.[154] It is thus only correct that the Italian Banca d'Italia states that a compliance officer who is at the same time part of the senior management should not have direct responsibilities with regard to operative areas.[155] Especially with regard to larger investment firms, appointing managing directors simultaneously as compliance officers should be avoided in order to prevent conflicts of interest.[156]

(b)   Legal Status

49   The compliance officer has an important position in the company: in order to ensure that he can act effectively he should have a high position in the company's hierarchy and be able to report directly to the management.[157] It is thus generally recommended that the compliance officer be placed at the top of the organisation under the direct authority of the senior management.[158] Furthermore, the principle of independence that applies to both the compliance function and the compliance officer requires that the compliance officer is not subject to instructions or otherwise influenced by other units of the investment firm.[159]

(aa)   Independence towards Senior Management

50   A number of interpretational difficulties arise with regard to the question of independence between the compliance officer and the senior management, the directives containing no provisions thereon. While the fact that measures adopted by the senior management are also subject to the compliance officer's supervision, indicating that

---

[152] CESR, *Technical Advice on Possible Implementing Measures of the Directive 2004/39/EC on Markets in Financial Instruments, 1st Set of Mandates*, CESR/05-024c, January 2005, p. 15, Box 2 No. 9a and Commission, *Background Note*, Sec. 3.2. The ESMA guidelines do not seem to address this issue.

[153] BaFin, *Rundschreiben* (circular) *4/2010 (MaComp)*, June 2011, BT 1.1.1 para. 2.

[154] In detail: J.A. Harm, *Compliance*, p. 65–66.

[155] Banca d'Italia, *The Compliance Function*, July 2007, p. 6; Basel Committee on Banking Supervision, *Compliance and the Compliance Function in Banks*, April 2005, Principle 5, para. 26.

[156] Cf. J.A. Harm, *Compliance*, p. 65–66.

[157] CESR, *Technical Advice on Possible Implementing Measures of the Directive 2004/39/EC on Markets in Financial Instruments, 1st Set of Mandates*, CESR/05-024c, January 2005, p. 15, Box 2 No. 9a ("direct reporting line"); Basel Committee on Banking Supervision, *Compliance and the Compliance Function in Banks*, April 2005, Principle 5, para. 24 ff. See also ESMA, *Guidelines on Certain Aspects of the MiFID Compliance Function Requirements, Final Report*, ESMA/2012/388, July 2012, general guideline 5, para. 43 and 48.

[158] Cf. Gabbi et al., *Managing Compliance Risk after MiFiD*, p. 5; Austrian Standard Compliance Code, *Grundsätze ordnungsgemäßer Compliance*, para. 5 and 6; R. Veil, WM (2008), p. 1093, 1097; D. Eisele, in: H. Schimansky et al. (eds.), *Bankrechts-Handbuch*, § 109 para. 125 ff.; J. Bürkle, in: C.E. Hauschka (ed.), *Corporate Compliance*, § 8 para. 31; T. Lösler, WM (2008), p. 1098, 1102–1103.

[159] BaFin, *Rundschreiben* (circular) *4/2010 (MaComp)*, June 2011, BT 1.1.1 para. 1.

---

the compliance officer should also be largely independent from the management,[160] Article 9 Organisational Requirements Directive assigns the final right and obligation to ensure compliance to senior management.[161] This leads to considerable tension between the principle of independence of the compliance officer on the one hand and the corporate and supervisory principle of an overall compliance responsibility of senior management on the other. The legal literature is thus embroiled in an intense debate on the legal nature and the status of the compliance officer, centring around the question whether this officer is bound to instructions by the management or is independent thereof.[162]

51   The discussion can be led back to the dual regulatory aim of the European compliance concept mentioned above.[163] The MiFID's concept of a compliance officer requires him to deal with conflicting interests:[164] as an employee of an investment firm it is obliged to act in the interest of the company. At the same time, his responsibility to monitor internal legality is in the public interest.[165] So far, the legal literature has placed a greater emphasis on the first aspect, understanding the compliance officer as a "man of the company"[166].[167] The enactment of the MiFID has, however, brought a change in the responsibilities of the compliance officer: the fact that one of the main regulatory objectives of the directive is to promote investor protection indicates that the compliance officer is now to be understood primarily as an advocate of public interest.[168] The compliance officer must thus be understood as having a special position in the company, based on the registration and approval requirements and his individual disciplinary independence.[169] His legal status is increasingly becoming comparable to that of a classical *Betriebsbeauftragter*, i.e. company representative, in German law who is independent in terms of performing his duties.[170]

52   The national supervisory authorities appear to follow the understanding that the compliance officer is bound by instructions given by the management,[171] his independence being nonetheless ensured by a number of additional measures. The BaFin, for example, does not only require notification and documentation when a compliance officer is dismissed, but further documentation whenever the man-

---

[160] Cf. ESMA, *Guidelines on Certain Aspects of the MiFID Compliance Function Requirements, Final Report*, ESMA/2012/388, July 2012, general guideline 7, para. 58, which clarifies that the tasks performed by the compliance function should be "carried out independently from senior management".

[161] See above para. 24.

[162] Cf. R. Veil, WM (2008), p. 1093 ff. on the one hand and T. Lösler, WM (2008), p. 1098 ff. and M. Casper, *Der Compliancebeauftragte*, in: G. Bitter et al. (eds.), *Festschrift für Karsten Schmidt*, p. 199 ff. on the other. See also J.A. Harm, *Compliance*, p. 64 ff.

[163] See above para. 12–13.

[164] Cf. R. Veil, WM (2008), p. 1093, 1096 ff.

[165] See above para. 12.

[166] T. Lösler, in: T. Hellner and S. Steuer (eds.), *Bankrecht und Bankpraxis*, para. 7/814.

[167] Cf. T. Lösler, WM (2008), p. 1098 ff. and M. Casper, *Der Compliancebeauftragte*, in: G. Bitter et al. (eds.), *Festschrift für Karsten Schmidt*, p. 199 ff.

[168] See above para. 7 and 12.

[169] See para. 53.

[170] Summarising the concept of a compliance officer under German law, T. Lösler, in: T. Hellner and S. Steuer (eds.), *Bankrecht und Bankpraxis*, para. 7/814. More details on this very complex question in R. Veil, WM (2008), p. 1093, 1096 ff. and J.A. Harm, *Compliance*, p. 67 ff.

[171] Cf. BaFin, *Rundschreiben* (circular) *4/2010 (MaComp)*, June 2011, BT 1.1.1 para. 1.

agement largely overrules a compliance officer's evaluation and recommendation.[172] This is in line with the recently published ESMA guidelines.[173] Such actions must be listed in the compliance report,[174] ensuring that they can be examined by the supervisory function. In practice this leads to a strengthening of the compliance officer's position. The Austrian financial supervision ensures an even farther-reaching independence, having recently explicitly opposed the concept of the compliance officer being bound by managerial instructions.[175]

(bb) Disciplinarian Independence and Protection against Dismissal

53   The independence from managerial instructions must be distinguished from the disciplinary independence of compliance officers.[176] This concept describes the fact that the compliance officer must be exempt from sanctions being imposed against him as a reaction to failure by the firm to comply with its obligations. Such sanctions are particularly likely to involve employment law-related measures. Whether the compliance officer should generally be exempt from the risk of dismissal has been much debated in the legal literature.[177] European law has not included this form of protection in its directives.[178] The BaFin suggests that a compliance officer should be appointed for at least 24 months in order to ensure independence, recommending a 12-month period of notice.[179] In France the AMF must be notified of any sanctions imposed against the compliance officer.[180] The ESMA aims to protect the independence of the compliance officer by suggesting that he should only be replaced by senior management or by the supervisory function.[181]

(c)   Responsibilities and Powers

(aa) Informational Rights and the Right to Issue Instructions

54   The compliance officer's powers can be divided into informational and investigative powers on the one hand and intervention powers on the other: just like other

---

[172] Ibid., BT 1.1.1 para. 5.

[173] ESMA, *Guidelines on Certain Aspects of the MiFID Compliance Function Requirements, Final Report,* ESMA/2012/388, July 2012, general guideline 7, para. 59. ESMA initially proposed that senior management shall only be allowed to issue "general instructions" to compliance staff and shall otherwise not interfere with the compliance function's day-to-day activities. As this may have been incompatible with the ultimate compliance responsibility of senior management, this sentence has been deleted in the final guidelines.

[174] On the compliance report see below para. 57–58.

[175] FMA, *Rundschreiben* (circular) *betreffend die organisatorischen Anforderungen des Wertpapieraufsichtsgesetzes,* May 2007, p. 9 with explicit reference to R. Veil, WM (2008), p. 1093. See also A. Fuchs, in: A. Fuchs (ed.), *Kommentar zum WpHG,* § 33 para. 86; D. Illing and K. Umnuß, CCZ (2009), p. 1, 4.

[176] The terminology is not yet uniform. Cf. T. Lösler, in: T. Hellner and S. Steuer, *Bankrecht und Bankpraxis,* para. 7/833.

[177] On this discussion see R. Veil, WM (2008), p. 1093, 1997–1998; M. Casper, *Der Compliancebeauftragte,* in: G. Bitter et al. (eds.), *Festschrift für Karsten Schmidt,* p. 199, 210–211; D. Illing and K. Umnuß, CCZ (2009), p. 1, 6 ff. J. Rodewald and U. Unger, BB (2007), p. 1629, 1633 requires the compliance officer to be protected from dismissal *de lege ferenda.*

[178] Commission, *Consultation Paper, Review of the Markets in Financial Instruments Directive (MiFID)* (December 2010), p. 67 submits the dismissal of the compliance officer to the approval of board and the notification of the supervisory authority.

[179] BaFin, *Rundschreiben* (circular) *4/2010 (MaComp),* June 2011, BT 1.1.1 para. 6. Similarly Standard Compliance Code, Grundsätze ordnungsgemäßer Compliance, No. 5.

[180] Art. 313-36 RG AMF.

[181] ESMA, *Guidelines on Certain Aspects of the MiFID Compliance Function Requirements, Final Report,* ESMA/2012/388, July 2012, general guideline 7, para. 57.

---

members of the compliance staff, a compliance officer must be granted unrestricted access to all information necessary in order to fulfil his compliance duties,[182] and furthermore must be permitted to report directly to senior management.[183] The ESMA guidelines suggest that the compliance officer should also be able to attend meetings of senior management or the supervisory function.[184]

55   The principle of effectiveness further requires compliance officers to have authority to terminate critical transactions at a very early stage.[185] The BaFin, for example, allows compliance officers to intervene in the process of signing and approving new products.[186] The European provisions do not, however, bindingly require that compliance officers be given the right to issue instructions and remedy infringements personally. This can be deduced *e contrario* from Article 6(2)(a) and (3)(b) of the implementing directive, which requires that the compliance function monitors and assesses the adequacy and effectiveness of the measures and procedures of the investment firm, and reports its findings to senior management. The compliance function is not, however, required to take the necessary corrective measures. The European understanding of the compliance officer is thus that it monitors legal risks and passes the information on to the senior management and in some cases to the supervisory authority.[187] Depending on the size and the risk structure of the investment firm, the compliance officer may have to be granted independent investigative powers and the right to issue instructions in some cases, in order to ensure an effective management of compliance risks and thereby a sufficient level of investor protection.[188]

56   The exact nature of the compliance officer's investigative powers and right to issue instructions is a matter of national company law. Due to the fact that the overall responsibility for the compliance organisation lies with the senior management, it must ultimately also decide how to prevent and sanction infringements of law. *De lege ferenda* and based on the MiFID's aim to enhance investor protection, however, it seems recommendable to strengthen the legal status of the compliance officer and to equip him legally with an independent right to issue instructions and intervene personally in certain cases. This would allow the prevention of conflicts of interest when the senior management, to which the compliance officer must report, is personally involved in any violation of the law.

---

[182] Art. 6(3)(a) Organisational Requirements Directive. See above para. 41.

[183] This can be deduced from the advisory function of the compliance officer and also, *e contrario*, from the reporting obligation described in Art. 9(2) Organisational Requirements Directive.

[184] ESMA, *Guidelines on Certain Aspects of the MiFID Compliance Function requirements, Final Report,* ESMA/2012/388, July 2012, general guideline 5, para. 48.

[185] R. Veil, WM (2008), p. 1093, 1098.

[186] BaFin, *Rundschreiben* (circular) *4/2010 (MaComp)*, June 2011, BT 1.2 para. 3. According to § 12(3)2 WpD-VerOV in its version as amended by the German Anlegerschutz- und Funktionsverbesserungsgesetz (German Investor Protection Enhancement and Improvement of the Functioning of the Capital Markets Act) the compliance officer must be permitted to take preliminary measures in order to prevent client interests from becoming affected.

[187] More details in M. Casper, in: Bankrechtliche Vereinigung (ed.), *Bankrechtstag 2008*, p. 139, 158 ff.

[188] On this compliance risk assesement by the senior management see above para. 23–25.

(bb) Compliance Reporting

(1) Internal Reporting

57 The compliance officer must submit internal reports to the senior management and—if existent—to the supervisory function[189] at regular intervals.[190] The directive does not contain details on the content and format of the report, merely stating that the reports should be submitted on a frequent basis, at least annually, and in writing.

58 The compliance report has three aims. The first is to ensure an information basis for the senior management who holds overall responsibility for monitoring that the investment firm is acting in conformity with the law and who is responsible for taking the necessary measures to rectify deficiencies discovered by the compliance function. The report must therefore contain information on the development of compliance risks and on measures that have been taken to mitigate these risks.[191] The second aim of the compliance report is to provide a written basis for the compliance officer to make suggestions to senior management—and if existent to the supervisory function—on possible measures to improve compliance management.[192] While the compliance officer's suggestions and recommendations are not binding for senior management, the management will nevertheless have to examine them closely and will often follow these recommendations.[193] In some Member States the compliance report also aims to support the supervisory tasks of the competent authorities. In France and Luxembourg, for example, the supervisory authorities can refer to the report for informational purposes.[194]

59 In practice, the compliance reports should be synchronised with the reports submitted by the risk management and the internal audit function as the three areas overlap.[195] The volume and frequency of the reports depends on the individual risk situation. In general, annual reports will be regarded as insufficient to supply the management with all necessary information in larger companies, quarterly reports having become most common in practice.[196]

60 The regular reports must be distinguished from so-called ad hoc reports that must be submitted if the investment firm violates the law. For more serious violations ad hoc reports are not a voluntary but rather an obligatory measure for the compliance

---

[189] Art. 9(2) and (3) Organisational Requirements Directive.

[190] Art. 6(3)(b), 9(2) and (3) Organisational Requirements Directive.

[191] Details regarding the content of the compliance reports are specified by ESMA, *Guidelines on Certain Aspects of the MiFID Compliance Function Requirements, Final Report*, ESMA/2012/388, July 2012, general guideline 3, para. 27–32 (especially para. 29). See also K. Muther-Pradler and M. Ortner, in: E. Brandl and G. Saria, *Praxiskommentar zum Wertpapieraufsichtsgesetz*, § 18 para. 33. Cf. D. Sandmann, CCZ (2008), p. 104.

[192] In more detail J.A. Harm, *Compliance*, p. 76 ff.

[193] As mentioned above, ESMA guidelines suggest that any deviations from important recommendations or assessments issued by the compliance function must be documented. See ESMA, *Guidelines on Certain Aspects of the MiFID Compliance Function Requirements, Final Report*, ESMA/2012/388, July 2012, general guideline 7, para. 59.

[194] Art. 1 instruction no. 2008-01 and CSSF, *Circular 04/155*, September 2004, para. 37.

[195] Cf. para. 36 ff. and § 28 para. 2–3.

[196] D. Sandmann, CCZ (2008), p. 104, 107. See also the empirical data in: M. Gallo, *Compliance Function*, p. 325 ff. (Italy); J. Oelkers, *Compliance in Banken*, in: O. Lucius et al. (eds.), *Compliance im Finanzdienstleistungsbereich*, p. 130, 174 ff. (Austria).

officer.[197] If the violation is less severe it will generally be sufficient only to inform the next higher level in the company.[198]

(2) External Reports

61 A controversial issue relates to the question of whether a compliance officer is obliged to inform external bodies, such as supervisory authorities, of legal violations (so-called external reports). The aim of effective capital market supervision and the principle of investor protection supports this idea. The disadvantage of this obligation would be that the reputation of the investment firms would suffer and they would no longer be able simply to sanction the violation internally.

62 The "Standards for Investor Protection" published by the CESR in July 2002 required an external reporting in cases of "serious breaches of conduct of business rules".[199] As opposed to this, the technical standards developed in the course of the MiFID implementation confirm that European law does not require reports to be submitted to supervisory authorities,[200] although the CESR did not rule out the possibility of introducing a legal obligation to this effect.[201]

63 The United Kingdom introduced external reporting obligations for compliance officers on the basis of the duty of firms to cooperate with the regulator, as described in Principle 11 of the FSA Handbook. The FSA has defined this obligation more concretely, stating that any significant breach of a supervisory rule by an investment firm or one of its employees must be reported to the respective authority.[202] In Germany the concept of external reports is controversial.[203] The legal literature largely assumes that there is no legal basis for such an obligation.[204] As described above, the supervisory authorities in France and Luxembourg are permitted to request compliance reports from the companies' compliance officers.[205]

3. Chinese Walls

64 Informational barriers or "Chinese walls" are an essential element of the compliance system.[206] The term refers to any internal policies and procedures that restrict the

---

[197] ESMA, *Guidelines on Certain Aspects of the MiFID Compliance Function Requirements, Final Report*, ESMA/2012/388, July 2012, general guideline 3, para. 30.

[198] For details see M. Casper, in: Bankrechtliche Vereinigung (ed.), *Bankrechtstag 2008*, p. 139, 158 ff.

[199] CESR, *A European Regime of Investor Protection—The Professional and the Counterparty Regimes*, CESR/02-098b, July 2002, para. 11.

[200] Notification obligations for possible breaches of the rules on insider dealings or market manipulation can be found in Art. 6(9) MAD and Art. 7–11 Implementing Directive 2004/72/EC.

[201] CESR, *Technical Advice on Possible Implementing Measures of the Directive 2004/39/EC on Markets in Financial Instruments, 1st Set of Mandates*, CESR/05-024c, January 2005, p. 12.

[202] SUP 15.3.11 FSA Handbook. Cf. S. Bazley and A. Haynes, *Financial Services Authority Regulation and Risk-Based Compliance*, p. 386 ff.

[203] Cf. R. Kittelberger, *Einführung einer neuen Berichtspflicht für Wertpapierdienstleistungsunternehmen und deren Folgen* (2005); T. Lösler, WM (2007), p. 676 ff.; M. Casper, *Der Compliancebeauftragte*, in: G. Bitter et al. (eds.), *Festschrift für Karsten Schmidt*, p. 199, 211.

[204] For banking supervision the "Mindestanforderungen an das Risikomanagement" (MaRisk—minimum requirements for risk management) contain a reporting duty of the internal audit function towards the supervisory authority should "severe violations" by the management become apparent. Cf. BaFin, *Rundschreiben* (circular) *11/2010 (BA)*, December 2010, BT 2.4. para. 5.

[205] See para. 58.

[206] Also termed "screens" in Anglo-American law. Cf. K.J. Hopt, in: S. Kalss et al. (eds.), *Festschrift für Peter Doralt*, p. 213, 214.

flow of information within the investment firm and prevent information which is confidential to one department from being passed freely to other departments.[207] Chinese walls follow two closely connected aims: the restricted flow of information aims to reduce conflicts of interest between the investment firm and the client or between two clients of the investment firm. Chinese walls are further supposed to safeguard inside or other confidential information from being traded or disseminated. The establishment of areas of confidentiality helps to ensure that inside information is only disseminated to other employees of the investment firm if authorised as described in Article 3(a) MAD and thus cannot be used to the detriment of clients.[208]

65   The concept of Chinese walls originated in US capital markets law[209] where it was first developed in a settlement made between the supervisory authority SEC and the brokerage Merrill Lynch, Pierce, Fenner & Smith, Inc.,[210] on the basis of the following facts (abridged): Merrill Lynch obtained inside information on the economic situation (negative profit expectations) of the aircraft manufacturer Douglas Aircraft in the course of its work as lead manager for the issuance of bonds. The "Underwriting Division" passed this information on to the investment department of the brokerage firm, which then informed selected customers of the negative profit expectations of the issuer. The SEC regarded this behaviour as a breach of the rules on inside information. Without confirming this legal assessment, Merrill Lynch committed itself to restricting the internal flow of information and thus preventing the abuse of inside information by taking certain organisational measures.[211] In the United Kingdom Chinese walls have been used to overcome conflicts of interest since the 1970s.[212] Based on the experience in the Anglo-American jurisdictions, Chinese walls have also become a common feature in continental European banks and investment firms.[213]

(a)   Legal Foundations

66   In the Recitals to the MAD, Chinese walls are explicitly mentioned as a preventive measure to combat market abuse.[214] As opposed to this, the MiFID and its implementing directive do not make any explicit reference to the establishment of Chinese walls. Nonetheless it can be assumed that European law demands that

[207] See also the definition offered by the Law Commission, Fiduciary Duties, p. 138: "Procedures for restricting flow of information within a firm to ensure that information which is confidential to one department is not improperly communicated … to any other department within the conglomerate."
[208] T. Lösler, in: T. Hellner and S. Steuer, *Bankrecht und Bankpraxis*, para. 7/8432. On the requirements for a dissemination of inside information see § 13 para. 84–93.
[209] On the legal developments in Anglo-American law see H. McVea, *Financial Conglomerates*, p. 171 and passim; N. Poser, 9 Mich. YBI Legal Stud. (1988), p. 91.
[210] *In re Merrill Lynch, Pierce, Fenner& Smith, Inc.* [1968], 43 SEC 933. In detail N. Poser, 9 Mich. YBI Legal Stud. (1988), p. 91, 105–106.
[211] The organisational measures are described in a "Statement of Policy", imprinted in H. McVea, *Financial Conglomerates*, Appendix II.
[212] The Law Commission's recommendations on the "Fiduciary Duties and Regulatory Duties" of 1992 play an important role in the development of the Chinese wall concept in the UK.
[213] On the legal developments in Germany see D. Eisele, in: H. Schimansky et al. (eds.), *Bankrechts-Handbuch*, § 109 para. 126 ff.; on Swiss law see S. Abegglen, *Wissenszurechnung bei der juristischen Person*, p. 363 ff.; on the legal developments in Spain see A.M. Andrés, 81 RDBB (2001), p. 49 ff.
[214] Recital 24 Directive 2003/6/EC.

investment firms control their internal flow of information through organisational arrangements: the Organisational Requirements Directive requires Member States to ensure that investment firms "establish, implement and maintain systems and procedures that are adequate to safeguard the security, integrity and confidentiality of information, taking into account the nature of the information in question".[215] This general principle is put into more concrete terms in Article 22(3)2(a) Organisational Requirements Directive with regard to the management of conflicts of interest without, however, describing in more detail how the control of the information flow should be organised.[216]

67   In some Member States Chinese walls are expressly mentioned as a tool to manage compliance risk: in France investment firms are required to establish informational barriers (*barrières à l'information*) in order to control the circulation of inside information.[217] This is to help identifying those departments of the company that are in possession of inside information and to separate them physically from other departments as far as possible. The compliance officer is to be notified prior to any dissemination of inside information. In Spain Article 83.1.b and c LMV contain rules on the establishment of Chinese walls (*murallas chinas*).[218] The German BaFin has included extensive guidelines on appropriate organisational measures preventing a free flow of information in the MaComp.[219] In Austria § 4 of the ECV of 2007 (Austrian Issuer Compliance Regulation) and Modul 2 (Insider Dealings and Market Manipulation) of the Standard Compliance Code of 2008 contain similar provisions. In the United Kingdom section 147 FSMA empowers the FSA to enact "control of information rules". Whilst the Handbook does not necessarily require the establishment of Chinese walls, it does contain rules on their legal effects.[220]

(b)   Elements

68   Firms use a combination of different measures in order to control the internal flow of confidential information effectively. Based on the concept of the "reinforced Chinese wall"[221] the restriction of the flow of information by means of informational barriers is supplemented by trading restrictions and further measures designed to prevent conflicts of interest and insider trading.[222] Chinese walls usually consist of the following elements.

---

[215] Art. 5(2) Organisational Requirements Directive.

[216] This is based on a deliberate decision by the legislator: the first CESR Consulation Paper of June 2004 suggested the establishment of informational barriers between proprietary trading, portfolio management and corporate governance (CESR/04-261b, Box 6 No. 7 and 8). This was criticised in the course of the consultation procedure, CESR consequentially introducing more flexible requirements regarding the control of the flow of information in the final version. This regulatory approach is reflected in the final version of the Organisational Requirements Directive, the term "informational barrier" having been replaced by a less stringent definition in Art. 22(3)2(a).

[217] Art. 315-15 RG AMF. Cf. R. Veil and P. Koch, *Französisches Kapitalmarktrecht*, p. 108.

[218] Cf. L.J. Cortés, *El mercado de valores (I): organización. La inversión colectiva*, in: A. Menéndez (ed.), *Lecciones de Derecho Mercantil*, p. 756.

[219] BaFin, *Rundschreiben* (circular) *4/2010 (MaComp)*, June 2011, AT 6.2 para. 3.

[220] SYSC 10.2. FSA Handbook. See below para. 80.

[221] Cf. M. Lipton and R.B. Mazur, 50 N.Y.U. L. Rev. (1975), p. 459 ff.

[222] D. Eisele, in: H. Schimansky et al. (eds.), *Bankrechts-Handbuch*, § 109 para. 36 ff.

(aa) Segregation of Confidential Areas

69   Confidential areas are those departments of a company that are continually or
      temporarily in the possession of inside information or other compliance-relevant
      information.[223] In investment firms this may include, inter alia, the underwriting
      division, the credit department or the department responsible for mergers and
      acquisitions.[224] Any such areas must be segregated from the other departments of
      the company by effective measures, ensuring that confidential information remains
      within this segregated area unless dissemination is necessary for operational rea-
      sons.[225] Depending on the size of a company, segregation is possible on a number of
      levels: the departments can be separated physically, for example, by situating them
      on different floors or in separate buildings. Further possible measures include the
      restriction of communication and access to databases.[226] Employees must undergo
      training in order to be sensitised regarding the importance of a restricted flow
      of information (*mental* Chinese wall). Further measures become necessary if an
      employee is removed from one confidential area to another (*personal* Chinese
      wall).[227]

70   The dissemination of confidential information cannot be prohibited without excep-
      tion as the establishment of informational barriers may conflict with the economic
      aim of efficient company communication and can even endanger the clients'
      interest.[228] A "wall crossing", i.e. exceptions from the informational barriers, must
      therefore be permitted if necessary to ensure the aims of capital market law or to
      fulfil a legal obligation.[229] A cross-departmental flow of information is, however,
      always subject to strict requirements and follows the "need-to-know" principle, only
      allowing the dissemination of information if absolutely necessary and only to the
      extent of absolute necessity.[230]

71   The restrictions on the flow of information further depend on the nature of the
      information involved: inside information as defined by the MAD may only be
      passed on to other employees under the conditions of Article 3(a) MAD, i.e. "in the
      normal course of the exercise of [a person's] employment, profession or duties".[231]
      As opposed to this, publicly known information may be passed on without restric-
      tion, unless other legal provisions state otherwise, for example for reasons of data

---

[223] Cf. § 3 No. 3 ECV 2007. Any information that may cause a conflict of interests can be described as
"compliance-relevant".

[224] A. Meyer and U. Paetzel, in: H. Hirte and T.M.J. Möllers (eds.), *Kölner Kommentar zum WpHG*, § 33
para. 70.

[225] T. Lösler, in: T. Hellner and S. Steuer (eds.), *Bankrecht und Bankpraxis*, para. 7/843.

[226] Cf. M. Kloepfer Pelèse, Bull. Joly Bourse (2009), p. 204, 210.

[227] Law Commission, *Fiduciary Duties*, p. 156 ff. Cf. C. Hollander and S. Salzedo, *Conflicts of Interest &
Chinese Walls*, para. 13–22; D. Eisele, in: H. Schimansky et al. (eds.), *Bankrechts-Handbuch*, § 109 para. 142–143.

[228] C.f. McVea, *Financial Conglomerates*, p. 201 ff.; T. Lösler, in: T. Hellner and S. Steuer, *Bankrecht und
Bankpraxis*, para. 7/843.

[229] An effective risk management may require that inside information is passed on to the risk control function
immediately. Cf. M. Jahn and N. Welter, in: O. Jost (ed.), *Compliance in Banken*, p. 175, 180 ff. with further
examples.

[230] Cf. C. Hollander and S. Salzedo, *Conflicts of Interest & Chinese Walls*, para. 13–22; A. Meyer and U. Paetzel,
in: H. Hirte and T.M.J. Möllers (eds.), *Kölner Kommentar zum WpHG*, § 33 para. 72–73. The requirements for
"wall crossing" remain unclear; P. Buck-Heeb, *Insiderwissen, Interessenkonflikte und Chinese Walls bei Banken*,
in: S. Grundmann et al. (eds.), *Festschrift für Klaus J. Hopt*, p. 1647, 1666 attempts to define these requirements
more concretely.

[231] See § 13 para. 86–88.

protection. "Confidential" information stands between these two extremes, the lack of price relevance preventing it from being classed as inside information, but its disclosure still constituting a potential risk to the clients' interests.[232] Whether "wall crossings" are permitted in these cases must be determined for each case individually, based on a consideration of the conflicting interests.[233]

72   Some Member States have introduced provisions on the requirements for "wall crossings". The German BaFin allows crossings, provided they are necessary for the investment firm to fulfil its obligations. The BaFin argues that if an investment firm is active in a number of different business segments, it may be necessary to disclose confidential information to staff members of other business areas, especially in complex business transactions.[234] The ECV of 2007 takes a similar stance in its principles regarding the disclosure of inside information.[235]

73   Any cross-departmental dissemination of information must be documented and monitored by the compliance function. The compliance officer holds a position above—or "on"—the wall, and acts as a "clearing house" for any compliance relevant information.[236]

(bb) Watch Lists and Restricted Lists

74   A watch list[237] is a highly confidential and regularly updated list of financial instruments on which the investment firm holds compliance-relevant information.[238] The list can then be used by the compliance function in order to examine proprietary, customer and employee tradings for possible insider dealings and conflicts of interest.[239]

75   The business activities of an investment firm are not affected by the fact that certain instruments are included in the watch list. These financial instruments can continue to be recommended to investors and still be an object of proprietary trading. However, if the watch list reveals gaps in the Chinese wall or gives rise to the suspicion that inside information is being used abusively, the compliance officer may cancel the respective transactions.[240] The watch list can only fulfil its aim if employees notify the compliance officer of compliance-relevant information.[241]

---

[232] BaFin, *Rundschreiben* (circular) *4/2010 (MaComp)*, June 2011, AT 6.1. lists the knowledge of customer orders that are used to the clients disadvantage through proprietary transactions as an example.
[233] K. Rothenhöfer, in: S. Kümpel and A. Wittig (eds.), *Bank- und Kapitalmarktrecht*, para. 3.346–347.
[234] BaFin, *Rundschreiben* (circular) *4/2010 (MaComp)*, June 2011, AT 6.2. para. 3(b).
[235] § 6 (2) ECV 2007.
[236] The importance of the compliance function for the supervision of the internal flow of information is emphasised in the SEC's paper *Broker-Dealer Policies and Procedures Designed to Segment the Flow and Prevent the Misuse of Material Nonpublic Information* (May 1990), p. 23. See also D. Eisele, in: H. Schimansky et al. (eds.), *Bankrechts-Handbuch*, § 109 para. 36 ff.
[237] On the relationship between watch lists and the insider lists as required by Art. 6(3)3 MAD and Art. 5 Implementing Directive 2004/72/EC see H. Renz and K. Stahlke, ZfgK (2006), p. 353.
[238] See SEC, *Broker-Dealer Policies* (May 1990), p. 4 ff. (USA); Law Commission, *Fiduciary Duties*, p. 159 f. (UK); BaFin, *Rundschreiben* (circular) *4/2010 (MaComp)*, June 2011, AT 6.2. para. 3(c) (Germany); Standard Compliance Code of 2008, Modul 2: Insider Dealings and Market Manipulation, No. 5.2.1.2 (Austria).
[239] T. Lösler, in: T. Hellner and S. Steuer (eds.), *Bankrecht und Bankpraxis*, para. 7/815.
[240] D. Eisele, in: H. Schimansky et al. (eds.), *Bankrechts-Handbuch*, § 109 para. 36 ff. This particularly applies, if the compliance officer has been awarded the power to personally take remedial measures. See above para. 54–55.
[241] BaFin, *Rundschreiben* (circular) *4/2010 (MaComp)*, June 2011, AT 6.2 para. 3(c).

Malte Wundenberg

76   Most investment firms have additionally introduced a so-called "restricted list" which—unlike the watch list—is freely accessible to all company employees.[242] Proprietary and third-party trading and the recommendation of financial instruments in this list is prohibited.[243] Investment firms may, however, with the authorisation of the compliance officer, make exceptions to these prohibitions.[244]

77   Restricted lists first became relevant in US law. In the case of *Slade v. Shearson, Hammill & Co.*[245] a brokerage house (Shearson, Hammill & Co.) had obtained inside information on the negative economic developments of a certain issuer (Tidal Marine International Corp.) but had nonetheless recommended the company's shares to clients. Shearson argued that the securities department had not known about the inside information due to the existing areas of confidentiality. In an *amicus curiae* brief the SEC recommended diffusing the conflict between the issuer and his clients by introducing restricted lists.[246]

78   Taking account of the far-reaching effects, the restricted list should only contain financial instruments on which an investment firm has inside information that is likely to have a considerable effect on the share price if it becomes public.[247] The inclusion of financial instruments in the restricted list should therefore be seen as an *ultima ratio* measure for situations in which the conflict of interests cannot be mitigated solely by the restriction of the internal information flow.[248]

(c)   Legal Effects

79   The legal effects of Chinese walls have always been a subject of controversy in the legal literature, primarily with regard to the question as to whether effectively established confidential areas protect the firms under civil law and criminal law from the accusation of having participated in insider dealings. Another question that remains unanswered is whether the implementation of informational barriers is sufficient to prevent an attribution of knowledge within the company.

80   These questions have been addressed in the United Kingdom. When a firm establishes and maintains a Chinese wall it may withhold the information and also permit persons employed in the respective part of its business to withhold the information from those employed in other areas.[249] Information may also be withheld between

---

[242] In legal practice there are a number of different restricted lists. The Standard Compliance Code of 2008, Modul 2: Insider Dealings and Market Manipulation, No. 5.2.1.2 distinguishes between selective lists (only applicable for certain departments) and comprehensive lists (applicable to all company employees). Cf. A. Meyer and U. Paetzel, in: H. Hirte and T.M.J. Möllers (eds.), *Kölner Kommentar WpHG*, § 33 para. 77.

[243] BaFin, *Rundschreiben* (circular) *4/2010 (MaComp)*, June 2011, AT 6.2 para. 3(c).

[244] Restricted lists are therefore also described as prohibitions subject to the possibility of authorisation. Cf. D. Eisele, in: H. Schimansky et al. (eds.), *Bankrechts-Handbuch*, § 109 para. 151.

[245] 517 F.2d 398 (2d Cir. 1974).

[246] Cf. L. Loss and J. Seligman, *Fundamentals of Securities Regulation*, p. 1008 ff. and C. Benicke, *Wertpapiervermögensverwaltung*, p. 753 ff.

[247] Cf. I. Koller, in: H.-D. Assmann and U.H. Schneider (eds.), *Kommentar zum WpHG*, § 33 para. 11 (possibility of a suspension of quotation); K. Rothenhöfer, in: S. Kümpel and A. Wittig (eds.), *Bank- und Kapitalmarktrecht*, para. 3.361 (immediate and considerable price change).

[248] The restricted list as a means to prevent insider dealings is seen critically, for example by H. McVea, *Financial Conglomerates*, p. 231–232 and D. Eisele, in: H. Schimansky et al. (eds.), *Bankrechts-Handbuch*, § 109 para. 156.

[249] SYSC 10.2 FSA Handbook. In detail C. Hollander and S. Salzedo, *Conflicts of Interest & Chinese Walls*, para. 13-01 ff. and R. Veil and M. Wundenberg, *Englisches Kapitalmarktrecht*, p. 145–146.

different parts of a business within the same group.[250] If the flow of information has been effectively restricted by the use of Chinese walls, this generally provides a defence against proceedings brought under section 397(2) or (3) FSMA on the basis of an alleged market manipulation.[251] The FSA Handbook further provides a defence for a firm against FSA enforcement action based on a breach of a relevant requirement to disclose or use this information.[252] The Handbook also contains detailed provisions on the effects of Chinese walls on an attribution of knowledge. Generally an investment firm will not be assumed to have acted knowingly if none of the relevant individuals involved on behalf of the firm acted with that knowledge as a result of established Chinese walls.[253]

81   Whilst the FSA's provisions provide a very far-reaching protection against supervisory sanctions, it is as yet unclear whether they also constitute a defence against a common law claim for breach of fiduciary duties.[254] Case law appears to be limited regarding a civil law acknowledgement of Chinese walls,[255] an attribution of knowledge not generally being prevented and liability not automatically being excluded by the establishment of Chinese walls.[256] In line with the prevailing view, the same applies with regard to German law.[257]

V.   Sanctions

82   The MiFID provides Member States with a large margin of appreciation with regard to the enforcement of the organisational obligations of investment firms, only requiring Member States to ensure that the appropriate administrative measures can be taken and administrative sanctions can be imposed, without defining the structure of the required sanctioning regime in detail. European law thus leaves the choice to the national legislator, provided the measures are sufficiently effective, proportionate and dissuasive.[258]

---

[250] SYSC 10.2.2(2) FSA Handbook which, however, only refers to the COBS section of the FSA Handbook (rules of conduct).

[251] SYSC 10.2.3(1) (G) FSA Handbook and sec. 397(4) and (5)(c) FSMA.

[252] SYSC 10.2.2(4) and 10.2.3(2) (G) FSA Handbook; sec. 118A(5)(a) FSMA. See also the "defences" in SYSC 10.2.3(3) (G) against other sanctions.

[253] SYSC 10.2.4 and 10.2.5 (G) FSA Handbook. SYSC 10.2.4. only states this explicitly with regard to the rules of conduct laid down in the COBS and CASS sections of the Handbook. SYSC 10.2.5 is merely a guidance that, however, appears to prevent an attribution of knowledge for all regulated areas.

[254] For an overview of this complex issue see C. Hollander and S. Salzedo, *Conflicts of Interest & Chinese Walls*, para. 13-07 ff.; H. McVea, *Financial Conglomerates*, p. 135 ff. and passim; Law Commission, *Fiduciary Duties*, p. 152 ff. See also K. Jarvis, 3 J. Financ. Crime (2007), p. 192–195.

[255] Cf. House of Lords judgment in the case *Prince Jefri Bolkiah/KPMG* [1999] 1 All ER 517.

[256] See K.K. Mwenda, *Banking Supervision*, p. 88: "Law courts have usually taken the view that Chinese Walls do not afford a solution to the attribution of knowledge"; C. Hollander and S. Salzedo, *Conflicts of Interest & Chinese Walls*, para. 13-08 ff. Seen restrictively by the Law Commission, *Fiduciary Duties*, p. 152 ff.

[257] Cf. P. Buck-Heeb, *Insiderwissen, Interessenkonflikte und Chinese Walls bei Banken*, in: S. Grundmann, et al. (eds.), *Festschrift für Klaus J. Hopt*, p. 1647, 1656 ff.

[258] Art. 51 MiFID; see also § 12 para. 4–5.

Malte Wundenberg

1.   Sanctions against Investment Firms

83   The Member States have developed different enforcement strategies for the compliance requirements.[259] All approaches centre on administrative enforcement by way of investigative and remedial measures and the power to impose administrative fines. The administrative enforcement of the organisational obligations is, however, constructed in different ways. In Germany § 33 WpHG did not initially impose any fines for breaches of the organisational obligations, relying on the general regulatory powers of the BaFin to remedy infringements of supervisory law.[260] Most recently the German Bundestag has, however, deemed certain breaches of the organisational requirements to be an administrative offence.[261] In Sweden the supervisory authority can demand any grievances to be redressed or impose fines (*straffavgift*) of up to 50 million SEK,[262] while the United Kingdom threatens investment firms with unlimited fines.[263]

84   In the United Kingdom the FSA has repeatedly sanctioned failings in the internal governance and control systems, a landmark decision being the case of *Carr Sheppards Crosthwaite Ltd.* (CSC), which occurred before the MiFID was implemented.[264] CSC, a subsidiary 100% owned by Investec plc, was specialised in asset management for private clients. The parent company had identified deficits in the internal control system during an internal audit and had informed the FSA thereof. The FSA regarded CSC's compliance system as insufficient and imposed a fine of £500,000. The FSA criticised the fact that the subsidiary's compliance department did not introduce a direct reporting line to the parent undertaking and that the compliance handbooks were incomplete. More recently the FSA imposed a considerable fine (£5.25 million) against the insurance company Aon Ltd. on the grounds that the company had not taken adequate measures in order to prevent corruption and bribery.[265] Compliance failings have also been sanctioned in the latest landmark decision against Barclays Bank plc:[266] Barclays was found to have manipulated submissions which formed part of Libor (the estimated interest rate at which banks can borrow funds from other banks in the London interbank market) between 2005 and 2009. According to the FSA, Barclay failed to conduct its business with due skill, care and diligence when considering issues raised internally in relation to its Libor submissions. Libor issues were escalated to Barclays' compliance function on three occasions during 2007 and 2008. In each case the compliance staff failed to assess and address these issues effectively. Due to these compliance failings (and other breaches of law)

---

[259] For an overview of the Member States supervisory powers and possible sanctions regarding the obligations laid down in the MiFID see CESR, *Supervisory Powers, Supervisory Practices, Administrative and Criminal Sanctioning Regimes of Member States in Relation to the Markets in Financial Instruments Directive (MiFID),* CESR/08–220, February 2009.

[260] Cf. A. Fuchs, in: A. Fuchs (ed.), *Kommentar zum WpHG,* § 33 para. 3.

[261] § 39 No. 17b WpHG as amended by the Anlegerschutz- und Funktionsverbesserungsgesetzes (maximum fines of €200,000).

[262] According to Kapitel 25, § 9(2) LVM this is restricted to 10% of the previous year's turnover.

[263] On the enforcement practice of the FSA see *Decision Digest,* p. 273 ff.

[264] FSA, *Final Notice,* 19 May 2004.

[265] FSA, *Final Notice,* 6 January 2009.

[266] FSA, *Final Notice,* 27 June 2012.

the FSA fined Barclays £59.6 million. For similar reasons, a fine of £160 million was imposed on the UBS, the largest FSA fine to date.[267]

85   Sanctions under civil law do not as yet appear to play any role in sanctioning breaches of compliance obligations; in fact, civil law sanctions have been expressly ruled out by some Member States.[268]

2.   Sanctions against the Senior Management and the Compliance Officer

86   The enforcement measures that can be taken against investment firms must be distinguished from measures addressed directly to senior management or to the compliance officer. This concept of a direct supervisory responsibility of senior management or the compliance officer is known, for example, in Sweden,[269] the United Kingdom[270] and—in principle—in Germany.[271] The breach of compliance obligations can further constitute a breach of internal duties of care, leading to damage claims for the investment firm against the management.[272] In the United Kingdom fines and other supervisory measures can be directed against both senior management and the compliance officer.[273]

87   In Germany the Bundesgerichtshof (BGH, German Federal Court of Justice) decision of 17 July 2009 has led to a controversial discussion on the criminal liability of compliance officers.[274] The 5th Strafsenat (criminal division) purported in an obiter dictum that the compliance officer will generally have a special responsibility as required by § 13(1) StGB (German Criminal Code) (so-called *Garantenstellung*, i.e. guarantor duty) to prevent employees of an investment firm from committing crimes related to the company's business. According to the BGH this constituted the necessary consequence of the compliance officers' obligation to prevent violations of legal provisions (particularly criminal offences).[275] The legal literature has strongly criticised the BGH's ruling.[276] Whether the compliance officer is to be regarded as criminally responsible for preventing breaches of the rules on insider dealings based on his *Garantenstellung* therefore appears doubtful. In the United Kingdom, the accountability of senior management

---

[267] FSA, *Final Notice*, 27 June 2012, para 17–18 and 162–184. Interestingly, the fine was imposed solely on the basis of the FSA Principles (Principles 2, 3 and 5) and not on the basis of MiFID rules.

[268] In the United Kingdom liability is excluded in SYSC Sch. 5.4 FSA Handbook (and in sec. 150 FSMA with regard to private damage claims). In Germany it is assumed that violations of compliance obligations (§ 33 WpHG) do not give rise to a private cause of action, cf. A. Fuchs, in: A. Fuchs (ed.), *Kommentar zum WpHG*, Vor §§ 31 bis 37a para. 83.

[269] Pursuant to Kapitel 25, § 4(2) LVM the FI can require the dismissal of the managing director and appoint a successor.

[270] Sec. 66 FSMA. See also fn. 287.

[271] This applies to investment firms that are credit and financial service institutions in the sense of the KWG, cf. § 25a(1)2 KWG. Breaches of the organisational obligations can lead to warnings or a dismissal of the management, cf. § 36 KWG.

[272] More details on this topic in German law in M. Wundenberg, *Compliance und die prinzipiengeleitete Aufsicht über Bankengruppen*, p. 132–136 and passim.

[273] Compliance officers are "approved persons" and as such must adhere to the FSA Handbook's "Statements of Principles", cf. APER 2.1.2 (P), especially Principle 5, see above para. 21 and 47. For details on the FSA's sanctioning powers towards approved persons see FSA, *Enforcement Guide*, October 2010, para. 9.1. ff.

[274] BGHSt 54, p. 44, 50.

[275] BGHSt 54, p. 44, 50.

[276] Cf. T. Rönnau and F. Schneider, ZIP (2010), p. 53 ff.

for compliance failings has recently been subject of the FSA decision against *John Pottage*. The FSA alleged that Pottage (who was in a controlling function of UBS Wealth Management Ltd.) failed "to take reasonable steps to identify and remediate the serious flaws in the design and operational effectiveness of the governance and risk management framework", issuing a fine of £100,000 for breaching APER Statement of Principle 7. However, this decision was overruled by the Upper Tribunal, which concluded that there was insufficient evidence to support the case, indicating that an approved person will only be in breach of the Principles where it is "personally culpable, and not simply because a regulatory failure has occurred in an area of business for which it is responsible".[277]

VI. Conclusion

88   The MiFID and the Organisational Requirements Directive have introduced a comprehensive regime regarding compliance, risk management and internal audit in investment firms. The European provisions reflect a regulatory trend that has also become apparent in other areas of supervisory law, namely to require supervised firms as well as their senior management to develop systems of internal control and governance arrangements in order to enhance investor protection and market efficiency. The European legislator opted for a principles-based approach to regulation, granting investment firms a large margin of appreciation regarding the implementation of the regulatory requirements. The European provisions do, however, explicitly require the establishment of an independent compliance function and the appointment of a compliance officer.

89   The European provisions are based on the Basel Committee on Banking Supervision's principles concerning the development of a risk-orientated compliance organisation and are an important contribution to the harmonisation of the organisational obligations for investment firms. Nevertheless differences in the legal practice of the Member States still exist, especially regarding the legal status of the compliance officer and the supervisory authorities' sanctioning powers. Against this backdrop, the recent attempts made by the ESMA to promote greater convergence in the interpretation of the organisational principles laid down in the MiFID, as well as the supervision of these principles by the competent national authorities, must be welcomed.

90   It seems recommendable, especially considering the recent experience gained during the financial crisis, to strengthen further the internal compliance and risk management function in order to increase investor protection and market efficiency. The European Commission's proposal to place a greater emphasis on the effectiveness of the compliance and risk management function and to ensure their independence towards senior management could therefore be a determining factor for future legal developments.[278]

---

[277] *John Pottage v. FSA*, FS/2010/0033 at para. 148.
[278] Cf. Commission, *Public Consultation: Review of the Markets in Financial Instruments Directive (MiFID)* (December 2010), p. 67–68 ("strengthening the involvement of board members in the functioning of the compliance, risk management and internal audit functions"). See § 28 para. 6.

7

Conclusion

---

§ 30   A Review of the Past and Suggestions for the Future

I.   Topics for Final Consideration

1   If one reviews the legislative process of capital markets law in Europe, it appears necessary to refer back to the initial question[1] of whether European capital markets law has become an independent field of law, perhaps even with first indications of a codified system.[2] The answer to this question can be found by examining the current European provisions, their structure and implementation into the national law of the Member States and the underlying concepts of enforcement. Further aspects also require consideration: in 2000 the Lamfalussy Committee complained that the European provisions on capital markets law were interpreted in many different ways throughout Europe.[3] Has this changed? A summary of the conclusions in the preceding chapters will not be offered here.[4] Rather, it should suffice to point out the main findings on unity and disparity in European capital markets law.

2   These insights enable a forecast regarding the challenges in the future: do European legislative acts need to be better adapted to each other? What are possible concepts for enforcement and sanctions? Which aspects should be regulated at a European level and which should rather be left to national legislation? A final question to be considered is the future role of legal experts in the legislative procedures, where their involvement has so far been neglected at a European level.

---

[1] See Preface and § 6 para. 40–43.
[2] See Preface.
[3] See § 1 para. 17.
[4] For further information on the following see the chapters on insider dealings § 13 para. 138–140, market manipulation § 14 para. 92–93, short sellings § 15 para. 21–22, prospectus disclosure § 17 para. 75–76, the disclosure of financial information § 18 para. 78–81, disclosure of inside information § 19 para. 144–146, disclosure of major shareholdings § 20 para. 140–143, directors' dealings § 21 para. 30–31, disclosure regarding control over a company § 24 para. 58–61, investment firms § 25 para. 14–15, financial analysts § 26 para. 88, rating agencies § 27 para. 67 and on the organisational requirements for investment firms § 29 para. 88–90.

II. Capital Markets Law(s) in Europe or European Capital Markets Law?

1. Degree of Existing Provisions

3   The number of existing European provisions on capital markets law is impressive: already the four framework directives comprise more than 100 articles which are complemented by more than 100 further articles in the implementing legislative acts. The Takeover Directive provides another 23 articles, the regulation on rating agencies more than 50, and over 80 provisions concern the new European supervisory authority, the European Securities and Markets Authority (ESMA). The extent and density of European capital markets legislation is, in other words, impressive. This has been confirmed in this book regarding the rules on market abuse, transparency regimes, informational intermediaries and the requirements regarding compliance in investment firms. Nearly all procedures on capital markets are subject to European legislation.[5]

4   This legal situation is the result of several decades of legislative proceedings. Originally the impulse came from the European Commission, which regarded harmonisation as essential for a uniform internal market. The more recent impressive increase in European provisions can, however, only be explained in terms of the financial crisis. Based on the insights gained during the crisis, the European legislature—partly under the influence of the Member States[6]—regarded it as necessary to regulate rating agencies[7] and short selling[8] at a European level and to establish a European supervisory authority.[9] Without the financial crisis, politics would have prevented these decisive steps in European capital markets law.

5   Capital markets law has matured considerably. Some areas, such as the provisions on insider dealings, prospectuses, the disclosure of inside and financial information and the organisational requirements for investments firms, have passed through two phases of legislation within only twenty years.[10] The experience gained with these first legislative acts enabled the European legislature to develop more refined directives, giving the regimes on insider dealings and disclosure clearer outlines. Other areas, such as the rules on market manipulation and financial intermediaries, were developed more recently and have not yet been subject to similar changes. Nevertheless they already appear well developed. The rules on market manipulation profited from the European legislature's experience regarding insider dealings, the regulatory concept following the same approach of first supplying general definitions and subsequently giving more precise examples of and signals for market manipulation.[11] The provisions on rating agencies also follow existing regulatory strategies. The

---

[5] Recently, even a new regulation on short sellings was introduced. See § 15 para. 9.

[6] The European Commission at first did not regard the regulation of short sellings as necessary. Only when a number of Member States began introducing provisions to this effect, did the Commission initiate a European regulation. See § 15 para. 8–9.

[7] See § 27 para. 11.

[8] See § 15 para. 9.

[9] See § 1 para. 35 and § 11 para. 37.

[10] See § 1 para. 5–27.

[11] See § 14 para. 25–27.

central rules on the duty of care when compiling a rating,[12] for example, are based on the regulatory approach developed with regard to financial recommendations and analyses.[13] The organisational requirements for rating agencies[14] are comparable to the provisions for investment firms contained in the Markets in Financial Instruments Directive (MiFID) and the implementing Organisational Requirements Directive.[15]

6　All areas are now once again being revised and the European Commission has started a consultation process on the revision of the framework directives.[16] An intense communication with capital market participants has helped the Commission determine the need for amendments and develop effective new rules. The amendments to the Prospectus Directive[17] brought a number of important new provisions[18] without, however, changing the overall concept of prospectus law. It is to be expected that the revision of the other framework directives will run a similar course.[19]

2.　Consistent Application of Law

7　The aim of ensuring a unified level of regulation is to reduce the costs of transactions on the European capital markets, thereby strengthening the allocative efficiency of capital markets. Additionally the purpose of the consistent application of law throughout the European Union is to protect investors, ensuring the institutional functioning of the capital markets—aims that would be endangered if the implementation, application and interpretation of the European provisions were to be handled differently in the individual Member States.[20] The European legislature has provided various legal structures in order to fulfil this aim.

8　Most requirements and prohibitions, especially those on market manipulation and transparency, are contained in detailed provisions, instead of mere general clauses that would require supervisory practice and the courts to develop case groups, putting the abstract requirements into a more concrete form. The European legislature has rather enacted additional implementing directives that provide definitions of the most important legal terms contained in the respective framework directives.[21] These provisions do not provide the answer to all questions regarding the interpretation of the directives: this is neither possible nor necessary as no set of rules will ever prove acceptable without additional interpretation. It is sufficient that the most relevant terms are defined in the directives, at least preventing a discussion on the interpretation of the most relevant terms. For all other terms, the interpre-

---

[12] See § 27 para. 40.

[13] See § 26 para. 28.

[14] See § 27 para. 25–33.

[15] See § 29 para. 29–41.

[16] The European Commission organised conferences and encouraged interested parties to submit written statements. The evaluation process is described on the Commission's website at: http://ec.europa.eu/internal_market/securities/news/index_en.htm.

[17] See § 17 para. 5.

[18] See § 17 para. 33 and 35.

[19] The European Commission plans to enact a regulation on market abuse in the future. See § 1 para. 41.

[20] ESMA's powers towards the national supervisory authorities for cases of an incorrect application of the law are, pursuant to Art. 17 ESMA Regulation, restricted to cases in which directly applicable provisions in regulations were applied incorrectly. See § 11 para. 58–61.

[21] A typical example is the term "inside information". See § 13 para. 32–48 and § 19 para. 32–48.

tational guidelines published by the Committee of European Securities Regulators (CESR) and the ESMA provide initial orientation. These guidelines must, however, be applied with care as they are not binding on the national courts of the Member States who sometimes deviate from the authorities' understanding of certain provisions.[22] At the same time, this is a common phenomenon and does not overly influence the consistent application of the law throughout the European Union, both civil and criminal jurisprudence helping to achieve a conclusive understanding of the provisions.

9   Other areas, especially the organisational requirements for investment firms, financial analysts and rating agencies, are subject to a principles-based approach to regulation. The respective provisions are abstract, leaving the persons to whom they are addressed with a choice of measures that fulfil the regulatory aim.[23] None of the European provisions, however, grants them *plein pouvoir*, always giving directions on possible measures. The principles are further put into more concrete terms by "circulars" and "letters" published by the national supervisory authorities.[24] This "guidance" is common throughout Europe. Nevertheless it is not uniform, the supervisory authorities sometimes applying and recommending diverse approaches and organisational measures.[25] These differences, however, usually only affect details. In general the principles-based approach has thus also improved the consistent application of the law.[26] A further aspect of this regulatory strategy is the fact that the approaches to interpretation taken by the supervisory authorities are usually undisputed, so that there is generally no discrepancy between the supervisory and the judicial understanding of the provisions.

3.   Supervision and Sanctions

10   When determining whether a European capital markets law has become an independent field of law one must also take into account the concept of supervision and the possible sanctions. The legal situation with regard to the supervision of the markets is disparate. The administrative powers of the supervisory authorities are only outlined roughly in the directives. The Member States must provide their authorities with general powers to take the necessary measures if legal provisions are violated. They must further supply them with informational and supervisory powers and allow them to prohibit certain behaviours. The authorities are, however, at the same time subject to the national constitutional and administrative provisions, which restrict the authority's enforcement possibilities to an extent that is as yet unclear. In some Member States the administrative enforcement is accompanied by different forms of private enforcement, a particularly impressive example being financial reporting, which can comprise various elements from different fields of law, such as audits by independent auditors as is common in stock exchange and

---

[22] Especially striking in the case of *Daimler/Geltl*, cf. § 6 para. 10.
[23] In more detail on this regulatory strategy § 4 para. 51–61 and § 29 para. 4–11.
[24] See, for example, § 29 para. 10.
[25] See, for example, § 29 para. 11.
[26] See in particular § 29 para. 89.

Rüdiger Veil

accounting law,[27] and financial accounting supervision by a private body[28] which is supplemented by the supervision through the administrative authority[29] and the shareholders.[30]

11   A clear statement on sanctions in European capital markets law is even harder to give, and as yet only the rating regulation[31] provides clear requirements.[32] According to the four framework directives, Member States shall ensure that the sanctions are effective, proportionate and dissuasive. The directives do not, however, provide any more specific requirements for the sanctions. It therefore comes as no surprise that the Member States operate with manifold sanctioning instruments,[33] the only common tendency being the use of criminal sanctions, which are primarily applied in cases of breaches of the rules on market abuse. The differences are nevertheless considerable—liability, for example, requiring anything from intent to gross or ordinary negligence.[34] The possible penalties and the sanctions imposed in reality also vary greatly.[35]

12   The most common supervisory sanctions are fines. They are often imposed on investors and issuers against breaches of notification and disclosure obligations, as described in Chapter 3. The degree of liability required and the possible sanctions once again vary between the Member States. Some Member States additionally provide the possibility of a private enforcement, either in the form of a loss of voting rights for breaches of notification obligations[36] or in the form of damage claims of investors against the issuer and its management on the basis of the disclosure of incorrect information.[37]

4.   Conclusions

13   Closer examination of the levels of sanction has proven that European capital markets law cannot yet exist without national legislation. Not only the legal consequences, however, but also the facts of a provision rely strongly on national law, more than 90% of European law still being enacted in the form of directives that are not directly applicable in the Member States but rather require implementation. As a result the European provisions are often not transposed one-to-one, the Member

---

[27] Audits are fully harmonised under European law. Cf. Directive 2006/43/EC of the European Parliament and the Council of 17 May 2006 on statutory audits of annual accounts and consolidated accounts, amending Council Directives 78/ 660/EEC and 83/349/EEC and repealing Council Directive 84/253/EEC, OJ L157, 9 June 2006, p. 87.

[28] In Germany the Deutsche Prüfstelle für Rechnungslegung e.V. (Financial Reporting Enforcement Panel) is responsible for balance sheet control. A similar system can be found in the UK where the Financial Reporting Review Panel ensures that the annual accounts of public companies and large private companies comply with the requirements of the Companies Act 2006 and the applicable accounting standards.

[29] The German BaFin plays a subsidiary role in financial reporting as opposed to the Deutsche Prüfstelle für Rechnungslegung e.V.

[30] The shareholders can file a suit against an annual financial statement. This question has not been harmonised at a European level.

[31] See § 27 para. 58–61.

[32] See § 12 para. 4.

[33] See § 12 para. 10–21.

[34] On insider dealings see § 13 para. 15–31.

[35] See § 12 para. 10, 12, 14, 16, 18 and 20, § 13 para. 124–126 and § 14 para. 85–86.

[36] See § 12 para. 7 and § 20 para. 91–95.

[37] See § 12 para. 7, § 17 para. 50–74, § 18 para. 63–71, § 19 para. 108–128 and § 20 para. 96–98.

States rather introducing rules,[38] definitions and terms[39] which are adapted better to their national systems. In some areas, especially with regard to the transparency of major shareholdings[40] and insider dealings[41] the Member States have even exceeded the European requirements, developing additional, farther-reaching rules.

14   The provisions in the numerous directives and regulations originating from Brussels can nevertheless collectively be regarded as an independent, European, field of law. The Member States' national capital markets laws nowadays centre on implementing provisions for European provisions, thereby mainly aiming to fulfil the requirements set out by the European rules. The considerable differences in legal application which the Lamfalussy Committee found to exist in 2000 can no longer be discerned. Whilst the financial crisis repeatedly led some Member States to press ahead, enacting stricter provisions, this does not change the conclusion that a European capital markets law has developed.

15   European capital markets law can certainly not yet be regarded as a full codification,[42] some provisions proving unsystematic and not well adapted to the concept as a whole. Additionally the European legislature has as yet not called for the development of exhaustive European rules. Nevertheless the European provisions show first elements of a codification:[43] the European approach is to prevent market abuse with a multitude of prohibitions—a concept that no longer contains significant gaps. Additionally notification and disclosure obligations ensure an efficient pricing by determining that informational intermediaries, such as financial analysts and rating agencies, evaluate the information in a way that enables investors to rely on their results. Both the rules on information and the rules on market abuse are subject to supervision by the authorities and to self-control by investment firms and issuers. The individual elements are thus closely connected in their overall aim to ensure the functioning of the markets by strengthening investor confidence.

III.   Prospects and Challenges

1.   Reorganisation of the European Sources of Capital Markets Law

16   In future the connections between the different areas of regulation could grow stronger at a European level. The four framework directives must be seen from a historical point of view—each having been enacted as an answer to current issues,

---

[38] Market manipulations, for example, have been regulated in a different way in Germany than envisaged by the MAD. In direct contrast to this, the Swedish legislature only introduced a single general clause. See § 14 para. 9.

[39] This is most obvious with regard to insider dealings and inside information. Cf. § 13 para. 15–31 and § 19 para. 34–36.

[40] Strict provisions apply with regard to transparency regarding the influence of voting rights (additional notification thresholds, different provisions on the attribution of voting rights), transparency of financial instruments, and investor intentions.

[41] The principle-based approach to legislation taken in the United Kingdom (§ 13 para. 31 and 119) has the effect that the rules on insider dealings are generally more strict than required by the MAD.

[42] German methodology defines codification as a collection of provisions on a certain area of law that attempts to regulate the area as completely as possible. Cf. F. Bydlinski, *Juristische Methodenlehre und Rechtsbegriff*, 2nd ed. (1991), p. 573.

[43] A systematic interpretation is therefore of particular importance, see § 5 para. 43–47.

Rüdiger Veil

rather than in a larger concept. The Market Abuse Directive (MAD), for example, provides rules for different areas of regulation, including market manipulation and insider dealing on the one hand, and financial analysts on the other. Additionally the obligation to disclose inside information and the notification obligations regarding directors' dealings would have been better suited for the Transparency Directive (TD) than for the MAD.[44] For now the Commission still plans to leave the content of the four framework directives largely unchanged,[45] although a systematic restructuring of the provisions, comparable to the European Commission's approaches to banking law,[46] appears far more recommendable.[47]

17   The notification and disclosure obligations spread out over the MAD and the TD should, for example, be incorporated into one single legislative instrument, separating the provisions on insider dealings and market manipulation. Comparable to the new provisions on rating agencies, the rules on financial analysts should also be implemented into a separate directive or regulation.[48] Such restructuring would render the regime more systematic and the different areas could be better adapted to each other. Introductory general provisions for all disclosure obligations could contain definitions of the most important terms and answer questions regarding the scope of application of the provisions or on the home Member State principle. Additionally a legal structure based on the underlying concept of the respective provisions would give the opportunity to develop general principles for the notification and disclosure of price-relevant information.

18   A final aspect that needs to be discussed concerns the question as to which areas should continue to be regulated by directives and for which areas regulations appear more suited. This distinction should be made based on the level of enforcement and particularly with regard to the possible sanctions. Market abuse provisions, which are traditionally subject to criminal law sanctions, should remain regulated by a directive, leaving the Member States the choice of whether to introduce additional prohibitions.[49] All other areas should, however, be incorporated into regulations, which clearly determine whether the Member States should be permitted to introduce additional stricter rules.[50]

---

[44] Some Member States have recognised this and implemented the MAD's provisions on inside information and directors' dealings in the sections of their statutes on transparency. See § 19 para. 4–6.

[45] Cf. Commission Proposal on the Revision of the Framework Directives (§ 1 para. 41 ff.).

[46] The European Commission is currently revising the Capital Requirements Directive which is in future to be divided into one large framework directive and a regulation (CRD IV).

[47] The ideal situation would be a uniform codification of the entire European capital markets law. Yet at the moment this is not realistic, which is why this book is recommending (at least) the "lesser approach".

[48] It would be effective to develop uniform legislation for financial analysts and rating agencies in which general questions relevant for both could be regulated in a general introductory section. The complexity of this project, however, makes it appear doubtful that the European legislature will opt for this approach, especially as legal literature provides no solutions as yet and it is unclear whether this approach would really help in legal practice.

[49] The draft proposal for a new Directive on criminal sanctions for insider dealing and market manipulations (cf. § 1 para. 41) only aims at minimum harmonisation of criminal provisions.

[50] The question regarding the remaining legislative powers of the Member States is complex. One must determine whether the Member States are to be prohibited from enacting any new provisions in an area regulated by European law (e.g. additional notification thresholds for major shareholdings, cf. § 20 para. 17–26), or whether they are not even permitted to enact further provisions in areas that are, as yet, unaffected by the European provisions (e.g. a notification and disclosure obligation with regard to an investor's intentions when acquiring major shareholdings, cf. § 20 para. 127–138). Until a full European codification exists, the latter is neither desir-

2. Regulatory Concepts Regarding Enforcement and Sanctions

19   Future developments regarding sanctions and enforcement will depend on the instruments the European legislature uses regarding substantive law. If the rules for issuers, investors and intermediaries are introduced by way of regulation, the ESMA should be responsible for supervision, as is the case regarding rating agencies.[51] This is not, however, mandatory; with regard to regulations, supervision does not necessarily have to take place at a European level. Neither does it appear realistic that the Member States will convey all powers from their national supervisory authorities to the ESMA within the next few years. The focus must therefore be drawn to the challenges to be met by the Member States in the context of a reform of the framework directives.

20   The powers of the national supervisory authorities as outlined by the framework directives must be the starting point of this examination. More precise requirements would be neither necessary nor adequate, based on a consideration of the fact that only the Member States can decide how far their supervisory authority's powers should reach and whether (additionally) elements of a principles-based supervision, as exists in the United Kingdom, should be introduced.[52] The Member States must decide on all these questions at a national level, taking into account their constitutional requirements.

21   The applicable sanctions are only outlined roughly at a European level. The European Commission justifiably wants to introduce clearer requirements and its envisaged concepts appear to be a step in the right direction: naming and shaming is to become a common practice and the fines are to be increased. Additionally, however, another instrument should be made more effective: disgorgement has not as yet reached its full effectiveness, although it can have considerable deterrent effects. The Member States should thus be obliged to develop independent rules, permitting the supervisory authorities to estimate and disgorge profits obtained illegally.

22   Furthermore it is to be expected that private enforcement will become increasingly important in Europe. The European legislature need not, however, develop harmonising rules thereon, national concepts appearing preferable. The experience of the past few years has shown that the Member States are aware of the competition between their legal systems. The United Kingdom, for example, which traditionally relied on supervisory measures, has only recently introduced rules on civil liability,[53] and is further planning provisions on class actions.[54] In order to gain investor protection and remain competitive on the European market the Member States will thus not be able to avoid developing the necessary substantial and procedural rules for damage claims. Neither damage claims nor other methods of private enforcement such as a loss of rights for investors breaching their obligations are, however, able entirely to replace measures of public enforcement.

---

able nor politically realistic. Short sellings have proven that often the incentive for a European legislation is given by the legislature of the Member States.

[51] See § 27 para. 52–57 and § 11 para. 60–61.
[52] Cf. F. Walla, *Die Konzeption der Kapitalmarktaufsicht in Deutschland* (2012).
[53] See § 19 para. 124.
[54] See § 12 para. 21.

Rüdiger Veil

3. Legislation 2015: Stronger Influence of Legal Knowledge

23   Since 2011 legislation in Europe has been following a new approach: the ESMA plays an important role in the Lamfalussy Process, next to the European Commission. Neither ministerial bureaucracy nor supervision, however, can do without external expert knowledge. The Commission therefore acts upon the capital markets practice and takes the practical view into account. The consultation procedure is open to all people and organisations. The Commission further relies on reports presented by expert groups[55] and selected organisations.[56] Legal experts have not, however, been involved—not one of the high-level experts in the most important groups was a legal professional. Legal experts are also rarely seen in the permanent groups of experts. All the members of the European Securities Markets Expert Group (ESME), responsible for advising the European Commission, have other professions. Whilst the ESMA does not have an advisory board as such, it has been assigned the so-called "Securities and Markets Stakeholder Group" which facilitates the consultations between the ESMA and stakeholders when drafting regulatory technical standards.[57] Only 4 of the 29 members of this group are academics,[58] the others belonging to practice.

24   Whilst any legal professionals are free to give their opinion during the consultation process,[59] European capital markets legislation should in the future make use of expert knowledge in a more institutionalised framework. The analysis of European capital markets law presented in this book has shown the complex nature of this concept. It is necessary to take all professional disciplines, legal systems and traditions involved into account if further harmonisation is to be achieved in the future. Any political steps towards a principles-based approach to regulation and a harmonisation of the sanctioning regime should in future only occur under consultation with experts from the legal profession.

---

[55] The most important expert groups in European capital markets legislation were the Segré Group, the Lamfalussy Group and the de Larosière Group. See § 1 para. 2, 16 and 33.

[56] The European Commission orders reports from private organisations such as auditing companies and law firms, as was recently the case with regard to the revision of the Transparency Directive (report by Mazars) and the Takeover Directive (report by Marccus Partners). The studies are to examine the general opinion of the market participants on the effectiveness of the directive.

[57] See information on the ESMA website.

[58] Aleksander Chlopecki, Professor of Law, University Warsaw; Jesper Lau Hansen, Professor of Financial Markets Law, University Copenhagen; Niamh Moloney, Professor of Financial Markets Law, London School of Economics and Political Science (LSE); Pierre-Henri Conac, Professor of Financial Commercial Law, Université du Luxembourg.

[59] To date only infrequent use of this possibility has been made—according to the website of the European Commission (http://ec.europa.eu/internal_market/securities/docs/transparency/transparency-consultation-summary_en.pdf) only one of 111 reports was submitted by an academic in the consultation procedure for the Transparency Directive.

Bibliography

Afrell, Lars et al., *Lärobok i kapitalmarknadsrätt*, 2nd ed. (1998).

Andersson, Sten et al., *Aktiebolagslagen. En kommentar på Internet* (2009).

Annunziata, Filippo, *La disciplina del mercato mobiliare*, 4th ed. (2008).

Assmann, Heinz-Dieter and Schneider, Uwe H. (eds.), *Wertpapierhandelsgesetz, Kommentar*, 6th ed. (2012).

Assmann, Heinz-Dieter and Schütze, Rolf A. (eds.), *Handbuch des Kapitalanlagerechts*, 3rd ed. (2007).

Baetge, Jörg et al., *Bilanzen*, 10th ed. (2009).

Bagge, James et al. (eds.), *Financial Services Decision Digest: FSA Final Notices and FSMT Decisions* (2007).

Baumbach, Adolf and Hopt, Klaus J., *Handelsgesetzbuch, Kommentar*, 34th ed. (2010).

Baums, Theodor and Thoma, Georg F. (eds.), *Kommentar zum WpÜG*, as of November 2010.

Beckman, Mats et al., *Lagarna på värdepappersområdet. En kommentar till insiderstrafflagen m. fl. lagar* (2002).

Bergmann, Cecilia et al. (eds.), *Karnov Lagkommentar på Internet, Lag (2007:528) om värdepappersmarknaden*, loose-leaf, as of 1 July 2009.

Bergmann, Cecilia et al. (eds.), *Karnov Lagkommentar på Internet, Lag (1991:980) om handel med finansiella instrument*, as of 2009.

Bergmann, Cecilia et al. (eds.), *Karnov Lagkommentar på Internet, Lag (2006:451) om offentliga uppköpserbjudanden på aktiemarknaden*, as of 1 July 2009.

Bieber, Roland et al., *Die Europäische Union*, 8th ed. (2009).

Birds, John and Boyle, A.J., *Boyle & Birds' Company Law*, 7th ed. (2009).

Blair, Michael (ed.), *Annotated Guide to the Financial Services and Markets Act 2000*, 2nd ed. (2005).

Blair, Michael (ed.), *Blackstone's Guide to the Financial Services and Markets Act 2000*, 2nd ed. (2010).

Blair, Michael et al. (eds.), *Financial Services Law* (2009).

Bonneau, Thierry and Drumond, France, *Droit des marchés financiers*, 2nd ed. (2005).

Brandl, Ernst and Saria, Gerhard (eds.), *Praxiskommentar zum Wertpapieraufsichtsgesetz*, 2nd ed. (2010).

Buck-Heeb, Petra, *Kapitalmarktrecht*, 5th ed. (2011).

Callies, Christian and Ruffert, Matthias (eds.), *Das Verfassungsrecht der Europäischen Union mit Europäischer Grundrechtecharta—Kommentar*, 3rd ed. (2007).

Campbell, Dennis (ed.), *International Securities Law and Regulation* (2008).

Carlson, Laura, *Fundamentals of Swedish Law* (2009).

Claussen, Carsten P., *Bank- und Börsenrecht*, 4th ed. (2008).

Coffee, John C., Jr., and Seligman, Joel, *Securities Regulation*, 9th ed. (2003).

Costi, Renzo, *Il mercato mobiliare* (2010).

Couret, Alain and Le Nabasque, Hervé, *Droit financier*, 2nd ed. (2012).

Cox, James D. and Hazen, Thomas L., *Corporations*, 2nd ed. (2003).

Bibliography

Dauses, Manfred A. (ed.), *Handbuch des EU-Wirtschaftsrechts*, as of June 2010.

Davies, Paul L., *Gower and Davies' principles of modern company law*, 8th ed. (2008).

Edwards, Vanessa, *EC Company Law* (1999).

Eidenmüller, Horst (ed.), *Ausländische Kapitalgesellschaften im deutschen Recht* (2004).

Eilers, Stephan et al. (eds.), *Unternehmensfinanzierung* (2008).

EWG-Kommission (ed.), *Der Aufbau eines Europäischen Kapitalmarkts: Bericht einer von der EWG Kommission eingesetzten Sachverständigengruppe (Segré-Bericht)* (1966).

Ferran, Eilís, *Company Law and Corporate Finance* (1999)

Fleischer, Holger (ed.), *Handbuch des Vorstandsrechts* (2006).

Franke, Günter and Hax, Herbert , *Finanzwirtschaft des Unternehmens und Kapitalmarkt,* 6th ed. (2009).

French, Derek et al. , Mayson, *French & Ryan on Company Law*, 27th ed. (2010).

Fuchs, Andreas (ed.), *Kommentar zum WpHG* (2009).

Goette, Wulf and Habersack, Mathias (eds.), *Münchener Kommentar zum Aktiengesetz*, Vol. 1, 3rd ed. (2010); Vol. 6 (2011); Vol. 9a, 2nd ed. (2004).

Grabitz, Eberhard and Hilf, Meinhard (eds.), *Das Recht der Europäischen Union*, Vol. 3, as of April 2009.

Groß, Wolfgang (ed.), *Kapitalmarktrecht—Kommentar zum Börsengesetz, zur Börsenzulassungs-Verordnung, zum Wertpapierprospektgesetz und zum Verkaufsprospektgesetz*, 4th ed. (2009).

Grunewald, Barbara and Schlitt, Michael, *Einführung in das Kapitalmarktrecht*, 2nd ed. (2009).

Gullifer, Louise and Payne, Jennifer, *Corporate Finance Law* (2011)

Haarmann, Wilhelm and Schüppen, Matthias (eds.), *Frankfurter Kommentar zum WpÜG*, 3rd ed. (2008).

Habersack, Mathias and Verse, Dirk A., *Europäisches Gesellschaftsrecht*, 4th ed. (2011).

Habersack, Mathias et al., *Unternehmensfinanzierung am Kapitalmarkt*, 2nd ed. (2008).

Habersack, Mathias et al. (eds.) , *Handbuch der Kapitalmarktinformation* (2008).

Haratsch, Andreas et al., *Europarecht*, 7th ed. (2010).

Hauschka, Christoph, E. (ed.), *Corporate Compliance: Handbuch der Haftungsvermeidung im Unternehmen*, 2nd ed. (2010).

Haynes, Andrew, *Financial Services Law Guide*, 3rd ed. (2006).

Hazen, Thomas L. Heinze, Stephan, *The Law of Securities Regulation*, 6th ed. (2009-2012).

Europäisches Kapitalmarktrecht, Recht des Primärmarktes (1999).

Hellner, Thorwald and Steuer, Stephan (eds.), *Bankrecht und Bankpraxis, loose-leaf,* as of October 2010.

Hernández Sainz, Esther, *El abuso de información privilegiada en los mercados de valores* (2007).

Hess, Burkhard et al. (eds.), *Kölner Kommentar zum KapMuG* (2008).

Hirte, Heribert and Möllers, Thomas M.J. (eds.), *Kölner Kommentar zum WpHG* (2007).

Hirte, Heribert and von Bülow, Christoph (eds.) , *Kölner Kommentar zum WpÜG*, 2nd ed. (2010).

Hopt, Klaus J., *Der Kapitalanlegerschutz im Recht der Banken* (1975).

Hopt, Klaus J. and Voigt, Hans-Christoph (eds.), *Prospekt- und Kapitalmarktinformationshaftung—Recht und Reform in der Europäischen Union, der Schweiz und den USA* (2005).

Horspool, Margot and Humphreys, Matthew, *European Union Law* (2010).

Kalss, Susannne et al., *Kapitalmarktrecht* , Vol. I (2005).

Kübler, Friedrich and Assmann, Heinz-Dieter, *Gesellschaftsrecht*, 6th ed. (2006).

Kümpel, Siegfried et al. (eds.) , *Kapitalmarktrecht*, looseleaf, as of January 2010.

Kümpel, Siegfried and Veil, Rüdiger, *Wertpapierhandelsgesetz*, 2nd ed. (2006).

Kümpel, Siegfried and Wittig, Arne (eds.), *Bank- und Kapitalmarktrecht*, 4th ed. (2011).

Langenbucher, Katja, *Aktien- und Kapitalmarktrecht*, 2nd ed. (2011).

Langenbucher, Katja (ed.), *Europarechtliche Bezüge des Privatrechts*, 2nd ed. (2008).

Lenenbach, Markus, *Kapitalmarktrecht und kapitalmarktrelevantes Gesellschaftsrecht*, 2nd ed. (2010).

Lenz, Carl-Otto and Borchardt, Klaus-Dieter (eds.), *EU-Verträge: Kommentar nach dem Vertrag von Lissabon*, 5th ed. (2010).

Lomnicka, Eva and Powell, John L. (eds.), *Encyclopedia of Financial Services Law*, looseleaf, as of December 2010.

Lord Millett et al. (eds.), *Gore-Browne on Comapanies*, looseleaf, as of January 2011.

Loss, Louis and Seligman, Joel, *Securities Regulation,* Vol. 1, 3rd ed. (1998).

Loss, Louis and Seligman, Joel, *Fundamentals of Security Regulation*, 5th ed. (2004).

MacNeil, Iain, G., *An Introduction to the Law on Financial Investment* (2005).

Marsch-Barner, Reinhard and Schäfer, Frank A. (eds.), *Handbuch börsennotierte AG*, 2nd ed. (2009).

Mathijsen, Petrus S.R.F., *A Guide to European Union Law*, 10th ed. (2010).

Menéndez, Aurelio, *Lecciones de Derecho Mercantil*, 6th ed. (2008).

Merkt, Hanno and Göthel, Stephan R., *US-amerikanisches-Gesellschaftsrecht*, 2nd ed. (2006).

Moloney, Niamh, *EC Securities Regulation*, 2nd ed. (2008).

Morse, Geoffrey (ed.), *Palmer's Company Law*, looseleaf, as of December 2010.

Oppermann, Thomas et al., *Europarecht*, 4th ed. (2009).

Panasar, Raj and Boeckman, Philip, *European Securities Law* (2010).

Park, Tido (ed.), *Kapitalmarktstrafrecht*, 2nd ed. (2008).

Raiser, Thomas and Veil, Rüdiger, *Recht der Kapitalgesellschaften*, 5th ed. (2009).

Rechtschaffen, Alan N., *Capital Markets, Derivatives and the Law* (2009)

Richter, Rudolf and Furubotn, Eirik G., *Neue Institutionenökonomie*, 4th ed. (2010).

Riesenhuber, K. (ed.), *Europäischen Methodenlehre—Grundfragen der Methoden des Europäischen Privatrechts*, 2nd ed. (2010).

Samuelsson, Per et al., *Lagen om marknadsmissbruk och lagen om anmälningsskylighet—En kommentar* (2005).

Schäfer, Frank A. and Hamann, Uwe (eds.), *Kapitalmarktgesetze, Kommentar*, 2nd ed., looseleaf, as of March 2010.

Schimansky, Herbert et al. (eds.), *Bankrechts-Handbuch*, 3rd ed. (2007).

Schmidt, K. (ed.), *Münchener Kommentar zum Handelsgesetzbuch*, Vol. 3, 2nd ed. (2008); Vol. 5, 2nd ed. (2009).

Schmidt, Karsten and Lutter, Marcus (eds.), *Aktiengesetz—Kommentar*, 2nd ed. (2010).

Schulze, Rainer et al. (eds.), *Europarecht, Handbuch für die deutsche Rechtspraxis*, 2nd ed. (2010).

Schwark, Eberhard and Zimmer, Daniel (eds.), *Kapitalmarktrechtskommentar*, 4th ed. (2010).

Schwarze, Jürgen (ed.), *EU-Kommentar*, 2nd ed. (2009).

Sealy, Len and Worthington, Sarah, *Cases and Materials in Company Law*, 9th ed. (2010).

Steiner, Josephine and Woods, Lorna, *EU Law*, 10th ed. (2009).

Streinz, Rudolf (ed.), *EUV/EGV: Vertrag über die Europäische Union und Vertrag zur Gründung der Europäischen Gemeinschaft*, Kommentar (2003).

Streinz, Rudolf et al., *Der Vertrag von Lissabon zur Reform der EU*, 3rd ed. (2010).

Swan, Edward J. and Virgo, John, *Market Abuse Regulation*, 2nd ed. (2010).

Tapia Hermida, Alberto J., *Derecho del Mercado de Valores*, 2nd ed. (2003).

Bibliography

Valette, Jean-Paul, *Droit de la régulation des marchés financiers* (2005).

Veil, Rüdiger and Koch, Philipp, *Französisches Kapitalmarktrecht* (2010).

Veil, Rüdiger and Walla, Fabian, *Schwedisches Kapitalmarktrecht* (2010).

Veil, Rüdiger and Wundenberg, Malte, *Englisches Kapitalmarktrecht* (2010).

Von der Groeben, Hans and Schwarze, Jürgen (eds.), *Kommentar zum Vertrag über die Europäische Union und zur Gründung der Europäischen Gemeinschaft*, 6th ed. (2003).

Weber, Stefan, *Kapitalmarktrecht* (1998).

Werlauff, Erik, *EU Company Law, Common Business Law of 28 Member States*, 2nd ed. (2003).

Winternitz, Christian P. and Aigner, Lukas, *Wertpapieraufsichtsgesetz* (2007).

Zib, Christian et al. (eds.), *Kapitalmarktgesetz Kommentar* (2008).

Zöllner, Wolfgang and Noack, Ulrich (eds.), *Kölner Kommentar zum Aktiengesetz*, Vol. 6, 3rd ed. (2004).

Zunzunegui, Fernando, *Derecho del Mercado Financiero*, 3rd ed. (2005).

Guidelines, reports and other CESR and ESMA documents cited in this book are available at: www.esma.europa.eu.

Subject Index

The numbers in bold type refer to §, the numbers in normal type refer to para.

Index of National Laws

Abbreviation/title	Full national title	Translated title	Country
ABGB	Allgemeines Bürgerliches Gesetzbuch	Austrian General Civil Code	Austria
ABL	Aktiebolagslag (SFS 2005:551)	Swedish Stock Corporation Act	Sweden
Act on the Prevention of Improper Securities and Derivatives Transactions	Gesetz zur Vorbeugung gegen missbräuchliche Wertpapier- und Derivategeschäfte	Act on the Prevention of Improper Securities and Derivatives Transactions	Germany
AktG	Aktiengesetz	German Stock Corporations Act	Germany
AnSVG	Anlegerschutzverbesserungsgesetz	German Investor Protection Improvement Act	Germany
AO	Abgabenordnung	German Act on the Administrative Procedures in Taxation	Germany
APER	Code of Practice of Approved Persons (FSA Handbook)		UK
årsredovisningslag	årsredovisningslag	Swedish Accounts Act	Sweden
BEHV–EBK	Verordnung der Eidgenössischen Finanzmarktaufsicht über die Börsen und den Effektenhandel	Swiss Regulation on Stock Exchanges and Securities Trading	Switzerland
Beteiligungsfondsgesetz	Beteiligungsfondsgesetz	Austrian Equity Participation Funds Act	Austria
BGB	Bürgerliches Gesetzbuch	German Civil Code	Germany
BilMoG	Gesetz zur Modernisierung des Bilanzrechts	German Accounting Law Modernisation Act	Germany
BörseG	Börsengesetz	Austrian Stock Exchange Act	Austria
BörsG	Börsengesetz	German Stock Exchange Act	Germany
BörsO FWB	Börsenordnung für die Frankfurter Wertpapierbörse	German Exchange Rules for the Frankfurter Wertpapierbörse	Germany
BörsZulVO	Börsenzulassungs-Verordnung	German Stock Exchange Admission Regulation	Germany
BrB	Brottsbalk (SFS 1995:1554)	Swedish Criminal Code	Sweden
C. com.	Code de commerce	French Commercial Code	France
C. mon. fin.	Code monétaire et financier	French Monetary and Financial Code	France
CASS	Client Asset Sourcebook (FSA Handbook)		UK
Cc	Code Civil	French Civil Code	France
CC	Código Civil	Spanish Civil Code	Spain
CJA	Criminal Justice Act 1993		UK
COBS	Conduct of Business Sourcebook (FSA Handbook)		UK
Codice Civil	Codice Civil	Italian Civil Code	Italy
Companies Act 2006	Companies Act 2006		UK

Index of National Laws

Abbreviation/title	Full national title	Translated title	Country
Company Act 1980	Company Act 1980		UK
Consiglio Nazionale degli Ordini dei Giornalisti	Consiglio Nazionale degli Ordini dei Giornalisti	The Italian National Council's Regulation of Journalists	Italy
CP	Código Penal	Spanish Criminal Code	Spain
Criminal Justice Act 1993 (Commencement No. 5) Order (SI 1994/242)	Criminal Justice Act 1993 (Commencement No. 5) Order (SI 1994/242)		
DTR	Disclosure Rules and Transparency Rules (FSA Handbook)		UK
ECV	Emittenten-Compliance-Verordnung of 2007	Austrian Issuer Compliance Regulation	Austria
FinAnV	Verordnung über die Analyse von Finanzinstrumenten	German Regulation on the Analysis of Financial Instruments	Germany
Finansinspektionen's regulation FFFS 2007:16	Finansinspektionen's regulation FFFS 2007:16	Shwedish MaComp	Sweden
Finanzmarktaufsichtsgesetz	Finanzmarktaufsichtsgesetz	Austrian Financial Market Supervision Act	Austria
FinDAG	Gesetz über die Bundesanstalt für Finanzdienstleistungsaufsicht	German Law on the Financial Services Supervisory Authority	Germany
FMABG	Finanzmarktaufsichtsbehördengesetz	Austrian Financial Markets Supervisory Authorities Act	Austria
FRUG	Finanzmarktrichtlinie-Umsetzungsgesetz	German Financial Market Directive Implementation Act	Germany
FSA Handbook	FSA's Handbook of Rules and Guidance		UK
FSMA 2000	Financial Services and Markets Act 2000		UK
Gesetz zur Stärkung des Anlegerschutzes und Verbesserung der Funktionsfähigkeit des Kapitalmarktes	Gesetz zur Stärkung des Anlegerschutzes und Verbesserung der Funktionsfähigkeit des Kapitalmarktes	German Investor Protection Enhancement and Improvement of the Functioning of the Capital Markets Act	Germany
GG	Grundgesetz	German Constitution	Germany
Grundsätze ordnungsmäßer Compliance	Grundsätze ordnungsmäßer Compliance	Austrian Standard Compliance Code	Austria
HGB	Handelsgesetzbuch	German Commercial Code	Germany
Investment Recommendations (Media) Regulations 2005	Investment Recommendations (Media) Regulations 2005		UK
Investmentfondsgesetz	Investmentfondsgesetz	Austrian Investmentfund Act	Austria
KapInHaG	Kapitalmarktinformationshaftungsgesetz	German Capital Markets Information Liability Act	Germany
KapMuG	Gesetz über Musterverfahren in kapitalmarktrechtlichen Streitigkeiten	German Capital Markets Model Case Act	Germany
KMG	Kapitalmarktgesetz	Austrian Capital Market Act	Austria
KuMaKV	Verordnung zur Konkretisierung des Verbots der Kurs- und Marktpreismanipulation	German Regulation for the Implementation of the Prohibition on Market and Price Manipulation	Germany
KWG	Gesetz über das Kreditwesen	German Banking Act	Germany

Abbreviation/title	Full national title	Translated title	Country
lag om anmälningssky-ldighet vissa innehav av finansiella instrument	lag om anmälningsskyldighet vissa innehav av finansiella instrument	Swedish Act on the Disclosure of Ownership regarding Certain Financial Instruments	Sweden
lag om börs- och clearing-verksamhet (SFS 1992:543)	lag om börs- och clearingverk-samhet (SFS 1992:543)	Swedish Act on Stock Markets and Clearing	Sweden
lag om investeringsfonds (SFS 2004:46)	lag om investeringsfonds (SFS 2004:46)	Swedish Investment Fund Act	Sweden
lag om offentliga upp-köpserbjudanden på aktiemarknaden (SFS 2000:1087)	lag om offentliga uppköpserb-judanden på aktiemarknaden (SFS 2000:1087)	Swedish Takeover Act	Sweden
lag om straff för marknadsmissbruk vid handel med finansiella instrument (SFS 2005:377)	lag om straff för marknadsmiss-bruk vid handel med finansiella instrument (SFS 2005:377)	Swedish Market Abuse Act	Sweden
lag om värdepappersrörelse (SFS 1991:981)	lag om värdepappersrörelse (SFS 1991:981)	Swedish Act on securities trans-actions	Sweden
lag omgrupprättegång (SFS 2002:599)	lag omgrupprättegång (SFS 2002:599)	Swedish Group Proceedings Act	Sweden
LHF	lag om handel med finansiella instrument (SFS 1991:980)	Swedish Act on the trading in Financial Instruments	Sweden
LMV	Ley 24/1988, de 28 de julio, del Mercado de Valores	Spanish Securities Market Act	Spain
LSA	Ley de Sociedades Anónimas	Spanish Stock Corporation Act	Spain
LVM	lag om värdepappers-marknadenv (SFS 2007:528)	Swedish Securities Market Act	Sweden
MaComp	Mindestanforderungen an Compliance	BaFin's Minimum Requirements for Compliance	Germany
MaKonV	Verordnung zur Konkretisierung des Verbotes der Marktmanipu-lation	German Implementing Regulation on the Prohibition of Market Manipulation	Germany
MAR	Code of Market Conduct/ Market Abused Regulation (FSA Handbook)		UK
MaRisk	Mindestanforderungen an das Risikomanagement	German Minimum Requirements for Risk Management	Germany
MVSV	Mindestinhalts-, Veröffentlichungs- und Sprachenverordnung	Austrian Ordinance on Minimum Contents, Publication and Language	Austria
öAktG	Österreichisches Aktiengesetz	Austrian Stock Corporation Act	Austria
öUWG	Unlauterer-Wettbewerbs-Gesetz	Austrian Act against Unfair Practices	Austria
OWiG	Gesetz über Ordnungswidrig-keiten	German Administrative Offenses Act	Germany
PRIN	Principles for Businesses (FSA Handbook)		UK
RD	Real Decreto	Spanish Royal Decree (Regula-tion)	Spain

Abbreviation/title	Full national title	Translated title	Country
RD 1310/2005	Real Decreto 1310/2005, de 4 de noviembre, por el que se desarrolla parcialmente la Ley 24/1988, de 28 de julio, del Mercado de Valores, en materia de admisión a negociación de valores en mercados secundarios oficiales, de ofertas públicas de venta o suscripción y del folleto exigible a tales efectos	Spanish Royal Decree (Regulation) on Prospectuses	Spain
RD 1333/2005	Real Decreto 1333/2005, de 11 de noviembre, por el que se desarrolla la Ley 24/1988, de 28 de julio, del Mercado de Valores, en materia de abuso de mercado	Spanish Royal Decree (Regulation) on Market Abuse	Spain
RD 1362/2007	Real Decreto 1362/2007, de 19 de octubre, por el que se desarrolla la Ley 24/1988, de 28 de julio, del Mercado de Valores, en relación con los requisitos de transparencia relativos a la información sobre los emisores cuyos valores estén admitidos a negociación en un mercado secundario oficial o en otro mercado regulado de la Unión Europea	Spanish Royal Decree (Regulation) on Transparency on Capital Markets	Spain
RD 217/2008	Real Decreto 217/2008, de 15 de febrero, sobre el régimen jurídico de las empresas de servicios de inversión y de las demás entidades que prestan servicios de inversión y por el que se modifica parcialmente el Reglamento de la Ley 35/2003, de 4 de noviembre, de Instituciones de Inversión Colectiva, aprobado por el Real Decreto 1309/2005, de 4 de noviembre	Spanish Royal Decree (Regulation) on Investment Firms	Spain
RD 1066/2007	Real Decreto 1066/2007, de 27 de julio, sobre el régimen de las ofertas públicas de adquisición de valores	Spanish Royal Decree (Regulation) on Takeovers	Spain
RE	Regolamento Emittenti	Italian Issuers' Regulation	Italy
	Real Decreto-ley 5/2005, de 11 de marzo, de reformas urgentes para el impulso a la productividad y para la mejora de la contratación pública	Spanish Royal Decree-Act (Regulation) on urgent reforms to increase productivity and to improve public procurement	Spain
Regolamento Congiunto	Regolamento Congiunto	Italian Compliance Regulation	Italy
Regolamento Intermediari	Regolamento Intermediari	Italian Regulation on Intermediaries	Italy
Regolamento Mercati	Regolamento Mercati	Italien Financial Markets Regulation	Italy

Abbreviation/title	Full national title	Translated title	Country
Regulation FFFS 2005:9	Regulation FFFS 2005:9	Swedish Regulations and general guidelines regarding investment recommendations directed to the general public and the management of conflicts of interest	Sweden
RG AMF	Règlement général Autorité des Marchés Financiers	General Regulations of the French Stock Market Authority	France
RRM	Reglamento del Registro Mercantil	Spanish regulation on Company Registries	Spain
SEC Rules	SEC Rules		USA
Securities Exchange Act 1934	Securities Exchange Act 1934		USA
SFS	Svensk förtfattningssamling	Swedish law gazette	Sweden
StGB	Strafgesetzbuch	German Criminal Code	Germany
SYSC	Senior Management Arrangements, Systems and Controls (FSA Handbook)		UK
Takeover Code	Takeover Code		UK
TUF	Testo Unico della Finanza	Italian Consolidated Laws on Finance	Italy
TUG	Transparenzrichtlinie-Umsetzungsgesetz	German Implementing Act on the Transparency Directive	Germany
ÜbG	Übernahmegesetz	Austrian Takeover Act	Austria
VAG	Versicherungsaufsichtsgesetz	German Law on Insurance Supervision	Germany
VMV	Veröffentlichungs- und Meldeverordnung	Austrian Disclosure and Notification Regulation	Austria
vædipapirhandelslov	vædipapirhandelslov	Danish Securities Trading Act	Denmark
WAG	Wertpapieraufsichtsgesetz	Austrian Securities Supervision Act	Austria
WpAiV	Verordnung zur Konkretisierung von Anzeige-, Mitteilungs- und Veröffentlichungspflichten sowie der Pflicht zur Führung von Insiderverzeichnissen nach dem Wertpapierhandelsgesetz	German Regulation on Disclosure of Securities Trading and Insider Dealings	Germany
WpDVerOV	Verordnung zur Konkretisierung der Verhaltensregeln und Organisationsanforderungen für Wertpapierdienstleistungsunternehmen	German Regulation Implementing the Rules of Conduct and Organisational Requirements for Investment Service Companies	Germany
WpHG	Gesetz über den Wertpapierhandel	German Securities Trading Act	Germany
WpHMV	Verordnung über die Meldepflichten beim Handel mit Wertpapieren und Derivaten	German Regulation on the Notification Obligations when Trading with Securities and Derivatives	Germany
WpPG	Wertpapierprospektgesetz	German Securities Prospectus Act	Germany
WpÜG	Wertpapiererwerbs- und Übernahmegesetz	German Securities Acquisition and Takeover Act	Germany

Index of National Laws

Abbreviation/title	Full national title	Translated title	Country
WpÜGAngebVO	Verordnung über den Inhalt der Angebotsunterlage, die Gegenleistung bei Übernahmeangeboten und Pflichtangeboten und die Befreiung von der Verpflichtung zur Veröffentlichung und zur Abgabe eines Angebots	German WpÜG Offer Ordinance	Germany
ZPO	Zivilprozessordnung	German Civil Procedure Code	Germany

Index of National Laws by Country

Austria

National title	Translated title	Abbreviation
Allgemeines Bürgerliches Gesetzbuch	Austrian General Civil Code	ABGB
Beteiligungsfondsgesetz	Austrian Equity Participation Funds Act	
Börsengesetz	Austrian Stock Exchange Act	BörseG
Emittenten-Compliance-Verordnung of 2007	Austrian Issuer Compliance Regulation	ECV
Finanzmarktaufsichtsbehördengesetz	Austrian Financial Market Supervisory Authorities Act	FMABG
Finanzmarktaufsichtsgesetz	Austrian Financial Market Supervision Act	
Grundsätze ordnungsmäßiger Compliance	Austrian Standard Compliance Code	
Investmentfondsgesetz	Austrian Investmentfund Act	
Kapitalmarktgesetz	Austrian Capital Market Act	KMG
Kuratorengesetz	Austrian Bond Act	
Mindestinhalts-, Veröffentlichungs- und Sprachenverordnung	Austrian Ordinance on Minimum Contents, Publication and Language	MVSV
Österreichisches Aktiengesetz	Austrian Stock Corporation Act	öAktG
Übernahmegesetz	Austrian Takeover Act	ÜbG
Unlauterer-Wettbewerbs-Gesetz	Austrian Act against Unfair Practices	öUWG
Veröffentlichungs- und Meldeverordnung	Austrian Disclosure and Notification Regulation	VMV
Werpapieraufsichtsgesetz	Austrian Securities Supervision Act	WAG

Denmark

National Title	Translated Title	Abbreviation
vædipapirhandelslov	Danish Securities Trading Act	

France

National Title	Translated Title	Abbreviation
Code Civil	French Civil Code	Cc
Code de commerce	French Commercial Code	C. com.
Code monétaire et financier	French Monetary and Financial Code	C. mon. fin.
Règlement général Autorité des Marchés Financiers	General Regulations of the French Stock Market Authority	RG AMF

Germany

National Title	Translated Title	Abbreviation
Abgabenverordnung	German Act on the Administrative Procedures in Taxation	AO
Aktiengesetz	German Stock Corporations Act	AktG
Anlegerschutzverbesserungsgesetz	German Investor Protection Improvement Act	AnSVG
Börsengesetz	German Stock Exchange Act	BörsG

Verordnung zur Konkretisierung von Anzeige-, Mitteilungs- und Veröffentlichungs-pflichten sowie der Pflicht zur Führung von Insiderverzeichnissen nach dem Wert-papierhandelsgesetz	German Regulation on Disclosure of Secu-rities Trading and Insider Dealings	WpAiV
Versicherungsaufsichtsgesetz	German Law on Insurance Supervision	VAG
Wertpapiererwerbs- und Übernahmegesetz	German Securities Acquisition and Takeover Act	WpÜG
Wertpapierprospektgesetz	German Securities Prospectus Act	WpPG
Zivilprozessordnung	German Civil Procedure Code	ZPO

Italy

National Title	Translated Title	Abbreviation
Codice Civil	Italian Civil Code	
Consiglio Nazionale degli Ordini dei Gior-nalisti	The Italian National Council's Regulation of Journalists	
Regolamento Congiunto	Italian Compliance Regulation	
Regolamento Emittenti	Italian Issuers' Regulation	RE
Regolamento Intermediari	Italian Regulation on Intermediaries	
Regolamento Mercati	Italien Financial Markets Regulation	
Testo Unico della Finanza	Italian Consolidated Laws on Finance	TUF

Spain

National Title	Translated Title	Abbreviation
Código Civil	Spanish Civil Code	CC
Código Penal	Spanish Criminal Code	CP
Ley 24/1988, de 28 de julio, del Mercado de Valores	Spanish Securities Market Act	LMV
Ley de Sociedades Anónimas	Spanish Stock Corporation Act	LSA
Real Decreto	Spanish Royal Decree (Regulation)	RD
Real Decreto 1066/2007, de 27 de julio, sobre el régimen de las ofertas públicas de adquisición de valores	Spanish Royal Decree (Regulation) on Takeovers	RD 1066/2007
Real Decreto 1310/2005, de 4 de noviembre, por el que se desarrolla parcialmente la Ley 24/1988, de 28 de julio, del Mercado de Valores, en materia de admisión a negociación de valores en mercados secundarios oficiales, de ofertas públicas de venta o suscripción y del folleto exigible a tales efectos	Spanish Royal Decree (Regulation) on Prospectuses	RD 1310/2005
Real Decreto 1333/2005, de 11 de noviembre, por el que se desarrolla la Ley 24/1988, de 28 de julio, del Mercado de Valores, en materia de abuso de mercado	Spanish Royal Decree (Regulation) on Market Abuse	RD 1333/2005
Real Decreto 1362/2007, de 19 de octubre, por el que se desarrolla la Ley 24/1988, de 28 de julio, del Mercado de Valores, en relación con los requisitos de transparencia relativos a la información sobre los emisores cuyos valores estén admitidos a negociación en un mercado secundario oficial o en otro mercado regulado de la Unión Europea	Spanish Royal Decree (Regulation) on Transparency on Capital Markets	RD 1362/2007

Index of National Laws by Country

Real Decreto 217/2008, de 15 de febrero, sobre Spanish Royal Decree (Regulation) on   RD 217/2008
el régimen jurídico de las empresas de servi-   Investment Firms
cios de inversión y de las demás entidades que
prestan servicios de inversión y por el que se
modifica parcialmente el Reglamento de la Ley
35/2003, de 4 de noviembre, de Instituciones
de Inversión Colectiva, aprobado por el Real
Decreto 1309/2005, de 4 de noviembre

Real Decreto-ley 5/2005, de 11 de marzo, de   Spanish Royal Decree-Act (Regulation) on
reformas urgentes para el impulso a la pro-   urgent reforms to increase productivity and
ductividad y para la mejora de la contratación to improve public procurement
pública

Reglamento del Registro Mercantil   Spanish regulation on Company Registries RRM

Sweden

National Title	Translated Title	Abbreviation
Aktiebolagslag (SFS 2005:551)	Swedish Stock Corporation Act	ABL
årsredovisningslag	Swedish Accounts Act	
Brottsbalk (SFS 1995:1554)	Swedish Criminal Code	BrB
Finansinspektionen's regulation FFFS 2007:16	Shwedish MaComp	
lag om anmälningsskyldighet vissa innehav av finansiella instrument	Swedish Act on the Disclosure of Ownership regarding Certain Financial Instruments	
lag om börs- och clearingverksamhet (SFS 1992:543)	Swedish Act on Stock Markets and Clearing	
lag om handel med finansiella instrument (SFS 1991:980)	Swedish Act on the trading with Financial Instruments	LHF
lag om investeringsfonds (SFS 2004:46)	Swedish Investment Fund Act	
lag om offentliga uppköpserbjudanden på aktiemarknaden (SFS 2000:1087)	Swedish Takeover Act	
lag om straff för marknadsmissbruk vid handel med finansiella instrument (SFS 2005:377)	Swedish Market Abuse Act	
lag om värdepappersmarknadenv (SFS 2007:528)	Swedish Securities Market Act	LVM
lag om värdepappersrörelse (SFS 1991:981)	Swedish Act on securities transactions	
lag omgrupprättegång (SFS 2002:599)	Swedish Group Proceedings Act	
Regulation FFFS 2005:9	Swedish Regulations and general guidelines regarding investment recommendations directed to the general public and the management of conflicts of interest	
Svensk författningssamling	Swedish law gazette	SFS

Switzerland

National Title	Translated Title	Abbreviation
Verordnung der Eidgenössischen Finanz-marktaufsicht über die Börsen und den Effektenhandel	Swiss Regulation on Stock Exchanges and Securities Trading	BEHV–EBK

United Kingdom

National Title	Translated Title	Abbreviation
Client Asset Sourcebook (FSA Handbook)		CASS

Code of Market Conduct/Market Abuse Regulation (FSA Handbook)		MAR
Code of Practice of Approved Persons (FSA Handbook)		APER
Companies Act 2006		
Company Act 1980		
Conduct of Business Sourcebook (FSA Handbook)		COBS
Criminal Justice Act 1993		CJA
Criminal Justice Act 1993 (Commencement No. 5) Order (SI 1994/242)		
Disclosure Rules and Transparency Rules (FSA Handbook)		DTR
Financial Services and Markets Act 2000		FSMA 2000
FSA's Handbook of Rules and Guidance		FSA Handbook
Investment Recommendations (Media) Regulations 2005		
Principles for Businesses (FSA Handbook)		PRIN
Senior Management Arrangements, Systems and Controls (FSA Handbook)		SYSC
Takeover Code		

USA

National Title	Translated Title	Abbreviation
SEC Rules		
Securities Exchange Act 1934		

Index of Supervisory and Court Rulings

The numbers in bold type direct to main reference.

511